THE
INSIDERS'®
GUIDE
TO

Denver

THE INSIDERS' GUIDE®

TO

Denver

by
Jana Miller
and
Sally Stich

The Insiders' Guide®
An imprint of Falcon® Publishing Inc.
A Landmark Communications company
P.O. Box 1718
Helena, MT 59624
(800) 582-2665
www.insiders.com

Sales and Marketing: Falcon Publishing, Inc.
P.O. Box 1718
Helena, MT 59624
(800) 582-2665
www.falcon.com

•

FOURTH EDITION
1st printing

•

©1999 by Falcon Publishing, Inc.

•

Printed in the United States of America

•

Cover photos: Skier, Daily Camera/Jay Quadracci; State Capitol, Denver Metro Convention &
Visitors Bureau; Denver at Sunset, Daily Camera. **Spine photo:** Bronco sculpture, Daily Camera.

•

Publications from *The Insiders' Guide*® series are available at special discounts for bulk
purchases for sales promotions, premiums or fundraisings. Special editions, including personalized covers, can be created in large quantities for special needs.
For more information, please contact Falcon Publishing.

ISBN 1-57380-093-7

Preface

Welcome to the Mile High City. Whether you're relocating or just visiting, we're sure you'll love it here. From our sweeping Rocky Mountain vistas to our casual hospitality, Denver is a place rich in history, beauty and excitement. And *The Insiders' Guide® to Denver* is designed to help you make the most of your time here.

For starters, chances are good that if you're already in Denver reading this book, the sky will be a startling shade of blue for at least part of the day. The sun shines at least a good part of 310 days a year here, and sunglasses are highly recommended. In fact, bad weather is perhaps the biggest misconception about Denver. Put simply, snow-capped peaks in the Rockies don't mean snow-covered streets in Denver. Sure, we get the occasional blizzard seen on national news, but there's nary a trace after the sun melts it away in a day or so.

Beyond the great climate, Denver is a vibrant, growing city. It's no surprise that Denver was the site of the 1997 Summit of the Eight, which brought together leaders of eight of the world's most economically powerful nations. President Clinton lauded Denver for its thriving economy, warm hospitality and breathtaking views. Wives of the summit leaders traveled by train to Winter Park Resort to lunch at the mountain-top Sunspot Lodge (you can too; just check our Skiing chapter for details). And leaders enjoyed the novelty of Western ways at the famous Fort restaurant in Morrison (check our Restaurants chapter for details). Japan's Prime Minister Ryutaro Hashimoto even donned a new pair of cowboy boots during his trip.

Denver is making a strong comeback from its bust in the early 1980s, when its reliance on oil triggered a downturn in the economy. Now, telecommunications is king, the Colorado Rockies are the pride that brings in baseball-loving tourists, and Denver boosters are beating their chests.

Even die-hard Denver lovers — as we are — find new things to treasure about our city. Our city parks, for instance, are vast expanses of green cut with walking and biking trails and flower beds that are a feast of splendor to stroll amid. If parks are too docile and what you really want is great shopping, you're in luck: besides the Cherry Creek Shopping Center (which stands as the area's top attraction, surpassing even the Mint, the Coors Brewery and the Denver museums in tourist draw!), Greater Denver has two new and swanky shopping attractions. Park Meadows, in southeast suburbia (take Interstate 25 south from Denver to the County Line Road exit), opened in August of 1996 to rave reviews and has maintained that positive momentum ever since. And the downtown shopping and entertainment offerings got a much-needed shot in the arm when the new Denver Pavilions opened last fall on the 16th Street Mall. (See our Shopping chapter for more information on all of these venues.)

There are so many things to do in or near downtown these days —with more being planned — that boredom is out of the question. Elitch Gardens amusement park recently relocated in the once-abandoned Platte Valley area just west of downtown. Brewpubs are a way of life — in or out of baseball season. And Larimer Square (Larimer Street between 14th and 15th streets downtown) is a year-round destination to experience Denver's flavor and appreciation for historical buildings and the lore that accompanies them.

While no book can ever capture everything great about a metropolitan area as diverse as Denver, this one attempts to distill the best of everything into a format that will give newcomers the inside scoop, offer visitors a guide on what to see and experience, and bring even more wisdom to longtime Denverites. So go forth and tour, buy a pair of cowboy boots, picnic in the park, gaze at the mountains from the middle of the city and savor the beauty. When you're done, let us know what you think. Did we leave out your favorite restaurant? Did we neglect to mention some really nifty place to visit, thing to do or fact worth knowing? Send suggestions for our yearly updates to the publisher, and we'll do our best to check them out. Send us your comments at Insiders' Guides, Falcon Publishing, P.O. Box 1718, Helena, MT, or visit us at our website at www.insiders.com, where comments and suggestions are welcomed and encouraged.

About the Authors

Jana Miller

Jana J. Miller moved with her family to Denver at the age of 8, and she swears she will never leave. She grew up in the suburbs, then sought a more fast-paced life in the heart of Denver's Capitol Hill neighborhood. She earned her undergraduate degree in journalism from Metropolitan State College of Denver and later earned her master's degree at Ohio State University, where she was awarded a Kiplinger Fellowship. In between, she wrote for newspapers as a beat reporter covering everything from higher education to the Colorado General Assembly. She also spent two years traveling Colorado and the rest of the mountain region as a correspondent for *USA Today*.

Her love of Colorado and the Denver area grew the more she discovered through her work and travel. She now lives in the quaint northwest Denver neighborhood called The Highlands, where she is reminded daily how much she loves this city. In addition to her freelance work, she is senior associate for Ciruli Associates, a well-respected political strategy firm specializing in public policy issues.

Sally Stich

Sally Stich grew up in Omaha, Nebraska, and lived there until the age of 18. Having visited a friend in Denver during her senior year of high school, she applied to the University of Denver, where she matriculated in 1968. After graduation in 1972, she decided that this was where she wanted to spend her adult life, a decision influenced by the fact that her college boyfriend, a native New Yorker, had also decided to stay in Denver. Armed with a degree in French, she got a job teaching at St. Mary's Academy, where she taught both English and French for seven years.

Returning to school in 1980, this time the University of Colorado, she got a master's degree in English literature and started teaching writing at the college level, until seven years later when she realized she didn't know if she could write the assignments she was asking her students to do. That's when she decided to start writing. Her first gig was writing a regular entertainment column for the *Denver Post*. That was in 1986. She continued with the *Post* for six and a half years and eventually branched out until she was writing for such national publications as *Ladies Home Journal*, *Redbook*, *Mademoiselle*, *Sunset* and *Continental Profiles*. Today she still writes for magazines and teaches graduate-level writing courses at her alma mater.

She and her college sweetheart — now her husband of 22 years — live in Denver, where they have raised their two kids, Max, 19, and Sarah, 15. She thinks Denver is just about a perfect place to live — if you don't have to take any of the highways too often.

Acknowledgments

Thanks first to Laura Caruso and Bob Ebisch, the authors of the first and second editions of *The Insiders' Guide®️ to Denver*. They have gone on to other projects but have left an indelible mark on this guide. The Real Estate chapter would not have been as complete without the help and knowledge of several experts: Jane Merrick and Jim Romano of Moore and Company in Littleton, who helped with neighborhoods in the southeast section of the metro area; Linda Simpson, of Moore and Company at the Ranch, who helped with neighborhoods in the north and west parts of town; and Susan Joslyn, at Century 21 Professionals Inc. in Lakewood, who offered advice on neighborhoods in the west. Thanks to Kiki Sayre, who knows everything about skiing in Colorado, and to the experts at Lower Downtown Development Inc., who provided assistance on the latest in LoDo. Thanks to editor Molly Perkins for her patience. And thanks most of all to my partner and best friend, Tim Mullin.

— Jana

A book such as this is naturally a collaborative effort. My thanks go to all the Insiders who provided me with material beyond the reach of my own experience. Special thanks go to two people: Jan Snyder, whose keen eye and sharp sensibilities kept me on track; and Tom Stich, who not only introduced me to Jan, but who also kept his eye out for every piece of written material that related to this great city.

— Sally

Table of Contents

Directory of Maps

Denver's Surrounding Counties

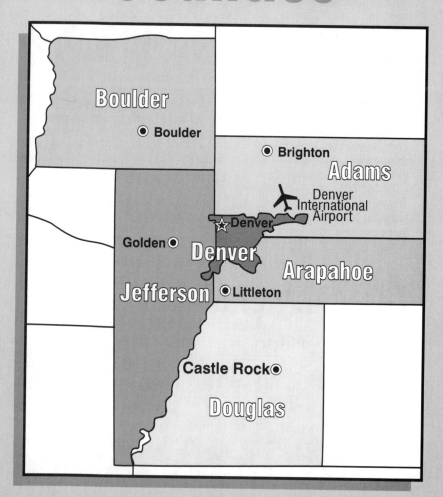

Denver

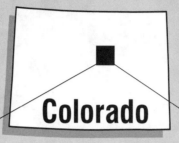

Colorado

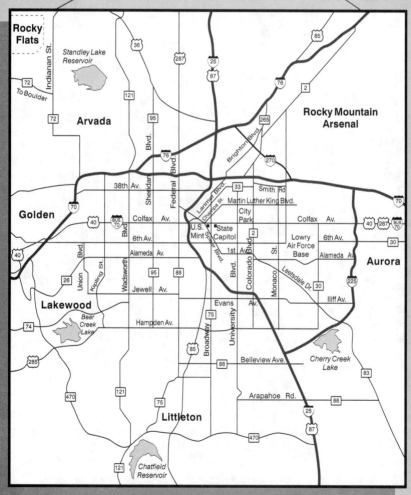

Rocky Flats

Standley Lake Reservoir

Indianan St.

36

287

25

87

85

I-76

2

72

To Boulder

72

121

Arvada

95

Sheridan Blvd.

Federal Blvd.

76

265

Brighton Blvd.

270

Rocky Mountain Arsenal

38th Av.

Larimer Blvd.

Champa St.

33

Smith Rd

Martin Luther King Blvd.

Golden

70

40

BUS 70

BUS 70 Blvd.

Colfax Av.

City Park

Colfax Av.

40 287 BUS 70

6th Av.

U.S. Mint

State Capitol

2

Lowry Air Force Base

6th Av.

30

40

Alameda Av.

1st Av.

Speer Blvd.

Colorado Blvd.

Monaco St.

Alameda Av.

Aurora

Union Blvd.

Kipling St.

Wadsworth

95

88

Leetsdale Dr.

30

225

26

Jewell Av.

Iliff Av.

Lakewood

Bear Creek Lake

Evans Av.

74

Hampden Av.

75

Belleview Ave.

Cherry Creek Lake

285

85

88

83

121

75

Arapahoe Rd.

88

25

470

Littleton

87

470

121

Chatfield Reservoir

The Colorado Rockies have set plenty of records in their years as a major-league team.

How to Use This Book

The Insiders' Guide® to Denver is designed to let you flip easily through pages and look for something specific or simply find something that catches your eye. For overall subject areas, such as nightlife or shopping, go to the Table of Contents. To find information on specific places, such as the name of a restaurant or a ski resort, consult the index.

This book is a guide and not a directory. So while we've made sure to include all the leading tourist attractions, restaurants, hotels and just about every other leading thing in Greater Denver, to a great extent our choices are personal ones. But that's one of the things that makes this guide so valuable. We give honest, knowledgeable Insider-based information on Denver and the surrounding counties of Adams, Arapahoe, Douglas and Jefferson. Although Boulder is sometimes considered part of the Denver metro area, its offerings are enough to fill a separate book. See our *Insiders' Guide® to Boulder and Rocky Mountain National Park*.

Denver, and Colorado's entire Front Range for that matter, is experiencing explosive growth. This has had positive results, such as the blossoming of cultural attractions and job markets. And it has negative results, too, such as the impact of a growing population on urban sprawl, increased traffic congestion and decreased wildlife habitat. But much of what makes people want to move here, or stay here, is intact. The climate is moderate, recreational activities abound, and some of the most beautiful scenery in the country is within a few hours' drive.

As much as this book isn't a directory, neither is it a novel. You don't have to pick it up and read it straight through. Check the Table of Contents and read selectively on a need-to-know or want-to-know basis. Each chapter has its own introduction, so it's clear what's included and how it's organized. However, if you are new to the area, begin by reading through the Area Overviews and Getting Around chapters.

This book is meant to be used. Carry it in your backpack, tuck it in the glove box of your car, put one of the kids in charge of carrying it. When you're touring around town and want to know where to stop for lunch, or whether the Denver Zoo is open on Sundays (it is), you'll be glad you have it nearby.

Throughout the book we've included Insiders' Tips, handy hints from those in-the-know for those who want to be.

Enjoy your stay, whether it be for a few hours or a lifetime.

Denver possesses a strong Western heritage but revels in its fast-growing high-tech economy and upscale, trendy feel.

Area Overviews

Let's get one thing straight right away: Denver is not a cowtown.

Sure, tourism promoters love to emphasize Western lore to potential visitors, and you're likely to encounter mounted police on downtown streets, but we don't all wear cowboy hats and keep our horses in back yard barns. Denver possesses a strong Western heritage but revels in its fast-growing high-tech economy and upscale, trendy feel.

OK, we feel better having said that. Now we can go on to brag about this great Western city and explain why metro Denver is one of the fastest growing localities in the nation.

It is today, as it was 100 years ago, the largest metropolis between California and Missouri and between Dallas and Seattle. An expansive self-regard still comes easily to the present inhabitants of Greater Denver, just as it did when Denver was being established in the mid-1800s.

The metropolitan area in general is defined by the City and County of Denver and its four suburban counties, Adams, Arapahoe, Douglas and Jefferson. Boulder County is close by but regarded as having its own identity.

Only about 40 percent of Greater Denver's present citizens were born here. An obvious testimony to their pride — and maybe a little resentment of all the newcomers — is the "Native" bumper sticker visible on cars. The other 60 percent of Greater Denver's residents came here by choice. Some of these may mock the natives' hubris with bumper stickers that are identical except for the disappearance of the "t," but they are no less bullish on the area's attractions and achievements.

Natives and newcomers alike are uneasy about the city's growth, which poses threats to their quality of life with real-estate developments that mar views or diminish open spaces. But boosterism runs rampant.

Because of its geographic location near the nation's center, Denver is already a major hub of the railroad, airline and highway systems. The new airport, Denver International, is supposed to transform Denver's position midway between Munich and Tokyo, Canada and Mexico, into a focus of worldwide trade and transportation.

Geography has a lot to do with Denver's historical image of itself at the hinge of the North American continent. No matter where you are in Denver, you have only to look west to see the Rocky Mountains running north and south like a wall dividing west from east. The first slopes of the Foothills begin at the edge of Greater Denver. Behind the Foothills and front ranges you can see the gray back ranges rising to the jagged spine of the North American continent, the Continental Divide.

Self-styled since the 1800s as the "Queen City of the Plains," Denver might lay equal claim to being the Monarch Metropolis of the Mountains. Its urban fabric extends into the mountains on the west and overlays the first swells of the Great Plains to the east. The mountains are what drew Paleolithic hunters to the sheltering slopes and fertile hunting grounds of the Foothills. Between the housing developments of Jefferson County on Denver's southwest fringe, archaeologists have found 10,000-year-old sites where mammoths and camels appear to have been killed by human hunters. Later, modern Indians, principally the Ute, Comanche, Apache, Arapaho, Cheyenne and Kiowa, gravitated to the area for hunting, trade and war.

Settling the Land

Non-native Americans came first from the south, beginning with Spanish expeditions in the 1600s. During the next two centuries a slow movement of mostly agrarian colonists from Mexico and New Mexico gave a distinctly Hispanic culture to the southern part of the state. The City of Pueblo, less than a two-hour drive south of Denver, was Mexican territory until the United States grabbed the Southwest in the war with Mexico in 1848. As Colorado grew, the ancestors of today's Hispanic citizens generated much of the sweat that built the state's mining, railroads and agriculture.

Invaders from the east came faster and hit harder. In 1858, little more than 50 years after the first mountain men began trapping furs in the Rockies, a party of prospectors panned gold from the Platte River in what is now the City of Englewood on Denver's southern edge. It wasn't enough to pay each man more than about $10 a day, but it was enough to start the rush.

The history of modern Denver began at the confluence of the South Platte River with tiny Cherry Creek, where cottonwood groves sheltered the camps of Indians and early explorers such as John C. Fremont. By the beginning of 1859, the City of Denver was established at the confluence by friends of James W. Denver, then governor of Kansas Territory. By the middle of 1859, the cottonwood groves had been axed into oblivion and replaced by some 400 cabins and a lot of bare dirt and mud. Today that area has been revamped into an urban playground where children swim in cool waters, and kayakers navigate a fast-running shoot.

Striking Gold

Gold strikes in the mountains brought not just a growing swarm of fortune-seekers from the east but also merchants, industry and other elements of a real city, including the bad elements in boom-town proportions. Denver had "more brawls, more pistol shots with criminal intent . . . than in any community with equal numbers on Earth," according to Horace Greeley. "Uncle Dick" Wootton, an early merchant, later recalled that "stealing was the only occupation of a considerable portion of the population, who would take anything from a pet calf, or a counterfeit gold dollar, up to a sawmill."

However, as Denver matured to become the capital of the new Colorado Territory in 1867 and capital of the State of Colorado in 1876, it acquired a certain air of refinement. "A shooting affray in the street is as rare as in

Buffalo Bill (William F. Cody) was one of early Denver's most famous citizens.

Liverpool," noted Isabella Bird in 1872, "and one no longer sees men dangling to the lamp posts when one looks out in the morning." Still, she noted, Denver was not a very pretty sight, a city that "lay spread out, brown and treeless, upon the brown and treeless plain, which seemed to nourish nothing but wormwood and the Spanish bayonet."

The kind of money needed to polish the city's rough edges was soon to come from Colorado's growing cattle, mining, railroad, steel, banking and other industries. Gambling houses and painted ladies still characterized the city in journalistic accounts of the time. Yet a new class of aristocrats began decorating Denver's Capitol Hill neighborhood with mansions that have now become tourist destinations. Silver strikes in the mountains in the late 1870s caused another mining boom that poured money into the city until the silver market collapsed in 1893 and threw Denver into a depression. But more gold strikes in the mountains, along with the growth of Colorado agriculture and manufacturing industries, brought Denver citizens into the 20th century more given to creating parks than cavorting in bawdy houses.

Still the Queen City of the Plains was more plain than queenly, as one visitor put it. Major credit for making the queen look like a lady generally goes to Mayor Robert Speer, who pursued his dream of a "City Beautiful" during the first two decades of this century with expanding neighborhood and mountain parks. He is also credited with the laying of hundreds of miles of sewers and paved streets, turning Cherry Creek from a garbage dump into the centerpiece of what is today Speer Boulevard, planting thousands of trees and promoting other projects that culminated in the Denver Civic Center, which was completed nearly two decades after his 1918 death. Civic Center today is a popular park located between the magnificent Capitol and City and County buildings downtown.

War Spurs Growth

Despite the Great Depression, Denver's population grew by more than 50 percent between 1910 and 1940. It was World War II that initiated the area's greatest surge of growth when fear of attack on the nation's coasts transformed the area into a center of military and other government functions. Within a year after Pearl Harbor, major employment bases appeared in facilities such as the Denver Federal Center, the Rocky Mountain Arsenal and Fitzsimmons Army Medical Center. Those who came for war-related opportunities stayed on when the war was done, and Greater Denver now contains some 50 percent of Colorado's population.

Optimism and Diversification

Since World War II, the local economy has had its ups and downs, but Greater Denver has never lost that growth momentum. The last slump came during the 1980s, while the rest of the nation was booming and Denver was reeling from an oil bust. Now the region has come back with a new and more diversified economy. Optimism is visible in unprecedented spending on transportation infrastructure, including Denver International Airport, the city's new light-rail transportation system and the rebuilding of the intersection of Denver's

two major interstates, I-70 and I-25, which had been nicknamed the "mousetrap" for its ability to foul traffic.

In many ways, Denver is reinventing itself in the '90s. The $126-million Colorado Convention Center opened in 1990 and already political talk has turned to expanding it to attract even bigger conventions. Also in 1990 came the opening of Cherry Creek Shopping Center, Greater Denver's prestige retail mall that boasts the state's first outlets of stores such as Lord & Taylor, Saks Fifth Avenue and Nieman Marcus. Upscale retail got another giant boost in 1996 when Park Meadows opened on the southern edge of town, and again in 1998 when Denver Pavilions arrived on the downtown scene.

Perhaps nowhere is revitalization more evident than in the area known as the Central Platte Valley, where the city began around the confluence of the South Platte River and Cherry Creek. As the railroads arrived in the 1870s and Denver grew up and grew outward, the Central Platte Valley became the rail and warehousing district. By the 1980s, the Central Platte Valley had become an urban wasteland, with a smattering of businesses in old buildings and a lot of trash-strewn vacant fields crisscrossed by railroad tracks. Now the area is rebounding as the focal point of the new Denver. City planners envision a planned community of green spaces and residential, retail, office and entertainment developments. Much of the vision is still blue sky, but some of its anchor developments are already in place. In 1995, the 50,000-seat stadium known as Coors Field opened on the edge of the Central Platte Valley as home for Denver's major-league baseball team, the Colorado Rockies. Just a half-mile southwest down the valley, Elitch Gardens, Denver's premier amusement park, opened its 60 acres of fun in 1995 after a move from the city's far west side, where it had been located since 1890. Another announcement in 1995 was the selection of a site just across the South Platte River from Elitch Gardens for the $67-million Ocean Journey aquarium, which opened in 1998.

Rebounding ahead of the Central Platte Valley has been Lower Downtown, the turn-of-the-century, red-brick business and warehousing district along the valley's edge. In the last decade, it has become a renovated historic district of restaurants and brewpubs, prestigious offices, condominiums and lofts around Denver's historic railroad terminal, Union Station. Lower Downtown is particularly hot since the opening of Coors Field, home of the Rockies. On the north side of Lower Downtown, the area becoming known as the ballpark neighborhood has seen the opening of hundreds of new housing units and a few dozen restaurants.

Big City Pains

Of course, not everything is perfect about Greater Denver.

Tourists strolling amid the stately buildings and luxuriant flower gardens of Denver's Civic Center might well be asked for money by transients who lounge in the shade. Petty crime is as prevalent in Denver as any mid-sized city. Yet, crime in Denver does not distinguish it from other metropolitan areas. In terms of its crime rate, Denver lies between Lubbock, Texas, and Springfield, Massachusetts. Denver is more dangerous than Des Moines, safer than Seattle.

One of Denver's most notorious negatives is what locals call "the brown cloud," the yellow-brown layer of air pollution often visible in the air above the city. Denver may be 1 mile above sea level, but it actually lies in a geographic depression. The High Plains rise for 50 miles or so as one travels to the east, and, of course, the mountains rise beyond 14,000 feet to the west.

Summer visitors may wonder, "What brown cloud?" During warm weather, convection carries the pollution up where the winds can carry it away. High-pollution days are most frequently announced during the winter, when temperature inversions trap and concentrate air pollution in the depression. Unfortunately, this means that those who buy a house with a wood-burning fireplace may be buying a house with wasted wall space; those nights on which a merry crackling fire would be most comforting often seem to be the same nights when it's against the law to build a fire. More irritating is feeling it in the lungs and eyes. Some of us don't even notice it. But those with allergies or respiratory conditions can find it distressing. It's ironic, considering that many of Greater Denver's early inhabitants — including Mayor Robert Speer — came here because the clean, dry air was celebrated as a cure for tuberculosis.

Still, those who compare Denver's air pollution to that of Los Angeles are stretching it; Denver rarely violates national clean air standards. Even without air pollution, breathing is a bit more difficult at 1 mile of altitude. This is typically a mild and temporary problem. Only during the first week or so in Denver do some visitors feel headachy and strangely out of sorts. Since Denver is a gateway to the mountains, however, visitors need to take seriously the dangers of acute altitude sickness, a collapse of the body's ability to take in and metabolize oxygen. Those who plan to exert themselves in the mountains need to take a few days to get used to the altitude and drink an abnormally large amount of water; otherwise they could find themselves beset by abdominal cramps and hyperventilation.

As the population grows, rush-hour traffic jams are worse than natives have ever known. If you're from Chicago or Los Angeles, you may find Denver's traffic jams unimpressive. Former Los Angelenos newly transplanted to Denver can be heard claiming to commute to downtown from homes in the mountains in the time it would take them to drive 1 mile at rush hour in L.A. Most people, however, find

INSIDERS' TIP

When traveling on Interstate 25 through the north side of the metro area, car pool to take advantage of HOV, or high occupancy vehicle lanes, during rush hours. You'll avoid the parking lot Denverites call I-25 and get where you're going with ease. Watch the signs carefully, as times and directions change according to traffic patterns.

Denver traffic tremendously unpleasant and getting worse.

One of the nation's biggest misconceptions about Denver concerns the weather. Seen from far away, Denver is hard to distinguish from the mountains that are so important to its national image. More than 80 percent of Colorado's population lives in the "Front Range," the increasingly interconnected metropolitan areas ranging from Greeley on the north to Pueblo on the south along the base of the mountains. Front Range weather is surprisingly mild. Someone in Chicago or Cleveland may hear of new snow falling on 6-foot snowpacks in the Rockies, then call a friend in Denver and find out the temperature here is 70 degrees.

Long cold spells do set in periodically from November to February. And Denver does get some whopping snowstorms, more in March than in any other month. Every year sees at least one storm that leaves highways littered with abandoned vehicles. But a few days later, don't be surprised to see people out working in their yards. On April 10, 1995, for example, a snowstorm dumped up to 15 inches on the Denver area. On the morning of April 11, people woke up to 20 degrees and knee-deep snow. Two days later it was 80 degrees, and birds were hopping on dry green lawns. Snow melts particularly fast during the late winter and early spring when Chinook winds come roaring down from the mountains at speeds that have been clocked as high as 143 miles per hour. These warm, dry "snow-eaters" literally suck the moisture out of the snow before it can reach the soil, and they have been known to raise Front Range temperatures by as much as 36 degrees within two hours. They've also been known to tear the roofs off houses, topple trees and blow semi-trucks right off the interstate.

Mild on average, Greater Denver is the land of weather extremes, one of the reasons why the National Center for Atmospheric Research is just up the road in the City of Boulder. Meteorologists joke that the area is ideal, because they can go golfing in the morning and chase thunderstorms in the afternoon. With Denver's weather extremes, it's easy to understand the common observation: "If you don't like the weather, wait 15 minutes."

Denver Suburbs

Much of what we've already said about Greater Denver has focused on the City of Denver, but the suburban counties have their own lives and characters. While the City and County of Denver's population declined by 32,000 during Colorado's recession in the 1980s, the population of Greater Denver's suburban counties — Arapahoe, Jefferson, Douglas and Adams — grew by 212,000. Now that Colorado's economy has begun attracting people and companies again, the suburban counties are reaping the lion's share of the growth.

Jefferson County, West of Denver

Among Greater Denver counties, Jefferson County is second only to the City and County of Denver in population. The county wraps around the western end of the metropolitan area and includes such mountain communities as Evergreen and Conifer and reaches into the Pike National Forest. Only Douglas County rivals Jefferson for scenic beauty. Located nearest the mountains, Jefferson tends to attract residents motivated by quality of life. Colorado's image is one of mountains, and when people immigrate here, those who can afford to locate in or near the mountains generally go that route. Jefferson County has a highly educated population and a high percentage of dual-income families.

Greater Denver's gateway to the mountains, Jefferson County is traversed by streams of skiers and other motorists on I-70 west or on U.S. Highway 6 through scenic Clear Creek Canyon, the historic main thoroughfare to the gold and silver meccas of the 1800s. Many of these passersby notice little more of Jefferson County than the City of Golden below to the north or the upscale homes of mountain communities that dot the hills along the route farther into the Foothills.

But "Jeffco," in the local slang, is also an urban county in which cities such as Arvada, Westminster, Wheat Ridge and Lakewood represent a continuum of the urban fabric reaching out from Denver.

Jefferson County is highly industrialized with an emphasis on high technology. Golden, the county seat, claims Greater Denver's highest population percentage of technology Ph.Ds. Up to a third of the students at Golden's Colorado School of Mines stay on in Jefferson County after they graduate. Jefferson County is the regional geotechnology, materials, mining and energy business cluster.

The U.S. government is the county's largest employer with the mammoth Denver Federal Center in Lakewood, Jefferson County's largest city, and the National Renewable Energy Laboratory in Golden.

Arapahoe County, East and South of Denver

Back when it was Arapahoe County of the Kansas Territory, it once covered nearly half of the present state of Colorado. Now Arapahoe County covers about 800 square miles reaching halfway from Denver to the Kansas border. Arapahoe holds the biggest part of Denver's eastern suburbs and folds under the south side of Denver to encompass such south Denver suburbs as Englewood, Cherry Hills Village and Littleton, the county seat.

Arapahoe contains most of the City of Aurora, and Aurora contains nearly 50 percent of the county's population as well. Aurora is the state's biggest city in area and its third-largest in population. Since World War II, Aurora has been heavily influenced by the military. It contains Fitzsimmons Army Medical Center (the city's second-largest employer), bordering the now-closed Lowry Air Force Base on the west and embracing Buckley Air National Guard Base (the city's largest employer) on the east. The closing of Lowry Air Force Base in 1994 slapped the city's economy in the face, as did the federal decision in 1995 to close Fitzsimmons, but Lowry is already attracting plenty of development interest. So is the old

Stapleton International Airport on Aurora's boundary.

The county's second- and third-largest cities, Englewood and Littleton south of Denver, also suffered from workforce reductions during the early 1990s at Martin Marietta, now Lockheed Martin, in nearby Jefferson County. At the decade's dawn, Martin Marietta was Littleton's largest employer. Littleton's employment base has become increasingly diversified. Littleton still has something of a small-town feel, but its school system has produced Scholastic Aptitude Test scores that rank in the top echelons of Greater Denver.

Englewood was a prairie when Colorado's first gold discovery occurred there in 1858. By the late 1800s, however, the fruit orchards of Englewood had given that city its modern name from the Old English words for "wooded place." Denver's ladies and gentlemen preferred it for Sunday carriage drives and picnics. Since that time, Englewood has developed a strong business community. Today Englewood has Colorado's largest concentration of biomedical/biotechnology companies.

Adams County, Northeast of Denver

Adams County ceded 53 of its approximately 1,200 square miles to the City of Denver so that Denver could build its new airport. But Adams County is still Greater Denver's largest county. Lying north of Arapahoe County, Adams County extends as far to the east as Arapahoe County but much wider north to south.

Adams County is perhaps Greater Denver's most economically diverse county, hosting agriculture, heavy industry, transportation and high-tech companies. It does have an image as Greater Denver's big-shouldered, blue-collar county, thanks to the spread of warehouses,

Greater Denver Vital Statistics

• Denver was named for James W. Denver, governor of Kansas Territory when the city was founded.

• Denver became the capital of the new Colorado Territory in 1867 and capital of the State of Colorado in 1876.

• Population: The Denver Regional Council of Governments on July 1, 1997, estimated the City and County of Denver at 497,625, Adams County at 308,425, Arapahoe County at 463,600, Douglas County 127,400 and Jefferson County at 510,600.

• Location: The city lies at the base of the Rocky Mountains about a third of the way across Colorado from Wyoming to New Mexico.

• Terrain: Rocky Mountain Foothills on the west, rolling plains on the east.

• Altitude: A bronze disk imbedded on one of the western steps of the State Capitol building proclaims "ELEVATION 5,280.000 FEET." The words, "ONE MILE ABOVE SEA LEVEL" are chiseled just below.

• Climate: Mild. Dry heat in summer makes days bearable, nights pleasantly cool. Snow seldom stays long on the ground during winter. Average maximum temperature in the summer is 85 degrees; minimum is 56. Average maximum winter temperature is 45 degrees; minimum is 18. Average annual rainfall is 11 inches. Average annual snowfall is 60 inches. Average number of days with snow, ice pellets or hail of 1 inch or more in depth is 18. Clear days: 115. Partly cloudy days: 130. Cloudy days: 120.

• Denver government consists of a mayor and a city council. The current mayor is Wellington Webb.

Wellington Webb (right) is Denver's mayor.

smokestack industries and oil refineries that can be seen steaming like volcanoes on winter mornings as you drive along interstates 70 and 270. At the same time, it has its share of communications, biopharmaceuticals, computer software and hardware companies in its eastern, urbanized zone. The county's square mileage is predominantly a rural area of farming and ranching. Even in Brighton, the county seat, one of the most celebrated citizens is the nation's most well-known "cowboy poet," Baxter Black.

Jumping out at anyone who looks at a map of Greater Denver is a large blank space east of Commerce City with a scattering of lakes and the lettering "Rocky Mountain Arsenal (Restricted Area)." Once the site of Cold War chemical weapons manufacturing, the arsenal is a 27-square-mile area often said to contain the most polluted square mile on earth. As a Superfund site, it's in the process of a federal cleanup effort exceeding $1 billion. Meanwhile, off-limits to hunters and other human intrusion, it has become the most impressive wildlife refuge in Greater Denver. A continuous traffic of weekend visitors and weekday school groups take the guided tours on double-decker buses to view eagles, elk and other wildlife that call the arsenal home.

While dealing gracefully with its past, Adams County is well positioned for its future. Surrounding the new airport, Adams County will be a primary beneficiary of economic spinoffs as well as a primary recipient of new airport noise. Not everyone wanted the Denver International Airport there, and not everyone is satisfied with how it has been developed. In return for 53 square miles of its land, Adams County is supposed to get economic growth related to development around the airport.

In the long term Adams County expects substantial benefits. Despite strong growth in Greater Denver, the county still has a good availability of land and buildings at affordable prices. Despite having Greater Denver's second-lowest population, the county's percentage population growth between 1990 and 2010 has been projected as Greater Denver's second-fastest after Douglas County. Adams County's own airport, Front Range Airport, is just 3 miles from the Denver International Airport and rather new itself, having begun operations in 1983. The abundance of air transportation has enhanced basic industries such as metalworking, food processing and wood products in Adams County's southwestern corner as well as the 120th Avenue corridor of high-technology companies in the county's northwestern corner.

Douglas County, South of Denver

Flowing through the Pike National Forest southwest of Denver, the South Platte River has some of the most celebrated trout fishing — it was once called "the St. Peter's Basilica of trout fishing" by *Time* magazine — on Colorado's Front Range. This is Douglas County.

Highlands Ranch — one of Greater Denver's most popular planned communities, offering mountain views and plenty of parks and walkways — is also Douglas County. The population of Highlands Ranch is expected to reach 100,000 by the year 2015.

INSIDERS' TIP

While Denver's weather is envied across the country, contrary to popular belief, the city doesn't have 300 full days of sunshine per year. Not long ago, the state climatologist's office tried to calculate how Greater Denver could live up to the claim and found that 300 days is an accurate figure if you count as a "day of sunshine" those days in which the sun shines for more than 45 minutes. In general, Denver summers start the day sunny, cloud over in the afternoon and end up clear. Denver does get more sunshine than Miami. It gets less than San Diego, but hey, who doesn't?

Photo: Daily Camera/Lourie Zipf

The Denver City and County Building is the hub of local government.

Including the three municipalities of Castle Rock, Larkspur and Parker as well as a piece of Littleton, Douglas County is the only metro county that does not share a boundary with the City and County of Denver. It's separated from Denver by a slice of Arapahoe County that wraps under the city's south side.

Douglas County is Greater Denver's southern frontier. It has some impressive planned communities such as Highlands Ranch and Castle Pines, but it's mostly open country. Douglas is the only Greater Denver county in which the vast majority of its population lives in unincorporated communities. It is one of Greater Denver's prestigious living zones, with the region's highest median income and home prices. Douglas County is also the region's major bedroom community, with by far the highest ratio of people commuting outside the county to reach their jobs.

As the focus of what local planners call the Denver/Colorado Springs Development Corridor, Douglas is also Colorado's fastest-growing county with a population that ballooned 230 percent between 1980 and 1990. With 29 planned communities and 319 subdivisions covering nearly 18 percent of the county, Douglas anticipates a half-million new residents by the year 2030.

Meanwhile, the county plans to keep as much as 70 percent of its 841 square miles as open space in the form of ranches, greenbelts and public parks. Taking the county as a whole, it sometimes seems almost as much a part of Colorado Springs as it is of Denver. The county seat of Castle Rock, so named for the monolith-capped hill that towers above it, is just short of halfway to Colorado Springs, and most of its workers commute to one metropolis or the other.

Rush hour comes early in Denver. Assuming all goes well, the highways have cleared by 9 AM, and the evening rush hour starts as early as 3 PM.

Getting Around

"If you get lost, look at the mountains." That's the mantra when it comes to getting around Denver. The mountains to the west can orient even the most turned-around visitor or resident, so take advantage of them as you're navigating your way around.

The second vital feature to remember is that unlike the rest of the metro area, downtown is parallel to the Cherry Creek. So at times downtown feels like a confounding mistake in the midst of streets otherwise neatly laid out in a north-south and east-west fashion.

Denver's first streets were designed to be parallel to Cherry Creek. Later, streets were laid out north-south and east-west. It helps to look at a Denver map to orient yourself. In general, from downtown Denver, Aurora is to the east; the Denver Tech Center, Englewood and Greenwood Village are to the south; Littleton is southwest; Lakewood, Wheat Ridge and Golden are to the west; Arvada, Broomfield and Westminster are to the northwest; and Commerce City, Northglenn and Thornton are to the north.

"Downtown" refers to the area that is roughly bounded by 13th Avenue on the south, Speer Boulevard (which follows Cherry Creek) on the west, the South Platte River on the north and Grant Street on the east. Most streets downtown run one way. Seventeenth Street, where most of the banks and big office buildings are located, is in many ways the heart of downtown. The 16th Street Mall is also an important pedestrian thoroughfare, as free shuttle buses run up and down its 1-mile length, connecting the two RTD (Regional Transportation District) bus terminals at Civic Center on Broadway and Market Street a mile away. The shuttle buses operate between about 5:30 AM and 1 AM on weekdays, from about 6 AM to 1 AM on Saturdays and from 7 AM to 1 AM on Sundays. Frequency depends on the time of day and ranges from one every 10 minutes to almost one a minute during the morning and afternoon rush hours. The 16th Street Mall is closed to auto traffic between Market Street and Broadway. Bikes and in-line skates also aren't allowed.

Somewhere around Market Street, downtown becomes Lower Downtown, or "LoDo" (say "low-dough"). Dana Crawford, who spearheaded the Larimer Street rejuvenation, defines the area narrowly as Larimer and Market streets west to Union Station, from 20th Street to Cherry Creek. A broader definition extends farther west to the Platte River. Well, at least you'll have an idea of what people are talking about when you hear them say LoDo. Coors Field isn't actually in LoDo, but it's close enough at the northern perimeter. Capitol Hill is the name given to the area just east of downtown.

Our Area Overviews chapter, which talks about the different counties that make up Greater Denver, should help you orient yourself. For descriptions of neighborhoods, see our Neighborhoods and Real Estate chapter.

Logistics: Finding an Address

In central Denver, the streets are laid out on a sort of cross: Broadway runs north-south and serves as the dividing line between east and west addresses, and Ellsworth Avenue runs east-west and serves as the dividing line between north and south streets and addresses. Broadway and Ellsworth Avenue are the "zero hundred blocks," meaning that street addresses get larger the farther away they get from these central streets.

Maps Unlimited, 899 Broadway, (303) 623-4299, has every kind of map you'll ever need to find your way around — topographic, recreational and illustrated. They also stock guidebooks.

Main Arteries and Thoroughfares

Interstate 25 runs north-south through Denver in a line from Colorado Springs to Cheyenne (and farther, of course, in each direction). Just north of downtown, it intersects Interstate 70, which runs east-west through the northern edge of the city and is the major route to the mountains. The always-busy intersection of these two highways is known as the Mousetrap, a testament to its congestion. In bad weather or at rush hour, avoid it if you can. However, extensive improvements have been made to the Mousetrap and more are being planned.

Interstate 225 makes a loop southeast of the city, passing through Aurora and hooking up again with I-25 near the Denver Tech Center area. Colorado Highway 470 (known as C470) rounds the west and south sections of the metro area, from I-25 at the Arapahoe County/Douglas County border, west past Littleton, then north to I-70.

Other major thoroughfares are Sixth Avenue (U.S. Highway 6), which joins up with I-70 at Golden; Santa Fe Drive (U.S. Highway 85), a north-south route that can be a good alternative to I-25; and Broadway. Colfax Avenue (Colo. Highway 40) is a major east-west route, but, like Broadway, it has a lot of traffic and traffic lights so it's hardly a quick way to get from one side of town to another. Speer Boulevard runs parallel to the Cherry Creek, and connects downtown with the Cherry Creek shopping area.

Rush hour comes early in Denver. Assuming all goes well, the highways have cleared by 9 AM, and the evening rush hour starts as early as 3:30 PM. As mentioned, the Mouse-trap is perhaps the most congested intersection, but traffic also runs heavy southbound on I-25 in the evening from downtown to the Tech Center. It's not quite Los Angeles, but it's threatening to be.

There are HOV (high-occupancy vehicle) lanes set up to encourage carpooling on several of Denver's major commuter routes, including S. Santa Fe Drive, eastbound U.S. Highway 36 and I-25 north of downtown. Watch for them and use them, they'll save you 15 to 20 minutes of stop-and-go in rush hours. To use these lanes, you must have at least two occupants per vehicle.

Denver's notorious "brown cloud" has prompted much hand-wringing about auto exhaust pollution. The pollution is worse in winter when temperature inversions clamp down on the city. A program called Clean Air Colorado monitors air quality between November and April of each year and declares voluntary "no drive" days when things look particularly bad. (On these high-pollution days, woodburning is banned.) News programs regularly broadcast the status, or you can call the Air-Quality Advisory Line, (303) 758-4848.

Parking is tight but not impossible downtown and much cheaper than in other big cities. Options for drivers are on-street meters and parking lots. Bring coins and small bills; you'll need to spend anywhere from $4 to $8 for an afternoon shopping or touring spree.

Public Transportation

Regional Transportation District
1600 Blake St. • (303) 299-6000

The Regional Transportation District, RTD, runs buses throughout the city and suburbs, and a light-rail leg in the downtown area.

INSIDERS' TIP

Ski traffic on I-70 has become a major problem, one that is predicted to worsen as the population grows. Prepare for the worst when day skiing: a trip from Denver to Breckenridge that used to take an hour and a half can take up to three hours during peak times and days.

Light Rail — Light rail runs along a central corridor (the Metro Area Connection, or MAC) from 30th Avenue and Downing Street through Five Points neighborhood, downtown Denver, the Auraria campus and then along railroad right-of-way to the Gates Rubber Plant at I-25 and Broadway. The 5.3-mile route includes 14 stations and connects with bus routes to the south at the I-25/Broadway station. Fares are the same as for local buses: $1.25 during peak times and 75¢ at off-peak times. The next extension of light rail will be from the I-25 and Broadway station, south along Santa Fe Drive to Mineral Avenue in Littleton. Completion is expected in July of 2000. The 8.7-mile line will include five stations and several bus route feeder connections.

Buses — RTD runs local, express and regional bus service. Local buses operate on many routes downtown and cost $1.25 during peak times, 75¢ at off-peak times. Express routes travel longer distances without as many stops; the basic fare is $2. Regional routes run to Boulder and other outlying areas; fare is $3. The regional buses are comfortably upholstered, with reclining seats and air-conditioning. In all cases, exact change is required. Tokens, ticket books and monthly passes are available at supermarkets, and many discounts apply (for senior citizens, students and the disabled). RTD offers a $3 day pass, good for unlimited travel on all local bus routes and light rail. It can be purchased at Market Street, the Civic Center Bus Terminal on Broadway and on the Cultural Connection Trolley. For schedule and route information, call (303) 299-6000, or stop in at the Market Street Station at 16th and Market streets.

RTD's Downtown Express service benefits commuters who live north of downtown. Two-way bus lanes run along the middle of I-25 from 58th Avenue to the downtown Market Street Station on a newly completed extension of the 16th Street Mall that runs past Union Station. In September 1995 the lanes were extended as far north as 70th Street, and carpools of two or more persons (in addition to buses) are now allowed to use the lanes.

For information about public transportation to and from the airport, see the airport sections later in this chapter. RTD also provides transportation to professional football and baseball games; check our Spectator Sports chapter, or call (303) 299-6000 for details.

Taxis

Generally, you don't just wave down a cruising taxi on a Greater Denver street, although it's possible downtown; you usually call ahead. In fact, it's a good idea to call 30 minutes ahead of time, especially on weekend nights. Five taxi companies serve Greater Denver and will take you out of the city if you wish, but it gets expensive. All taxi services provide rides to and from DIA for around $35.

Metro Taxi, (303) 333-3333, charges a $1.60 entry fee and $1.60 a mile.

Zone Cab, (303) 444-8888, charges $1.20 to enter and $1.40 a mile.

Yellow Cab, (303) 777-7777, charges $1.40 to enter, and $1.40 a mile.

American Cab, (303) 321-5555, is $1.40 to enter and $1.40 a mile.

Freedom Cab, (303) 297-8200, is $1.40 to enter and $1.40 a mile.

Leaving Town: Trains and Buses

Trains

Union Station
1701 Wynkoop St. • (303) 534-2812

Like many cities in the West and Midwest, Denver has a Union Station that dates back to the 19th century and used to be much busier than it is now. Among the east-west trains that still run through Denver is the famous *California Zephyr*, which travels an amazingly scenic route across the Continental Divide and through Glenwood Canyon on its way to Salt Lake City and, eventually, Oakland, California. In the winter, a ski train makes the round trip to Winter Park; see our Ski Country chapter for details. Union Station is in Lower Downtown at Wynkoop and 17th streets. For Amtrak information, call (800) USA-RAIL. For recorded

Art at the Airport

As one of the largest public construction projects in recent years, with an original budget of more than $3.2 billion, Denver International Airport had a correspondingly large amount of money to spend on art. That's because Denver, like so many other cities, has a percent-for-art ordinance that specifies that an amount equal to 1 percent of the total costs of new city construction be set aside for art at the site. This added up to about $7.5 million worth of art commissions divided among 25 projects.

Close-up

That sounds like a lot of money and a lot of art — and it is — but DIA is so big that the art still can seem tucked away. It's an airport, not a museum, and nobody would ever mistake the two. Still, a traveler is unlikely to pass through DIA without at least noticing some of the art. The main areas to look for art are in the center and wings of each concourse, along the underground train passages and throughout the main terminal.

Here are a few of our favorites pieces:

A 30-foot-high fiberglass blue mustang is the first piece of art people see as they come into the airport via Peña Boulevard. Made by well-known New Mexico artist Luis Jiminez, the rearing horse has eyes that shoot out laser-like beams of red light.

Near the carousels in the baggage claim area, check out the two whimsical suitcase gargoyles by Terry Allen. They go by the name "Notre Denver."

Also in the baggage claim area are two colorful murals painted by Denver artist Leo Tanguma, a Chicano activist-artist who likes to involve the community in creating his murals.

Across the main terminal from Tanguma's murals is Gary Sweeney's "America, Why I Love Her," two big photomural maps of the United States with the artist's small framed snapshots of odd bits of Americana (ever seen the Frog Fantasies Museum in Eureka Springs, Arkansas?) tacked onto the appropriate locations. Sweeney used to work as a baggage handler for Continental Airlines. On Denver's spot on the map, he included a little sign that says: "You are here . . . but your luggage is in Spokane." Needless to say, not everybody was amused, especially when glitches in the automated baggage system caused multiple delays in the airport opening date.

— continued on next page

Photo: Daily Camera

Denver International Airport opened February 28, 1995.

On the balustrade at the top of the escalators that connect Level 5 and Level 6 in the main terminal, are 28 glossy, vibrant ceramic vases by internationally known ceramicist Betty Woodman. Although Woodman has exhibited widely in the United States and Europe, this was her first public commission.

One of our favorite pieces is the interior garden created by Michael Singer in Concourse C. These mossy ruins are visible from below as you exit the train and from above in the concourse.

Artists have worked on the floors of DIA in several places, including the main terminal and Concourse B, so if you watch where you're walking, you'll see pictographs, fossils and more inlaid in the terrazzo floor. In the food court areas in Concourse A, you'll notice colorful tile patterns that appear to be abstract — but go up the escalator, take a look from above and you'll see that they form foreshortened figures of people. Barb McKee and Darrell Anderson collaborated on this project.

Finally, on the way out of the airport you may notice a line of rusted farm implements. It's not that there wasn't time to clean up — this is part of an art project created by Sherry Wiggins and Buster Simpson to acknowledge that agriculture was historically one of the primary uses of the land on which DIA was built.

Curious passersby can get a brochure that identifies and locates the art at DIA in the information booths in the main terminal and in concourses A and C.

information about Amtrak departures and arrivals in Denver, call the Denver Amtrak ticket office, (303) 534-2812.

Buses

Greyhound Bus Terminal
1055 19th St. • (303) 293-6555, (800) 231-2222

The Denver terminus for Greyhound and other private bus lines is at 20th and Curtis streets, only a few blocks away from RTD's Market Street Station. Generally, RTD provides bus service to points less than an hour away, such as Boulder and Longmont. See the section on public transportation in this chapter. Longer trips, including trips to Fort Collins and the mountains, originate at the 20th and Curtis station. Because both stations are downtown, make sure you know whether someone is talking about the RTD Market Street Station or the Greyhound station. For Greyhound fare and schedule information, call one of numbers above. As seems to always be the case with big-city bus terminals, this one is not in the

nicest part of town. There's no reason to avoid it; just be alert.

Airports

Denver International Airport
8500 Peña Blvd. • (303) 342-2000

Is there anybody out there who hasn't heard about Denver International Airport and can't recite at least one joke about the baggage system or what DIA stands for? Its postponed opening dates (four, before it opened on February 28, 1995), distance from downtown (24 miles) and escalating price tag ($4.9 billion is a modest estimate) generated no respect from the rest of the nation. Denverites are, however, learning to live with it, and some claim to love it. DIA is larger than Dallas-Fort Worth Airport and Chicago's O'Hare Airport combined, extending over an area of 53 square miles. It is the first major U.S. airport to be built from the ground up in nearly 20 years. DIA's five runways can land three aircraft at once using state-of-the-art radar, an improve-

Denver's infamous Mousetrap, I-70 and I-25 north of downtown, has been redesigned, but is still tricky to navigate.

Photo: Daily Camera/Lourie Zipf

ment over Stapleton International Airport, which closed for business when DIA opened.

RTD still uses Stapleton as a transfer center for skyRide, its service to DIA, and skyRide passengers can park at Stapleton for free. The remainder of Stapleton's 4,700 acres will likely be developed as some kind of commercial mix, with an urban park component, but all that's still up in the air.

DIA is situated to the north and east of Denver and is accessed via Peña Boulevard. Peña Boulevard can be reached via Exit 284 off I-70. Travelers from the north can get to the new airport by taking 104th Avenue or 120th Avenue to Tower Road and then driving south to Peña Boulevard. There are numerous stoplights on this route, however.

If you're dropping someone off or picking someone up, there is no charge for the first 70 minutes you spend after passing the DIA toll booth, although there have been proposals to change that, so be aware. After that, charges for short-term parking run from $2 an hour, up to a maximum of $10. Long-term parking costs $5 a day in the uncovered lot or $10 a day in the covered lot.

You could let RTD do the driving. skyRide operates five major routes, from Boulder along U.S. Highway 36 to Stapleton and DIA (Route AB); from Cold Spring Park-n-Ride in Lakewood through downtown to Stapleton and DIA (Route AF); from Stapleton and Montbello to DIA (Route AS); between Highlands Ranch and the Denver Tech Center to DIA (Route AT); and from Northwest Jefferson and Adams counties (Route AA). One-way fare for the sub-

urban routes is $8; from downtown, $6; and from Stapleton, $4. skyRide passengers can park their cars at Stapleton for free. For skyRide information, call RTD at (303) 299-6000.

DIA is a handsome airport, with a dramatic tented roof of Teflon-coated fiberglass fashioned into 34 peaks symbolizing the Rocky Mountains. From a distance, the roof also looks like an encampment of tepees, a nod to the site's historical usage as American Indians' migratory land. Inside, many surfaces are brushed steel, and $7.5 million worth of commissioned art adorns the floors, walls and ceilings (see our close-up in this chapter for a fuller description of the art).

DIA has three concourses and a main terminal, all of which are connected by underground trains. There is also a pedestrian bridge between Concourse A and the main terminal that provides a good view of the airfield.

Travelers should appreciate DIA's retail shops and restaurants, which, by the terms of their concession contracts, are prevented from charging more than 10 percent above what comparable prices are elsewhere in Denver. Also, there are more brand-name stores and food outlets than in Stapleton. Benjamin Books, with branches in all concourses, has a fine selection of hardcover and paperback books that's far superior to the usual newsstand fare.

Ground transportation from DIA into Greater Denver is plentiful. Taxis can be hailed outside the baggage claim area and cost around $40 to downtown, more if you're going farther (see the taxi section in this chapter). Shuttle buses are provided by many major hotels, so check

with your hotel. Otherwise, there are 364 "commuter" services operating out of DIA. Call (303) 342-4059, and you will be connected with the one right for you. You must have a destination in order to get a price quote, but DIA to downtown will cost around $15. Out of Colorado, you can call (800) AIR-2-DEN to make arrangements ahead of time.

Pick any rental car service, and it is available at DIA. Rental car counters are near baggage claim, and there are signs leading you to them. Rental agents recommend making arrangements before you arrive, as many agencies run out of cars during peak times.

Advantage Rent-A-Car, (303) 342-0992
Avis, (303) 342-5500
Budget, (303) 341-2277
Dollar, (303) 342-9099
Enterprise, (303) 342-7350
Hertz, (303) 342-3800
National, (303) 342-0717
Payless Car Rental, (303) 342-9444
Thrifty, (303) 342-9400

Colorado Springs Airport
7770 Drennan Rd., Colorado Springs • (719) 591-1293

We've included the Colorado Springs airport because of the potential money-saving deals. Many Greater Denverites opt to fly in or out of the Springs because fares have been as much as 50 percent lower into and out of this airport about 90 miles south of Denver. The best thing to do is to check with your travel agent. Shuttle service is available to a variety of locations in the Denver area for around $30 to $40. Call (719) 597-4682 for shuttle information.

Centennial Airport
7800 S. Peoria St., Englewood • (303) 790-0598

This suburban airport southeast of Denver is among the busiest general aviation airports in the country. It features three lighted runways, no landing fees and an instrument landing system for bad weather. Two full-service fixed-base operators are on hand for fueling. Ground transportation is limited to taxis and crew cars for corporate pilots.

Accommodations

Greater Denver is a community of travelers, those who traveled here to live, those who travel here for vacations and, increasingly, those who travel here on business. It's a popular spot for conventions, and it's one of those places where the residents seldom have any trouble convincing people from other states to come and visit.

The appetites of travelers for good accommodations are well-matched by more than 16,000 hotel and motel rooms in the Denver area. Whether your tastes tend toward the magnificent or the humble, you'll find plenty of choices. One thing you might note if you're considering staying downtown: all downtown hotels underwent complete renovations in 1997, not coincidentally before the Summit of the Eight, so your downtown choices are sure to be updated, modern and generally pleasant.

In its infancy stage is a new convention center hotel, planned across the street from the existing Colorado Convention Center. It isn't likely to be built in 1999, but once done will serve the throngs that meet downtown at the center.

One good general source of hotel information is the Colorado Hotel and Lodging Association Inc. It has a Colorado Accommodations Guide that you can get by writing them at 999 18th Street, Denver 80202, or by calling their Colorado service line, (800) COLORADO. You can also get information on availability and make reservations at hotels anywhere in the state by calling (800) 777-6880.

Lodging prices in the mountain resorts show amazing bargains in the off-seasons of spring and fall, but Denver hotels, tending to be less vacation- and more commerce-oriented, don't show that much variation year round. As commercial hotels, however, they do tend to give much better rates on weekends than during the week, which is, of course, a boon for the working person who wants a weekend getaway.

Price Code

Our listings rate hotels according to a three-symbol price key, representing average room cost per night during the week for a double occupancy.

$	Less than $80
$$	$81 to $120
$$$	More than $120

The average room rate is not what you'll pay all the time, of course. Most hotels have a wide range of rates on any specific day, and, in addition to good weekend rates, most offer special package deals. Romantic weekend packages are popular with hotels, often lumping together such things as tickets and a limousine ride to a show, carriage rides or dinner at a local fine restaurant into a single price.

At the more moderately priced downtown hotels, you might want to check and see what kind of conventions they have going. Nothing is more disruptive to a vacation than lying down for a good night's sleep only to discover there are 500 high school debaters at a regional competition in the same hotel, and it sounds like they are all in the room next door.

The two biggest sources of hotel bookings are business, including conventions, and tourism. Business travelers stay in the greatest numbers at hotels in downtown Denver, the Denver Tech Center to the southeast and points in between. Tourists will generally stay anywhere they can get a good price, but near downtown is the preferred location for seeing the sights of Denver.

If you're interested in seeing Rocky Mountain National Park and want Denver to be part of your trip, choose from the many lodgings on Denver's northwest quadrant. The near-east side of Denver is the most convenient place to stay if you're visiting the Denver Museum of Natural History, Colorado's second-most popular attraction. Lodgings on the west side of Denver provide the best access to Golden, the home of the Coors Brewery. The west side also allows for fast access to downtown and makes for a speedy mountain getaway via I-70. Sporting events are another big attraction, and the downtown or the near-west side are prime lodging locations for ready access to the Colorado Rockies at Coors Field or the Denver Broncos at Mile High Stadium.

Big news for Denver is that hotels are finally going up around Denver International Airport. In fact, one Insider says it looks like someone waters the soil along Peña Boulevard at night since on any given day you can see new construction popping up. The first hotel opened in January of 1996 — a Fairfield Inn by Marriott, part of an eventual $1 billion Denver International Business Center being constructed along Tower Road between 64th and 72nd avenues, just a few miles from the terminal.

According to the Metro Convention and Visitors Bureau, the number of tourists to Denver who stayed overnight continues to climb — from 5.9 million in 1996 to 6.4 million in 1997. And that doesn't count business travelers. Add an additional 2.4 million business visitors, and Greater Denver hosted 8.8 million people in 1997. All of that adds up to some big money. In 1997, those 8.8 million overnight visitors spent $2.1 billion dollars, making tourism the second largest industry in the city, after manufacturing. Statewide, 25.1 million pleasure and business travelers pumped $7.1 billion into the economy in 1997.

www.insiders.com

See this and many other **Insiders' Guide®** destinations online.

Visit us today!

Though we get more tourists in the summer, skiers are bigger spenders. On the other hand, skiers do most of their spending in the mountains, tending to hop the first rental car or resort shuttle they can catch out of town. So for the skiers, for attendees at the many conferences held at mountain resort areas and for all those who want a place to stay in the mountains in the summer, we need to point out that you don't have to do much touch-tone punching to find lodgings.

Besides calling the toll-free reservations number listed above for the Colorado Hotel and Lodging Association, you can call a central reservations number at every major resort for help with prices and availability. See the Ski Country chapter in this book. Also consult the white pages of the Denver phone book.

Hotels in the southeastern part of Greater Denver, especially around the Denver Tech Center area, seem far from the new Denver International Airport northeast of the city. But they're actually closer in terms of time and traffic than many more central areas, thanks to I-225 that runs up the east side of the metro area to connect with I-70. Hotels in that area are also closer than it would seem to the mountains via I-70, thanks to C-470, the completed southwest quadrant of Denver's future beltway. C-470 offers a low-traffic highway across the south side of Greater Denver, curving up along the edge of the Foothills to meet I-70 west near Golden. It's a faster and less nerve-wracking route than you would otherwise take from the southern half of Greater Denver, which re-

INSIDERS' TIP

File this one under ancient secrets of the Brown Palace Hotel. The Navarre Building, 1727 Tremont Place, across the street from the Brown Palace, was built in 1890 as the Brinker Collegiate Institution, the first coeducational college west of the Missouri River. Nine years later, it was converted into the Hotel Richelieu, the city's most elegant gambling house and brothel. In its basement, you can still see rails disappearing into the wall where rail carts once traveled a tunnel beneath Tremont Place, delivering fine foods from the Brown Palace kitchens. Legend has it that these carts also delivered Brown Palace patrons too discreet to be seen above ground entering and leaving the Hotel Richelieu.

quires you to travel I-25 through the most congested parts of the city before you reach I-70.

A lot of hotels have free continental breakfast, free transportation, free newspapers delivered to your door, free attached parking, free or discounted access to a nearby athletic club. In most of our listings, we haven't detailed all the freebies, but do make a point of asking when you check in. Sometimes they may forget to tell you that you don't need to buy breakfast in the morning.

All hotels, bed and breakfasts, and hostels in this chapter accept credit cards.

One fact that you may not notice in looking for a hotel, but of which you should be aware to save yourself confusion and possible grief, is that many Englewood addresses are not in Englewood. They actually are in unincorporated parts of Arapahoe County, which includes Englewood, and therefore have an Englewood mailing address. We've noted this up-front in each such listing.

Hotels

Denver

Adam's Mark Denver Hotel
$$$ • 1550 Court Pl. • (303) 893-3333

A complete 1997 renovation of The Adam's Mark expanded this downtown property to more than 1,200 rooms and placed it among the 25 largest hotels in the nation. The concierge level is the top two floors of the hotel and offers panoramic views of the city. The Concorde Club, exclusively used by guests, is a central area with seating for up to 75 where there's daily continental breakfast, afternoon tea, hors d'oeuvres and a nightly dessert service. Every room in the hotel is equipped with work space, and the phones have speed dial, speaker action and dataports. The hotel has more than 125,000 square feet of meeting space, three restaurants, two bars and a nightclub with live entertainment nightly, a florist, a gift shop, a business center, a beauty salon and barber shop. There's also a fitness center with steam room, exercise equipment, an outdoor heated pool and a sundeck. It's on the 16th Street Mall a block away from the Denver

Civic Center, four blocks from the Colorado Convention Center and a few blocks from Denver Pavilions Shopping Center.

Best Western Executive Hotel
$ • 4411 Peoria St. • (303) 373-5730

Originally built to serve the old Stapleton Airport (although not very close to Stapleton), Best Western Executive now serves Denver International. It capitalized on its serendipitous proximity to DIA with a $4 million sprucing up. It now has 200 rooms, each featuring work areas and small sitting areas. It operates the Cockpit Grill restaurant, an outdoor courtyard pool and a fitness center.

Best Western Landmark Hotel
$ • 455 S. Colorado Blvd. • (303) 388-5561

This is Best Western's most central hotel, within walking distance of the Cherry Creek Shopping Center (about a mile away). It was completely redecorated in 1997 and now houses 280 rooms, a restaurant, meeting space for 600, an attractive indoor pool and hot tub with skylights and a poolside lounge.

Brown Palace Hotel
$$$ • 321 17th St. • (303) 297-3111

This is Denver's most famous hotel, and deservedly so. If you want a central downtown location, prestige accommodations and a historic experience all in one, you can't do better than the Brown Palace. The list of celebs and potentates who have stayed here since Henry C. Brown opened the doors in 1892 includes every U.S. president since Teddy Roosevelt, except for Jimmy Carter; the Beatles and Elvis Presley; British royalty; kings from Sweden and Romania; Japan's emperor; and entertainment industry names ranging from Lionel Barrrymore to Bruce Willis. Flo Ziegfield wanted to stay there but they wouldn't let him bring his dog in, so he stormed off in a huff.

When the Brown Palace opened, it represented the state of the Victorian art in Italian Renaissance hotel design, with a sunlit, eight-story atrium lobby and tiers of balconies above white onyx walls. It has 230 rooms and 25 suites, more than 13,000 square feet of meeting space; an elegant dining room; an award-winning restaurant, The Palace Arms (described in our Restaurants chapter); a tavern; a lounge and, once again, a central location at the head of 17th Street.

The Burnsley
$$ • 1000 Grant St. • (303) 830-1000

Equipped for and specializing in the extended stay, the Burnsley also compares with the finest Denver hotels in its offering for even the one-night visitor. All the rooms are apartment-style suites, and each tastefully furnished unit has a fully equipped kitchen, separate living room, dining area and bedroom with king-size bed. The Burnsley also has an on-site, self-serve business center and outdoor pool, as well as complimentary passes to a nearby fitness center. In case you don't want to cook in your kitchen, there's also a restaurant. There's a complimentary buffet breakfast, happy hour and parking. We've put the $$ symbol on this entry because it costs between $99 and $145 per night for stays of one to seven days, but as an extended-stay hotel it costs more like $85 per night when you're there for 30 days or more.

The Cambridge
$$ • 1560 Sherman St. • (303) 831-1252

On the upslope of Capitol Hill just two blocks from the head of 17th Street, "the Wall Street of the Rockies," the restaurant, lounge and 27 individually decorated suites of this hotel have an atmosphere of senior executive elegance. It bills itself as "Denver's Personal Hotel." It's an exclusive, fine European sort of place, with complimentary continental breakfast and newspaper.

Cherry Creek Inn
$$ • 60 S. Colorado Blvd. • (303) 757-3341

Although located on a busy boulevard, this inn has one of Denver's nicer locations on the Cherry Creek greenbelt and near the Cherry Creek shopping/arts/dining area. It's something of a business-traveler hotel, emphasiz-

ing desks in the rooms and a business center that can help with such things as laptop computers, faxes and aid in preparing presentations for the 10,000 square feet of meeting/social space. It has a heated outdoor pool, restaurant, gift and sundry store and beauty shop as well as complimentary passes to a nearby health club.

Comfort Inn Downtown Denver
$ • 401 17th St. • (303) 296-0400

You can see the big yellow letters, "Comfort Inn," high on the side of this 229-room downtown hotel. Although it's an economy hotel, it's connected by a skywalk across Tremont Place to the Brown Palace Hotel, one of Denver's luxury inns. That means the Comfort Inn can offer as amenities the restaurants, lounges, meeting spaces and elegant lobby of the Brown Palace.

The Comfort Inn is near the head of 17th Street, where the State Capitol and Civic Center and Denver Art Museum are a short walk away, and where you can hop one of the free shuttles on the 16th Street Mall to Larimer Square and Lower Downtown.

Courtyard by Marriott
$$ • 7415 E. 41st Ave. • (303) 333-3303

Aside from the trademark gazebo by the indoor pool in the courtyard, the Courtyards by Marriott are the basic upscale hotels for the discerning business traveler. Positioned off I-70 on Denver's northeast side, it is one mile from the old Stapleton International Airport and 17 miles from the new Denver International Airport.

Courtyard by Marriott
$$ • 6901 Tower Road • (303) 333-0300

Billing itself as one of the closest hotels to DIA, this Courtyard property also features a full-service restaurant and bar. One important distinction for all-night travelers: room service ends at 9:30 PM, so late night dinner is out.

INSIDERS' TIP

Many of the hotels near Denver International Airport offer a convenient low-cost shuttle to and from. Check with the reservation desk for details.

Denver Marriott City Center
$$ • 1701 California St.
• (303) 297-1300

Marriott's flagship hotel in the city, the Denver Marriott City Center lies in the thick of downtown activities. Within a block of 17th Street, less than two blocks from the 16th Street Mall and less than four blocks from the Colorado Convention Center, it has prestige accommodations in 612 rooms. The fitness center has an indoor pool, exercise room, whirlpool and sauna. The hotel is a big meeting center, with more than 25,000 square feet of space.

Denver Marriott Southeast
$$ • I-25 at Hampden Ave.
• (303) 758-7000

The Denver Marriott Southeast is about halfway between downtown Denver and the Denver Tech Center. It's a big place, with 595 guest rooms and nearly 16,000 square feet of meeting space. Inside the hotel, there are two restaurants and a sports bar, indoor and outdoor pools, a hydrotherapy pool and an exercise room. You've got the Wellshire Municipal Golf Course a little more than a mile west and a lot of theaters and restaurants within a couple of miles.

Denver Marriott Tech Center
$$$ • 4900 S. Syracuse St.
• (303) 779-1100

On the edge of the City of Denver's farthest southeast corner, and right off I-25, this hotel is well-named for its access to the Denver Tech Center area. There are good views of the mountains here. Recreational facilities include not only a workout room, indoor and outdoor pools, a sauna, a steam room and a whirlpool, but also racquetball and handball courts, massage and tanning beds. The hotel has 625 rooms, more than 35,000 square feet of meeting space, three restaurants and a deli.

Doubletree Hotel Denver
$$$ • 3203 Quebec St. • (303) 321-3333

One of the finer "airport hotels," the Doubletree is just off I-70 at near the old Stapleton International Airport and offers ready access to the new Denver International Airport as well (via free shuttle). Until June 1998, it was known as the Red Lion Hotel. It has an outdoor hot tub, an indoor pool and exercise equipment for the guests in its 574 rooms. As with other large hotels, it's a major meeting venue with 26,000 square feet of space as well as two restaurants, a cafe and a lounge.

Drury Inn Denver Airport
$ • 4400 Peoria St. • (303) 373-1983

A well-situated inn for the price-conscious traveler, the Drury Inn is off I-70 between the old Stapleton International Airport and the new Denver International Airport. A free breakfast bar and evening cocktails and snacks are available in the lobby Monday through Thursday. This hotel has a heated outdoor pool and meeting rooms. A renovation was completed in 1998.

Embassy Suites Denver Southeast
$$ • 7525 E. Hampden Ave.
• (303) 696-6644

Of four Embassy Suites hotels in Greater Denver, this one is near the intersection of Hampden Avenue and I-25 — just 2 miles from DTC with fast access to downtown as well. Each suite has a living room as well as a bedroom, and guests can enjoy exercise facilities, an indoor pool, banquet facilities and free cooked-to-order breakfast in the atrium.

Embassy Suites Hotel Downtown
$$$ • 1881 Curtis St. • (303) 297-8888

This fine, big beauty of a hotel is Embassy Suites' downtown flagship. It's a little more than two blocks from the 16th Street Mall and all its attractions. It's also close to the pubs and shops and galleries of Lower Downtown. The hotel has 337 suites with one or two bedrooms and a living room and also has 193 furnished apartments for longer stays. The hotel has an outdoor swimming pool. A highlight of the hotel is its Athletic Club at Denver Place.

It costs $10 extra for hotel guests, but it's a 65,000-square-foot, three-tier facility with an indoor swimming pool; racquetball, squash and basketball courts; what the hotel claims is the longest indoor running track in Denver; cardiovascular equipment and circuit training area; aerobic and conditioning classes; and a masseuse. There's also a deli, cafe and restaurant at the hotel.

Embassy Suites–Denver Airport Hotel
$$ • 4444 N. Havana St. • (303) 375-0400

Amid construction of a new generation of airport hotels at the new Denver International Airport, this property closer to old Stapleton offers fine accommodations. Located 12 miles west of the new airport, it is near I-70 for connections west and close to I-225 for connections south. It has 212 suites, a restaurant and lounge, indoor pool, steam room, sauna, whirlpool, exercise equipment, outdoor sundeck, grand ballroom, 12 executive meeting suites, complimentary cooked-to-order breakfast in the atrium and complimentary cocktails and nonalcoholic beverages for two hours every evening.

Executive Tower Inn
$$ • 1405 Curtis St. • (303) 571-0300

Near the Denver Performing Arts Complex and two blocks from the 16th Street Mall and the Colorado Convention Center, the Executive Tower Inn is in a convenient location. Its 336 guest rooms are luxurious. It has two restaurants, a lounge and 22,000 square feet of meeting space. Its Tower Athletic Club is an outstanding exercise and relaxation center. You'll find an Olympic-size indoor swimming pool, steam rooms, saunas, indoor and outdoor jogging tracks, exercise rooms, aerobic classes, a whirlpool and courts for tennis, racquetball, squash and volleyball.

Fairfield Inn By Marriott
$ • 1680 S. Colorado Blvd.
• (303) 691-2223

Just a block north off I-25 on Colorado Boulevard, the Fairfield Inn by Marriott is midway between downtown Denver and the Denver Tech Center. Three miles to the north and west is Cherry Creek. The hotel packs 166 rooms into 10 stories, with three levels of covered parking, an indoor pool, exercise facility and continental breakfast served in the lobby.

Fairfield Inn By Marriott–DIA
$ • 6851 Tower Rd. • (303) 576-9640

Oh joyous day for the business traveler! This was the first DIA airport hotel to open. It was a modest beginning to the ongoing hotel development around DIA, with 161 rooms and a free continental breakfast but no restaurant (although you can dine at the Courtyard by Marriot next door).

Midday and evening food are available in the form of microwavable vending-machine fare. For relaxation, it has a heated pool and Jacuzzi. It's also got a meeting room and van transportation to and from the airport.

The City of Denver is still fiddling with Peña Boulevard intersections though, and it can get confusing out there on the plains. Directions are necessary: Coming south from the airport on Peña Boulevard, you can exit on Tower Road and go south to the hotel (it's about four miles from DIA). Coming north from the city toward the airport take I-70 to the Tower Road exit, and go north for 4.5 miles, where you'll see the hotel on the left.

Four Points Hotel Denver Cherry Creek
$-$$ • 600 S. Colorado Blvd.
• (303) 757-3341, (800) 325-3535

A Sheraton hotel, the Four Points Hotel Denver Cherry Creek features 320 guest rooms, a heated outdoor pool, a full-service restaurant and lounge, and ample meeting and conference space. It's within walking distance of the upscale Cherry Creek Shopping Center and many of Denver's finest restaurants and entertainment venues. Guests enjoy a courtesy shuttle within 5 miles of the hotel, and all rooms feature a mini-refrigerator, coffee maker, hair dryer, and iron and ironing board.

Hampton Inn Denver–Airport/I-70
$ • 4685 Quebec St. • (303) 388-8100

This Hampton Inn offers 138 rooms near the former Stapleton International Airport. At 18 miles from Denver International Airport, it is still convenient when DIA hotels fill up. It offers a complimentary continental buffet breakfast.

Holiday Inn Denver Downtown
$$ • 1450 Glenarm Pl. • (303) 573-1450

This downtown Denver hotel is centrally situated 1½ blocks from the 16th Street Mall and an equal distance from the U.S. Mint. Holiday Inn's city center prestige hotel, it's a 21-story highrise with 389 rooms, a restaurant, lounge, banquet capabilities, conference rooms for up to 500 and an outdoor, rooftop pool open in season.

Holiday Inn
Denver International Airport

$$ • 15500 E. 40th Ave. • (303) 371-9494

The closest Holiday Inn to DIA has 256 guest rooms and 66,000 square feet of meeting space and public areas. Located north of the Chambers Avenue Exit from I-70, almost in the City of Aurora, it also has a restaurant and lounge, indoor pool, whirlpool, sauna and fitness room.

Holiday Inn Denver–North/Coliseum

$ • 4849 Bannock St.
• (303) 292-9500

You'll see it on the west side of I-25 as you drive just north of I-25's intersection with I-70. That intersection is not the most scenic place in the area, but you can't find a better location for immediate access to all four points of the city compass. In addition to 215 rooms and eight two-bedroom suites, they've got an outdoor heated pool with a wading pool for the kiddies, a full-service dining room, a deli and a tavern, Teddy's, that got Channel 7's nod as one of the top seven clubs in Colorado (see our Nightlife chapter).

Holiday Inn–Denver Central

$$ • 4040 Quebec St. • (303) 321-6666

Among one of many hotels near Stapleton that continue to do well, this hotel now serves the new airport and the west side of Denver. It's just off I-70, so there's also fast access to downtown Denver and points west. It has a restaurant, outdoor pool and 4,000 square feet of meeting space.

Holtze Executive Hotel

$$$ • 818 17th St. • (303) 607-9000

One of Downtown Denver's newer hotels, opened in 1995, is a 244-room extended-stay hotel resulting from a $20 million renovation of one of 17th Street's oldest buildings, the American National Bank Building at 17th and Stout streets. The one- and two-bedroom suites, with full kitchen and dining room, go for $129 to $159. Many of the rooms have big windows overlooking 17th Street, while others look into an interior atrium with a rock garden and waterfall beneath skylights. The hotel does not serve meals, but nearby restaurants will deliver meals to guest suites (menus are

in the suites for guest convenience). The Holtze also includes street-level retail including the La Salsa restaurant and Starbucks Coffee.

Hotel Monaco Denver

$$$ • 1717 Champa St.
• (303) 296-1717

Offering guests a "world of hip, high style luxury," Hotel Monaco came on the scene October 1998 in the renovated 1917 Railway Exchange and 1937 Moderne Title buildings. Similar to properties in San Francisco, Seattle, Chicago and Salt Lake City, Hotel Monaco offers 189 rooms decked in plush interiors designed to create a residential feeling. Included are two phone lines with dataport, and CD players. Fourteen of the thirty-two suites contain whirlpool spas. Fifi is welcome here, too, or if you're traveling petless, Hotel Monaco will deliver a goldfish to your room to keep you company. On-site exercise facilities and an Aveda Lifestyle Spa pamper guests.

Howard Johnson Lodge West

$ • 4765 Federal Blvd.
• (303) 433-8441

Off I-70 at Federal, Howard Johnson Lodge West is next to Rocky Mountain Park and Lake, an easy walk from Regis College and $1\frac{1}{2}$ miles from Lakeside Amusement Park. Close to the business areas around I-25 and on the near-west side convenient to downtown, this Howard Johnson has 92 guest rooms, an outdoor pool, a restaurant and cocktail lounge.

Hyatt Regency Denver Downtown

$$$ • 1750 Welton St.
• (303) 295-1234

Looking down from high-rises on the northeastern end of Capitol Hill, the eye is immediately attracted to a large outdoor jogging track and tennis court next to a pool on one of the rooftops in downtown Denver. That's a part of the Hyatt Regency Denver Downtown, which offers guests a "Colorado theme," including a vast Colorado sandstone fireplace in the lobby, a restaurant called "1876" and 25 deluxe suites. In all, the Hyatt has 511 rooms, with 40,000 square feet of meeting space, the previously mentioned rooftop recreational facilities and special rates at one of Denver's best health clubs a block away.

The Tabor Center is also home to the Westin Hotel.

Hyatt Regency Tech Center
$$$ • 7800 E. Tufts Ave.
• (303) 779-1234

The Tech Center Hyatt is an outstanding visual landmark in this part of the Tech Center because it's surrounded by a lot of open ground and because, of course, it's a Hyatt. The landscape is so open around it, you have great views of the Rockies even if you're standing in the parking lot. A majestic 450-room facility, it's designed to give you the sense of being inside a large old Colorado train station. But it doesn't look old at all, and its grand ballroom, four banquet rooms and four meeting rooms make it a favorite meeting place for the business/convention crowd. A rooftop restaurant and lounge makes for scenic dining, and relaxation opportunities include an indoor pool, sauna, hot tub, exercise room and lighted tennis court.

La Quinta Inn–Airport
$ • 3975 Peoria Way • (303) 371-5640

This is one of the hotels that benefited from proximity to Denver International. Located on I-70, west of the intersection with I-225, it's also convenient to the Denver Coliseum and the city of Aurora. It's a typical moderately-price business-traveler hotel. The 112 rooms are attractive but basic affairs with small work tables. You can go for a little extra with "King Plus" rooms with king-size beds, recliners and two telephones, one of which is accessible to a computer. Complimentary airport shuttle is available. The hotel was completely renovated inside and outside in the mid-90s. It has a heated outdoor pool, free continental breakfast and a guest laundry facility.

La Quinta Inn–Central
$ • 3500 Park Ave. W. • (303) 458-1222

Just north of downtown Denver, La Quinta Inn–Central is a three-story hotel of 106 rooms with an outdoor swimming pool and a renovated lobby. A continental breakfast is offered. It's right next to Coors Field, close to Elitch Gardens amusement park, and convenient to downtown, the west side and the sports complexes of Mile High Stadium and McNichols Arena.

La Quinta Inn–South

$ • 1975 S. Colorado Blvd.
• (303) 758-8886

It's nice to find an inexpensive but pleasant place to stay in the central business location of I-25 at South Colorado Boulevard, midway between downtown Denver and the Denver Tech Center. La Quinta Inn–South is such a place, with the dependable La Quinta features of quiet, comfortable rooms with the "King Plus" features mentioned in the entry above, an outdoor heated pool, a continental breakfast and a guest laundry facility. This particular area of Colorado Boulevard also has a lot of mid-range and chain restaurants to choose from.

Loews Giorgio Hotel

$$$ • 4150 E. Mississippi Ave.
• (303) 782-9300

There's enough elegant Italian styling to make your head swim at this 12-story hotel near the intersection of Colorado Boulevard and Mississippi Avenue. Inside the lobby, library, 7,000 square feet of meeting rooms and 200 guest rooms, all you see is custom furnishing, marble, murals, frescoes and continental antiques. The Tuscany Restaurant has exclusively Italian wines. Guests interested in exercise can take advantage of the aerobic center, which has equipment such as exercise bikes and rowing machines.

Oxford Hotel

$$$ • 1600 17th St. • (303) 628-5400

The 81-room Oxford Hotel is in the heart of Lower Downtown's recently renovated redbrick district, one block from Union Station, a block from the fabulous Wynkoop Brewing Company's restaurant, bar, cabaret and billiard parlor; across the street from an antique shop and adjacent to an art gallery. The Oxford was built a year before the Brown Palace Hotel, by the same architect, and was once the preeminent lodging for travelers arriving in Denver by rail. It's not as beautiful as the Brown Palace Hotel, but the surroundings are more historic. The Cruise Room bar contained in the hotel is a popular nightspot; and the Oxford is easy walking distance from the other nightspots of Lower Downtown and Larimer Square. And, it's just three blocks away from the new Coors Field, home of the Colorado Rockies. McCormick's Fish House and Bar, also in the same building, is one of Denver's best places to eat (see our Restaurants chapter). Next door on the other side of the art gallery is the Oxford Club, a very nice health club with barbering and styling available upstairs at the Oxford Aveda Salon.

Quality Inn and Suites

$ • 4950 Quebec St. • (303) 320-0260

Just north of old Stapleton International Airport, this hotel is also a good bet for travelers coming into the new Denver International Airport because I-70 whizzes right past the hotel. DIA is 13 miles away. It has 195 rooms, an outdoor pool, dining and conference center space for 300, and a restaurant that serves dinner only.

Quality Inn Denver South

$$ • 6300 E. Hampden Ave.
• (303) 758-2211

At the intersection of Hampden Avenue and I-25 north of the Denver Tech Center, and less than 2 miles from I-25's intersection with I-225 north toward the airport, the Quality Inn South is well positioned for travel. Besides its 185 guest rooms, restaurant, lounge and banquet facilities, this newly refurbished hotel has an outdoor pool, sauna and hot tub.

Ramada Inn Downtown

$ • 1150 E. Colfax Ave. • (303) 831-7700

East Colfax is not the most scenic street in Denver, but you're in the Capitol Hill area here, and you're about halfway between the city center and the Colfax/University Avenue area. There are some fine restaurants within a few blocks, not to mention the attractions of the

Denver Botanic Gardens and City Park, with the Denver Zoo and Denver Museum of Natural History. The Ramada has 146 rooms at very reasonable prices and a heated outdoor pool with a hot tub.

Ramada Inn Denver Airport
$ • 3737 Quebec St. • (303) 388-6161

An airport-accessible location is the main feature of this Ramada, along with a restaurant, lounge, meeting rooms and 148 guest rooms, including 90 king rooms. There is also a heated outdoor pool and complimentary transportation to Denver International Airport, 17 miles away.

Ramada Mile High Stadium
$$ • 1975 Bryant St. • (303) 433-8331

One of the most convenient hotels to Denver sporting events, this 13-story, circular tower of 167 rooms is separated from McNichols Sports Arena only by Mile High Stadium. And those sports venues are right across I-25 from downtown Denver. The restaurant and lounge is on the 14th floor, with great views of the area, including downtown Denver. The hotel also has an outdoor pool, exercise facilities and more than 2,100 square feet of meeting space.

Red Lion Hotel
See Doubletree Hotel Denver

Regency Hotel
$ • 3900 Elati St. • (303) 458-0808

On the heights across the South Platte River and I-25 from downtown Denver, the Regency is one of the near-west side's visual landmarks, thanks to the spherical spaceframe dome of its Picadilly Rotunda. It's a convention hotel, with 342 rooms and 63,000 square feet of conference space, but the regular Joe and Jane can enjoy its amenities, including restaurant, piano lounge, indoor and outdoor pools, exercise areas and sauna.

Renaissance Denver Hotel
$$$ • 3801 Quebec St. • (303) 399-7500

Formerly the Stouffer Concourse Hotel, this is another hotel that has in the past focused on business from Stapleton International Airport. Now it continues to offer high-end accommodations to air travelers from the new airport as well as people doing business in the north and east sides of Greater Denver. Just south of I-70, it has great connections to downtown Denver and the west. It has 400 guest rooms, three Club Floors with enhanced facilities and service, a restaurant, a health club with spas and indoor and outdoor pools, and more than 25,500 square feet of meeting space. DIA shuttle is $10.

Residence Inn By Marriott–Denver Downtown
$$ • 2777 N. Zuni St. • (303) 458-5318

Residence Inns are equipped as extended-stay accommodations, with per-night prices dropping substantially if you're there more than a week. Each unit has a fully equipped kitchen and living room area; either one-bed studio suites or two-bed, loft-style penthouse suites. This one lies just off Speer Boulevard across the Central Platte Valley and I-25 from downtown Denver. It has a heated outdoor swimming pool, one hot tub and an exercise room. There's a central dining room with complimentary breakfast and dinner, and they'll do your grocery shopping for you for free (you just pay for the groceries). It offers great access to Elitch Gardens and downtown.

Sheraton Four Points Inn
$ • 3535 Quebec St. • (303) 333-7711

Sheraton's bow to the importance of northwest Denver's air-travel corridor, this 196-room hotel off I-70 is a fast, clean, highway-ride away from takeoffs and touchdowns at Denver International Airport. The hotel recently underwent a top to bottom renovation, completed in January 1999. The indoor swimming pool, hot tub and exercise area are in a pleasant two-story space with two walls of windows to the outside. Just outside the glass doors from the pool is an 18,000-square-foot courtyard with gazebo and picnic tables, often used for barbecues and company picnics. The Sheraton also has a restaurant and 7,500 square feet of meeting space. Airport shuttle costs $8.

Stapleton Plaza Hotel and Fitness Center
$$ • 3333 Quebec St. • (303) 321-3500

The full title of this hotel says a good deal

about the health club amenities available. The health club has fitness consultants, aerobics classes, racquetball courts, a heated outdoor pool, a whirlpool, a steam room/sauna and very nice exercise equipment. The hotel's 300 guest rooms are arrayed around a striking, 11-story atrium lobby. Boardrooms are available on each floor, and the hotel has an 18,000-square-foot conference center, a business-services center, a restaurant and a lounge.

Teatro, A Wyndham Grand Heritage Hotel
$$$ • 1100 14th St. • (303) 228-1100

Denver's newest luxury property, Teatro has made grandeur out of the historic Tramway Tower built in 1911. The downtown property caters to the luxury business and upscale leisure market with 116 rooms featuring Asian and European appointments, two phone lines, fax, copier and scanner. The hotel also houses two restaurants by well-known local chef Kevin Taylor, as well as a private wine cellar. Meeting space is limited to less than 2,000 square feet, but does include an executive boardroom with mountain view and a fireplace. Fitness center and 24-hour room service available.

Warwick Hotel
$$$ • 1776 Grant St. • (303) 861-2000

The accommodations shine in this tony hotel on Capitol Hill. All of the 194 rooms have Thomasville furniture. The hotel features a number of romantic and night-on-the-town weekend packages and free car service to downtown and fashionable Cherry Creek. The open-air, rooftop pool is nice, and there are complimentary health club privileges.

Westin Hotel Tabor Center
$$$ • 1672 Lawrence St. • (303) 572-9100

Although the alphabet places this downtown hotel at the bottom of our list, it really deserves to be near the top, if not the first on the list. All downtown hotels can claim a central location, but the Westin is truly central to the best shopping, entertainment and nightlife of downtown Denver. It's on the 16th Street Mall, at the Tabor Center complex shopping mall, and it's a short walk away from the historic buildings, wonderful shops and fine dining of Larimer Square and Lower Downtown

Denver. The hotel itself is palatial, with 420 rooms, including 13 guest suites of up to 1,700 square feet, a great restaurant and lounge, and enough ballroom and meeting space (19,400 square feet, including a 200-seat auditorium) to make it one of the city's preferred gathering spots. The lobby lounge is a great place for people-watching. There's a health club, racquetball courts, an indoor/outdoor pool with a channel that allows you to swim between them, a sauna and a nice hot tub on the western sundeck by the outdoor pool. The swanky Palm restaurant in the hotel is the place to power lunch.

Wyndham Garden Hotel–Denver Southeast
$$ • 1475 S. Colorado Blvd.
• (303) 757-8797

Just north of I-25 on Colorado Boulevard, this hotel offers fast access to downtown and the Denver Tech Center, and it's also in a commercial area with a lot of restaurants and movie theaters an easy walk away. Besides 240 rooms, it has a cafe and lounge on the lobby level. The Skyline Ballroom on the top floor has commanding views of the Front Range.

Adams County

Quality Inn at the Mart
$ • 401 E. 58th Ave. • (303) 297-1717

Though Denver is the mailing address, the Quality Inn at the Mart is actually in a patch of unincorporated Adams County. That's a relatively unimportant distinction, though, because it's on I-25 north of I-70 and well-connected to Denver and its environs. It's also adjacent to the Merchandise Mart, a prime business venue from which the hotel takes its name. It has 161 rooms, a restaurant, a lounge, a balcony on every room above the second floor, an outdoor heated pool, a beauty/barber shop and a post office. They also offer ATM service and an exercise facility.

La Quinta Inn–North
$ • 345 120th Ave. W., Westminster
• (303) 252-9800

When you stay this far north on I-25, you're putting yourself in a position convenient not just to Greater Denver but to the northern attractions as well: Weld County, Fort Collins, Cheyenne, Rocky Mountain National Park via U.S. Highway 36, Big Thompson Canyon via U.S. Highway 34 out of Loveland, etc. Still, the Westminster La Quinta is near to commercial areas and companies, such as the headquarters of Gerry Baby Products.

Rooms are basic but tidy and attractive, and you can opt for a "King Plus" room with a king-size bed, recliner chair and two telephones. One of those phones is a dataport phone, accessible to computer. This is the only La Quinta in Greater Denver with privileges at a nearby health club, and it also has a heated outdoor pool, free continental breakfast and guest laundry facility. Nearby restaurants include Applebee's, Village Inn and Perkins.

Radisson North Denver Graystone Castle
$ • 83 E. 120th Ave., Thornton
• (303) 451-1002

You can't miss this place, because it is in fact a gray stone castle. The medieval theme is carried out in some of the interior decoration, but it's a modern hotel with close to 9,000 square feet of meeting space and 137 rooms. Enjoy controlled access to the "Camelot Level" on the fifth floor, a restaurant, a pub lounge, an indoor heated swimming pool, a hot tub, sauna and an exercise room.

Ramada Limited Denver North
$ • 110 W. 104th Ave., Northglenn
• (303) 451-1234

If you want a Greater Denver address but also ready access to Fort Collins and points north, or to Rocky Mountain National Park, this is a dandy location. And it's still just 10 miles north of downtown Denver. Its 140 rooms have in-room refrigerators. It has a self-service laundry facility on site as well as an on-

site Applebee's restaurant and a free breakfast bar in the lobby. There's a weight room facility and an outdoor swimming pool in an interior courtyard in addition to a special small pool for kids. The hotel has meeting and banquet rooms for up to 150 people. Within walking distance are a shopping mall, night clubs, other restaurants, movie theaters and bowling.

Arapahoe County

AmeriSuites
$$ • 8310 E. Crescent Parkway
• (303) 804-0700
$$ • 9030 Westview Ave., Littleton
• (303) 662-8500
$$ • 16250 W. 40th Ave., Aurora, near DIA • (303) 371-0700

AmeriSuites is new to Denver, although corporate travelers may be familiar with their consistent accommodations and little extras that help make doing business easier. and All three properties are identical, and feature 128 suites with refrigerator, microwave, coffee maker, iron and ironing board, VHS and dataports for computers (some with two phone lines). There also is a business center with computers, Internet access, copiers and faxes. For pleasure, there is an indoor pool, fitness center and continental breakfast.

Courtyard by Marriott
$$ • 6565 S. Boston St., Englewood
• (303) 721-0300

As we warned at the beginning of this chapter, many Englewood mailing addresses are not in Englewood. This is one of them. The Courtyard by Marriott is in Greenwood Village's southeastern tip, near the intersection of I-25 and Arapahoe Road. This Courtyard bills itself as "the hotel designed by business travelers," and that's appropriate for its setting in the Den-

---

INSIDERS' TIP

A few years ago, urban archaeologists went probing to find an underground tunnel that supposedly used to exist between Union Station and the Oxford Hotel. They didn't find the tunnel, but according to local legend, Teddy Roosevelt's aides once used it to whisk him from Union Station to the hotel when they decided he'd had too many spirits to be seen by the public.

Denver's Most Famous Hotel

Quite simply, the Brown Palace — known locally as "The Brown" — is Denver's most famous hotel. Opened on August 12, 1892, it has conducted business every day since — never even stopping to catch its breath during one of its many renovations.

Close-up

It was the brainchild of Henry Brown, a real estate mogul from Ohio, who came to Denver in 1860 and purchased acres of land, including the triangular plot at the corner of Broadway, Tremont and 17th streets, where the hotel stands today. (Not surprisingly, the hotel is also triangular.)

Brown decided Denver needed a grand hotel, and, sparing no expense, he hired Denver architect Frank Edbrooke, who'd also designed the State Capitol. Edbrooke designed the hotel in the Italian Renaissance style. The grand exterior was matched by an equally grand interior. In fact, the lobby boasted the country's first atrium with

balconies rising eight floors above ground. Cast-iron railings with ornate grillwork panels surround each floor. (Two of the grillwork panels are upside down — no one knows if this was an accident or intentional.)

The hotel opened in 1892 with 400 guest rooms that rented for between $1 and $4 a night. It had no restaurants (today there are four), but it did have at least 18 stores (today there are two gift shops, a flower shop and an art gallery).

The hotel has always had its own water supply, using artesian wells that provide water to every faucet in the hotel. The hotel also produces all its own baked goods in a carousel oven that is only one of three in the world. The Brown's Melba toast, served in the restaurants, is considered one of its specialties.

Over the years, The Brown has housed its share of famous guests. President Dwight Eisenhower not only stayed here, he also left a dent in the fireplace molding when his erratic golf ball hit the

The Brown Palace Hotel, built in 1892, is Denver's most famous hotel.

Photo: Brown Palace Hotel

wall. The Beatles stayed in 1964, and the Brown received a slew of applications from young girls to be housekeepers. Even the singer formerly known as Prince spent a few days at the Brown. He requested that the bed be stripped to the frame so that he could place his own water-filled pad on it.

Naturally, a hotel of this caliber has had its share of unusual situations. At one time, pets were allowed in the hotel. One of the first canine visitors was a fox terrier from Philadelphia who'd inherited $50,000 from his owner and on the advice of his veterinarian came to the Rocky Mountains to cure his consumption. The pooch and the daughter of his master, as well as a nursemaid, took a seven-room suite for an indefinite period.

Another wealthy visitor arranged for his dog to be fed on hotel china with silver domes. The pampered canine did, however, have to eat on the sidewalk since his visit came after dogs were prohibited from sleeping in the hotel. Where'd this pup take naps? In a rented limo outside the hotel.

The hotel is still the palace that Henry Brown envisioned. But it doesn't necessarily mean those without deep pockets can't enjoy it. For many locals, taking afternoon tea in the lobby is urbanely sophisticated. Tea and an individual platter of sandwiches and sweets runs around $16.

If you don't want to drop a dime, you can still enjoy the Brown. Free tours are offered every Wednesday and Saturday at 2 PM. Depending on whether it's occupied or not, the Presidential Suite where Eisenhower stayed is on the tour. Even if you don't get to see that room, the tour offers a great anecdotal history of the hotel and a chance to see exactly which two cast-iron panels are upside down. (You can try to figure it out yourself, but chances are you'll fail.)

---

ver Tech Center area. The hotel has large rooms, most with king-size and double rooms and suites with closed-out bedroom and living room area. The hotel offers a minigym, indoor pool and Jacuzzi and, of course, the courtyard with gazebo and barbecue grills. The Courtyard Cafe serves breakfast buffets, and the hotel also has a lounge bar open Sunday through Thursday.

Crystal Inn at DIA
$$ • 330 N. Ouray St. • (303) 340-3800

Opened in 1997 to serve DIA, the Crystal Inn is located in Aurora near the airport. It houses 157 rooms, 16 of which are suites with a living area, refrigerator and microwave; some have Jacuzzis. Amenities include an indoor pool and Jacuzzi, laundry facilities and a fitness area. Breakfast is served daily, and there is free shuttle service to DIA.

Denver Hilton South
$$ • 7801 E. Orchard Rd., Englewood • (303) 779-6161

Again, this hotel is not in Englewood, but in Greenwood Village on the southern border of the Denver Tech Center. It has 302 rooms, a restaurant, a lounge, an exercise room, a pool and sauna, a boardroom, meeting suites and a grand ballroom. This is a very attractive suburban hotel — a feeling of elegance greets you when you enter its polished lobby and see the multi-story, sunlit open spaces of its central lounge.

Doubletree Hotel Denver Southeast
$$ • 13696 E. Iliff Pl., Aurora • (303) 337-2800

On I-225 in Aurora, the Doubletree–Southeast has the best of that side of town and fast connections south toward the Denver Tech Center and north to the airport. The Doubletree–Southeast offers 248 rooms, a restaurant with a very impressive upscale atmosphere as well as cafe, bar, executive conference suites, health club and indoor pool. All the rooms have two double beds or king-size beds.

Embassy Suites
Denver Tech Center
$$ • 10250 E. Costilla Ave., Englewood • (303) 792-0433

Another property in unincorporated Arapahoe County, this hotel is close to the Denver Tech Center, Inverness Business Park and I-25 and a half-block from Southshore Water Amusement Park. It has 236 two-room suites that each include a separate living room with a sofa bed and a dining/work table. The restaurant has Southwestern and traditional cuisine, and you can work your meal off at the fitness center, indoor pool and whirlpool or at a nearby full-service health club.

Hampton Inn Denver/Aurora
$ • 1500 S. Abilene St., Aurora • (303) 369-8400

Serving a central location in the City of Aurora, this hotel is also located along I-225 for fast access north to the Denver International Airport and south to the Denver Tech Center and Colorado Springs. The hotel has 132 rooms with coffee makers, ironing boards and irons. The hotel also provides a free continental breakfast buffet, outdoor swimming pool and conference space.

Hampton Inn Denver/Southeast
$ • 9231 E. Arapahoe Rd., Englewood
• (303) 792-9999

The Hampton Inn Denver–Southeast is in the hotel cluster on the southeastern tip of Greenwood Village, adjacent to the intersection of Arapahoe Road and I-25, south of the Denver Tech Center. The hotel has 152 rooms, an outdoor swimming pool, workout facilities, in-room coffee service, ironing boards and irons in all rooms, and a free continental buffet breakfast. It offers great access to Park Meadows shopping center.

Holiday Inn Denver South/ Centennial Airport
$$ • 7770 S. Peoria St., Englewood
• (303) 790-7770

Located in unincorporated Arapahoe County, this Holiday Inn is conveniently situated at the Centennial Airport, near the Denver Tech Center and Inverness Business Park and on the way to Colorado Springs. It's close to C-470 around the southwest side of Greater Denver and has good connections to Denver International Airport via I-25, I-225 and I-70. This hotel has 119 guest rooms, 50 of which are suites with separate bedrooms and living rooms. It has a cafe and lounge, an outdoor pool, a health club with sauna, a ballroom and six flexible meeting/banquet rooms.

Holiday Inn South Denver
$ • 3200 S. Parker Rd., Aurora
• (303) 695-1700

The Holiday Inn's Parker Road address is right on I-225, connecting north to I-70 and south to I-25. It's also right on the edge of Cherry Creek Reservoir State Recreation Area, in case you can work in some time for swimming, boating or bike riding. There is also a rifle range. The hotel has 479 rooms, a restaurant and special rates at an adjacent fitness center with racquetball courts, exercise equipment, indoor running track, swimming pool and saunas.

The Inverness Hotel and Golf Club
$$$ • 200 Inverness Dr. W., Englewood
• (303) 799-5800

It's not in Englewood but in unincorporated Arapahoe County just west of Centennial Airport. At the intersection of I-25 and County Line Road, one of I-25's last major intersections before it heads south through Douglas County to Colorado Springs, it's centrally located in the "Piedmont Megalopolis," as some are beginning to call the increasingly interconnected Front Range urban landscape. Absolutely stunning from the outside, the Inverness Hotel's high-tech/high-style exterior fits the state-of-the-art conference facilities in the interior, with 33 meeting rooms including auditoriums, conference rooms, boardrooms and breakout rooms with sophisticated audiovisual accommodations built in and aided by audiovisual specialists in a central control room. The hotel was named as "Best Conference Facility" in *Colorado Business Magazine*'s February 1995 "Best of Colorado Business" feature.

You don't have to attend a conference to enjoy the adjoining Inverness Golf Course, home of the Colorado Open. The hotel has its own pro shop as well as a billiards room, three lighted tennis courts, indoor and outdoor pools, saunas, indoor and outdoor whirlpool baths, health club with aerobics studio, exercise circuit and exercise equipment. Guests in the 302 rooms can also enjoy four fine restaurants, including the award-winning, four-diamond The Swan Restaurant.

INSIDERS' TIP

Can't travel without your beloved Fifi? Not problem at the new Hotel Monaco Denver, (303) 296-1717. Or, if you prefer company, the hotel will provide a pet goldfish during our stay.

Denver is the legislative hub of Colorado.

La Quinta Inn–Aurora
$ • 1101 S. Abilene St., Aurora
• (303) 337-0206

Aurora Regional Medical Center is right across I-225 from this centrally located Aurora hotel, and I-225 provides quick access north to the airport and south to the Denver Tech Center, Douglas County and points south. It has a heated outdoor pool and laundry facilities and includes a free continental breakfast and free cable TV. Nearby restaurants include Coco's, Bennigan's, Black-eyed Pea and The Italian Fisherman. Rooms are basic but tidy and attractive, and you can opt for a "King Plus" room with a king-size bed, recliner chair and two telephones, one of which is a dataport phone, accessible to computer.

Radisson Hotel Denver South
$$ • 7007 S. Clinton St., Englewood
• (303) 799-6200

No, it's not in Englewood. It's just off I-25 at the far southeastern tip of Greenwood Village between the Denver Tech Center and Centennial Airport, and near Park Meadows.

It's a good place to stay if your Denver stay includes business or pleasure in Castle Rock or Colorado Springs. It also has great access to shopping at the Castle Rock Factory Outlet stores. Like other big hotels in this burgeoning part of town, it has great views of the mountains, especially from the Plaza Club levels on the ninth and 10th floors, where you have concierge service, complimentary complete breakfast in the morning and cocktails and hors d'oeuvres in the evening. The rooms total 263; the conference center meeting space totals 8,100 square feet. The hotel has a restaurant, lounge, exercise facility, outdoor heated pool and whirlpool.

Residence Inn by Marriott–Denver South
$$ • 6565 S. Yosemite, Englewood
• (303) 740-7177

This hotel is actually on the border of unincorporated Arapahoe County and Greenwood Village in the Denver Tech Center area. That needs to be said for the benefit of those who want to find this tasteful, extended-stay hotel in the Denver Tech Center area. Even the "studio suites" include a fully equipped kitchen. Set in a neighborhood environment, the hotel has an outdoor swimming pool, heated spa and complimentary passes to a nearby fitness club. There also is a fair amount of strip mall shopping, including coffee and bagel shops, nearby.

Jefferson County

Broomfield Guest House
$$ • 9009 W. Jeffco Airport Ave., Broomfield • (303) 469-3900

The Broomfield Guest House could almost be listed in our Bed and Breakfasts section, with its quiet country-inn ambiance, its complimentary breakfast, its "great room" with fireplace and collection of books. Then again, it has amenities similar to those found in a hotel, such as a laundry room, conference and meeting rooms, an on-site catering and special events coordinator and a corporate atmosphere. One might describe it as a "corporate B&B," although it's not just for the business crowd. The great room and patio are good places for wedding-related events as well as corporate cocktail parties. Each separate suite has its own private entrance and fireplace, kitchenette, private bath and king bed. Some have whirlpool baths and separate sitting rooms.

Broomfield Manor Hotel
$ • 570 Hwy. 287, Broomfield • (303) 466-7311

This is our only hotel listing in Boulder County, but Broomfield is also a part of Jefferson County, and the Broomfield Manor Hotel has long been the city's workhorse economy hotel. It has 60 rooms, along with a restaurant, lounge and banquet room. In the same building is a beauty shop, barber shop, nail shop and insurance agency.

Comfort Inn Southwest Denver
$ • 3440 S. Vance St., Lakewood • (303) 989-5500

On the south end of Lakewood, less than a mile from the Foothills Golf Course and just south of U.S. 285 west to C-470 and the mountains, the Comfort Inn is one of the cost-conscious alternatives for lodging in the southwest metro area. Each room has contemporary furnishings and a king-size bed or two queens. Four of the rooms are two-room suites. The hotel has a small fitness center with a rowing machine, exercise bike, stair climber and sit-up bar; an outdoor heated pool with a hot tub; free continental breakfast; and guest laundry and valet service. In 1998, they received a Gold Award, for the fourth year in a row, from Choice Hotels International.

Days Inn Denver West
$ • 15059 W. Colfax Ave., Golden • (303) 277-0200

Another cost-conscious alternative on the west side, this Days Inn sits at a major node of the west side's transportation web. You can go straight west to Golden, hop on I-70 west or east, or jog south to catch U.S. Highway 6 for a fast (unless its morning rush time), no-stoplight run to downtown Denver. This Days Inn has 155 rooms, a restaurant, heated outdoor swimming pool, hot tub and sauna and exercise area and meeting/banquet facilities.

Denver West Marriott
$$ • 1717 Denver West Blvd., Golden • (303) 279-9100

One of the first places people mention when asked about fine accommodations on the far-west side, Denver West Marriott is set in the Denver West Office Park just off I-70 in Golden. Guests in its 307 rooms are 20 minutes from downtown Denver. Only 10 minutes on I-70 west and you'll be in the mountains. It has an indoor and outdoor pool, exercise equipment, saunas, a hydrotherapy pool, restaurant, lounge and 9,000 square feet of meeting/banquet space.

Four Points Denver West
$$ • 137 Union Blvd., Lakewood • (303) 969-9900

On the far western side of Lakewood, between the Denver Federal Center and Red Rocks Community College, the Four Points Denver West, a Sheraton hotel, is a great staging point for business and tourism excursions around the west side of Greater Denver. A straight shot west for a couple of miles on U.S. Highway 6 connects you to I-70. This hotel has 170 rooms, complimentary transportation within a 5-mile radius, a dining room, exercise room, outdoor pool, sauna and whirlpool. New in 1998 are 25-inch televisions in all the rooms, a new phone system that includes dataports and dual lines in business class rooms.

Foothills Corporate Lodging
$ • 420 Corporate Cir., #Q, Golden
• (303) 232-2932, (800) 456-0425

You can't take advantage of the extended-stay accommodations at Foothills unless you commit to at least 7 days, but you get a full apartment for what a room of equivalent quality would cost you at most hotels. More important is that this family-owned company has 15 different lodging sites around the Denver area. Locations range from Highlands Ranch to Broomfield; there are over 125 units in all. You can choose between one-, two- and three-bedroom units. All complexes have outdoor pools. Most have workout rooms, but if yours doesn't, Foothills Corporate Lodging can arrange for local health club memberships.

Hampton Inn Denver–Southwest
$ • 3605 S. Wadsworth Blvd., Lakewood
• (303) 989-6900

South of U.S. Highway 285, on the southern tip of Lakewood where it borders unincorporated Jefferson County, the Hampton Inn Denver–Southwest is convenient to the mountains and to the big employers of southwest and western Jefferson County such as the Denver Federal Center, Martin Marietta, US West, Coors and Manville. It has 148 rooms, an outdoor swimming pool, free continental breakfast, meeting rooms, neighborhood surroundings and the Foothills Golf Course nearby.

La Quinta Inn–Golden
$ • 3301 Youngfield Service Rd., Golden
• (303) 279-5565

This is a great location for access to the mountains on I-70 west or to the business and tourist attractions of Jefferson County. Practically out its front door, 32nd Avenue winds west past the Adolph Coors Co. brewery to the City of Golden. On the other side of I-70, an extensive shopping center has nearly everything you might need, including a Starbucks Coffee shop. The hotel has 129 rooms on three floors and a heated outdoor pool.

La Quinta Inn–Westminster Mall
$ • 8701 Turnpike Dr., Westminster
• (303) 425-9099

Just south of U.S. Highway 36, east of Sheridan Avenue, this hotel puts you in an intermediate location between Denver and Boulder. And Sheridan, of all the north/south thoroughfares on the west side, is one of the fastest moving, so that means a decent connection with I-70 to the south. You're also right next to some of the west side's biggest shopping and entertainment areas along north Sheridan and Wadsworth, including the Westminster Mall Shopping Center on the other side of Sheridan. The hotel has 130 rooms, a heated outdoor pool, continental breakfast and guest laundry facilities. Rooms are basic but tidy and attractive, and you can opt for a "King Plus" room with a king-size bed, recliner chair and two telephones, one of which is a dataport phone, accessible to computer.

Doubletree Hotel Denver/Boulder
$$ • 8773 Yates Dr., Westminster
• (303) 427-4000, (800) 868-4001

Perched on a nice Rocky Mountain vantage point just north of U.S. Highway 36, this is a good hotel for those seeking ready access both to Greater Denver and Boulder County to the northwest. It's a classy place with complimentary continental breakfast, cocktails and hors d'oeuvres served Monday through Friday in the private Summit Club on the concierge floor. In addition to its 180 rooms, including "Jacuzzi suites," it has more than 8,000 square feet of meeting space, a restaurant, a lounge and a very nice whirlpool, sauna, indoor swimming pool and exercise room.

Ramada Inn–Denver West
$ • 7150 W. Colfax Ave., Lakewood
• (303) 238-1251

Formerly known as Denver Lakewood Inn, this is a nice, inexpensive hotel for business and vacation travelers. Just off of two major east-west thoroughfares, W. Colfax Avenue and U.S. Highway 6, and less than 5 miles east of I-70, it's a good location for access to both downtown Denver and the mountains. There's an onsite restaurant, Sammy's, a heated outdoor pool and free coffee 24 hours a day in the lobby. That's about it for amenities, but the 122 rooms were totally remodeled in the summer of 1997.

Sheraton Denver West Hotel & Conference Center
$$ • 360 Union Blvd., Lakewood
• (303) 987-2000

Aimed at the business traveler, with a full-service business center and 18,000 square feet of meeting space in 16 meeting rooms, this 242-room hotel is also one of the nicest places to stay on your vacation. Right off U.S. Highway 6, it's a great staging point for trips to the mountains; it's also in a thriving business and commercial area of western Greater Denver.

The Sheraton has its own restaurant and an in-house health club, weight room, indoor pool and sauna. If you want to go whole hog, the oversized rooms on the concierge floor have whirlpool tubs and other amenities.

Table Mountain Inn
$$ • 1310 Washington Ave., Golden
• (303) 277-9898

The Table Mountain Inn shares an important characteristic with the Westin Hotel Tabor Center in our Denver listings: the alphabet places it at the bottom, but it ranks at the top for the county. First of all, it's very charming with its Santa Fe-style architecture and interiors. Second, its Southwestern-cuisine restaurant, The Mesa Bar & Grill, is not just a hotel restaurant but a westside treasure that people drive from other nearby cities just to enjoy. Third, it's right on the main street of downtown Golden in the midst of the neighborly, small-town atmosphere. It's within walking distance of the Coors Brewery and the Colorado School of Mines to boot. In August 1999, the hotel will expand from 32 rooms to 74 and add a new parking area and weight room.

Bed and Breakfast Inns

There are some who don't care for the bed and breakfast experience; they want a modern room, a pool, a restaurant, a gift shop and a lobby. But others enjoy the charm, personal touch, intimacy and often historic surroundings of a bed and breakfast inn. Greater Denver has such inns that compare with the best anywhere.

In the use of our price-key symbols ($, $$ or $$$), representing double occupancy during the week, we've tried to represent an average price of accommodations for each bed and breakfast inn, but remember that the inns often have a limited number of rooms and have widely varying price ranges.

All of the bed and breakfasts in our listing accept credit cards, and none of them accept pets. None of them will turn away people with children, but in some cases, as indicated, children may be difficult to accommodate due to limits on the number of people allowed in rooms or the inability to add an extra bed to rooms.

Denver

Capitol Hill Mansion
$$$ • 1207 Pennsylvania St.
• (303) 839-5221

All the fineries you expect from a bed and breakfast inn can be found in this mansion of ruby sandstone, along with all the sense of place and history you expect in the historic inn experience. The mansion is on the National Historic Register, having been built in 1891 as one of the last great mansions raised before the silver crash put a temporary damper on local development. It's in an area near the State Capitol, surrounded by ornate historic structures built when Capitol Hill was known as "snob knob." The exterior is a turreted, balconied affair with a grand curved porch. The interiors live up to even the most aristocratic expectations, with crafted, patterned plaster and golden oak paneling opening to a dramatic sweeping staircase with stained and beveled glass windows. The public parlors are inviting, and each room is individually decorated with such touches as brass beds, claw-foot tubs, private balconies, curved-glass windows, high ceilings, fireplaces, oak floors, a solarium and a hand-painted mural. Soothing music, soft lighting and jetted tubs are among the other attractions. There are eight guest rooms in all, each with a private bath, some with whirlpools. Those with kids should know

that Capitol Hill Mansion has only one room in which it allows children younger than 15 years of age.

Castle Marne
$$$ • 1572 Race St. • (303) 331-0621

Victorian architecture with an eccentric flair is the charm of this bed and breakfast on Denver's near-east side, 20 blocks from downtown and an easier and more scenic walk from the Denver Zoo, the Denver Museum of Natural History and the Denver Botanic Gardens. Built in 1889, Castle Marne really looks like a small castle. Its designer was eclectic architect William Lang, who also designed Denver's famous "Unsinkable" Molly Brown House, now a major landmark and tourist attraction. Castle Marne is striking on the outside, stunning on the inside.

Some of the guest rooms have their own Jacuzzi tubs for two. Three of the rooms have private balconies with hot tubs for two. All have furnishings chosen to bring together authentic period antiques, family heirlooms and exacting reproductions to create a mood of tranquil and elegant charm. You can find that same mood in the parlor, a serene retreat of high ceilings and glowing, dark woods and the cherry-paneled dining room. The castle's big visual treasure is what they call their Peacock Window, a circular, stained-glass beauty part-

way up the grand staircase. The castle also has a gift shop, game room, Victorian garden, an airy veranda and a guest office for the business traveler, including computer. Generally, only well-behaved children older than 10 are allowed. Although that is the only restriction on children at Castle Marne, most rooms are subject to a maximum occupancy of two persons per room.

Franklin House
$ • 1620 Franklin St. • (303) 331-9106

You may find fancier bed and breakfasts in Denver, but you won't find one at such inexpensive prices in such a great location. Franklin House's hosts, George and Sharon Bauer, describe it as Denver's only European-style inn. By that they mean that it's nothing fancy, just comfortable rooms with a nice breakfast and homey charm rather than Victorian charm, even though the building itself is an 1890s home. It has eight rooms, a sitting room with a TV, books, music and a backyard patio. The Bauers speak German, Spanish and a little French, although they don't get enough French visitors to keep real sharp on the latter. If you drew a triangle with points at downtown Denver, the Denver Botanic Gardens and City Park, with its Denver Zoo and Denver Museum of Natural History, Franklin House would be just about in the middle of the triangle.

Haus Berlin
$$ • 1651 Emerson St.
• (303) 837-9527, (800) 659-0253

Haus Berlin is an 1892 Victorian townhouse, which has traditionally been known as the Haskell House because it was built for Thomas Haskell, founder of Colorado College in Colorado Springs. It's on the National Historic Register and sits on a tree-lined street surrounded by similar structures. That's about as Victorian as Haus Berlin gets, however, because the interior is mostly northern European furnishings with just a few antiques. Christiana Brown, co-owner and host with her American husband, Dennis Brown, is a native of Berlin. The original paintings and other works of art that decorate Haus Berlin are a mixture picked up by the couple in their European and Latin American travels and during the 12 years they lived in the Virgin Islands. All linens used in the hotel are cotton, and there's a pretty backyard with flower gardens where guests can opt to enjoy their breakfast in the warmer months. Haus Berlin is between downtown and City Park, an easy walk from the Denver Zoo and the Denver Museum of Natural History. It's just a couple of blocks from the medical cluster of Saint Joseph Hospital, Children's Hospital and the Presbyterian/St. Luke's Medical Center. There are also some nice restaurants along the nearby stretch of 17th Street. It's hard to accommodate children here as there are no futons, cots or rollaway beds.

Holiday Chalet
$ • 1820 E. Colfax Ave. • (303) 321-9975

Though each suite has its own kitchen, Holiday Chalet serves a continental breakfast. This Victorian-charm hotel is a restored, three-story brownstone mansion built in 1896 for a prominent Denver jeweler. The present owners represent the third generation of the same family that has served guests here. It's situated for easy walking to the Denver Zoo, the Denver Museum of Natural History and the Denver Botanic Gardens. It's about 10 blocks from downtown.

Lumber Baron Inn
$$$ • 2555 W. 37th Ave. • (303) 477-8205

One of Denver's newer bed and breakfast inns, the Lumber Baron was refurbished and opened for business in the summer of 1994. But it goes way back before that, being an 1890s brick mansion built by John Mouat, a Scottish immigrant who ran a major millwork and construction supply company. He put six different kinds of wood into his house's fancy woodwork. The first two floors have 12-foot ceilings, there's a 2,000-square-foot ballroom on the third floor, and there is space for banquets and event rental. The Lumber Baron has five suites, all of them with Jacuzzis for two. All the suites, as with the entire house and grounds, are pure Victorian elegance. A full breakfast is part of the package.

Merritt House
$$-$$$ • 941 E. 17th Ave. • (303) 861-5230

Four blocks east and three blocks north of the State Capitol, the Merritt House is about as historic as a bed and breakfast can get. It was designed by Frank Edbrooke, the same architect who designed the Brown Palace Hotel, the Oxford Hotel, the Tabor Grande Opera House and a lot of other historic treasures. It's also in the Swallow Hill District, which is on the National Register of Historic Places and is named for its original real-estate developer, not because it was buzzing with swallows. The 1889 Merritt House has 10 guest rooms which, along with the common areas, reflect the elegance of 1880s era. All the rooms, however, have a telephone and cable TV, and some of the private bathrooms include whirlpool Jacuzzis. Otherwise, they have antiquarian furnishings such as queen-size, four-poster beds or brass beds, brass chandeliers, wing-back chairs and Oriental carpets. Full breakfast is included.

Queen Anne Inn Bed & Breakfast
$$ • 2147 Tremont Pl. • (303) 296-6666

The Queen Anne Bed & Breakfast Inn is in a restored area on the edge of downtown: the Clements Historic District, Denver's oldest continuously occupied residential neighborhood. The Queen Anne itself consists of two adjacent Victorian buildings in the Queen-Anne style of architecture, of 1879 and 1886 vintage, both of which are on the National Historic Register. They give you a list of guidebook editors to write to, and that's because they know they're a good bet for favorable review with their elegantly restored interiors, period furnishings, eager service and 14 quaintly homey rooms featuring individual baths, writing desks, piped-in chamber music at your control and fresh flowers. Rooms range from $75 to $175. This inn has been rated one of the best of Denver by *Westword* and among the seven most romantic destinations in Colorado by a local television station. The new Coors Field is also about a 15-minute walk away, which hasn't hurt the bed and breakfast's business.

Victoria Oaks Inn
$ • 1575 Race St. • (303) 355-1818

Guests rate this as a pearl, largely due to its welcoming and gracious owners and homey ambiance. It's a restored 1896 mansion with just nine rooms and a lot of atmospherics such as antiques, leaded-glass windows, original oak woodwork and tile fireplaces. It's nicely located, too, for easy access to some of the finest amenities of Denver's near-east side. Little more than a mile west is the State Capitol, and beyond it, downtown Denver. Less than a mile of pleasant walking can take you to Cheesman Park, City Park and three of Denver's finest attractions: the Denver Botanic Gardens, the Denver Zoo and the Denver Museum of Natural History. Due to some bad experiences with children, the owners prefer not to have them as guests, however they will consider it on a case-by-case basis.

Jefferson County

On Golden Pond
$ • 7831 Eldridge St., Arvada
• (303) 424-2296

"European hospitality and a relaxing blend of country comfort" are promised in this bed and breakfast's brochure. You drive semi-rural roads to a long gravel drive leading up past a horse pasture on the left and goats on the right, through a lane overhung by bushes, trees and flowers, to the entrance. Neighbors are far away, and the 10 acres truly offer a quiet, country atmosphere. There are five rooms, four of which look south on manicured grounds with a duck pond and gazebo. Your host, Kathy Kula, is a native of Germany, and

this is the only accommodation with German speakers on the west side of Greater Denver. But it's great for every nationality, and for some reason they get a lot of British visitors who are in Colorado for the bird-watching. Among the amenities of this location are a hot tub and pool, and you can bicycle and walk the country roads and ride horseback in the Foothills. Breakfast is served on the deck or indoors, and there is a traditional late-afternoon kaffeeklatsch with coffee and pastries. Although the room average is less than $80, there is also the lovely Peacock Room for $120 per night and the Blackbird Room at $100.

The Cliff House Lodge & Cottages
$$$ • 121 Stone St., Morrison
• (303) 697-9732

In the charming town of Morrison amid the red-rock splendor of the Morrison Geological Formation, this bed and breakfast is housed in a sandstone Victorian built in 1873 by Morrison's founder, George Morrison. George built an addition for his quarry miners back around the turn of the century, and his house became a hotel. Now it's a bed and breakfast, although it's really more properly described as a country inn. Only two suites are actually in George's house. The rest are private, separate cottages, where candlelight breakfasts are brought to the cottage door. Special offerings are the honeymoon suites, which include private hot tubs, entertainment centers and woodburning fireplaces. Accommodating children may be difficult here, since the Cliff House does not have futons, cots or rollaway beds.

Antique Rose
$$ • 1422 Washington Ave., Golden
• (303) 277-1893

The Antique Rose Bed & Breakfast Inn has just four rooms in an 1880s Queen Anne Victorian home, with gables, dormers and fishscale and diamond-shaped shingles. Originally the home of Senator and Mrs. Richard Broad Jr., it later became a boarding house for Colorado School of Mines students. It has historic designation and was opened as a bed and breakfast in 1993 and taken over by a new owner in 1996. In the southern end of Golden's historic business district, it is an easy walking distance from Golden's many historic

and tourist attractions. Office services are also available. Children are difficult to accommodate because no room has more than one bed, and there are no cots or rollaways. A full breakfast is served.

Hostels

Hostels are for the truly cost-conscious traveler who is not looking for frills or even a bathroom in the room. If you're traveling on a budget and love an offbeat atmosphere and what might seem like bohemian accommodations to the folks at the Westin and the Hyatt, there's nothing like that special camaraderie that prevails in the hostel environment.

They used to call these things "youth hostels" because older folks tended to think they were OK for kids but declassé for adults, or that they were just plain dives for hippies and the down-and-out. Now, in a more enlightened era, we know that all ages can enjoy the hostel experience. OK, hostels sometimes look like flop houses from the outside, and they're sometimes in seedier parts of town. Then again, some of them are unexpectedly attractive. One thing for sure is they tend to be close to the center of town, with prices that allow you to stay for a week on what would be one

night's price at a reasonably fancy hotel. Our price key, explained in the beginning of the chapter, doesn't really tell you how cheap they are, because prices for the following hostels can be under $10 per night. Denver has several choice venues for the hosteler.

You can get the full scoop on hostels in the Denver area and the rest of Colorado by calling American Youth Hostels–Hostelling International at (202) 783-6161, for anywhere in the United States. There's also a Boulder number, (303) 442-1166, that's good for Colorado hostels. We've listed below the downtown Denver possibilities.

The Hostels listed below all accept major credit cards but no personal checks. There are no age restrictions on occupants, except that people younger than 18 cannot check in without a parent or guardian.

Denver Central YMCA
$ · 25 E. 16th Ave. · (303) 861-8300

The Y is just off the Civic Station bus terminal for the 16th Street Mall, a prime location. The Y has 189 rooms, with no phone and no TV, ranging from a single without a bathroom to a double with a bathroom. One thing about the YMCA is that few hotels can claim a health club that is nearly as extensive as the Y's.

Exercise facilities are free for residents and include an indoor pool, two gyms, two indoor running tracks, a Nautilus center, other exercise equipment and handball and racquetball courts. No alcohol is allowed, and pets aren't welcome either. The rooms are clean, secure and comfortable.

Denver International Youth Hostel
$ • 630 E. 16th Ave.,
• (303) 832-9996

The Denver International Hostel is just six blocks east of Broadway and the edge of the downtown. It's all dormitories, meaning you share bedrooms with other people, but the dormitories are separated into men's and women's sections. How many people share a room? It depends on the night. Bathrooms are down the hall. They have showers, a kitchen you can use and a common room with a TV, library and stereo, balconies, storage and sports equipment. You have to check in between 8 and 10 AM or between 6 and 9 PM, when the office is open. There's no curfew; you get keys to come and go when you please.

Melbourne Hotel & Hostel
$ • 607 22nd St. • (303) 292-6386

An old hotel, the Melbourne is a member of the American Youth Hostel Association. Rooms have sinks and beds. Bathrooms are off the hall. Ten of the 16 rooms in this hotel are not a part of the hostel but simply hotel rooms. The six hostel rooms are dormitories, meaning you share a room with three to five people. Wine and 3.2 beer are allowed, but no hard liquor. The Melbourne is Denver's most child-accommodating hostel. It has four family rooms, each of which has a double bed plus a set of bunk beds.

Hostel of the Rocky Mountains
$ • 1530 Downing St. • (303) 861-7777

One of the newest hostels in the area, this one offers rooms with four beds (36 beds in all), each room having its own bath and shower and kitchen. Every room also has TV with HBO. The location is great, with easy bus access and dozens of restaurants within 1 mile. They also offer bikes for rent, Internet access and tours to mountain locations.

A number of Denver restaurants pride themselves on what they're able to do with buffalo meat.

Restaurants

Dining out, like shopping, is an area in which Greater Denver excels. Lots of hot young chefs are busy in the kitchens here, enough so that their food has collectively earned the name "Rocky Mountain cuisine."

What this means is an emphasis on game and other local products, like trout and lamb. (Colorado has the country's fourth-largest population of lamb and is the country's largest processor of lamb.) Southwestern influences abound; many of the new chefs are liberal in their use of chiles, cilantro, tomatillos and black beans.

Of course, there's plenty of old-fashioned Rocky Mountain cuisine to be had too. A number of restaurants pride themselves on what they're able to do with buffalo meat. Buffalo, along with other game such as elk and pheasant, has long been on the menu at Denver's oldest restaurant, The Buckhorn Exchange. Leaner than beef, buffalo is enjoying a resurgence of popularity nationwide, and Colorado restaurateurs, such as Sam Arnold of The Fort are leading the way. The strong-stomached Denver diner may want to sample Rocky Mountain oysters, which are — how shall we put it? — the testicles of the male buffalo or male cow, sautéed or breaded and deep-fried. Believe us, not everyone eats the stuff.

Getting fresh seafood used to be a problem in Denver, but no more. Pacific Coast fish such as salmon and river fish such as trout are widely available and consistently good. Maine lobster isn't hard to find either, but fans of clams and oysters on the half-shell will have a more difficult (though not impossible) time fulfilling their desire; those are about the only things that Denver restaurants are lacking. Fresh sushi is all the rage and easy to find.

As for ethnicity, Greater Denver counts among its blessings several Ethiopian eateries and topnotch Vietnamese, Japanese, Korean, Mexican, Peruvian and Brazilian restaurants. There are also plenty of California-influenced bistros, especially in the Cherry Creek

Price Code

To give an idea of price, we've used the following symbols. These price codes are based on the average price of two entrees, excluding alcohol, dessert, tax and tip.

$	less than $14
$$	$15 to $22
$$$	$23 to $32
$$$$	$33 and higher

area. Most serve pastas, burgers and pizzas, many made in on-site woodburning ovens.

In this section we've left out chain restaurants such as Chili's and Pizza Hut, not because we have anything against them, but on the assumption that readers already know what to expect at these places. Locally owned chains that operate within the Greater Denver area only are included, as visitors couldn't be expected to know their fare. A national chain may have slipped into the listings here and there, either inadvertently because we didn't know it was one of many, or because to omit it would leave a particular geographic area under-represented. In the case of exceptional merit, we've bent our rules on chains.

As you can imagine, no one book could ever describe all of Greater Denver's restaurants. We've picked out the best and the brightest, as is our mandate throughout this guide. Some are special-occasion places, others are neighborhood joints. Some are widely known local institutions, others much less so. We also tried to be clear about whether it's the food, the ambiance, the crowd, the service or all of the above that makes a place worth a visit. Obviously we don't expect everyone to agree with all our choices, and restaurants are notoriously mutable creatures, apt to get better or worse or go out of business without warning. Hours and days of operation change, too, so we suggest you call before you go. Also, while some restaurants serve continuously, others close between lunch and dinner, so if it's a mid-afternoon bite that you're after, definitely call first.

For dining out with children, take a look at our Kidstuff chapter, where we have described restaurants that cater to kids or places where the entertainment is at least as much of a draw as the food. If you're looking to combine eating with music, or if you're more in the mood for a bar than a restaurant, check our Nightlife chapter.

We've listed restaurants alphabetically by category, based on our experience that Denverites, like most Westerners, are more inclined to drive to a destination than to pick a restaurant on the basis of what's within walking distance. At the end of each listing, however, we've given an indication of location. Downtown restaurants are all within walking (or free shuttle bus) distance of downtown hotels. Restaurants we've described as being central are usually more than a half-mile walk from downtown. Each restaurant is in Denver unless otherwise noted.

Listing by category has its own set of problems, of course. In Denver, it seems that every third restaurant has at least a few Mexican-inspired items on the menu, and steakhouses and seafood restaurants usually cross over into each other's territory. We placed restaurants by their specialty, but if you read the descriptions themselves you'll get a better sense of what else each offers.

Denver is a very casual city and the suburbs even more so. It's possible to eat a $100 dinner in shorts and sandals and not feel like the waiter is looking down at you. But, Denverites generally do dress up for a nice meal, especially at trendy bistros. In general, price is a good guide as to how formal a restaurant is: the more expensive, the more dressed-up the clientele. Consider location, too. At virtually all the restaurants we've listed in West Denver, a person who shows up dressed to the nines is going to feel very much out of place. Another rule of thumb is that restaurants that don't take any credit cards tend to be the most casual and located in neighborhoods that aren't the most fashionable. (This isn't necessarily true of coffeehouses and bakeries, however.)

Most of the restaurants listed in this chapter accept major credit cards; we have specified those that do not.

Unless we've noted otherwise, all restaurants are open for lunch and dinner. Many downtown restaurants serve lunch on weekdays only.

Most Greater Denver restaurants accept local (but not out-of-state) checks. Occasionally a check guarantee card is required, and, of course, there are some restaurants that don't take checks at all. Policies change, so call first if this is important to you.

Also, the nonsmoking movement is strong along Colorado's Front Range (especially in Boulder), and a growing number of restaurants are totally nonsmoking. Once again, if this is an issue for you, it's best to call ahead. Or, you can get a copy of the Colorado Guide to Smoke-Free Dining by calling the Group to Alleviate Smoking Pollution (GASP) at (303) 444-9799.

Remember that lunch at an expensive place is likely to be quite a bit less costly than dinner, although the price difference varies from restaurant to restaurant. Happy dining!

African

The Ethiopian Restaurant
$-$$, no credit cards • 2816 E. Colfax Ave. • (303) 322-5939

How's this for choice: We give you two Ethiopian restaurants to choose from, both located on Colfax Avenue from downtown east almost to Aurora. The first is the small, homey Ethiopian Restaurant with a warm pink dining room serving lunch and dinner at reasonable prices. This is a nonsmoking establishment, and it serves beer and wine only (including Ethiopian honey wine). Lunch and dinner daily. (Central/East)

Queen of Sheba Ethiopian Restaurant
$, no credit cards • 7225 E. Colfax Ave. at Quebec St. • (303) 399-9442

This is a casual and small spot that offers

the same smiling service as its counterpart to the west. Prices at Queen of Sheba are rock bottom. A favorite with meat eaters is the shish-kebab. Smoking is not allowed, and beer and wine only are served. The Queen of Sheba serves lunch and dinner and is closed on Monday. (Central/East)

Mataam Fez Moroccan Restaurant
$$$$ • 4609 E. Colfax Ave.
• (303) 399-9282

A meal at Mataam Fez is more than a meal, it's an experience. A five-course Moroccan feast (priced at $23.95 per person) is served in sumptuous, tented surroundings with entertainment on the weekends. Patrons dine using their fingers, while sitting on the floor with their shoes off. This nonsmoking restaurant is open for dinner only. There is also a location in Boulder. (Central)

American

Aubergine Cafe
$$ • 225 E. Seventh Ave.
• (303) 832-4778

Sean Kelly, formerly of Barolo Grill, is the mastermind behind this nifty little spot. "Aubergine" is French for eggplant, and while grilled, roasted and pureed eggplant — and sometimes eggplant risotto — are on the menu, the restaurant also serves meat and fish. Still, it's vegetarian heaven. There's an outdoor patio, and the restaurant serves beer and wine only. It's closed on Monday, but serves lunch and dinner Tuesday through Friday and dinner only Saturday and Sunday. (Central)

Augusta
$$$$ • at the Westin Tabor Center, 1672 Lawrence St. • (303) 572-7222

Named for the first wife of 19th-century silver tycoon Horace Tabor, Augusta has a Manhattan-style dining room with a wall of curved windows overlooking the downtown skyscrapers. The interior is sleek and dark, hung with Erte prints and draws almost as much praise as its inspired updating of traditional hotel dining-room fare. Service is topnotch. Reservations are recommended.

Breakfast only daily; brunch on Sundays. (Downtown)

Avenue Grill
$$-$$$ • 630 E. 17th Ave.
• (303) 861-2820

Denver's young movers-and-shakers gather at the long bar here and do business at the banquettes with their cellular phones. This is not a place to hide out in a dark corner, as there are none. So what's to eat? Salads, sandwiches, burgers, a few Southwestern dishes, a tasty cioppino and some killer desserts. It's a great people-watching spot on Denver's "restaurant row." Lunch and dinner are served daily, except Sunday when it's open for dinner only. (Central)

Bayou Bob's
$ • 1635 Glenarm St. • (303) 573-6828
$ • 5650 Greenwood Plaza Blvd.,
Greenwood Village • (303) 740-7772

Itching for some jambalaya, red beans and rice, a po'boy sandwich, shrimp gumbo or fried catfish? Bayou Bob's is one of the few places in town that serves authentic Louisiana Cajun food. The downtown restaurant moved from its 17th Street location around the corner to the Paramount Building in the fall of 1995. The Greenwood Plaza location near the Denver Tech Center is geared more toward family dining. Bayou Bob's doesn't serve lunch on Sunday, but otherwise serves lunch and dinner daily. (Downtown, Southeast)

Brasserie Z
$$-$$$ • 815 17th St. • (303) 293-2322

This is one of Denver's newer, hipper spots serving American cuisine in an energetic atmosphere. The 24-foot-long burnished bar is a great gathering spot. Lunch is served Monday through Friday for the downtown work crowd, and dinner is served every night. (Central)

Breckenridge Brewery
$-$$ • 2220 Blake St. • (303) 297-3644

The emphasis here is on the microbrewed beers and ales, but no one need go hungry with a menu that includes hearty pub fare — burgers, chicken sandwiches, salads, soups — for lunch and dinner daily. Close to Coors

Field, it's a great place for an after-game brew. (Downtown)

The Broker
$$$-$$$$ • 821 17th St. • (303) 292-5065
$$$-$$$$ • E. 39th Ave. and Peoria St.,
Aurora • (303) 371-6420
$$$-$$$$ • 5111 DTC Pkwy., Greenwood
Village • (303) 770-5111

The downtown Broker is situated in what was once a bank — some tables are in the old vault. All Brokers serve classic and contemporary American entrees and are known for their steaks, ice-cold peeled shrimp, good wine lists and excellent desserts. The downtown location is a popular place for a business lunch. The Brokers serve lunch and dinner during the week and dinner on the weekends. This is one of the rare Denver dining spots where the attire tends to be somewhat dressy, though it's not required. (Downtown, East and Southeast)

Cafe Bohemia
$$ • 1729 E. Evans Ave. • (303) 777-7222

A touch of new American influences the classic French bistro style cuisine in this excellent spot away from the downtown scene. The decor is thrift-store comfortable. The food is fresh and creative. The dinner menu is limited to four choices to keep things simple. And dinner is served only Thursdays through Sundays. Lunch served Tuesday through Saturday. Closed Sunday and Monday. (South)

Cafe Odyssey
$$-$$$ • 500 16th Street, in Denver
Pavilions • (303) 260-6100

This chain restaurant offers diners a fun experience in one of three theme dining rooms: Serengeti, Atlantis or Machu Pichu. Lunch and dinner are s erved daily and offer a vast array of foods, including pastas, burgers, chicken enchiladas, N.Y. strip, pork chops, rice, pizza

and sandwiches. A children's menu is available.

Cafe Paradiso
$$$ • 2355 E. Third Ave. • (303) 321-2066

This small, popular Cherry Creek eatery distinguishes itself from the crowd by its no-butter, no-cream preparation of eclectic salads, pasta dishes and entrees. However, anything goes when it comes to the luscious desserts. Reservations are recommended at this nonsmoking restaurant. Cafe Paradiso is closed on Sunday and Monday and serves dinner only. (Cherry Creek)

Champion Brewing Company
$-$$ • 1442 Larimer St. • (303) 534-5444

Part of the same family of restaurants as the Mexicali Cafe, Tommy Tsunami's Pacific Diner, the Cadillac Ranch and Josephina's, Champion has prime sidewalk seating in Larimer Square. Count on this young, fun place for terrific munchies, beer brewed on the premises and a menu that runs the gamut from Jamaican jerk chicken to fajita salad. Champion serves lunch and dinner daily. (Downtown)

Cheesecake Factory
$$ • 1201 16th St. • (303) 595-0333

If you like lots of choices and your plate piled high, Cheesecake Factory is for you. A dizzying menu of 150 items (not including 35 cheesecake flavors) might send up red flags for discriminating palettes, but the long lines waiting for a table appear endless. Then again, there are 35 cheesecake flavors. Reservations not accepted. Lunch and dinner daily; weekend brunch. (Downtown)

The Cherry Cricket
$-$$ • 2641 E. Second Ave.
• (303) 322-7666

The Cherry Cricket is known for its fa-

INSIDERS' TIP

Denver has always been a town whose inhabitants enjoyed dining out. But with today's booming economy, restaurants are often filled all week long. If a restaurant takes reservations, make them. Otherwise, count on long wait lists or plan to dine very early or late.

A heady experience for carnivores, the Buckhorn Exchange will make vegetarian plates on request.

mously juicy burgers and its extensive roster of microbrews. The salads are substantial, fresh and quite good. This is a loud neighborhood joint that goes crazy on St. Patrick's Day. It's open for lunch and dinner daily. (Cherry Creek)

Cliff Young's Restaurant
$$$$ • 700 E. 17th Ave.
• (303) 831-8900

Cliff Young's is one of Denver's most innovative restaurants and has maintained its status even after the departure of its namesake owner. The food has always been astonishingly creative, but the prices are high, making this a special-occasion choice for Denverites and out-of-town visitors. The restaurant recently downsized its private banquet space in order to make room for a sports grill (see Dante Bichette's Sports Grill). Reservations are recommended. Attire can be very dressy. Dinner

only is served Monday through Saturday. (Central)

Crocodile Cafe
$$ • 1630 Market St. • (303) 436-1144

A high-energy restaurant with brick walls, a big bar and a 20-foot-long fake crocodile suspended from the ceiling, "Croc's" serves mainly Mexican food at reasonable prices. There are also burgers, seafood and a wall-to-wall happy hour. Lunch and dinner are served daily in addition to a weekend brunch of Mexican omelettes, huevos rancheros and breakfast burritos. (Downtown)

Dante Bichette's Sports Grill and Roadhouse
$ • 700 17th Ave. • (303) 861-1010

Located in the former dining room of Cliff Young's Restaurant (Cliff Young's is still open, just smaller), the grill bills itself as the only "upscale" sports bar and restaurant. Judge for yourself. The restaurant features televisions in every corner, yet small bistro-style tables. Fare is Mexican standards and sandwiches, with more ambitious items such as chicken and salmon. Lunch and dinner daily. (Central)

Dick's Last Resort
$-$$ • 1743 Wazee St. • (303) 292-1212

Set your inhibitions free — this is no place for the stodgy. Dick's promises to show everyone a great time at this concept restaurant out of Dallas. Diners from other cities — San Antonio and Cleveland among them — will recognize the scene at Dick's, where diners sit at long tables with strangers (not for long), and the servers help you get to know one another. Upstairs is the gameroom with pool and shuffleboard. Outside is the largest patio in LoDo with 250 seats. Oh yes, and there's food: burgers, pork ribs, roasted chicken, shrimp and 78 different beers. Lunch and dinner are served daily. (Downtown)

Dixons Downtown Grill
$-$$ • 1610 16th St. • (303) 573-6100

Dixons is the place to go when everyone is hungry for something different. You'll find steaks, seafood, a chili plate, Southwestern fare, pastas, burgers and more. The atmosphere is relaxed, with large booths and an oak bar area. Popular items include the penne pasta with sausage, the peppercorn steak and the herb-baked salmon. Dixons is owned by the same folks who own Goodfriends on E. Colfax Avenue and Racine's on Bannock. It's open for breakfast, lunch and dinner Monday through Friday and brunch and dinner on weekends. (Downtown)

El Rancho Restaurant & Mountain Lodge
$$$ • El Rancho Exit 252 off I-70 • (303) 526-0661

A restaurant and lodge about 18 miles west of Denver near Genesee, El Rancho has a rustic atmosphere and seven fireplaces. The main dining room has a view of the Rocky Mountains and serves such regional specialties as prime rib and trout. The cinnamon rolls are locally famous. Open since 1948, El Rancho serves lunch, dinner and a Sunday breakfast buffet. Live entertainment is offered on some weekend nights. The outdoor patio with its great views makes a meal special. The eight lodges are fun for a weekend getaway or for out-of-town visitors. (West suburbs)

Fourth Story
$$-$$$ • 2955 E. First Ave. • (303) 322-1824

The Fourth Story is turning out to be one of Denver's finest restaurants. The setting is elegant: Windows frame the dining area and offer stunning views from this fourth-floor eatery. The decor is warm and muted, and the bar is a rich centerpiece. It's located above the popular Tattered Cover Bookstore and has a simply wonderful front lounge with overstuffed couches and cozy chairs. The food keeps getting better and better. Fare is creative American, emphasizing fresh ingredients and unusual combinations. Entree offerings are clever. The wait staff is friendly, unpretentious and knowledgeable about the menu and the superb wine list. Lunch and dinner served daily. Sunday brunch was voted "best of" in 1998 by local weekly newspaper, *Westword*. (Cherry Creek)

Giggling Grizzly
$-$$ • 1320 20th St. 297-8300

From the big Grizzly (yes, giggling) painted outside, you can tell this will be a fun place. It's really more of a bar than a restaurant, but you can get burgers, sandwiches and the like. The crowd tends to be young, the music rockin' and on the loud end. Giggling Grizzly does a robust business, especially during Rockies games. It's a good place to sample LoDo fever, and, well, drink lots of alcohol. The Grizzly serves dinner nightly and lunch daily except Sunday. (Downtown)

Goodfriends
$ • 3100 E. Colfax Ave. • 399-1751

The name says it all: here's an easygoing place to get together with friends and enjoy sandwiches, burgers or Southwestern food, with virtually everything on the menu prepared in low-fat fashion upon request (not a bad idea, given the generous portions and heavy hand with such things as cheese). Lunch and dinner are served daily. (Central/East)

Govnr's Park
$-$$ • 672 Logan St. • (303) 831-8605

Named for its proximity to the governor's mansion across the street, this is a popular spot with the Friday night crowd looking for the relaxed after-work scene. Once a dry cleaners, Govnr's Park is now a big, boisterous neighborhood restaurant and tavern with sandwiches, burgers and tavern dishes on the menu. The front patio, shaded by a large awning, is especially nice for an informal Sunday brunch. Lunch and dinner are served every day. Half of Gov's is a pool room that draws a mainly twenty-something crowd. (Central)

Gunther Toody's
$ • 4500 E. Alameda Ave., Glendale
• (303) 399-1959
$ • 9220 E. Arapahoe Rd., Englewood
• (303) 799-1958
$ • 7355 Ralston Rd., Arvada
• (303) 422-1954
$ • 8266 W. Bowles Ave., Littleton
• (303) 932-1957

You'll feel like you're in a scene of the movie *Grease* at this '50s-concept diner with gum-chewing waiters and waitresses. The food is classic American fare, and the milk shakes will bring out the kid in you. We highly recommend it for children. Breakfast, lunch and dinner are served every day. (East, Southeast and West suburbs)

Hard Rock Café
$$ • 500 16th St. • (303) 623-3191

Traditional American burgers (at least a half dozen variations, including veggie) share the menu with barbecue items. But the real attraction is the rock memorabilia culled mostly from the collection of longtime Denver concert promoter Barry Fey. The signature shop sells the usual Hard Rock paraphernalia, such as fanny packs, sweat shirts and T-shirts. Lunch and dinner daily. (Downtown)

Highlands Garden Cafe
$$-$$$ • 3927 W. 32nd Ave.
• (303) 458-5920

Simple, fresh American cuisine is served in the charming surroundings of this converted Victorian home. The menu changes daily depending on what the chef finds fresh at the market, whether that's fish, chicken or produce. Diners can enjoy a flower-filled patio from Memorial to Labor days, when Sunday brunch is also served. Otherwise, lunch and dinner are served Tuesday through Saturday. (Northwest)

Hugh's (Formerly Greens)
$$-$$$ • 1469 S. Pearl St. • (303) 744-1940

Formerly a humble natural-foods joint on East Colfax, Greens, as it was known, edged upscale in decor and cuisine when it moved to South Pearl Street, in a yuppified area of town. The urbane interior features saffron-hued walls in the dining room and a rubbed-denim color in the bar. Although there are still plenty of vegetarian dishes, the menu includes contemporary American presentations of steaks and lamb chops, too, often with a Southwestern twist. The menu changes seasonally. On weekends it serves dinner only, but it serves both lunch and dinner on weekdays. (South central)

LoDo's
$$ • 1946 Market St. • (303) 293-8555

The rooftop deck of this spot near the homeplate entrance to Coors Field lets you drink in the view while enjoying your meal. Reservations for rooftop are accepted most days (except game days). Inside, there's a 60-inch television to keep you abreast of games. Twenty-four tap beers will stave off your thirst. Eats include fish and chips, shrimp, fajitas, pasta, sandwiches and salads. Lunch and dinner daily. (Downtown)

Maria's Bakery & Deli
$, no credit cards • 3705 Shoshone St.
• (303) 477-3372

A delightful, out-of-the-way spot located in an old Denver neighborhood, Maria's serves sandwiches so thick you have to eat them with a fork and knife (oh, that meatloaf and avocado . . .). The self-service bakery and deli doubles as the owners' home. You order in the garage, eat in the beautiful large garden or, during cooler weather, inside the greenhouse. It serves lunch only, Tuesday through Friday. Enter through the wrought-iron gate on 37th Avenue. This is a truly charming place and worth the trip. (West Denver)

Marlowe's

$$$ • 511 16th St. • (303) 595-3700

The epitome of Denver's singles scene in the '80s, Marlowe's remains a popular gathering spot for lunch, dinner or after work. The restaurant serves steaks, chops, seafood, salads, pasta and fresh Maine lobster. Marlowe's features an extensive martini list as well as daily happy hour specials. Saturday night offerings include live music and dancing. The restaurant, located across from Denver Pavilions, boasts a good patio on the 16th Street Mall with prime people-watching. Lunch and dinner are served daily. (Downtown)

Mel's Bar & Grill

$$$ • 235 Fillmore St. • (303) 333-3979

Mediterranean fare and an upscale, yet comfortable atmosphere are on the menu at Mel's. A prime Cherry Creek location, good wine list and creative beef, chicken and pasta choices make this a popular spot. The cozy bar draws folks in their 30s to 50s. Live jazz is performed most nights. Lunch and dinner daily except Sunday, which is dinner only. (Cherry Creek)

Mercury Cafe

$-$$, no credit cards • 2199 California St. • (303) 294-9258

In addition to hosting one of the best and most eclectic performing-arts series in town, the funky, friendly Mercury Cafe serves late breakfast, lunch, dinner and weekend brunch, with an emphasis on natural foods. The food is as varied as the entertainment lineup; a meal here might include tofu enchiladas, steaks, salmon or sandwiches. Closed Mondays. (Downtown/Central)

Mesa Bar & Grill at the Table Mountain Inn

$$-$$$ • 1310 Washington Ave., Golden • (303) 271-0110

Enter this adobe-style inn for a variety of southwest dishes. Here you'll find such dinner specialties as prime rib of buffalo, cowboy chops and grilled salmon. For lunch, choose among buffalo burgers, chicken, salads and daily specials — all spiced and prepared with southwest flair. Breakfast, lunch and dinner served daily; brunch is available on Sunday.

The Moondance

$$ • 1626 Market St. • (303) 893-1626

Chef Michael Sarlo promises to treat you like you live next door to this intimate, "comfortable den." While you're there, he'll serve you from his menu of salads, fish, steaks or the house specialty, gumbo. Moondance prides itself on catering to the individual diner's needs, so if you're hankering for something you don't see, he'll try to accommodate. The atmosphere is casual, and the impressive art is from the gallery next door, Knox Gallery. It's open for lunch weekdays and dinner nightly. Enjoy the piano bar Wednesday through Sunday. (Central)

Mustard's Last Stand

$, no credit cards • 2081 S. University Blvd. • (303) 722-7936

You can't get more American than hot dogs, french fries and root beer floats, all of which this plain little joint does to perfection. Its location near the University of Denver guarantees a steady clientele, but older folks sneak over for the Polish sausage too. The original Mustard's Last Stand is at 1719 Broadway (at Arapahoe Avenue) in Boulder, (303) 444-5841. It's open daily. (South central)

My Brother's Bar

$ • 2376 15th St. • (303) 455-9991

The entrance to this corner tavern looks less than inviting, but everyone is welcome. A mixed crowd gathers here for burgers (a tasty vegetarian version is available) and beers. The pleasantly shaded patio out back is a hidden delight. It's a good place to keep in mind when you're hungry late at night, as they serve past midnight. It's closed on Sunday. (Downtown/Platte River area)

Palace Arms

$$$$ • at the Brown Palace Hotel, 321 17th Ave. • (303) 297-3111

The poshest of the Brown Palace's four restaurants, the Palace Arms is one of the very few places in Denver where gentlemen are required to wear jackets and ties. The setting and service are superb, holdovers from a more formal era. The room is decorated with antiques dating from the 17th century, including a pair of dueling pistols said to have belonged

Chefs in Greater Denver help charitable causes with culinary creations, such as this all-chocolate armadillo.

to Napoleon. The fare is contemporary regional cuisine, and the award-winning wine list features close to 1,000 titles. Reservations are strongly recommended. Lunch and dinner served daily, along with Sunday brunch. (Downtown)

The Palm
$$$$ • 1201 16th St. • (303) 825-7256

This is the place for the gigantic-martini power lunch. The Westin Hotel at the Tabor Center provides the backdrop for this top-notch restaurant, where Denver's business set devours thick slabs of dry-aged beef as heartily as its talk of mergers and acquisitions. Lobsters are so big they once needed their own apartment. Caricatures of Denver's noted and notorious hang on the wall. Everything is à la carte, so bring your American Express. Lunch and dinner Monday through Friday; dinner only on weekends. (Downtown)

Paramount Cafe
$-$$ • 511 16th St. • (303) 893-2000

A favorite for people-watching, the Paramount's outdoor seating area extends into the 16th Street Mall. This casual lunch or dinner spot serves burgers, sandwiches and Tex-Mex food at low prices in a setting reminiscent of a '50s diner. Happy hour after work is a lively scene. Lunch and dinner are served daily. (Downtown)

Pearl Street Grill
$-$$ • 1477 S. Pearl St. • (303) 778-6475

A big, friendly bar and restaurant with a particularly nice outdoor patio, the Pearl Street Grill serves soups, salads, sandwiches, burgers, etc., along with a large selection of beers on tap. It serves lunch and dinner every day and offers brunch on the weekends. No reservations are taken. (South central)

Potager
$$ • 1109 Ogden St. • (303) 832-5788

Every so often you come across a restaurant you can't wait to tell your friends about. Potager is one of them. It's everything a great restaurant should be: intimate, friendly and unpretentious. And the food, sublime. Potager opened in 1997 in the heart of Capitol Hill and is drawing raves from everyone who discovers this elegant, yet cozy neighborhood spot. Chef Teri Rippeto is creative and bold in her choices. The flavors of her food dance across your tongue. The decor is stark yet soft, with natural wood and nearly bare walls. For breakfast, the feel is more relaxed, with fresh-baked goods and cereals on the patio, at the breakfast bar, or on a comfy couch if you prefer.

The Augusta, in the Westin Hotel in the Tabor Center, is one of Greater Denver's finest restaurants. It's open weekdays for breakfast only and brunch on Sunday.

Breakfast, lunch and dinner are served Tuesday through Saturday. On Sunday, it's breakfast and lunch only. It's closed Monday. (Central)

Racine's
$-$$ • 850 Bannock St. • (303) 595-0418

Housed in a former auto-dealer showroom, Racine's is a big, laid-back place that's fun for breakfast, weekend brunch, lunch, dinner or anything in between. The menu has something for everyone, from sandwiches to pastas to a selection of Mexican entrees. An in-house bakery makes carrot cake, muffins and Racine's locally famous brownies (in addition to the usual chocolate with or without nuts, flavors include white chocolate, peanut butter and German chocolate) — all ready to be packaged up and taken home. The patio deck offers a retreat from busy nearby Speer Boulevard. (Central)

Rainforest Cafe
$$ • 3000 E. 1st Ave. • (303) 355-8500

The motto here is "a wild place to stop and eat." They're right. It is an event that kids will enjoy. There are fake waterfalls, bird shows, robots and exotic fish tanks. This place, in short, is all about fun and flash. Food? Pastas, chicken, seafood, etc. Lunch and dinner daily. (Cherry Creek, inside the shopping center.)

Reiver's
$$ • 1085 S. Gaylord St. • (303) 733-8856

A popular watering hole in the Washington Park neighborhood, Reiver's is best known for its burgers and casual atmosphere. The delicious shepherd's pie is packed with potatoes. After your meal, stroll around the neighborhood and window shop. Reservations are accepted, except on Fridays. Lunch and dinner are served every day. It's also a great place for a casual Saturday or Sunday brunch. (South central)

Rialto Cafe
$$$$ • 934 16th St. • (303) 893-2233

Housed in the former Joslins department store building, this great-looking restaurant features dark woods, a pressed-tin ceiling and motifs from the 1920s and '30s. Food resembles today's hip spots that offer New American cuisine, all served by a well-trained and attentive staff. Here you'll find such treats as roasted elephant garlic, peppered ahi appetizer, grilled strip steak and pan-roasted mussels. Friday and Saturday evenings are good for martinis. Breakfast, lunch and dinner served daily. (Downtown)

Rock Bottom Brewery
$$ • 1001 16th St. • (303) 534-7616

A huge brewpub with outdoor seating on the 16th Street Mall, the Rock Bottom Brewery is related to the Walnut Brewery in Boulder. It's popular from lunch well into the evening, and the extensive menu includes salads, pastas, barbecued meats and sandwiches.

It's an all-around favorite with locals, whether the action is on the patio or around the impressive bar. It's open seven days. (Downtown)

Rocky Mountain Diner
$-$$ • 800 18th St. • (303) 293-8383

A retro-Western diner with handsome green-leather booths, the Rocky Mountain Diner serves big portions of meat loaf, chicken-fried steak and pot roast with mashed potatoes and vegetables. Save room for the white chocolate banana cream pie and the many old-fashioned soda-fountain drinks available too. Smoking is allowed at the bar only. Lunch and dinner are served daily. (Downtown)

The Rose Tea Room
$-$$ • 7425 Grandview Ave., Arvada • (303) 420-3333

A very prettily decorated tea room housed in a 100-year-old former print shop in historic Olde Town Arvada, The Rose Tea Room is a wonderful spot for a ladies' lunch or afternoon tea. It even does a proper English high tea, with a pot of tea, sandwiches, pastries, scones and fruit, but you must reserve your place 24 hours in advance. Lunch is served Tuesday through Saturday. Breakfast is available by reservation. (West suburbs)

Ship Tavern
$$$ • at the Brown Palace Hotel, 321 17th St. • (303) 297-3111

In the Brown Palace Hotel (but accessible through its own entrance off Tremont Place), the Ship Tavern is modeled after a classic English pub and is crammed with replicas of actual ships from America's Clipper period. The food is classic too: prime rib, fish, chicken,

lamb chops and sandwiches. Breakfast, lunch and dinner served daily. (Downtown)

The Sports Column
$-$$ • 1930 Blake St. • (303) 296-1930

This traditional sports bar hops during all sporting events for the Colorado Rockies, Colorado Avalanche, Denver Broncos and Denver Nuggets. The menu is fairly extensive for a sports bar and includes variations on burgers, sandwiches, pastas, salads, appetizers and burritos. And they serve late: until midnight daily. Happy hour caters to the after-work crowd from 4 to 7 PM. Enjoy lunch or dinner daily with good views of several big-screen televisions. A nice summertime feature is the rooftop deck with views of city lights. (Downtown)

Strings
$$$ • 1700 Humboldt St. • (303) 831-7310

Diners rate this classy spot as one of Denver's best. They like its distinctively eclectic California-Italian menu of pasta, seafood, warm salads and grilled dishes; they appreciate the artistic presentation; they enjoy its extensive wine list; and they like its friendly owner, Noel Cunningham. The place is a perfect example of the vibrant spirit that typifies Denver, where more casually dressed diners mingle with the "Dynasty" set. Strings underwent a renovation recently that included a face-lift and changes to the menu. Lunch and dinner are served every day except Sunday when it's dinner only. Reservations are recommended. (Central)

Trinity Grille
$$$ • 1801 Broadway • (303) 293-2288

A popular spot for lunching lawyers, the Trinity Grille is brisk and shiny with polished wood, brass railings and a black-and-white tile floor. Steaks, soups, sandwiches, fish and homemade pasta dishes are the mainstay of the menu. The Cobb salad, in particular, is highly recommended. It's closed Sunday, serves dinner nightly and offers lunch on weekdays only. (Downtown)

Vesta Dipping Grill
$$-$$$ • 1822 Blake St. • (303) 296-1970

Kudos to owner Josh Wolkon's great con-

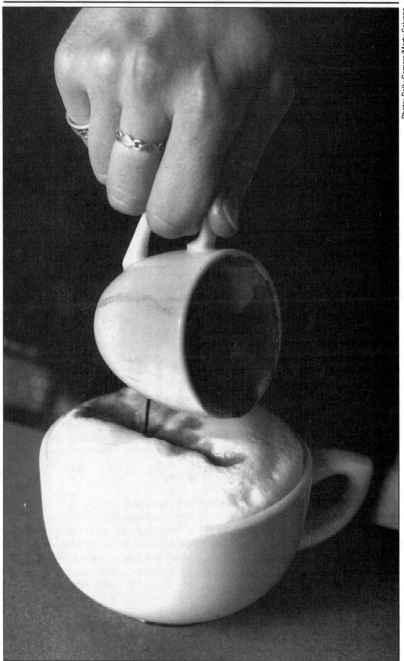

Photo: Daily Camera/Marty Caivano

Fine coffeehouses abound in Greater Denver, providing a daylong experience from breakfast to lunch and evening entertainment.

cept in relaxed yet upscale dining. Vesta Dipping Grill is housed in a stunning space in a renovated warehouse, with exposed brick walls, high-backed booths and funky lighting. So stunning, in fact, that the American Institute of Architecture saw fit to single it out among Colorado restaurants. Vesta is a creative and welcome addition to the familiar brewpubs around Coors Field. Wolkon has brought a hip elegance along with a new dining experience to LoDo. Start off with a variety of appetizers (the melt-in-your-mouth sesame-crusted tuna roll in a kickin' wasabi cream sauce is a personal favorite). Then choose a skewer dinner or a traditional "knife and fork" entree, including a great-tasting pork tenderloin served with apple roasted mashed potatoes and veges. The "dipping" comes in the form of your choice of three homemade sauces that give the meal spice, pizazz and variety; sharing is definitely in at the Dipping Grill. Dinner is served nightly; Thursdays feature live jazz. (Central)

Wazee Lounge & Supper Club
$ • 1600 15th St. • (303) 623-9518

It's back to the '40s, or some other unspecified prior decade, at this laid-back pizza-and-burgers joint. A Lower Downtown favorite for years, it's hard to say just what makes this place so neat. The diverse crowd? The bohemian ambiance? The pizza? Regardless, it remains popular year after year. It's closed on Sunday, but serves lunch and dinner otherwise. (Downtown)

Wolfgang Puck Café
$$ • 500 16th St. • (303) 595-9653

Puck loaded his Denver menu with beef, thinking we cowpokes would want our meat, then opened his restaurant to find we eat like Californians: more pasta than meat. Both are found on the menu at this popular Denver Pavilions spot where lines are loooong. Two open kitchens keep things interesting, and produce Puck's famed pizza pies from wood-fired ovens. The scale here is grand: four sushi chefs

serving 30 at the sushi bar, and up to 70 servers at every shift. Lunch and dinner daily. (Downtown)

Wynkoop Brewing Company
$-$$ • 1634 18th St. at Wynkoop St.. • (303) 297-2700

Housed in the historic J.S. Brown Mercantile Building, the Wynkoop led the way in the resurgence of Lower Downtown. Denver's first brewpub, it was founded in 1988 and serves a variety of handcrafted ales and pub fare, such as pot pies with quinoa crust, at reasonable prices for lunch and dinner. The main dining area is noisy, crowded and often smoky — not necessarily a reason to stay away, we're just warning you. Upstairs is a classic pool hall that hops with the 20-30 set. Reservations are accepted for large groups only. Sunday breakfast/lunch starts at 11 AM, and lunch and dinner are served daily. (Downtown)

American/Steaks

Aurora Summit
$$$$ • 2700 S. Havana St., Aurora • (303) 751-2112

A classic steakhouse, with a dark, woodsy, masculine ambiance, the Aurora Summit serves only the finest grade of U.S.D.A. prime, aged, corn-fed beef. In the tradition of steakhouses, the menu also includes seafood entrees. In the large front lounge, there's a piano bar Monday through Saturday nights with a small dance floor. Aurora Summit serves dinner seven days a week. Reservations are preferred. (Southeast)

Beacon Grill
$$$-$$$$ • 303 16th St. (second level) • (303) 592-4745

This isn't strictly a steakhouse, but what is, anymore? And they do make a big deal out of their Double-J Limousin beef, a breed of cattle raised on Colorado's Western Slope that's naturally lower in fat. The smoked salmon

---

INSIDERS' TIP

A good way to sample Greater Denver's better — but more expensive — restaurants is to go for lunch instead of dinner. You'll enjoy the same great quality at lower prices.

cheesecake appetizer draws raves. A great big patio overlooks the 16th Street Mall, and there's piano music Thursday through Saturday. Dinner is almost twice the price of lunch, something to keep in mind if you're on a budget. Beacon Grill is closed Sunday (but may open when Pavilions opens); reservations are recommended, even for lunch, which is served Monday through Friday only. (Downtown)

The Buckhorn Exchange
$$$$ • 1000 Osage St. • (303) 534-9505

The Buckhorn Exchange is Denver's oldest restaurant. It was founded in 1893 by "Shorty Scout" Zeitz, who, along with his family, amassed an astounding collection of animal trophies, including moose, elk, buffalo and bear. More than 500 stuffed animals and birds are displayed — it's sort of like dining in a natural history museum. The menu, accordingly, runs to traditional Western fare: beef, barbecued pork ribs and game meats. For something more unusual, try the rattlesnake or alligator tail appetizers. Vegetarian alert: you may feel a little squeamish here, but if you can put up with the dead heads on the wall, call ahead and the restaurant will put together a vegetarian plate just for you. Dinner entrees are expensive ($20 and up), but lunch is quite reasonable, with almost everything priced at $10 and less. Thursday through Saturday nights feature folk and cowboy music in the saloon upstairs. It's probably more popular with tourists than locals, but there's no other place like it. Reservations are recommended for dinner, which is served daily. Lunch is served Monday through Friday only. (Central)

Cadillac Ranch
$$-$$$ • 1400 Larimer St. • (303) 820-2288

The Cadillac Ranch prides itself on its Texas-size certified Angus steaks and its howdy-pardner friendliness (without overdoing the western angle). The fun, colorful decor consists of cowboy boots, saddles, horseshoes and car parts. There's a second-floor patio with a view of the Rocky Mountains. In addition to steaks, try the Route 66 Rotisserie Chicken or a variety of sandwiches and salads. Reservations are suggested. Cadillac Ranch serves dinner nightly, lunch on weekdays and brunch on weekends. (Downtown)

Denver Buffalo Company
$$$ • 1109 Lincoln St. • (303) 832-0880

More than just a restaurant, the Denver Buffalo Company complex includes a trading post, art gallery, deli and food mart in addition to the Western-style main dining room. A nicely appointed private dining room that seats up to 30 can be reserved in advance for special occasions. Buffalo is, as you might have guessed, the No. 1 choice here, all of it raised on the company ranch near Kiowa in eastern Colorado. There are chicken, seafood and pasta entrees as well. The restaurant serves lunch and dinner every day except Sunday, when it's dinner only. (Central)

The Denver ChopHouse & Brewery
$$$ • 1735 19th St. • (303) 293-3628

For years there were few places to eat in Lower Downtown. Then, as Coors Field was built, sports bars, brewpubs and steakhouses sprang up on every corner. The Denver ChopHouse is one of the most successful; reservations are suggested for weekends. The outdoor barbecue area, with its patio and rolling roof, is a big draw. The decor is rich with dark wood and high booths. The food is inventive; try the Portobello mushrooms dipped in Worcestershire and garlic, then grilled. The ChopHouse is affiliated with Boulder's Walnut Brewery. Lunch and dinner are served daily. (Downtown)

The Fort
$$$$ • 19192 Rt. 8, Morrison
• (303) 697-4771

The Fort combines Wild-West flair with classy fare: Where else do waiters dressed in leather vests and beads open bottles of champagne with a tomahawk? Located in the Foothills, the restaurant is a full-size adobe replica of Bent's Fort, Colorado's first fur-trading post. Owners Sam and Carrie Arnold were among the first restaurateurs to feature buffalo meat on the menu; other unusual entrees include elk, quail, rattlesnake and Rocky Mountain oysters (rolled in seasoned flour and deep-fried). More traditional preparations of trout and steak are available, and for those who wish to sample a little bit of everything, there's a game plate. As we said about the Buckhorn Exchange, there's no place else like it. Reservations are recommended. The Fort serves dinner nightly. (West suburbs)

Morton's of Chicago
$$$$ • 1710 Wynkoop St.
• (303) 825-3353

One of the last holdouts in Denver's Tivoli Center, a brewery turned shopping mall turned community-college student union, Morton's finally moved to Lower Downtown, across from Union Station. A classic, classy steakhouse, Morton's is always mentioned when people talk about where to get great steaks. Only U.S.D.A. prime served here. If surf and turf is what you're after, Morton's flies live lobster in from Maine daily. It serves dinner nightly; reservations are recommended. (Downtown)

Ruth's Chris Steak House
$$$-$$$$ • 1445 Market St.
• (303) 446-2233

Ruth's Chris is a steak-lover's steakhouse (only prime served here). The atmosphere is relaxed with plenty of dark wood, the booths are big and private, and cigars are allowed in the bar area. The 20-ounce T-bone is the biggest; the 8-ounce filet the smallest. Also available are lobster, veal, chicken and halibut. Dinner is served nightly, and reservations are recommended. (Downtown)

Asian

Akebono
$$-$$$ • 1255 19th St. • (303) 295-1849

Located in colorful Sakura Square, Akebono is a handsome, coolly lit Japanese restaurant with a sushi/sashimi bar and a full menu including gyoza, fried oysters, teriyaki and tempura dishes. It's closed Monday and serves dinner only the other six days. (Downtown)

L'Auberge Zen
$$$-$$$$ • 9955 E. Hampden Ave.
• (303) 751-3571

We feel pretty confident stating that L'Auberge Zen is Greater Denver's only French and Japanese restaurant, with a sushi bar located next to a rather continental-looking dining room. Go ahead and order French if that's

what you're in the mood for, but the critics have generally lavished their praise on the Japanese entrees. In fact, L'Auberge Zen emphasizes its Japanese fare. It's closed Monday and doesn't serve lunch on weekends. (Southeast)

Busara
$ • 1435 Market St. • (303) 893-2884

What sets this attractive LoDo restaurant apart in a sea of brick-walled renovated loft spaces? It's not only good, it's priced right. Now that's a treat in spendy LoDo. Thai food is the specialty here. Spring rolls are crispy, sauces are spicy (or mild, if you prefer) and food combinations are clever. Lunch Monday through Saturday. Dinner only on Sunday. (Downtown)

Chao-Praya Thai
$$ • 5411 Quebec St., Commerce City
• (303) 287-2210

Some of the best Thai food in the area can be found at this surprisingly gracious truck-stop location. The family-owned restaurant traces its history back to Laiad Chittivej, a remarkable immigrant who opened the first Thai restaurant in Denver. Hot means hot, so don't be shy about asking for the level you feel comfortable with. Virtually everything on the menu can be made vegetarian. Lunch and dinner are served daily. (Northeast)

Domo Restaurant
$ • 1365 Osage St. • (303) 595-3666

No sushi! No upscale see-and-be-seen surroundings. Domo is all about an authentic Japanese country food experience. Teriyaki meats and fish, for example, are flavored like the real thing, not layered in gooey sauce. Domo proves good doesn't have to be expensive.

Closed Sunday and Wednesday. Lunch and dinner otherwise. (Central)

BD's Mongolian Barbecue
$ • 1620 Wazee St. • (303) 571-1824

Once you choose your meats, vegetables and sauce, the cook stir-fries it while you watch. BD's is a no frills way to dine when you're tired of all the upscale joints around town. Lunch and dinner daily. (Downtown)

Imperial Chinese Restaurant & Lounge
$$ • 431 S. Broadway • (303) 698-2800

Imperial does indeed live up to its name, with opulent decor that resembles the set for *The Last Emperor*. And better, the food matches the quality decor. The restaurant specializes in seafood, but don't pass up the sesame chicken, or, if you're in the mood for the royal treatment, the fabulous Peking duck. Reservations are accepted for parties of four or more only. Lunch and dinner are served daily, except Sunday, which is dinner only. (Central)

J's Noodles
$, no credit cards • 945-E S. Federal Blvd. • (303) 922-5495

Many of Greater Denver's best and most authentic Asian restaurants are located along South Federal Boulevard. For many aficionados of Thai food, this plain storefront restaurant tops the list for its combination of outstanding Thai food and low prices. Try a noodle bowl at lunch or a curry for dinner. J's Noodles is open every day. (Southwest)

Long Binh
$ • 940 S. Federal Blvd. • (303) 935-4141

Long Binh is a modest Federal Boulevard eatery that is often mentioned when you ask Denverites about their favorite place for Vietnamese food. The noodle bowls and the crispy egg rolls are special favorites. The staff receives compliments for their friendly manner; eat here more than once and you might be recognized. Lunch and dinner are served every day. (Southwest)

Mori Sushi Bar & Tokyo Cuisine
$$-$$$ • 2019 Market St. • (303) 298-1864

Just a baseball's throw from Coors Field on the corner of Market Street and 20th Avenue, Mori Sushi offers a great selection of sushi, noodle dishes (the seafood udon noodles are a personal favorite) and other Japanese specialties in a pleasant setting that includes a small aquarium. The restaurant is popular with downtown workers at lunch. At dinner the menu expands into what seems like a book, but rest assured, you're unlikely to make a bad choice. Lunch and dinner are served daily except Sundays when it's closed. (Downtown)

New Orient
$$ • 10203 E. Iliff Ave., Aurora • (303) 751-1288

A small, simply decorated restaurant, New Orient serves Vietnamese, Chinese and "Amerasian" cuisine, updating traditional recipes with creative touches. What this means is that you can have roast-duck soup and pineapple-paprika shrimp for lunch with cappuccino mud torte for dessert. Seafood is a specialty at this nonsmoking restaurant. Reservations are recommended on the weekend. It's closed on Monday. (Southeast)

New Saigon
$$ • 630 S. Federal Blvd. • (303) 936-4954

Yet another Federal Boulevard restaurant, New Saigon is a perennial winner in local weekly *Westword*'s "Best Vietnamese Restaurant" category. One of Denver's first Vietnamese restaurants, it's been in business more than 10 years. Despite tons of competition, its loyal fans can't be lured away from the spicy beef and the acclaimed fish dishes. New Saigon offers great food in slightly more upscale surroundings than its Federal Boulevard counterparts. Lunch and dinner are served daily. (Southwest)

P.F. Chang's China Bistro
$$ • 1415 15th St. • (303) 260-7222

Don't expect the usual sweet and sour chicken at Chang's. In fact, don't expect the usual Chinese fare at all; Chang's does it with a stylish twist. From crab wontons to mouth-melting flourless chocolate cake, P.F. Chang's serves flavorful meals to the LoDo crowd. And the decor speaks LoDo's elegant language: exposed brick, polished woods and ornate sculptures. Our only gripe: entrees can be a bit heavy on the sweet sauce. Enlist the excellent wait staff to help ensure the best combination of items. Appetizers are a must. Our favorites: shrimp dumplings and lettuce cups stuffed with chicken. And don't forget the garlic snap peas — a P.F. Chang signature side dish. Lunch and dinner daily. (Downtown) Also a Park Meadows location, 8315 S. Park Meadows Center Drive, (303) 790-7744. (Southeast)

Seoul Food

$ • 701 E. Sixth Ave. • (303) 837-1460

A friend who has lived in Korea swears that the most authentic Korean food in town is cooked and served at this casual eatery. The bee bim bob (a mixed vegetable dish available with chicken and tofu) and the bulgogi (Korean beef) are favorites, as is the barley tea. The beef can be fatty, which is typical for Korean fare. Seating is available at tables, the main counter or outdoor on the patio. It's closed Sunday and open for lunch and dinner otherwise. (Central)

Sonoda's

$$$ • 3108 S. Parker Rd., Aurora
• (303) 337-3800

Proprietor Kenny Sonoda calls his casual restaurant a "Japanese seafood house and sushi bar," and, indeed, the menu features changing seafood specials depending on what's fresh and available. Local restaurant critics are fond of the sushi, which wins praise for freshness. The sushi lunch offers six to eight types, including a tuna roll. There are two other locations: the new Sonoda's Sushi & Seafood downtown and one at Park Meadow's Shopping Center. Both receive good reviews for freshness and flavor. Sonoda's serves lunch and dinner daily and dinner only on Sunday. (Southeast)

Sushi Den

$$$ • 1487 S. Pearl St. • (303) 777-0826

A chic, modern restaurant that just happens to be a sushi bar, Sushi Den does a superb job with cooked fish too. The standout is the steamed fresh fish in a bamboo basket. The sushi bar is a visual feast, and the dining room is modern with lots of black, granite and concrete. Presentation here is artful, from decor to plate.

Dinner is served nightly, and lunch is served only on weekdays. (South Central)

Sushi Heights

$$ • 2301 E. Colfax Ave. • (303) 355-2777

A tidy Japanese restaurant with classical music playing in the background, Sushi Heights gets raves for its sushi. It's also known for its reasonably priced lunch specials, usually around $5 to $10, such as teriyaki, tempura

and rice bowls. It's closed Sunday and doesn't serve lunch on Saturday. (Central)

T-Wa Inn

$$ • 555 S. Federal Blvd. • (303) 922-4584

The T-Wa Inn was Denver's first Vietnamese restaurant. It has a huge menu that emphasizes seafood — a point driven home by the foyer's aquarium filled with giant silver arrow wanna fish (for decoration only). The Asian decor is exotic without being overwhelming. Lunch is as low as $4.95, and dinner offers a variety of vegetarian and meat dishes; both meals are served daily. Should you desire Vietnamese coffee, it will be French-pressed for you right at the table.

Lunch and dinner served everyday. (Southwest)

T-Wa Terrace

$$$ • 6882 S. Yosemite St., Englewood
• (303) 741-4051

Located in the Southgate shopping center just south of Arapahoe Road, the T-Wa Terrace was started by one of the founders of the T-Wa Inn. Recommended dishes include the Vietnamese egg rolls and the soft-shell crab. Dinner is served nightly, and lunch is served every day but Sunday. (South/Greenwood Village)

Tommy Tsunami's Pacific Diner

$$$ • 1432 Market St. • (303) 534-5050

You'll be dazzled by the decor when you walk in this hip and trendy LoDo spot, and the food will make you happy, too. Appetizers are especially good here: try the ahi roll or wrapped and fried coconut shrimp. Choose between such dishes as noodle bowls, shushi boats or Chilean sea bass. There also is a sushi bar. Lunch and dinner served daily. (Downtown)

Yoisho Restaurant

$, no credit cards • 7236 E. Colfax Ave.
• (303) 322-6265

A tiny Japanese restaurant — only three tables and bar seating — with a devoted following, Yoisho has a simple menu with mostly fried Japanese dishes (no sushi here) and notable gyoza dumplings. There's no smoking and no alcohol. Yoisho serves lunch and dinner every day except Sunday. (East)

Barbecue

Sam Taylor's Bar-B-Q
$ • 435 S. Cherry St. • (303) 388-9300

Is Sam Taylor's smoky-sweet and spicy barbecue the best in town? Lots of folks say it is. For years, Taylor's restaurant was located on the links at City Park Golf Course, but, due to differences with the landlords at the city of Denver, moved to a new location. The atmosphere is still ultra-casual family style, with picnic tables on the patio. The amazing, melt-in-your-mouth barbecue is served daily for lunch and dinner. (Central/East)

Wolfe's Barbeque
$ • 333 E. Colfax Ave. • (303) 831-1500

Here's hope for committed vegetarians: in addition to Wolfe's scrumptious traditional barbecued meats, you can get smoked, grilled tofu and vegetarian baked beans at this eatery a block from the State Capitol. For the carnivores, the barbecue is first-rate. Wolfe's serves lunch and dinner Monday through Friday only. (Central)

Bistros

Bistro Adde Brewster
$$ • 250 Steele St. • (303) 388-1900

Bistro Adde Brewster serves unpretentious lunches and dinners in an intimate setting. Entrees include grilled duck, bistro burgers and baked eggplant. The Bistro does a great steak, and a truly wonderful tuna appetizer. Service here is always friendly and professional. The bar is small and almost always full of regulars. Low-fat HealthMark selections are available.

It's closed Sunday but serves lunch and dinner otherwise. (Cherry Creek)

Papillon Cafe
$$$$ • 250 Josephine St. • (303) 333-7166

For standout French fusion, try the highly regarded Papillon. It's clearly one of Denver's best, thanks to chef Radek Cerny whose cooking pedigree is impressive. His classic French dishes are Asian-influenced and artfully prepared. The decor is a bit stuffy and the wine list spendy, but hey, it's French. Lunch and dinner served daily. (Cherry Creek)

Pour la France
$ • 730 S. University Blvd. • (303) 744-1888

A likable French cafe and bakery with branches in Aspen and Boulder, Pour la France offers light lunches and dinners — perhaps a Mediterranean salad — and excellent pastries and desserts. The dense, dark melt-in-your-mouth chocolate truffle cake is a chocoholic's fantasy come true. This is also a good spot for breakfast, a mid-morning coffee break or a late-night glass of champagne. Breakfast is traditional egg dishes; all meals are served daily. (South central)

Sfuzzi
$$ • 3000 E. First Ave. • (303) 321-4700

Sfuzzi bills itself as an Italian bistro, although more than one local restaurant critic has noted the California influence on the decor and the menu. Located in the posh Cherry Creek Shopping Center, Sfuzzi features a central woodburning pizza oven and an open kitchen. Specialties include grilled and smoked meats and, of course, pizzas. The young and the beautiful eat here, and the restaurant is noted as much for its people-watching as its food. Reservations are accepted. Lunch and dinner are served daily. (Cherry Creek)

Continental

The Swan
$$$$ • 200 Inverness Dr. W., Englewood • (303) 799-5800

Inside the sprawling Inverness Hotel and Golf Club south of the Denver Tech Center, The Swan is sophisticated but light and open in its decor. The cuisine is traditional continental, with knockout presentations of lamb, lobster and steaks. The restaurant is consistently an award-winner. It's open for dinner only Tuesday through Saturday. (Southeast)

Briarwood Inn
$$$$ • 1630 18th St., Golden • (303) 279-3121

The Briarwood Inn isn't that far from downtown, and not far at all for those who live in

Denver's western suburbs, but it's a world away from the hustle-bustle. A romantic getaway, the formal, old-fashioned Briarwood Inn is Victorian in its decor and continental in its cuisine. Complete meals are served, including appetizers, dessert and entrees such as prime rib and fresh seafood, at prices ranging from $22 to $39 per person. Dinner is served nightly, and lunch is served on weekdays. It's especially nice for a sumptuous Sunday brunch or when it's decorated for the winter holidays. (West suburbs)

The Burnsley Hotel
$$$-$$$$ • 1000 Grant St.
• (303) 830-1000

The intimate dining room at this small Capitol Hill hotel is extravagantly wallpapered and almost fussily furnished. This is the place to go when you don't want to run into everyone you know and would rather sink into a banquette and sip a martini than schmooze. The food is Americanized continental cuisine of lamb, chicken and seafood with frequ ently changing specials. We've been hearing good things about the $7.95 breakfast buffet, served Monday through Friday until 9:30 AM. It serves dinner nightly, breakfast daily and lunch on weekdays only. (Central)

Chinook Tavern
$$$ • 265 Detroit St. • (303) 394-0044

There's always a hot new place in Cherry Creek, and in the spring and summer of 1995 it was the Chinook Tavern. But unlike many Cherry Creek spots that fold after their 15 minutes of fame, this one has lasted. The menu is German-influenced, but the translation is a very contemporary one, and the warm decor avoids any Bavarian cliches. The grilled fish dishes are flavored with delicious sauces. Lunch and dinner are served Monday through Saturday. (Cherry Creek)

European Cafe
$$$ • 1040 15th St. • (303) 825-6555
$$$ • 5150 S. Quebec St. (I-25 and Belleview) in the Denver Tech Center, Greenwood Village • (303) 770-6500

European Cafe moved in January 1997 to its new location closer to Denver's Performing Arts Center, making it popular with the theater crowd (theater-goers say it does a good job of getting you to the show on time). Simply put, this is one of Denver's best restaurants and a personal favorite of ours. Its French/continental cuisine is exquisitely conceived and executed; the presentation is artful but not forced; the service is impeccable; and the surroundings are elegant. It is still paired with Al Fresco, which is adjacent and under the same ownership, but serves excellent northern Italian cuisine. The original European Cafe, at 2460 Arapahoe Avenue in Boulder, (303) 938-8240, is still going strong, and there's now a third location at the Denver Tech Center, however the surroundings are much more suburban bland than downtown. Reservations are recommended. (Downtown, Southeast)

Little Russian Cafe
$$-$$$ • 1424 Larimer St. • (303) 595-8600
$$-$$$ • 2500 E. Orchard Rd., Greenwood Village • (303) 347-0300.

The Little Russian Cafe serves hearty peasant fare such as stuffed cabbage, dumplings and borscht in a smashing red dining room. Stroll by while shopping, and the aroma will tempt you inside.

You can simply stop in for apple strudel and tea served Old-World style in silver-handled glasses, or for a shot of ice-cold homemade flavored vodka. There is also a Little Russian Cafe in Boulder. Reservations are recommended on the weekend. Lunch isn't served at the downtown location but is at the new Orchard Road location in Cherry Hills

INSIDERS' TIP

The Seattle-style coffee shop is all the rage in Denver, as it is in other big cities. Many of Denver's are a great spot to take a break, experience a local neighborhood and have a light meal. Most serve bagels, scones, desserts and other treats as well as light sandwiches.

southeast of town. Dinner is served nightly. (Downtown, Southeast)

The Manor House
$$$ • No.1 Manor House Rd., Littleton
• (303) 973-8064

In a beautiful setting perched atop Ken Caryl Ranch, the Manor House serves Colorado continental cuisine, including roast duck, lamb chops, steaks and prime rib on weekends. Salmon is a specialty. The 1914 Southern-style mansion was the original manor home for Ken Caryl Ranch. Dinner only is served Tuesday through Sunday (closed early at 8 PM Sundays). Reservations are requested. (Southwest)

Wellshire Inn
$$$-$$$$ • 3333 S. Colorado Blvd.
• (303) 759-3333

Housed in an English Tudor mansion on the grounds of the Wellshire Municipal Golf Course, the Wellshire Inn is richly decorated with 100-year-old tapestries, stained glass and handsome wood paneling.

Owner Leo Goto serves sophisticated continental fare, including rack of lamb and salmon. There are nightly specials. Breakfast, lunch, dinner and Sunday brunch are served. The eggs Benedict is the specialty, but the French toast with vanilla ice cream melted into the batter could tempt you away from the standard. (Southeast)

Delicatessens

The Bagel Deli
$-$$ • 6439 E. Hampden Ave. at Monaco St. • (303) 756-6667

A big, family-style kosher-style restaurant and deli that serves breakfast, lunch and dinner until 7:30 PM, The Bagel Deli has been in business in Denver since 1967. Never mind nouvelle; come here when you want chopped liver, Dr. Brown's sodas, gefilte fish, knishes, blintzes and oversized deli sandwiches including, of course, corned beef on rye.

Open for lunch and early dinner every day until 7 PM or 8 PM, depending on the day. (Southeast)

Laughing Dog Market
$ • 1925 Blake St.
• (303) 293-2364

Variety is the key here. Love hummus? They've got it. Been bugging for a burrito? It's here. Want a pound of salad? Look no further. You'll also find plenty to look at if you're waiting for take-out. The art-covered brick walls set a nice stage.

It's open Monday through Saturday for breakfast, lunch and an early dinner (it closes around 5 PM). (Downtown)

New York Deli News
$ • 7105 E. Hampden Ave.
• (303) 759-4741

Similar in offerings, prices and easygoing style to The Bagel Deli, The New York Deli News also serves breakfast, lunch and dinner daily. You'll enjoy great pumpernickel bread, pastrami, bagels, corned beef, all flown in from New York, and — loosen your belt — genuine New York-style cheesecake. (Southeast)

Zaidy's Deli
$-$$ • 121 Adams St.
• (303) 333-5336

Zaidy's may very well be the closest thing to an authentic New York Jewish deli as can be found in Greater Denver. This is a prime source for potato latkes, smoked fish and matzoh ball soup just like your grandmother used to make. Come for breakfast or lunch daily, dinner Wednesday through Sunday. (Cherry Creek)

French

La Coupole
$$$ • 2191 Arapahoe St.
• (303) 297-2288

Situated in the old brick Hotel Paris building, La Coupole boasts one of the most beautiful dining rooms in Denver, with its old wood floors and stained-glass ceiling. At the entrance is a lovely enclosed courtyard with several tables shaded by umbrellas. The fare is classically French, with a country touch. This is a terrifically romantic restaurant but not too fussy for business lunches either. On Friday and

Saturday evenings starting at 8 PM there's live jazz; reservations are essential at these times. Lunch and dinner are served Tuesday through Sunday, except Saturday and Sunday when it's dinner only. Closed Monday. (Central/Downtown)

Le Central

$$ • 112 E. Eighth Ave. • (303) 863-8094

Le Central styles itself as "the affordable French restaurant" and does a good job of living up to that claim without skimping on quality. The restaurant is a charming series of low-ceilinged rooms; the food is country French. Lunch and dinner are served daily in addition to brunch on Saturday and Sunday. (Central)

Tante Louise

$$$$ • 4900 E. Colfax Ave.
• (303) 355-4488

Often called the most romantic restaurant in Denver, Tante Louise is known as much for its extensive, award-winning wine list with more than 600 selections and its attentive service as for its contemporary French-American cuisine. Located in a lovely old home, the restaurant has lots of little private nooks that are renowned for encouraging marriage proposals. Tante Louise has been in business since the early 1970s. Dinner only is served every night except Sunday. Reservations are recommended. (Central)

Greek

Central 1

$$ • 300 S. Pearl St. • (303) 778-6675

A nothing-fancy Greek restaurant not far from the Mayan Theatre, Central 1 has been pleasing customers with its souvlaki and gyros since the early '80s. The Greek and chicken salads are popular for lunch. Central 1 serves lunch and dinner every day except Sunday. (Central)

Yanni's

$$ • 2223 S. Monaco Pkwy.
• (303) 692-0404

This is a classic Greek family-run taverna, with a blue-and-white interior and outdoor tables with umbrellas. The menu leans heavily on traditional, hearty dishes such as moussaka and pastitsio. On Friday, Saturday and Sunday nights, they spit-roast a lamb. Everything here is fresh, including the homemade bread. Knock back a shot of ouzo and let the feasting begin! Lunch is served Monday through Saturday, dinner nightly. (Southeast)

Health Food/ Natural Foods

The Harvest Restaurant & Bakery

$-$$ • 430 S. Colorado Blvd.
• (303) 399-6652
$-$$ • 7730 E. Belleview Ave., Greenwood Village • (303) 779-4111

The Harvest had its start as a natural foods restaurant in Boulder and has since branched out into Denver. There are many vegetarian items on the menu as well as chicken and meat salads and sandwiches plus lots of homemade baked goods and a potent, aromatic spice tea. The low-key Harvest is particularly good for breakfast and for solo diners, who can choose to sit at a shared community table. Breakfast, lunch and dinner are served daily at this nonsmoking restaurant. (Cherry Creek, Southeast)

Healthy Habits

$-$$ • 865 S. Colorado Blvd.
• (303) 733-2105
$-$$ • 14195 W. Colfax Ave., Lakewood
• (303) 277-9293

The casual Healthy Habits, just east of the Cherry Creek neighborhood, offers an all-you-can-eat salad buffet plus soup and pastas. The muffins are a standout. And despite the name, desserts are not banished from the premises. There are plenty of HealthMark items for people watching their diet, but non-dieters will be in heaven with dozens of salad choices and great pastas too. Lunch and dinner are served daily. There's also a Boulder location. (Cherry Creek, West suburbs)

Indian

Delhi Darbar
$$$ • 1514 Blake St. • (303) 595-0680

Downtown's only Indian restaurant is refined in its decor and in its wide range of tandoori dishes, which include two kinds of Cornish game hens and quail in addition to the more standard chicken. We're particularly fond of the murgh tikka saag, chicken in a spinach sauce. The $5.95 lunch buffet is an especially good value, with a choice of four entrees and as many as 22 items in all. Vegetarians will appreciate the many meatless entrees. Lunch and dinner are served daily. There is also a Delhi Darbar in Boulder. (Downtown)

India's
$$-$$$ • 3333 S. Tamarac Dr.
• (303) 755-4284

India's is a feast for the senses, with its tantalizing aromas, colorful cloth hangings and hypnotic Indian music. Located in a strip shopping mall just behind Tamarac Square, India's is Denver's oldest Indian restaurant and one of the finest you are ever likely to encounter. The curries are hot and spicy, and the tandoori dishes are very popular. Reservations are recommended. Dinner is served nightly, lunch Monday through Saturday. (Southeast)

International/Eclectic

Saffron Restaurant
$$$ • 6600 S. Quebec St., Englewood
• (303) 290-9705

A quiet, elegant little restaurant, Saffron uses a Mediterranean style of seasoning in all its dishes, which range from pastas to beef, lamb and chicken preparations. Saffron, mint, curry and lemon are common flavorings. Prime rib is served on Saturday nights; on Sundays

the restaurant is closed. Lunch is served Monday through Saturday; closed Sunday. Reservations are requested on the weekend. (Southeast)

Italian

Al Fresco
$$$ • 1040 15th St. • (303) 534-0404

In the same renovated brick building that houses the European Cafe, the sophisticated Al Fresco specializes in Northern Italian food and was Denver's first restaurant to feature a woodburning pizza oven. Dinner is served nightly, but there's no lunch on weekends. Reservations are accepted. (Downtown)

Amadeo's
$, no credit cards • 5025 W. 44th Ave.
• (303) 455-5078

Amadeo's is a homey Italian restaurant with a big glass case of bakery items, including pies and cookies for eat-in or take-out. Amadeo's is open for lunch Monday through Friday and dinner from 5 PM to 8 PM Thursday and Friday. Look for the cheery red, white and green awning about two blocks south of Sheridan Boulevard. (West Denver)

Barolo Grill
$$$ • 3030 E. Sixth Ave. • (303) 393-1040

Since its opening in 1992, Barolo has skyrocketed into the ranks of the hottest of the city's hot spots. The food in this chic restaurant could be called "Cal-Ital," combining as it does Northern Italian recipes with California ingredients. Barolo does several good fish dishes with great sauces. Wines are an especially good value. It serves dinner only, Tuesday through Saturday; reservations are strongly recommended. (Central)

Basil Ristorante
$$ • 846 Broadway • (303) 832-8009

The only gripe about Basil's used to be its cramped space. That problem was solved in 1998 when it moved to new digs down the street. Now, more diners can enjoy the build-your-own entrees, chosen from several pastas, sauces, meats and veggies. The hand-rolled ravioli and fresh pastas are made on the premises, as are the breads and desserts. Basil's does pizza one better with its panini, bread dough wrapped around vegetables and cheeses and topped with marinara sauce. Basil's has lots of vegetarian selections. (One warning: Basil's is cigar friendly.) Dinner only, daily. Basil's serves beer and wine only. (Central)

Bella Ristorante
$$ • 1920 Market St. • (303) 297-8400

One of the original LoDo creations, Bella has the LoDo look of chic, renovated warehouse. Food portions are grande and the in-house bakery is sumptuous. Try the family style, six-course meal, including appetizer and dessert, for $19.95 a person. *Abbondanza!* Another location at 8405 Park Meadows Center Drive, (303) 768-8400, serves the southeast area. Lunch and dinner Monday through Sunday. (Downtown)

Carmine's on Penn
$$ • 92 S. Pennsylvania Ave.
• (303) 777-6443

Make a reservation; this place is way too popular to expect a table during the civilized dinner hour without one. And for good reason. Piles of homemade pasta form the bed for spicy and flavorful sauces. The portions are enough to feed two, plus lunch the next day. Wine list is adequate, if not expansive. The atmosphere bustles with an eclectic neighborhood scene. Carmine's is fast becoming a Denver institution. Dinner only Tuesday through Sunday. (Central)

Dario's
$$ • 2011 E. 17th Ave. • (303) 333-5243

An old-fashioned, cozy little Swiss-Italian neighborhood restaurant with traditional red-and-white checked tablecloths, Dario's serves veal, seafood, poultry and, of course, pasta dishes. Everything is made from scratch.

Dario's serves dinner nightly and lunch during the week only. (Central)

Il Fornaio
$$$ • 1631 Wazee St.
• (303) 573-5050

A deliciously elegant LoDo spot, Il Fornaio is a California-based restaurant whose specialty is its breads and baked goods (*il fornaio* means "the baker"). Meals can be quite good, too, though not always up to par with the prices and surroundings. Ask the server what's good and fresh to make the best selection. Lunch and dinner daily. (Downtown)

Josephina's
$$ • 1433 Larimer St. • 623-0166

A longtime Larimer Square favorite, Josephina's is known for its pizza and live jazz. In warm weather patrons try for a table on the sidewalk that provides a better spot from which to watch the comings and goings on this pedestrian-friendly block. The food at Josephina's is consistent, and the location on historic Larimer Square is worth the visit. Lunch and dinner are served daily. (Downtown, Southeast)

Little Pepina's
$$-$$$ • 3400 Osage St.
• (303) 477-3335

A veritable institution in West Denver, Little Pepina's has been around since 1938, and it looks it; the lavish maroon and pink decor is the height of mid-century style. But we mean this in the most complimentary way and hope they never change a thing. The generously proportioned fare includes pastas, fish, chicken, veal and an assortment of classic desserts highlighted by cheesecake, cannoli and the layered Sicilian cake called zuccata. Lunch and dinner are served on weekdays, but on weekends it's dinner only. It's closed on Monday. (West Denver)

INSIDERS' TIP

In 1944, Louis Ballast grilled a slice of cheese onto a hamburger at his Denver drive-in restaurant and patented the invention as "The Cheeseburger." Other claimants can take up their case with the Denver Metro Convention & Visitors Bureau, which stands by this bit of trivia.

Maggiano's Little Italy
$$ • 500 16th St. • (303) 260-7707

Dark woods, brass and red-checkered tablecloths give the feel of Little Italy in the 1940s at this family style newcomer located in the Denver Pavilions. The place is friendly and the large food portions are served with gusto. Salads are simple but fresh and crisp. Lunch and dinner daily. (Downtown)

Pagliacci's
$$ • 1440 W. 33rd Ave. • (303) 458-0530

Family-run for 50 years, Pagliacci's is another West Denver institution. The neon clown on the roof is famously visible from I-25 but not from the restaurant itself, which has a handsome, grotto-like interior. If you can't stay for a meal, you can get the famous minestrone to go. The food is excellent and sure to please for family dining or for romantic dates in one of the many red booths. It serves dinner only and is closed Monday. (West Denver)

Panzano
$$$ • 1717 Chama St. • (303) 296-3525

Housed in the new Hotel Monaco Denver, Panzano is a trip into calming dark woods and earth tones. Two open kitchens fill the air with scents of baked goods. Appetizers are especially good here, but watch out for Americanized Italian fare on the entree palette. Reservations, especially at the bustling noontime, are recommended. Breakfast, lunch and dinner daily. (Downtown)

Pasta's
$$$ • 9126 W. Bowles Ave., Littleton • (303) 933-2829

Pasta's is a big, friendly, family-run southern Italian restaurant that specializes in big portions and solicitous service. The staff will treat you like a relative as you enjoy their pastas, chicken, veal and seafood entrees. Pasta's serves lunch and dinner daily, except Sunday when it's dinner only. (Southwest)

Pasta, Pasta, Pasta
$-$$ • 278 Fillmore St. • (303) 377-2782

The food at this small, casual spot is far more creative than the name. Pasta, of course, is the focus. There is no set menu, so offerings depend on what's available. Eat in the sparse dining area, or on the small deck while shopping in North Cherry Creek; take out is available, too. Prices are reasonable in an otherwise expensive, tony area. Service is minimal (order at the counter), but friendly. Coffee drinks and mouth-watering desserts round out the meal. Lunch only weekdays till 5 PM and weekends till 4 PM. (Cherry Creek)

Ranelle's
$$$ • 1313 E. Sixth Ave. • (303) 831-1992

A tiny and loved northern Italian restaurant, Ranelle's is known for its sophisticated pasta dishes and its excellent soups and wine list. Reservations are strongly recommended. Ranelle's serves large enough portions to skip the entree and make a meal out of salad and a pasta.

It's closed Mondays and serves lunch weekdays and dinner on weekends. Reservations are recommended. (Central)

Sostanza
$$ • 1699 17th St. • (303) 292-4682

This recent addition to LoDo dining offers Old World Northern Italian cuisine with a contemporary flair. The dishes remain authentic to Italy. Try the popular Penne Russa, a two-pasta dish with a hint of vodka just like you'd get in the old country. The wine list is extensive; some go for its merits alone. The dining room is comfortable, simple and warm, with long windows in the bar area kept open during warm weather. You can smoke in the bar. It's closed on Sunday. Dinner is served the other six nights and lunch is served Monday to Friday. (Downtown)

Mexican

The Blue Bonnet Lounge
$ • 457 S. Broadway • (303) 778-0147

This Mexican joint was "discovered" by Denver yuppies in the '80s and remains popular — prepare to wait a while for a table. There's nothing fancy here, but there's lots of it with great big margaritas to wash it all down. The refried beans are a standout. Lunch and dinner are served daily. (Central)

Casa Bonita

$ • 6715 W. Colfax Ave., Lakewood
• (303) 232-5115

Unaccompanied adults take note: the food is decent at this place, but not the real attraction, which is the Disneyland-like entertainment geared toward children. Divers entertain daily by jumping from faux cliffs into a pool. For details, see our Kidstuff chapter. Lunch and dinner are served daily. (Southwest)

El Noa Noa

$ • 722 Santa Fe Dr.
• (303) 623-9968
$ • 1920 Federal Blvd., Westminster
• (303) 455-6071

The Denver location is in an authentic Mexican-American neighborhood, which is the site each year of a Cinco de Mayo parade and street festival, and in good weather, you can enjoy the large patio with wrought-iron chairs and a fountain. Both El Noa Noas dish out tasty enchiladas, burritos, tacos and rellenos. Lunch and dinner are served daily. (Central, North)

El Taco de Mexico

$, no credit cards • 714 Santa Fe Dr.
• (303) 623-3926
$, no credit cards • 2463 Sheridan Blvd., Edgewater • (303) 237-7174

This simple joint holds its own, despite stiff competition from larger and better-known El Noa Noa next door. Dining here is ultra-casual with a few tables and bar seating. It's open for breakfast, lunch and dinner daily. (Central, North)

La Estrellita

$ • 7617 W. 88th Ave., Westminster
• (303) 422-3700
$ • 45 N. Main St., Brighton
• (303) 654-9900

There are three Mexican restaurants owned and operated by the Montoya family; the other

is in Boulder. The award-winning green chile is available hot, medium, mild or vegetarian. Buy it by the quart for take-out. The atmosphere is casual. Breakfast is served all day. It's open seven days for all meals. (West, North)

La Loma Restaurant

$-$$ • 2527 W. 26th Ave.
• (303) 433-8300

In the up-and-coming Diamond Hill neighborhood just west of I-25 at Speer Boulevard, La Loma is rather incongruously housed in an 1887 Victorian home that's been renovated into a sprawling restaurant with a series of dining rooms. The restaurant is known for its big Margaritas and authentic food. Lunch and dinner are served every day except Saturday, which is dinner only. (West Denver)

Las Delicias

$-$$ • 439 E. 19th Ave. • (303) 839-5675
$-$$ • 50 E. Del Norte St. • (303) 430-0422
$-$$ • 1530 Blake St. • (303) 629-5051
$-$$ • 19553 Main St., Parker
• (303) 840-0325

This family-run restaurant has expanded to four locations, and loyal customers still can't get enough of their Michoacan-style carnitas and fajitas, carne adobada, taquitos, carne asada and steak ranchero. It offers great breakfasts in addition to lunch and dinner every day. (Central, North, Downtown, South)

Mexicali Cafe

$-$$ • 1453 Larimer St.
• (303) 892-1444

This is a big, fun, colorful place with a nice location in Larimer Square. They describe themselves as a "Bordertown Diner" and make an especially big deal about their fajitas. There's a good selection of barbecue items, more than at most Tex-Mex places. The outdoor tables are prized for people-watching. Lunch and dinner are served daily, and there's a special weekend brunch menu. (Downtown)

INSIDERS' TIP

If you're on the lookout for a low-fat, low-sodium meal, check your menu for HealthMark selections. HealthMark is a Denver organization that analyzes recipes and gives its stamp of approval to those that meet its criteria.

Mexico City Lounge & Cafe
$, no credit cards • 2115 Larimer St.
• (303) 296-0563

Denverites make a big fuss about authenticity when discussing the comparative merits of restaurants. No argument here: this is the real thing. The green chile and burritos are favorites, and breakfast is a real eye-opener. If you're a fan of menudo, this is the place to go. It's closed Mondays, but serves breakfast and lunch on the other days. (Downtown)

Morrison Inn
$-$$ • 301 Bear Creek Ave., Morrison
• (303) 697-6650

This is a fun, Americanized restaurant in an 1885 building in the heart of the Foothills town of Morrison. It's known for its custom-made (not pre-mixed) margaritas and for being a beginning — or ending — spot for mountain bikers and hikers. The fare is standard Mexican served for lunch and dinner daily. (West suburbs)

Rosa Linda's Mexican Cafe
$ • 2005 W. 33rd Ave.
• (303) 455-0608

You say you want a neighborhood restaurant? Check out this one. Run by the Aquirre family since 1985, Rosa Linda's is a small, plain place with great burritos, enchiladas and soft chile rellenos. Rosa Linda's wins awards for its shredded beef burritos, chile rellenos and other specialties. There are a few tables on the sidewalk. It's open daily for lunch and dinner. (West Denver)

Taqueria Patzcuaro
$, no credit cards • 2616 W. 32nd Ave.
• (303) 455-4389

An ultra-casual restaurant in a Spanish-speaking neighborhood, Taqueria Patzcuaro draws fans of its green chile and soft tacos from all over the city. The neighborhood around Taqueria is alive with Mexican music.

Lunch and dinner are served daily, and there's no alcohol. (West Denver)

Z-Teca
$ • 550 Grant St. • (303) 765-5878
$ • 1531 Market St. • (303) 629-1300
$ • 8246D W. Bowles Ave., Littleton
• (303) 948-2000
$ • 5188 S. Broadway, Lakewood
• (303) 806-9500
$ • 8719 E. Dry Creek Rd., Englewood
• (303) 221-7200

Interested in a burrito the size of your head? Try Z-Teca. This made-to-order Mexican fast food place serves a great burrito stuffed with fresh ingredients and flavors bursting from the giant flour tortilla (or you can get it "naked"). The grilled chicken or barbacoa is just the right amount of meat, rice, beans, cheese and salsa to keep you happy all day long. There's also a potato/veggie combo that zings, and the margaritas are quite good. Lunch and dinner served daily. (Central, Downtown, Southwest, South, Southeast)

Middle Eastern

Cedars
$$-$$$ • 1550 S. Federal Blvd. at Florida Ave. • (303) 936-2980

A Lebanese family owns and operates this attractive 100-seat restaurant, which serves terrific falafel, tabbouleh and more sophisticated Middle Eastern fare. Save room for the baklava. It's open for lunch and dinner Monday to Saturday. (Southwest)

Jerusalem Restaurant
$ • 1890 E. Evans Ave.
• (303) 777-8838

A tiny, eight-table restaurant that does a bustling take-out business, Jerusalem is popular with students from the University of Denver campus nearby. Everything is good here, in-

Cadillac Ranch in downtown Denver's Larimer Square prides itself on its Texas-size certified Angus steaks.

Photo: Daily Camera/Lourie Zipf

cluding the kebabs, hummus, baba ghanouj and phyllo pastries. Students cramming for an exam no doubt also appreciate the fact that Jerusalem is virtually always open, from about 9 AM to as late as 4 AM. The space crunch is eased in the summer by the outdoor patio. Alcohol is not served. (South central)

Pizza

Armando's of Cherry Creek
$ • 201 Milwaukee St. • (303) 320-6300

This casual New York-style pizzeria in the heart of Cherry Creek North has many fans, and the double-crusted spinach pizza with black olives is especially well-thought-of. The lasagna would make mom proud. Take-out is available. There is a $10 minimum for credit card purchases. Lunch and dinner are served daily.

There's also a franchise location, not associated with the Cherry Creek store, in Aurora at 16611 E. Smoky Hill Road, (303) 690-6660. (Cherry Creek, East)

Beau Jo's Pizza
$-$$ • 2700 S. Colorado Blvd.
• (303) 758-1519
$-$$ • 7805 Wadsworth Blvd., Arvada
• (303) 420-8376.

The original Beau Jo's is still in Idaho Springs and is a beloved stopping point on the way home from skiing for Denverites who crave thick-crusted pizza loaded with toppings. While diners wait for the pizza (good things take time), they can draw on napkins and pin them on the wall along with the thousands of others. Finally, Beau Jo's opened up branches in southeast Denver, Arvada and Boulder. All are open for lunch and dinner daily. (South central, West suburbs)

Bonnie Brae Tavern
$-$$ • 740 S. University Blvd.
• (303) 777-2262

The crowds! The noise! The pizza! This astoundingly popular, 60-year-old neighborhood pizza joint is locally famous and always busy, busy, busy. It's a fun place, but don't come here if you're in a hurry. It serves lunch and dinner daily except Monday. Take-out is available. (South central)

Pasquini's Pizzeria
$ • 1310 S. Broadway • (303) 744-0917

A nifty little pizzeria with an artsy interior and mosaic-topped tables, Pasquini's serves New York-style thin crust, sauceless Bianca and thick-crust Sicilian-style pizzas and individual pizzettas with interesting toppings. Also on the menu are calzones and subs. Pasquini's is nestled amid the antique stores on South Broadway at Louisiana Avenue. Lunch and dinner are served daily except Sunday, which is dinner only. Take-out and delivery are available. (South central)

Pizza Colore Cafe
$-$$ • 1512 Larimer St. • (303) 534-6844

The Rocky Mountain offshoot of a small New Jersey chain, Pizza Colore has a menu that's built around a clever gimmick: pizzas come with sauces of red, green or white, the three colors of the Italian flag. Other Italian entrees, plus calzones, are available. Smoking is allowed on the patio, which is where you'll want to be anyway in good weather. Pizza Colore has an upscale cousin in Cherry Creek, Cucina Colore, at 3041 E. Third Avenue, (303) 393-6917. Both locations open seven days for lunch and dinner. (Downtown, Cherry Creek)

Seafood

Fresh Fish Company
$$$ • 7600 E. Hampden Ave.
• (303) 740-9556

The aquatic theme extends to the decor at this big restaurant, which consists of walls of beautiful tropical aquariums. Mesquite grilling is a specialty here, and the $16.95 Sunday brunch, with all-you-can-eat crab legs and shrimp, is very popular. On Sunday nights there's a lobster bake, with discounts on lobster. Lunch is served Monday through Friday, dinner nightly. (Southeast)

Jax Fishhouse
$$-$$$ • 1539 17th St. • (303) 292-5767

Jax won't slip a skimpy slice of fish on your plate. Here, you'll get a hearty slab of fresh fish, seasoned well and served with a nice variety of side dishes. The raw oysters, stone crab claws and crawfish are all delicious and succulent. Non-fish eaters can opt for a burger or steak, but fish is truly the dish. The place is hopping, too, so don't expect to be seated right away. Just take your time and enjoy the buildup. Jax serves dinner only, every night. (Downtown)

McCormick's Fish House & Bar
$$$ • 1659 Wazee St. • (303) 825-1107

In McCormick's elegant dining room can be found some of the freshest fish in Denver. If oysters are in season, this is one of the few places in town to get them. McCormick's "The Time Is the Price" menu, available from 5 to 6 PM, is one of the best bargains going (if you order one of the evening's special selections at 5:45 PM, you pay $5.45). And for one of the best deals around, try the happy hour bar menu of seafood appetizers for only $1.95 from 3 to 6 PM or 9 to 11 PM. This is a great deal and a good choice for pre- and post-theater meals (the Denver Performing Arts Complex is just a few blocks away). Private dining rooms are available; call for information. Breakfast, lunch and dinner are served daily. (Downtown)

240 Union
$$-$$$ • 240 Union Blvd. at Sixth Ave., Lakewood • (303) 989-3562

The menu changes seasonally at this creative restaurant, which specializes in seafood. Pastas and pizzas round out the offerings. It has a fine pedigree: two of its three owners are Noel Cunningham, of Strings restaurant fame, and executive chef Matthew Franklin, who did a stint at the original Rattlesnake Club, Denver's most innovative restaurant of the 1980s. The restaurant has recently undergone a face-lift and now sports blue skylights and wooden dividers that represent "the city meeting the Foothills." There's a nice enclosed patio and a wall-to-wall open grill. 240 Union serves dinner nightly and lunch on weekdays. (West suburbs)

Wahoo's Fish Taco
$ • 1521 Blake St. • (303) 623-0263

Hey surfers, missing the scene on the

Baja? Then stop into Wahoo's for your fix. And while you're at it, try their unique and tasty — really — fish tacos. The mild white fish is flaky and full of flavor. Chicken and steak are also available in burritos, bowls and sandwiches. This restaurant is styled after a surfer joint and owned, not coincidentally, by old surfers. Beer, margaritas and wine are served. The patio is small, but great for people-watching. Lunch and dinner are served daily. (Downtown)

South American

Cafe Brazil
$$$, no credit cards • 3611 Navajo St. • (303) 480-1877

Cafe Brazil is a tiny, intimate restaurant in what used to be an Old World Italian neighborhood that has become more ethnically mixed. The neighborhood has a strong artistic inclination with an alternative gallery and theater space in the same block. It may not look like much from the outside, but trust us, the food is terrific. Try the feijoada completa, Brazil's national dish. It combines black beans, meat, fruit and rice in a most delicious way. Cafe Brazil is open for dinner only and is closed Sunday and Monday.

Reservations are recommended on the weekends. (West Denver)

Sabor Latino
$-$$ • 4340 W. 35th Ave. • (303) 455-8664

A charming place in an interesting neighborhood, Sabor Latino serves South American and Mexican cuisine. Sabor Latino recently went upscale, at least in its new, expanded digs. But the food is still the same, and still good. Specialties of the house include Colombian tamales and South American empanadas, baked or fried. A nice selection of Chilean wines is available. It serves lunch and dinner Monday through Saturday and is closed on Sunday. Reservations are not accepted. (West Denver)

Less Than a Meal: Coffeehouses, Ice Cream Parlors, etc.

All For the Better
$, no credit cards • 3501 S. Clarkson St., Englewood • (303) 781-0230

This is a sweet, old-fashioned ice-cream parlor that also serves soup and sandwiches. Ice cream is homemade, and flavors vary daily. It's across the street from Swedish Medical Center. It's open during lunch and dinner hours seven days a week. (Southeast)

Bluepoint Bakery
$, no credit cards • 1307 E. Sixth Ave. • (303) 839-1820

Bluepoint devotees are fierce in their praise of this bakery's bread, which ranges from densely brown and chewy to light as a feather. The sourdough is great, and there are more unusual breads, too, such as tomato-basil or olive. Rather than the giant cookies you'll find elsewhere, Bluepoint's are petite treats. The granola is a great for breakfast. Bluepoint opens early (7 AM) and closes in the early evening Monday through Saturday. It's closed Sundays. (Central)

Common Grounds
$, no credit cards • 3484 W. 32nd Ave. • (303) 458-5248

A coffeehouse in the European tradition, Common Grounds doubles as a community center for the west Highlands neighborhood. Lots of free reading material, board games and a piano for would-be Liberaces make this a place to stop and sit a spell. Pastries, cakes, muffins and bagels are available. In the evenings, there might be poetry readings or jazz concerts. Sign of the times: this coffeehouse prohibits smoking.

It's open seven days until 11 PM. (West Denver)

Economy Greek Market
$ • 1035 Lincoln St.
• (303) 861-3001

A Denver institution since 1901, the Economy Market stocks hard-to-find varieties of imported feta cheese and olives as well as other Greek and Mediterranean specialties. It's open every day except Sunday for breakfast and lunch, featuring gyros and other deli items. (Central)

Highland Grounds Corner Coffee House
$ • 3301 Tejon St. • (303) 433-4626

The anchor to an ever-improving neighborhood, Highland Grounds is the essence of a neighborhood gathering spot. Coffee drinks are the focus, along with fresh bagels and pastries from Denver's Bluepoint Bakery. Sandwiches are also available (as is a selection of fine cigars). Historic photos of Highland fill the walls and frame comfortable booths and chairs. All it takes is a few visits to this friendly spot and owners Shelly and Jamy Garcia will treat you like family. Open Monday through Friday at 6:30 AM; Saturday and Sunday at 8 AM. Closes between 7 PM and 9 PM Monday through Saturday, and 2 PM on Sunday.

Josh & John's Naturally Homemade Ice Cream
$, no credit cards • 1444 Market St.
• (303) 628-0310

Started by two boyhood friends in their 20s, Josh & John's now has stores in Boulder, Colorado Springs and Denver. About 13 flavors are available at any given time. Try the coffee crunch, citrus bliss or the Rocky Roy, named after Colorado's Gov. Roy Romer. You can also get a cup of coffee, but no fancy lattes or anything like that. It's open from 11 AM to midnight daily. (Downtown)

Le Delice
$-$$ • 250 Steele St.
• (303) 331-0972

Actually, you can get lunch here, a slice of quiche or a salad to fortify you in the midst of a Cherry Creek shopping excursion. You can even get a light dinner most evenings until 9 PM. But our primary reason for including this very French bakery is the extravagant array of mouthwatering tortes, cookies and pastries. The visual feast alone will put weight on you.

It's closed Sundays and early, at 6 PM, on Mondays. (Cherry Creek)

Liks
$, no credit cards • 2039 E. 13th Ave.
• (303) 321-1492

Take a number and get in line for this well-known Denver spot. Formerly known as Lickety Split, this old-fashioned ice cream parlor is the place to go for a New York egg cream or a fabulously indulgent sundae. The homemade ice creams come in such tempting flavors as Almond Roca and Cheesman Park (a strawberry-cheesecake concoction named for the park a few blocks away).

Don't fret if they're out of your favorite flavor; they'll put it on the request list and call you when it's available. It's open seven days. (Central)

The Market
$ • 1445 Larimer St.
• (303) 534-5140

Come to The Market for great food and desserts or just a cup of coffee and amazing people-watching. It's all here, from gourmet pasta to killer cakes, to black-leather-clad bikers and CEOs. You can make a meal out of the gourmet offerings, which include made-to-order deli sandwiches and a changing variety of soups and salads. It's not really a restaurant, so we've included it in this category. The baked goods, top-of-the-line chocolates and shelves of imported food items make this as much a shopping destination as a dining spot, and the espresso bar is always busy. Bring a cup of cappuccino and a plate of biscotti out to a table on the sidewalk and watch the world go by. It's open seven days a week. (Downtown)

Moe's Broadway Bagel

$ • 550 Grant St. • (303) 733-7331

$ • 745 Colorado Blvd. • (303) 322-2966

Schmears, sandwiches and homemade ice cream make Moe's a popular spot for lunchers and munchers. At least a dozen bagel flavors tempt diners, along with an array of meat and veggie fillings and cream cheese smeared on thick as a brick. Monday through Saturday, 6 PM to 8 PM, Sunday closes at 5 PM. (Central)

Newsstand Cafe

$ • 630 E. Sixth Ave. at Washington St.

• (303) 777-6060

A wonderful sip-and-read coffeehouse a few blocks from the famed Esquire Theatre, the Newsstand attracts an interesting, literary crowd. Sandwiches and pastries are available in addition to espresso drinks. With more than 1,000 magazines, newspapers and books (including audio, travel and Internet books) for sale, no one need suffer for lack of reading material. It's open seven days. (Central)

Omonia Bakery

$, no credit cards • 2813 E. Colfax Ave.

• (303) 394-9333

This authentic Greek bakery will satisfy a craving for baklava, koularakia, kataifi or galataboureko. A napoleon is available, too, and, of course, there's strong coffee to go with whatever sweet your heart desires. It's open daily until 10 PM. (Central)

Paris on the Platte

$ • 1553 Platte St. • (303) 455-2451

Popular with neighborhood artists, some of whom exhibit their paintings here, Paris on the Platte is connected to a used bookstore. If coffee isn't enough, sandwiches, salads and soups are available as well as pastries and bagels.

It's open till 1 AM Sunday through Thursday and 3 AM Friday and Saturday. (Downtown/Platte River)

Pasquini's Baking Company

$ • 1710 S. Broadway • (303) 698-9393

The rustic breads are manna for those who appreciate a real, hard crust. Formerly known as Campagna Baking, they also make muffins and pastries and sell Italian meats and

cheeses. Coffee is available too. The bakery is open every day except Monday and its products are widely carried in local supermarkets. (South)

Rheinlander Bakery

$, no credit cards • 5721 Olde Wadsworth Blvd., Arvada • (303) 467-1810

$, no credit cards • 8025 N. Sheridan Blvd., Unit U • (303) 427-5664

Authentic German rye bread tops the list at this charming family-run Old World bakery in Arvada's historic Olde Town district. Coffeecakes, Danish pastries, European-style tortes and cookies are available too. The Sheridan location specializes in wedding cakes. Both locations are closed Sunday. They're open until 6 PM on weekdays and 5 PM on Saturday. (Western suburbs)

Rosales Mexican Bakery

$, no credit cards • 2636 W. 32nd Ave.

• (303) 458-8420

This family-operated bakery features 80 varieties of authentic Mexican pastries and bread baked fresh daily as well as a selection of imported Mexican items. On weekends Rosales serves carnitas, tortas and tamales. It's open daily from 6:30 AM to 10 PM. Checks are not accepted. (West Denver)

St. Mark's Coffeehouse

$, no credit cards • 1416 Market St.

• (303) 446-2925

$, no credit cards • 2019 E. 17th Ave.

• (303) 322-8384

The bohemian alternative to the much more crowded Market on Larimer Street, St. Mark's serves coffee, cappuccino and baked goods from 7 AM to midnight on weekdays and until 1 AM on weekends. Patrons sit outside for people-watching or inside on folding chairs and former church pews. It's open daily. Checks are not accepted. (Downtown) The location on 17th Avenue opened in August 1997.

Stella's Coffeehouse

$ • 1476 S. Pearl St.

• (303) 777-1031

Stella's is almost certainly the only Denver coffeehouse with a branch in Amsterdam —

the owner's family runs a cafe by the same name in that European city. Stella's has lots of outdoor seating and scrumptious baked goods and desserts. It also serves a light lunch menu. The adjoining Amsterdam Room has live entertainment on weekends and can be booked for private meetings and parties. No smoking is allowed, a custom we suspect doesn't hold true for the trans-Atlantic Stella's. It's open seven days a week, until 1 AM on weekends. (South Central)

Breakfast

Benny's Central
$ • 301 E. 7th Ave.
• (303) 894-0788

Benny's is actually a full-service Mexican food joint with as much history as flavor in its food. But we've listed it under breakfasts because, it serves the best breakfast burrito known to humankind. Fat and filled with eggs, potatoes and a choice of menudo, sausage or meat, it's served smothered in green chili with tender chunks of pork. It's no diet plate, mind you, but great comfort food. And while you wait you can munch chips and salsa (also among the best in Denver). There are other breakfast items, all with Benny's Mexican flare. For lunch or dinner, choose from a variety of combos and à la carte items. If you go on the weekend, plan on slurping a few margaritas while you wait an hour for a table. Breakfast, lunch and dinner served daily. (Central)

Dozen's
$ • 236 W. 13th Ave.
• (303) 572-0066

Want a breakfast that will stay with you, but don't want to ingest too much grease? Dozen's is the place. Located in a quaint, renovated house on the outskirts of downtown, Dozen's serves a traditional American breakfast of wonderful omelets, griddle combinations, waffles and pancakes. Homemade baked goods are served, too. Dozen's bustles weekdays with a business crowd and on weekends, albeit more relaxed, with the coffee-drinking, paper-reading crowd.

Dozen's serves breakfast and lunch daily. (Central)

Egg Shell and Incredibles Cafe
$ • 1520 Blake St.
• (303) 623-7555

Homemade soups, desserts and an extensive breakfast menu provide something for everyone. And it's in a great downtown location across from the Farmer's Market (summer weekends). Platter-sized pancakes, omelets of every combination and even some breakfast pasta make the Egg Shell good. Atmosphere is just right to wake you up: busy and often loud. Breakfast and lunch daily. (Downtown)

Delectable Egg
$ • 1642 Market St. • (303) 572-8146
$ • 1625 Court Pl. • (303) 892-5720

Traditional breakfast choices including omelets, eggs benedict, waffles, french toast and pancakes fill customers at this spot. Similar to the Egg Shell, Delectable Egg is housed in an old warehouse, which makes it look a little like greasy-diner-gone-chic (although the food isn't unusually greasy). Otherwise, Delectable Egg is standard, but good, breakfast stuff. Breakfast and lunch daily. (Downtown)

Ellyngton's
$$$$ • at the Brown Palace Hotel,
321 17th St. • (303) 297-3111

Best known for its lavish champagne brunch (with Dom Perignon, if you've got the bucks for it), the classy and urbane Ellyngton's also serves a tasteful breakfast and lunch, but no dinner. Sunday brunch is an extravagant buffet with impressive displays of food. (Downtown)

Le Peep Restaurant
$ • 3030 E. 2nd Ave. • (303) 394-2040
$ • 1699 S. Colorado Blvd.
• (303) 759-3388
$ • 2456 S. Parker Rd. • (303) 369-5404
$ • 7400 E. Hampden Ave.
• (303) 694-3456

There's a small selection of sandwiches, but Le Peep is all about breakfast. Omelets, pancakes, french toast, you get the picture. There's nothing gourmet here, but it's tasty. Coffee drinkers will like the self-serve pot left on the table. Breakfast and lunch daily. (Cherry Creek, South, Southeast, East)

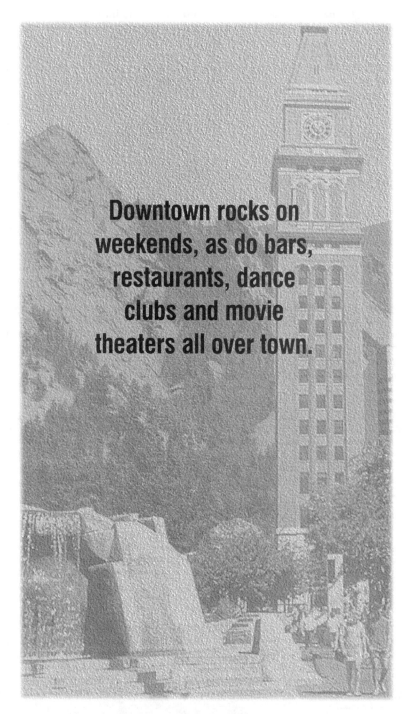

Downtown rocks on weekends, as do bars, restaurants, dance clubs and movie theaters all over town.

Nightlife

Visitors who haven't strolled Denver streets for a few years will notice something remarkably different about downtown these days: the city hops until the wee hours. As recently as the early 90s, downtown Denver businesses were scheming ways to keep people in the city after dark. Today, parking rates are at a premium (when you can find it) and waiting for a restaurant table is part of the experience. But don't let that dissuade you from venturing downtown; it's an experience not to be missed.

Downtown rocks on weekends, as do bars, restaurants, dance clubs and movie theaters all over town. Thanks to a booming economy, when the sun goes down this town is once again exciting, eclectic and electrifying.

In this chapter we survey Denver's nightlife, stopping in at a few of our favorite bars, brewpubs, live music venues, comedy clubs and movie houses. This isn't meant to be a comprehensive listing; for that kind of inclusiveness, the best place to turn is *Westword*, Denver's free weekly paper. The Friday editions of *The Denver Post* and *Rocky Mountain News* carry weekend entertainment listings, as does the *Daily Camera* with Boulder's happenings as well. The newspaper *Out Front* is a good source of information about gay and lesbian nightlife. The paper is free and widely distributed in most coffee and sandwich shops.

Because people interpret "nightlife" so broadly — it includes everything from a coffeehouse with live poetry readings to an outdoor rock concert at a stadium — there is some inevitable overlap with other chapters. A brewpub such as the Wynkoop that serves dinner also draws a late-night billiards crowd. Martini and wine bars house the chic set (get to the Cruise Room early for a sought-after booth). If a listing in this chapter has an asterisk (*) after its name, that means it's described in further detail in our Restaurants chapter.

Theater and dance performances and concerts, such as those at the Denver Performing Arts Complex, are covered in our Arts chapter. We direct your attention to such popular in-town music venues as the Paramount Theatre, the Ogden Theatre and the Swallow Hill Music Association.

As opposed to concert halls, where advance ticketing is recommended, most of the live music venues described in this chapter serve food and drink and can be visited on a drop-in basis, although this is no hard-and-fast rule. Finally, you'll find family attractions that don't shut down at dusk, such as Elitch Gardens, described in the Tours and Attractions chapter.

Keep in mind, too, that today's hot spot could be tomorrow's Siberia. No guidebook could ever hope to keep up with the strange twists of taste that make one place worth lining up for and another worth taking pains to avoid. It seems every bar in town added a pool table in 1993; whether this is a trend with staying power or whether we'll see them replaced with aquariums or climbing walls is anybody's guess. And, of course, music and dance clubs change their format and hours frequently. If you're looking for a specific kind of music, it's always best to call ahead.

After years of a system that permitted individuals 18 and older to buy 3.2 percent beer but nothing stronger, the Colorado legislature simplified matters by raising the drinking age for any kind of alcoholic beverage to 21. Closing time at bars and nightclubs is generally 2 AM, but most restaurants stop serving food at 11 PM or even earlier.

Colorado is not a state that takes drunk driving lightly. Penalties for driving under the influence or driving while impaired are severe. If you've had too much to drink, any restaurant or bar will call a taxi for you. If you're headed up to Central City and Black Hawk for an evening of gambling (see the end of this chapter), we strongly recommend that you avail yourself of one of the shuttle services rather than driving your own car.

Bars and Other Gathering Spots

Duffy's Shamrock Restaurant & Bar
1635 Court Pl. • (303) 534-4935

Duffy's Shamrock Restaurant & Bar really comes into its own on St. Paddy's Day, but it's a classic Irish drinking establishment the rest of the year too. In fact, so rowdy is its St. Patrick's Day crowd that the bar used to close that day. A full menu includes sandwiches, steaks, prime rib and shrimp. And there are plenty of Irish beers on tap and by the bottle. Nothing fancy, mind you, but a right neighborly place.

Cruise Room
1600 17th St. • (303) 628-5400

The restored Oxford Hotel, one block away from Union Station, boasts a restaurant and bar complex that's among the city's best. The intimately sized Cruise Room was modeled after a lounge on the Queen Mary and has a wonderful art-deco interior that dates back to the lifting of Prohibition in 1933. A favorite with visiting authors, the Cruise Room is a great place for a late-night drink, especially if your taste runs to martinis. The bar doesn't have live music, but the jukebox is well-stocked with jazz and Big Band music. Be forewarned: it can be tough to get a seat on the weekends unless you arrive early and stake your spot.

Fado Irish Pub
1735 19th St. • (303) 297-0066

A welcome departure from the LoDo brewpub scene, Fado brings Ireland to Denver. Most of this authentic Irish pub really is authentic — built in Ireland and brought to Denver piece by piece. Relax in one of nearly a dozen cozy nooks, or be in the middle of the crowd that surrounds the large central bar.

There's a full Irish menu too, with appetizers are served until midnight.

McCormick's Fish House and Bar*
1659 Wazee St. • (303) 825-1107

For more-public occasions, the roomy corner bar at McCormick's attracts a big crowd after 5 PM for Guinness Stout on tap and other libations. If you decide to stay for dinner, some of the freshest fish in town can be had in McCormick's main dining room just across the hallway. Check out their well-priced happy hour appetizers after work and late night.

The Brown Palace
321 17th St. • (303) 297-3111

The grande dame of Denver hotels, The Brown Palace has three dining rooms, including Ellyngton's* and the formal Palace Arms*, where gentlemen diners are requested to wear jackets and ties. The Ship Tavern* is the most casual (though not necessarily the least expensive) of the trio and a good place to stop in for a drink or a bite to eat. It's more restaurant than bar, but with its dark wood and nautical decor, it has the feel of an English pub. The walls and ceiling are hung with models of actual ships from America's clipper period. The Ship Tavern can be entered through the Brown Palace Hotel lobby, at 321 17th Street, or from the street at Tremont Place.

The Buckhorn Exchange*
1000 Osage St. • (303) 534-9505

The upstairs bar at The Buckhorn Exchange has been a Denver institution for more than 100 years — Colorado's first liquor license is posted on the wall. The handcarved, white-oak bar dates from 1857 and was brought over from Germany. Weekends, there's live music in the adjacent Victorian parlor. The Buckhorn is also famous for its vast collection of animal heads mounted on the walls.

INSIDERS' TIP

For nightlife with a relaxed twist, try securing a seat at one of the outdoor restaurants on Larimer Square, sit back and people-watch the night away. You'll see it all, from weekend warriors in black leather on Harleys to clubbers in a mini-skirt parade to lovers strolling arm-in-arm.

Live Music

Bluebird Theater
3317 E. Colfax Ave. • (303) 322-2308

For a diverse range of musical acts in a gritty neighborhood, try the Bluebird. Located on Denver's infamous East Colfax Avenue, the Bluebird opened as a movie house in 1913 and has since had several incarnations (including a stint as a porn house). Local bands as well as up-and-coming acts share the marquee. There's a balcony for the under 21 set, 550 seats on the main level and several tables arranged to accommodate the evening's musical attraction (arrive early to secure a table). A dance floor sometimes serves as a mosh pit, depending on the act. Hours and ticket prices vary depending on who's playing.

El Chapultepec
1962 Market St. • (303) 295-9126

Once on the edge of gentrified Denver, El Chapultepec used to be a slightly dangerous place to drink beer, eat a burrito and listen to jazz. It now finds itself in the rising shadow of Coors Field and encroached upon by brewpubs, art galleries and designer tile shops. So far, the essential attraction — sizzling jazz — has remained the same. El Chapultepec is open every night; there's no cover charge, and they don't take reservations.

Brendan's Market Street Pub
1624 Market St. • (303) 595-0609

Brendan's Market Street Pub serves up live blues every night at a subterranean lair in lower downtown (LoDo to Insiders). Monday nights are set aside for an all-comers-welcome blues jam. A pub menu is available. Brendan's happy hour lasts from 4 to 7 PM Monday through Thursday. Cover charge is usually $3 to $5.

Moondance Café*
1626 Market St. • (303) 893-1626

If you want a pure piano bar, this is your place. You can sit at the piano and interact with the pianist at this neighborhood place that prides itself on welcoming everyone. A full menu is served, and the age range tends toward 30 and older.

Trios Enoteca LoDo
1730 Wynkoop St. • (303) 293-2887

The popularity of Trios Enoteca has waned with the whims of trendy bar life, but it's still a great place to order from more than 300 wines. The cigar room draws the 30- and 40-something crowd. Live music is performed five nights a week. Decor is elegant, light woods with comfortable couches and high-backed chairs. A light menu is also served.

Soapy Smith's Eagle Bar
1317 14th St. • (303) 534-1111

During most of the week, Soapy Smith's Eagle Bar is popular with students from the nearby Auraria Campus, who come to drink a beer and enjoy live music. It's not exclusively the college T-shirt crowd, but they dominate. You'll find live tunes seven nights a week — from jazz bands to funk and ska. Cover charge is usually $1 to $3.

Purple Martini
1358 15th St. • (303) 820-0575

In the mood for an exotic martini? The Purple Martini offers 80 different kinds as well as live jazz Wednesday, Thursday and Saturday. Acid jazz is played the other nights (although not live). Look for a 30-something crowd dressed in "business casual." Half-off happy hour is from 4 PM to 6:30 PM.

La Coupole*
2191 Arapahoe St. • (303) 297-2288

Although the skyscrapers of downtown Denver are visible from the windows of La Coupole, the lace curtains, wood floors, snippets of overheard French and gracious outdoor courtyard make patrons feel like they're dining in Paris. This elegant French restaurant is one of the most beautiful rooms in Denver

INSIDERS' TIP

If a listing in this chapter has an asterisk (*) after its name, that means it's described in further detail in our Restaurants chapter.

Movies Filmed in Denver

Even if you've never been to Denver, you may have seen it in the movies. The hit movie *Die Harder*, starring Bruce Willis, had major scenes filmed at the old Stapleton Airport. Portions of Woody Allen's 1973 film *Sleeper* were shot in Denver and vicinity, including the exterior of the National Center for Atmospheric Research in Boulder and a modernist home visible from I-70 near Genesee that's known locally as the Sleeper house.

Between July 1996 and June 1997, 188 film productions took place in Denver, including eight feature films, according to the Mayor's Office of Art, Culture & Film, which keeps tabs on such things. All this production activity tucked $32.8 million into Denver's coffers.

Among the films being shot in Denver in past years were Warner Brothers' *Under Siege II: In Dark Territory*, with Steven Seagal; and Boat Drink Productions' *Things to Do in Denver When You're Dead*, starring Andy Garcia. *In Dark Territory* has scenes in Lower Downtown (LoDo), including around Union Station and Coors Field. *Things to Do* was shot largely in the Five Points neighborhood at 26th and Welton streets, including the historic old Rossonian Hotel. For some key scenes, the Rossonian's bar was transformed into a malt shop. *Elephant Man* (also known as Nickel and Dime), with Bill Murray, was also filmed in Denver and Colorado.

Recently, the made-for-TV film *Asteroids* was filmed in downtown Denver and prominently displayed the campus of East High School, one of Denver's beautiful, old schools. The remake of *The Shining* (also

Photo: Mayor's Office of Art, Culture and Film

The bar at the old Rossonian Hotel in Five Points was transformed into a malt shop for the film *Things to Do in Denver When You're Dead.*

made for TV) was shot in Denver and Estes Park. And not surprisingly, *The Ellen Hart Peña Story* (she's the wife of former mayor Federico Peña), was filmed in Denver.

in which to enjoy a meal and, on Thursday through Saturday nights from 7:30 to 11 PM, live jazz. Reservations are recommended.

Jimmy's Grille
320 S. Birch St., Glendale • (303) 322-5334

Jimmy's Grille packs 'em in for reggae and Tex-Mex food and burgers. Some of reggae's biggest stars have played here on Thursday through Saturday nights. There's also jazz on Tuesday nights.

Josephina's*
1433 Larimer St. • (303) 623-0166

There's no cover and no minimum drinks charge at Josephina's, where there's live entertainment every night of the week. Bands and musicians — mostly classic rock and R&B — have the stage.

Josephina's offers fine Italian food including pizza and pastas. Reservations are suggested as it gets pretty packed, but you can typically find standing room.

DESTINATION
DOWNTOWN
DENVER
& LODO

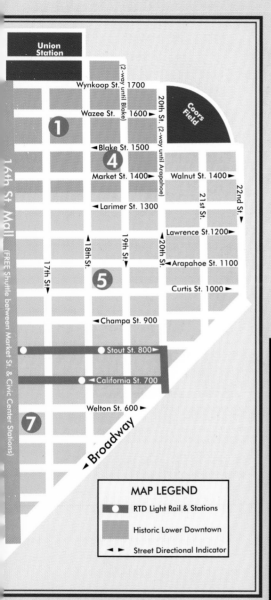

Union Station

Wynkoop St. 1700

(2-way until Blake)

Wazee St. 1600 ►

①

20th St. (2-way until Arapahoe)

Coors Field

◄ Blake St. 1500

④

Market St. 1400

Walnut St. 1400 ►

Larimer St. 1300 ►

21st St.

22nd St. ▼

Lawrence St. 1200 ►

18th St.

19th St.

20th St.

◄ Arapahoe St. 1100

Curtis St. 1000 ►

17th St.

⑤

◄ Champa St. 900

Stout St. 800 ►

◄ California St. 700

Welton St. 600 ►

⑦

Broadway

16th St. Mall

(FREE Shuttle between Market St. & Civic Center Stations)

MAP LEGEND

● RTD Light Rail & Stations

■ Historic Lower Downtown

◄ ► Street Directional Indicator

MAP INDEX

① JAX FISH HOUSE

② LARIMER SQUARE

③ TIMBUKTU STATION

④ VESTA DIPPING GRILL

⑤ EMBASSY SUITES

⑥ RIALTO CAFE

⑦ MARLOWE'S

⑧ MAGGIANO'S LITTLE ITALY

LO
DO
DENVER
old. New. Now.

GETTING HERE Parking & Access in Downtown Denver

Parking

Whether you're going to Larimer Square, Lower Downtown, the Denver Performing Arts complex, Denver Pavilions, The Shops at Tabor Center, Writer Square or any other Downtown destination, you'll find plenty of parking within a block or two of the 16th Street Mall. Garage spaces are usually more expensive than those in surface lots, and be aware of events and activities that may affect parking costs and availability.

16th Street Mall Shuttle

Once you've arrived, you can hop on the FREE 16th Street Mall Shuttle to access all of Downtown's shops, restaurants and other holiday attractions. The shuttle stops at every intersection along 16th Street between the Civic Center and Market Street bus stations.

Transit

You can park for free at the Alameda & Broadway or I-25 & Broadway park-n-ride lots and take RTD's light rail right into the heart of Downtown Denver. Dozens of bus routes also come into Downtown from all over the metropolitan area. Contact RTD at 303-299-6000 for more details on fares and schedules.

At Maggiano's, you'll find generous portions of outstanding Southern Italian cuisine served Family-Style. Reminiscent of a Little Italy Dinner House, you can choose from a delicious array of Salads, Soups and Antipasti, Pasta dishes, Prime Steaks, Chicken, Lamb, Fresh Fish and more.

MAGGIANO'S
LITTLE ITALY®

"You just can't get more Italian."

Lunch and Dinner daily. Reservations accepted.
500 Sixteenth Street, Denver, CO
303-260-7707   Fax: 303-260-7683

Ogden Theatre
935 E. Colfax Ave. • (303) 830-2525

Another of Denver's famed former movie houses, the Ogden attracts a wide range of acts, from the likes of Offspring to a more sedate Jackson Browne. The Ogden often has the best ticket in town, aside from major concert venues. Hours and ticket prices vary.

Sing Sing
1735 19th St. • (303) 291-0880

Located beneath The Chop House, Sing Sing offers dueling pianos in a relaxed setting and a chance to sing your heart out. This is definitely a more mainstream crowd that enjoys the likes of Billy Joel tunes. It's also not for the frail, as the improvisational songs can lean toward the raunchy. Food is limited to popcorn, peanuts and hotdogs.

Soiled Dove
1949 Market St. • (303) 299-0100

Sing along with the dueling piano players — jazz, rock 'n' roll — whatever you want. A recent addition is the full Caribbean style menu from the upstairs restaurant, Above the Dove.

Vartan's Jazz Club and Restaurant
1800 Glenarm Pl. • (303) 399-1111

Vartan's is well-known among jazz-loving Denverites. This location, opened in 1997, features the same great acts that locals are used to, plus more space and a full menu. Depending on who's playing, the cover charge can be steep ($10-$20), but worth it for great music. Reservations are suggested.

Beacon Grill*
303 16th St. • (303) 592-4745

Beacon Grill offers jazz piano Thursday, Friday and Saturday nights from 5 to 8 PM. There's no cover and a great free buffet from 3 to 6 PM every day except Saturday.

Dancing

I-Beam
1427 Larimer St. • (303) 534-2326

I-Beam presents live entertainment, Top-40 and disco music, dancing and billiards for the 20-something set. There's no cover on Fridays from 8 to 10 PM and a minimal cover on Saturdays.

Market 41
1941 Market St. • (303) 292-5641

Market 41 attracts a dancing crowd, somewhere in the age range of 21 to 50. Tuesday through Sunday it offers different kinds of music: rockabilly, disco, DJ music — even a live jam on Sunday night.

Market 41 has a limited menu — hot dogs, bratwurst and the like — and on a night when the Rockies are playing, it opens two hours prior to the game for early birds who want a little nosh.

9th Avenue West
99 West 9th Ave. • (303) 572-8006

Catch the Latin, salsa and swing craze at this neighborhood spot where a full food and bar menu are served. The 14-piece salsa band is mucho popular, as are the salsa and swing lessons, offered prior to dancing (call for times). The decor is fun, too, with comfy couches for resting between steps.

Polly Esther's
2301 Blake St. • (303) 382-1976

A dance card wouldn't be complete without a trip into the 70s. Luckily, Polly Esther's features the groovy mirrored ball, 70s garb scene (not required, but a good option). Cover runs up to $7, and lines can be long as this is newer among the dance clubs.

Ziggies Saloon
4923 W. 38th Ave. • (303) 455-9930

A popular R&B joint, Ziggies Saloon is regarded by many as a great blues bar. There's live music Wednesday through Sunday nights (possibly additional nights depending on the lineup) and a dance floor for those who rock. On Sunday afternoons there's a no-cover-charge acoustic jam.

Seven South
7 S. Broadway • (303) 744-0513

For live alternative rock, try Seven South on Friday and Saturday nights; for live jazz, come on Wednesday. Regulars say the jukebox is a fine substitute the rest of the time.

Plan on a $4 cover charge on Friday and Saturday nights.

Cosmo Lounge
1523 Market St. • (303) 607-9270

Prepare to dress for a night of dancing at Cosmo (formerly Club Velvet). Not much has changed since it was the popular Club Velvet; it's still a trendy dance scene. The rules are: no shorts, no T-shirts, no sneakers, no jeans. An in-house DJ plays acid jazz on the main level. Dinner is available on the second level until 11 PM. Dancing on the third level is available Wednesday through Saturday. Couches upstairs are the most desirable place to sit — they make Cosmo look like a darkened set of *Friends*.

The Church
1160 Lincoln St. • (303) 832-3528

Take an old cathedral and transform it into a dance club, complete with stained glass windows and an elevated altar area, and you've got Denver's hottest club. The Church attracts dancers of all ages (of course, the weekends tend toward the younger set) mainly because it is large enough to offer a variety of music styles. Wednesday nights are Big Band swing, and Thursdays are disco, with a live band. The weekends offer techno music, retro and industrial — all in different rooms. There is a full sushi restaurant.

Expect to pay a $10 cover at The Church, unless you arrive before 9 PM.

Sky Box
1520 20th St. • (303) 298-7625

A great place to dance to Top 40s, hip hop and alternative music, The Sky Box attracts a youngish crowd — ages 21 to 30. There's a $5 cover after 9:30 PM (women get in free until 11 PM). It's open Friday and Saturday.

Roadhouses

Herman's Hideaway
1578 S. Broadway • (303) 777-5840

Herman's Hideaway is a live music showcase with a large dance floor. The entertainment can vary from rock to zydeco. As you might expect of a roadhouse, decor is casual and the atmosphere is laid back. The crowd is 20s to 40s. Advance ticketing is advisable for special bookings of nationally known acts; call Herman's or TicketMaster, (303) 830-TIXS.

Buffalo Rose Saloon
1119 Washington St., Golden • (303) 279-5190

Buffalo Rose Saloon was established in 1851. The saloon presents a variety of musical acts, from well-known rock groups to folk singers, Wednesday through Saturday nights. Cover charge for lesser-known acts is around $3. Otherwise, tickets are available from TicketMaster, (303) 830-TIXS. Buffalo Rose serves a full menu until 10 PM and a late-night menu until closing.

Little Bear
28075 Colo. Hwy. 74 (Main St.), Evergreen • (303) 674-9991

Even folks from the plains brave the narrow mountain roads to make the scene at the Little Bear. Neither the route nor the rollicking roadhouse atmosphere is for the timid, but it's a fine place to listen to national and local rock, folk and blues musicians. Advance tickets for special bookings are available at TicketMaster, (303) 830-TIXS. Pizza and burgers are served from 11 AM, and it's open every day. There's a $3 to $5 cover charge on the weekends.

Country-and-Western Nightclubs

Grizzly Rose Saloon & Dance Emporium
5450 N. Valley Hwy. • (303) 295-2353, concert line (303) 295-1330

Grizzly Rose Saloon & Dance Emporium was voted the nation's No. 1 country music dance hall by the Country Music Association, and it's where the big names come to play when they're in town. With a 5,000-square-foot dance floor and headliners such as Willie Nelson, Waylon Jennings and Toby Keith, it's not hard to see why the Grizzly Rose is the undisputed favorite in the live-music C&W category. Advance ticketing is recommended for national acts; call the Grizzly Rose or

TicketMaster, (303) 830-TIXS. Sunday night is family night, when all ages are welcome.

Stampede Mesquite Grill & Steakhouse
2430 S. Havana St., Aurora
• (303) 337-6909

Stampede Mesquite Grill & Steakhouse is a club with a giant racetrack dance floor, line dancing and lessons, a yuppie clientele and an antique bar. Call ahead for reservations at the restaurant, which is on a second-floor balcony overlooking the nightclub and offers well-priced dinner specials.

Teddy's Restaurant and Lounge
4849 Bannock St. • (303) 292-9500

Teddy's Restaurant and Lounge, in the Denver North Holiday Inn near the intersection of I-70 and I-25, has a different musical format every night. Tuesday and Sunday nights are reserved for country. Other nights are disco, oldies or top-40. Happy hour with free hors d'oeuvres runs from 5 to 7 PM. Teddy's is a full-service restaurant serving breakfast, lunch and dinner.

Brewpubs, Sports Bars and Pool Halls

Wynkoop Brewing Company*
18th and Wynkoop Sts. • (303) 297-2700

After 5 PM is a busy time for the Wynkoop Brewing Company, Denver's first brewpub. Opened in 1988, the Wynkoop offers comedy downstairs, dining on the first floor and pool upstairs, all in the historic J. S. Brown Mercantile Building, c. 1899. Regulars like the Railyard Ale. Wynkoop also brews its own root beer. The billiards room has 22 pool tables, dart lanes and shuffleboard as well as a full-service bar. Cue rentals and lessons are available; call for more information. Comedy in the basement is offered Thursday through Saturday for $12 and a one-drink minimum.

Sports Column*
1930 Blake St. • (303) 296-1930

Billing itself as "major league excitement," Sports Column joins the ranks of lower down-

Red Rocks Amphitheater is a beautiful natural setting for an outdoor concert.

town sports bars. It has the requisite pool tables, foosball, and food. It also features five big screens and plenty of video games.

Champion Brewing Company*
1442 Larimer St. • (303) 534-5444

A microbrewery/sports bar/restaurant in a great location in Larimer Square, Champion Brewing Company has the requisite pool tables and big-screen TVs. But there's also plenty of outdoor seating for prime people-watching. You might opt for a mug of the Home Run Ale, a gold-medal winner in the 1994 American Beer Contest.

Rock Bottom Brewery*
1001 16th St. • (303) 534-7616

Yet another brewpub and pool hall, the huge, sunny Rock Bottom Brewery is popular with the young lawyers and bankers who work on 17th Street. Try the Red Rocks Red Ale — the popular brew here. The large patio affords some of the best people-watching on the 16th Street Mall. The food's pretty good, too. And, of course, you can shop at the in-house boutique for T-shirts and the like.

The Breckenridge Brewery*
2220 Blake St. • (303) 297-3644

The Breckenridge Brewery, opened in

1992, makes the same beers and ales as its Summit County cousin. Pub fare is served, and there's beer drinking and billiards late into the evening (and early into the morning). Tuesday evenings are set aside for a blues jam, and there's live music on weekends on the patio, weather permitting. There is no cover charge.

Wazoo's on Wazee
1819 Wazee St. • (303) 297-8500

One of the restaurants and gathering spots that's been getting good word-of-mouth for its pizza and hamburgers, Wazoo's on Wazee has nine pool tables, three bars, 13 TVs and an outdoor patio that's within cheering distance of Coors Field.

Shakespeare's
2375 15th St. • (303) 433-6000

This restaurant/bar/pool hall opened in 1995 and has been packing 'em in ever since. Shakespeare's offers 19 pool, two snooker and four billiard tables. A full menu is available, and all ages are welcome.

All-Ages Nightlife

Rock Island
1614 15th St. • (303) 572-7625

Rock Island was cool before LoDo was hot. Opened in 1985, it's always attracted a younger crowd that not only likes to dance to alternative music but also believes that black is the best color of clothing. One of Rock Island's great attractions is that each Saturday it offers a 16-and-older night for the younger crowd. Cover charge is $8, and anyone under 18 must clear out by 11:30 PM.

Mercury Cafe
2199 California St. • (303) 294-9281

The reincarnation of a legendary Denver nightclub of the '70s and early '80s, the Mer-

cury Cafe offers everything from swing dancing and Big Band music to performance art, comedy, theater and lectures. Mercury Cafe serves lunch, dinner and weekend brunch, with an emphasis on natural foods. It doesn't accept credit cards.

Muddy's Java Cafe
2200 Champa St. • (303) 298-1631

Similar in inclusiveness to the Mercury Cafe (and just a block away) is the Bohemian Muddy's Java Cafe. Muddy's offers comedy on some nights and poetry readings on others. Over the course of a week, expect to find theater, jazz, folk and blues. Open until 4 AM on Fridays and Saturdays, this is a great late-night hangout for dedicated coffee drinkers.

Club Synergy
3240 Larimer St. • (303) 296-9515

Club Synergy rocks for the 16 and older crowds that want techno bands and a resident DJ. The club is open from 9 PM to 5 AM Fridays through Sundays. Plan on paying up to $8 cover charge. Friday is 16 and older night until 11:30 PM. After that, it's 18 and older.

Coffee on the Z
1412 Wazee St. • (303) 592-1962

Coffee on the Z is in the Core Art Space, offering a chance to sip a latte while gazing at cool art Monday through Friday. It serves pastries and deli sandwiches in addition to caffeine-fixes and makes a great place to rest awhile on a Friday night Art Walk (see the Arts chapter).

Comedy Clubs

Chicken Lips Comedy Theater
1624 Market St., Ste. 301 • (303) 534-4440

Chicken Lips Comedy Theater hosts improvisational comedy and offers musical, po-

---

INSIDERS' TIP

If you like the nightlife but aren't into the hyper-mini skirt crowd, try Fado Irish Pub at 19th and Wynkoop. You'll find cozy spots for conversation and enjoy the authentic decor, much of which was shipped over from Ireland.

Some coffeehouses offer inexpensive entertainment with
poetry nights and acoustic music.

litical parody along the lines of Capitol Steps, only funnier. Call ahead for a new schedule. Ticket prices average $15, and advance reservations are suggested. They also perform for private parties. Chicken Lips differs from the other comedy clubs listed here in that it is an all-ages club. It does serve alcohol, however. Improvisational comedy classes are offered; call for information.

Comedy Works
1226 15th St. • (303) 595-3637

Roseanne (formerly Barr and Arnold) is among the many comics who made appearances early in their careers at Comedy Works. Tuesday night is new talent night; Wednesday through Sunday nights are for established performers. Ticket prices vary, but $13 is about the upper limit unless a headliner is on the ticket, which could cost up to $25. Reservations are recommended, and it's for ages 21

and older only. Ask about nonsmoking performances.

Comedy Sports
1634 18th St. • (303) 297-2111

Comedy Sports, billed as Denver's longest-running comedy show, occupies the lower level of the Wynkoop Brewing Company with performances Thursdays, Fridays and Saturdays. Don't expect stand-up. This place does skits, scenes and ensemble comedy similar to "Saturday Night Live." And customers really feel like they're attending a sporting event since they decide which "team" is funnier. Reservations are recommended. Tickets cost $12.

Wits End Comedy Club
8861 Harlan St., Westminster
• (303) 430-4242

Wits End Comedy Club offers the comic hijinks of local, national and international jokemeisters. The humor tends toward the clean side, but you still have to be 21 or older to attend. There are no nonsmoking performances, though there is a nonsmoking section on Friday and Saturday nights. Tickets run $8.

Movies

United Artists Denver Pavilions
16th Street Mall and Tremont Pl.
• (303) 454-9032

The newest member of the "stadium seating" theaters, Denver Pavilions offers a central location and 15 screens. Four hour validated parking is available at the 15th and Welton streets entrance to the Pavilions.

Landmark Mayan
First Ave. and Broadway • (303) 744-6796

Denver's finest art movie house is the Mayan. This 1930s-era movie house is decorated on every inch of its wall and ceiling surface with wonderful Mayan figures and other designs. Everything is classy here: the decor, the audience, the films, even the espresso and pastries served in the second-floor cafe. There's one large screen on the main level and two smaller ones above. The Landmark Chez Artiste Cinema, at 2800 S. Colorado Boulevard, (303) 757-7161, and the Esquire Theater, (303) 733-5757, at 590 Downing Street, are owned by the same company. Discounted multiple admission tickets are available that can be used at all three locations. Be sure to buy popcorn at any of these theaters: they use real butter!

Landmark Esquire
590 Downing St. • (303) 733-5757

Home of limited-release films, the Esquire is a favorite of urban moviegoers looking for a more old-fashioned experience. *The Rocky Horror Picture Show* plays every Saturday at midnight at the Esquire.

Continental Theater
I-25 and Hampden Ave.
• (303) 758-2345

This recently renovated theater (June 1996) has long been one of Denver's most comfortable. Roomy seats and wide aisles make viewing a pleasure. Once a single theater, the Continental is now six theaters, the smallest with 200 seats; the largest, 869 seats. The bulk candy sold in the lobby offers one of the best selections around.

Tivoli 12
901 Larimer St. • (303) 790-4262

For an urban movie-going experience, try the 12-plex at the Tivoli, which also houses the Student Union for Auraria Higher Education Center, so expect a certain youngish crowd. The Tivoli 12 is the location for the Denver International Film Festival in October. One warning: the screens are small.

Gambling

Since gambling was legalized in 1991, casinos have replaced nearly every retail shop, restaurant, snack shop and business in the historic mining towns of Central City and Black Hawk, a little more than 30 miles from downtown Denver.

To get there, take U.S. Highway 6 W. through Clear Creek Canyon to Colo. Highway 119 and follow the signs, or take I-70 westbound to the Central City/Colo. 119 Exit and head north. Better yet, let someone else do the driving. If you're just visiting, ask at your

---

INSIDERS' TIP

A few restaurants that are equally good spots for a pre-dinner or late-night drink and a nosh are: Marlowe's* at 16th Street and Glenarm Place, (303) 595-3700; The Paramount Café*, next door to Marlowe's at 511 16th Street, (303) 893-2000; the glitzy Texas-style Cadillac Ranch*, 1400 Larimer Street, (303) 820-2288; and the Avenue Grill*, 630 E. 17th Avenue, (303) 861-2820, the choice of Denver's young movers and shakers.

hotel about transportation, or check the Yellow Pages under "Buses — Charter and Rental" for the names of companies that offer roundtrip bus and shuttle service to Central City and Black Hawk.

A few shuttle services you might look into are the Black Hawk and Central City ACE Express, (303) 421-2780, and the People's Choice, (303) 936-1117.

Once you get there, one casino is pretty much the same as the next. The biggest decision is whether to stay in Black Hawk, which is right on Colo. 119, or turn in on the spur road and travel 1 mile farther to Central City. Shuttle buses connect the two, but if you're only up for the evening you probably won't want to spend your time going back and forth. If you'd like to mix your gambling with a little history, head into Central City. It's been tarted-up a lot since its mining days, but you can still get a sense of what it used to be like.

Limited stakes gambling is the rule here, with $5 being the maximum bet. Only poker, blackjack and lots of one-armed bandits are allowed at the nearly 40 parlors that operate between 8 AM and 2 AM.

The Gilpin County Chamber of Commerce, (800) 331-LUCK, and the Central City Information Center, (800) 542-2999, can help you pick out a casino that has the kinds of games and amenities you want. *The Colorado Gambler*, a free newspaper, is also a good guide. It's widely available in the gambling towns and often in Denver, especially at hotels. Be prepared to pay for parking, which can get expensive if you want to be close-in. Parking is at a premium and difficult to find close-in, but the good news is that it's validated as long as you gamble.

Otto's
260 Gregory St., Black Hawk
• (303) 642-0415

Otto's is kind of a mom-and-pop casino with blackjack and slot machines. For 36 years, this was a five-star restaurant, the Black Forest Inn. The owners have expanded into gambling with Otto's and the Rohling Inn.

The Gilpin Hotel
111 Main St., Black Hawk
• (303) 582-1133

The Gilpin Hotel has poker tables, something not all the casinos can claim. Its Mineshaft Bar long predates gambling — it has been a local hangout for 100 years.

Canyon Casino
131 Main St., Black Hawk • (303) 582-1171

Canyon Casino is more of a Las Vegas-style casino and is well-supplied with slot machines, blackjack and poker tables. As for entertainment in addition to gambling, well, this ain't Vegas by a long shot, so you won't find any here.

Harvey's Wagon Wheel Hotel & Casino
321 Gregory St., Central City
• (800) HARVEYS

This is one of Colorado's largest hotels and casinos, with 117 rooms. Look for live entertainment, live casino action, slots and a restaurant that serves barbecue.

WHERE WESTERN
CIVILIZATION BEGINS.

Shopping

With a booming economy that doesn't seem to have an end in sight, Denver's shopping scene keeps growing and getting more sophisticated.

Cherry Creek's swanky shops ushered in an era of excess in Denver that was matched by Park Meadows in 1996 and, in November 1998, was extended with the opening of Denver Pavilions, 350,000 square feet of entertainment, restaurants and retail. The Pavilions location will fill a void in urban shopping left over from the bust-days of the late '80s. Denverites hope Pavilions, located about mid-downtown, will revive the ailing (though still popular) 16th Street pedestrian mall, which offers more T-shirts and sports paraphernalia than upscale goods.

The center features a variety of offerings, among them a Virgin Records Megastore, Hard Rock Café, NikeTown, United Artists movie theater and a Wolfgang Puck Café. Denver Urban Renewal Authority kicked in $24 million of the $101.5 million price tag — an amount that represents the "culmination" of Denver's downtown revitalization efforts, according to Mayor Wellington Webb.

Beyond the retail, restaurant, entertainment offerings, Pavilions is creating a buzz around the city with its proposed 40-foot tall, lighted "DENVER" sign. Boosters call it art, and say it will add identity to downtown. Detractors call it promotional schlock, and say Denver knows what it is.

Meantime, shoppers flock to the Cherry Creek Shopping Center when they simply must have their Gucci. The mall (with more low-cost fare than famed boutique brands) attracts 16 million visitors a year and is in the top 1 percent of all shopping centers in the United States in sales per square foot. In fact, the Cherry Creek mall is the area's No. 1 attraction, outdrawing the U.S. Mint, Coors Brewery and the Denver museums.

Park Meadows, also a recent addition to Greater Denver's shopping scene, isn't far behind. In its first year of business, it attracted 13 million visitors. It continues to grow today, adding tentacles of big box and off-price stores such as the Great Indoors, Home Depot and Designer Shoe Warehouse.

As in many other cities, large department stores left Denver's downtown in the 1970s and '80s as malls were built in outlying areas. Smaller specialty stores moved in instead on downtown's major shopping thoroughfare, 16th Street. And Tabor Center, an urban mini-mall, now anchors the lower end of 16th Street. Larimer Square remains one of the city's best shopping meccas, with interesting boutiques and restaurants in a historically rich area. To the north and west of Larimer Square, in what's called LoDo (Lower Downtown), are many galleries, restaurants and sports bars. South Broadway is the site for dozens of antique and folk-art stores, and, of course, there are islands of delight scattered throughout the city and its suburbs.

In this chapter we've focused on three major shopping areas that have a great concentration and variety of stores: Cherry Creek North; Downtown, LoDo and Larimer Square; and South Broadway. The Cherry Creek and Larimer Square areas are small enough to walk around, and that's how we've written those sections, with directions from one place to the next. South Broadway is more spread out — we survey the shops from north to south, but you'll want to travel by car or bus rather than on foot to cover the whole span.

To finish off your introduction to Denver shopping, we've included a roundup of where to go for arts and crafts, books, clothes, food and gourmet cooking supplies, furniture, gifts and outlet and bargain stores.

Most stores are open daily and accept credit cards, but call ahead to be sure.

But first, the basics — department and grocery stores. Major department stores with more than one location in Greater Denver include Foley's, Joslins, JCPenney and Mervyn's. For Western wear, both Miller Stockman and Sheplers have locations throughout the metro area. Gart Brothers, Recreational Equipment Inc. (REI) and Eastern Mountain Sports (EMS) stores supply Denverites with gear for camping, hiking, biking, rafting and other outdoor stuff.

New to the Denver area is Jumbo Sports, which has opened two 60,000-square-foot megastores in Littleton and Westminster. Jumbo Sports offers a comprehensive selection of brand-name sporting goods at discount prices as well as equipment and clothing for tennis, golf, fishing, hunting, scuba diving, team sports and just about anything you can think of. The south store is at 7848 County Line Road in Littleton and the north store is at 9219 N. Sheridan Boulevard.

A top source for consumer electronics, including stereos, televisions, VCRs and cellular phones, is SoundTrack. There are several SoundTrack stores throughout the metro area. You'll find their Denver location at 1370 S. Colorado Boulevard.

The big supermarket chains include King Soopers, Safeway and Albertsons. For natural foods, visit any of the several Alfalfa's or Wild Oats markets.

Major Shopping Areas

Cherry Creek North

The neighborhood directly to the north of the mall, Cherry Creek North, is a delightful mélange of interesting shops, galleries and restaurants. The showpiece here is the **Tattered Cover Book Store**, 2955 E. First Avenue. With four floors of books, thousands of titles in stock at any given time, cozy armchairs for undisturbed reading and great service, the Tattered Cover is the bookstore of your dreams. The Tattered Cover stocks many out-of-state newspapers and foreign magazines as well as hard-to-find literary journals.

Watch the Sunday papers or call (303) 322-1965 ext. 7446 for information on book signings and other special events. The Tattered Cover also has a branch in Lower Downtown Denver at 1628 16th Street (at Wynkoop), near Union Station.

Down the block at the corner of Milwaukee Street and Second Avenue are two furniture stores, each with a different emphasis. At **Roche-Bobois International Design Center**, 201 Milwaukee Street, the look is sleek and European. Across the street at **Expressions**, 3007 E. Second Avenue, a custom furniture store, there's more fabric and less leather. If you're looking for something to hang above the sofa, **Saks Galleries**, 3019 E. Second Avenue, carries 19th- and 20th-century representational art.

Pismo Contemporary Art Glass, 235 Fillmore Street, stocks an unmatched selection of art glass by Coloradans Brian Maytum, Kit Karbler and internationally known glass artist Dale Chihuly in its luxurious gallery. (Pismo also has a furniture gallery of wonderful one-of-a-kind chairs, bureaus, headboards and the like around the corner at 2727 E. Third Avenue.) More art glass can be found at **International Villa**, 262 Fillmore Street.

Some of Colorado's best crafts artists exhibit their works at **Panache**, 315 Columbine Street. Here you'll find feather necklaces, handmade jewelry, award-winning ceramics by Steve Schrepferman and larger-than-lifesize papier-mâché and mixed-media critters by local artist DeDe Larue. **Show of Hands**, 2610 E. Third Avenue, and **Artisan Center**, 2757 E. Third Avenue, have more utilitarian crafts.

The belts and jewelry at **Body Art**, 250 Fillmore Street, are expensive but unusual and classy. For young, up-to-the-minute designer clothing for women, visit **Ma Lex**, 2825 E. Third Avenue. The store also carries a small selection of men's wear. **Tapestry**, 286 Fillmore Street, has women's clothing, jewelry and accessories with an ethnic flair. Some items are one-of-a-kind. Another source for funky clothing and inexpensive jewelry for men and women is **Eccentricity**, 2440 E. Third Avenue. The highlights at **Applause**, 2827 E. Third Av-

Photo: Daily Camera/Jay Quadracci

Free shuttle buses stop at every block in the 16th Street Mall.

enue, are the unique selection of kids' clothing and the handpainted children's furniture.

More kids' stuff can be found at **The Wizard's Chest**, 230 Fillmore Street, which in addition to children's toys carries grown-up games and an attic full of costumes and masks. **Kazoo & Company,** 2930 E. Second Avenue, has educational games and toys.

Gardeners will love the **Smith & Hawken** store at 268 Detroit Street. Shop for high-quality gardening tools, workwear, containers, plants and garden furniture.

Hermitage Antiquarian Bookshop, 290 Fillmore Street, is a pleasant spot with neat library stacks of first editions and other rare or old books. And **Shalako East**, 3023 E. Second Avenue, has a fine selection of Native American arts and jewelry.

Downtown, LoDo and Larimer Square

Downtown Denver's main shopping thoroughfare, 16th Street was transformed into a tree-lined pedestrian mall in 1980 through 1982. Free shuttle buses run the length of the mall, connecting Lower Downtown with the Civic Center area. Many of the stores along 16th Street are touristy, but it's worth strolling the mile-long stretch to see what's here. A

relatively new arrival, **MediaPlay**, at the corner of 16th and California streets, has a large selection of discounted books and music. With the recent additions of **TJMaxx** and **Ross**, the corner has become a mini off-price mecca in downtown. Restaurants along the mall often have outdoor seating — great for people-watching — and there are shaded benches for those who've brought their own lunch. If you haven't planned ahead, buy a to-go lunch from a street vendor or fast-food restaurant.

More traditional shopping takes place at the glass-enclosed, three-story **Tabor Center**, (303) 572-6868, which extends along 16th Street from Arapahoe to Larimer. A top Tabor Center attraction is the **Sharper Image** store, which carries high-tech gizmos and gadgets you didn't know you needed until you saw them. **Africa House** has wonderful African arts and crafts including fine textiles. There's a food court here, too, should you feel a little peckish.

The heart of Larimer Square is Larimer Street between 15th and 14th streets. From Tabor Center, walk one block south through the cluster of stores and restaurants called **Writer Square**, and you'll be standing on the spot where Denver got its start in 1858. It was on this block that Denver's first bank, bookstore, photographer and dry-goods store were located. The original buildings were made of wood and destroyed in a fire in 1863; the brick structures that now line the street were erected for the most part in the 1870s to '90s, and the entire area was renovated in the mid-1970s. Interested visitors can pick up a walking-tour brochure and information on the individual buildings at the kiosk on the east side of the street. (It's open 8 AM to 5 PM daily.)

Larimer Square has a nice mix of shops and restaurants, including a branches of **Talbot's**, **Ann Taylor** and **Williams-Sonoma**. **Cry Baby Ranch** has Western furnishings and trinkets, while the **Squash Blossom Gallery** is known for its outstanding selection of Southwestern jewelry and crafts. **J. Howell Gallery** spotlights fine crafts by Coloradans, and **The Market** has an exhaustive selection of gourmet goodies as well as coffee, deli and bakery items to take out or eat on the premises. **Z Gallerie**, on the corner of 15th and Larimer streets, has contemporary home furnishings and accessories.

American Costume at 1526 Blake Street has more than 10,000 costumes in stock. Whether you're looking for something offbeat for Halloween, or are slated to play Santa at the office party, they'll suit you up. At this point you're just a few blocks from the **Tattered Cover Book Store**'s LoDo branch, at 16th and Wynkoop streets.

As you move into LoDo, check out **Bouquets**, 1525 15th Street, for the most unusual flowers and flower arrangements in town. Head over to **Stuart Buchanan**, 1530 15th Street, for 18th- and 19th-century European country antiques and furnishings.

The 1700 block of Wazee Street was once the heart of Denver's contemporary art district, and it still is, in a sense, although closures and additions have shifted the emphasis away from the avant garde. We write more about that in our Arts chapter.

If you're more in the mood for furniture, specifically art deco, stop in at **Wazee Deco**, 1730 Wazee Street, which carries some of the best classic pieces around. A few doors away is **Spinners**, 1743 Wazee Street, a place that specializes in refurbished old gas pumps (yes, they are in demand!) and jukeboxes — bits of Americana.

A bit farther uptown, collectors of Native-American crafts head for one of the two Denver outlets of the **Mudhead Gallery** in the Hyatt Regency Hotel, 555 17th Street, or the Brown Palace Hotel, 321 17th Street.

The Native American Trading Company, a fine source for pots, textiles and Edward S. Curtis photogravures, is across from the Denver Art Museum at 1301 Bannock Street.

On the upper, southern edge of downtown is one of Denver's most venerable stores. **Gart Brothers Sporting Goods** is at 10th Avenue and Broadway, in a wildly extravagant building known as the Sportscastle. This seven-level store stocks everything including tents, cameras, bicycles and tennis shoes. Gart Brothers has dozens of other locations throughout the state, but none so architecturally distinctive as this one.

A few blocks away at 1109 Lincoln Street is the **Denver Buffalo Company**, a sort of mini-mall that includes a trading post, art gallery, food market, deli and restaurant. You can find anything from cowboy-hat bottle openers to Western clothing to fine traditional and contemporary Western art. There's even a teepee inside the store. The food market stocks such indigenous delicacies as buffalo sticks and hickory-smoked bison jerky.

South Broadway

Because Broadway runs one-way from north to south until it becomes a two-way street south of the I-25 interchange, we've arranged our selections from north to south — the way a car or bus would travel the route.

Manos Folk Art, 101 Broadway (across the street from the Mayan Theatre), has a magical selection of Ocumicho devil ceramics, Zapotec rugs and all kinds of masks, mirrors and furniture from Mexico and Latin America.

Mecca Modern Interior, 21A S. Broadway, is the avant-garde kid on the block, with furniture and accessories that are recognizable modern classics.

Sheptons Antiques, 389 S. Broadway, also has an international selection of furniture and salvaged architectural elements including carved wood doors and portions of wrought-iron fences.

At Popular Culture, 1150 S. Broadway, the "antiques" are younger than many people alive today. The store focuses on deco moderne and other mid-20th-century styles.

This shop is noted for its collection of 1950s furniture and Russel Wright dinnerware.

The entire block of South Broadway between Arizona and Louisiana avenues is lined with antique stores. **The Antique Market**, 1212 S. Broadway, and **The Antique Guild**, 1298 S. Broadway, consolidate the wares of many dealers under one roof.

A few blocks farther south is **Hooked on Glass**, 1407 S. Broadway, which specializes in Depression glass and other collectibles.

Denver Pavilions

On the 16th Street Mall between Tremont and Welton sts. • (303) 260-6000

The Pavilions doesn't fit into traditional "mall" or shopping area categories because it offers more than retail. In fact, some of the longest lines are found at **Wolfgang Puck's Café**. Pavilions bills itself as the new wave of retail, restaurant and entertainment. You can browse **Banana Republic**, indulge in something decadent at the **Corner Bakery**, then take in a flick at the United Artist theater (all high-backed stadium seating).

Pavilions boasts several anchor attractions, including Wolfgang Puck's, a **Virgin Records Megastore**, **Barnes & Noble** and **Hard Rock Café**, along with more familiar shops, such as **Bath and Body Works**, **Gap** and **The Limited**. A 30,000-square foot **NikeTown** will open in 1999 (one of only 15 in the U.S.).

Mall crawlers used to the confines of suburban malls will be surprised at the Pavilions' open air setting. But with a yearly average of 325 days of sunshine, outdoor shopping is rarely a problem in Denver.

Shopping Malls

Following are the locations and phone numbers of the major outlying shopping malls.

Cherry Creek Shopping Center
3000 E. 1st Ave. • (303) 388-3900

Anchored by Lord & Taylor, Saks Fifth Avenue, Nieman Marcus and Foley's, the specialty stores in the Cherry Creek Shopping Center tend to be on the high end — Louis Vuitton, Bally of Switzerland, Abercrombie &

Fitch. Even the restroom is above average: Clad in marble, with automatic fixtures, it was written up in *Time* magazine! There is a dining area with quick food, or several upscale restaurants, such as Sfuzzi, for Northern Italian.

The center expanded just in time for Christmas 1998 with 25 new stores. New tenants include Tiffany & Co., a Rainforest Café (plan ahead for long lines during peak season) and the Learning Center. The bigger, better Lord & Taylor anchors the addition. Also fairly new to the mall is an elaborate play area for kids with seating for adults near the mall entrance to Foley's. The area features super-sized, colorful breakfast food items for the kids to crawl on. Kids can't resist sliding down the bacon into an egg yolk. The attraction is so popular that mini playgroups have formed for regular visits.

Aurora Mall
Off I-225 at Alameda Ave., Aurora • (303) 344-4120

Aurora Mall has the look and feel of a fairly typical suburban mall. Anchored by Foley's, Sears and JCPenney, it offers recognizable stores like The Disney Store and Eddie Bauer, as well as smaller, more boutique-like shops. It recently installed a beautiful carved carousel where kids (and adults) can take a spin. And the movie theaters, once full-priced, now offer 50¢ movies.

Buckingham Square
Havana St. and Mississippi Ave., Aurora • (303) 755-3232

Buckingham Square is anchored by Joslins at one end and Montgomery Ward at the other. Mervyn's fills out one of the arms of the mall. The small stores in-between tend toward lower-end retail. A few food joints dot the mall, but there is no food court, per se. What Buckingham Square offers is a different show every weekend — antique shows, car shows, community bake sales, arts and crafts festivals and more.

Tamarac Square
Hampden Ave. and Tamarac Dr. • (303) 745-0055

Tamarac Square is a destination mall, not a mall you go to "hang around." Barbara &

Company is a high-end women's clothing store, and The Regiment, a classic men's clothing store. Hyde Park Jewelers is also here and offers fine jewelry and wonderful gift items. (They're also in Cherry Creek Shopping Center.) Other stores include the biggest Gap in Denver and small boutique-type stores. The mall has a movie theater with six screens.

Tiffany Plaza
Hampden Ave. and Tamarac Dr. (across from Tamarac Square) • (303) 771-8210

The parking lot here is always full, in part due to the AMC movie theaters and the variety of restaurants here (Le Peep, Ciao! Baby, Uno's, among others). Shoppers come here for Loehmann's, Walgreen's, and T and C, a men's discount clothing store.

University Hills Shopping Center
S. Colorado Blvd. and Yale Ave. • (303) 759-8000

Once one of Southeast Denver's great malls, University Hills fell into decline in the 1980s. But after a complete renovation, it reopened in 1997 as a strip center (the former mall is now a parking lot). It still remains a neighborhood center as opposed to a large mall with regional draw. Main stores include Home Place, Office Max and a King Soopers grocery store. Smaller stores include Starbucks Coffee and Einstein Brothers Bagels.

Villa Italia
Wadsworth Blvd. and Alameda Ave., Lakewood • (303) 936-7424

With more than 140 stores, including Foley's, Joslins, Montgomery Ward and JCPenney, Villa Italia draws shoppers from Lakewood as well as all over Denver. Not one of the newer, glitzier malls, this is still a reliable shopping center.

Lakeside Mall
Off I-70 between Sheridan Blvd. and Harlan St. exits (entrance 44th Ave.), Lakewood • (303) 455-7072

One of Greater Denver's older and smaller malls, Lakeside is anchored by Target and Montgomery Ward. Stores tend to be on the lower-end of retail, and there are a few fast food joints. The $1 store can be fun (warning: many items are more than $1).

Southglenn Mall
S. University Blvd. and Arapahoe Rd., Littleton • (303) 795-0856

The main reason for shopping at Southglenn is that you'll pay lower sales tax here than anywhere else (3.8 percent as compared to 7.3 percent at Cherry Creek Shopping Center, for example.) Expanded four years ago, Southglenn is a clean, pleasant mall anchored by Sears, JCPenney, Joslins and Foley's. (Until Park Meadows opened, this Joslins was the flagship store.) Other shops include typical mall offerings — The Limited, Gap, Eddie Bauer and Victoria's Secret.

Park Meadows
8401 Park Meadows Center Dr., Littleton • (303) 792-2999

Park Meadows is anchored by Nordstrom, Dillard's and Foley's. Many stores here are Colorado firsts — Crate and Barrel and Restoration Hardware, for example. The food court is huge and the restaurants are on the swanky side. Park Meadows grows ever-larger each year with the addition of retail around its perimeter. It's a great mix of low-, mid- and high-end retail.

Southwest Plaza
Wadsworth Blvd. and W. Bowles Ave., Littleton • (303) 973-5300

Once Denver's largest mall, Southwest Plaza serves Jefferson County's booming population. Anchored by Foley's, JCPenney, Joslins, Montgomery Ward and Sears, Southwest Plaza has almost every type of clothing, food, music and shoe store. There are even a couple of furniture and accessories stores and a Target.

Northglenn Mall
Off I-25 at 104th Ave. W., Northglenn • (303) 452-5683

Built in the late 1960s, Northglenn Mall is an amalgam of 30 stores, mostly mom-and-pop type places that sell gifts and jewelry. Mervyn's is the only anchor, and while there's no food court, there are a few independently owned restaurants.

Thornton Town Center Mall
10001 Grant St. (Off I-25 at 104th Ave. E.), Thornton • (303) 252-0007

This fairly small mall (25 stores) is unusual for its anchor: bigg's Hypermarket, a combination grocery store, video store, pharmacy and almost anything else you can put a price tag on. There's also a Home Depot and a 64,000-square-foot Half Price Store.

Westminster Mall
Sheridan Blvd. and 88th Ave., Westminster • (303) 428-5634

Westminster Mall is the only mall in the area with six anchor stores, making it officially a Super Center. With 170 to 200 stores, Westminster draws from all over the state, especially folks from the mountain communities. Though 20 years old, this mall renovates frequently, so it's up-to-date.

Antiques

The South Broadway area, described earlier in this chapter, has the greatest concentration of antique stores in the Greater Denver area. In addition to the stores we mention by name, you're sure to find more, especially continuing farther south. And if you're willing to travel out of Denver 30 to 40 minutes, you might want to check out the town of Niwot and its two-block main street filled with antique shops. Auctions are sometimes held on Sundays. To get there, take I-25 north to Colo. Highway 52 W. to connect with Colo. Highway 119. Niwot is about 1 mile north of the intersection of highways 52 and 119.

Even farther afield is the town of Lyons, which lies at the mouth of St. Vrain Canyon on the way to Estes Park, about 45 minutes from downtown Denver. Antique stores dot both sides of the old-fashioned Main Street. You'll find a few that specialize in Western memorabilia. To get there from central Denver, take I-25 north to the Colo. Highway 66 Exit, then go west about 17 miles.

Closer to town check out the following shops.

Elegant Glass Antiques
7501 Grandview Ave., Arvada • (303) 424-9330

Elegant Glass deals in Depression glass as well as art china and art glass. This is where people come to fill in missing pieces of old china patterns. The store also sells collectibles, such as marbles and clocks.

Olde Wadsworth Antiques
7511 Grandview Ave., Arvada • (303) 424-8686

Opened under new ownership in September of 1996, Olde Wadsworth Antiques carries oak, walnut and mahogany furniture as well as books, glassware and collectibles. The store has been completely remodeled and offers more variety than before.

Arvada Antique Emporium
7519 Grandview Ave., Arvada • (303) 422-6433

Colorado's oldest antique co-op, Arvada Antique Emporium houses seven dealers who sell everything from pre-Columbian artifacts to *Star Wars* memorabilia. The Emporium is open seven days a week.

Antique Mall of Lakewood
9635 W. Colfax Ave., Lakewood • (303) 238-6940

This "mall" has about 105 dealers under one roof. In addition to a cafe, there's also a dealer who specializes in books — both old books and reference books about antiques.

INSIDERS' TIP

One of the great respites from shopping with the kids is Cherry Creek Shopping Center's play area. Located outside the mall entrance to Foley's, kids can romp into the evening on overstuffed, cushioned "breakfast foods" while parents sit back and watch, read a magazine, make new friends or just relax.

Park Meadows Draws Shoppers from Afar

When Park Meadows opened in August of 1996, it was hailed as a shopping center unlike any ever built. In fact, it was described as a retail "resort." Whether or not shoppers feel like they're on vacation is uncertain, but what is known is that the mall has attracted visitors as if it were a vacation spot. In its first year, 13 million people came to check out Metro Denver's largest mall — all 1.5 million square feet of it.

Close-up

With three top-drawer anchors — Colorado's first Nordstrom, Denver's first Dillard's and Colorado's largest Foley's — the mall is a shopping mecca for a seven-state region.

In its first year, Park Meadows has managed to perform well above the national average for sales — averaging around $415 per square foot. And this mall is fast becoming one of the must-see places in Denver, though it's not exactly right in the hub of activity, as is Cherry Creek Shopping Center. Rather, it was built in Douglas County, the area's fastest growing county and an area not previously known for its great shopping opportunities.

What makes it different from other malls is its "feel." While most malls are conglomerates of stores, Park Meadows was designed to feel like a mountain ski lodge (a very, very busy one!). Massive natural wood-beam cathedral ceilings soar above the second-level of stores, and the mall is bathed in natural light. Strategically located throughout are large stone fireplaces, and in winter, when the air outside is frosty, the mall offers free hot chocolate to be sipped in front of a roaring fire. Best of all, the mall offers overstuffed leather chairs and couches at frequent intervals so weary shoppers can have a rest.

Hahn Company, the developer of Park Meadows, also commissioned eight Colorado artists to create $2 million worth

Photo: Park Meadows

Park Meadows was designed to have the look and feel of a rustic ski lodge.

of artwork for the mall. "We were going for a 'WOW!' factor," says Janet Beaudry, Marketing Director for Park Meadows. "We want people to look up and around, not just ahead."

The mall is home to 120 stores, many of which are new to Colorado — Crate and Barrel, Restoration Hardware, Nordstrom. And while the obligatory food court is located right near the center, Park Meadows also houses "better" restaurants: California Cafe, Bella Ristorante and Alcatraz Brewing Company. Even the United Artists Movie Theater here is a little bigger and a little glitzier. In addition to the multi-screen movie theater, there are four virtual reality experiences, including, "Virtual Hanglider."

— continued on next page

What also distinguishes Park Meadows as a shopping "experience" are the four districts. The Lifestyle District revolves around stores like Eddie Bauer and J. Crew. The Fashion District is dominated by Nordstrom and Crate and Barrel (fashion for the home). The Family District revolves around Warner Brothers and Dillard's. (Look for the overstuffed leather animals here where kids can climb.) Finally, the Entertainment District houses the movie theaters and food court.

Whether shoppers notice exactly where they are or not, the psychology of the design is pure '90s: The mall is no longer a place to stop and shop; it's a place to stop and shop, stop and eat, stop and be entertained. It's also a place to be educated in Shopping Mall 101. If you really want to understand the mall from a developer's and architect's point of view, call the marketing department, (303) 792-2999, and arrange a behind-the-scenes tour, which will not only point out all the indigenous materials used to build the mall, but also why it was built as it was. It may make spending your hard-earned dollars that much easier.

Grandpa's Depot
1616 17th St. #267 • (303) 628-5590

This is the place for railroad memorabilia. You can find dining-car china, lanterns, silver and just about anything associated with trains and their accessories.

Arts and Crafts

For arts and crafts, make Cherry Creek North your first stop (see Major Shopping Areas at the beginning of this chapter). Additional resources include the following.

Akente Express
919 Park Ave. W. • (303) 297-8817

Akente Express is an African-American heritage shop that stocks original fabrics from Africa, handmade clothing, jewelry, artwork, sculpture and all-natural, alcohol-free essential oils.

The Clay Pigeon
601 Ogden St. • (303) 832-5538

The Clay Pigeon is Denver's oldest gallery specializing exclusively in handmade works of clay, including both stoneware and porcelain. This is a great place to buy unusual serving pieces and wedding gifts.

Galeria Mexicana
3615 W. 32nd Ave. • (303) 964-9050

Galeria Mexicana specializes in Latin American crafts and collectibles. The prices are unbelievably affordable, and the selection

of goods from jewelry to clothing to art is extensive.

Old Santa Fe Pottery
2485 S. Santa Fe Dr. • (303) 871-9434

Old Santa Fe Pottery houses two rows of shops filled with Oaxacan wood carvings, painted Talavera ceramics, furniture, rugs and all sorts of pottery. You'll enjoy a pretty central courtyard reminiscent of a Mexican village.

Skyloom Fibres
1705 S. Pearl St. • (303) 777-2331

Skyloom Fibres, the largest weaving, knitting, yarn, basketry and bead store in the Rocky Mountain area, is also a friendly, mellow place with a 20-page catalog of classes. It's easy to find; just look for the purple building. It's recently expanded to include clothing and gifts.

Pearls & Jewels
1457 S. Pearl St. • (303) 744-6944

Pearls & Jewels is a nifty little bead store that also offers classes in everything from basic bead-stringing to creating your own lampshade. It also has a gift shop and specializes in beaded curtains.

Books

The behemoth Tattered Cover Book Store, with its Cherry Creek and LoDo branches, dominates Greater Denver's literary scene, but Denver's readers are avid enough to support more than one general-interest bookstore. Large chains such as Waldenbooks and B. Dalton Bookseller have branches in many regional shopping malls. And Barnes & Noble Booksellers is found all over town. Another good all-around bookstore, the Book Rack, has two locations in Denver at 2382 S. Colorado Boulevard and in Lakewood at 1535 S. Kipling Parkway. Then there are the specialty bookstores, a few of which we list here.

ABC Books and Posters
2550 S. Colorado Blvd. • (303) 759-0250

This small shop carries a little bit of everything, including children's books, Spanish-language books, travel guides and best-sellers in hardcover and paperback. The shop prides itself on special orders, which usually arrive within about three days.

Brentanos
3000 E. First Ave. • (303) 337-4432

Brentanos sells what they call "hot and easy" titles, meaning front-list newer releases. With these as the main focus and the small size of the store, not many older titles are available. You'll find sections of fiction, history, social science, audio, poetry, self help and travel, among other things.

Cultural Legacy Bookstore
3633 W. 32nd Ave. • (303) 964-9049

Cultural Legacy Bookstore is the only bookstore in Colorado to specialize in Latino literature, with Spanish, English and bilingual books and magazines for children and adults. Ask about book signings and other special events.

The Gallagher Collection
1298 S. Broadway • (303) 756-5821

Located at the Antique Guild on Denver's famed antique row, The Gallagher Collection is a member of the Rocky Mountain Antiquarian Booksellers Association. The shop features rare and out of print books, books and posters on WWI and WWII, fine binding and other specialty items.

The Hue-Man Experience
911 Park Ave. W. • (303) 293-2665

The Hue-Man Experience is an African-American bookstore that also sells African cards, jewelry and fabrics. They have the largest collection of African-American titles in the country as well as a children's story hour.

Murder by the Book
1574 S. Pearl St. • (303) 871-9401

Murder by the Book, a cozy store in a former home, specializes in new and used mystery novels. If your kids love mysteries, check out the children's selections.

Neighborhood Bookstore
8200 S. Quebec St., Englewood
• (303) 721-7882
16728 E. Smoky Hill Rd., Aurora
• (303) 766-9491

The Neighborhood Bookstores are your basic general-use bookstores. You'll find mostly modern, currently popular titles in just about every genref. About 20 percent of the titles are new; the rest are used books. Ask about their trade-in system for used books.

Reel Books Audio Bookstore
1512 Larimer St. • (303) 629-5528

Reel Books has thousands of books on tape, for adults and children, to buy or rent. Whether you want mysteries, self-help, the classics or biographies, chances are you can find it on tape here.

The Bookies
4315 E. Mississippi Ave., Glendale
• (303) 759-1117

Though The Bookies is primarily known for its great children's selection, it also carries most best-seller titles too. Better yet, every book is sold at a discount — at least 15 percent off.

Clothing

See our Cherry Creek and Larimer Square sections earlier in the chapter for a good overall roundup of clothing stores. Here are some more options to consider.

Auer's
210 St. Paul St. • (303) 321-0404

Auer's is for the woman who wants elegant designer clothes with according prices. With

You'll find bookshops, cafes, restaurants and upscale shopping in the Downtown and Larimer Square areas.

brands like Armani, Escada, and YSL, Auer's carries clothes you won't see everywhere else. The sales staff also helps customers put together perfect outfits.

Barbara & Company
7777 E. Hampden Ave. • (303) 751-2618

Funky yet classic clothes in beige, white, black and brown make up the mainstay of Barbara & Company's clothing. If you're unable to put things together, let the knowledgeable staff outfit you from head to toe. But plan to pay high prices for the clothes and accessories.

Iris Fields
1099 S. Gaylord St. • (303) 777-0516

At Iris Fields you'll find contemporary women's clothing that is unusual but comfortable, affordable but not cheap. Better yet, you won't see everyone else in the same outfit.

Food and Gourmet Cooking Supplies

Don't forget the Market in Larimer Square. But keep in mind these other spots as well.

Asian Market
333 S. Federal Blvd. • (303) 937-1431

If you're in the market for Asian fruits and vegetables, exotic brands of soup and noodles, check out the Asian Market. It's a good source for hard-to-find items for true Asian cooking located in the Asian Center, a two-story shopping center specializing in Asian businesses.

Cook's Mart
3000 E. Third Ave. • (303) 388-5933

Cook's Mart has an enormous selection of pots, pans, casseroles, whisks, imported knives and just about everything you could think of to set up a fully equipped semiprofessional kitchen. It also includes unusual table accessories — salt and pepper shakers, serving spoons and casseroles.

Pacific Mercantile Co.
1925 Lawrence St. • (303) 295-0293

Pacific Mercantile Co., in the heart of Denver's Japanese community, offers an astonishing selection of Asian foods, many of which will be unrecognizable to the average American cook. For chefs looking for a specific, hard-to-find ingredient, this is a tremendous resource as well as a cultural minivacation.

Stephany's Chocolates
4969 Colorado Blvd. • (303) 355-1522

Stephany's Chocolates, with several locations, are a Colorado tradition and a popular gift for visitors to take home. (They're readily available at the airport.) The Denver Mints — get it? — are a big seller.

Stephany's has stores in the Tabor Center and the Cherry Creek Shopping Center, among other locations.

European Mart
5225 Leetsdale Dr. • (303) 321-7144

When you're in the mood for Hungarian salami or hearty sausage, the European Mart is the place to stop. Filled with eastern European delicacies — meats, fish, candies, cookies — this shop is the real thing. The Russian owners are helpful and eager to please. The food is great.

Denver Bread Company
3200 Irving St. • (303) 455-7194

For fabulous and unusual bread, Denver Bread Company is the newest bakery of choice. Look for hearty rustic breads, garlic twists and three-seed rye.

INSIDERS' TIP

Don't miss the newest addition to the region's shopping attractions, Denver Pavilions in the heart of downtown. Opened in November 1998, Pavilions offers shoppers as much entertainment as shopping, with a movie theater and Hard Rock Café.

A street musician serenades shoppers in downtown Denver.

Boyer's
747 S. Colorado Blvd. • (303) 289-3345

Boyer's, a Denver-based coffee roaster and packager, offers its coffee and related items at lower-than-supermarket prices at two factory outlets in Greater Denver. There are stores at 747 S. Colorado Boulevard and 7295 N. Washington Street in Northglenn.

Furniture

A number of furniture warehouses, including **Sofa Mart**, 5445 N. Bannock Street and **Super Dave's Furniture Discount City**, 300 W. 53rd Place are along the west side of I-25 (take the 58th Avenue exit and go south). Quality and prices vary, but it's worth stopping to at least comparison shop. We've also mentioned a few furniture stores in our Cherry Creek section. Elsewhere in the city, you might consider the following.

Decor Southwest
9100 W. Sixth Ave., Lakewood
• (303) 233-5405

Decor Southwest specializes in handcrafted Southwestern furniture, accessories and lighting. Prices range from medium to high, and if you don't see what you want, just ask. They do custom work.

Howard Lorton Galleries
12 E. 12th Ave. • (303) 831-1212

If you're into traditional, classic, expensive furniture, Howard Lorton is one of Denver's premier galleries. Open since 1927, this shop offers top-of-the-line furniture, lamps, carpeting and draperies.

Lakewood Furniture
8990 W. Colfax Ave., Lakewood
• (303) 233-5811

Lakewood Furniture features unfinished furniture in a variety of styles, including Mexican, country, Shaker, Russian and barn-wood. If you don't see what you want, they'll build it for you.

Whitney's of Cherry Hills
5910 S. University Blvd., Littleton
• (303) 794-0990

Whitney's features 500 furniture manufacturers from around the world. From traditional to contemporary furniture and accessories, Whitney's also offers a staff of interior designers who can help with a room or a whole house.

Kacey Fine Furniture
1201 Auraria Pkwy. • (303) 571-5123

Though Kacey Fine Furniture is in several locations (there's even one in Frisco), this main store is the largest with floor after floor of everything from leather couches to traditional bedroom sets to funky coffee tables. Kacey has a great selection and reasonable prices. Better yet, every year on the owner's birthday, she offers a discount equal to her age. She's currently in her mid-40s.

▲ Authentic Gifts

▲ Colorado Gourmet Foods

▲ Corporate Gift Solutions

FREE GOLD PANNING

4840 W. 29TH AVE.
DENVER, CO 80212-1511

303-480-9050
http://www.madeincolorado.com

Gifts

In a sense, this category exists for stores we couldn't fit anyplace else because at this point in the chapter, we've listed dozens of places to buy gifts — from gourmet food stores to arts and crafts cooperatives. But here are five more of our favorites that you won't want to miss.

Colorado in a Basket
6005 E. Evans Ave., No. 101
• (303) 756-4778

Colorado in a Basket is the place to look for that quintessential Colorado gift. This com-pany prepares a variety of baskets filled with Colorado products, or you can make up your own selection. Prices begin at $25. Stop by the showroom or call (303) 756-4778 for a brochure.

Kobun Sha
1255 19th St. • (303) 295-1845

Kobun Sha is in colorful Sakura Square. It carries futons, Japanese shoji screens, lamps, ukiyo-e print postcards and cards, dolls, kites, tea sets and other Japanese gift items as well as an extensive line of English-language books on Japanese subjects.

Made in Colorado
4840 W. 29th Ave. • (303) 480-9050

Gifts, collectibles and foods from 250 Colorado regional artisans and craftspeople are featured in this northwest Denver store. The works encompass the artistic, the whimsical, the edible, the decorative, the readable, the touchable. Their "unusual" gift collection includes a gold panning kit — everything you need to strike it rich in the hills.

The Perfect Setting
5042 E. Hampden Ave. • (303) 759-1200

The Perfect Setting specializes in classy wedding gifts as well as gifts for other occasions. The store pays great attention to detail, displaying china, glass and gewgaws in artful ways. Though the store looks high-end, there are many affordable gifts. Gift wrap is free.

Thistle & Shamrock
407 17th St. • (303) 292-6522

Thistle & Shamrock features Scottish and Irish imports, including kilts, jewelry, fine china and assorted collectibles. Look for Beleek china and Edinburgh crystal. As you shop, enjoy lovely Scottish or Irish music in the background.

Kathie's Import Chalet
3971 S. Broadway, Englewood
• (303) 761-8038

Kathie's Import Chalet is a treasure trove for collectors of figurines (Hummel, Armani and Swarovski crystal). It also stocks music boxes, cuckoo clocks, nutcrackers and Christmas ornaments as well as Boyd's Bears and Cherished Teddies.

Bargain Shopping

Denver has its share of off-price retailers, including **Loehmann's**, 7400 E. Hampden Avenue, which sells primarily name-brand women's clothing at low prices. Beyond that, there are several great consignment and near-new stores, such as the following.

The Snob Shop
2804 E. Sixth Ave. • (303) 355-6939

This one's been around for a while and is known for its discriminating selection of clothing for men, women and children plus shoes and accessories. Check it out for anything from casual to dressy.

Rich Rags
600 Downing St. • (303) 861-2130

This consignment shop deals only in women's clothing. As its name implies, it features labels like Carole Little, Donna Karan, Armani and the like.

Gumballs
5787 S. Gallup St., Littleton
• (303) 795-6557

Tired of paying top dollar for kids' blue jeans? Gumballs often has a rack of them priced around a dollar. But that's not all; go here to find a lot of gently used children's clothing.

Outlets

Castle Rock Factory Shops
Exit 184, Meadow Parkway (off I-25 S.),
Castle Rock • (303) 688-4494

The largest outlet mall in the Front Range, Castle Rock has 110 stores — everything from designer clothes to electronics. Open seven days a week, the outlet has an easy and convenient layout and a central food court with the usual fast food offerings.

Rocky Mountain Factory Stores
I-25 N. to Exit 257B, Loveland
• (970) 663-1717

With 82 stores, Rocky Mountain Factory Stores has the Front Range's only Speigel and Bose (stereo equipment). There's the standard offering of clothes and kitchenwares, with savings up to 70 percent off everyday prices. Though there is no food court onsite, the outlet has several restaurants within walking distance.

Silverthorne Factory Stores
I-70 W. to Exit 205, Silverthorne
• (970) 468-9440

Started as a fashion and active outerwear outlet, Silverthorne's 80 stores now include kitchenwares and shoes. It offers 30 to 70 percent off regular prices and is surrounded by restaurants in this small mountain town.

The city's full of special-interest museums devoted to such diverse subjects as fire fighters, railroads, African Americans in the West, dolls and English painter J.M.W. Turner.

Tours and Attractions

In this chapter we've rounded up our favorite museums, gardens and historic houses. What Greater Denver has to offer in this category may surprise newcomers: The Museum of Natural History is the fifth largest of its kind in the country, and the Denver Art Museum is the largest such institution between Kansas City and the West Coast. Denver's Zoo and its Botanic Gardens are both highly respected, and the city is full of special-interest museums devoted to such diverse subjects as firefighters, railroads, African Americans in the West, dolls and English painter J.M.W. Turner. Among the most popular tourist attractions in the area are the tours at the United States Mint in Denver and Coors Brewery in Golden.

We've organized this chapter by category: first museums; then historic houses and other historic sites; parks and gardens; and finally, tours. Readers with a particular interest in the arts may also want to check our Arts chapter, as community art centers and galleries are listed there. At the end of the chapter, we suggest ways of combining visits to different sites that are near each other or that tie in thematically (for example, if you want to spend a day immersing yourself in Western history).

Hours and admission prices are subject to change. Also, be aware that some Greater Denver attractions either have shorter hours or are closed during winter. Please call before planning a visit.

RTD runs a Cultural Connection trolley that stops every half-hour at or near more than a dozen of Greater Denver's most popular cultural attractions, including the Denver Museum of Natural History and the Denver Botanic Gar-

dens as well as sites downtown. For $3 a day, you can get on and off as often as you like. You can buy tickets and pick up a map at the Visitors' Information Center at 225 W. Colfax Avenue, the downtown RTD stations on 16th Street at Market Street and Civic Center or on the bus itself (exact fare required). Make sure to pick up a map that shows the route or call (303) 299-6000 for up-to-date schedule information. The trolley operates between 9:30 AM and 6:30 PM seven days a week from mid-May through Labor Day weekend. Your trolley pass is also good on local buses and light rail.

Attractions listed below that are on the Cultural Connection trolley route are indicated by the notation "CC trolley stop." In some cases attractions aren't directly on the route but are within walking distance, so we've provided directions.

Museums

Colorado's Ocean Journey
700 Water St. (in the Platte River Valley just west of downtown)
• (303) 561-4450

Denver's newest attraction isn't exactly a museum, but it fits well under the category of other top-notch local and tourist spots in this chapter. Due to open in summer 1999, this long-awaited addition to the Central Platte Valley promises a unique experience in the arid west (far from the under-sea land of coastal areas).

Advance press dubs Ocean Journey a "world-class aquarium offering the wonders of water on two journeys: from the Continental Divide to the Sea of Cortez, and from an Indonesian Rainforest to the Depths of the Pacific." Located across the Platte River from Elitch Gardens, its $93 million price tag ensures hours of interactive fun. The 17 acre-complex will include 15,000 specimens of fish, mammals and birds; 1,000 plants; an 80-foot tall structure of red brick, glass and metal; and more than one million gallons of water recycled throughout the facility.

www.insiders.com

See this and many other Insiders' Guide® destinations online.

Visit us today!

Features include five major indoor exhibits: Colorado River Journey, a trip along the grand river including trout streams, wetlands, beaver ponds and waterfalls; Sea of Cortez, a journey of salt marshes, dunes and tide pools where you'll see starfish, eels, underwater caves and other exotic crustaceans at the touch pool; Indonesian River Journey, a glimpse at the second-largest rainforest on earth and its exotic species; Depths of the Pacific, a look at a coastal lagoon from a fish's perspective, including coral reef, sharks and eels; and Ocean Discovery Plaza, an exploration of various weather and water through wind, rain and fog, and a display of the playful antics of orphaned California sea otters.

The Denver Museum of Natural History
2001 Colorado Blvd. (in City Park, at Colorado Blvd. and Montview)
• (303) 322-7009, (303) 370-8257 (Hearing-impaired TDD), (800) 925-2250
• www.dmnh.org

The Denver Museum of Natural History is the largest cultural attraction in the Rocky Mountain region, with an average of 1.7 million visitors annually. In addition to more than 90 dioramas depicting animals from around the world, the museum's permanent exhibitions include a Hall of Life devoted to studying the human body, a planetarium and a fine gem and mineral collection that includes examples of Colorado gold and the largest rhodochrosite gem in the world. Other highlights include the Hall of Ancient Peoples, which deals with early man and early civilizations. Don't forget to take

a look at the re-designed Egyptian Mummies exhibit.

The museum also houses the award-winning dinosaur exhibit, the $7.7 million "Prehistoric Journey." It includes walk-through "enviroramas" complete with controlled lighting and temperatures, sounds, vegetation and even bugs!

Watch for special exhibitions, which in the past have included artistic and archaeological blockbusters such as "Ramses II" and "Imperial Tombs of China" and entertaining fare such as "Star Trek: Federation Science."

The museum also houses the Gates Planetarium and an IMAX theater. The planetarium features changing star programs and classes. Admission to IMAX is $6; planetarium admission is included in the museum admission price. Call the recorded information lines listed above for details.

The museum is open 9 AM to 5 PM from Labor Day to Memorial Day. Summer hours are 9 AM to 5PM Sunday through Wednesday and 9 AM to 7 PM Thursday, Friday and Saturday. Admission is $6 for adults and $4 seniors 60 and older and children 3 to 12. Combination museum and planetarium or IMAX theater tickets are available for $9; call or ask at the museum for more information. Also, some special exhibitions require an additional charge and advance reservations. The museum has a cafeteria-style restaurant and "T-Rex" cafeteria. (CC trolley stop)

The Denver Art Museum
100 W. 14th Ave. Pkwy.
• (303) 640-4433 (recorded information), (303) 640-2793

The Denver Art Museum is the largest art museum between Kansas City and the West Coast and is especially noted for its superb collections of Native American, pre-Columbian and Spanish colonial art. Its seven floors also house impressive displays of American, Asian and contemporary art and galleries devoted to design, graphics and architecture. See our Arts chapter for more details. (CC trolley stop)

Museum of Outdoor Arts
7600 E. Orchard Rd., Englewood
• **(303) 741-3609**

More than 50 outdoor sculptures comprise this "museum without walls" in the 400-acre Greenwood Plaza Business Park in the Denver Tech Center area. The museum is a collection of buildings, plazas and sculptures that combine into an artistic setting. (See our Arts chapter.)

Colorado History Museum
1300 Broadway • **(303) 866-3682**

The Colorado History Museum offers permanent and changing exhibitions about state history. The museum has an outstanding collection of William Henry Jackson photos, a large diorama of Denver as it appeared in 1860 and a comprehensive research library that is free and open to the public Tuesday through Saturday from 10 AM to 4:30 PM. Special exhibits have included everything from photography retrospectives to a display of Vatican treasures that coincided with Pope John Paul II's visit to Denver in 1993. As part of what is called the Civic Center Cultural Complex, the history museum, the library and the art museum collaborate on programs and share resources. Exhibits include the annual "Artists of America," which showcases artists from all over the nation, and others such as a 1960s and '70s retrospective featuring hippie and Vietnam-era artifacts. The museum is open 10 AM to 4:30 PM Monday through Saturday and noon to 4:30 PM on Sunday. Admission is $3 adults, $2.50 for seniors 65 and older and for students with ID, $1.50 for kids 6 to 16 and free for children younger than 6. (CC trolley stop)

Fort Vasquez
13412 U.S. Hwy 85, Platteville
• **(970) 785-2832**

Forty miles downstream from Denver on the South Platte River lies Fort Vasquez, a reconstructed 1830s fur-trading post operated with a museum by the Colorado Historical Society. The museum features exhibits and dioramas depicting the trading era. In summer, "mountain men" entertain visitors with re-enactments of old west trading days. A buffalo teepee will interest youngsters. Admission is free; hours are 10 AM to 4:30 PM Monday through Saturday year-round. In summer, Sunday hours are 1 PM to 4:30 PM.

The Black American West
Museum and Heritage Center
3091 California St. • **(303) 292-2566**

The Black American West Museum is a small but fascinating place that sets a lot of records straight and provides a long-buried picture of the role played by black Americans on the frontier. For example, few people know that the first black mayor of a major American city was Francisco Reyes, owner of the San Fernando Valley until he sold it in the 1790s and became the mayor of Los Angeles. The 1950 Van Heflin movie *Tomahawk* featured white actor Jack Okie playing explorer Jim Beckwourth, who discovered Beckwourth Pass through the Sierras. The movie's only problem: Beckwourth was black, as were up to one-third of all cowboys in the early West. The museum is housed in the former home of Dr. Justina L. Ford, Colorado's first licensed African-American female doctor. It is open 10 AM to 5 PM Monday through Friday and noon to 5 PM on Saturday and Sunday. Winter hours are shorter, with the museum closed Monday and Tuesday and open only from 10 AM to 2 PM Wednesday through Friday and noon to 5 PM Saturday and Sunday. Admission is $3 adults, $2 seniors and students, $1 for students ages 13 to 17 and 50¢ for children 4 to 12.

Museo de las Americas
861 Santa Fe Dr. • **(303) 571-4401**

This is the first museum in the Rocky Mountain region dedicated to Latin-American art, history and culture. The Museo de las Americas showcases art from all the Americas, including the Caribbean, in changing exhibitions. See our Arts chapter for more information.

Colorado Railroad Museum
17155 W. 44th Ave., Golden
• **(303) 279-4591**

One of our personal favorites, this museum houses more than 50 historic locomotives and cars as well as additional exhibits in a 12-acre outdoor setting. Don't miss the D&RG Engine No. 346, the oldest operating locomotive in Colorado. The museum is open daily from 9 AM to 5 PM (until 6 PM June through August). Admission is $4 for adults, $3.50 for seniors older than 60 and $2 for kids younger than 16. Family admission is $9 (two parents and children younger than 16). To get to the museum, take Exit 265 off I-70 W. and follow the signs. The No. 17 bus stops at the museum hourly on weekdays only; call RTD at (303) 299-6000 for schedule information.

Forney Transportation Museum
4303 Brighton Blvd. • (303) 297-1113

This longtime Denver favorite will move to its new location near the Denver Coliseum in 1999, but its exhibits will remain the same. It is scheduled for a late spring or early summer opening. The Forney Museum displays all kinds of old vehicles, including a number of one-of-a-kinds. Of special interest are the world's largest steam locomotive, Prince Aly Khan's Rolls Royce Phantom I and an original McCormick reaper. The museum is scheduled to be open 10 AM to 5 PM Monday through Saturday and closed on Sunday, but hours are subject to change so call ahead. It's closed on Christmas, Thanksgiving and New Year's Day. Admission prices in 1998 were $4 adults, $3.50 for seniors, $2 ages 12 to 18 and $1 ages 5 to 11, but also could change with the new location, so call ahead.

Buffalo Bill
Memorial Museum and Grave
987½ Lookout Mountain Rd., Golden
• (303) 526-0747

Dramatically located on top of Lookout Mountain, this fascinating museum is filled with memorabilia honoring the famous frontier scout, showman and Pony Express rider William F. Cody, colloquially known as Buffalo Bill. Included are gun collections, costumes and posters from the Wild West show and a collection of dime novels. The grave site affords an expansive view of the plains to the east and mountains to the west (and, less attractively, the rampant construction of large houses on the nearby hillsides). The museum is open 9 AM to 5 PM daily from May through October; 9 AM to 4 PM the rest of the year. It's

closed on Monday in the winter. Admission is $3 adults, $2 seniors, $1 for children 6 to 15 and free for children younger than 6.

Denver Firefighters Museum
1326 Tremont Pl. • (303) 892-1436

Housed in Station No. 1, which was built in 1909, the museum has a collection of original hand-drawn firefighting equipment, two engines from the 1920s and various antique firefighting memorabilia, including helmets, uniforms and trophies. The museum is open from 10 AM to 2 PM Monday through Saturday. Admission is $3 for adults and $2 for seniors and children 12 and younger.

(CC trolley stop — Get off at 14th and California streets at the Colorado Convention Center and walk two blocks ahead (east); turn right on Tremont.)

Denver Museum of
Miniatures, Dolls and Toys
Pearce-McAllister Cottage, 1880 Gaylord St. • (303) 322-1053

The two-story Pearce-McAllister Cottage, built in 1899, is of interest for its architecture and original decor and for its changing displays of vintage dolls, dollhouses, toys and miniatures. The museum offers year-round workshops for adults and kids on dollmaking, toys, and arts and crafts in miniature. There are three free days in the summer sponsored by the Scientific and Cultural Facilities District; call to find out when. The museum is open 10 AM to 4 PM Tuesday through Saturday and 1 to 4 PM Sundays (closed major holidays). Admission is $3 for adults, $2 for senior citizens and $2 ages 2 to 16, and includes a tour of both the cottage and museum. A group discount rate is available. (CC trolley stop)

Mizel Museum of Judaica
560 S. Monaco Pkwy. • (303) 333-4156

This, the Rocky Mountain region's only museum of Judaica, was established in 1982. Special programs, workshops, speakers, seminars and films are designed to complement the museum's changing exhibitions, whether drawn from its own collection or borrowed from such prestigious institutions as the Israel Museum and the Smithsonian Institution. Hours

Six Flags Elitch Gardens Thrills Visitors in New Home

There are those who say the beloved original Elitch Gardens, situated in an established Denver neighborhood covered by an emerald canopy of trees, can never be topped by the new park sandwiched between skyscrapers and Mile High Stadium.

Apparently they haven't ridden the 22-story free-falling Tower of Doom.

"It's the best," says Chris Roth, 17. "When you ride it, everything inside you disappears — like everything drops to the bottom and it's gone."

Roth ought to know. As official switch-flipper for local favorite roller coaster Twister II, Roth is no stranger to thrills. He sees visitors day after day scream in delight at the park's expanding lineup of dare-devil rides.

Close-up

The expansion is all part of a bigger, better Elitch's that began in 1994 when the park closed its doors after 104 years as a west Denver institution. The closing was mourned by longtime Denverites as the end of a treasured institution. The park reopened in 1995 in the city's Central Platte Valley, in the shadow of Coors Field and Denver's skyline. In 1998, Elitch's was sold to "Six Flags."

Elitch's started in 1890 when John and Mary Elitch turned a small apple orchard into picnic areas and ball fields open to the public. It later boasted Denver's first zoo. In 1891,

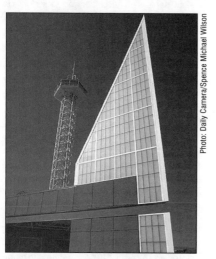

Photo: Daily Camera/Spence Michael Wilson

The observation tower (background) is a favorite at Six Flags Elitch Gardens.

the Elitch Theatre opened its first season and for 96 years hosted such luminaries as Sarah Bernhardt, Cecil B. DeMille, Grace Kelly and Edward Robinson. In 1925, the treasured carousel with 67 handcarved horses and chariots was installed. The restored carousel is a focal point of the new park.

Over the years, Elitch's became known for its signature gardens, a sprawling collection of impressive flowers, trees and shrubs. It will take many years before the "gardens" in the new Elitch Gardens come anywhere close to the impressive foliage tenderly raised at the old site. Meantime, efforts have been made to capture some of the nostalgia of the old Elitch's. A Victorian-style promenade with colorful storefronts and restaurants harkens to the old Elitch days. The Trocadero Theater, built in honor of Elitch's famed Trocadero Ballroom at the old park,

seats 700 and feature live shows.

Despite a greater emphasis on high-quality rides, visitors still might find Elitch's minuscule compared to such mega-theme parks as Walt Disney World, Paramount's King's Island and Cedar Point (both in Ohio) or any of the Six Flags operations. But it seems to be winning converts in Colorado and surrounding states.

Although the park opens weekends in May, Memorial Day is the official launch of the

— continued on next page

season. It was the perfect time for Sidney, Montana, resident Colton Martini to test his queasiness quotient. A ride on Twister II was fun, but his sights were set elsewhere.

"That didn't take my stomach like I thought it would, but I think that will," he said, pointing toward scream-inducing Mind Eraser. The $10 million twisted steel coaster ride consists of two 16-passenger trains suspended over 2,172 feet of steel track. Secured by space-age harnesses, riders ascend a 100-foot hill before blasting almost straight down the other side to enter a breathtaking corkscrew that hurls the train upside down –twice. In all, Mind Eraser is two minutes of dives, rollovers and spins. The screams are hair-raising the entire time.

"That was a total rush," exclaimed Andrew Sartorio, 18, of Denver. "Total adrenaline the whole way."

If you go, be sure to check out Shipwreck Falls, a splashy water ride that sends riders of all ages over a 50-foot waterfall, and Island Kingdom, a 10-acre tropical paradise theme area packed with all types of water adventure for all ages.

are Monday through Friday 10 AM to 4 PM and Sunday noon to 4 PM.

Rocky Mountain Quilt Museum
1111 Washington Ave., Golden
• (303) 277-0377

As much a resource center for quilters as a museum, the tiny Rocky Mountain Quilt Museum has more than 150 old and new quilts in its collection. Exhibits change every two months. Quilts and other needlework are offered for sale at the museum, which also conducts classes and outreach programs. The museum is open noon to 4 PM Tuesday through Saturday. Admission is $3 for adults and free for children younger than 6.

Historic Houses/ Museums and Other Historic Sites

Byers-Evans House and Denver History Museum
1310 Bannock St. • (303) 620-4933

John Evans was Colorado's second territorial governor. William Byers founded the *Rocky Mountain News*. Both men and their families were prominent during Denver's early years, and their names appear on avenues and mountain peaks. This house, built by Byers in 1883 and sold to Evans's son in 1889, has been restored to the 1912-24 period. The two

rooms at the entrance (the former service wing) now house the Colorado History Museum and its interactive video displays. The house and museum are open from 11 AM to 3 PM Tuesday through Sunday. Admission is $3 adults, $2.50 seniors 65 and older and $1.50 for kids 6 to 16. Combination tickets including entrance to the Colorado History Museum are $5 for adults, $4 for seniors and $2 for kids 6 to 16. (CC trolley stop)

Molly Brown House Museum
1340 Pennsylvania St. • (303) 832-4092

Only Baby Doe Tabor can match Molly Brown for name recognition among turn-of-the-century Denver women. Each has had her life memorialized in song: Baby Doe, in the opera *The Ballad of Baby Doe*, and Molly Brown, in the Broadway musical *The Unsinkable Molly Brown*. Molly was one of early Denver's more flamboyant characters, who achieved true heroine status for her actions during the sinking of the *Titanic*, which she survived. Her Victorian home has been restored and furnished in period style with many personal mementos and possessions.

Due to the popularity of the movie *Titanic*, the Molly Brown House sold out fast in summer 1998 (usually by 2 PM). Museum officials suggest arriving early as they do not take reservations. The museum is open in summer from 10 AM to 5 PM Monday through Saturday and noon to 5 PM on Sunday. Winter hours are 10 AM to 4 PM Tuesday through Saturday, noon to 4 PM on Sunday. The museum is

Photo: Daily Camera/ Spence Michael Wilson

The Twister is one of the highlights at Six Flags Elitch Gardens.

closed on all major holidays. Admission is $5 for adults, $3.50 for seniors, $1.50 for kids 6 to 12 and free for children younger than 6. A number of special dinners, teas, readings and workshops are scheduled throughout the year; call for more information. (CC trolley stop)

Colorado State Capitol
Broadway and Colfax Ave.
• **(303) 866-2604**

The Colorado State Capitol stands exactly 1 mile above sea level. On the 15th step there's a carving stating the elevation as 5,280 feet high, but a small brass plaque on the 18th step corrects the carving and proclaims itself the true mile-high marker. Inside the capitol building, free tours lasting about 45 minutes are given weekdays from 9 AM to 3:30 PM and in the summer on Saturdays too (from 9:30 AM to 2:30 PM). Those with strong legs and lungs can climb the 93 steps to the top of the gold-plated dome for a view over the plains and mountains. Although the gold on the out-side of the dome tends to receive more attention from casual passersby, the real precious mineral is on the inside of the building, where rose-colored Colorado onyx was used as wainscoting. The onyx came from a small quarry in Beulah, Colorado, and has never been mined elsewhere. (CC trolley stop)

Colorado Governor's Mansion
400 E. Eighth Ave.
• **(303) 837-8350, (303) 866-3682 (tours)**

Completed in 1907, the governor's mansion was originally the private residence of the Walter Scott Cheesman family. In 1927 the house was sold to the Boettcher family, and in 1960 the Boettcher Foundation gave the property to the state to use as the governor's mansion. The Colonial Revival structure contains artwork from all around the world and a Waterford chandelier that once hung in the White House. The mansion can be visited on Tuesday afternoons between noon and 2 PM June through August. Tours leave every 10 minutes. Two evening tours are offered from 5 to 7 PM on the last Tuesday of the month, June through August. The mansion is open to the public for a week during December when it's decorated for Christmas. Call for dates, as they vary every year.

Four Mile Historic Park
715 S. Forest St. • (303) 399-1859

Designated a Denver Landmark in 1968, Four Mile Historic Park commemorates the site of a former stagestop and contains the oldest home still standing in Denver. In addition to the 1859 log home, visitors can tour the living history farmstead and, on nice days, have a picnic here. Stagecoach rides are available every weekend between 11 AM and 2 PM, for $1 a person. Special events days are held about six times a year and include horsedrawn wagon rides and demonstrations of blacksmithing, butter churning and other chores. There are living history re-enactments of Civil War events during the spring and summer. Hours are 10 AM to 4 PM Wednesday through Sunday from April through September. Admission is $3.50 for adults, $2 for seniors and students 6 to 15 and free for children younger than 6. Winter hours are Friday through Sunday, 11 AM to 3 PM.

Fairmount Cemetery
430 S. Quebec Ave.
• (303) 399-0692

This 360-acre privately owned cemetery dates back to 1890 and is the final resting place for many former mayors, socialites, gunfighters, madams and Civil War veterans. An infamous "resident" is Col. John M. Chivington, responsible for the massacre of defenseless Indians at Sand Creek in 1864. The grounds contain more than 200 types of trees, and tours are given twice a year by the Denver Botanic Gardens for those interested in this aspect of the cemetery. Self-guided tours are possible anytime (a guidebook can be purchased at the site), and free guided tours are conducted from 10 AM to noon on Saturdays after Memorial Day and continuing through October. Call ahead to reserve a spot on the tour.

Riverside Cemetery
5201 Brighton Blvd., Commerce City
• (303) 293-2466

Denver's oldest cemetery, founded in 1876, contains the graves of three Civil War medal-of-honor winners; Augusta Tabor, the first wife of turn-of-the-century silver baron Horace Tabor; and Colorado's first black ballplayer, Oliver E. Marcel. Visitors can pick up a booklet and map for $2 during office hours, 8:30 AM to 4:30 PM Monday through Thursday and 10 AM to 4:30 PM Friday. The office is closed weekends. The cemetery is on Brighton Boulevard about 2 miles north of I-70.

Littleton Historical Museum
6028 S. Gallup St., Littleton
• (303) 795-3950

This living history museum consists of a reconstructed 1860s homestead and a turn-of-the-century farm that re-creates pioneer life. Among the original buildings on the 14-acre site are a 1910 ice house, a sheep and goat shelter originally built as a settler's cabin in the 1860s, an 1890s farmhouse and the first schoolhouse in Littleton. Three galleries in the main museum building feature changing exhibits. Outdoors, costumed staff and volunteers care for the chickens and livestock and go about the business of tending a 19th-century farm. They're not too busy to stop and explain things to visitors, however. Admission is free (large groups are charged a small fee and should call first). The museum is open 8 AM to 5 PM Tuesday through Friday, 10 AM to 5 PM on Saturday and 1 to 5 PM on Sunday; it's closed on Monday and major holidays.

Lakewood Heritage Center
797 S. Wadsworth Blvd., Lakewood
• (303) 987-7850

A historic site and museum with several

structures, including an 1880s farmhouse and a 1920s schoolhouse, Lakewood Heritage Center also has a barn gallery with changing exhibits. The visitors center has a permanent exhibit on May Bonfils, daughter of one of the founders of *The Denver Post*, and exhibits of work by local artists that change monthly. Admission, which includes a tour, is $2 for adults, $1 for children and free for kids younger than 3. Admission is free every third Sunday of the month. Hours are 10 AM to 4 PM Tuesday through Friday and noon to 4 PM Saturday and Sunday. Ask about special children's programs. Groups of five or more should make reservations.

Parks and Gardens

The Denver Zoo
City Park, E. 23rd Ave. and Steele St.
• (303) 331-4100

Easily combined with a trip to the Natural History Museum, the Denver Zoo has the usual complement of lions and tigers and (polar) bears as well as monkeys and birds, in a mix of enclosed and open habitat areas. Perhaps the most famous creatures to come from the Denver Zoo are Klondike and Snow, the adorable polar bear siblings who made national news while being nursed to health by zoo officials. Klondike and Snow have since moved on to another home.

The $10 million Tropical Discovery exhibit is designed to re-create a rainforest habitat inside a glass-enclosed pyramid. More than 240 animal species live here, nearly double what the zoo had previously. There is a separate nursery area where new arrivals needing human help get their first taste of what it's like to be in the public eye. Primate Panorama, a 5-acre, all-natural habitat is the latest crowd-pleaser. For those who can't or don't feel like walking the zoo, a fun train circles the major outdoor exhibits frequently throughout the day. The zoo is open daily, including all holidays, from 9 AM to 6 PM in summer, 10 AM to 5 PM in winter. Tropical Discovery and Bird World close at 4 PM. Admission is $8 for adults ($6 in winter), $6 for seniors, $4 for children ages 4 to 12 and free for children 3 and younger. About seven free days for Colorado residents are scheduled throughout the year; call for exact dates. (CC trolley stop)

Denver Botanic Gardens
1005 York St. • **(303) 331-4000**

One of Greater Denver's most lovely refuges, the Botanic Gardens encompasses 21 acres and includes a rose garden, herb garden and other specialty gardens. The 1-acre rock alpine garden is considered one of the finest in the country. Our personal favorite is the lovely Japanese Shofu-en (Garden of Pine Wind) designed by America's foremost Japanese landscaper, Koichi Kawana. It is complete with an authentic teahouse. Local residents look to the water-saving xeriscape demonstration garden and the home demonstration garden for ideas they can put into use in their own yards.

A tropical conservatory and pavilion houses orchids, bromeliads and other warmth-loving species. Outdoor concerts are held here in the summer; come early and bring a picnic dinner. Schedules are available at the gate in early June.

The Botanic Gardens are open May through September (summer hours) from 9 AM to 8 PM Saturday through Tuesday, and from 9 AM to 5 PM Wednesday through Friday. Winter hours (October through April 30) are 9 AM to 5 PM seven days a week. Admission (May through September) is $5.50 for adults, $3.50 for seniors and students with ID, $3 for ages 6 to 15 and free for children younger than 6 when accompanied by an adult. Reduced admission prices (50¢ to $1 off) apply October through April. (CC trolley stop)

Six Flags Elitch Gardens
I-25 and Speer Blvd. (Exit 212 A)
• **(303) 595-4386**

For more than 100 years, Elitch Gardens was a west Denver tradition. Opened in May 1890 as Elitch Zoological Gardens by John and Mary Elitch, it boasted three thrilling roller coasters: the Wildcat, the wooden Twister and the Sidewinder.

In the spring of 1995, Elitch Gardens reopened in a larger, 68-acre location in the Central Platte River Valley just off the Speer Boulevard Exit from I-25. (At night, all lit up, it's a beautiful and memorable sight for anyone driving through Denver on the interstate.) In 1998, the park was sold and renamed Six Flags Elitch Gardens. A rebuilt, 100-foot-high Twister II is one of the top attractions. There are 49 major rides in all, including several added in 1997: a water ride featuring a 50-foot plunge; a 210-foot free fall from the Tower of Doom; and a 60 mph ride through rollovers and corkscrew spins in the Mind Eraser (fast becoming the top attraction). For tamer pursuits, there's a 300-foot high observation tower with a panoramic view. The 1925 carousel made the move downtown.

In general, Elitch's is open daily from 10 AM until 10 PM from Memorial Day through Labor Day. There are shortened hours for the few weekends before and after Memorial and Labor days; call for times.

Admission for the 1998 season (including all rides and entertainment) was $26 for adults; $16 for kids less than 48 inches tall; $16 for seniors 55 to 69; and free for seniors 70 and older and kids 3 and younger. Parking is $5 per vehicle.

Lakeside Amusement Park
4601 Sheridan Blvd.,
(I-70 and Sheridan)
• **(303) 477-1621**

An all-ages amusement park, Lakeside has a merry-go-round, a Ferris wheel, a roller coaster and other exciting rides. One of the best things to do at Lakeside is to ride the train around the lake after dark. The park is open from May through Labor Day weekend. In May, the park is open on weekends only. It is open seven days a week June 6 through mid-August. Kids younger than 8 are welcome in the kiddie playland from 1 PM on weekdays, but the major rides don't begin operating until 6 PM weekdays and noon on weekends. Gate admission is $1.50 a person. An unlimited ride ticket costs $10.75 a person weekdays; $12.75 Saturdays, Sundays and holidays. Individual ride coupons can also be purchased. Prices are the same for adults and children.

Tours

United States Mint
320 W. Colfax Ave. • (303) 405-4761

One of Denver's most popular tourist attractions, the Mint produces 10 billion coins each year. Free tours are conducted weekdays from 8 AM to 2:45 PM except for the last Wednesday of the month, when tours begin at 9 AM. The 15-minute tours are first-come, first-served and leave every 15 to 20 minutes from the Cherokee Street entrance. Children younger than 14 must be accompanied by an adult. Wheelchairs are OK but cameras are not. No photos can be taken inside the building. Hours for coin sales are the same as tour hours. The Mint is closed on all legal holidays and for one week in summer, usually in late June, for inventory. (CC trolley stop: Get off at the Visitor's Bureau; the Mint building is visible across Colfax Avenue)

Coors Brewery
13th Ave. and Ford St., Golden
• (303) 277-BEER

Colorado is the second-largest producer of beer in the United States, and most of it comes from the Coors Brewery in Golden, the world's largest single-site brewing facility. The free tour and tasting ranks as one of Greater Denver's top tourist attractions; more than 10 million people have taken the 30-minute tour. Tours run from 10 AM to 4 PM Monday through Saturday and end with free beer sampling.

Hakushika Sake U.S.A. Corporation
4414 Table Mountain Dr., Golden
• (303) 279-7253

Tours at Golden's newest brewing facility — the first brewery outside Japan for this 300-year-old company — illustrate the process of making sake, but many people take the tour just to see the company's gorgeous collection of Japanese art, including 19th-century woodblock prints. Advance reservations are necessary; call one to two days ahead. Free tours last about 45 minutes and are conducted every hour between 10 AM and 3 PM Monday through Friday, except noon. Tours end with free samples at the gift shop.

Suggested Outings

One-day family outing . . .

Visit the Denver Museum of Natural History and the Denver Zoo. Take in a show at either the Gates planetarium or the IMAX theater. Then, if you have time, the Denver Museum of Miniatures, Dolls and Toys isn't far away.

Within walking distance downtown . . .

The Denver Art Museum, the Museum of Western Art, the Colorado History Museum, the U.S. Mint, the Colorado State Capitol, the Molly Brown House, the Firefighters Museum and the Colorado History Museum (Byers-Evans House) are all within walking distance of each other downtown. Don't try to see all these sights in one day, but pick the ones that interest you most; plot a route and save the rest for another afternoon.

For art lovers . . .

The Denver Art Museum and the Western Art Museum can be visited in one day if you don't try to see the whole art museum (save the non-American art galleries for another day). If you're at the Denver Art Museum at lunchtime, eat in their cafe. If you're over by the Western Art Museum, try the Trinity Grille next door at 1801 Broadway, (303) 293-2288. Or, if it's getting late, stop in at the Brown Palace Hotel across the street for afternoon tea in their elegant lobby.

INSIDERS' TIP

Denver's newest attraction, Denver Pavilions, offers an array of familiar shops in an accessible outdoor setting downtown. See our Shopping chapter for more information. When the weather is chilly, don't forget your coat to stay warm as you walk between stores.

Colorado Railroad Museum or, for the more artistically inclined, the Foothills Art Center, a small community arts center at 809 15th Street. We've fully described the art center in our Arts chapter. You may also want to visit the Rocky Mountain Quilt Museum, 1111 Washington Avenue.

History buffs . . .

Don't miss the Black American West Museum. A visit there combines well with visits to the Colorado History Museum and/or the Denver History Museum. Another possible combination is with the Western Art Museum.

Ethnic heritage tour (half-day) . . .

Divide your time between the Black American West Museum and the Museo de las Americas. Grab a snack at the Panaderia and Pastelaria Santa Fe, 750 Santa Fe Drive — it's recommended by the Museo staff for authentic Mexican pastries.

Art and garden tour . . .

Spend half the day at the Denver Art Museum, the rest at the Denver Botanic Gardens (via CC trolley).

Fauna and flora . . .

Spend half the day at the Denver Zoo, the rest at the Denver Botanic Gardens. Take the CC trolley.

Trains and automobiles . . .

Greater Denver has three museums of special interest in this category: the Forney Transportation Museum, the Colorado Railroad Museum and the Denver Firefighters Museum. With a car, all could be visited in one day.

One-day outing in Golden . . .

Start with a tour of the Coors Brewery (or end here if you're afraid the free beer samples will make you too sleepy to enjoy what comes next). Then drive up to the Buffalo Bill Memorial Museum and Grave and, if it interests you, nearby is the Mother Cabrini Shrine, which honors the first American saint (see our Worship chapter for more information). For lunch, take a picnic to Red Rocks Park if the weather's nice or eat Southwestern food at Silverheels Southwest Grill, 1122 Washington Avenue, in downtown Golden. In the afternoon, visit the

Walking tours . . .

A booklet of six downtown walking tours collectively called The Mile High Trail is available for $1.50 at the Greater Denver Chamber of Commerce, 1445 Market Street, (303) 534-8500. The information booth at Larimer Square can provide historical and architectural information about buildings in the 1400 block of Larimer Street. The Denver Metro Convention and Visitors Bureau conducts walking tours of Denver; call (303) 892-1505 for details. "Discover Denver" classes that include guided walking tours are offered several times a year through Colorado Free University, (303) 399-0093. Despite the school's name, the classes aren't free of charge — but prices are quite reasonable.

Public art tour . . .

The Mayor's Office of Art, Film and Culture, 280 14th Street, (303) 640-2696, can provide a brochure identifying public art throughout the city. The brochure contains a suggested walking tour and driving tour. Don't miss the outdoor murals on the 15th Street viaduct and Barbara Jo Revelle's vast tile mural of photographic images of people from Colorado's history, at the Colorado Convention Center (Welton Street side). The brochure is also available at the Denver Visitors Information Center, 225 W. Colfax Avenue, (303) 892-1112, and at public libraries in the Greater Denver area.

We think of Denver
as kids' country.

Kidstuff

We think of Denver as kids' country. Greater Denver offers a multitude of activities for the younger set — but we admit we like the outings too. Best of all, Denver's laid-back attitude says kids are welcome just about anywhere — assuming they aren't totally untrained, of course.

One of the first pieces of advice anyone in Greater Denver should heed to find ways for kids to have fun: take them out to play with Mother Nature. It doesn't matter what trail or mountainside you take them to; short hikes or climbs for smaller kids are found in the same places where adults and older kids go to get serious. There's an abundance of trails and natural beauty close to Greater Denver. Go to a local bookstore and pick up a copy of *Best Hikes With Children in Colorado*, by Maureen Keilty, and you can get good directions to a lot of kid hikes on the edge of the metro area. When hiking, make sure to protect yourself and your kids by using sunscreen and taking water bottles.

Mother Nature is only one of the kid-friendly attractions around Greater Denver. Check the other chapters of this book for ideas, especially Tours and Attractions, Spectator Sports, Annual Events, Parks and Recreation, and Daytrips.

What follows is limited to a reasonable number of unique attractions aimed at the younger set, but there are others too numerous to mention. Many of the following entries are generally desirable for all ages and only incidentally for kids. Take the kids fishing at any of the many reservoirs and rivers along the Front Range and in the nearby mountains. Go horseback riding at any of the stables around Greater Denver. Walk or ride bicycles on trails, usually along creeks, rivers, canals and lakeshores that thread the greenbelts of Greater Denver.

Call nearby public libraries about story hours and other child-oriented activities. Call city and county departments of parks and recreation in your area to see about kid activities ranging from soccer and baseball to art classes. Departments of parks and recreation are listed in our Parks and Recreation chapter.

One of your best comprehensive local resources to kid activities is *A Colorado Parent Directory*, available at local bookstores for $4.95. This annual directory is a comprehensive family resource guide and has just about everything a parent would want to know about the area; it's a good place to go for entertainment as well. It's produced by *Colorado Parent Magazine*, (303) 320-1000, a free monthly publication that can be found at 800 locations ranging from bookstores and libraries to doctors' offices and day-care centers.

Another great kid reference is *Kids Discover Denver and Boulder*, by Sara Goodman Zimet. At $12.95, with more than 200 pages, it's full of suggestions about playgrounds, entertainment centers, amusement parks, wildlife watching, museums, arts, sports, story reading and storytelling, and it also has a calendar of kid-friendly events. You should be able to find it at local bookstores, but you can also order it from Discovery Press Publications, P.O. Box 201502, Denver 80220-7502; (303) 355-9689.

Places to Go With Children in Colorado, by Patti Thorn and Marty Meitus, is another good source. It covers a range of opportunities from museums and fun parks to whitewater rafting and dude ranches. Almost one-third of the information covers opportunities specifically in Greater Denver. You should be able to find it in most significant local bookstores for $10.95.

Wet 'n' Wild

There are swimming pools all over the place, and some of them go the extra mile to be kid-friendly.

Westminster City Park Recreation Center
10455 Sheridan Blvd., Westminster
• **(303) 460-9690**

This indoor pool has a large children's pool with a tile beach sloping gently at one end, a fountain and a slide just for kids. The main pool for lap swimmers bulges out at one side under a waterfall. You can go behind the waterfall and look through windows to get an underwater view of the next pool, one floor above and dedicated entirely to swinging out on and dropping from a rope fastened at the ceiling three stories up. Above the rope-swing pool is the beginning of a water slide that ends with a splash in the main pool. Admission ranges from $2 to $4.25.

www.insiders.com
See this and many other
Insiders' Guide®
destinations online.
Visit us today!

The Bay Aquatic Center
250 Lamar St., Broomfield
• **(303) 469-5825**

This outdoor city facility is strictly for kids; there's no lap pool like there is at the indoor Westminster City Park Recreation Center. But kids will surely enjoy it. The tot pool has straight slides. The main pool has larger straight slides and spiral slides, and it also has a jungle gym in the water where kids can climb around and release sprays of water by pulling on ropes. This pool never gets deeper than 5 feet, and the jungle gym is in less than 1 foot of water. Admission ranges from $2.50 to $7. Children younger than 4 get in free.

Thornton Recreation Center
11151 Colorado Blvd., Thornton
• **(303) 252-1600**

In October 1994, the Thornton Recreation Center opened a fantastic new indoor 15,000-square-foot aquatics center, which includes artificially generated waves, lap swimming, a raindrop play area with waterfall and Jacuzzi, a lazy river and a water slide. Admission ranges from $2.50 to $7.

The Golden Community Center
1470 10th St., Golden • (303) 384-8100

The Golden Community Center has an indoor pool that kids will love, with a raindrop play area, water slide and hot tub as well as a lap pool and leisure pool. Admission ranges from $1 to $4.

Water World
88th Ave. and Pecos St., Federal Heights
• **(303) 427-7873**

Greater Denver's bigger outdoor water park, Water World offers more than 60 acres of aquatic fun. Float down a circular series of chutes and pools on an inner tube. Ride a huge rubber raft down a torrent. Sit on a plastic sled that plunges almost straight down and builds up enough speed to aquaplane across the pool at the bottom. Water World has it all. The park also recently added a Journey to the Center of the Earth ride, in which you cruise through caves where moving dinosaurs menace you. From late May to the end of summer Water World operates from 10 AM to 6 PM every day. Admission is $19.95 for adults and $18.95 for kids 4 to 12. If you're 60 and older or 3 and younger, it's free. Resident admission for people presenting a valid Highland Hills or City of Westminster resident ID card is $10 for adults and $9 for children. All eyeglasses must have safety straps.

Eating Out

Kids are welcome at just about any restaurant in town. Still, we've listed those that have true kid appeal.

Casa Bonita
6715 W. Colfax Ave. • (303) 232-5115

Rising from the JCRS Shopping Center in Lakewood, the distinctive steeple of Casa Bonita has become a Greater Denver landmark. Although this is a perfectly good Mexican restaurant with American dishes, too, people come here more for the play than for the food. It's like eating in a cave with huge chambers and a complex labyrinth of tunnels and hidden nooks, with strolling mariachis and other features. Kids love Black Bart's cave, a series of creepy scares in tunnels sized for kids. There's a video arcade and other entertainments. The crowning glory is the 30-foot waterfall, where divers plunge into a pool below while performances at the top of the waterfall involve cowboy gunfights and explorers tangling with a gorilla. Every performance ends with somebody falling 30 feet into the pool. It's a popular place for kid birthday parties and for parents who want to kick back while their kids run wild. Admission is the price of a meal, which for adults ranges from $5.49 to $8.49 with an $8.39 all-you-can-eat binge. Children younger than 12 can get $2.99 meals. Hours are 11 AM to 9:30 PM Sunday through Thursday, 11 AM to 10 PM Friday and Saturday.

Gunther Toody's
4500 E. Alameda Ave., Glendale
• (303) 399-1959
9220 E. Arapahoe Rd., Englewood
• (303) 799-1958
7355 Ralston Rd., Arvada • (303) 422-1954
8266 W. Bowles, Littleton • (303) 932-1957

The staff all dress like characters from *Grease* at this 1950s-concept restaurant, and they usually do such a good job of acting their sassy, gum-chewing parts that there must be a Gunther Toody's acting school somewhere. The only games are a few classic pinball machines, and it's not exclusively a kid restaurant. But that's why we're mentioning it here, because it deserves wider recognition as a great, non-arcade dining place for kids and their families. Entrees mostly range between $5 and $7, although prices go as high as $9 for a double diner — a big double cheeseburger platter.

Trail Dust Steak Houses
7101 S. Clinton St., Englewood
• (303) 790-2420
9101 Benton St., Westminster
• (303) 427-1446

Kids love the two-story slide that empties onto the hardwood dance floor at the Trail Dust Steak Houses, and they'll howl when a waitperson cuts off someone's tie. The steaks are good, as are all the fixin's.

Piccolo's
3563 S. Monaco Pkwy. • (303) 757-5166
1744 E. Evans Ave. • (303) 722-4955
7585 S. University Blvd., Littleton
• (303) 797-0686
12325 W. 64th Ave., Arvada
• (303) 424-3700

This neighborhood restaurant is packed with families, not only because their Italian and Mexican food is good but also because they know kids' eyes are often bigger than their stomachs. To that end, they offer half-portions of any pasta — even quarter-portions if your child so desires.

Original Pancake House
5900 S. University Blvd., Englewood
• (303) 795-0573

Go to this breakfast/lunch place at 9 AM on Saturday or Sunday and you'll see a mess of families — so many you can easily plan on an hour's wait. But it's worth it. The variety of pancakes and waffles is mind-boggling, and kids love the huge apple pancake, which is the house specialty.

Planes, Trains and Boats

Colorado Railroad Museum
17155 W. 44th Ave., Golden
• (303) 279-4591

A lot of Western city parks used to have trains that kids could climb around on, but now they're mostly surrounded by fences to keep the kids out. None of that nonsense here! The Colorado Railroad Museum is mentioned in our Tours and Attractions chapter, but at 12.5 acres, with more than 50 pieces of "rolling stock," it's so fantastic for kids that it bears repeating. Kids can climb up and walk through the antique railway cars, climb into the cupolas of the cabooses to look out the windows and climb up on the big engine right outside the museum building and pull the rope and ring the awesome bell. You have to be a bit older to appreciate most of the two floors of memorabilia inside the museum building, but kids love the enormous model train setup in the basement, which you can run by plugging in a quarter. Several times a year the museum fires up and runs the state's oldest railway engine. The first week of December, Santa Claus parks inside a caboose and receives children between the hours of 10 AM and 4 PM. Admission is $3.50 for adults, $1.75 for kids younger than 16 accompanied by a parent, $3 for people older than 60 and $7.50 for a family, which the museum defines as two adults and children younger than 16. Hours are 9 AM to 6 PM every day of the week in June, July and August, and 9 AM to 5 PM the rest of the year.

Platte Valley Trolley
2785 N. Speer Blvd. • (303) 458-6255

To get to the trolley, park at the Denver Children's Museum (see our listing in this chapter) and walk from the museum east to the Platte River. This turn-of-the-century streetcar tour is for all ages. Small tykes may recognize its near-exact resemblance to the streetcar on the *Mister Rogers' Neighborhood* TV show. Kids 6 years of age and younger may prefer the half-hour tour to the hour tour. You'll enjoy a narrated tour along the Platte River, with bits of history and expositions on present and future features of this area such as Mile High Stadium and Golda Meir's former residence. The hour tour goes up Lakewood Gulch, along the tracks where the interurban trolley used to run from Denver to Golden.

Admission for the half-hour tour is $2 for adults and $1 for kids and seniors. The hour tour costs $4 for adults, $3 for seniors and $2 for kids. Hours are 11 AM to 4 PM. June through September, there are tours every day; September and October, every day but Monday, weather permitting, and November through March, weekends only, weather permitting.

Pikes Peak Cog Railway
U.S. Hwy. 24 W. from Colorado Springs to the Manitou Exit, west on Manitou Ave. and left onto Ruxton Ave., Colorado Springs • (719) 685-5401

Adults become kids again during this delightful experience. We've covered this in greater detail in our Daytrips chapter, yet this is one of the greatest kid activities on the Front Range: a $3^1/_2$-hour trip to the top of Pikes Peak on the highest cog railway in the world. All this presumes, of course, that your kids are of an age and temperament to tolerate the long ride. Reservations are required. The train costs $21.50 for adults, $10 for kids ages 5 to 11.

Wings Over The Rockies
7750 E. Irvington Pl. • (303) 360-5360

The closing of Lowry Air Force Base in the fall of 1994 was accompanied by the opening a few months later of what is now one of Greater Denver's greatest museums. Wings Over the Rockies does for aviation what the Colorado Railroad Museum does for the railroads: puts the biggest and best of the historic hardware on very impressive display for the public. With the exception of the Space Station Module, you can't actually go inside the displays, but up close and gargantuan, they have a tremendous, visceral impact. Among the 20 aircraft on display in the museum are big bombers, racy fighter jets and helicopters — a scan of aviation history. You've got civilian and military aircraft, models, simulations, photographs and space-related ob-

---

INSIDERS' TIP

For cold-weather fun with the kids, take them tubing down a ski slope at Keystone. For around $10 per hour for adults and about half that for kids, you get a gondola ride to the tubing spot and rope-tow rides back to the top. See our Ski Country chapter or call the Keystone Activities Center at (970) 668-0866.

jects so visitors can experience scientific discovery. It's all contained in the vast interior of Lowry's Hangar 1. Since it's all indoors, it's particularly nice on a winter day when outside activities are curtailed. This excepts the B-52 bomber on display outside. There are also a variety of historic aviation artifacts and a museum store. Admission is free to museum members, and for others it costs $4 for adults, $2 for children ages 6 to 17 and seniors older than 60, and it's free for kids 5 and younger. Wings Over the Rockies is open from 10 AM to 4 PM Monday through Saturday and 12 to 4 PM on Sunday.

From I-225, take Sixth Avenue west to Lowry Boulevard, turn left at the dead end and proceed until you see the hangars. It's the first one to the west. Or you can take Alameda west to Fairmount Cemetery and turn right on Fairmount Drive. Straight ahead you'll see the two hangars, and it's the first one to the east.

Kids cool off in the fountain of the Denver Museum of Natural History.

Punt the Creek
1666 S. University Blvd. • (303) 698-1322

One of Denver's newest attractions, Punt the Creek is a great way to see Lower Downtown from the vantage point of a boat — or punt, in this case. A punt is a flat-bottomed boat, similar to a gondola. You can take a five-block ride downstream and back up while hearing the history of Cherry Creek and the history of punts. Get your ticket at the kiosk on Larimer Street between 14th Street and Speer Boulevard. Take a few steps down to the pedestrian path and follow it one block to Market Street where you'll embark. The punts operate from 4 to 9 PM Tuesday through Sunday in June, July and August. Boats leave every 10 minutes. Tickets cost $7 per adult, $3.50 per child ages 12 and younger and $6 per senior. Or pay $18 for a family of four. All children must wear life jackets, which are provided by your guide.

Nightlife for the Younger Crowd

Club 22
Northglenn Recreation Center, 11801 Community Center Dr., Northglenn • (303) 450-8800

Club 22 stands for "2 old for a sitter and 2 young to drive." This is safe and supervised nightlife for adolescents of middle-school age. Parents check their kids in, and the kids don't leave until the parents check them out. In between, there's music and dancing, swimming and other activities, such as volleyball and wallyball in the Rec Center's athletic facilities. There are contests, food and beverage concessions and always some sort of special event, such as a movie or an entertainer or demonstrator. Admission is $3 per night. Club 22 takes place on the first and third Saturdays of each month from 7 to 10:30 PM.

Friday Night Live
Westminster City Park Recreation Center, 10455 Sheridan Blvd., Westminster
• **(303) 322-9317**
Goodson Recreation Center, 6315 S. University Blvd., Littleton
• **(303) 322-9317**

Friday Night Live features safe and supervised weekend nightlife for adolescents ages 9 to 14. Depending on where one attends, it may be on Saturday instead of Friday. The phone number above is for Friday Night Live of Colorado, the franchisor for the program at the different rec centers. It's turned out to be a popular program, and it takes place during the school year.

You'll typically find games, dancing and music with a live DJ; a gym is open for such activities as basketball, dodgeball, wallyball and volleyball; concessions for pizza and soft drinks; movies, contests and special guests. There is one adult counselor for every 25 kids, a uniformed policeman on hand at all times and parental check-in and check-out. Admission in 1997 was between $6 and $6.50 for the rec centers. Hours are 7 to 11 PM.

The Plant and Animal Kingdom

Denver Botanic Gardens
1005 York St.
• **(303) 331-4010**

Kids of all ages enjoy these lovely gardens and the tropical conservatory. We've described the gardens in detail in our Tours and Attractions chapter. Most likely, however, children will be more interested in the changing menu of year-round kid activities, such as the Halloween jack-o'-lantern show and the summer evening concerts listed in our Annual Events chapter. It's also a pretty place to run around, with a couple of grassy knolls that small kids love to climb on and roll down. It's a nice place for a picnic, like being out in the country when you're in the city. Admission is $5.50 for adults and $3 for kids. The gardens are open from 9 AM to 8 PM Saturday through Tuesday and 9 AM to 5 PM Wednesday, Thursday and Friday.

Mile High Greyhound Park
6200 Dahlia St. at Colorado Blvd., Commerce City • **(303) 288-1591**

See our Spectator Sports chapter for details, but don't forget that this is a great place to go to entertain your kids for just $1 a head for parents, with kids younger than 18 getting in free. You don't even have to bet. Kids who love dogs will love this show, and smaller children can always take an interest in Rusty, the white mechanical bunny that never gets caught. It's a lovely outing on a warm summer evening, and it's a fascinating spectacle for kids and parents alike. Races take place at 1 PM on Monday, Wednesday, Friday and Saturday as well as at 7:30 PM every evening except Thursday and Sunday.

The Denver Museum of Natural History
2001 Colorado Blvd. (in City Park, at Colorado Blvd. and Montview)
• **(303) 370-6357**

See our Tours and Attractions chapter for more detail on this museum, but don't forget it's one of the greatest places around for kids. We know one woman from Montana who recalls the museum as a favorite childhood memory from the time her family came down specifically to visit it. When you walk under the claws of the huge Tyrannosaurus Rex skeleton as you enter the front door you know you've entered a place of wonder. Sure, kids have to be older to appreciate a lot of things here, but the exhibits of dinosaurs and Pleistocene megafauna, such as the two saber-toothed tigers attacking the giant sloth, are sure winners. So are the many dioramas showing different kinds of fauna in exquisitely crafted natural settings that blend so flawlessly into painted backdrops that you really feel like you're on a mountain top with the eagle family or at the seashore with the sea lions. A number of the woodland backdrops have elves painted into them or elf figurines hiding in the foreground foliage or under rocks or logs. A real challenge is trying to find the elves; we've only managed to spot a couple of them. The IMAX theater with its four-story-high screen is a treat some Denverites enjoy taking their kids to frequently. The museum also has some great children's educational programs, al-

Safe in the shadow of city skyscrapers, Denver kids get active.

though they fill up frighteningly fast once their scheduling becomes public knowledge. Admission to the museum is $6 for adults; $4 for ages 3 to 12. IMAX is the same. However you can buy a museum/IMAX ticket for $9 for adults; $6 for kids. The museum is open from 9 AM to 5 PM from Labor Day to Memorial Day, and in the summer from 9 AM to 5 PM Sunday through Wednesday and 9 AM to 7 PM Thursday through Saturday.

The Denver Zoo
City Park, E. 23rd Ave. and Steele St. (near the Denver Museum of Natural History)
• **(303) 331-4100**

You can't miss with a zoo, and The Denver Zoo may well be Greater Denver's most popular kid place of all. For more on this wonderful place, see our Tours and Attractions chapter and also our Annual Events chapter. The Zoo has some wonderful special events around the seasons. Admission to the zoo is $8 for ages 13 to 61 ($6 in the winter); $3 for ages 4 to 12. The zoo is open every day of the year from 9 AM to 6 PM.

Butterfly Pavilion & Insect Center
6252 W. 104th Ave., Westminster
• **(303) 469-5441**

If your child loves butterflies, this place is a perfect destination. More than 1,200 butterflies live in a 7,200-square-foot tropical forest. At the emergence viewing area, you can watch the last tow stages of metamorphosis as butterflies emerge from their chrysalids. Outside is a butterfly garden, with flowers designed to attract butterflies. The Pavilion is open Tuesday through Sunday from 9 AM to 5 PM year-round. Admission is $6.50 per adult, $3.50 per child ages 4 to 12 and $4.50 for seniors.

Rocky Mountain Arsenal National Wildlife Refuge
72nd and Quebec sts., Commerce City
• **(303) 289-0232**

Take a two-hour bus tour of one of the country's former toxic waste sites, now overrun with all kinds of wildlife. On this free Saturday tour, from 9 to 11 AM, you hear the history of the area as well as its environmental cleanup. If you're lucky, you'll also see eagles, hawks, mules, white-tailed deer and prairie dogs. If the wildlife is out romping, this will be one of those "WOW!" experiences. Though the tour is free, reservations are a must.

Hudson Gardens
2888 W. Maplewood Ave., Littleton
• **(303) 797-8565**

Metro Denver's newest public gardens, this is a beautiful place to walk on a clear, warm day. Sixteen different "rooms" make up this floral wonderland, and kids can sniff at the "Fragrance Garden," wander through the "Secret Garden" and look for butterflies in the "Butterfly Bank Garden." The gardens are open year-round from 10 AM to 5 PM Wednesday through Sunday. Adults pay $4; children, $2.

Museums

Children's Museum of Denver
2121 Children's Museum Dr.
• **(303) 433-7444**

There's a wealth of things to do here, all of it aimed specifically at kids and all of it educationally oriented. There's a miniature grocery store, where kids can shop or be the checkout person, and a Denver Nuggets exhibit, where kids can compare their sizes to basketball players' sizes, shoot baskets, etc. There are laboratories where kids can work with earth sciences and natural phenomena and play educational games on computers. You'll find a light room and sound room, plant and animal exhibits, woodworking and a traveling exhibit that changes every three months. Play Partners is a special toddler play area set up like The Three Bears' house. Kids can ski year round on the KidSlope, although reservations are recommended. It's a great museum, but a very busy one that's often crowded. The museum recommends coming between 2 and 5 PM on weekdays, when it's least crowded. Admission is free for kids younger than 1, $2 for ages 1 to 2, $5 for ages 3 to 59 and $3 for ages 60 and older. Hours are 10 AM to 5 PM Tuesday through Sunday during the school year, plus 10 AM to 5 PM on Mondays throughout the summer. The museum is also open on Mondays that are school holidays.

Worthy of note is the museum's annual Halloween party, Trick-or-Treat Street, which runs for nearly a week including Halloween. This is Denver's non-scary trick-or-treat alternative. Multitudes of kids show up in costumes to pass through the many exhibits and receive candy. The event includes pumpkin carving, performances and other activities.

The museum can be a little tricky to reach, so here are some directions: it's right off 23rd Avenue and I-25. If you exit from I-25, go east on 23rd and take the first right on Seventh Street and then an immediate right onto Children's Museum Drive.

The Denver Art Museum
100 W. 14th Ave. Pkwy. • **(303) 640-KIDS**

On the first Saturday of the month, the Denver Art Museum features free family workshops in which kids can explore the galleries while learning and creating. They'll also enjoy the all-the-time features such as "eye spy" games on every floor. Available every second, third, fourth and fifth Saturday of the month is a free Family Backpack, which is a backpack kids can check out, containing games and activities relating to exhibits. There's Kids Corner on the main-floor lobby, but a lot of kids, of course, will also be interested by the museum itself. See our Tours and Attractions chapter for more on this great museum. Call (303) 640-KIDS for specific information on children's and family programs. The museum is open from 10 AM to 5 PM Tuesday through Saturday and 12 to 5 PM on Sunday. Admission is $4.50 for adults and $2.50 for kids and seniors. On Saturday Colorado residents get in free.

Littleton Historical Museum
6028 S. Gallup St., Littleton
• **(303) 795-3950**

This museum is covered in our Tours and Attractions chapter, but it's one of our favorites for kids. As a living-history museum, it's particularly fascinating to kids interested in the past. But it's also a great way to let the kids see lots of animals and explore a fantasy world of the past. It's a working homestead and farm, with sheep, oxen, pigs, cows, chickens, horses and other animals. Costumed staff and volunteers go about their antiquarian life chores, keeping to the roles and speaking in the manner of people from the late 19th century. As you walk around, you may encounter them working in a garden or barn or fields, cooking in the house, blacksmithing in the 1903 blacksmith shop or teaching in the 1860s schoolhouse. If you're lucky in the winter, you may catch them harvesting ice from the lake for the 1900 ice house, although the ice in recent years often has not been thick enough to harvest. Admission is free. Hours are 8 AM to 5 PM Tuesday through Friday; 10 AM to 5 PM Saturday and 1 to 5 PM on Sunday.

Four Mile Historic Park
715 S. Forest St. • (303) 399-1859

This museum is covered in our Tours and Attractions section but should be noted here as well. Kids enjoy walking through the living history farmstead, where they can see old machinery, reconstructed barns, outhouses (not for use and odor-free), root cellars, chickens, ducks, calves and horses. Older kids may also enjoy the tour of Denver's oldest house, led by costumed tour guides. In 1995, the park added a guided tour via stagecoach on weekends only. During special events, there are more kid attractions such as demonstrations of blacksmithing, butter churning and other crafts of yesteryear as well as horse-drawn wagon or stagecoach rides. The number of events annually varies, but the museum has a few standard events: a July Fourth old-fashioned family picnic; two spooky theme nights on the weekend before Halloween; and the holiday open house in December. Admission is $3.50 for adults, $2 for kids and seniors, and free for kids younger than 6. The park also does special programming with special rates for groups of 10 or more.

In 1995 for the first time, the park went to year-round operation. Summer hours are still 10 AM to 4 PM Wednesday through Sunday. Call the park for winter hours.

Making Money

Young Americans Education Foundation
311 Steele St. • (303) 321-2954

This foundation was launched in the late 1980s by Bill Daniels, one of Denver's most famed citizens for his role as the pioneer of

the cable TV industry, an industry in which Denver now plays a leading role. Daniels, now chairman of Daniels Communications Inc., a broker/dealer of major cable systems around the country, started the foundation to give kids an early grounding in the business culture. Most widely known is the Young Americans Bank, a real FDIC-insured bank of which the foundation is the nonprofit holding company. Designed for ages 0 to 21, it's the only bank in the world exclusively for kids. They can have their own savings and checking accounts, ATM and credit cards, and mutual funds. It emphasizes individual attention to children, with small teller booths designed with steps so kids can look the teller in the eye, and tellers who teach the kids one-on-one about deposit slips, interest and so on.

Be Your Own Boss is a program, started in 1994, for kids interested in starting and/or owning their own companies. This program is offered during the summer as a week-long day camp for ages 12 to 14. Kids are taken step-by-step through the entrepreneurial process, from basic education on things like financing to the writing of their own business plans.

Young AmeriTowne is another nifty program, involving students role-playing in 16 different jobs and running their own town. It's accessed through schools, but parents can help by hustling their children's teachers to get their classes involved. During the school year, students learn first in their classrooms before coming in for a one-day program. Kids can also go to Young AmeriTowne on an individual basis during its summer programs: the Undergraduate Program (ages 10 to 12), the Girls Can Program (girls only, ages 10 to 12); the Executive Program (for experienced Young AmeriTowne citizens, ages 10 to 14), and the Junior AmeriTowne (for kids who have just completed 2nd, 3rd or 4th grades).

The United States Mint
320 W. Colfax Ave. • (303) 844-3582

Ever wondered what 40 million coins look like? Take the 30-minute tour of the U.S. Mint and you may get some idea. This free tour starts with an exhibit on the history of money and then to the observation room where you can look down on 60 high-speed presses that produce as many as a billion coins a month.

In the next room, you see machines count, sort and bag coins. You learn that 70 percent of the coins stamped in Denver are pennies. Stop in at the Numismatic Sales Room where you can gaze on — even purchase — special coins, medallions and commemorative coins. Tours start at 8 AM and go every 15 minutes until 2:45 PM Monday through Friday.

Amusement Parks (Indoors and Out)

Funplex
9670 W. Coal Mine Ave., Littleton
• (303) 972-4344

This is a 3¹/₂-acre indoor fun center for all ages. Activities include 40 lanes of bowling, roller-skating, one 18-hole miniature golf course, more than 150 video games, two restaurants, an ice-cream shop, a sports bar and Laser Storm, a light tag game. There's also the Pirate Cove Kids Corner, which includes a pool of balls and a slide. Also new are six major rides. There's no admission fee; you pay by activity, which ranges from $2.25 to $6. Hours begin at 11 AM daily in the summer and 4 PM the rest of the year. Closing varies from 10 PM to 1 AM, depending on the day of the week.

Discovery Zone
14281 E. Exposition Ave., Aurora
• (303) 340-1619
7510 Parkway Drive, Littleton
• (303) 649-1831

Discovery Zones are designed for kids ages 18 months to 12 years. They feature an obstacle course, slides and nets and bins of plastic balls connected by human-size gerbil tunnels. A separate play area for babies and toddlers makes sure they won't get trampled by the big kids. The game room includes 26 games such as whack-an-alligator, skee ball and basketball. Right next to the games is a cafe, with food and drink of the pizza/hot dog variety and tables. Since our last edition, the Discovery Zones have eliminated the quiet room, surrounded by windows, where parents used to be able to get away from the noise. All-day admission is $5.99 for ages 3 and older;

$3.99 for kids ages 1 to 3, and parents get in free. Hours are 9 AM to 8 PM Monday through Thursday, 10 AM to 9 PM Friday and Saturday and 11 AM to 7 PM Sunday.

Funtastic Fun
3085 S. Broadway, Englewood
• (303) 761-8701

This used to be called Funtastic Nathan's when it was located in the Cinderella City mall, but in 1994 it moved and changed its name. It's popular among kids of Greater Denver's south side. This fun center includes a Ferris wheel, a carousel, a train, swings, a cave, an air castle and a lot of things kids can do on their own. A room of plastic balls with slides and games such as skee ball and air hockey will also keep the kids happy. Funtastic Fun also has a room for younger kids, which includes a smaller air castle, so the squirts don't get roughhoused by the bigger kids. Individual admission is $5.99 for all day, except on Tuesdays and Wednesdays, when it's $3.99. The group rate is $3.99 per head every day. Hours are 10 AM to 9 PM daily.

Six Flags Elitch Gardens
I-25 and Speer Blvd. • (303) 595-4386

Elitch Gardens is Denver's oldest fun park, dating from 1890 when it began as a botanical and zoological gardens and had no mechanical rides. Since then, it has become Denver's flashiest amusement park. Now it's even bigger, expanding in 1995 from its old 28-acre site to a new 68-acre site along the South Platte River across from the Children's Museum. In 1997 it was purchased by Premier Parks, Inc., the fourth-largest theme park company in the United States. The new Elitch Gardens has more than 40 rides, including a wonderful Kiddieland. Among the rides is an absolute horror called the Avalanche, in which rows of strapped-in riders are carried several stories into the air and turned upside down and flipped around. It's a nightmare. Disaster Canyon is another beauty, a raft ride on white water and through a spray tunnel that will soak you. One of the great new features is the Total Tower, which reminds one of Seattle's Space Needle. It's 300-feet high with a 360-degree viewing platform. In 1997, the park added the Mind Eraser, a steel, looping suspended roller

A Day in the Park

For many Denverites, the way to spend a perfect day with the kids is at one of Denver's wonderful parks. Thanks to the vision of Robert Speer (after whom Speer Boulevard is named), Denver has a system of parks and greenways that is the largest in the nation.

The story goes that Speer attended the 1893 Chicago Exposition where he gathered ideas for turning Denver into a beautiful city of open spaces intended for public use. Elected mayor in 1904, he went to work convincing his fellow politicians of the need for the city to buy land for recreational use. In 1868, the first park opened at 31st and Curtis Streets. Mestizo-Curtis Park (originally called Curtis Park after postmaster Samuel Curtis) is still a vital part of this north Denver neighborhood.

Today, 94 years after Speer was elected, the city and county of Denver has 281 urban parks, 125 miles of hiking and biking paths, 100 miles of parkways and 20,000 acres of mountain parks. And that only includes those areas administered by the city of Denver. Go to the suburbs and you'll find many more.

— continued on next page

Photo: Denver Metro Convention & Visitors Bureau

Head to Denver's Genesee Park to see the buffalo.

Though all the parks are soothing oases, the following are particularly beloved by kids.

Washington Park
Louisiana Ave. and Downing St.

This is one of Denver's most popular park destinations. Originally a prairie, it has two lakes that allow fishing (don't forget your license) and a lawn bowling/croquet green. Best of all, most of the streets are closed to vehicle traffic so your family can in-line skate, bike or walk without fear of being mowed down.

City Park
17th Ave. and Colorado Blvd.

This park just east of Downtown is full of possibilities, not the least of which are visits to the Zoo and the Denver Museum of Natural History. A lake in the park offers paddleboating. A rose garden close to the museum provides a great picnic site. Need more activity? The park has a public golf course and tennis courts. And in the summer, it's easy to find a free concert in the bandshell near the lake.

Cheesman Park
E. 12th Ave. and Humboldt St.

Cheesman Park has some terrific playground equipment (not to mention a pretty spectacular view of the mountains). Kids love the castle structure for climbing and hiding, and the jungle gym is one of the best around. Most striking is the Cheesman Park Pavilion, a Parthenon-like structure perfect for running around or watching the sunset.

Genesee Park
I-70 W. to the Genesee Exit

How many cities boast parks that house a herd of buffaloes? The best reason to head here is to see the 30 or so bison roaming right off the highway. Once you see these gentle giants, you won't care that there aren't all the other fancy trappings of city parks.

Belleview Park
5001 S. Inca St., Englewood

Belleview is simply one of the most fun family parks around. Often called Airplane Park, it has two playgrounds filled with space-related jungle gyms, slides and swings. It also has a miniature train that takes visitors around the park and a petting zoo with cows, pigs, goats and rabbits. If that's not quite enough, a clear, shallow stream runs through the park, and it's perfect for wading.

Cushing Park
795 W. Eastman St., Englewood

This is the site of one of Denver's first gold discoveries. Not surprisingly, its playground is reminiscent of the Old West with a stagecoach, a tepee, a jail, and a horse and buggy — all of which keep active buckaroos busy while their parents lounge under a tree and relax. Cushing is also the only park in Englewood with an area specifically for skateboarders.

coaster and the 200-foot free-falling Tower of Doom. Admission for the 1998 season (including all rides and entertainment) was $26 for adults; $16 for kids less than 48 inches tall; $16 for seniors 55-69; and free for seniors 70 and older and kids 3 and younger. Parking is $5 per vehicle. Elitch's opens in May on weekends only. After Memorial Day, it is open daily 10 AM to 10 PM until Labor Day.

Getting to Elitch Gardens is no problem, since it now has its own exit from the Speer Boulevard viaduct, with its own traffic light intersection on Speer. Coming across the viaduct toward downtown Denver, it will be a right turn. Coming from downtown, it will be a left turn. There is also an access from 15th Street.

Lakeside Amusement Park
Just south of I-70, 4601 Sheridan Ave., Lakeside • (303) 477-1621

Amid the grand hoopla of Elitch Garden's whopping new amusement park that opened in 1995, don't forget Lakeside. It remains an old-fashioned amusement park, with art deco that marks it as having changed little since the 1940s, although, of course, it has more recent rides. Among the sentimental favorites of Greater Denverites are the little trains that run around the lake, and everybody likes to scream when they go through the funky old tunnel. It has an extensive kiddieland with 15 rides sized for the tots. Lakeside still lets you bring in your own food for a picnic, and you don't have to pay big bucks to get in. Admission is $1.50. Inside, you pay 25¢ per coupon, and it takes two to five coupons per ride. Sometimes we just like to swing in for a ride on the Cyclone, the big roller coaster, and then call it a day. Unlimited ride passes are $10.75 during the week and $12.75 on Saturday, Sunday and holidays. It opens weekends in May and full time in June and closes after Labor Day weekend. The kiddie playland opens during the week from 1 to 10 PM and on Sundays and most Saturdays from noon to 10 PM. The rest of the park rocks and rolls from 6 to 11 PM during the week and from noon to 11 PM on Sundays and most Saturdays. Parking is free.

Heritage Square
I-70 W. to Exit 259; go right for 1 mile, Golden • (303) 279-2789

Out in the open all by itself, up against the Foothills, Heritage Square is a great place to go for family entertainment. It's what appears to be a small Western town, with porticoed boardwalks along the front of retail stores, restaurants and entertainment options lining its streets. The hill on the west side of town has an Alpine slide that operates in summer, and it's just the greatest fun; except that all too often, if you don't go fast enough, some gungho geek comes racing up behind you with a bump. Heritage Square claims more than 40 attractions counting stores, restaurants and amusement rides. It has bumper boats, go-carts and a family arcade. The Heritage Square Music Hall usually has a fun show to offer, and you can rent the town hall and wedding chapel for parties. You might also want to check out The Lazy H Chuckwagon Show and Dinner, a dinner show and hayrack ride that costs $15 for adults, $10 for kids ages 3 to 10 and nothing for little pardners younger than 3.

Admission to Heritage Square is free, as is the parking. It's fun just to stroll around. Hours are 10 AM to 9 PM every day during the summer. Spring, fall and winter hours are 10 AM to 6 PM every day except Sunday, when it's noon to 6 PM.

And Finally . . .

These entries defy categorization. They're still great fun, so check them out!

Renaissance Festival
I-25 about 25 minutes south from Denver to Larkspur (Exit 173), then follow the signs • (303) 688-6010

See our Annual Events chapter for more on the Renaissance Festival, but it's such a killer kid-pleaser that it cannot be omitted from this section. It's a dizzying fantasy world full of battling knights and cavorting jesters and associated monsters and grotesques, where hundreds of attractions attendants, food vendors,

Roller hockey is a favorite pastime for urban kids.

craftspersons and performers dress, act and speak appropriately to their setting in this recreated 16th-century village. It's an event rather than a place, however, so remember it's only around for eight weekends in June and July. Admission is $12.95 for adults; $5 for children ages 5 to 12. Kids younger than 5 get in free. Discount tickets are available at King Soopers supermarkets.

Tiny Town
6249 S. Turkey Creek Rd., Morrison
• (303) 697-6829

Hidden away in a mountain canyon southeast of Greater Denver, this is a curious and charming town of 110 miniature buildings constructed at one-sixth scale on 6 acres. Kids can actually go inside some of the buildings, but it's a place where families enjoy just walk-

INSIDERS' TIP

The Tattered Cover Book Store, 2955 E. First Avenue in Cherry Creek, has a whole floor devoted to children's books. There are also little tables and chairs where kids can sit and read or look at pictures.

ing around. You can ride a miniature train pulled by a real — but tiny — steam engine over a mile-long course. They have a snack bar, a gift shop and puppet shows on weekends. Part of the magic of this place is that it looks rather ancient, and it is. It's the oldest miniature town in the United States. George Turner was the owner of a Denver moving and storage business just after the turn of the century, and this was his mountain property. His granddaughter was chronically ill, so he built a few miniature houses in the pasture for her to play in, then kept adding to the tiny town. Turkey Creek Road was dirt then, and people would stop their cars and delight their kids with the magic little town. By the 1920s and 1930s, it was one of Colorado's major tourist attractions. After World War II, it went through several decades of decline, including a flood and a number of failed attempts to make it a profitable tourist business. Now it's operated by the Tiny Town Foundation, which donates 30 percent of the profits to charities and uses a lot of volunteers. Admission is low: $2.50 for adults and $1.50 for kids ages 3 to 12, and children younger than 3 get in free. Pay an extra $1 if you want to ride the train. It's open 10 AM to 5 PM weekends only in May, September and October and daily Memorial Day through Labor Day. Take C-470 to U.S. Highway 285, travel about 4 miles southwest on U.S. 285, turn left on Turkey Creek Road, and go about .25 of a mile. You'll see Tiny Town on the right.

Denver Puppet Theatre
3156 W. 38th Ave. • (303) 458-6446

The Denver Puppet Theatre is a delightful experience for kids ages 3 and older. With six different plays performed each year — classics, world stories, new plays — kids can come back every two months for a new show. Marionettes and shadow puppets make up the characters and visitors can see all the puppets after each performance. (No autographs, however.) Performances are on Thursday and Friday at 10 AM and 1 PM, on Saturday at 11 AM and 1 PM and on Sunday at 1 PM. Tickets are $3 per person.

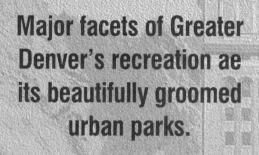

Major facets of Greater Denver's recreation ae its beautifully groomed urban parks.

Parks and Recreation

Greater Denver is a recreational heaven. Where else can you enjoy some of the best skiing in the world on Saturday, then play 18 holes of golf on Sunday — all on a sunny March weekend?

It doesn't stop there. We've got biking trails, hiking trails, climbing spots and picnicking galore. You can boat, swim, fish, snow ski, water ski or windsurf. You can hunt wildlife or simply admire it from afar. You name it, we've got it. And it's all in the city or just minutes outside its limits.

We have organizations, facilities, rental companies and tour guides for everything — bicycling, climbing, fishing, hunting, running, in-line skating, sailing, water-skiing and horseback riding, to name a few. We even have ranges for skeet, trap, pistols and rifles. Skiing, of course, is Colorado's most popular and famous form of recreation as well as one of the state's biggest money-earners. In addition to some brief tips in this chapter, we've given skiing a chapter of its own called Ski Country.

Major facets of Greater Denver's recreation are its beautifully groomed urban parks. The ones listed below will add a delightful serenity to your day. In general, Denver's parks are open from 5 AM until 11 PM and do not allow camping.

Parks
Urban Parks

City and county parks and recreation departments are much more than fabricated facilities and structured activities. The parks themselves offer pleasant havens throughout Greater Denver's urban fabric. Pockets of greenery, playing fields, playgrounds and surfaces for running, biking and skating are just some of the amenities. We've mentioned several of the area's parks in relation to activities described previously.

The city parks offer a lot more than we sometimes suspect. Denver Parks and Recreation, for example, is the responsible agency for such widely varied facilities as the Denver Zoo, Mile High Stadium, the city's golf courses and 100 miles of foliated center strips on major streets.

Denver has about 250 parks, ranging from small triangles to enormous open spaces, as well as a trail system guesstimated at about 130 miles. And, of course, there are the 14,000 acres of Denver Mountain Parks, including a variety of named and about 25 unnamed parcels of natural area.

The Plains Conservation Center
21901 E. Hampden Ave., Aurora
• **(303) 693-3621**

This is a 1,900-acre Colorado Prairie Natural Area just east of the eastern edge of the urban fabric of Aurora. Take Parker Road off Interstate 225, go south to Hampden Avenue, then east. After a few miles you come suddenly to the end of the housing developments; the road turns to gravel, and in a few miles you find the center on top of a ridge to the left. The center has a museum, monthly moonlight walks, Saturday night wagon rides from June through September and other attractions. But you need reservations to go out there and for their activities.

Chatfield Arboretum
Off Wadsworth Blvd. south of Colo. Hwy.
470, Littleton • (303) 973-3705

This little gem is operated by the Denver Botanic Gardens and offers historic sites, trails and naturalist guides. It's a great place for a picnic, and the traditional playground next to the historic schoolhouse is fun for kids. Down the path along Deer Creek you can see the foundation where the schoolhouse was before they moved it. Look for the piece of chain on one of the cottonwood branches above the path, the remnant of the swing where kids played 100 years ago. Chatfield Arboretum is just off Wadsworth Boulevard south of C-470.

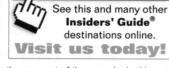

www.insiders.com
See this and many other
Insiders' Guide®
destinations online.
Visit us today!

Dinosaur Ridge
Outside Red Rocks Amphitheater,
Morrison • (303) 697-DINO

This unexpected park is a treasure of exposed dinosaur bones and tracks, along with plant and other fossils. The best way to get there is to take I-70 west to the Morrison Exit, and head south on Colo. Highway 26. A couple of miles downhill, you'll see the right turn that takes you to Red Rocks. Don't take that! We're offering it only as a landmark to help you identify the turnoff across the road (which will be a turnoff to the left) on West Alameda Parkway. At that left turnoff, there is a sign that says Natural National Landmark, which is Dinosaur Ridge. The road swings uphill, and on the north side of the road, you'll see a stone building and barn. That's the Dinosaur Ridge Visitor Center, where you can get information about Dinosaur Ridge hours, tours and directions as well as buy T-shirts, books, casts of dinosaur footprints and other dinosaur-relevant things. Dinosaur Ridge is essentially an outdoor experience, however. Continuing east on West Alameda Parkway, you'll find on the uphill slope exposed dinosaur bones in the hillside. This is where the first dinosaur bones in the Western United States were found in 1887. It's wheelchair accessible. Over the hill and starting down, you come to another display, this one of exposed dinosaur footprints. It can be a little irritating visiting this display because

usually you have to park and walk along a narrow ditch beside a narrow road where cars are whizzing by. You stand in the ditch and look at the footprints. It's particularly scary when you have small children along because they tend to jump around erratically and bolt in unexpected directions. However, the Friends of Dinosaur Ridge hold "Open Ridge Day" one Saturday each month from April through October, when the road is closed to cars and volunteers station themselves at the various stops along the road to tell you what you're looking at. You can also join one of the Dinosaur Ridge guided tours. Call the visitor center, (303) 697-DINO, for information. Admission is free, but donations are accepted.

As long as you're out there, you may want to combine your Dinosaur Ridge visit with a visit to the Morrison Natural History Museum, where they have some of the original bones that were taken out of the first dinosaur dig site as well as other exhibits. To get to the museum, get back on Colo. Highway 26 and go south into the town of Morrison, turn right in the center of town at the intersection by the Morrison Inn (a great place to stop for American-Mexican food, by the way; see our Restaurants chapter), go about a half-mile to the last stoplight and turn left onto Colo. Highway 8 and go about a half-mile to the museum. You'll see the log-cabin structure on your right.

Cheesman Park
Between 8th and 13th aves.,
east of Lafayette St.

Cheesman Park is a Denver jewel just east of downtown. This vast oasis in town features a great one-and-a-half-mile walking/jogging path, enormous trees throughout, manicured flower gardens and an impressive pavilion at the eastern edge. And the mountain view from the pavilion is stunning. The compressed dirt jogging path is easy on the body, and popular with nearby residents. The park was established in 1892 on the city's former first cemetery lot. The park is adjacent to the Denver Botanic Gardens, which charges a small entry fee and is open daily.

To get there, take 14th Avenue east out of

downtown to Lafayette, then head south one block to the park.

City Park
17th Avenue Pkwy. and Colorado Blvd.

The lake at City Park is ringed by acres of grass and mature trees that offer wonderful picnicking and relaxing. There also is an extensive path great for biking/walking/in-line skating. The historic City Park Pavilion was recently restored and features musicians in the bandstand on the lake's west shore. In the summer you can rent paddleboats seven days a week for only $5 an hour. The east end of the park is home to the Denver Zoo and the Museum of Natural History. To get there, take 17th Avenue east out of downtown to York Street. The park lies between York Street and Colorado Boulevard.

Sloan Lake Park
17th Ave. and Sheridan Blvd.

Sloan Lake is one of the more popular lakes/parks in the north end of town. Like other Denver parks, it is dotted with trees and offers a great place to have a picnic, play Frisbee or just hang out. A running trail circles the park and soccer fields. A large playground is great for kids. To get there, take Colfax Avenue west out of town to Sheridan Boulevard, then right to 17th Avenue.

Washington Park
Louisiana Ave. and Downing St.

This is perhaps the most popular park for a variety of sporting events. For starters, there's a great path around the park for bicycling, walking/jogging and in-line skating. In the middle are two lakes for fishing (especially good for kids). There are soccer games and impromptu volleyball games nearly every warm, sunny weekend of the year. The flower gardens on the western edge, along Downing Street, are perfection and the backdrop for great tourist photographs. But most of all, "Wash Park," as it's known, is a wonderful spot to relax and enjoy Denver's blue skies and manicured parks.

State Parks and Recreation Areas

Moving farther out from the urban area, you encounter county park and open-space systems. Jefferson County has the largest, but Adams, Douglas and Arapahoe also have their county park systems. As you get into the mountains, you also encounter the Denver Mountain Parks system, 14,000 acres of mountain parks scattered through four counties. Red Rocks Park is one of these, as is the Winter Park ski area (see our Ski Country chapter for details). When people want to enjoy the great outdoors without driving way into the mountains, the first places they often think about are the four state parks and two state recreation areas right in Greater Denver. We've already mentioned two of them — Chatfield State Recreation Area and Cherry Creek Reservoir State Recreation Area — in relation to a number of the activities covered above. But they're all exceptionally fine, and you can get more information by calling each park or by contacting the Colorado Division of Parks and Outdoor Recreation's Metro Region office, (303) 791-1957. All state parks charge a $4 admission fee per vehicle.

Red Rocks Park
Off Morrison Rd., Morrison
• (303) 791-1957

Entrance to Red Rocks is free and open year round (when there's not a concert going on) and definitely worth the visit. The natural rock formations are splendid to see. Much of the area is wheelchair accessible too. You can even bring a guitar and play on the natural amphitheater's stage. To get there, just take I-70 west to Morrison Road, go south and follow the signs.

Barr Lake State Park
Northeast of Denver about 20 miles, near Brighton • (303) 659-6005

Barr Lake State Park near Brighton is a 2,600-acre state park surrounding a 1,900-acre prairie reservoir. Decades ago, the reservoir used to be something of a sewage dump, and people would roll up their car windows when they drove past on I-76. But please, that was long ago. Today it's a charming and tranquil place with more than 300 species of birds. It's the greatest place around here to watch eagles that hunt around the lake and nest in the trees at the lake's southern half, which is designated as a wildlife refuge (no pets allowed in this area). It's also the biggest lake in the Denver area where you can canoe, kayak or otherwise go boating without being buzzed by Jet Skis, powerboats and water-skiers. The only boats allowed on the lake are sailboats, hand-propelled craft and boats with electric trolling motors or gas engines of 10 horsepower or less. Hiking here is pleasant because the lakeshore is lined with cottonwoods. There are plenty of aquatic plants and marshes, where it's always interesting to watch the big carp rooting and sucking. On both the north and south ends of the lake you can walk out on wooden boardwalks extending into the lake and watch wildlife from the gazebo at the end. Bring binoculars; it's fun to watch the eagles from the southern gazebo. Camping is not allowed at Barr Lake. To get there, take I-76 northeast out of Denver about 20 miles to Exit 22, Bromley Lane, east to Picadilly Road and south to the park entrance. There's also a nature center with displays and information and a bookstore.

Castlewood Canyon State Park
South of Denver near Castle Rock • (303) 688-5242

Castlewood is one of those delightful discoveries that people often make only after years or decades of living in the area. To those used to thinking of Colorado as a mountainous place, this may seem more like some hidden natural gorge refuge on the far plains of Kansas. Part of Colorado's Black Forest, it's a popular place for short- and medium-range hiking and bird-watching. There are viewpoints and hiking trails aplenty. You can follow Cherry Creek along its scenic cut in the landscape and visit the old stone ruins of Castlewood Canyon Dam, which look like something left over from the Egyptians. There's also a nifty trail that leads up to a cave, a small cave, but very delightful for kids. Dogs are allowed on a 6-foot leash. No camping is allowed. Take I-25 south to Castle Rock, go west on Colo. 86, turn south just before Franktown on Douglas County Road 51, and you'll see the park entrance after about 3 miles.

Chatfield State Recreation Area
Off Colo. 470 and Wadsworth Blvd. • (303) 791-7275

Here you'll find Greater Denver's widest range of outdoor experiences from power-boating to appreciating nature in remote surroundings. The northern end is the reservoir, a place popular with boaters, water-skiers, swimmers and anglers (check our boating section in this chapter for details). It's probably the area's greatest general recreational resource in terms of variety and scenery. As you get toward the south end, where the South Platte River flows into the reservoir, and head on south from there, you're in the nature part of the park. The South Platte Valley along here is heavily wooded beneath a striking canopy of old-growth, riverbottom cottonwoods. People bike, hike and horseback-ride on the paths following the river, and the river here is also a charming place to cast a line. On the west side, between the river and U.S. Highway 75, the Chatfield Wetlands is a newly created area with ponds and flora engineered to be a natural Colorado wetland. There are lots of waterfowl and animals. You can walk the wetlands from either side. There's a viewing platform just off U.S. Highway 75 on the west side. And if you keep on U.S. Highway 75 farther south, you get to the Waterton Canyon Recreation Area, about 4 miles south of C-470. You can take a trail up the canyon, where there are lots of nature observation opportunities (including the canyon's own bighorn sheep

Tree-shaded green spaces abound in Denver.

herd), picnic spots, fishing, historic spots and ultimately a connection into the Colorado Trail, which goes all the way to Durango.

The north end of Chatfield, however, is where you'll find the more civilized activities concentrated. The swimming beach is large and first-rate. The campgrounds have more than 150 sites with all the amenities, but we suggest reservations, (303) 470-1144. The Chatfield Marina, (303) 791-5555, has extensive facilities and extensive capacity for renting boats, as outlined in our Boating and Windsurfing entry above. You can also rent paddleboats, water toys and pontoon boats there, and you can ride on a hot-air balloon that takes off near the swimming beach. The U.S. Army Corps of Engineers has also been offering summer tours of the Chatfield Dam.

The B&B Livery, (303) 933-3636, offers horseback riding. Note that dogs are not allowed in Waterton Canyon Recreation Area. Dogs are allowed in Chatfield on a leash not longer than 6 feet, and there is a dog exercise area where they're allowed off-leash on the north side of the dam, in Chatfield State Recreation Area. To get to Chatfield, take I-25 or I-70 to C-470, and C-470 to the Wadsworth Boulevard Exit. Or just take Wadsworth Boulevard south, if you're near it on the west side. Just south of C-470 on Wadsworth, you'll see the park entrance on the left.

Cherry Creek State Recreation Area
I-225 and S. Parker Rd.
• (303) 690-1166, (303) 699-3860.

Like Chatfield, Cherry Creek is based on the existence of a large reservoir, in this case Cherry Creek Lake. It's less nature-oriented and more activity-oriented than Chatfield. However, there are wetlands, including beaver ponds that kids can enjoy by seeing the beaver pop up out of the water now and then. The recreation area gets a lot of school groups for its trails and guided nature walks. The south end is the most nature-oriented, where Cherry Creek and Cottonwood Creek flow into the reservoir. There is a mountain-bike trail and a lot of cottonwood trees and aspens. Along the trail systems you may see mule deer and white-tailed deer, owls, coyotes, foxes and the like.

One of the big advantages of this recreation area is that it's so centrally located. It's right off I-225, surrounded by Aurora, Denver, the Denver Technological Center and Centennial Airport. A lot of people coming here to visit friends or family opt to stay at the recreation area where they can camp or park their RVs. Cherry Creek Lake is not much smaller than Cherry Creek Reservoir, and the folks at Cherry Creek Rec think their campground is nicer. Call (303) 470-1144 for camping reservations, and plan to make them at least 3 or 4 days ahead of time. It has 102 campsites on five loops, and most of them are shaded by trees. It has a marina, (303) 779-6144, which we describe in our Boating and Windsurfing entry in this chapter. Cherry Creek Rec has riding stables, (303) 690-8235, and a gun club, (303) 693-1765. The recreation area is 1 mile south of I-225 on Parker Road.

Golden Gate Canyon State Park
Outside of Golden off Golden Gate Canyon Rd. • (303) 582-3707

This is the mountainous park among Greater Denver's six nearby state parks and recreation areas. It's where you go for vistas, and it's heavy on the aspens, which means you're not likely to find a nearby place with better viewing of the autumn gold — from Panorama Point especially, on the top of the park at its northern edge. A lot of people like to drive up to Panorama Point on those autumn days of blue skies and green and gold mountains. A little path from the parking lot and picnic area leads to a multilevel, mega-gazebo on the brim of a westward-sloping mountainside, where you can look across deep valleys and up to more than 100 miles of snowcapped peaks along the Continental Divide. The park's 14,000 acres range from 7,600 to 10,400 feet in altitude, and it has 35 miles of trails for foot and hoof, 275 picnic sites and more than 140 campsites as well as backcountry shelters and tent sites. Reservations are recommended and can be made by calling (303) 470-1144 or (800) 678-2267. Once there, your first stop is always at the visitors center on the park's lower east end, where there's a pond full of big, tame trout to watch and a museum to browse through. Right outside the visitor center is a nature trail designed for accessibility to the physically impaired. You can reach the park by turning west off of Colo. Highway 93 onto Golden Gate Canyon Road and driving about 15 winding miles to the park.

Roxborough State Park
South on Santa Fe Dr., past Littleton • (303) 973-3959

Roxborough is the most natural of Greater Denver's local state parks. It was Colorado's first state park to be designated both a Colorado Natural Area and a National Natural Land-

mark. There is only one building, the visitor center. Camping, rock climbing and pets aren't allowed. What you do have is the opportunity to take a number of lovely hikes/walks through some dramatic and unique natural terrain. The hikes are gentle; a brochure is available at the visitor center at the entrance. The geology is spectacular. The Dakota Hogback runs north-south along the west side of the metro area. The park hides behind it to the west with the spectacular red-rock moonscape of the Fountain Formation. You can see this more easily to the north by driving through the Ken Caryl Ranch development north of Deer Creek Canyon, but you can see it in the undeveloped natural state here. There has been some controversy about new housing developments going up just outside the boundaries of Roxborough that destroy the sense of being in a remote place. You can't really see the development from the bulk of the park. The way the park is sequestered behind the Dakota Hogback makes it one of those special places where you can feel remote even though you're close to the metro area. The park is in a transition zone between mountains and plains and has an interesting mixture of mountain and prairie species. You have scrub oak, prairie grass, wet meadows, cottonwoods and box-elders. You'll find some aspen groves, ponderosa pine and Douglas fir on Carpenter Peak. The highest point in the park, Carpenter Peak is on one of the trails and offers some great views. The Fountain Valley Loop and the South Rim Trail are also wonderful ways to spend a good part of your day. Bring a backpack with a picnic lunch, and, of course, plenty of water.

There are numerous guided nature hikes and nature programs. The park also has an "extended golf cart" ride, known as The Rocks Ride, that can cover some of the trails and is available to people who can't hike because of health reasons or disabilities. But it has a limited schedule, and reservations are required. So call ahead. Reach Roxborough by U.S. Highway 85 (Santa Fe Drive) south from Denver to Titan Road, take a right on Titan and go 3.5 miles. Follow Titan Road left onto Rampart Range Road. Go 3 miles and turn left onto Roxborough Park Road; then take an immediate right onto the park access road. The entry fee is $4 per car and well worth it.

Public Recreation Centers and Programs

Public parks and recreation departments are your greatest resource for year-round recreation, so use them often. Public recreation centers, ubiquitous throughout Greater Denver, are your best bets for finding indoor and outdoor swimming pools. No matter where you are, there is more than one nearby. If you're a member of the community, the cost is minimal. If you come from another community, the cost is only slightly higher. Parks and recreation departments are also your best bet for youth team sports ranging from basketball to soccer, and if they don't run their own programs in some sport — T-ball for the kiddies or tennis for adults — they will certainly be able to refer you to the nearest local organizations that do.

The offerings at the following public centers are too vast to catalog here, so we've just listed the numbers for you to call. However, we have listed specific programs under other headings, tennis or climbing, for example, to steer you in the right direction.

Denver
Denver Parks and Recreation Department, (303) 964-2500

Adams County
Adams County Parks and Community Resources Department, (303) 637-8000
Aurora Parks and Recreation Department, (303) 695-7200
Brighton Recreation Center, (303) 659-7088
Commerce City Parks and Recreation Department, (303) 289-3766
Hyland Hills Park and Recreation District, Federal Heights, (303) 428-7488
Northglenn Parks and Recreation Department, (303) 450-8721
Thornton Parks and Recreation Department, (303) 538-7300

Arapahoe County
Arapahoe Park and Recreation District, (303) 730-6109
Aurora Parks and Recreation Department, (303) 695-7200
Cherry Creek Vista Park and Recreation District, (303) 779-4525
Englewood Parks Department, (303) 762-2541
South Suburban Park and Recreation District (also covers a small area of Douglas County), (303) 798-5131

Douglas County
Castle Rock Recreation Center, (303) 660-1036
Parker Recreation Center, (303) 841-7191

Jefferson County
Arvada Parks and Recreation Department, recreation handled by North Jeffco Park and Recreation District (below), (303) 424-7733
Broomfield Recreation Center, (303) 469-5351
Edgewater Recreation Center, (303) 237-4817
Foothills Park and Recreation District, (303) 987-3602
Golden Recreation and Parks Department, (303) 384-8100
Lakewood Recreation Department, (303) 987-7800
North Jeffco Park and Recreation District, (303) 424-7733
Westminster Parks and Recreation Department, (303) 430-2400
Wheat Ridge Parks and Recreation Department, Anderson Community Building, (303) 421-0700

Recreation

Bicycling

Pavement Bicycling

Cities in the Greater Denver area have put significant effort and money into building superb trails that allow bicyclists to take rides that can last all day long. These paths were designed both for bicycling and in-line skating so rather than repeat our listings, we've described several paths in our "In-line Skating" section in this chapter.

For bicycling in Denver, your first resource should be a Denver Bicycle Touring Club Map, available at most bike shops for around $3. To get one mailed to you, call (303) 756-7240. In addition, consider the following for relaxing or challenging rides (you set the pace).

Arapahoe Greenway Trail in Littleton

This is a major bike trail in Greater Denver that runs from Chatfield Reservoir in the southwest to the city of Thornton in the upper north metro region. The trail passes through more than a dozen parks. Access points are legion; consult the Touring Club Map for details. Two popular accesses are Confluence Park at 15th and Platte streets near Lower Downtown and Ruby Hill Park near Evans and Broadway.

East Seventh Avenue Bike Route

This ride takes you through city streets, so watching for traffic is a must. But if you're more interested in sampling Denver's scenery and architecture than getting a real workout, this is a nice ride. Start just south of downtown at Broadway and East Seventh Avenue, then head east on Seventh and follow the bike route signs. You can take it for several miles through Denver's oldest neighborhoods, replete with mansions and stunning old trees.

The Highline Canal

This Denver-area highlight was built in the 1880s and is now lined by huge cottonwoods in what amounts to a river of ancient trees through the city. This favorite trail runs from Aurora Reservoir in the eastern suburb to Chatfield Reservoir in the southwest suburbs. Depending on the time of year, the canal will either be swollen with spring runoff or bone dry. Watch for horses, as the dirt areas are popular with equestrians.

Clear Creek Bike Path

This bike path runs from Lowell Boulevard in Denver west along Clear Creek all the way to Golden to about 44th Avenue and Youngfield Street. Our only wish is that it connected from Lowell Boulevard to Confluence Park so bicyclists wouldn't have to ride city streets in between. The incline heading west is gentle, but a reminder that you're climbing.

Resources

The State of Colorado has urban trail maps for four different areas of the state. One of those is for the metropolitan Denver area: Urban Trails in Colorado, Denver Metro Area. The state also has a very useful Colorado Trails Resource Guide. These references are available free if you stop by or write: Trails Guides, 1313 Sherman Avenue, Room 618, Denver 80203. Provide a self-addressed, stamped return envelope with six first-class stamps; the envelope should measure at least 6 by 9 inches. Some bike shops will have urban trail maps available as well.

A nonprofit group called **Bicycle Colorado**, (303) 756-2535, is perhaps the biggest single source of bicycling information. It has a general guide to public-lands trails and other tips, and it also has a beautiful publication called *Bicycle Colorado Magazine*.

Among the other bicycling resources that may be helpful are **The Denver Bicycle Touring Club**, (303) 756-7240; **Team Evergreen**, (303) 674-6048, one of the friendlier of local bicycle clubs with about 700 members, weekly road-bike and mountain-bike rides, its own newsletter and other attractions; and the **Bicycle Racing Association of Colorado**, (303) 440-5366.

Rentals

There are numerous bike rental shops in the Denver area; your best bet is to consult the Yellow Pages. Expect to pay from $15 to $25 a day depending on the quality and expense of the bike. We'll give you an idea of a few good shops that have been around for a long time.

Englewood Bicycle Company
3546 S. Logan • (303) 781-1162
This shop rents everything from trail bikes for pavement to high-performance mountain bikes and has maps and brochures for sale.

Adventure Cycling
4361 S. Parker Rd. • (303) 699-2514
Adventure Cycling rents bikes and is convenient to those in the southeast part of town.

Cycle Analyst
722 S. Pearl St. • (303) 722-3004
Cycle Analyst is closed Sundays and Mondays, but it's a great shop otherwise. It is close to many paved trails as well as Washington Park (see our In-line Skating section).

Sports Rent
8761 Wadsworth Blvd. • (303) 467-0200
This shop rents three types of bikes, depending on the terrain you plan to tackle.

Mountain Biking

If any outdoor sport could be said to define Colorado, mountain biking would probably run a close second to skiing. Hikers are still the primary users of Colorado backcountry, but increasingly they are having to share the path with mountain bikers. Mountain bikes are a return to sanity, rather like the fat-tire bikes we older people had as kids before skinny-tire bikes became the norm. Of course, mountain bikes are a quantum leap ahead of the old fat-tire bikes, with super-light frames and gearing low enough to ride up the steepest hills.

Mountain bikers can pretty much go on any hiking trail and off-trail as well. Well, we have to qualify that. Since the mountain bikes have become a boom sport, a lot of hikers and horseback riders have begun to feel the same revulsion when they see a mountain bike coming that they often feel when they see a motorized dirt bike. Mountain biking is not as noisy, but some "extreme" mountain bikers do tend to race toward and past hikers at

breakneck speed. Some hikers or horseback riders will glare and act surly or superior in the presence of even the most polite mountain bikers. Polite bikers slow when passing hikers, or get off the trail for people on horses. In fact, consideration for others is among the International Mountain Biking Association's official Rules of the Trail: 1) Ride on open trails only, 2) Leave no trace, 3) Control your bicycle, 4) Always yield the trail, 5) Never spook animals, and 6) Plan ahead.

Where trails are closed specifically to mountain biking, in places like Boulder Mountain Parks, it's most likely because mountain bikes in excessive numbers are viewed as destructors of trails. Mountain bikes don't drop road apples all over the trails, but they erode trails in ways that horses do not. At any rate, you can't mountain bike in Roxborough State Park, in City of Boulder open space or on about half the trails in Golden Gate State Park. Then again, the other half of the trails in Golden Gate are open to bikes, as are virtually all national forests along the Front Range and nearby areas over the Continental Divide. Generally, if you don't see a sign prohibiting mountain biking, you can take to the trails.

A lot of great mountain-biking rides are available right in Jefferson County on Denver's immediate west side. These are wonderful places for their terrain, scenery and/or technical aspects. All of them are accessible to anyone with reasonably fit lungs and legs.

Waterton Canyon
Take Wadsworth Boulevard south from its junction with C-470, 4 miles to the Waterton Canyon Recreation Area sign, and turn left to park. You are now at the South Platte River just upstream from Chatfield Recreation Area. There are lovely and gentle trails around the recreation area, but up the canyon, it gets a little more dramatic. No dogs are allowed; there's a herd of bighorn sheep up this canyon. A 6-mile dirt road heads up past Cottonwood Gulch, Mill Gulch and Stevens Gulch to the Colorado Trail. You can keep going on the Colorado Trail if you want to, but the 6-mile stretch is technically intermediate as far as bike-handling skills and average as far as lungs and legs. Some people like to go about a mile beyond Stevens Gulch and turn left on the

Roxborough Loop, which can take you around and back down to Waterton Canyon Road.

Mount Falcon

Take U.S. 285 W. past C-470 to the Morrison exit, then right. Follow the clearly marked signs. From the Morrison Trailhead, you can head up the Castle Trail to the pavilion at the Walker's Dream Shelter. You can ride several loops above this point, with moderate technical skills and high exertion.

Deer Creek Park Trail

This area is about 4 miles up Deer Creek Canyon from Wadsworth Boulevard, in Jefferson County Open Space. Steeper areas like Deer Creek aren't for beginners, or those who haven't been working out. It might be fun for a while, but you'll tire and lose interest too soon if you aren't in shape for it.

Hayden/Green Mountain Park Trails

These intermediate trails also challenge riders. They wind through the park before climbing 1,200 feet to the Green Mountain summit. To get there, take Sixth Avenue west to the Union Street Exit, go south to Alameda Avenue, then right. The park is on the right side.

References

One of the best overall references for these and other rides is a book, *The Best of Colorado Biking Trails*, published by Outdoor Books & Maps Inc., of Denver, and available in many local bookstores, bike shops and outing stores. Other good mountain-biker references include: *Denverides: The Mountain Biking Guide to Denver, Colorado*, by Dave Rich; *Mountain Bike Rides in The Colorado Front Range*, by William L. Stoehr; *Bicycling the Backcountry*, also by Stoehr; *Bike With a View*, by Mark Dowling; *Ride Guide*, by *Rocky Mountain News* columnist David Nelson; and *Colorado Gonzo Rides*, by Michael Merrifield.

Boating and Windsurfing

Boaters and windsurfers have a lot of lakes and reservoirs to choose from around Greater Denver, but if you're into powerboating there are only a few select places that are either large enough or allow enough horsepower to do more than putt from one fishing spot to the next.

The most popular lakes for power boating are the big boys, **Cherry Creek Lake** and **Chatfield Reservoir**, the focuses, respectively, of Cherry Creek Reservoir State Recreation Area and Chatfield State Recreation Area. Both of them are big reservoirs and, as part of state recreation areas, are just nice environments in which to split the water. You can find more general descriptions of these recreation areas in our State Parks and Recreation Areas entry in this chapter, but boaters will be interested to know that both of them have extensive marinas offering a lot of rentals.

The Cherry Creek Marina
Aurora • (303) 779-6144

The marina is on the west side of the reservoir, just follow the signs after entering. It has slips, water access and rentals of canoes, motorboats, sailboats, rowboats, pontoon boats and bicycles. This marina also has a little restaurant. It's open weekdays from 10 AM to 8 PM and weekends from 8 AM to 8 PM April 1 through October 31, weather permitting. Rental prices vary greatly. Sailboats, for example, rent for $17 an hour, fishing boats for $25 an hour and 10-person pontoons for $65 an hour. Discounts often apply to multiple-hour rentals.

Chatfield Marina
11500 N. Roxborough Park Rd., Littleton • (303) 791-5555

This marina for the Chatfield Reservoir includes a store with boating and fishing supplies, groceries and take-out food. It's Denver's only on-the-water grill and deli restaurant with a patio and an observation deck. The season runs from April 1 to October 31. Hours are 9 AM to 7 PM, Monday through Thursday; 9 AM to 8 PM on Friday; 8 AM to 8 PM Saturday; and 8 AM to 7 PM on Sunday. Rental for sailboats and fishing boats, paddleboats, water toys and pontoon boats is run out of Little Ships, (303) 791-6104, next to the marina. Little Ships is open 9 AM to 6 PM on weekends and 10 AM to 6 PM on weekdays. Prices vary, but run around $90 an hour for a ski boat, $50 to $60 for a pontoon and $10 for paddleboats. It's best to make reservations in advance.

Aurora Reservoir Marina
5800 Powhatan Rd., Aurora
• **(303) 690-1286**

This newer facility is 7 miles east of Quincy Reservoir in Arapahoe County. Powerboaters pay it little attention, since gas motors aren't allowed on the water. But the water is clean, and it's popular with sailors and windsurfers. There's a little marina with a general store, where you can rent electric motorboats, rowboats, sailboats, sailboards, paddleboats and canoes. You'll find the reservoir by driving about 2 miles east of Gun Club Road on E. Quincy Avenue and turning right at Powhatan Road. Hours vary depending on sunrise and sunset, but generally run from 7 AM to 5 PM. Electric boats cost $11 an hour, sailboats are from $13 to $17, and paddleboats are $10 an hour.

Bear Creek Lake Park
Off Morrison Rd. near Colo. 470, Lakewood • (303) 697-6159 (park rangers)

There are three water areas here: Bear Creek Lake, Little Soda Lake and Big Soda Lake. Bear Creek is mainly for fishing as it allows no motors greater than 10 horsepower. There also is some sailing. Hours are 6 AM to 10 PM from Memorial to Labor days, and admission is $3 per car. There are no rentals at Bear Creek Lake. The access point is easy to see off Morrison Road, once you exit off C-470.

Big Soda Lake is open to the public for powerboats and has its own **Soda Lake Marina**, (303) 697-1522, where you can rent paddleboats, kayaks, sailboats, sailboards, canoes and bicycles for $10 an hour (Sunfish sailboats are $12 an hour). The marina is open

noon to 7 PM weekdays and 10 AM to 7 PM weekends. Big Soda recently added a swim area. Admission to the lake is $3 per car. Big Soda Lake also is the base of operations for Greater Denver's only accredited windsurfing school, Chip Graham Windsurfing Academy, (303) 426-6503.

Little Soda Lake isn't open for public boating. However, it is open for the Soda Lake Ski School, (303) 697-0121. Hours and costs vary.

Standley Lake
9805 W. 88th Ave., Westminster
• **(303) 425-1097**

Standley Lake, the big north Jefferson County lake bordered on the north and east by Westminster and on the south by Arvada, is a popular location for windsurfing. Motorboats are allowed there, but you need a permit for boats with more than 20 horsepower ($500 a year for residents, $600 for nonresidents), and the number of permits is limited. Boats with less than 20 horsepower can use the lake for $10 per day. Call the City of Westminster's office at the lake at the number above. There are no rental facilities at Standley.

Climbing

Climbing isn't exactly the kind of sport you just decide to try on a Saturday morning. It can be dangerous — and deadly — even for those who've been doing it for years. But it also can be an unparalleled challenge for people into getting the most from their workout.

There are many climbing opportunities in Colorado. Most require getting out of the Denver area, but you can start by taking lessons and learning the ropes in town. A number of businesses and recreation centers have their own in-house climbing walls. From there, you can graduate to climbing areas just outside of

---

INSIDERS' TIP

One of the best bargains in fitness is the Denver Parks and Recreation membership. Depending on the recreation center and the offerings chosen, Denver residents can lift weights, play basketball and swim for less than $20 a year. Check with your nearest rec center for details.

Boulder, where the terrain is internationally known. There also are climbing groups that put together excursions. One to try is **Stone Karma Guides**, (303) 733-9732, which is run by employees at the Paradise Rock Gym.

Paradise Rock Gym
6260 N. Washington St., No. 5
• **(303) 286-8168**

This is an indoor rock-climbing gym built around technical climbing, with 6,000 square feet of climbing wall and structure as well as lessons, a small amount of climbing accessory retail and cross-training facilities such as weight machines, stationary bicycles and stair machines. Beginners are welcome here for lessons. The Monday night lesson is for beginners and costs only $20, including equipment. More advanced lessons are offered in a complete instruction program; call for information.

Thrillseekers Inc.
1912 S. Broadway • (303) 733-8810

This climbing gym offers more than 9,000 square feet of climbing space (with more on the way), 40 top ropes, three lead caves where climbers can get horizontal and a separate "bouldering" rate where you can free climb. A complete lesson program is available for all levels, and a full retail section will fill your every climbing need. Lesson prices vary depending on level and number of people so call ahead. Thrillseekers offers a team-building seminar.

Recreational Equipment Inc. (REI)
4100 E. Mexico Ave. • (303) 756-3100

This gigantic store tempts visitors with its climbing wall at the entrance to the store. REI offers classes that run four nights for all levels. Cost is around $100 for members and $140 for nonmembers. Kids climb free on Saturdays, but call for details and times. REI's wall is designed for introductions to climbing so it isn't equal to the rock gyms mentioned above. Beyond the wall, it offers a full range of retail equipment for climbing and mountaineering. Walls and lessons also are available at REI stores at 8991 Harlan Street, Westminster, (303) 429-1800, just west of the Westminster Mall; and 5375 S. Wadsworth Boulevard, Lakewood, (303) 932-0600.

City Park Recreation Center
10455 Sheridan Ave., Westminster
• **(303) 460-9690**

City Park has its own climbing wall in its gymnasium, where people can practice climbing or take climbing lessons while the basketballs bounce behind them. Classes are offered for beginner, intermediate and advanced climbers. Or you can take a short orientation, then pay a low drop-in fee of $2.75 for residents or $4.25 for nonresidents.

Colorado Mountain Club
710 10th St., No. 200, Golden
• **(303) 279-3080**

Technical climbing instruction is available from the grandfather of Colorado mountaineering organizations, the Colorado Mountain Club. But classes are offered only once a year. Basic rock climbing is offered in May and June, and the intermediate class is usually in August or September. Membership is required, and runs about $70 for year-round, instate membership and about $50 for a "Friends of Colorado Mountain Club" membership for out-of-staters. From there, you will receive a schedule of events, including climbing excursions, twice a year. Their new climbing wall was completed in summer 1998.

Fishing

One-third of the state's land area is open to public hunting and fishing. Colorado is a national destination for these activities, the kind of place where people come from the Midwest and both coasts to cast a fly in rushing mountain streams.

Fishing in Colorado, of course, isn't just a matter of mountain trout streams. The state has flatland rivers, large lakes and reservoirs aplenty. The state's 6,000-plus miles of streams and 2,000-plus lakes and reservoirs open to public fishing include high-country fishing for cutthroat, brook, brown, lake and rainbow trout. There's also a lot of warm-water quarry such as walleye, largemouth and smallmouth bass, catfish, crappies, yellow perch, wipers, bluegill and muskie. A lot of warm-water fishing is available right in Greater Denver. The state's record tiger muskie (40 pounds, 2 ounces) was caught in Quincy Reservoir in

Aurora, a half-mile east of Buckley Road on Quincy Avenue in Aurora.

The Denver daily papers publish a weekly fishing and stocking report provided by the Colorado Division of Wildlife. In *The Denver Post*, it's called "Colorado's Best Bets," and in the *Rocky Mountain News*, it's called "Colorado's Hot Spot." Both offer anglers up-to-the-minute scoops on hot spots.

Recorded information on fishing is available 24 hours a day from the Division of Wildlife, (303) 291-7533; for information on fishing conditions, call (303) 291-7534.

Licenses

Fishing licenses are required; you can get yours at most major sports and outdoors stores. Cost is $20.25 per year for Colorado residents, $40.25 for nonresidents. A day license costs $5.25 for residents or nonresidents, and a five-day license is $18.25 residents or nonresidents. There are discounts for senior citizens and people with disabilities; and children younger than 16 do not need a license. Anglers receive a complete rules and regulations brochure when they purchase a license. Brochures are usually available where you buy your license. Colorado's excellent fishing opportunities are made even better by the efforts of the Colorado Division of Wildlife's 15 hatcheries. The division stocks 3.5 million 10-inch fish every year plus another 43 million warm-water fish and 11 million subcatchable cold-water fish. The Colorado DOW reminds anglers that it costs 90¢ to raise a catchable fish, including stocking, and anglers are asked to conserve fish resources by immediately returning fish not intended for consumption. There are various size and fish limits as well as rules on allowable bait, depending on the waters and type of fish. Consult the brochure you receive during licensing or call the DOW at (303) 291-7533.

Fishing Spots

Trout enthusiasts may want to try Colorado's Gold Medal waters, so designated because they have a high-quality aquatic habitat, a high percentage of trout 14 inches or longer and a high potential for trophy fish. The Colorado Division of Wildlife has a booklet on the state's 10 Gold Medal waters; call (303) 297-1192, and they'll send you one. It also has another booklet, *Colorado's Fishing Hot Spots*, featuring a number of hot spots right around Denver.

Cherry Creek Reservoir offers premier trophy walleye fishing, nestled in a natural prairie environment. The best fishing here is mid-May to early June with jugs, bait and plugs along the dam and island. Anglers also find crappies, wipers and catchable stocked trout. Take I-225 to Parker Road and go south on Parker Road to the east entrance off South Yosemite Street. There is a nominal fee to enter the park.

Aurora Reservoir is an oasis providing 820 acres of water for the outdoor enthusiast. There are plenty of game fish, including rainbow trout, brown trout, walleye, wipers, largemouth bass, yellow perch and crappie. The reservoir is open year round from dawn until dusk. Aurora Reservoir is 2.5 miles east of Gun Club Road on Quincy Avenue in Aurora. Fees are the same as the entrance to the park; usually about $5 to $8 a carload.

Chatfield Reservoir is one of the metro area's most popular recreation areas. The reservoir is developing a good walleye population, with many fish in the one- to three-pound class. There also are yellow perch, rainbow trout, tiger muskie, smallmouth bass and crappie. Night fishing lands channel catfish, particularly in the Plum Creek area. From Colo. 470 W., go south on Wadsworth to the park entrance. You'll pay to get into the park, usually about $5 to $8 a carload.

Standley Lake is popular in west Denver for its deep (80-plus feet) reservoir with excellent habitat for rainbow trout, wiper, walleye, smallmouth bass and yellow perch. Only walk-in access is allowed, and it's open in spring and fall. Standley Lake is at West 88th Avenue and Kipling Street.

The **Big Thompson River** is just east of Estes Park, about an hour's drive north and west from Denver. Stocked rainbow trout and natural brown trout populations provide good fishing from May through September. Salmon eggs, various lures and worms work best during the spring runoff; flies are best during late July, August and September. Take I-25 N. out of Denver to Colorado Highway 34, then west into the Big Thompson Canyon.

Golf

Nothing enhances a golf game like beautiful scenery, and in Greater Denver you always have the mountains for a backdrop. No matter where you live or stay, you're always near a golf course because Greater Denver has nearly 70 of them, with more on the way. The most prestigious courses are those at Cherry Hills Country Club in Cherry Hills Village and Castle Pines in Douglas County. Unfortunately, those are private clubs; unless you've got connections and/or a membership, forget about them.

But you can enjoy Castle Pines as a spectator each August at the Sprint International, Colorado's biggest pro golfing event. And the Colorado Open takes place each July at the Inverness Golf Course near the Denver Tech Center; it's really one of the better state opens in the nation.

But playing is more fun than watching. The main thing you have to know, if you're coming to Colorado as a visitor and want to play golf, is that you need a tee time in advance. The courses are usually jammed. Unfortunately, an outsider can't just waltz in and get an advanced tee time at many local golf courses because Denver and Aurora golf courses operate according to a computerized reservation system. You need a pre-purchased $10 reservation access card with an individual code to use these systems. If you call in and try to make a reservation without a pre-authorized code, the computer will thank you nicely and hang up.

If you're in town for more than a fast swing-through, go ahead and get a card because Denver has several fine courses. Call Denver's Golf Line, (303) 964-2563, for details.

Of course, you certainly don't have to confine yourself to Denver and Aurora. There are plenty of other courses around the area that don't have this reservation-card requirement.

Even with a reservation card, you're typically not allowed to make a reservation at most golf courses more than a couple of days ahead of time. During the summer, a lot of the more

prestigious golf courses are locked up a week or two in advance. A real golfer is not going to go on vacation without tee times locked in upfront. One suggestion: if you're coming for a vacation from outside Colorado and you're interested only in golf in the mountains, call the Colorado Golf Resort Association, (303) 699-GOLF. The Colorado Golf Resort Association also has a *Colorado Golf Vacation Guide* that is aimed strictly at destination vacationers. It's mailed only out of state. You can't get it in state. It lists all the courses in Colorado with greens fees, yardages, information on hotels and tee time preferences, etc.

The same phone number, (303) 699-GOLF, is also the phone number for the *Colorado Golfer Newspaper*. The newspaper sells an annual issue that has listings and fees of all the courses in Colorado. A subscription to the *Colorado Golfer Newspaper* costs $6 for a year of six issues, including the annual guide.

Another golfing organization you might want to know about is the Colorado Golf Association, (303) 779-4653. It's an organization for amateurs with some 40,000 members, and it serves as an information clearinghouse for all the amateur tournament events in the state. It also has a fine publication informally known as its "SHAG book" and formally known as the *Schedule Handicap and Association Guidebook*. This booklet is a golf course directory with information covering all the courses in Colorado, including handicap information, tournament schedules and other features, such as handicap conversion tables. It lists golfing organizations and has maps of Colorado and a blowup map of Greater Denver showing course locations. You need to be a member to get it, but if you contact the CGA early in the year before all the booklets have been mailed out, you may be able to get one as a non-member.

Another excellent publication is *The Guide to Golf in the Rockies*, which includes a color photo, description and information on fees, yardages, slopes and other features for the best golf courses in the mountains and on the

Front Range. This book is published by Breckenridge Publishing Company, (970) 453-5512.

We can't tell you all the great places to golf around Greater Denver; there are just too many of them. But here are a few hot tips. The greens fees listed are for 18 holes for non-members or nonresidents. Residents, in general, will pay a few dollars less.

Arrowhead
10850 W. Sundown Tr., Littleton
• **(303) 973-9614**

Designed by Robert Trent Jones, Arrowhead winds through a landscape of scrub oak and towering red sandstone rocks. *Golf Digest* ranks it among the state's top-20 courses. The par is 72 on this 6269-yard, 18-hole course. Keep an eye out for rattlesnakes, as they are plentiful at Arrowhead, and watch out for the 13th fairway, which drops from a cliff off the tee to a 174-yard par 3. To get to Arrowhead, don't go to Littleton; that's just the mailing address. It is in unincorporated Douglas County next to Roxborough State Park, which is a clue that the scenery is spectacular. Take Exit C-470 S. on Santa Fe Drive to Titan Road then go west on Titan Road for about 8 miles. The course entrance will be on the left. Greens fees are $85 including a cart.

Fox Hollow
13410 W. Morrison Rd., Lakewood
• **(303) 986-7888**

Another golf course ranked as one of Colorado's top-20 courses by *Golf Digest*, Fox Hollow has become a real hit since it opened in 1993. The 27-hole course, consisting of three nines, is a nice place to play because it's well-designed. You have everything from high greens with wonderful views of the whole area, to low-down play among the trees, ponds, lakes and meadows. It was ranked the No.1 public course four years in a row (1993-97) by Colorado golfers in an annual statewide poll. Greens fees are $30, and carts are $10 per person.

Inverness Golf Club
200 Inverness Dr. W., Englewood
• **(303) 397-7878**

Guests of the Inverness Hotel in Englewood or guests of the club's members may play at this private resort club featuring a park-style course designed by Press Maxwell. It's a par 70, 6073-yard, 18-hole course. Players like the 3rd hole, which features a long par 3 where you hit over a lake, with water on the right and bunkers to the left. The club and resort are first-class, designed with a rugged Colorado style and plenty of two-story windows to draw your attention to awesome views. Greens fees are $60, and carts are $14 per person.

Legacy Ridge
10801 Legacy Ridge Pkwy., Westminster
• **(303) 438-8997**

For the feel of a country-club course with lots of water and sand traps and a challenging variety of terrain, Legacy Ridge is a good course to try. The 18-hole course opened in September 1994 and was designed by Arthur Hills, a big-name course designer based in Toledo, Ohio. It's just off 104th Avenue between Sheridan and Federal boulevards. The 13th hole will challenge you with its 45-degree slope down the fairway, protected by trees on either side. Greens fees are $32, and carts cost $10.75 per person.

Meridian Golf Club
9742 S. Meridian Blvd., Englewood
• **(303) 799-4043**

Commonly esteemed as a good place to play, Meridian Golf Club is a links-style course designed by Jack Nicklaus. It's also the home of the Meridian Golf Learning Center, run by the renowned teaching pro Mike McGetrick. This course is a typical Nicklaus course with lots of water and bunkers for a challenging day on the links. The course also features plenty of native rough along its 6500 yards. Greens fees are $50, and carts are $12 per person.

Lone Tree
9801 Sunningdale Blvd., Littleton
• **(303) 799-9940**

Formerly a private country club but now under the South Suburban Recreation District, Lone Tree is popular with southeastern metro residents. This Arnold Palmer/ Ed Seay design, built in 1984, is a links-style course out in the open with a minimum of trees. The 6033-yard, par 72 course features water and long, narrow fairways. Although the address is Littleton, the course is actually in Douglas County. Take I-25 S. past C-470 to Lincoln Avenue, then exit west on Lincoln Avenue. Less than 2 miles of driving from Lincoln Avenue will take you to the course. Greens fees are $45, and carts cost $10.

Plum Creek Golf Club
331 Players Club Dr., Castle Rock
• **(303) 688-2611**

Fitting right in with public courses that seem private is the links-style Plum Creek Golf Club. Prior to going public, it was a tournament players' course and was owned by the PGA tour. Plum Creek offers stunning views of the mountains and a nice escape from the city. The back nine has a few trees, but for the most part it's wide open. Golfers like the 13th hole for its novelty — you'll see a dead tree with a hangman's noose dangling from it. Greens fees are $65 on weekdays and $75 on weekends. Carts are included in those prices.

Raccoon Creek
7301 W. Bowles Ave., Littleton
• **(303) 973-4655**

Just below the City of Denver's southwest corner lies the 18-hole Raccoon Creek. The course was designed by Dick Phelps, a well-known course designer based in Evergreen. It's fun, interesting and challenging and features mature trees that make the course gorgeous. There are 14 holes with water, creeks throughout the course and a hole (No. 17) that stretches 225 yards over water from the tee. Greens fees are $28 on weekdays and $32 on weekends. Carts cost $11 per person.

Riverdale
13300 Riverdale Rd., Brighton
• **(303) 659-4700**

Also known as Riverdale Dunes, this is a wonderfully challenging links-style course designed by Pete Dye. It was the site of the USGA Public Links Championship in 1993. *Golf Digest* places it among Colorado's top 20 courses. The 15th hole, a 426-yard par 4, makes things interesting with a dogleg left bordered by water and the right side out of play.

You may need a little more direction than the above address to find it. Take I-25 north to 120th Avenue, then go east to Colorado Boulevard and take a left. Go to 128th Avenue, then east until 128th ends at Riverdale Road. Turn left and go a half-mile to the clubhouse. If you're coming from U.S. Highway 85, exit west on 124th Avenue to Riverdale Road, turn right and drive 1 mile to the clubhouse. Greens fees are $27, and carts are $10 per person.

Thorncreek Golf Course
13555 Washington St., Thornton
• **(303) 450-7055**

This course is not exactly links-style or park-style. It's a pro-level 18-hole course and a public course that feels like a country club. It's a young course with many smaller trees, some water and sand. A favorite hole is the 165-yard par three 12th hole, with an elevated tee box facing the mountains with a view that might take your mind off golf. Greens fees are $28. Carts cost $12 per person.

Westwoods Golf Club
6655 Quaker St., Golden • (303) 424-3334

Westwoods is another public course with that country-club feel. Also known as the Westwoods Ranch, this 18-holer opened in June 1994. The terrain gets pretty high, with a few water hazards, and is esteemed for its spectacular views. The course is walkable but not considered the easiest to walk. No. 16 is a short par 4 in a beautiful setting by a peaceful wooded area. Greens fees are $26, and carts are $10 per person.

Hiking

Hiking is the most common way of enjoying Colorado's backcountry. For information on hiking safety and our favorite places to hike, see our Great Outdoors chapter.

Horseback Riding

What's more quintessentially Western than an outing on the back of a horse, especially when you're riding on the prairies or Foothills of the Rockies? Riding in the Denver suburbs may not compare with the more remote horse

Photo: Daily Camera/David P. Gilkey

Colorado may not have an ocean, but lakes and reservoirs offer opportunities for water recreation.

experiences in the high country and points west, but it beats a canter through Midwestern cornfields.

A lot of people on the outskirts of Denver have their own horses, but if you don't, there are some fine stables to choose from for a daily rental ride. The two state recreation areas on Greater Denver's south side are nice places to ride, simply because they have large and carefully cultivated natural areas and their own stables on site where you can pay to ride the nature trails.

Paint Horse Stables
4201 S. Parker Rd., Aurora
• (303) 690-8235

At the Cherry Creek Reservoir State Recreation Area, this is a great spot for a ride. The area is wooded and has lots of open meadows with natural grasslands. You need reservations to ride here; a day or two in advance is fine. Cost is $14 for one hour or $26 for two hours. It's open from 9 AM to 6 PM year round (typically only on weekends in winter).

B&B Livery
11500 N. Roxborough Park Rd., Littleton
• (303) 933-3636

These stables at the Chatfield State Rec-

reation Area provide a serene riding setting with great foothill views. Rides are available beginning in March or April, depending on how wet the spring is, and usually end around October or November, again depending on weather. Reservations are needed for rides, which cost $12.50 for an hour-long walking tour or $40 for a walking/trotting ride. B&B is open every day from 9 AM to 5 PM but might close on Mondays, so call ahead. Rides are provided until November, and hay rides are available year round, weather permitting. To get there from Colo. 470, take the Wadsworth Exit S., then left at the third stoplight, into the park. From there follow the signs.

Stockton's Plum Creek Stables Ltd.
7479 W. Titan Rd., Littleton
• (303) 791-1966

Plum Creek also has access to the 7,000 acres of Chatfield State Recreation Area via its own private entrance. The area is beautiful, with plenty of bird-watching opportunities on native prairie grasses. Find Stockton's by going about 4 miles south of C-470 on Santa Fe Drive and turning right on Titan Road. Rides are provided from 9 AM to 3 PM and cost $15 an hour; children must be 9 or older. Tours are guided through the wooded area of the recreation area.

A Worthy Ranch & Stables
West Parker Rd., Parker • (303) 841-9405

On the other side of Greater Denver's south side are a couple of stables in the town of Parker, which you can reach by taking I-25 a little more than a mile south of its intersection with C-470, then traveling east about 2.5 miles on Lincoln Avenue (Exit 193) before turning right on a little dirt road called West Parker Road. A Worthy Ranch & Stables is about 2 miles down West Parker Road on the left. It offers lessons as well as riding, with miles of trails. Guided rides are given by reservation and cost $22.50 for an hour and a half or $30 for two hours.

Old West Stables
14700 Morrison Rd., Morrison
• (303) 697-1416

At the corner of Foxton Road and U.S. Highway 285 in Morrison, these stables offer horse rides, guided and self-guided, in the 2,700 acres of Lakewood's Bear Creek Lake Park. It also offers half-day and full-day rides in the mountain community of Conifer. Old West's Conifer rides take place on the 460 acres of Beaver Ranch, which is a children's summer camp. Old West offers horse-drawn sleigh rides at Beaver Ranch in the winter, the closest mountain sleigh rides to Denver. Rides cost $14 an hour per person, and children must be at least 7. Reservations are needed; rides begin at 9 AM and end at 4:30 PM during the week and 6 PM on weekends.

Hunting

Hunting, together with fishing, is a $3 billion a year industry in Colorado. That's second only to the ski industry in terms of economic impact. As vast as the numbers are, so are the locations and types of hunting avail-

able in Colorado. Hunting is legal on certain public lands as well as on private land with permission. In fact, you might see bumper stickers that say "Ask first . . . before hunting or fishing on private land."

Licenses and Seasons

All hunting, including on public land, requires licenses that can be purchased at any major sports and outdoors stores (such as Kmart or Gart Bros. Sporting Goods stores). The cost varies depending on the game hunted.

For example, a resident deer license costs around $20; nonresidents pay $150. Rare game such as moose will cost much more to hunt — $200 for residents and more than $1,000 for nonresidents. There are limits on the number of licenses issued, with more reserved for residents. A lottery is held for some big-game hunting where numbers are kept to a minimum. Call the Division of Wildlife, (303) 297-1192, for a complete list of prices and limitations. Brochures for the various types of hunting are available from the DOW beginning in February and March, depending on the game. The yearly updates spell out the rules and regulations.

Most hunting is confined to specific seasons, whose dates vary from year to year. To find out the parameters of specific game, contact the Division of Wildlife at (303) 297-1192 or use the following recorded information lines: big-game hunting, (303) 291-7529; small game, (303) 291-7546; game birds,(303) 291-7547; and waterfowl, (303) 291-7548.

The state is most famous for big game, including elk, mountain lion, black bear, mule deer, bighorn sheep, mountain goat, white-tailed deer and pronghorn antelope. But 105 of the state's 113 species of sport game are small game, including ducks and geese, wild turkey, ring-necked pheasant, mourning dove, band-tailed pigeon, quail, grouse, rabbit and coyote.

INSIDERS' TIP

The must-see view of Greater Denver and the Rocky Mountains is from the entrance to the Denver Museum of Natural History, in City Park at Colorado Boulevard and Montview. The sweeping vista of treetops, skyscrapers and snow capped peaks is the best in town.

There's a lot of winter trapping as well for beaver, muskrat, bobcat, weasel, marten, mink, badger and fox.

In-Line Skating

Commonly called Rollerblading for the trademark brand name, this sport is more properly called "in-line skating" for the same reason you say "copying" instead of "Xeroxing." In-line skates differ from traditional roller skates in that the wheels are in a single line rather than being set foursquare like the wheels of a car. This makes in-lines go a little faster than ordinary roller skates and work a little better for outdoor use, since they are better at traversing cracks and other surface glitches. If you're a beginner, you might want to try the safe route of renting in-lines at a local indoor roller rink, where there are music, lights and other amenities. Roller Express, 8412 N. Huron Street, Thornton, (303) 428-5061, is the big rink in north Greater Denver. Here, too, you can rent both in-line and traditional rollers in a safe, indoor atmosphere of neon lights and music. This rink features teen nights, adult nights and family nights.

Outdoors is a different story; it's where you go when you want to get a little more serious about in-line skating. Outdoors, there's the temptation to go faster, which in-lines can do, and the tendency to fall harder with rougher landings. Experts always recommend wearing helmets, knee pads and wrist guards.

There are plenty of places around Greater Denver where in-lining can be slow and easy, where people of all experience levels can enjoy the sport. Check Denver's city bicycle maps (see the Pavement Bicycling entry in this chapter) for the city bike paths where Rollerblading is good. If it's a good pavement biking path, then it's a good blading path.

Colorado Highway 470 Path
Various access points along C-470, from Highlands Ranch to I-70

One place that's "totally happening," according to one in-liner jock, is the bike path that follows C-470 along its eastern side in Jefferson County. It has good uphills and downhills, sharp corners and a smooth surface built for speed. The path parallels C-470 on the east side all the way to I-70.

The Cherry Creek Greenbelt Path
Various access points from Confluence Park to Cherry Creek Reservoir

This miles-long cement path begins (or ends, depending on your perspective) at Confluence Park, which is the confluence of the South Platte River and Cherry Creek, off 15th Street just west of Lower Downtown. It follows the Cherry Creek past the Denver Country Club, through the Cherry Creek neighborhood to the east side of town and out to Cherry Creek Reservoir. The entire length is approximately 15 miles of smooth surface and quiet spaces. It's one of the most esteemed blading zones due to its pleasant and fashionable location and the many connecting bike paths along its length. The streets of Cherry Creek also have a great reputation: it's a fun place to be, and the streets tend to be new and smooth.

South Platte River Path
Access Points from downtown Denver through Littleton

This path also starts (or ends) at Confluence Park and travels the other way, along the Platte, to Chatfield State Park. It's just as good as the Cherry Creek; wide open and lots of smooth skating. This one might be slightly slimmer than Cherry Creek.

Washington Park
Between S. Franklin and S. Downing streets just north of I-25

Washington Park is always filled with skaters, bikers, walkers and joggers. An asphalt street rings the park and has lanes for bikers and skaters, walkers and joggers. Inside the park the scenery is interesting, with soccer and volleyball games going on, and colorful flower beds and two lakes along the way.

Crown Hill Park
On the east side of Kipling St. between 32nd and 26th aves., Wheat Ridge

This is popular for the seamless concrete path surrounding Crown Hill Lake. Again, the park atmosphere is friendly and inspiring for all the amateur athletes who take to the path year round. You'll share the path with bikers and joggers, but mostly joggers, and like all Denver-area paths it can get crowded at times. Just watch out for speed demons.

Cherry Creek Reservoir State Recreation Area
South on the Parker Rd. Exit off of I-225

Just follow the signs off Parker Road to enter the paths that wind through this state park area. The terrain is smooth and flat and surrounded by prairie grasses and groves of trees where you can rest and cool off. The path is open year-round, and it's great on sunny winter days too. One word of warning, watch for park traffic on cross streets, especially on weekends.

Chatfield State Recreation Area
South on Wadsworth Blvd. off C-470

Follow the signs to this state park area for smooth in-line skating. As with other paths, you'll share this with bikers and joggers, but there's plenty of room. The mountain views are better here than at Cherry Creek, but both are perfect spots for people of all levels of expertise. There aren't too many shady spots on the Chatfield path, so brings lots of water. As with Cherry Creek, watch for park traffic on cross streets.

Rentals

In-line skating rentals can be found in every area of town. Reservations aren't necessary as most places rent by the hour on a first come, first served basis. The cost will vary, so you need to check with the individual shops. You can expect to pay at least $4 an hour and up to $8 (24-hour rentals priced as low as $15). Ski Tech, a store at 700 S. Pearl Street in Denver, (303) 777-3380, rents to a lot of Washington Park skaters. So does Sports Plus, 1055 S. Gaylord, Denver, (303) 777-6613. The Skate Shop, 5050 S. Federal, No. 6, Englewood, (303) 730-1344, rents largely to skaters on the South Platte River and Cherry Creek trails. Grand West Outfitters, 801 Broadway, Denver, (303) 825-0300, is an outdoors store that rents a lot of in-lines to people skating on the Cherry Creek greenbelt path. Many of these stores carry brochures and maps of paths.

Running

Runners are everywhere in Greater Denver, in the streets of downtown and the suburbs, in the city parks and greenbelts and along the mountain paths. You can run anywhere. Most people run in their own neighborhoods. But there are some popular running venues for those who want to run where others are running, in pleasant settings and on motorist-free trails.

Washington Park, between S. Franklin and S. Downing streets just north of I-25, probably has Denver's highest runner density. That may be because it's one of Denver's biggest and most pleasant parks, or it may be because it's in an area with a lot of upscale empty-nesters who believe in exercise and don't have to get it by pushing their kids on the park's swings. Closer in, City Park, between Colorado Boulevard and York Street, two blocks north of E. Colfax Avenue, is another popular running area where folks can get away from cars and run through some semblance of foliated quietude. Greenbelts, including the popular Highline Canal in Littleton, the Cherry Creek Bike Path and the South Platte River trails in Chatfield Reservoir, are particularly nice places to run for that same aesthetic. If you like running on natural terrain, which is healthier because it avoids the repetitive, one-dimensional joint-pounding of flat terrain, you may want to try the many fine trails along the Front Range. See some of our suggested mountain biking trails outlined in our Mountain Biking entry.

A lot of runners are solitary souls. You see them at dawn while you're driving to work, and you see them in the evening when you're coming home, running alone and happy about it. But for those who enjoy the group experience, there are plenty of events and clubs. Greater Denver's largest annual running events include the 5-mile Cherry Creek Sneak in April, (303) 394-5152; the Governor's Cup 5K in September, (303) 727-8700; the Run for the Zoo, a 5K and 10K in October, (303) 331-5800; the Race for the Cure 5K in October, (303) 727-8700; and the 4-mile Turkey Trot on Thanksgiving morning, (303) 433-8383.

Among the larger running clubs are the Colorado Masters, for the older-than-30 crowd, (303) 751-4284 or (303) 232-1308; and the

Rocky Mountain Road Runners, (303) 871-8366. Don't forget that walkers have found increasing acceptance in the area's big running events. The Front Range Walkers, (303) 377-0576, is perhaps the area's biggest walking club.

Some running stores also serve as information clearinghouses on running clubs, events and race series and are places where you can sign up for races. These include Mongoose Runners Den, 8877 Harlan Street, Westminster, (303) 657-0225; and Runners Roost Ltd., 1685 S. Colorado Boulevard, Denver, (303) 759-8455. A store called Fleet Feet has outlets around the Greater Denver area, but its main information and race sign-up center is Fleet Feet's Cherry Creek North store at 2760 E. Second Avenue, (303) 320-0750.

Skiing

You'd expect skiing to be the top entry in any guide to Greater Denver recreation, but we're placing it down here because it's well-covered in our Ski Country chapter. That chapter gives you an abundance of information on all the major ski areas near Denver, along with plenty of tips on tickets, lessons and the ski season.

Skiing is certainly recreation, however, and if you're a beginner or a want-to-be beginner, you may want to know about a couple of the information sources that can help you get into the sport.

Colorado Ski Country USA, (303) 837-0793, a trade association for all the ski resorts in the state, publishes the *Colorado Ski Country Consumer Guide*. Within about 130 pages, it contains a lot of the information you want to know about skiing in Colorado. Colorado Ski Country USA will mail it to you free if you give them a call. Colorado Ski Country USA also sponsors a major consumer show every fall at one of Denver's big convention spaces, where you can find out about the latest in gear, apparel and accessories.

You may also want to know about Sniagrab (bargains spelled backward), the big annual ski equipment and apparel sale held every year by Gart Brothers Sporting Goods outlets around Greater Denver. It starts on the Saturday before Labor Day and runs through much of September. You can find some fine deals on new and used equipment.

One of the best ways to get into skiing is to link up with a ski club. It's not only a social event, but a way of letting the more experienced take you under their wing via group outings to local ski areas where all you have to do is show up, get on the bus and have a good time. A lot of health clubs and recreation districts have ski clubs, and it's not unlikely that you'll find a ski club at your place of employment.

But if you want the best overall source of local ski clubs, try the *National Ski Club News*. This is a newsletter about ski clubs nationwide, and it's published in Denver. To get a list of local ski clubs, all you have to do is send your request and a self-addressed, stamped envelope to National Ski Club News, P.O. Box 17385, Denver 80217.

Tennis

Greater Denver has plenty of tennis facilities, both private and public. Of course, you don't have to contact any organizations or join any leagues to play tennis. You can find courts in just about any major city park.

In Denver try Washington Park, between S. Franklin and S. Downing streets just north of I-25, and City Park, between Colorado Boulevard and York Street, two blocks north of E. Colfax Avenue. Park play is free and usually runs on a first-come, first-served basis as long as there are no tournaments or lessons going on.

Beyond public courts, there are many organized centers and city recreation departments that offer players a chance to join group play, take lessons and play in tournaments.

Greater Denver's central tennis resource is the Colorado Tennis Association, (303) 695-4116. If you're looking for courts or are interested in finding out how to get into organized tennis leagues or sanctioned tournaments, the CTA can help steer you to the right place. It also has copies of tournament schedules for adults and juniors as well as general information brochures. It's the local branch of the U.S. Tennis Association as well, so you can get USTA memberships and publications through the CTA.

Photo: Daily Camera/Crissy Pascual

Tennis ladders are available through recreation centers, tennis associations and country clubs.

Gates Tennis Center
100 S. Adams St. • (303) 355-4461

This popular facility is just south of the Cherry Creek mall and consistently rated as one of the top public tennis facilities in the country. You don't need a membership, court times are reasonable, and lessons are competitively priced. It has one of the nation's largest tennis ladders, a challenge arrangement in which you sign up at a certain level and begin to play and move up and down the ladder. Gates has more than 1,000 people on its computerized ladder, enough to offer specialized ladders for singles, doubles, etc. There's even a coed ladder reputed as a good place for singles to meet. It's a 20-court facility complete with clubhouse, locker room and pro shop. Pros will teach you, and ball machines will test you.

Denver Parks and Recreation
Denver area parks • (303) 331-4047

The city recreation district maintains a few dozen courts across the city for daytime play.

There are junior programs and adult lesson programs throughout the Denver area. The USTA youth tournament program costs about $30 and runs seven weeks of instruction in the summer and one week of tournaments beginning in early June. Adults 18 and older can join the Congress Park (Eighth Avenue and York Street east of downtown) program, or the Berkley Park (46th Avenue and Sheridan Boulevard northwest of town) program in June and July for around $52 resident and $64 nonresident. Call for information on other programs.

Aurora Parks and Recreation
Aurora area parks • (303) 695-7201

Aurora has a good reputation for its public tennis program. Pros offer beginning, intermediate and advanced lessons for one-week or two-week sessions as well as evening and Saturday lessons. Tournament play is available too; check the summer brochure. Aurora maintains 72 courts on a first-come, first-served basis. Very few courts are lighted; one example is Del Mar Park at Sixth Avenue and Peoria Street. Lessons range from $16 to $39 for residents and up to $65 nonresidents.

The Chatfield/Columbine YMCA
10393 W. Alamo Pl., Littleton
• (303) 979-3707

This YMCA offers six outdoor courts in a lovely setting with views of the foothills. Four courts are outside and lighted. Programs include lessons, tournaments, drills and leagues for adults and children. Cost depends on the program. For example, 90 minutes of drills run $15, and tournaments are about $22 for singles and $26 for doubles. Call for a complete list of programs.

Holly Tennis Center
6651 S. Krameria Wy., Englewood
• (303) 771-3654

Holly offers the most USTA-sanctioned tournaments in Colorado. It offers programs on a total of 40 courts, including use of courts in the South Suburban Recreation District. Six of Holly's courts are lighted. League play varies from $35 to $50 and includes practice and matches. Junior and adult private and group lessons cost between $30 and $50.

Ken Caryl Ranch Community Center
1 Club Dr., Littleton • (303) 979-2233

Ken Caryl has four indoor courts and six outdoor courts. You won't find prettier surroundings; the Ken Caryl Ranch community is in the red-rock moonscape of the valley hidden behind the Hogback Formation that runs north/south along C-470. The facility is actually owned by Jefferson County Open Space. Offered here are leagues, tournaments and lessons for resident and nonresident youth and adults. You also can purchase a membership to the center. Cost varies depending on the program. Tennis clinics, for instance, vary from $20 to $70 per person.

Arvada Tennis Center
Corner of 65th and Miller sts., Arvada
• (303) 420-1210

This is a fine public facility with eight courts and sanctioned USTA play. If you want to take to the courts, we suggest making reservations in advance. It is open from about 4:30 till 10 PM nightly and on Saturdays and Sundays from 7 AM until noon.

Wildlife Watching

While hunting wildlife is more traditional, recent years have seen a tremendous growth in the stalking of wildlife either to photograph or just for the joy of seeing it as close as is possible or safe. There are few things as magical as watching a herd of elk feeding in a mountain field, or catching a glimpse of a red fox as it darts amid trees. Colorado offers more than 100 places to view wildlife year round. The best time to view is early morning and late evening (dawn and sunset).

As you travel Colorado's roads and highways, watch for signs that depict a pair of binoculars and say "Wildlife Viewing Area," then follow the signs. One such area is just outside Denver International Airport. Another is in the mountains, along I-70, just east of Georgetown (about an hour and a half from Denver). But there are dozens more. Contact the Division of Wildlife at (303) 297-1192 for a list or pick up a wildlife viewing book at any major bookstore. The *Colorado Wildlife Viewing Guide* is available through the Colorado Wildlife Heritage Foundation for $8.95. Call (303) 291-7212.

By the way, wildlife viewing has its own set of etiquette that keeps wildlife — and people — safe and healthy. For instance, keep binoculars handy because wildlife should be viewed from a distance. Of course, never chase or spook animals; not only is it frowned upon, but also it's illegal. And don't approach wildlife too quickly, as you can scare them away and ruin everyone's enjoyment.

Hiking — with backpack, daypack, no pack or leading a laden llama — is the most common way of enjoying the backcountry.

The Great Outdoors

As a diverse three-dimensional universe, the mountains offer unparalleled opportunity for adventure. You can venture deep into the Colorado Rockies for long trips or drive less than a half-hour and be surrounded by great exploring territory.

Camping, hiking and biking abound in Colorado's great outdoors, and we've offered a few tips to enjoy them.

More than one-third of Colorado's land area is owned by and is available to the public, including 8.3 million acres of Bureau of Land Management tracts and 14.3 million acres of national forest. There are 11 national forests in Colorado, covering major parts of the state. One can't point to specific attractions in the national forests as easily as one can in the state parks and recreation areas because the national forests are basically undeveloped areas where you can hike, fish, hunt, ride and camp just about anywhere. They are also where the vast majority of wilderness can be found, and if you want to hike to some remote and beautiful backcountry refuge anywhere in the United States, the likelihood is that you'll do it in a national forest.

National Forests

While national forests are open generally to timber sales, mining and other activities that purists might find at odds with the idea of a natural setting, wilderness areas are those set aside specifically under the 1964 Wilderness Act, allowing no permanent roads, structures, timber sales or mining other than those that already exist. These areas are wild country, accessible only by trail and closed to motorized transport.

Three of Colorado's national forests are located immediately to the west, northwest and southwest of Greater Denver: Pike National Forest, Arapaho National Forest and Roosevelt National Forest. You can seek information on these from the National Forest Service's Denver Regional Office, (303) 275-5350, or call each National Forest office itself.

Arapaho and Roosevelt National Forests

Arapaho and Roosevelt National Forests, (970) 498-2770, are a combined jurisdiction that span the Continental Divide from the Wyoming border to just south of I-70, west of Denver. Roughly speaking, the Roosevelt National Forest comprises that section east of the Continental Divide. The Arapaho National Forest lies west of the Continental Divide, although it comes east to cover the area south of I-70 to mid-Jefferson County.

Together they make up some 1.3 million acres in the Rocky Mountains and Foothills, wrapping around Rocky Mountain National Park and including 47 National Forest camp-

---

INSIDERS' TIP

Bring mosquito repellent on those backpacking trips. It makes a big difference in your level of enjoyment.

grounds and a number of wilderness areas such as the Rawah Wilderness on the Wyoming border, the Indian Peaks Wilderness west of Boulder and the Cache La Poudre Wilderness around the Cache La Poudre River that flows through Roosevelt National Forest and down to Fort Collins.

Pike and San Isabel National Forests

www.insiders.com

See this and many other **Insiders' Guide®** destinations online.

Visit us today!

Another combined jurisdiction, the Pike and San Isabel National Forests, (719) 545-8737, consist of 2.3 million acres. The San Isabel is, at its closest, about 100 miles of winding, two-lane U.S. Highway 285 away from Denver; at its farthest, it winds south almost to New Mexico.

The Pike National Forest, at 1.1 million acres, is Greater Denver's national forest neighbor south of I-70 and west of I-25, reaching to the southwest of Colorado Springs (Pikes Peak is part of this national forest). It contains several converging sources of Greater Denver's South Platte River as well as that river's most scenic stretches before it reaches the Flatlands. It has a half-dozen of the state's peaks higher than 14,000 feet, sharing Mount Evans with Arapaho National Forest. Its vegetation is drier than Arapaho and Roosevelt National Forests, with more juniper, oak brush and bristlecone pine. Its major wilderness area is the Lost Creek Wilderness, 106,000 acres where Pikes Peak granite has been eroded into domes, spires, turrets and crests, with a lot of big-boulder slopes. Lost Creek is less popular than Indian Peaks and the other big wilderness areas to the north, and it's a good place to backpack and find a bit of solitude. One unique feature of the Pike is 118 miles of motorcycling trails in a designated area around Sedalia.

Hiking

Hiking — with backpack, daypack, no pack or leading a laden llama — is the most com-

mon way of enjoying the backcountry. The most important rule is to be prepared and have fun.

You can hike just about anywhere on national forest land as long as it isn't posted as off-limits. Wherever you hike, things get more beautiful the higher you get. You will probably start climbing in the lower forests of aspen and ponderosa pines or dark, moody groves of spruce and fir, but eventually, as you rise, the forest will break open into the "krummholz," or crooked wood zone, where trees stunted by altitude and twisted by relentless winds make a border before the alpine meadows above. When you're above treeline, you're in alpine meadows, and you're also in the heights of drastic weather.

After advising you not to drink the river water without using disinfectant pills or passing it through a disinfectant pump, the second piece of advice that mountain-savvy folks will give you is to dress in layers. When you start hiking down low, shorts and T-shirt are probably what you'll want to be wearing. But there are few things more miserable than someone who takes nothing warmer or drier and reaches 14,000 feet as the weather moves in, dropping temperatures into the 40s or lower with high winds, sometimes a cold rain or snow and usually a good afternoon lightning storm. In a sizeable backpack, if you're hiking high, bring a long-sleeved shirt, something warm such as wool or flannel. Bring a sweater or sweatshirt to put over that and a windbreaker/raincoat to put over that. A hood is always nice, but you should at least have a knit cap and warm gloves. Bring trousers, or at least sweatpants, to put on over or instead of the shorts. Those are the minimum pieces of clothing you'll need along with a sizeable water bottle, water disinfectant tablets and some snacks (high carbohydrates such as trail mix are good). And don't forget hiking boots if you plan a lengthy hike. Wear two pairs of thick socks to prevent blistering. With two pairs of socks, the socks rub against each other instead of the shoe rubbing through one sock against your foot.

We always hear stories about people who

started hiking, miserable with the heat, and wound up huddling in a snowstorm on some alpine boulder field, unable to go on or back because the snow had made the boulders too slippery, thanking their lucky stars that they had brought enough clothes, or cursing their luck that they hadn't.

Another piece of advice you hear from the medical community is to drink a lot of water. Dehydration seems to be a contributing factor in whether altitude sickness sets in — and how severely you'll have it if you do get it. Altitude sickness can be deadly; at the very least it's miserable for the sufferer and ruins the day for companions. There's about half as much oxygen at 14,000 feet as at sea level. Consequently, Coloradans have a lot more red blood cells than people living at lower levels.

Also, make sure to get a map — a good map. Get yourself one of those "quadrangle" maps on a 1:24,000 scale, where an inch equals about 0.4 miles. You may need more than one of them to cover the area of your interest. Another great resource is the *Colorado Atlas & Gazetteer*, a road-atlas-size book that consists of topographical maps of the entire state. Here the scale is more like 1 inch equals 2.5 miles, but you still get good detail, contour lines and trail routes. You can find quadrangle maps and the *Colorado Atlas & Gazetteer* in well-stocked outdoor/camping stores, bookstores and even some gas stations. You can also get maps from the Bureau of Land Management in Lakewood, (303) 239-3600, or from the U.S. Geological Service at the Denver Federal Center in Lakewood, Map and Book Sales, (303) 202-4700. You need topo maps if you're hiking far off-road; don't expect to find signs in the midst of the forest.

While few things are grander than the mountains in the varying moods of daytime, even fewer things are more eerie or romantic than hiking by moonlight. Plan a hike for a night that's close to a full moon. You may not want to do any hiking off-trail, but where there are trails, it's a beautiful way to spend a night and a morning. We've done the full-moon hike of Longs Peak, beginning before midnight and climbing the last rock slopes while the first orange sunbeams were making the mountains glow like neon. Another advantage is that, by

reaching the top in the early morning, you avoid the more common experience of reaching the top from midday to afternoon, when the thunderclouds often close in.

One-way, long-distance hiking is a lot of fun. Drive two cars to the trailhead at one end of your trail of choice that crosses, say, a mountain range. Then both drivers, or as many more as are in the group, get into the other car and drive around to the other side of the mountain range. You get a good hike in without having to retrace your steps.

One of the most impressive places in which to try this maneuver is Rocky Mountain National Park. From Bear Lake on the east side of the park to the city of Grand Lake on the west side of the park is about 18 miles. You'll get a map at the entrance to the park that will show you several great hiking trails. If you're in good shape and energetic, it's fun to hike across the entire national park in one day, and it's easier than it sounds. You spend the early part of the day doing about 4.5 miles of steep uphill to the Continental Divide on Flattop Mountain; the rest of the day is an easy downhill amble. The only problem with this hike is that you may overestimate it and wind up in Grand Lake too early for your dinner reservations.

Another good hike of this kind is through the Indian Peaks Wilderness of Arapaho National Forest, just south of Rocky Mountain National Park. Start at scenic Brainard Lake, which you reach via a turnoff to the west from Colo. Highway 72 just north of Ward. Head west from Brainard Lake on the South St. Vrain Creek trail, up and over the Continental Divide and down to Lake Granby's Arapahoe Bay. Say two couples want to do this hike. Both can drive their cars to Brainard Lake. Couple No. 1 does the hike west to east while couple No. 2 splits up and drives both cars around through Rocky Mountain National Park. Everybody has a camping vacation at the wonderful campground at Arapahoe Bay or stays at any of the more civilized accommodations in the area. Going back, couple No. 1 drives the cars while couple No. 2 gets to do the hike back to Brainard Lake.

You don't have to be a technical climber with ropes, beaners, ice axes and all the other gear and specialized knowledge to mount

A 19th-century Perspective of Denver

In 1873, British traveler Isabella Bird spent some time in Denver and other areas of Colorado. Her account of her travels, *A Lady's Life in the Rocky Mountains*, is still in print today and easy to find at Denver bookstores and libraries.

Isabella was an intrepid traveler and a keen observer. She came to town after passing a summer in Estes Park, a summer that included a dramatic climb up 14,255-foot-high Longs Peak in what is now Rocky Mountain National Park. The peak had been scaled for the first time only five years before Isabella was hauled up it by a true character named Rocky Mountain Jim. Isabella missed being the first woman to stand on its summit by about three weeks. American writer and orator Anna Dickinson got credit for that.

Isabella was surprised by Denver, which she called a "great, braggart city." Here, as recounted with permission from the biography *Amazing Traveler: Isabella Bird*, is her description of the streets of Denver:

"Hunters and trappers in buckskin clothing; men of the Plains with belts and revolvers, in great blue cloaks, relics of the war; horsemen in fur coats and caps and buffalo-hide boots with the hair outside; Broadway dandies in light kid gloves; rich English sporting tourists, clean, comely and supercilious-looking; and hundreds of Indians on their small ponies, the men wearing buckskin suits sewn with beads, and red blankets, with faces painted vermilion, and hair hanging lank and straight, and squaws much bundled up riding astride with furs over their saddles."

Readers interested in learning more about Isabella Bird and her adventures are directed to *A Lady's Life in the Rocky Mountains* by Isabella Bird and also to *Amazing Traveler: Isabella Bird*, by Boulder author Evelyn Kaye (Blue Penguin Publications, 1994.)

Photo: Denver Public Library - Western History Dept.

British traveler Isabella Bird
visited Denver in 1873.

most of the highest peaks in Colorado. You can certainly take any of the many courses available around the area if you want to do technical climbing. A lot of gyms and recreation centers nowadays have their own climbing walls (simulated rock faces) to practice on. See our Parks and Recreation chapter for details.

Most people, however, just want to climb

mountains, not scale them. You can do it the easy way on any of Colorado's 500 or so peaks higher than 12,000 feet (56 of them higher than 14,000 feet). People feel themselves part of a special club when they have done all of Colorado's "14ers." The average person can do many of them, and there are some relatively easy ones close to Denver.

Grays Peak and Torreys Peak are two very

accessible 14ers near Denver. Grays Peak, at 14,270, is the state's ninth-highest mountain, and Torreys Peak, at 14,267, is the 11th-highest. The hike to the top of either peak is about 4 miles. The two peaks are also just a half-mile apart, separated by an easily walkable saddle, so this is really a good opportunity to do two 14ers in one day. On this, like many high-altitude hikes, you're likely to encounter mountain goats along your path. To find the hike, take I-70 about 6 miles west of Georgetown to the Bakerville exit; take the road south for about 3 miles up Stevens Gulch to the Stevens Mine. You'll probably see cars belonging to other hikers parked up ahead. Cross the creek from where the cars are parked, and you'll find the trail heading 4 miles uphill to Grays and Torreys.

The easiest way to do a 14er, as we mention in our Daytrips chapter, is to simply drive up to the top of Mount Evans from Idaho Springs. If you like to hop boulders as well as walk on trails, one of the most fun excursions you can have in Colorado is to drive to the top of Mount Evans and then hike from there to the top of neighboring Mount Bierstadt and back. Like Grays and Torreys, the two mountaintops are quite close, and the sawtooth ridge saddle between them is quite negotiable. It's a wonderful way to enjoy the top of the world. We've made it from the top of Mount Evans to the top of Mount Bierstadt in less than 1½ hours.

On the way back, however, we were charmed to see a lovely cloud bank floating toward us until it arrived and closed us in a dense, deathly chilly fog that soaked, turned to snow and covered the boulders with ice. We got so exhausted from the struggle and so cold that we began imagining ourselves succumbing to hypothermia. As we say, come prepared. And watch those cliffs; not just on Mount Evans but everywhere in the mountains. Every year unprepared hikers become lost or die on what should have been an easy hike; many others are injured. We just can't stress enough the difference in hiking at lower and higher elevations. No matter how good of shape you're in, you will feel the effects of less oxygen and need to slow down and drink plenty of water.

Bierstadt is perhaps a more traditional climb from the parking area at Guanella Pass, 3 miles of trail. You reach Guanella Pass by driving south from Georgetown on the Guanella Pass Scenic Byway.

Longs Peak is the most famous 14er hike, easily reached by trail. That is, it's easy in that the trail is easy to follow, but the climb is a long one. You gain 4,800 feet over 8 miles to the top, and then, of course, you have to hike 8 miles back down. It's truly amazing how many people you encounter up there. Longs Peak is the big one that people point to from Denver. It's probably the most famous and popular big hike in Colorado, and it's close to Estes Park, the tourist city that everyone drives through on their way to Rocky Mountain National Park. To start your hike, drive 10 miles south from Estes Park on Colo. Highway 7, then turn west to the Longs Peak campground and ranger station, where you can start hiking. Typically, the best time is late July and early August. The rest of the year, snow and ice make Longs a technical climb. You might want to check with the rangers at Rocky Mountain National Park before heading out.

For other hiking opportunities, read *A Climbing Guide to Colorado's Fourteeners*, by Walter R. Borneman and Lyndon J. Lampert. Fourteeners aren't the only mountains around, of course, and there are plenty of 13ers and 12ers that put you at the top of the world. We've always been fond of the hike to the top of Mount Audubon, a 13,223-footer that's about a 4-mile slog uphill from Brainard Lake, just off of Colo. Highway 72 north of Ward. The last long slope of this climb is pure boulder-hopping, but at the top it's a beautiful view into the Lake Granby/Grand Lake area to the west, not to mention everything else for 70 miles in every other direction. For adventures such as this, Walter R. Borneman wrote a worthwhile book, *Colorado's Other Mountains: A Climbing Guide to Selected Peaks Under 14,000 Feet*.

You don't have to confine yourself to one-day peak assaults, since the bulk of the state's trails wind along the shoulders of mountains, through their valleys and over the passes between them. *Hiking Trails of Central Colorado* by Bob Martin and *Northern Colorado Hiking Trails* by Don and Roberta Lowe highlight a lot of opportunities not far from Denver. One other book we mentioned in our Kidstuff chapter that bears mentioning again here is *Best Hikes With Children in Colorado* by Maureen Keilty. It has a lot of easy but scenic and enjoyable hikes close to Denver, and it's not just for kids. Adults will enjoy it too.

A popular approach to hiking or horsepacking in the mountains is the get-high/ stay-high philosophy. If you're going to gain a lot of altitude, you want to stay up there a while and not go way down and have to hike back up. You may want to camp at some high mountain lake and spend a few days exploring the neighboring peaks and valleys or you may want to move from one high mountain lake to another. Some people do the latter by taking the trail down from the lake until it intersects another trail to another lake and then hiking back up. A more scenic way, which is easy if you have a topo map, is to simply hike over the ridges between the lakes. A week spent ridge-hopping from lake to lake along a mountain range is memorable indeed.

Among our favorite high-mountain camping areas along the central/northern Front Range are the Rawah Wilderness west of Fort Collins; the Never-Summer Range just east of Rocky Mountain National Park's northern end; and the Indian Peaks Wilderness, along the Continental Divide just south of Rocky Mountain National Park. A very lovely area for backpacking to the heights is the Collegiate Peaks area, uphill to the west from the city of Buena Vista, about 120 miles southwest of Denver on U.S. Highway 285.

Don't think just in terms of summertime hiking. The trails of summer are the cross-country ski trails of winter. Lisa Stanton's *Colorado Cross-Country Skiing* will be a valuable reference for those of you who take on the winter trails. Also, check our Ski Country chapter for suggestions on where to cross-country ski.

Camping

Finding a location to camp on national forest land is simple once you've determined whether you want to "car camp," as it's called, or backpack in for a more remote location. The main distinction is simple: Car camping usually means you'll be near your car, won't

have to hike in and will likely be at a designated campground with amenities such as outhouses and running water. If you car camp, you'll likely be near others — anywhere from 50 feet to a few hundred feet depending on the campground — and have a designated fire pit. You'll also pay a small daily fee of around $7 per site. If you backcountry camp, you can go virtually anywhere on national forest land and camp for free, but you won't have any amenities.

The rules for backcountry camping are fairly simple, but important: you must pick a spot at least 100 feet from a roadway, trail or stream and at least a half-mile from standing water; fires are allowed for cooking and warming and must be in a contained pit (large rocks formed into a ring work well), and you must restore the fire area when you leave; your car can be as much as 300 feet off the road but not parked in a bog; if you have a catalytic converter, do not park over grass as it can start a fire.

Making a reservation for car camping in designated campgrounds is recommended and nearly imperative on holiday weekends (see our list of phone numbers below). Backcountry camping does not require a reservation and can be done anywhere as long as the rules are followed.

If you car camp, you can get to a campground early and take your chances at cruising around looking for an empty space or finding somebody who looks like they are about to leave. Usually, you need to show up by 7 PM, or your reserved spot could be taken. The rules are somewhat loose and depend on individual campgrounds. The national forests have a toll-free number, and in any part of Colorado a certain percentage of the forest service campgrounds are part of that reservation system. Call (800) 280-2267 or (800) 365-2267, but make sure to have ready not only the name of the campground you want but also a selection of other campgrounds in the vicinity. Many times they'll tell you the one you want is not open to reservations but operates on a first come, first camp basis. The person you're talking to on that 800 number is actually sitting in Cumberland, Maryland, where Biospherics, the company that has the contract with the federal government, is located. If you ask the reservationists at Biospherics to suggest another reservations-accessible campground nearby, they will know as much about Colorado campgrounds as they do about campgrounds in Australia.

Following is a helpful list, by name, of national forest campgrounds in Colorado that are under the Biospherics reservation system. Note that a road atlas or Colorado state map is likely to have a little tree symbol representing each campground but no name. The *Colorado Atlas & Gazetteer* often has the name of a lake or creek that coincides with the nearby tent symbol indicating a campground. But there's one resource that names each campground on the map, and that's the National Forest visitor map, one for each national forest, produced by the National Forest Service itself and available for $3. You can get such maps from the National Forest Service's Denver Regional Office. You can either call them at (303) 275-5350 and ask that they fax or send you an order form, or you can drop in to the Regional Office at 740 Simms Street, Lakewood, and pick up the map(s) of your choice. You can also find these maps selling at some outing stores. Call the outing stores in your area first to make sure they have the maps you need.

Campgrounds

Arapaho/Roosevelt National Forest
Main Number, (970) 498-2770

Boulder Ranger District, Boulder,
(303) 444-6600
Campgrounds:
Kelly Dahl
Olive Ridge
Pawnee

Clear Creek Ranger District,
Idaho Springs, (303) 567-2901
Campgrounds:
Cold Springs
Echo Lake
Guanella Pass
West Chicago Creek
Pickle Gulch (Group Campground)

Estes-Poudre Ranger District, Fort Collins,
(970) 498-2770
Campgrounds:
Mountain Park

Redfeather Ranger District, Fort Collins,
(970) 498-2770
Campgrounds:
Chambers Lake
Dowdy Lake
West Lake

Sulphur Ranger District, Granby,
(970) 887-4100
Campgrounds:
Arapahoe Bay
Green Ridge
Stillwater

Pike National Forest
Main number (719) 545-8737

Pikes Peak Ranger District, Colorado
Springs, (719) 636-1602
Campgrounds:
 Meadow Ridge
Thunder Ridge
Pike Community (Group Campground)
Red Rocks (Group Campground)

South Platte Ranger District, Morrison,
(303) 275-5610
Campgrounds:
Buffalo
Kelsey
Lone Rock
Meadows (Group Campground)

South Park Ranger District, Fairplay,
(719) 836-2031
Campgrounds:
Aspen
Jefferson Creek
Lodgepole

One further note on national forest campgrounds: There are many, many more. For a full list, you can call the National Forest Service's Denver Regional Office at (303) 275-5350. They'll mail you the free brochure, "Rocky Mountain Region Campgrounds." Not only does it list all the campgrounds in Colo-

Photo: Daily Camera/Crissy Pascual

Kayakers navigate Colorado's rivers and creeks when snow melts in the high country.

rado, but it also lists campgrounds in national forest and national grasslands in Wyoming, Kansas, Nebraska and South Dakota. This brochure indicates which campgrounds are in the reservation system, and it also carries the reservations 800 number. It's a good idea to get it, because the campgrounds covered by the reservations system can change from year to year.

You can find a lot of books about camping, but a good basic reference is *The Complete Colorado Campground Guide*, by Outdoor Books Inc. of Denver, available at local bookstores and outing stores. For more information about recreation in other areas of Colorado, pick up copies of *The Insiders' Guide®to Boulder and Rocky Mountain National Park* and *The Insiders' Guide® to Colorado's Mountains*.

Resources

There are umpteen books on how to enjoy Colorado's recreational, scenic and natural opportunities. A pass through a major bookstore will load you down with more than you need. Following are a few other informational resources.

Colorado State Parks (camping, boating and recreation), (303) 866-3437

U.S. Forest Service camping reservations, (800) 280-2267

National Park Service camping reservations, (800)365-2267

Cabins and Lodge Association, (303) 499-9343

Colorado Division of Wildlife, Headquarters, Denver, (303) 297-1192; Central Region, Denver, (303) 291-7230; Northeast Region, Fort Collins, (970) 484-2836; Northwest Region, Grand Junction, (970) 248-7175; Southeast Region, Colorado Springs, (719) 473-2945; Southwest Region, Montrose, (970) 249-3431

Colorado Dude and Guest Ranch Directory Service (serving Colorado exclusively), (970) 887-3128

Dude Ranchers Association (serving all western states including Colorado), (970) 223-8440

Colorado Mountain Club, (303) 279-5643

Denver Audubon Society, (303) 696-0877

Colorado Dept. of Regulatory Agencies (outfitters registration office for hunting and fishing), (303) 894-7778

Colorado Outfitters Association, (303) 841-7760

"Lakes of Colorado" is a set of two one-hour videos oriented toward family vacations. They cover 40 lakes and provide relevant information on things such as camping and fishing. Produced by Tenderfoot Productions, 45 Plainsview Road, Boulder, (303) 444-7780, the videos cost $19.95 each or $35 for the set. They're available at local Gart Brothers and other outing stores, or by calling (800) 484-2458.

Although Denver is on the plains, it's only a little more than an hour or so from some of the best skiing on the continent.

Ski Country

Admit it. You've envisioned spending your days gliding down pristine, sunlit mountains and your nights snuggled cozily, brandy in hand, by a roaring fire. In Colorado Ski Country USA, the dream is just moments away from downtown Denver.

Although Denver is on the plains, it's only a little more than an hour or so from some of the best skiing on the continent. In good snow years (and with the help of snowmaking) the ski season stretches from mid-October through June. Remember, snow can be falling like crazy in the mountains while it's 60 degrees and sunny in Denver. Ski season traditionally runs from Thanksgiving to mid-April.

Colorado is home to 26 ski areas, ranging from rope-tows to world-famous resorts such as Aspen and Steamboat Springs. Seven major areas are daytrips from Denver, including Vail, one of the country's premier destination ski resorts. Overnight trips offer even more variety, but it's nice to be able to avoid the cost of lodging and still ski a variety of slopes.

If, despite all the descriptions of champagne powder and unbelievable scenery, downhill skiing just isn't your thing, don't despair. The resorts have realized that not everybody skis, and they've come up with winter activities for nonskiers. Sans skis, you can ride the chairlift up to the Lodge at Sunspot at Winter Park simply to enjoy the view and have lunch, then ride back down again. Other widely available winter activities include ice skating, snowmobiling, snowshoeing, horse-drawn sleigh rides and dogsledding.

Cross-country skiing is very popular and getting more so. Groomed cross-country tracks are available at most downhill areas and many backcountry trailheads — including some that connect with the 10th Mountain Trail Association Hut System, which was built to train the U.S. elite ski corps for World War II alpine assault. Some of these are within a few hours' drive from Denver.

All the big ski areas offer adult and child lessons, childcare and specialized lessons; call the general information number given for each resort for prices and special packages. We've given prices for the 1998-99 season. At press time, 1999-2000 prices hadn't been announced yet, but they typically go up $1 to $2 every year. Discounted lift tickets are sold at Front Range King Soopers, Albertsons and Safeway supermarkets, Total gasoline stations and REI sporting goods stores. Availability varies, so call ahead.

The fun doesn't stop when the snow melts. There are as many things to do and sights to see in summer as in winter. Mountain biking? How about an easy lift up with your bike on the gondola and a wild ride down. Music festivals? Ski slopes make great outdoor amphitheaters in the summer. Boating? There's nothing like a mountain lake or reservoir ringed in jagged peaks.

During the past 10 years or so, most of Colorado's ski areas have concentrated on becoming year-round resorts. In fact, says Colorado Ski Country spokesperson Lynn Bronikowski, Colorado resorts consider cruise vacations to be their stiffest competition so they're doing all they can to make sure the slopes remain the vacation of choice. As a result, ski resorts account for about $3.3 billion a year in tourism dollars.

To appeal to a wide audience, resorts have developed golf courses and established annual festivals and events such as the annual WestFest at Copper Mountain and A Taste of Vail. Drifting over the Vail Valley in a hot-air balloon is a great way to spend the afternoon. And the more than 50 miles of paved bike paths that extend from Breckenridge to Vail are unsurpassed.

It's crucial to take altitude into consideration when traveling to the mountains. Even folks accustomed to Denver's 5,280 feet above sea level can get dizzy after a high-speed chairlift ride to 12,000 feet. Drink plenty of water, give yourself time to adjust, and slow down if you get a headache or nauseated. Alcohol makes matters worse, so take it easy.

Also, no one should set out on backcountry trails, either on foot or on skis, without sound knowledge of avalanche awareness, direction-finding skills and adequate clothing, food and water. Even people going on daytrips should be prepared to spend a night outside, as weather conditions in the mountains change in seconds. Local bookstores are filled with trail guides — buy one that has basic safety information as well as backcountry routes. And always let someone know where you're going and when you expect to be back. If you want to enjoy the great outdoors when the snow is gone, see our Great Outdoors chapter for hiking, mountain biking and climbing information.

Eldora Mountain Resort, near Boulder, is covered in *The Insiders' Guide® to Boulder and Rocky Mountain National Park*. For more information on ski areas, see *The Insiders' Guide® to Colorado's Mountains*.

We've listed and described below some ski areas that make feasible daytrips from Denver. We've included information about winter and summer activities, dining, shopping and accommodations, should you decide to extend your daytrip into a weekend or longer.

Skiing is certainly recreation, however, and if you're a beginner or a want-to-be beginner, you may want to know about a couple of the information sources that can help you get into the sport.

Colorado Ski Country USA, (303) 837-0793, a trade association for all the ski resorts in the state, publishes the *Colorado Ski Country Consumer Guide*. Within about 130 pages, it contains a lot of the information you want to know about skiing in Colorado. Colorado Ski Country USA will mail it to you free if you give them a call and ask for it.

You may also want to know about **Sniagrab** (bargains spelled backward), the big annual ski equipment and apparel sale held every year by Gart Brothers Sporting Goods outlets around Greater Denver. It starts on the Saturday before Labor Day and runs through much of September. You can find some fine deals on new and used equipment.

One of the best ways to get into skiing is to link up with a ski club. For the best overall source of local ski clubs, try the **National Ski Club News**. To get a list of local ski clubs, all you have to do is send your request and a self-addressed, stamped envelope to National Ski Club News, P.O. Box 17385, Denver 80217.

We've given resource phone numbers in each section and at the end of the chapter as well. Most phone numbers are in the (970) area code, although a few resorts retain Denver direct-dial numbers and some have toll-free (800) numbers. In general, for activities on the ski mountain itself, call the resort; for lodging, dining and other activities, call the chamber of commerce.

Loveland

The closest major ski area to Denver, Loveland is at the Eisenhower Tunnel, an easy hour's drive west on I-70. Take Exit 216, just before the tunnel entrance. Loveland, the ski area (as opposed to the town, which is miles away on the plains), is strictly for skiing — there's no lodging, and there's very little in the way of restaurants. However, a traditional cafeteria-style lunch is available on the mountain with deli fare, soups, baked goods and specialty pizzas.

New since 1998 is a 5,000 square foot shopping space that sells everything ski and snowboard related. Here you'll find clothes, gloves, skis, boards and the like.

Loveland also grew in 1998 with the addition of the world's highest quad lift: more than 12,600 feet above sea level. It serves 450 acres of expert terrain, bringing the total to 1,265 acres served by lifts.

With an average annual snowfall of 385 inches and lower prices than other close-in areas, there's plenty to pull you off the highway before the tunnel. Snowboarders enjoy a snowboard-only park. Ladies get special treatment weekly January through March with a women's-only lift ticket and all-day instruction and video analysis for $54. Loveland opened an expanded and renovated rental shop in 1997, featuring the addition of telemark rentals. Loveland also offers an end-of-day bonus — no tunnel traffic. One-day lift tickets are $37 adult, suggested Front Range discount price $29. The direct-dial phone number from Denver is (303) 571-5580.

Berthoud Pass

After closing in 1993 due to lawsuits, fines and, finally, bankruptcy, Berthoud Pass reopened in January 1998. The terrain is perched at the top of Berthoud Pass, a winding mountain pass over which skiers must traverse to reach Winter Park resort.

The base area sits at 11,340 feet, and affords truly spectacular views of surrounding mountains. The base also is where winter and summer vacationers stop to take a picture and experience the dizzying effects of oxygen deprivation. But the altitude doesn't stop the brave at heart, who enjoy Berthoud's challenging and seriously steep terrain (not the place for neophytes with only one green run).

The 1998-99 season opened with two lifts and four shuttle buses serving 1,000 acres of terrain on 65 runs. Seventy percent of Berthoud's runs are expert. The 1998-99 price of $28 is a bargain by ski resort standards, but likely will rise. The resort phone number is (970) 726-0287.

Food choices are limited to a cafeteria in the baselodge and **Pauly's Grill**, where you can get a 99-cent bowl of chili or something else off the full-service restaurant and bar menu. There also are a few good options in Empire, located about 30 minutes east of the ski area. **The Peck House**, 83 Sunny Avenue, is fine dining, while **Jenny's**, 4 W. Park Avenue, is more laid-back standard American fare. Or in nearby Georgetown (off I-70), try the **Happy Cooker**, 412 6th Street, for traditional American breakfast; **The Raven Hill Mining Company**, 612 6th Street, for lunch or dinner barbecue and the like; or **The Red Ram**, 606 6th Street, a neighborhood-type joint with burgers and other basic fare

Getting There

To get to Berthoud Pass from Denver, take I-70 west to the Empire exit. (Watch for Empire's famous speed traps!) Follow U.S. Hwy 40 north up the switchbacks to the top of Berthoud Pass, where you'll find the baselodge.

Winter Park

Although it's 70 miles away from Denver (less than two hours from DIA), Winter Park is a City of Denver park — hence the name. The resort (Colorado's fifth-largest in skier visits and a favorite with Front Range skiers) was developed in the 1940s and doubled its capacity in the '70s. In 1997-98, Winter Park launched its terrain opening: 435 acres of ungroomed backcountry called Vasquez Cirque. The 1992 opening of Parsenn Bowl, a treeless, sunny alpine expanse of largely ungroomed terrain, added 200 acres. Winter Park is among the more friendly and laid-back of Colorado resorts and doesn't suffer from some of the snobbery of other destinations, such as Vail and Aspen.

In all there are three interconnected mountains, a high alpine bowl and Vasquez Cirque, all accessible with one lift ticket. Winter Park and Vasquez Ridge offer a mix of beginner, intermediate and advanced cruising runs. Mary Jane is where mogul enthusiasts test their knees (No Pain, No Jane, as the advertisement goes). The high-alpine Parsenn Bowl, at 12,060 feet, is known for its gladed tree skiing and above-timberline vistas.

Useful Numbers

Winter Park Resort, (970) 726-5514; direct dial from Greater Denver, (303) 892-0961

INSIDERS' TIP

Buy reduced-price lift tickets at Greater Denver locations including King Soopers, Albertsons and Safeway supermarkets; Total gasoline stations; and Gart Bros., Christy's and REI sporting goods stores.

Snow Conditions, (303) 572-SNOW

Winter Park/Fraser Valley Chamber of Commerce, (970) 726-4118; direct dial from Greater Denver, (303) 422-0666

Getting There

To get to Winter Park from Denver, drive west on I-70, exit onto U.S. Highway 40 W. at the Empire town exit (watch out for those speed traps) and continue over the majestic Berthoud Pass to Winter Park, which sits at the base of the north side of the pass. There are two entrances to the ski area. Expert skiers turn off at Mary Jane, while beginners and intermediates start the day at the main Winter Park base. The town of Winter Park is another few miles down the road. Fraser, where locals shop for necessities (Safeway, a supermarket, is located there) is 5 miles farther. There's plenty available for lunch on the mountain, and dinner options are to be found in town. Virtually all lodging, dining and shopping is situated along U.S. Highway 40 and is visible from the road.

If you balk at driving over a pass, you can make the trip by train. On weekends, the **Denver Rio Grande Ski Train** departs Denver's Union Station at 7:15 AM, dropping skiers within walking distance of the lifts, and leaves Winter Park at 4:15 PM just after the lifts close. The train runs weekends only during ski season and Friday and Saturday during February and March. The trip takes two hours each way and passes through the Moffat Tunnel. Originally, trains traveled over the Continental Divide via the Rollins Pass Road over Corona Pass. The 6.2-mile Moffat Tunnel was completed in 1927, drastically shortening travel time between Denver and the mountains. Cost is $35 to $40 same-day roundtrip for adults, depending on the month, and $60 to 65 in first-class. Discounted lift tickets are available on the train. For information and reservations call (303) 296-I-SKI.

Skiing

The town of Winter Park has grown up alongside the resort, but both the town and ski area remain casual. A free shuttle connects Winter Park and nearby Fraser, a great place to party aprés-ski and get a local taste of Colorado resort towns.

Seven high-speed quad lifts carry skiers and snowboarders to more than 2,500 acres of terrain. Snowboarders have three terrain stations ranging from beginner to advanced, plus two halfpipes. Non-skiers can ride the Zephyr Express lift to the top of Winter Park ski area and meet the rest of the group for lunch at the beautiful Lodge at Sunspot. One-day lift tickets are $50 adult (1998-99 price).

Winter Park is renowned for its ski program for the disabled and is home to the National Sports Center for the Disabled. Its 39 full-time staff members and more than 1,000 volunteers can handle the needs of more than 40 different disabilities.

Cross-Country Skiing

Downvalley from the downhill area is a top-notch **cross-country center** called Devil's Thumb Ranch, (970) 726-8231 or (800) 933-4339. Skate-skiers love the 105 kilometers of groomed trails at Devil's Thumb, which fan out into the forest from an expansive meadow. To get there, drive west from Winter Park to the town of Fraser and turn right onto County Road 83. Tickets are $12 for adults, $10 for ages 7 to 12 and seniors 60 and older, and free for children 6 and younger. Lessons and equipment rental are available. Devil's Thumb Ranch is open year round, with hearty dining in the Ranch House Restaurant & Saloon and private or bunkhouse-style accommodations available. Ask about moonlight sleigh rides and dogsled rides in the winter and horseback riding and trout fishing in the summer.

Backcountry skiers like the trails on top of Berthoud Pass and the Jim Creek Trail that

INSIDERS' TIP

With ski traffic mounting every year, think about renting a condo for the weekend to avoid day-skiing hassles. Sleep in on Saturday and take a shuttle to the slopes. On Sunday, be the first on the slopes — and the first to leave — to miss the Sunday afternoon rush.

Photo: Daily Camera/Jay Quadracci

Skiers have their choice of runs or trails within a few hours' drive of Denver.

begins directly across from the Winter Park ski area. No one should set out on these trails without knowledge of avalanche awareness, adequate clothing, food and water and a trail guide or maps.

Dogsled Rides and Other Winter Activities

Dogsled rides are a newly popular winter activity in Winter Park. The price is high, but Insiders say it's worth it. Dog Sled Rides of Winter Park, (970) 726-8326, charges $140 for two people for a one-hour ride; a child can accompany you for another $10. If you'd rather be pulled by horses than dogs, go for a **sleigh ride**. Jim's Sleigh Rides, (970) 726-0944, takes as many as 20 bundled-up guests per sleigh past the historic Cozens Ranch, along the Fraser River, with a stop in the woods for refreshments. Cost is $14 for adults, $11 for ages 12 and younger. Toddlers 2 and younger ride free. There's also Dinner at the Barn, (970)

726-4923, and Dashing Through the Snow, (970) 726-5376. They do hot chocolate tours and dinner tours for around $50 per person, BYOB.

Winter Park also has a free public **ice-skating** rink (rentals can be arranged at a nearby store). Ice skaters can try the Fraser Ice Rink, 601 Zerex (U.S. Highway 40 just before the Safeway Plaza), (970) 726-8882. The rink is outdoors and features bonfires at night.

You can also ride a **snowcat** to the top of the mountain for $22 for adults and $17 for kids (3 to 13) and seniors (62 and older). There are three tours that offer lunch stops; call (970) 726-5514 ext. 1727.

Snowshoe tours, including shoes and poles, offer a ride up on the lift and a gentle descent through wooded terrain. Cost is $25 per person and not recommended for kids younger than 7. Call (970) 726-5514 ext. 1727.

Snowmobile dinner tours start at 5 and 7 PM and run over three mountains then back to the Lodge at Sunspot for dinner in the lounge. Cost is $45 to $65 depending on dinner. Call (970) 726-5514 ext. 1727.

Summer Fun

Every summer the green slopes of Winter Park are the site of acclaimed musical events. **The American Music Festival** has featured such popular performers as Bonnie Raitt, John Prine and the Nitty Gritty Dirt Band, while the **Winter Park Jazz Festival** attracts an equally stellar lineup of great jazz musicians, including Harry Connick Jr. The American Music Festival is usually the second weekend in July, and the Jazz Fest follows the next weekend. If you go, bring rain gear.

Other summer activities available for less than $10 — check 1999 summer prices at (970) 726-5514 — include the **Alpine Slide** at the base of the mountain (Colorado's longest); **Mountainside Mini-Golf**, located at the base of the Zephyr lift, offering a Winter Park Valley history theme with railroad and mining holes; and the **Human Maze**, also located at the base of Zephyr, known for trapping adults while kids get through in record time.

Mountain Biking

Winter Park has worked hard to attract mountain bikers and is known as Mountain Bike Capital USA. More than 600 miles of marked, mapped and maintained trails wind through the Fraser Valley. At the ski area itself, riders can take the easy way up via the Zephyr Express chairlift to connect with another 45 miles of steep, exciting trails. Pick up a trail map at local bike stores or the Chamber of Commerce Visitor Center on the east side of U.S. Highway 40 downtown. Bike rentals are available at any number of local stores. Try the Winter Park Sports Shop, in town at 78336 U.S. Hwy 40, (970) 726-5554, with a good selection and knowledgeable staff, or Winter Park Rental and Repair Shop, at the base of the mountain, (970) 726-5514 ext. 1809. Tips on where to go are free from knowledgeable staff.

The Fraser River Trail is paved and the easiest, most mellow ride for families; it's good for in-line skaters too. Valley trails go up from there, to rides even locals find frightening. Helmets, of course, are highly recommended. A

Park Pass for all activities, including the Zephyr lift for mountain biking, is $35 for all day or $25 for a half-day. Otherwise, a Zephyr ticket for mountain biking is $16 all day or $6 for one ride.

Golf and Other Recreation

Golfers will enjoy the beautiful 18-hole Pole Creek Golf Club, (970) 726-8847, about 10 miles northwest of Winter Park in the town of Tabernash. Pole Creek consistently rates as the No. 1 public course in Colorado. There also is the Grand Lake Golf Course, (970) 627-8008, about 40 miles farther west. It's not quite Pole Creek, but it's easier to get on.

Non-golfers can choose among **fishing, hiking, horseback riding, jeeping** and **rafting**. Much of the Fraser Valley that isn't privately owned falls within the boundaries of the Arapaho National Forest. The Winter Park/ Fraser Valley Chamber of Commerce can provide more information, or contact the National Forest Service in Denver at (303) 275-5350.

Dining

Winter Park has traditionally been a day-use area for Denver families and doesn't have the range of restaurants and stores that the Summit County areas or Vail can offer. But things are picking up. **Dinner at the Barn** sleighrides, mentioned earlier, provide more than a meal: It's a horse-drawn sleigh ride through the woods and meadows of an 80-acre ranch, where dinner — with linens and china — is eaten by the light of a kerosene lantern in the horse stalls. After dinner there's live musical entertainment (guitars, harmonica, washboard, banjo). In summer, you make the trip by horse-drawn show wagon. Advance reservations are required. Cost is $49 for adults, $39 for children ages 4 to 12. There's a $5 lap fee for ages 1 to 3, and it's free for those younger than 1. Prices are slightly higher with a credit card, lower in the summer and don't include tip. Group discounts are available. Call (970) 726-4923. If you go and want to enjoy a bottle of wine or other spirits, you're encouraged to bring your own.

Gasthaus Eichler, in downtown Winter Park on U.S. Highway 40, (970) 726-5133, is noted for its Austrian and German specialties.

Across the street is **Arpeggios**, (970) 726-5402, which offers wonderful Northern Italian fare. Try the Chicken Fantasia, with a cream sauce, nuts and grapes tossed with pasta. Reservations are suggested at either place.

Fontenot's Cajun Cafe, (970) 726-4021, is a local favorite located downtown in the Park Plaza (on U.S. 40), serving lunch and dinner, including fresh fish, pasta dishes, crawfish and gumbo. **Lodge at Sunspot**, (970) 726-5514 ext. 1727, at the top of Winter Park mountain, serves a four-course dinner ranging from $40 to $65. It's open Thursday through Saturday nights and more during holiday seasons. Reservations are suggested. It's a great experience if you're looking for something a little more memorable.

The **Moffat Bagel Station** at 78437 U.S. 40, (970) 726-5530, serves great bagels with tons of varieties. Try the cinnamon crust, which tastes like a donut without all the fat. The coffee's good too. **The Shed** at 78672 U.S. 40, across from the Motel 8, (970) 726-9912, is a popular margarita-drinking, pool-playing hangout. Happy-hour margarita prices are good, and the Southwestern-Mexican fare is original and filling.

For more casual dining and nightlife — actually it can get wild at times — there's the **Crooked Creek Saloon & Eatery** at 401 Zerex Avenue off U.S. 40 in Fraser (970) 726-5727, which serves Mexican and American food and no small amount of beer. **The Last Waltz Restaurant**, 78336 U.S. 40, (970) 726-4877, has great green chili and other Mexican specialties as well as a continental menu and killer desserts baked by owner Nancy Waltz. Waltz also owns Arpeggios. A nice touch is the senior citizen's menu with reduced prices.

Shopping

The stores in Winter Park provide essentials if you've forgotten your hat or goggles or want to rent skates, snowshoes or a mountain bike. There's a nifty little bookstore, **Curiosity Books** at 519 Zerex in Fraser, and a sweet bakery, **Carver's** (tucked near the back of Cooper Square in the center of town). There are other small boutiques, but nothing on the order of Breckenridge or especially Vail, where shopping is an event unto itself. Watch for great deals on ski equipment and clothing in summer or at the end of ski season.

Accommodations

Accommodations in Winter Park range from condominiums on the mountainside to bed and breakfasts in town. **Winter Park Central Reservations**, (303) 892-0961 (direct dial from Greater Denver) or (800) 453-2525, can arrange lodging in more than 50 condominiums, motels, hotels, lodges, inns and bed and breakfasts.

Engelmann Pines, (970) 726-4632 or (800) 992-9512, a bed and breakfast run by a friendly couple, is pleasant and moderately priced ($65 to $115 double). Heinz and Margaret Engel have furnished the place with heirloom furniture brought from Europe, and they offer guests a separate kitchen and reading/TV room. If full-service hotels are what you're after, check into the **Vintage Hotel**, (800) 472-7017. There's a pool and restaurant on site. The closest thing in Winter Park to ski-in/ski-out is the **Iron Horse Resort and Retreat**, (970) 726-8851. Its restaurant, **Winston's**, is known for Beef Wellington, creative pasta dishes and single-malt scotches (you don't have to stay there to eat there). The bulk of available lodgings are condominiums in larger complexes. **Beaver Village Resort**, (800) 666-0281, is one well-run and centrally located although not lavish choice. **The Viking Lodge**, (970) 726-8885, is great for small budgets, and it's clean and well-maintained.

Summit County

The Summit County ski areas include Breckenridge, Keystone, Arapahoe Basin and Copper Mountain. Collectively, these four areas attract more skiers than any other ski destination in North America. And why not? There's tremendous variety, good shopping and restaurants, dependably fine snow and easy access from Greater Denver.

In years past, skiers could buy one ticket for A-Basin, Breckenridge and Keystone. Now, only Breckenridge and Keystone are interchangeable. To ski Copper, you must buy a Copper Mountain lift pass. The 1998-99 ticket price was $52 for adult one-day at Keystone,

Breckenridge or Copper Mountain. A-Basin is only $40. If you plan to be a frequent user, check out the Ski 3 card (available at Christy Sports stores in the Front Range and Frisco), or the money-saving Copper Card (800) 458-8386, which costs only $15 at King Soopers stores in Denver. Front Range skiers know that discount cards are a great way to save cash.

Summit County is about 1¹/₂ hours west of Denver on I-70. The Eisenhower Tunnel, opened in 1973, saves motorists 10 miles of driving over Loveland Pass on U.S. Highway 6, a steep, twisting road. Still, U.S. 6 is hard to beat for sheer scenic grandeur, as it crosses the Continental Divide and drops down past Arapahoe Basin before flattening out as it heads toward Keystone and the towns of Dillon and Silverthorne. When time permits and road conditions are favorable, this is a recommended alternate route and the most direct approach to Arapahoe Basin.

The crowds have been coming to Summit County in the summer in record numbers. Among other things, they come for the more than 50 miles of well-marked, paved bike path that winds through Summit County from Breckenridge to Frisco to Copper Mountain and beyond. It is an unmatched public amenity in Summit County, luring even daytrippers from Denver with its motor vehicle-free lanes and grand mountain scenery.

If you're planning a trip to Summit County, you might find it worth your while to read through the entire Summit County section that follows. We've treated each Summit County area separately, listing first ski information, then other winter and summer activities, and finally restaurants, shopping and lodging. But things are close enough so that a person might ski at Breckenridge, eat in Dillon and stay overnight in Frisco. An excellent free public transportation system, the **Summit Stage**, makes getting around without a car easy; pick up a schedule at the Visitors Center in Frisco, 011 S. Summit Boulevard (at the intersection of Summit Boulevard and Main Street) or Dillon, on U.S. Highway 6 about 1 mile south of I-70 at the Dillon Dam Road. The visitors centers are open daily year round.

Breckenridge

Useful phone numbers

Snow Conditions, (970) 453-6118

Breckenridge Ski Resort General Information, (970) 453-5000, (800) 789-SNOW

Breckenridge Outdoor Education Center (Disabled Skiing), (970) 453-6422

Breckenridge Resort Chamber, (970) 453-6018, (800) 221-1091

Breckenridge Resort Chamber Guest Services & Activities, (970) 453-5579

Town of Breckenridge Trolley Information, (970) 453-2251

Getting There

To get to Breckenridge, take the Frisco Exit from I-70 and drive south on Colo. Highway 9 for 9 miles.

Skiing

Breckenridge, the oldest and largest of the Summit County communities, is a former mining town that got its start when gold was discovered nearby in 1859. A national historic district, Breckenridge boasts a Main Street lined with handsome Victorian buildings that now house great shops, art galleries and restaurants. Breckenridge has 18 lifts and more than 2,000 skiable acres spread over four distinct peaks. It's the second-most popular ski mountain in North America. Snowboarding is permitted. There's close-in pay parking near the Peak 9 base, but most skiers park in one of the town's public lots and take the free shuttle to the slopes.

Vail Resorts spent $14 million at Breckenridge during the summer of 1998, adding TenMile Station, a 300-seat restaurant at Peak 9 midstation.

Cross-country Skiing and Other Winter Activities

There is a **Nordic skiing center** adjacent to the ski area; call (970) 453-6855 for more information. Other winter activities in Breckenridge include the usual — sleigh rides, snowmobiling, ice skating — and the unusual — the annual **Baileys International Snow Sculpture Championships** every January.

Ice-skating is available at Maggie Pond at the Village Hotel, (970) 453-9601, and Breckenridge Ice Rink, a new rink built in 1997, (970) 547-9974.

Snowmobilers can book rides with Good Times at (970) 453-7604 or (800) 477-0144; Tiger Run (970) 453-2231 or (800) 318-3186; or Eagle's Nest, (970) 468-0677. **Snowcat** tours are out of Ski Cooper, a resort in Summit County, (970) 486-2277.

For **disabled skiers**, adaptive skiing with special seats and equipment is offered by the Breckenridge Outdoor Education Center (Disabled Skiing), (970) 453-6422.

Summer Fun

In summer, there's **hiking** in the Arapaho National Forest and outstanding **golf** at the Jack Nicklaus-designed municipal course, the Breckenridge Golf Club. In 1991, *Golf Digest* named the Breckenridge Golf Club the top public course in Colorado. Call (970) 453-9104.

The Pioneer Trail is an easy and popular trail for **mountain bikers**. Start at the top of the Colorado SuperChair and wind down the front side of Peak 8, through thick forests and wide-open ski runs. Breckenridge offers lift rides up for mountain bikers.

The **Breckenridge Recreation Center** at 880 Airport Road, (970) 453-1734, is open every day and has indoor and outdoor tennis courts, a pool, racquetball courts, a steam room, a hot tub and separate locker room facilities for men and women. Visitors can purchase a daily admission.

If you'd like to see the Ten Mile Range of the Rockies from the back of a horse rather than on foot, **Breckenridge Stables**, (970) 453-4438, prides itself on its gentle horses. Several different rides are available, including two-hour rides for $32, a breakfast ride and a gourmet dinner ride for $40.

The Blue River, which runs through Breckenridge, is a favorite **fly-fishing** locale. Fishing licenses are required and can be purchased at various locations in town, i.e., sporting goods stores where fishing equipment and bait are sold. A water activity in Breckenridge that's fun for the whole family is **paddleboating** on Maggie Pond in The Village at Breckenridge.

Several once-booming townsites near Breckenridge still hold allure for visitors. Also within the town itself are a number of buildings reputed to be haunted. Call the resort's main number for information, (970) 453-5000.

The **Breckenridge Outdoor Education Center**, (970) 453-6422, also offers disabled visitors summer recreation events such as kayaking and ropes courses.

Dining

Breckenridge has superb dining and shopping. Among the fine restaurants in town are the **St. Bernard Inn**, 103 S. Main Street, (970) 453-2572, for northern Italian food (dinner only); **Pierre's River Walk Cafe**, 137 S. Main Street, (970) 453-0989, the creation of a French-trained chef, serving contemporary French and American cuisine with a seasonally changing menu; and **Cafe Alpine**, 106 Adams Street, (970) 453-8218, noted for its tapas bar, which features appetizers and 40 wines by the glass. Reservations are strongly suggested at all of these places. One of the state's first brewpubs, **Breckenridge Brewery & Pub**, is at 600 S. Main Street, (970) 453-1550 — try the Avalanche Ale or their pub-brewed root beer. Locals favor the **Blue Moose Restaurant**, 540 S. Main Street, (970) 453-4859, for its affordable natural food and friendly atmosphere; and **Mi Casa Mexican Restaurant & Cantina**, 600 Park Avenue, (970) 453-2071, for its Mexican lunch and dinners (no reservations) with daily specials.

Shopping

Breckenridge's shopping also rates superlatives. A few hours spent walking up and down Main Street will acquaint you with the best the town has to offer. Of course there's the usual array of T-shirt and souvenir shops, but there also are numerous spots that offer something special. Two galleries that would stand out anywhere are **Hibberd McGrath**, 101 N. Main Street, for fine crafts; and **Kinkopf Gallery**, 320 S. Main Street, for contemporary fine art, including paintings, sculpture, glasswork and pottery. You can get a complete list of local galleries at the Visitor Information Center, 309 N. Main Street.

You won't want to miss **The Twisted Pine**, 411 S. Main Street, for Western apparel, especially men's clothing and hats. For women's gear, check out their shop at 100 S. Main Street.

Blue Harry, 421 S. Main Street, is a unique clothing store that offers unisex jackets, belts, jewelry and other accessories, including their own exclusive shirts. Their men's and women's clothing has a distinctive Western, outdoorsy look. They also have a store in Vail. For a free catalog, call (800) 548-0480. **Goods**, 105 S. Main Street, is the most popular basic clothing shop in town.

Accommodations

Accommodations in Breckenridge range from luxury condominiums to Victorian-style bed and breakfasts in historic homes. The **Williams House Bed & Breakfast**, 303 N. Main Street, (970) 453-2975, is an especially well-appointed 19th-century home with period furniture and antiques, but guests also enjoy the modern pleasure of an outdoor hot tub. A wheelchair-accessible Victorian cottage with Jacuzzi, fireplace and sitting area is also available. Winter rates range from $100 to $250, and it's for nonsmoking adults only. The Breckenridge Resort Chamber can provide information about the other bed and breakfasts in town or book a condominium or hotel room. The **Village at Breckenridge**, (800) 800-7829, is a huge complex with athletic facilities. **Pine Ridge Condominiums**, (800) 333-8833, have full kitchens and washer/dryers in the units. The complex has two common hot tubs and a pool. The **Lodge at Breckenridge** has the distinction of being the world's highest athletic club and spa. The fitness center features individualized training for all levels, (970) 453-9300. The new **River Mountain Lodge**, (970) 453-4711, offers the convenience of being in town and is of high quality. **Allaire Timbers**

Inn, (970) 453-7530, is a high-end bed and breakfast with each room decorated individually. **Beaver Run Resort**, (800) 525-2253, is a ski-in/ski-out resort that's popular with visitors.

Keystone, Frisco, Dillon, Silverthorne

Getting There

The exits for Dillon and Frisco are directly off I-70. For Keystone, exit onto U.S. Highway 6 at the Dillon/Silverthorne Exit 205. Keystone is 6 miles down the road.

Skiing

Keystone is a self-contained resort, but what contains it are the municipalities of Dillon, Silverthorne and Frisco. When Keystone opened for business in 1969-70, it was widely considered a good spot for beginners and intermediates but not challenging enough for experts. The addition of steep and bumpy North Peak in 1984 and the expansion into the powder-filled glades of The Outback and The Outback Bowls in the '90s have greatly changed the character of the area and made it more attractive to advanced skiers. Keystone is noted for its snowmaking capability, which often allows it to open earlier than its neighbors. It is also the only ski area in Summit County to offer night skiing, until 9 PM. New in 1996-97 was the availability of snowboarding, including specially designated terrain, which is also lit. In summer 1998, Keystone owner Vail Resorts spent $18 million on the mountain. The biggest project was Keystone's fifth high-speed quad, which replaced the Santiago triple chair.

Keystone runs daily NASTAR races, including a self-timing system that allows skiers to improve with practice runs.

Keystone is in the midst of a multi-year $400 million base-area development that will add hundreds of residences, shops and a planned 250-room grand hotel. Called the Village at River Run, the multiphase project will include five different residential communities and facilities such as a library and community center.

Cross-Country Skiing and Other Winter Activities

A **Nordic center** at Keystone provides 18 kilometers of groomed trails and access to 57 kilometers of backcountry trails in the Arapaho National Forest. Rentals, lessons and tours are offered, including a full-moon tour with après-ski beverage. The Keystone Cross Country Center is 2.2 miles east of Keystone on Montezuma Road next to the Ski Tip Lodge. The Keystone Activities Center, (970) 668-0866, can provide more detailed information. There is a Nordic center, designed by Olympic silver-medalist Bill Koch, in Frisco, too, with 35 kilometers of trails near Dillon Reservoir. Call (970) 668-0866 for prices and rental information.

If you'd rather strike out on your own, some of the best cross-country skiing in Summit County is found by continuing along the road to Montezuma past the Ski Tip Lodge. Peru Creek (for beginners) and St. Johns and Wild Irishman Mine (for intermediates) are favorite tours for Front Range skiers. Remember to take precautions: let someone know where you're going and when you expect to return.

As for other winter activities, Keystone is home to Keystone Lake, the largest maintained outdoor **skating** lake in the country. It's right in the center of the village, and skate rentals are available. **Sleigh rides** and **snowmobiling** can be arranged by calling the Keystone Activities Center, (970) 668-0866. For a chilly thrill ride that all ages will love, try **tubing** in Keystone's designated area. For about $10 (adult price), you get to slide down the mountain on an inner tube and catch pulley rides back to the top.

Summer Fun

In summer, Dillon Reservoir — locally known as Lake Dillon — provides landlocked Coloradans with one of the state's greatest recreational assets, a 3,000-acre reservoir (the country's highest) ringed by mountains. The lake can accommodate sailboats, kayaks and fishing boats; charters are available. Weather and water level permitting, the marina is open from the end of May through the last weekend in October.

Swimming is allowed but only for the hearty as this mountain reservoir is ice-cold even in August. For information, call the Dillon Marina at (970) 468-5100.

There's **golf** at the Keystone Ranch Golf Course, (800) 451-5930, designed by Robert Trent Jones Jr., and at the more mountainous Eagles Nest Golf Club in Silverthorne, (970) 468-0681.

The main **fishing** artery in Summit County is the Blue River, where anglers hope for trout. Contact a local fishing shop or the Colorado Division of Wildlife for more information, (303) 291-7533.

Mountain bikers can sign up for a Dirt Camp weekend, in which elite-level coaching and training techniques are taught by world-class professionals. Cost is nearly $300 and includes meals and lodging. Call (800) 711-DIRT.

New in summer 1997 were **llama lunch treks**, where you have the fun and the llama carries your lunch. The trek stops for hiking along the way. Call (800) 354-4FUN. Prices for the 1998 summer season were $38 for adults and $24 for kids.

Keystone offers **International Cuisine cooking classes** in winter and summer, (800) 354-4FUN. The Thursday evening class is $50 and includes the meal you prepare. Multi-day classes are more elaborate. For around $525 per person, they include three nights' lodging, breakfasts and dinners.

Women of all fitness levels will find a summer program tailored to their needs at Keystone Resort's Women's Mountain Tune-Up Mini Spa. Cost hovers around $900 and includes four nights' lodging, meals and activities. Call (800) 354-4FUN.

Dining

The **Alpenglow Stube**, atop Keystone's North Peak, serves Bavarian-accented contemporary cuisine for lunch and dinner and is reached via enclosed gondola chairlift. The Stube is closed during the spring and autumn shoulder seasons, when the gondola doesn't operate. The rustic **Keystone Ranch**, a restored ranch with six-course dinners, is another very classy place to eat. It's open year round. To make a reservation at either restaurant (required), call Keystone's Dining & Ac-

Photo: Ski The Summit/Bob Winsett

Colorado's ski country resorts offer winter sleigh rides.

tivities Center, (970) 468-4130 or (800) 451-5930.

The **Old Dillon Inn**, (970) 468-2791, on Colo. Highway 9 in Silverthorne, is always packed on weekends with skiers who come for the Mexican food and margaritas, the impressive 19th-century bar and the rollicking music. For a quieter evening, cook your own steaks on the grill at **The Mint** in Silverthorne, 341 Blue River Parkway, (970) 468-5247. In one of the oldest buildings in Summit County, The Mint is a fun-for-the-whole-family dining spot. For a hearty pre-ski or pre-sail breakfast, take your appetite to the **Arapahoe Cafe**, 626 Lake Dillon Drive, Dillon, (970) 468-0873. The **Snake River Saloon**, 23074 U.S. Highway 6 in Keystone, (970) 468-2788, is locally famous for its spirited aprés-ski and late-night entertainment. The **Ski Tip Lodge**, (970) 496-4950 or (800) 354-4FUN, offers American regional cuisine, including several wild game dishes, in a rustic atmosphere. This historic spot was Colorado's first skiers' lodge.

Der Fondue Chessel, (800) 354-4FUN, entertains diners with Bavarian music while serving them a Swiss-style four-course fondue dinner. Dinner sleigh and hay rides (winter and summer), (800) 354-4FUN, pull riders up to the **Soda Creek Homestead** and serve a Western-style meal while a cowboy performer leads the crowd in a sing-along. **Garden Room Steak House**, (970) 496-4386 or (800) 354-4FUN, is in the village at Keystone.

Shopping

The factory outlet stores in Silverthorne are reason enough to drive up from Denver. Clustered in three malls just off I-70 at Exit 205 are bargain outlets for 80 well-known manufacturers, including **Bass Shoes**, **Liz Claiborne**,

Starter Sports, Nike, OshKosh B'Gosh and **Miller Stockman Western Wear**. The stores are open seven days a week and claim a 40-percent average savings over retail. For information, call (970) 468-9440.

Accommodations

Accommodations in Keystone include the luxurious **Keystone Lodge** and the truly deluxe **Chateaux d'Mont**. There are also condominiums of all sizes and private homes available for rent. Contact Keystone Reservations, (970) 496-4242 or (800) 222-0188. The **Paradox Lodge**, (970) 468-9445, features a secluded 10,500-foot elevation and reasonable rates. The **Ski Tip Lodge**, (970) 496-4950, offers good access to cross-country trails in a funky, authentic Colorado setting.

Simpler but charming and comfortable lodging can be found in Frisco, Dillon and Silverthorne. The **Galena Street Mountain Inn**, (970) 668-3224 or (800) 248-9138, is a pretty, modern bed and breakfast in Frisco, tucked a half-block back from Main Street and near the bike path. Rooms cost around $80 to $150, depending on the season. Summit County Central Reservations, (970) 468-6222 or (800) 365-6365, can provide more possibilities.

The **Best Western Ptarmigan Lodge**, (970) 468-2341 or (800) 842-5939, is on Lake Dillon at 652 Lake Dillon Drive (take Exit 205 off I-70). The lodge has deluxe motel accommodations, kitchenettes, condominiums with fireplaces and serves continental breakfast year round. Rates vary, depending on the season and type of accommodation selected, but are generally mid-range for this area. Kids younger than 12 stay free. In the height of ski season, a five-night minimum stay may be required. Newly remodeled to be more wheelchair-accessible, the lodge now has a hot tub, sauna and more cable TV channels.

There is a second Best Western lodge in Summit County, the **Best Western Lake Dillon Lodge**, at 1202 N. Summit Boulevard in Frisco, (970) 668-5094 or (800) 727-0607. More of a full-service hotel than the Ptarmigan Lodge, it has large rooms, an indoor pool, a hot tub, a restaurant, a ski shop and a lounge on-site. It also has family rooms available with three double beds. Kids 18 and younger stay free.

Again, rates vary tremendously, but are moderate for the area and comparable with the Holiday Inn, described below.

The 215-room **Holiday Inn**, at 1129 N. Summit Boulevard in Frisco (across the street from the Best Western Lake Dillon Lodge), provides comfortable overnight accommodations in a location just off I-70 that's more convenient than scenic. There's an indoor pool, sauna, hot tub, restaurant, lounge, gift shop and ski shop on the premises, and you are also within walking distance of Frisco shops and restaurants. Rooms can cost anywhere from $60 to $175, depending on the season. Kids 18 and younger stay free. For reservations, call (800) 782-7669, or from Denver, (303) 573-6345. The local phone number is (970) 668-5000.

Both the Best Western Lake Dillon Lodge and the Holiday Inn are close to the bike path and a Summit Stage bus stop. To reach either hotel, take Exit 203 off I-70.

Arapahoe Basin

Useful Phone Numbers

Main number, (970) 486-0718
Reservations, (888) ARA-PAHO
Nursery/day care (18 months and older), (970) 468-0718

Getting there

To get to Arapahoe Basin, take I-70 to exit 205, Dillon/Silverthrone. Follow U.S. Highway 6 for 11 miles; Arapahoe Basin is 5 miles past Keystone.

Once part of Keystone, A-Basin, as it's called, was sold in 1998 to Dundee resorts. Situated 5 miles away from Keystone at a (gasp) base altitude of 10,800 feet above sea level, Arapahoe Basin is where Insiders head for unbeatable spring skiing. A-Basin is known for its late-season skiing. (It stayed open until August 10 in 1995 due to late snows.) It's not unusual late in the season to see skiers in shorts and T-shirts. A-Basin is characterized by tough terrain and tough weather conditions — but a good day here is a great day. Don't forget the sunscreen.

A-Basin is a full-service resort, if not a glam destination on par with Vail and Winter Park.

The most important thing you'll find here is great skiing (490 acres; 40 percent expert). There also is a cafeteria, bar, ski school, rental shop and retail store. For information, call the main number.

Copper Mountain

Useful Phone Numbers

Snow Report, (970) 968-2100 or (800) 789-7609

Copper Mountain Resort general information, (970) 968-2882 or (800) 458-8386

Getting There

Copper Mountain is about 75 miles west of Denver. To get there, take I-70 west and get off at Exit 195.

Skiing

Copper Mountain was constructed as a self-contained resort in the early 1970s. It is the home of Club Med's first North American ski center, and it's a very enticing place for intermediate and expert skiers, as more than half the trails are rated advanced.

In January 1996, Copper opened a new double lift that serves the 700-acre Copper Bowl. A second lift was opened in 1997, bringing the total to 21 lifts (three high-speed quads). The expansion makes Copper the biggest ski area in Summit County with more than 2,400 acres.

Copper spent $66 million on improvements in the summer of 1998. Most notable is the new six-passenger, high-speed chairlift, Super B. There's also a new daylodge at the base.

Copper has also put a great deal of effort into its ski school program, so beginners will feel comfortable here as well. Sometimes Copper even offers free skiing on its easiest lifts.

Rides on the K and L lifts are often free in January and April for those learning to ski or for parents teaching children. In all, K and L lifts access 53 acres of terrain. To find out when tickets are free, call (970) 968-2318.

The mountain is naturally divided between harder and easier skiing. Still, Copper has a reputation as a prime destination for serious skiers who are looking to maximize time on the slopes and are turned off by the glamorous atmosphere of Vail. Snowboarding is permitted; the resort's first snowboard park opened in 1996-97 and its second opened in 1999. A one-day adult lift ticket to Copper Mountain costs $52 (1998-99 price). "Copper Cards" cost only $15 at King Soopers grocery stores in Denver and are a great way to save up to $15 a day on tickets.

Cross-country Skiing and Other Winter Activities

The **cross-country skiing tracks** at Copper Mountain begin near the Union Creek base area and branch off into the rolling, wooded valleys of the Arapahoe National Forest. You can book rentals, lessons and overnight hut trips by calling (970) 968-2318 ext. 6342.

Dinner **sleighrides** are offered nightly in winter and in summer (on wheels) and include a gourmet meal mid-mountain. Call the Copper Mountain Stables at (970) 968-2318.

Summer Fun

The Copper Creek Golf Club is the highest-altitude championship **golf course** in America. (Elevation is 9,650 feet, meaning your ball will fly 15 to 20 percent farther than at sea level.) **Hikers, backpackers** and **horseback riders** enjoy challenging themselves on the Wheeler-Dillon Pack Trail, which begins across the highway from Copper Mountain and climbs rapidly into the rugged Gore Range in the Arapaho National Forest. You can arrange

INSIDERS' TIP

If you'd like to hike or ride a mountain bike into the wilderness around the Holy Cross Wilderness area near Vail, Aspen or Copper Mountain but aren't keen on sleeping in tents, the 10th Mountain Division Hut Association huts are open in the summer from July 1 through September 30. Call (970) 925-5775 for more information or to make reservations.

pack trips through Copper Mountain Stables, (970) 928-2318. The Colorado Trail, a 469-mile trail that extends from Denver to Durango, passes near Copper Mountain too. You can also arrange a breakfast or dinner horseback ride out of Copper Mountain Stables.

In the summer you can ride the American Eagle lift free daily from mid-June to about Labor Day. For information about any summer activity at Copper Mountain, call Copper Mountain Resort, (800) 458-8386.

Frisbee golfers will love the new 18-hole course through the base of the village. It's a disc-thrower's delight — and free!

Mountain bikers enjoyed one of the best ski resort deals with a ride up the lift, including bike, for free in 1998. But due to construction, the ride might not be available during summer 1999. Call ahead to check. Bike rentals are easily found. Try Christy Sports, (970) 968-6250. Intermediate riders might want to try the Ten Mile Canyon ride, which follows the old railroad grade along Ten Mile Creek.

Dining

O'Shea's, (970) 968-2318 ext. 6504, in the Copper Junction Building at the base of the American Eagle lift, has been satisfying hungry skiers with its nachos, burritos and hamburgers for years. Locals also like **Farley's Prime and Chop House**, 104 Wheeler, for steaks, ribs and seafood, (970) 968-2577. **Pesce's Fresco**, (970) 968-2318 ext. 6505, in the Mountain Village, is better than burgers, but not quite posh. On the changing menu are soups, salads and pastas.

Shopping

While Copper Mountain has enough shops to provide the necessities and a few that provide delight, its offerings are eclipsed by what Vail, just a half-hour away, has to offer. Still, there are spots to buy ski and snowboard clothing and equipment. The biggest is **Christy Sports** in the center of the village, (970) 968-6250, also well-known in Greater Denver.

Accommodations

Virtually all the overnight lodging at Copper Mountain is in condominiums. Call **Copper Mountain Resort**, (800) 458-8386, for rental information.

Vail Valley

Useful Phone Numbers

Vail Associates/Ski Area information, (970) 476-5601

Snow Report, (970) 476-4888 or (800) 525-2257

Vail/Beaver Creek Reservations, (970) 845-5745 or (800) 525-2257

Vail Valley Tourism & Convention Bureau, (970) 476-1000 or (800) 525-3875

Getting There

Vail is along I-70 about 100 miles west of Denver; Beaver Creek is 11 miles farther west.

Skiing

The big — and sad — news for Vail was the summer 1998 fire that destroyed three buildings, including the majestic Two Elks Lodge at the summit of the mountain. The good news is that skiing has not been impacted. Virtually no trees were burned and no runs were affected.

Past visitors to Vail likely will remember the lodge, which opened in 1991 and seated 550 people at mealtime. The fire decimated the lodge and two other structures: ski patrol headquarters and a smaller restaurant called Camp One. The latter two buildings aren't yet scheduled for renovation, but Two Elks will be rebuilt. It is scheduled for a November 1999 ski season opening. The arson fire is still under investigation and as of early 1999, no one had been charged.

For as long as Vail has been a playground of plenty, Front Range residents have had a love-hate relationship with it. They love the skiing — acres and acres of varied, magnificently designed slopes — but hate the crowds, glitz and high prices. Driving to Vail from Denver also means navigating Vail Pass, which can be treacherous in bad weather and an incentive to exit at Copper Mountain or sooner. Still, every self-respecting skier should try Vail. It's the largest single ski-mountain complex in North America: three base areas, more high-speed quadruple chairlifts than any other ski area and vast powder-filled back bowls that spread out over 4,700 acres of spectacular alpine terrain. China Bowl alone is as large as many ski areas. Intermediates especially can ski all day and never go down the same run twice. A heated and lighted gondola, called the Eagle Bahn, was added in 1996. During the summer of 1998, Vail spent $10 million to improve its on-mountain restaurants and its Adventure Ridge mountaintop activity center featuring, an outdoor skating rink, snowmobile tours and other winter fun. New in 1999 will be Chaos Canyon for kids only, which features an obstacle course and other kid-friendly attractions.

A ticket at Vail is interchangeable with one at Beaver Creek, Vail's little (but even richer and more exclusive) sister 11 miles farther west on I-70. First opened in 1980-81, elegant Beaver Creek attracts an international elite clientele as well as local skiers who praise the area for its spectacular natural beauty, lack of crowds, free parking and intimate feel. About 80 percent of the runs at Beaver Creek are intermediate or advanced. Snowboarding is permitted at Vail and Beaver Creek.

One-day adult lift tickets are $59 to $61 (1998-99 rate), depending on whether it's a holiday or regular season (spring break weeks are considered holiday time). Kids do not ski free here: A child ticket for ages 12 and younger is a hefty $37. There are, however, a total of 12 kids-only areas (in addition to the large Chaos Canyon) featuring historical Indian teepee villages, a mountain lion's den, ski-through mock goldmines and a fort. Parking can add another $10 to your Vail tab, so carpool if you can. With more than 4,600 acres of trails and only 100 miles from Denver, Vail remains a top destination for serious skiers. Its international clientele means that you never know who might be in the gondola with you — a neighbor from Denver or a visitor from Europe or Mexico.

Modeled after a Tyrolean village, Vail is a charming town that caters to pedestrians. Free buses link all the base areas and run from morning to late night. Vail is home to the **Colorado Ski Museum**, at the Vail Transportation Center, (970) 476-1876, and is the frequent site of World Cup ski races.

Cross-Country Skiing and Other Winter Activities

Vail and Beaver Creek operate three **cross-country ski centers**: a Nordic center at the Vail Golf Course, (970) 479-4391, for track skiing and skating; the Golden Peak Cross Country Ski Touring Center, (970) 845-5313, at Vail with backcountry access to Vail Mountain and the White River National Forest; and the Beaver Creek Cross Country Ski Center, (970) 845-5313, at the bottom of Strawberry Park lift (chair 12). At Beaver Creek, skiers ride the lift up to McCoy Park, which sports a system of groomed trails. Equipment rentals, tours (including snowshoe tours) and lessons are available at all three areas. On Thursdays you can take an all-day nature tour from Golden Peak that includes a gourmet lunch (about $65); advance reservations are required.

There are abundant opportunities for **backcountry touring** throughout the Vail Valley; the summit of Vail Pass itself is often the first ski tour of the year for many Denver backcountry enthusiasts, as it receives plentiful early snow. The town of Vail and Vail Pass are the starting or ending points for several overnight tours to 10th Mountain Trail Association huts, including the luxurious (well, for a hut) Shrine Mountain Inn. Reservations are essential; call the 10th Mountain Trail Association, (970) 925-5775.

The **bobsled run** at Vail is a thrilling ride. Snowmobile and sleigh rides can be booked

---

INSIDERS' TIP

Go off the beaten path — and far away from the ski resort crowds — at the Frisco Nordic Center, alongside Dillon Reservoir about 5 miles before Breckenridge. Snowshoers and cross-country skiers find serenity among snow-covered evergreens and sloping trails. Stop at the horse barn and have lunch on the seat of a sleigh. Rentals and maps are available at the center's outpost. Call (970) 668-0866 for more information.

through local companies, and Vail's world-class John A. Dobson Ice Arena is open for public **skating** (admission: $4 for adults, $3 for children younger than 12 and $2 for skate rentals). Children 4 and younger are admitted free. Call (970) 479-2271.

Adventure Ridge, (970) 476-9090, is a new mountain-top activity center featuring an outdoor **skating rink, tubing hill, snowmobile tours** and **snowboarding halfpipes**. It's open in winter only until 10 PM and includes three restaurant choices.

Summer Fun

Summer is glorious in the Vail Valley. In fact many Denverites who avoid Vail's winter glitz look forward to Vail's more laid-back summer style. **Hikers** and **backpackers** can explore a large network of trails, either on foot or on horseback. Most of these trails lead rather rapidly up to the Continental Divide and are fairly steep, but the many lakes and waterfalls provide lots of resting and picnic spots. Much of the land around Vail is part of the White River National Forest; call or visit the Holy Cross Ranger District Office (off the West Vail exit ramp) for suggested routes and maps, (970) 827-5715.

Four chairlifts on Vail and Beaver Creek mountains make it easy to reach new **mountain biking** heights and nearly 100 miles of world-class trails. Rentals are easy to find at any number of shops in town or at the Wildwood Shelter on top of the Wilderness Express lift at Vail.

There are several public and private **golf courses** in the Vail Valley, the most touted of which is the Beaver Creek Resort Golf Club, (970) 949-7123, a Robert Trent Jones Jr. course. The par 72 Cordillera Golf Club opened in July 1997 with both mountain and valley courses, (970) 926-5100. A fun and affordable option is the Eagle-Vail Golf Course located between Vail and Avon, (970) 949-5267. Site of the Jerry Ford Invitational Golf Tournament is Vail Golf Club, a par 71 public course with spectacular views of the Gore Range, (970) 479-2260.

Vail offers several **summer getaway packages** starting as low as $60 a night based on double occupancy. For reservations and information, call the tourism bureau at (800) 525-3875. If you're looking for Vail glamour, try the Spa at the Sonnenalp Resort, offering the ultimate relaxation with a Scandinavian touch, (800) 654-8312. For the musically inclined, the **Colorado Vail Valley Music Festival** will be in its 12th season in July and August 1999, featuring an array of classical music and jazz, (970) 827-5700.

Dining

Two of the finest restaurants in the state are in Vail: **Sweet Basil**, 193 E. Gore Creek

Drive, (970) 476-0125, and the **Wildflower Inn**, 174 E. Gore Creek Drive in the Lodge at Vail, (970) 476-5011. Both are expensive but well worth it for special occasions; reservations are recommended. Sweet Basil serves inventive American cuisine in a pretty spot by Gore Creek. The Wildflower Inn offers up superbly creative American cuisine in an elegant setting. Less expensive is **Los Amigos**, (970) 476-5847, at the top of Bridge Street, which serves standard Mexican fare in a bustling atmosphere. Also more for the budget-minded, **Blu's**, 193 E. Gore Creek Drive, (970) 476-3113, is a longtime favorite serving breakfast, lunch and dinner. The food is eclectic American cuisine, including soups, salads, pizzas, great desserts and coffee.

Dining in Beaver Creek is even more heavily tilted toward the expensive than Vail, and reservations are *de rigueur*. **Mirabelle**, located in a former home at 55 Village Road, (970) 949-7728, receives high praise for its romantic ambiance, excellent service and French cuisine with a twist. It's closed briefly during the spring and fall, between ski season and summer. Up on the slopes of Beaver Creek, **Beano's Cabin** offers more than just a meal. Reached by sleighride, this elegant log-and-glass lodge offers six-course gourmet meals as well as entertainment for adults and children. In the summer, you can get there via horseback or horse-drawn wagon (about a one-hour trip) or by shuttle van (a 10-minute trip). Naturally, an experience like this doesn't come cheap: adults pay $75 (tax, tip and alcoholic beverages extra); children 12 and younger, $46. For reservations call (970) 949-9090.

For more casual, less-expensive meals, head to **Chili Willy's**, 101 Main Street in Minturn (7 miles west on I-70, 2 miles south on U.S. Highway 24), (970) 827-5887. You'll find great Tex-Mex fajitas, margaritas and a fun atmosphere.

Shopping

Vail and Beaver Creek are known for their fine selection of shops and galleries. But this is not bargain shopping. Sticker-shock is common, as are full-length furs, custom-designed jewelry and designer labels. For colorful, contemporary regional art, visit **Vail Village Art**, 194 E. Gore Creek Drive. The Vail Valley Gallery Association publishes a guide to area galleries that you can pick up at any member gallery or by calling (970) 949-1626. Ask about their Saturday evening gallery walks in the summer.

Vail and Beaver Creek offer resort-town shopping at its finest. **The Golden Bear**, 286 Bridge Street, has ladies' clothing and men's and ladies' jewelry, including earrings, pendants, bracelets and other accessories featuring its trademark golden bear (available in sterling silver too). **Gorsuch Ltd.**, 263 E. Gore Creek Drive, has been supplying Vail Valley residents and visitors with ski clothing and other sportswear — including biking and fly-fishing gear for the summer — for more than 30 years. **Pepi Sports** at 231 Bridge Street, is another longtime source for outerwear and sportswear as well as ski, bike and in-line skate rentals. There's also **True North**, at 100 E. Meadow Drive, which stocks an array of Canadian-designed outerwear, sweaters, pants and boots. **Slifer Collection**, 230 Bridge Street, carries gorgeous furniture and home furnishings, including the Ralph Lauren Home Collection.

Accommodations

A reasonably priced room can be hard to come by in the Vail Valley. When money is no object, grand lodges and luxury hotels are happy to oblige. Try the **The Lodge at Vail**, (970) 476-5011 or (800) 331-5634; **Beaver Creek Lodge**, (970) 845-9800 or (800) 732-6777; and the truly special **Lodge at Cordillera**, (970) 926-2200 or (800) 548-2721. But the price will be steep, ranging from around $100 a night in the off season to $500 in high season. A bed and breakfast somewhat off the beaten track is the **Eagle River Inn**, 145 N. Main Street in Minturn, (970) 827-5761 or (800) 344-1750, an enchanting Santa Fe-style hostelry with 12 rooms ranging in price from $75 to $180 a night. **The Roost**, (970) 476-5451, touts itself as the least expensive lodging in Vail and offers continental breakfast. Visitors can stay at **The West Vail Lodge** for about $200 for a room that sleeps four. U.S. Highway 24 runs right through Minturn. Many hotels offer greatly reduced rates in summer. Check the Denver newspapers for special packages, or call Vail/Beaver Creek Reservations, (800) 525-2257.

Ski Country Resources

Colorado Cross-Country Ski Association
For brochures on cross-country centers, (800) 869-4560

Colorado Ski Country
Daily Ski Conditions/Reports (statewide), (303) 825-7669

National Weather Service
Denver and central mountains, (303) 398-3964

Road Conditions within 2 hours of Denver, (303) 639-1111

National Forest Service
Denver Regional Office, 740 Simms St., Lakewood, (303) 275-5350

Arapaho National Forest
Dillon District Office, 680 Blue River Parkway, Silverthorne, (970) 468-5400

White River National Forest
Holy Cross Ranger District Office, 24747 U.S. Highway 24, Minturn, (303) 827-5715

Colorado Division of Wildlife
Fishing information, (303) 291-7533

10th Mountain Division Hut Association
Aspen, (970) 925-5775

U.S. Geological Survey
Topographical maps, (303) 202-4700

Recommended Guidebooks

Rocky Mountain Skiing by Claire Walter (Fulcrum Publishing)

Skiing Colorado's Backcountry by Brian Litz and Kurt Lankford (Fulcrum Publishing)

The Hiker's Guide to Colorado by Caryn and Peter Boddie (Falcon Press)

Denver and its surrounding communities offer enough parades, concerts, rodeos, art shows and ethnic celebrations to keep your calendar full year round.

Annual Events and Festivals

Love a lively parade or jumpin' jazz fest? Denver and its surrounding communities offer enough parades, concerts, rodeos, art shows and ethnic celebrations — pick a reason, we've got a festival — to keep your calendar full year round. And we've included as many as possible, from those with instantaneous name recognition, like the Cherry Creek Arts Festival, which draws a quarter-million people every July 4th weekend, to the lesser known ones, like the Fall Fest, held in September in downtown Golden.

The following list should be viewed as a practical guide to those festivals and events with a designated date and location, but a few words of warning: dates can change from year to year, often well after this guide is published, so an event listed in September, for example, may actually turn out to be in October; telephone numbers can also change after this guide has been published, although the old number can usually steer you toward the new number.

A good hedge against late changes in dates and information phone numbers, and just a useful thing to acquire anyway, is the *Denver Events Guide 1999* (updated annually) available from the Denver Metro Convention & Visitors Bureau, (303) 892-1505. Or if you find that one of our information phone numbers has gone bad by the time you try to use it, just call the bureau and ask for the correct number. Folks there may have it.

While the bureau's events guide is not as extensive as the subsequent listings, it has one significant advantage. Our listings include only annual events, those that happen every year. The bureau's guide includes many events that happen just once, such as a performance by a specific musical or dance group.

Many events in this chapter are not one-of-a-kind, and similar events can be found throughout the year. Between the City of Golden, the Buffalo Bill Memorial Museum and the Buckhorn Exchange, for example, you can find enough Buffalo Bill events to keep you buffalo crazy all year. There are mountains of mountain-man rendezvous. Nearly every community has its own yearly celebration, from the Carnation Festival in Wheat Ridge to Western Welcome Week in Littleton. Mountain communities and ski areas, ditto. Remember that whenever you go to an event in some community or ski area, you're also placing yourself in a position to enjoy the other attractions there and nearby.

Some festivals and events, such as the Bolder Boulder 10K run, are one-shot deals. Others, such as the "World's Largest Christmas Lighting Display" at the Denver City and County Building, may stretch out over weeks.

For the most part, these entries are confined to the Greater Denver area, but you'll notice that we've also covered events during the year at nearby ski areas and mountain communities. This list goes as far afield: Cheyenne, Wyoming; Estes Park; and Colorado Springs — all easy daytrips.

In some cases, you can expect to experience exactly what we have described in the following entries. We can't guarantee that a festival or event will be exactly the same every year, but we can tell you what to expect based either on promises by the organizers or on the experiences of past years.

Once again, we certainly haven't covered

everything there is to do. On the Fourth of July, for example, communities and organizations all over Greater Denver and the surrounding landscape have fireworks shows. Looking out across the plains from the mountains, the entire landscape seems to be erupting in fireworks. We recommend driving up in the evening to any Foothills road with an east-facing view, parking and enjoying the show.

And of course, if you're looking for festivals and events, you may want to go beyond those annual events that a book like this clearly can provide. Many of the organizations and communities included here have events that are not offered every year, while many other organizations and communities have the same event on a regular basis. Take the **Colorado Rockies** baseball team (call (303) 762-5437 or ROCKIES) as an example. They're playing constantly from spring to fall. The **Centro Cultural Mexicano**, (303) 331-1870, every month presents art exhibits and storytelling and features Hispanic artists. Fashionable **Cherry Creek** has what it calls summer strolls from June through August and gallery walks in February, May, September and December. The **Colorado Railroad Museum** at several points throughout the year has what it calls "steam ups," in which it fires up and moves Colorado's oldest locomotive, *No. 346.* The **Denver Botanic Gardens** offers a wonderful series of concerts during summer, too many to list individually here. These are just a few of countless sources of entertainment.

Beyond this list, the best advice we can give is that you should check your Friday weekend sections of *The Denver Post, Rocky Mountain News* and Boulder's *Daily Camera,* where the goings-on are listed in considerable detail. And don't miss the impressive events and activities section each week in *Westword,* Denver's leading weekly news publication that's available free in newspaper dispensers all over Greater Denver beginning on Wednesday and continuing until the dispensers are empty.

Use this list and take this advice, and you'll have more events and festivities than you could

attend if you split into 10 copies of yourself and every danged one of you spent the year at a dead run in pursuit of fun.

January

Denver Boat Show
**The Colorado Convention Center,
700 14th St. • (719) 590-7717**
This is boathead heaven in early January. The year's big boat show usually lasts four days, spanning a weekend and jammed with aquatic craft, rubber rafts, gear and accessories fore and aft. It's great fun to goggle at the huge luxury boats. Tickets are $5.50 for adults; $3.50 per child.

Chef's Cup Race and Benefit Dinner Dance
West Portal Station at the base of Winter Park Resort, Winter Park • (303) 892-0961
Ski competition is followed by gastronomy in early January. The West Portal Station is where the Moffat (train) Tunnel under the Continental Divide comes out on the west side, right by the base lodge of Winter Park. You can watch the ski racing from the base lodge, and that's where the dinner dance is held. Each of the featured chefs from around the Fraser Valley (the region from Winter Park to Fraser) prepares one specialty dish, and visitors thereby can get a sampling of the regional fare. While watching the race is free, attending the dinner costs $28 for one person and $43 for a couple.

Ullr Fest
Locations throughout Breckenridge • (970) 453-6018
Helmets with horns on them are the height of fashion at this free festival in honor of Ullr (pronounced "oo-ler"), the Norse god of snow. If you don't have a horned helmet, it will be a miracle if you can't find somebody selling them. (They are also handed out free at the parade.) Ullr Fest starts on a Monday and runs into the following weekend, usually the third

week in January. It includes a parade, fireworks on the mountainside near the ski area and a variety of different events daily. There are World Cup Championship freestyle competitions at the ski area, including events in ski ballet, mogul skiing and aerial jumping. Other activities include concerts and the opportunity for kids to go ice skating with cartoon characters. A dating game is hosted by Biff America. And the Ullympics feature coed teams competing in crazy events, such as Broom Ball and volleyball with snowshoes, on the first day of the festival.

National Western Stock Show & Rodeo
Denver Coliseum, 4600 Humboldt St.
• (303) 297-1166
National Western Complex, 4655
Humboldt St. (take Brighton Blvd.
exit off I-70) • (303) 297-1166

Get out of Dodge and get into Denver for this one. Everybody else does, or at least what seems like half the population of the American West. At over 90 years of age, the National Western is the largest annual event in Denver — and it's growing. You'll be in the company of more than 600,000 people, but the National Western is spaced over 16 days in mid-January, so there's plenty of room and time to tour the show competitions of everything from horses, sheep and cattle to chickens and rabbits in more varieties than you dreamed existed on the planet.

Rodeo events go on every day, with the nation's top horse and bull riders, calf ropers, you name it, competing for nearly $500,000 in prizes. Between the big events, you can see all kinds of oddball fun: western battle re-creations (cover the kids' ears if loud noises scare them); a sheepdog herding sheep with a monkey in a cowboy suit riding on its back; and rodeo clowns. General admission is $7 on weekends, $5 on weekdays, and rodeo tickets range from $8 to $15. The National West-

ern begins with a colorful parade through downtown Denver.

You might also want to check out what Denver calls the World's Largest Display of Christmas Lights at the City and County Building downtown. The lights are on from the first Thursday in December until January 1, but they're turned on at night during the stock show as well.

The Denver Sportsmen's Show
The Colorado Convention Center,
700 14th St. • (800) 343-6973

Not just for sportsmen, mind you, this is a family-oriented trade show held in mid- to late January with hundreds of exhibitors in outdoors activities including hunting, fishing, camping, hiking, horseback riding, boating and recreational vehicles. It's especially heavy on the hunting and fishing. Admission is $7 for adults, $4 for children.

The Annual Colorado Cowboy Poetry Gathering
The Arvada Center for the Arts and
Humanities, 6901 Wadsworth Blvd.,
Arvada • (303) 431-3939

Tales grow tall under a wide-open sky, and nobody spends more time under a wider sky than cowboys and cowgirls. Once a year in mid-January, the poetic cream of the ranching and cowpunching community brings its western oral tradition of tales and humor to Arvada from Colorado and beyond. Expect about 40 poets performing in three evening sessions as well as daytime events in which the public is sometimes invited to join in. There are also performances by cowboy musicians. Admission is from $8 to $13.

International Snow Sculpture Championships
Locations throughout Breckenridge
• (970) 453-6018

The City of Breckenridge lends its front-

INSIDERS' TIP

Easter sunrise service at Red Rocks Park (take the Morrison Road exit off of I-70) is a stirring nondenominational event that draws upwards of 12,000 people. In its 50-plus year history, it's been cancelled only five times due to inclement weather.

end loaders to fill wooden forms with 20-ton blocks of snow. Four-person sculpting teams from around the world climb on top and tromp and stomp until the snow is packed tight. The forms are removed, and what happens to each big block of snow is up to the contestants, who use only hand tools. Sculptures run the gamut from geometric to free-form to recognizable shapes and scenes. The sculptures can last up to 10 days, depending on the weather. The event is held in mid-January and is free whether you participate or just watch.

Colorado RV Adventure Travel Show

Currigan Exhibition Hall, 1324 Champa St. • (303) 892-6800

This is Greater Denver's version of hog heaven for the recreational-vehicle enthusiast. Admire and wander through the shining state-of-the-art in anywhere from 100 to 200 new recreational vehicles; see the latest in RV accessories and meet exhibitors from lodges and resorts that cater to the RV crowd. This event is held in late January, and the cost is $6 for adults; kids younger than 12 get in free.

February

Registration for Ride the Rockies

See the June entry, Ride the Rockies, for more on the largest and longest public group bicycling tour of the year, but right now is when you need to register if you're interested in taking part. It's a lottery, and you need to get on the stick if you want in. *The Denver Post*, sponsor of the ride, usually makes applications available in the first week of February, and they're due by the last week of February. Call (303) 820-1338 for information.

Wells Fargo Bank Cup

Winter Park Resort, Lower Hughes Ski Trail • (970) 726-1540

Winter Park bills this as the longest continuous professional ski event in the country. Actually consisting of a number of free events that visitors can enjoy from the base area over a three-day period in early February, along with evening functions, it is a fund-raiser for the National Sports Center for the Disabled

(NSCD), also in Winter Park. Events vary somewhat from year to year, but typically expect to see pro slalom races along with the occasional downhill race. Other events include the Pro HandiCup, in which some of the pro skiers put on the outriggers that disabled skiers use and compete with disabled skiers who train at the NSCD; the Bronco Alumni Challenge, in which former Denver Broncos football players compete with each other; and another racing competition featuring 20 and 30 teams, each composed of four amateur racers and one pro racer.

Senior Games

Breckenridge Ski Area, Breckenridge Nordic Center and Breckenridge Ice Rink, Breckenridge • (970) 668-5486

Open to anybody older than 55, the Senior Games are held the first part of February and feature competitions in Nordic events, alpine events, ice skating, snowshoeing and biathlon. There is usually a welcoming dinner too. If you're not in the competition, which costs $25 to enter, you can watch free.

Denver Auto Show

The Colorado Convention Center, 700 14th St. • (303) 831-1691

Shop among, or just enjoy looking at, all the new cars under one roof. (No driving from lot to lot and being stalked by salespeople.) The show includes imports and domestics, sometimes exotics, futuristics and prototypes. Attendance at this five-day affair in late February or early March has exceeded 170,000. Plan to pay $7 at the door to get in.

International Sportsmen's Expo

Currigan Exhibition Hall, 1324 Champa St. • (800) 545-6100

This is a pure hunting and fishing show sometime in early to mid-February that features products and services related to archery, firearms and fishing paraphernalia. This is a how-to show with a lot of educational aspects geared toward stimulating you to hunt and fish. You can sit in a U-shaped theater-seating section, for example, to watch a presenter on stage explaining as he ties flies or wraps fishing rods. Video monitors allow you to see the small work. Top-name seminar speakers from magazines such as *Field and Stream* or *Outdoor Life* will be here. Expect around 350 exhibitors and crowds in the low 30,000s. Price is $8 for adults; $5 for seniors and kids.

CHSAA State Wrestling Championships
McNichols Sports Arena, 1635 Clay St.
• (303) 344-5050

Don't expect to see bellowing mesomorphs in outlandish costumes. Do expect to see real mainstream wrestling, as the top high-school contenders square off for the state titles. At any one time, you will be able to see simultaneous contests on 10 different mats. The competition starts in mid- to late February and runs on a Thursday, Friday and Saturday. General admission is $5; reserved seats run $6 to $8.

Columbia Crest Cup
Lower Hughes Ski Trail, Winter Park Resort • (970) 726-1540

Part of the National Handicapped Sports Qualifications Series, this is a three-day qualifying race for disabled skiers working their way up the competitive ladder toward the U.S. national championships. It is usually held in late February or early March. See some of the best disabled skiers in the Rocky Mountain region in the super giant slalom, the giant slalom and the slalom. Benefiting the National Sports Center for the Disabled, this event is free to watch; to enter it costs $78.

Fat Tuesday Celebration
Bars and restaurants throughout Breckenridge • (970) 453-6018

Breckenridge hosts a modest version of Mardi Gras, which consists of ceremonies around the village. Beads, costumes and seafood abound on Fat Tuesday, usually in late February. Food and drink prices vary; everything else is free.

KBCO Cardboard Downhill Derby
Arapahoe Basin Ski Area, Summit County • (303) 444-KBCO

This is one of those fun, flaky ski-area events that provide comic relief in the Warren Miller ski films. Sometime around the last Saturday in February, people build crafts out of cardboard, string, tape, paper and glue, and then they ride them down a ski slope in the Downhill Derby. Not infrequently, the crafts disintegrate before they stop moving. It's not a race. Judging is based on originality, theme, costumes and engineering. Past derby themes include takeoffs on the Pope's 1993 visit to Denver and Lorena Bobbitt. "A-Basin," as the locals like to call it, has discounted skiing for this event. You can ski and stop to watch the antics in early afternoon. Afterward there's an award ceremony and live band. There's a $10 entry fee for the Derby plus $6 per pilot, but you can watch the whole zany event for free.

Buffalo Bill's Birthday
The Buckhorn Exchange, 1000 Osage St.
• (303) 534-9505

This is the first of Greater Denver's many annual celebrations of Buffalo Bill, a celebrated local citizen. The Mountain Man Association descends in full costume in the Buckhorn Exchange, Denver's oldest restaurant (see our Restaurants chapter), to celebrate Bill's February 26th birthday. Everybody at the restaurant dresses in costume too. The costumes are around pretty much all day. You can come for lunch or dinner, enjoy the color, and enjoy staged gunfights on the hour during the afternoon. Reservations are suggested for supper, if you want to get a table. This event is usually held the last Saturday in February. There is no price to come watch any of the events. If you stay to eat, plan to pay the price of dinner.

Buffalo Bill's Birthday Celebration
The Buffalo Bill Memorial Museum on Lookout Mountain, 987½ Lookout Mountain Rd., Golden • (303) 526-0744

This celebration takes place on the grounds of the Buffalo Bill Museum on Lookout Mountain, where the Buffalo meister's grave is located. Past celebrations included bluegrass music, free ice cream and cake and a birthday ceremony. Buffalo Bill look-alikes lend atmosphere and give talks about Bill's early years. In past celebrations, they've even had a guy who remembered Bill. This party is held on a weekend close to Bill's February 26 birthday.

Take I-70 west to Exit 256, where the sign says "Lookout Mountain" and "Buffalo Bill's Grave," follow the well-placed signs to the top of Lookout Mountain. The celebration is free.

March

Colorado RV, Sports, Boat and Travel Show
The National Western Complex, 4655 Humboldt St. (take the Brighton Blvd. exit off I-70) • (303) 892-6800

This is a general outdoor product show (it's mainly related to fishing and boating) with the largest display of RVs in the region. It's in early March. Adults pay $7, and kids younger than 12 are free.

CHSAA State Basketball Tournament
McNichols Sports Arena, 1635 Clay St. (for the big schools)
Denver Coliseum (for the smaller schools)
CU-Boulder Colorado State University, Fort Collins Fort Collins High School, Fort Collins • (303) 344-5050

See the final competitions of Colorado's high school basketball season. General admission is $5; reserved seats are $6 to $8.

St. Patrick's Day Parade
Streets of downtown Denver
• (303) 789-3333

This is big, folks, the second-largest St. Patrick's Day parade in the country (New York City is first). The divil, you say. Yes, it's true. It never seems to end. Past parades have taken more than four hours for 250 floats, bands and other colorful entrants to pass as clowns, leprechauns and vendors ply the awesome crowds of spectators. There are ancillary events during the entire week, including Irish entertainment at various pubs and other locations.

Annual Spring Home & Patio Show
The National Western Complex, 4655 Humboldt St. (take the Brighton Blvd. exit off I-70) • (303) 892-6800

There's nothing like a nice trade show in late March to get you in the mood for whatever slice of life they're selling. So get in the mood for the spring cleaning and summer grooming of house and yard by visiting the 300 exhibitors of home and garden products and services. Adults get in for $7; kids younger than 12 are free.

Denver March Pow-Wow
The Denver Coliseum, 4600 Humboldt St. (take the Brighton Blvd. exit off I-70)
• (303) 455-4575

Don't miss this one in mid- to late March. More than 1,000 Native Americans of tribes from most of the United States as well as Canada dancing simultaneously in full costume will stuff your eyes with enough chromatic spectacle to last all year. At the edges of the dancing, groups of men surround huge drums and make the whole coliseum vibrate. The big en masse dancing, the Grand Entry, happens Friday and Saturday at noon and 7 PM, and Sunday at noon, with other activities scattered throughout those days. And you'll get plenty of opportunities to see the costumes close up: The seats around you will be filled with Native American families related to the dancers. Costumed competitors will be sitting next to you and walking past you. That's one of the reasons why this event is such a find. It hasn't been "discovered" yet by the kinds of crowds that attend the National Western Stock Show & Rodeo (see the January entry), so you feel more completely immersed in authenticity. Kids love it.

There's a modest Native American market downstairs. Expect between 40 and 50 drum groups to be at the Pow-Wow, along with representatives of 60 to 70 tribes and a total three-day crowd in the neighborhood of 80,000 (not including children younger than 6 and adults older than 60, who get in free). For everyone else, a one-day pass is $5; a three-day pass is $10.

Rocky Mountain Home Show
Currigan Exhibition Hall, 1324 Champa St.
• (303) 778-1400

Domestic engineers take note. This regional trade show in March and its 300-some exhibitors feature the latest home-building and remodeling products and materials. You'll find interior design, energy conservation and about 50 seminars for your illumination. General admission is $7.

April

Breckenridge Beach Daze
Locations throughout Breckenridge
• (970) 453-6018

No, there's no beach, but the month of April is usually pretty warm, and this is a chance to enjoy the spring skiing and discounted lodging and lift tickets in the context of daily Beach Daze events, which include a parade, volleyball, races and a crawfish festival. All events, except skiing, of course, are free.

Easter Sunrise Service
Red Rocks Amphitheatre (north of Morrison on Hogback Rd.; take I-70 W. to the Morrison exit, then go south)
• (303) 892-1505

One of the most inspirational places you'll ever find for an Easter sunrise service is this gargantuan natural amphitheater of red sandstone facing east over the plains. The event is nondenominational, free and open to the public.

Spring Splash/Closing Day
Winter Park Resort, Lower Hughes Ski Trail, Winter Park • (303) 892-0961

This is one of those events that public relations people love because they get to use the word "zany." If you've ever seen the part of a Warren Miller ski movie where the sun is out, everybody wears sunglasses, and ski-babes in bikinis and ski-bozos in goofy costumes come barreling down the hill trying to hydroplane across a puddle of ice water and belly flop with a big splash — you've been looking at Spring Splash in Winter Park, which is always the closing Sunday of the season (typically mid-April). It has become one of the quintessential Colorado images — kind of an outdoor spectacle that people try to get a good view of by jockeying for position on the balconies of the base lodge. Spectating is free; participating will cost you a lift ticket plus an entry fee of $30.

Children's Day Celebration
Currigan Exhibition Hall, 1324 Champa St.
• (303) 331-1870

Children's Day is an old Mexican tradition, like Father's Day or Mother's Day in the United States. In Mexico the date is April 30, but here it's on the last Saturday in April. In Mexico, they take kids on field trips and have other festivities at school. Here, you can come and enjoy entertainment for kids, including clowns, piñatas, prizes, balloons, puppet shows, booths and mechanical games. Admission is free, but some rides and booths have moderate costs.

The Denver Art Museum Antiques Show & Sale
Hellenic Community Center,
4610 E. Alameda • (303) 640-2793

For nearly 15 years, The Spalding Rehabilitation Center sponsored this popular antique show and sale. In 1996 the Denver Art Museum took it over and now hosts the three-day event featuring formal and country American, Asian, English and Continental antique furniture. You'll see rare books and old maps, along with beautiful silver and pewter pieces. Always held in either April or May, the event in 1999 was in late April. Ticket price for all three days is $6. (The organizers plan to move the sale into the museum.)

May

Denver Botanic Gardens Plant and Book Sale
The Denver Botanic Gardens,
1005 York St. • (303) 331-4000

Plants and books are for sale, and proceeds benefit the DBG. You can buy thousands of flowers, herbs and vegetables. There are speakers and demonstrations going on in appropriate parts of the gardens: a bonsai-tree demonstration is in the bonsai section, for example; an expert on roses might hold forth in the rose garden. This makes a perfect Mother's Day weekend outing; plus admission is free.

The KBCO/Budweiser Kinetic Sculpture Challenge
The Boulder Reservoir, 51st St., Boulder
• (303) 444-KBCO

This has become one of the biggest and most colorful annual events in the Denver area, and it's certainly the looniest event of its size. The hijinks at the Boulder Reservoir pulled around 20,000 in attendance in 1996. The kinetic conveyances, sometimes called kinetic sculptures, are crafts powered by human muscle. They must be capable of going on land and water; and at the Challenge, they are required to go through a mud pit as well. The competition is judged not just on speed but also on creativity, team costumes and team spirit. There's also a beach volleyball tournament, live music and a food court. A warning: expect a big crowd, small access roads that are often muddy and limited parking. Car pooling is a good idea. An even better idea is to park somewhere nearby, or even in Boulder, and bicycle the rest of the way.

A parade is held in downtown Boulder on the Saturday preceding the Challenge. The festival now has two locations (University of Colorado campus and Crossroads Mall) where you can park and ride a shuttle bus for $2. Bring binoculars since a lot of the race takes place way out on the reservoir. The event is held on the first Saturday of May, weather permitting; otherwise, it's held the next Saturday. To enter the reservoir area to watch, the price is $2 per pedestrian or $25 per carload.

Spring Mountain Man Rendezvous
The Fort Restaurant, 19192 Colo. Hwy. 8, Morrison • (303) 697-4771

This free event features re-enactors of the 1830s and '40s dressed in buckskins and behaving like mountain men. There are competitions for best costume, tomahawk and knife throwing, black-powder target shooting, fire-starting with flint and steel and survival skills. There's also a mountain-man run. Held on a Sunday in early May, this event also features Native American trading tables where you can buy and trade for the works of Colorado Native American artisans.

Historic Denver Week
Larimer Square, Larimer St. (between 14th and 15th sts.) • (303) 296-9887

This festival is a weeklong salute in early May to historic Denver and historic Larimer Square featuring a variety of activities. There are historic preservation awards and historic

walking tours (East Colfax, the South Platte Valley, etc.) as well as a bus tour of historic police and fire department facilities. There is always a "Box City" where elementary school students build a city out of donated boxes. There's also a Queen for a Day event at the Molly Brown House Museum (see our Attractions chapter), where tea is served with scones and cream and preserves. Prices for walking tours and seminars range from $5 to $15.

Cinco De Mayo
Civic Center Park, between Colfax Ave. and 14th St. • (303) 534-8342

This is Denver's celebration of its enormous Hispanic heritage. Many confuse this with Mexican Independence Day, which is on September 16. Cinco de Mayo is actually a big celebration that has grown from a small event, although the original event had big meaning: la Batalla de Puebla, the Battle of Ciudad Puebla, which took place during the Mexican battle for independence from France.

Mexicans, equipped with little more than farm implements, whipped one of the greatest armies on Earth, although the French came back five days later and made up for it. Still, it's a spiritual moment for Mexico and a big holiday in Denver. It starts with the Celebrate Culture parade, intended to celebrate diversity, and a traditional Mariachi mass. Past celebrations included about 200 different booths with arts and foods, entertainment on six stages, ethnic-fashionwear showings and Latin, jazz, rap and contemporary music. There's also a children's area with stage including clowns, rides, dancing and all that jolly kidstuff. The event is free.

Copa Mexico Cinco De Mayo
Fort Logan Mental Health Center Facility, Oxford St. and Federal Blvd., Lakewood • (303) 331-1870
Greyhound Park, 6200 Dahlia St., Commerce City • (303) 331-1870

Copa Mexico means trophy Mexico. The best Hispanic soccer teams in Colorado participate in this May tournament, and the two playoff finalists square off in Greyhound Park. After the championship game, the park hosts a game between the Colorado Foxes or the Rapids and a professional soccer team from another city. The event is free except for the final game, which costs $5 per person.

Cinco De Miles
City Park, Colorado Blvd. • (303) 978-1698

Part of Greater Denver's general Cinco de Mayo festivities, and held on the weekend closest to May 5, this event is a 5-mile and 5K run, a 5K walk and a 1K family fun run. The entry fee for adults is $17; kids younger than 12, $15.

Kops 'n Kids
East High School and City Park, across 17th St. from City Park • (303) 399-5584

This law enforcement expo and family-entertainment event benefits the children of officers killed in the line of duty. There are six events on the third Sunday in May: a 10K run, a 5K run/walk, a 1K fun run, a 15-mile bike ride, a 50-mile bike ride and the Iron Mouse Biathlon, an event that combines the 15-mile bike ride with the 1K fun run. The bike rides are not competitions, but rather recreational rides. Along with food and beverage vendors, law enforcement people put together fun things to see and take part in, such as free canine exhibitions. The entry fee is $17 per person.

Taste of Breckenridge
Beaver Run Resort, Breckenridge • (303) (970) 453-5970

Chefs from the best restaurants in the Breckenridge area each prepare one of their specialties. The idea is to go and taste the food (and wine). Participants vote for their favorite independent restaurant and hotel restaurant. The charge has been $30 per person in the past. The event is held on Saturday of Memorial Day weekend.

Boulder Creek Festival
Downtown Boulder, Canyon Blvd. (along the Boulder Creek Path), Central Park and the Library-Municipal Building Complex, Boulder • (303) 449-3825

The Boulder Creek Festival expanded to two weekends in 1995. The weekend before Memorial Day weekend is the kickoff, with activities including the Creek Clean-Up and a community barbecue. On Memorial Day weekend, there's a rubber duck race on the creek, an International Folk Festival, five stages with free entertainment, Kids Place in the Park and other merriment. Attendance at the whole thing has been more than 100,000. The festival is free.

Bolder Boulder
Bank of Boulder, 30th & Iris sts., Boulder • (303) 444-RACE

There's no limit on the number of runners for this 10K race as in previous years, and you can even enter on the day of the race. Except, there is a $5 late fee if you register after a certain date (around May 19) and a $10 late fee if you register on race day. If you don't register late, it's $24 including a T-shirt ($15 without) and a bag lunch. What you mainly are paying for, however, is participation in what may be the most fun race you've ever run or spectated (37,785 people took part in 1996). There's a race for pros, the "elite" race, including many of the world's leading runners. And there's a "citizens' race," in which anybody can take part.

Most of the race is along small streets that go up and down through the charming small town of Boulder. It's not that small of a town anymore, but it has that feel. The locals put on quite a show along the route. On the curbs along the course is a never-ending succession of string quartets, jazz bands, belly dancers, you name it, and a lot of runners and groups of runners dream up theme costumes in which to run. You also can go just to enjoy the spectacle. Get there early in the day, though, because the traffic gets horrendous.

The Parade of the Years
Loveland to Estes Park • Contacts: Frank Hicks, (970) 586-4407, or Richard Paynter, (970) 832-6400

Antique-car buffs love this old-car rally. It commemorates the beginning of the tourist season, when people used to take their flivvers out of the barn and start using them. This was the weekend when the Stanley Hotel opened each year, and F.O. Stanley, who invented the Stanley Steamer auto and developed an auto road up the Big Thompson Canyon around 1908, took cars from Estes Park down to Loveland and Lyons to pick up guests at the railroad stations. People congregate in Loveland on a Friday night for an informal get-together, then parade through Loveland on Saturday morning and stop at the railroad station, where the public can inspect the cars; then they head up the Big Thompson Canyon on U.S. Highway 34. Sunday, there's a car rally in the morning and an exhibition in the evening at the Estes Park Historical Museum. There's a banquet Sunday night and a rally Monday morning, and that's that. You may enter the parade for $75 or watch for free.

June

Capitol Hill People's Fair
Civic Center Park, between Colfax Ave. and 14th St. • (303) 830-1651

Capitol Hill is a colorful and historic neighborhood that ranges from the funky to the aristocratic, and this is its annual celebration, held on the first weekend in June. Organizers claim this event is Colorado's largest arts and crafts festival, with about 500 exhibitors as well as food, dance, entertainment on six stages and kids' activities such as putt-putt golf, face painting and more. Crowds have swelled to about 250,000; admission is free.

The Elephant Rock Century Bike Tour
Registration at the Douglas County Courthouse, Castle Rock • (303) 688-4597

Bike tours of various lengths — 15-mile, 27-mile, 32-mile, 68-mile and 100-mile — around county roads end in a celebration with food booths in Courthouse Square. The Shimano Youth Race, on a special loop around the area, is for younger people. The fun takes place on the first Sunday in June and has a $25 entry fee.

Anniversary of Buffalo Bill's Burial
The Buffalo Bill Memorial Museum on Lookout Mountain, 987½ Lookout Mountain Rd., Golden • (303) 526-0744

This is a commemoration of Buffalo Bill's burial, one of the biggest events in Colorado history. Bill Cody died in January 1917, but he lay in state in the Colorado State Capitol Building while 50,000 mourners and gawkers filed by over one weekend. At his interment on June 3, next to what is now The Buffalo Bill Memorial Museum, 25,000 people walked or rode horses up the narrow Lookout Mountain road. Bill had once said he wanted to be buried in Cody, Wyoming, a town he founded, and the Wyomingans thought that was a good idea. There were threats of stealing the body, so Denver stationed a military tank at the grave. It was a colorful event, and today people make it a colorful celebration. It includes a mock funeral, with a procession of old cars and motorists who blunder into the procession and get trapped in it. The procession winds up the Lariat Trail on the east side of Lookout Mountain facing the plains. Somebody from the Masonic Temple (which handled part of the funeral for Bill) explains the funeral. A representative of Horan Funeral Home in Aurora, which embalmed and re-embalmed Bill while he lay in state, gives a talk on how the body was kept and buried. Guys in mountain-man costumes show up with horses and tepees. There's a Buffalo Bill-look-alike contest, buffalo-burger barbecue and children's activities. Since Bill was buried June 3, this free event is held on a weekend close to that date.

First Fest
The Arvada Center for the Arts and Humanities, 6901 Wadsworth Blvd., Arvada • (303) 424-0313

This is a celebration of the business communities in Arvada and Westminster, but it's not just for the business crowd. There are usually around 200 exhibits, food booths and activities for grownups and children. Police and fire departments sponsor exhibits. It also includes a 5K family fun run and live entertainment. Admission is free, and the event is usually the second Saturday in June.

Bethesda Dutch Festival
Columbia Behavioral Health Services, 4400 E. Iliff Ave. • (303) 759-6040

This free event has become a favorite. In typical Dutch tradition, the streets are scrubbed at the opening ceremony, usually held mid-June. Look for a "grocery store" with Dutch

The Colorado Renaissance Festival rings with the sound of jousting each summer.

goodies, a flower shop with tulips, Delft china displays, a parade and, of course, music and entertainment.

Estes Park Wool Market
Estes Park Fair Grounds, Community Dr. off U.S. Hwy. 36, Estes Park
• (970) 586-6104

Sheep ranching is a big part of Colorado's history and agriculture, and here's an event, held the second weekend in June, dedicated to its product. You'll find: spinning and weaving classes; dyeing classes; showings of sheep, llamas and alpacas; spinning and weaving demonstrations and contests; spinning wheels for sale; and commercial exhibits related to the wool industry. All events are free.

Gold Rush Days
Downtown Idaho Springs, (303) 567-2079 (toll call from Denver; dial 303 first)

This 75-year-old event held in mid-June celebrates mining history. Past Gold Rush Days included bands and other entertainment,

a country-fair theme, a pie-baking contest, food and crafts booths, a Sunday parade, mining demonstrations, a pony express, children's games, dancing and antique fire equipment. There is no charge.

Colorado Renaissance Festival
Off I-25 S., Larkspur • (303) 688-6010

Renaissance festivals are ripping good fun, and this is truly one of the most fun things you can do during the year. Spread out over a huge site beneath the greenwood trees, the festival re-creates a 16th-century marketplace filled with costumed characters and ruled by King Henry and Queen Anne. More than 200 costumed crafters sell handmade goods. One of the main attractions is the battling, strutting and jousting by knights on foot and horseback. You'll also enjoy strolling minstrels, jesters, jugglers, medieval food, rides and games galore for eight weekends in June and July. Admission is $12.95 for adults; $5 for children, ages 5 to 10. From Greater Denver, take I-25 S. to the Larkspur exit, then follow the signs to the festival.

Opera Pops Picnic Without Ants
Usually at the downtown Marriott Hotel, 17th and California Sts. • (303) 292-6700

A benefit for the Central City Opera, this event involves a picnic in a ballroom followed by a preview of all the artists who will be performing in Central City during the summer in addition to the opera's full orchestra. Held the third week in June, this is an evening of the opera's "greatest hits." The picnic supper tickets run $30 for dinner and the performance.

The Breckenridge Music Festival
The Riverwalk Performing Arts Center, Park Ave. and Four O'Clock Rd., Breckenridge • (970) 453-2120

Pretty much every day from mid-June to mid-August, visitors can enjoy performances by the National Repertory Orchestra and the Breckenridge Music Institute. Some days, it's

INSIDERS' TIP

Festivals and events any time of year are great opportunities to get the jump on Christmas shopping. They often feature the work of local artists and craftspeople.

just practice, but that can be even more interesting — and you get in free. Tickets for the regular performances run from $10 to $20.

Madam Lou Bunch Day
Teller House, 120 Eureka, Central City
• (303) 582-5322

Madam Lou Bunch was a scarlet woman who ran a herd of brazen bawds, prancing harlots and painted hussies in the mining boomtown days of Central City. The main event of this celebration, held on the Saturday and Sunday of Father's Day weekend, is a race on Main Street between brass beds on wheels, each of which is pushed by a brace of men in period costumes and carries a woman in full strumpet regalia.

There are also costume contests and other activities including music, an evening ball and trophy ceremony. The daytime activities are free; the ball costs $5.

Juneteenth
The Five Points Business District, Welton St. (between 24th and 28th sts.)
• (303) 832-3770

A major festivity of Denver's black community, Juneteenth stands for June 19, which was the day that slavery ended in Texas. For about three days, there are booths with food, arts and crafts, games and other activities. There is also a baseball tournament, exhibits at the Black American West Museum (see our Attractions chapter), a senior luncheon, large parade, Sunday gospel fest and more. The event is free.

LoDo Brewfest
Lower Downtown, Between the newer downtown area and the Central Platte Valley • (303) 698-HOPS

This is two days of opportunity in mid-June to sample more than 30 kinds of beer from Colorado brewpubs and microbreweries, of which the festival organizers claim Colorado has more than any place in the world. Colorado boasts about 90 microbreweries and brewpubs. Five Colorado wineries also will be present. The festivities include a street/block party with food and entertainment. Five bucks will get you in; then plan to pay $1 per 6-ounce taste.

Summer Pops Concert Series
The Arvada Center for the Arts and Humanities, 6901 Wadsworth Blvd., Arvada • (303) 431-3939

For a mixture of country, Big Band, jazz and Cajun music, come to the Arvada Center's outdoor amphitheater from the third weekend in June to the third weekend in August. You can picnic on the grounds before the shows and browse the art gallery. You can bring your picnic inside for the concert. There's also a musical every year, usually the last week of July and first week of August. Ticket prices range from $8 to $20.

Ride the Rockies
Statewide, a different route every year
• (303) 820-1338

If you have thighs like Tyrannosaurus Rex, Ride the Rockies is for you. At the very least, you should be in shape. This event lasts six to seven days, during which time a stream of about 2,000 jolly, miserable, laughing, moaning, exuberant bicyclists push their pedals for more than 400 miles. You will go through resort towns like Steamboat Springs or Vail, and more "everyday" towns like Walsenburg, Durango and Granby. You'll be riding up and down a lot, probably crossing the Continental Divide about three times and doing plenty of relatively lesser mountain passes as well. At night, you'll probably camp on high school sports fields or in their gyms. Communities nightly provide low-cost meals and various forms of entertainment. Not everyone can take part.

The event's title sponsor, *The Denver Post*, holds a lottery in February. If you win, you're in. The registration fee has been around $160 and usually includes something like a cycling jacket, jersey or shorts.

Children's and Adult Concerts
Denver Botanic Gardens, 1005 York St.
• (303) 331-4000

Sitting on the grass in the midst of the Denver Botanic Gardens on a summer evening is a great way to listen to jazz and classical music. This series of outdoor concerts is aimed at families in an informal setting. Bring a picnic and a blanket and you're set for a fun evening. Tickets range from $10 to $18.

Scandinavian Midsummer Festival
Bond Park, Virginia St. and Elkhorn Ave.,
Estes Park • (970) 586-9203

June 24 is midsummer in the Scandinavian countries. This prompts their biggest celebration next to Christmas. This big, traditional Scandinavian festival features arts, crafts, ethnic foods, educational mini-seminars and demonstrations, and the raising of the maypole with appropriate cavorting of Scandinavian folk dancers every hour. At least one dance group usually comes all the way from Scandinavia. There's also a bonfire, which is how Norwegians celebrate midsummer. Not surprisingly, this free festival is held the last Friday and Saturday of June, closest to June 24.

Summer Nights
Larimer Square, Larimer St. (between 14th and 15th sts.) • (303) 534-2367

On four nights, at varying dates from late June through late August, Larimer Square hosts a free concert series featuring rhythm and blues, jazz and Big Band music. It's open to the public, featuring national talent such as the Nylons and Beausoleil plus spirits and edibles. Concerts happen from 7:30 to 11 PM.

Greek Marketplace
The Assumption Greek Orthodox
Cathedral, 4610 E. Alameda Ave.
• (303) 388-9314

Assumption Greek Orthodox Cathedral, with its gold dome, is a familiar landmark. Denver's Greeks and Grecophiles convene here on the church grounds each year in mid-June for "wonderful food prepared by the ladies of our church," live music and Greek dance shows done by groups ranging in age from children to adults. Calamari, Aegean beer, wine and beverages are served, and there is usually a gift shop and a small carnival area for kids. All proceeds benefit the church. Admission is $1; the price for food and drink varies.

The Yellow Rose Ball: Opening Night
Central City Opera House, 124 Eureka,
Central City • (303) 292-6700

In late June or early July, the Central City Opera's season begins, usually with the annual presentation of the Central City Flower Girls followed by a dinner at the Teller House and a performance. Tickets for both are $175; for the performance only, $28 to $52.

International Buskerfest
16th Street Mall, Curtis to Larimer sts.
• (303) 534-6161

Buskers are street entertainers. This free event in late June features more than 200 lively shows by world-class jugglers, mimes, sword swallowers, magicians, tightrope artists, singers and dancers. After 8 PM, all buskers move to Larimer Street (it's closed to traffic for this event) to perform.

American Red Cross Fat Tire Classic
Locations throughout Winter Park and
Fraser Valley • (303) 722-7474

This two-day mountain-bike pledge tour is held the last weekend in June to benefit the American Red Cross. It's not a race; it's just a tour, and it has events for all levels of riders. You should be in shape, though. Even the beginner's ride is a 15-mile off-road event. All events include additional challenges along the way for those who want more fun/pain. You'll find gourmet food, live musical entertainment on Saturday night, prizes for different categories of riders and a raffle at this event. Along with the $55 registration fee, each rider must raise $175 in pledges.

Lady Foot Locker 5K
Pulaski Park, Alameda St. and Cherry
Creek Dr. N. • (303) 863-1633

Usually held the last Sunday in June, this one-day event includes a 5K run and walk for

---

INSIDERS' TIP

Find specifics on festivals and events each week by looking at the Friday sections of *The Denver Post*, *Rocky Mountain News* and Boulder's *Daily Camera*. Also check the activities/events listings in Denver's weekly newspaper, *Westword*.

girls and women only. The cost is $18 for women; less for girls. Proceeds benefit Gateway, a shelter for battered women and their children. Anyone can participate in Raymond's Fun Run, which is free and open to the whole family. The Lady Foot Locker 5K is one of the largest women-only events in the nation.

Bike to the Zoo Day
The Denver Zoo in City Park, E. 23rd Ave. and Steele St. • (303) 331-4100

In conjunction with Denver Bike Month, everybody who rides their bike to the zoo on the last Sunday in June gets in free and receives a bike-to-the-zoo button and free valet bike parking.

July

Summer Nights
See June entry.

Renaissance Festival
See June entry.

Summer Pops Concert Series
See June entry.

Children's and Adult Concerts
See June entry.

Breckenridge Music Festival
See June entry.

Cherry Creek Arts Festival
Cherry Creek North (bordered by St. Paul St. on the east and Clayton St. on the west, Second St. on the south and Third St. on the north) • (303) 355-2787

Pulling some 300,000 visitors for this event,

Denver's upscale retail shopping area hosts a sidewalk festival during Fourth of July weekend featuring fine arts and crafts, with 200 artists from around the nation and Mexico. National and international performers provide entertainment. Local chefs cook up their best for a block-long culinary-arts extravaganza where food vendors line the street. Browsing is free.

The Independence Day Celebration
Four Mile Historic Park, 715 S. Forest St. • (303) 399-1859

The Four Mile Historic Park, Denver's living-history park, gives good old-fashioned Fourth of July fun in the wholesome family manner. This is a day of patriotic music, games and activities featuring re-enactments by historically costumed people, stagecoach rides and food. Past events also included historic and craft demonstrations such as blacksmithing, quilting, weaving, lacemaking and butter churning. Admission is $5 per adult, $3 per child.

Race to the Clouds
Pikes Peak, outside Colorado Springs • (719) 685-4400

You can enjoy this famous annual Fourth of July Pikes Peak Hill Climb even if you're not one of the top race-car drivers who come here to test their skills on one of Colorado's 14,000-foot peaks. But you do need tickets ($25) ahead of time to drive up, park and watch the race from designated areas on the mountain. There are also numerous other races and events in the weeks surrounding this big one.

Freedomfest
Main St., Central City • (303) (800) 542-2999

Central City's patriotic celebration features bands playing American-style music, food

---

INSIDERS' TIP

Nature puts on her own annual events: the changing of the aspen in the fall, which draws Denverites out of the city to high-country roads; the ritual of elk bugling from mid-September to mid-October at Rocky Mountain National Park; and the blooming of a sea of irises at Long's Iris Garden, 3240 Broadway, Boulder, in late May/early June, where you can gaze, photograph or dig your own clumps for a reasonable price.

booths, a beer garden, hay-wagon and carriage rides and fireworks. It is held around the Fourth of July and is free.

Genuine Jazz in July
Maggie Pond at the base of Peak 9 Ski Area, Breckenridge • (970) 453-6018

Breckenridge's three-day, mid-July jazz festival features Colorado artists. Evening sessions take place at local bars. Free daytime performances occur at Maggie Pond, where a stage is built over the water and spectators sit on the shore. Evening events cost as much as $25 for a weekend pass. Attending a single performance runs around $8.

OBON: Gathering of Joy
Sakura Square, Lawrence St. (between 19th and 20th Sts.) • (303) 295-1844

A gathering in honor of those who have passed away, the OBON service is held at 10 AM in the heart of the Japanese cultural and business center. The event is usually held the second Sunday of July, but the date depends on when the Colorado Rockies are playing.

Rooftop Rodeo
Estes Park Fairgrounds, Community Dr. off Hwy. 36, Estes Park
• (970) 586-6104, (800) 44-ESTES

A rodeo plain and simple, this four-day event in mid-July offers a rodeo parade and six PRCA (Professional Rodeo Cowboy Association) rodeos, along with Western Heritage Day ($5 admission) including mountain-man rendezvous, an Indian village, gold panning, western entertainment on stage and so on. Other past attractions include cowboy cartoonists and poets, a dirt dance and concerts. The rodeo parade is free; each rodeo's admission is $7.

Buffalo Bill Days
Locations throughout Golden
• (303) 279-3113

The Buffalo Bill Days Corp. hosts this western celebration, which started in Buffalo Bill's honor but is now a celebration held every year (usually the third weekend in July) to promote the City of Golden. The event in the past has included a parade and other activities on Main Street and in Parfet Park and Clear Creek Living History Park. There has been musical entertainment, a golf tournament, country and western dance contests, living history re-enactments, a talent contest, a burro race and the Golden Derby for Young Racers. In years past, there was also a 6K and 10K race. Admission is free.

Buffalo Bill Day
The Buffalo Bill Memorial Museum on Lookout Mountain, 987½ Lookout Mountain Rd., Golden • (303) 526-0744

We just can't get enough of Buffalo Bill. The Buffalo Bill Memorial Museum celebrates its namesake with wagon rides, Indian dancers, music, an outdoor barbecue and demonstrations of old daily-life techniques such as weaving, spinning, making saddles, preparing foods, preserving foods and making bullets. Held in mid- to late July, this event is free.

Keystone Arts & Crafts Celebration
Keystone Village at Keystone Resort, Keystone • (800) 354-4FUN

This event features artists, live entertainment and booths. It is usually held the second weekend in July. Admission is free. Keystone is Exit 205 off I-70 W.

Drums Along the Rockies
Mile High Stadium, 2755 W. 17th St.
• (303) 424-6396

This is a booming good time in mid- to late July. It is the annual regional drum and bugle corps championships. Mile High Stadium usually is sparsely filled, mainly by alumni of the corps as well as friends and families of those competing, so there's plenty of room to spread out and relax. About eight of the best drum and bugle corps from the western United States and Canada compete in the Drum Corps Regional Championships, usually including four or five of the top-ranked corps in the world. Tickets range from $10 to $50.

Molly Brown's Birthday
The Molly Brown House Museum, 1340 Pennsylvania St. • (303) 832-4092

Outcast from high society though she remained, the Unsinkable Molly Brown was a celebrity, and her house is a museum. It celebrates her birthday on July 18 with an authentic 19th-century summer-evening ice cream social/garden party at which servers wear period costumes and attendees are welcome to do likewise. The price of admission — $7 for adults, $1.50 for kids and $5 for seniors — benefits the museum.

Mopar Parts Mile-High Nationals
Bandimere Speedway, 3051 S. Rooney Rd., Morrison • (303) 697-6001

This is motorhead heaven. Between 600 and 700 cars and the nation's top racers compete in pro-stock dragsters, top fuel cars and nitro funny cars in mid-July. Tickets range from $35 to $50, and all seats are reserved.

Theater in the Park
Greek Amphitheatre in Civic Center Park, between Colfax Ave. and 14th St. • (303) 770-2106

Twelve performances over four weeks (the last two weekends in July and the first two weekends in August) grace this wonderful outdoor amphitheater. Previous shows include the musical *Oliver!*, *Peter and the Wolf* in pantomime, the female version of the *Odd Couple* and flamenco ballet. Admission is free; picnics are encouraged.

Winter Park American Music Festival
Winter Park Resort, Winter Park • (303) 892-0961

This festival features two days of great music in a great setting. People sit on Lower Parkway, a ski run, and look down on the stage. Winter Park switches around concerts and contents every year, but you're likely to see some combination of top national country, folk, western, jazz, easy listening, instrumental, vocal and light-rock acts. Past performers include Hiroshima, Sarah McLachlan, David and Tab Benoit, the Brian Setzer Orchestra, George Benson, Bonnie Raitt, Lyle Lovett, Big Head Todd and the Monsters and Little Feat. There are usually vendors of food and trinkets. Tickets for this mid-July event range from $25 for one day to $45 for two days.

Alpine Artaffair
Main St., Winter Park • (800) 903-7275

At this two-day, outdoor, judged and juried art event, you can expect about 90 booths, exhibiting artists and craftspersons, photography, oil painting, pottery, jewelry and more. Live entertainment and craft demonstrations keep things upbeat at this third-weekend-in-July event. Admission is free.

Cherry Blossom Festival
Sakura Square, Lawrence St. (between 19th and 20th sts.) • (303) 295-1844

This celebration of Japanese culture is held in the heart of Denver's Japanese Community. If you love Japanese food, check out the food bazaar. Also watch martial arts displays, an Akita dog show, bonsai demonstrations and traditional folk dancing. The free event is held in mid-July, but the date varies depending on when the Colorado Rockies are playing.

Cheyenne Frontier Days
Frontier Park, Cheyenne, Wyo. • (800) 227-6336

This is a 10-day western theme event centered around rodeo events, but it also includes a carnival, evening shows by some of the biggest names in country-western music, parades, free pancake breakfasts, a chili cook-off, a performance by the Air Force Thunderbirds team and a free entertainment area with music and other acts. Cheyenne is only 100 miles from Denver, so it's a nice way to spend a day. About 300,000 people show up during the 10 days, but parking is generally no problem in the gravel lots around the Frontier Park stadium. The event is held the last full week in July. Gate admission is $2; rodeo tickets range from $8 to $20; night shows range from $14 to $18. To get to Frontier Park, take I-25 N. to Central Avenue Exit. Go south to Eighth Avenue and go west on Eighth to Frontier Park.

CAP the Rockies Ride for AIDS
Start at Kenosha Pass, finish in Denver • (303) 837-0166 • www.capride.org

As a fundraiser for the five different AIDS organizations in Colorado, riders gather a minimum of $2,000 in pledges and participate in a five-day, 300-mile bike ride through the Rockies.This year's event will be held from July 27 to August 1. Colorado AIDS Project hosts informational meetings, fundraising workshops and training seminars. Visit their web site for more information.

August

Summer Nights
See June entry.

Summer Pops Concert Series
See June entry.

Children's and Adult Concerts
See June entry.

Breckenridge Music Festival
See June entry.

Weld County Fair
Island Grove Regional Park,
425 N. 15th Ave., Greeley
• (970) 356-4000 Ext. 4465

County fair! Weld County, north of Adams County, ranks fourth among counties nationwide in agricultural revenues. Weld County contains the world's two largest feedlots and accounts for about a quarter of Colorado's agriculture. Its county fair does not have a carnival midway, but it does have a lot of animal showings and competitions, including about 1,400 4-H and FFA kids, with an animal-catching contest, food booths, a fun fair and a concert night. The fair is held in early August and is free to the public.

Rocky Mountain Wine and Food Festival
Winter Park Resort, Winter Park
• (970) 726-1540

This is mainly a weekend affair — always in early August — with wine and beer tasting and food tasting of creations prepared by some of Colorado's finest chefs. But the festival does start earlier in the week with evening events such as dinners at restaurants in the valley, where winemakers representing their products provide different wines throughout the evening to go with the meals. These events are sold out ahead of time, so get on the stick if you want a reservation. There are also wine and beer seminars. A fund-raiser for the National Sports Center for the Disabled, this event

costs $30 for all seminars and tastings, but if you buy your ticket in advance, it's $27.50.

Sculpture in the Park Show and Sale
Benson Park Sculpture Garden, 29th St.
and Taft St., Loveland • (800) 551-1752

Loveland bills this as one of the largest exhibitions of sculpture in the United States. The Benson Park Sculpture Garden ordinarily has about 40 sculptures, but on this day during the second weekend in August, it attracts about 180 artists from around the United States and Canada who show and sell their pieces. The event features entertainment, demonstrations by artists, a silent auction and speed-sculpting (artists who sculpt while you watch) demonstrations. Proceeds from this event buy new art for the Sculpture Garden. Tickets are $5.

Colorado Scottish Festival and Highland Games
Highlands Heritage Park, Quebec St. and
Lincoln Ave., Highlands Ranch
• (303) 238-6524

Wake up and smell the heather on the second weekend in August. Enjoy the competitions: bagpiping and drumming, highland athletic events and highland dancing. You'll also find vendors selling merchandise from the British Isles, exhibitions of highland cattle and dogs, and authentic food and beverages. Admission is $8 for adults, $4 for seniors and children. Take Colo. Highway 470 (on the south side of Denver) to Quebec Street and go south to the intersection with Lincoln Avenue.

Douglas County Fair
Douglas County Fairgrounds, 410
Fairgrounds Rd., Castle Rock
• (303) 688-4597

This is an old-fashioned August shindig with a rodeo, carnival and all the accoutrements of county fairdom. Simultaneously with the county fair, Castle Rock holds a community fair that includes a parade to celebrate the 4-H winners, with more than 100 parade entries and a barbecue in the Courthouse Square. The fair is free. The rodeo costs $8 for ages 13 and older, $6 for ages 6 to 12, and free for kids younger than 6. Tickets purchased

Photo: Daily Camera

Cowboys compete all year long, from summer rodeos to the Colorado
State Fair to the National Western Stock Show and Cheyenne Frontier Days.

in advance are discounted 25 percent. Call the number above to find where discounted tickets are sold.

Adams County Fair and Rodeo
Adams County Fairgrounds, 9755 Henderson Rd., Brighton • (303) 637-8000

Adams County claims the largest county fair in Colorado, and it has included such attractions as rodeos, tractor pulls, more than 150 exhibits and livestock shows, 4-H events, a children's pavilion, petting zoo, multicultural village, artisans bazaar, free entertainment and top-name concerts. Past celebrity entertainers include Alan Jackson and Mel Tillis. There's also a Mexican Cultural Day at the fair. Look for this event the first weekend in August. Admission to the fair is free; parking costs $3.

No Man's Land
Locations throughout Breckenridge • (970) 453-6018

From a fluke of history, a celebration is born. In 1936, the story goes, a local women's club discovered that Breckenridge had been left off various maps and treaties. So they had a flag-raising attended by Colorado's governor and invested Breckenridge into the United States. Still, for four days in August every year, Breckenridge likes to pretend that it is not part of the United States and calls itself the Kingdom of Breckenridge. The city celebrates its independence with the International Woodcarving Competition, historic walking tours, gold-panning demonstrations and other eccentricities plus concerts. Events are free, except for concerts ($10 to $20).

Western Welcome Week
Various locations in Littleton
• **(303) 797-5774, (303) 730-7369**

This is Littleton's big yearly celebration of itself. It runs for 10 days, beginning the second Friday in August. You'll find arts and crafts and continuous entertainment on Littleton's Main Street, with concerts, fireworks, a barbecue, pancake breakfasts, a chili cook-off, circus, used book sales and 5K and 15K races. There's also a canine Frisbee competition. Most events are free.

The Miner's Music and Jazz Festival
Main St., Central City • (800) 542-2999

Colorado's gambling mecca gets down with a weekend featuring hot jazz by renowned musicians plus an art festival, hay-wagon rides, a beer garden and dancing on historic Main Street. The free event is held in mid-August.

Winter Park Famous Flamethrower High Altitude Chili Cookoff
Main St., Winter Park • (800) 903-7275

This is a one-day opportunity to sample different types of chili and salsa produced for this regional competition. Costumed chili chefs vie for the Flamethrower title and the opportunity to represent the Rocky Mountain Region in the World Chili Cookoff. One hot prospect, tasty samples are available at a mere two bits a taste.

The Sprint International
Castle Pines Golf Club,
1000 Hummingbird Dr., Castle Rock
• **(303) 660-8000, (800) 755-1986**

A special afterlife for golf-watchers might look something like this Colorado golf event of the year. One of the world's great courses hosts one of the most unique and challenging tournaments of the Professional Golf Association's finest. An international field presents the best golfers from around the world. You're welcome to walk the holes with the golfers, thrill to their mighty drives and stand behind ropes at each hole and clap or moan as they sink or muff their putts.

You can attend golfing clinics, and if the pros are good Joes, you may even be able to talk with them and get your picture taken with them. This event is held the third week in August, Monday through Sunday. It's $150 to watch the whole week, and tickets are only sold in weeklong packages, though you can divide that package amongst your golf-loving friends.

Carnation Festival
Albert E. Anderson Park,
44th and Field sts., Wheat Ridge
• **(303) 422-0326, (303) 235-2806**

The fine community of Wheat Ridge has a jolly small-town parade along 38th Street from Harlan to Upham streets on the third weekend in August. Floats are invited to cover themselves with carnations, though a lot of them don't. The carnival in the park has rides for children, and the carnival midway has food, arts and crafts, the usual offerings. There's also a rubber duck race on Clear Creek; you buy sponsorship of a rubber duck — a fundraiser for Family Tree, a battered-women's shelter program. Admission is free.

Colorado State Fair
State Fairgrounds, 101 Beulah Ave.,
Pueblo • (800) 444-3247

The City of Pueblo is the farthest away of any listing in this guide for Annual Festivals and Events (it's two hours south of Denver on I-25), but this is the state fair. And who wouldn't want to know about that? It's one of the state's largest annual events as well as a big-time Colorado tradition.

It's rather huge, so let's just say there are all the rodeo events, livestock sales, horse shows, cooking competitions, midway carnival rides, games and lots of good food that we as Americans have come to expect from this distinctive piece of Americana known as the state fair. There are also concerts with big-name country-western singers who in the past included Garth Brooks, George Strait and Vince Gill. There are plenty of performers of other types of music as well. Julio Iglesias even came one year.

The first day of the fair is Fiesta Day, a Mexican heritage day. The fair runs for two weeks, late August to early September. General admission runs around $6. Plan to buy tickets for concerts and rodeos.

King of the Rockies
Mountain Bike Festival
Base of the Winter Park Ski Area, Winter Park • (970) 887-2519

This festival in mid- to late August features races and guided mountain-biking tours for all levels of mountain bikers as well as a mountain-bike and summer-sports expo. Tickets to enter range from $10 to $20 depending on the number of competitions you participate in.

Rocky Mountain Folks Festival
U.S. Hwy. 36, Lyons (on the way to Estes Park) • (800) 624-2422

This festival in mid-August features folk-music performers, in the past including artists Michelle Shocked, John Gorka, The Story, and Lowen and Navarro. There is also the Song School, with workshops and activities geared toward future musicians, and a song seminar that includes sessions on songwriting, copyrighting, bookkeeping, scoring and other elements of being a professional singer/songwriter. Last year, festival tickets were $60. Admission to the Song School is around $300.

Lakewood on Parade
Lakewood Park, Kipling St. and Cedar St., Lakewood • (303) 987-7800

The City of Lakewood's hour in the community-festival sun, this free event on the weekend before Labor Day weekend typically combines food, a bike race, games, entertainment, a parade, tennis tournament, golf tournament, car show and art show.

September

12th Annual AIDS Walk Colorado
Cheesman Park, central Denver
• (303) 837-0166
• www.capwalk.org

Every year, more than 15,000 people converge in Cheesman Park to raise money for Colorado AIDS Project and other AIDS organizations throughout the state by walking 10 kilometers. The 1999 event is scheduled for September 1. Volunteers are usually needed, along with walkers. For more information see their web site.

The Festival of Mountain and Plain:
A Taste of Colorado
Civic Center Park, between Colfax Ave. and 14th St. • (303) 534-6161

It's the Promised Land for gourmet and gourmand, and for those seeking fun, it's equally grand. Running about four days around the Labor Day weekend, this is one of Denver's largest annual gatherings, attracting more than 400,000. Organizers usually even block off a street or two. You can sample culinary delights from Greater Denver restaurants, so it's a good way to find new restaurants dear to your tastes. It's also about five festivals in one: not only a food festival, but also a children's festival, an arts and crafts festival, a carnival midway, stages with live entertainment and a kaleidoscope of buskers, vendors and other jollies.

The Festival of Mountain and Plain actually began in the 1800s and was named to celebrate Denver's dual personality as the Queen City of the Plains and the Monarch Metropolis of the Mountains. Entertainment is free; food can be purchased with tickets.

Colorado Springs Balloon Classic
Memorial Park, Pikes Peak Ave. and Union Blvd., Colorado Springs
• (719) 471-4833

This is a grand spectacle. Typically about 125 hot-air balloons from around the nation ascend en masse at 7 AM on Saturday, Sunday and Monday of Labor Day weekend. They are preceded by the "dawn patrol," about five balloons going up at 5:30 AM and dangling strobe lights, just to let folks know that the big event is coming. About 50 balloons light up Saturday night in the "Balloon Glo." (Albuquerque trademarked the name "Balloon Glow," so the folks in the Springs had to drop the "w.") In 1995 the festival added a new event, the Sunday night "glo" over the downtown area. Kiwanis Country Breakfast is served in a big tent from 5:30 to 9:30 each morning. There is a model hot-air balloon competition. Sky divers jump onto the site every morning and Saturday and Sunday evenings.

Past years included cloggers, an orchestra and a children's chorale. Plus there's a concert Saturday night. Admission is free.

Longs Peak Scottish-Irish Highland Festival

Various locations in Estes Park
• (800) 44-ESTES

Held the weekend after Labor Day, the Celtic tradition goes bananas for four straight days — Thursday night through Sunday night — with performances and competitions by bagpipe bands, highland dancers, Irish step dancers, highland dogs herding sheep, and Scottish athletes throwing the hammer and the caber. There is a parade, medieval re-enactments and folk concerts, performances on the Celtic harp and fiddle and tin-whistle contests. There's also a seminar on tartans and other necessities of the Celtic aesthetic. Expect a $10-per-day gate fee.

Fall Fest

Downtown Golden • (303) 279-3113

This used to be Oktoberfest, but organizers decided to broaden the scope. It's two days of food, entertainment, arts and crafts, a farmers' market, kids' activities, games, a mini-carnival and rides. And let's not forget a hometown parade. Look for this event in early to mid-September.

Castle Rock ArtFest

Old Courthouse Square, 301 Wilcox St., Castle Rock • (303) 688-4597

This arts festival is held the weekend after Labor Day, with family entertainment, continuous musical performances, children's entertainment and food. It features artists displaying, selling and working in the full range of media. Admission tends to run around $2.

Senior Citizens' Day at the Zoo

The Denver Zoo in City Park, E. 23rd Ave. and Steele St. • (303) 331-4100

Seniors 55 and older get into the zoo free, with entertainment, tours and free refreshments on the second Tuesday in September.

Summerset Festival

Clement Park, Bowles Ave. and Pierce St., South Jefferson County
• (303) 973-9155

This end-of-summer (second weekend after Labor Day) outdoor celebration has included a parade, hot-air balloon rides, a pancake breakfast and other food, a volleyball tournament, entertainment, booths, games, an arts and crafts show, golf tournament, softball tournament, concert-in-the-park picnic, 5K run and fishing derby. Admission is free.

Gateway to the Rockies Parade and Festival

Colfax Ave. (between Dayton and Florence sts.), Aurora • (303) 361-6169

This is Aurora's mid-September party. Folks on the west side of Denver like to think of Jefferson County as the gateway to the Rockies, but Aurora also makes that claim. Aurora's reason is that E. Colfax Avenue is the original U.S. Highway 40 into the Rocky Mountain area, and until I-70 was built, Aurora was the first city that westbound travelers hit on their way into Greater Denver. The free party has in the past included a parade, a farmers' market, arts and crafts, food booths with Colorado produce, on-stage entertainment, clowns, face painting, a petting zoo and pony rides.

Miniatures, Dolls & Toys Fall Show and Sale

Holiday Inn DIA, I-70 and Chambers Rd.
• (303) 322-1053

This is a benefit for the Denver Museum of Miniatures, Dolls & Toys, though the show and sale is never held there. Usually it's at some place with conference-room space. It typically includes more than 100 national artists who specialize in making miniatures, dolls, teddy bears and toys. They display and sell their wares during a two-day weekend in mid-September. There are also workshops Wednesday through Sunday that are open to the public, but interested folks must preregister. Admission is $3 to $5.

The Gilpin County Historical Society's Annual Cemetery Crawl

Various historic cemeteries in Central City • (303) 582-5283

Lend an ear to the living dead at this entertaining and educational event portraying the life of Gilpin County 100 years ago. Members and friends of the Gilpin historical society transform into "spirits" of former residents, leaders

Photo: Courtesy of the Larimer Group, Inc.

Denver has many celebrations of its diverse heritage throughout the year.

and movers and shakers of the period. The spirits share their stories as visitors walk through different historic cemeteries in mid-September. Admission is $5.

Mexican Independence Day
Civic Center Park, between Colfax Ave. and 14th St. • (303) 331-1870

Held in conjunction with the Mexican Consulate, this free event celebrates Mexican Independence Day, which is September 16. There is Latino entertainment including con-

tinuous live music, dancers, artists and food vendors. Performances on the Civic Center's Greek Amphitheatre stage usually crank up around 6 PM. Past events included a 5K run.

Taste of Keystone and Colorfest
Keystone Village at Keystone Resort, Keystone • (800) 354-4386

Held the second weekend in September, this includes the Taste of Keystone — food booths from all the Keystone restaurants — along with a raffle and musical entertainment, all on Saturday, with a golf tournament on Sunday. Food tickets will be available at the event for $1 each.

Breckenridge Festival of Film
Various locations in Breckenridge
- **(970) 453-6200**

This three-day fest in mid-September includes premieres of documentaries, feature films and children's features as well as parties in local clubs and bars. Past years have seen visits by James Earl Jones, Mary Steenburgen, Elliott Gould and Angie Dickinson. A VIP pass is $110; individual movie tickets are $6 each.

Fall Colorfest
Downtown Winter Park
- **(970) 726-4118**

This mid-September celebration marks the logging history of the Fraser Valley and the changing of the aspens as the scenic mountain community enters the fall season. A weekend highlight is the Scheer's Lumberjack Show of Champions, and you can take part in other activities such as mountain biking and hiking. All events are free.

Oktoberfest
Larimer Square, Larimer St. (between 14th and 15th sts.) • (303) 534-2367

Denver's main bow to the famous harvest festival of Munich is filled with polka bands and beer-drinking and sausage-eating fun. You'll see plenty of jolly Germanic costumes. This is one of the highlights of Larimer Square's festival year, and it's free, unless you eat and drink. Oktoberfest includes Kinderplatz, a kids area that has included "Prince Ludwig's castle," where kids can enjoy the Black Forest Maze and German storytellers, and "the world's shortest parade." It is usually held for two full weekends in mid-September.

Rocky Mountain Snowmobile Winter Recreation Exhibition
The National Western Stock Show Complex, 4600 Humboldt St. (take the Brighton Blvd. exit off I-70)
- **(303) 892-6800**

If Greater Denver hasn't had at least a trace of snow by the third weekend in September, it's an unusual year. And if you don't make a point of enjoying snow, you won't enjoy winter. Snowmobiles are one way of enjoying snow, so you may want to check out the latest in snowmobiles and accessories, snowmobile services and snowmobile travel destinations. Admission is $7 for adults; kids younger than 12 are free.

Fall Festival
Northridge Park & Recreation Center, 8801 S. Broadway, Highlands Ranch
- **(303) 791-8958**

This crafts show in late September features more than 100 crafters. You'll find a crafts bazaar, entertainers and exhibitors, a pumpkin-carving contest, food and kid activities.

October

Central City Opera Gala
Central City Opera House, 124 Eureka St., Central City
- **(303) 292-6700**

The historic opera house in Central City starts its season in summer, but it likes to remind people as early as October that there's some good singing to come in the summer to follow. This is an evening of dancing, cocktails, dinner, a silent auction and cabaret performance. Tickets are $150 per person.

Colorado Performing Arts Festival
Denver Performing Arts Complex, Speer Blvd. and Arapahoe St. • (303) 640-2678

Sample the performing arts in this free festival held the first weekend of October outside the buildings and inside the theaters of the Denver Performing Arts Complex. There is a daylong theater marathon of nonstop theater, music, dance, cowboy poets and kids' entertainment. Performers from around the state attend and sponsor hands-on art activities on the grounds for kids.

Cider Days Harvest Festival
Lakewood's Heritage Center, 797 S. Wadsworth Blvd., Lakewood
- **(303) 987-7850**

On the first weekend in October, craftspersons re-create historic farm and domestic activities. You'll see antique farm machinery, a vintage tractor-pull competition, food vendors and live music. Admission is $1.

Fall Mountain Man Rendezvous
The Fort Restaurant, 19192 Colo. Hwy. 8, Morrison • (303) 697-4771

Re-enactors of the 1830s and 1840s dress in buckskins and behave like mountain men. Competitions include best costume, tomahawk and knife-throwing, black-powder target shooting, flint and steel fire-starting and survival-skills demonstrations. There's also a mountain-man run. Stop by Native American trading tables where you can buy and trade for the works of Colorado artisans. This free event happens the first week of October.

Great American Beer Festival
Currigan Exhibition Hall, 1324 Champa St. • (303) 447-0126

This is America's biggest beer bash, held in early October. Bring a designated driver because there are more than 1,600 beers to taste, the product of some 300-plus American breweries, microbreweries and brewpubs. Tickets run from $28 to $30.

Chatfield Arboretum Pumpkin Festival
Chatfield Arboretum, Deer Creek Canyon Rd., unincorporated Jefferson Co. • (303) 973-3705

Bring a wheelbarrow and pick your own pumpkin(s) from the pumpkin patch. From tennis-ball sized ones to behemoths, the sale of these orange globes raises money for the Arboretum. There are also hay-rack rides, booths, crafts and food. This event is usually the second Saturday in October and costs $4 per adult; $2 per child. (The price of a pumpkin is extra.) Take Wadsworth Boulevard just south of Colo. Highway 470, then go west on Deer Creek Canyon Road for just more than a quarter-mile.

Denver International Film Festival
Various Denver locations • (303) 595-3456

The late Raymond Burr didn't just shoot all those Perry Mason TV movies in Denver because he liked the local sausage. Denver has an impressive community of film compa-

nies, technicians and artists, and this is that community's finest annual hour. The festival showcases more than 120 top feature, documentary and short films from around the world, screened at the Tivoli Theaters (Ninth Street and Auraria Parkway). The festival, usually held the second week in October, draws a host of actors, directors and producers. Celebrities roam the streets like cattle. Previous festivals have drawn celebrities such as Robert Altman, Geena Davis, Lillian Gish, Peter Bogdanovich, Stockard Channing, John Sayles and Gena Rowlands.

After some film showings, enjoy a question-and-answer session with the director, producer, actors or others involved in the film's genesis. Often, there are seminars for interested regular Joes and Janes on subjects such as screenwriting. Tickets range from $5 to $7.50.

Annual Ski Swap Extravaganza
Winter Park (exact location determined a month before the event) • (970) 726-1590

Winter is knocking at the door. Here's a chance to get new equipment, clothing and accessories — anything related to skiing or snowboarding — and a chance to dump your old stuff. Ski shops from around the Rocky Mountain region put their goods on sale in mid-October and proclaim, "Outstanding bargains with prices reduced up to 60 percent." Guys and gals just like you will be selling their equipment, and you can too. You just have to check in several days before the sale starts. The Friday evening preview costs $2 per individual or $5 per family; Saturday and Sunday are free.

Scuba ExtaSea
Denver Coliseum, 46th and Humboldt sts. • (303) 892-6800

Denver has more divers than any land-locked area in the country, claims the local dive community. Here's a chance to immerse yourself in Denver's biggest annual diving show, with the latest in scuba equipment along with exhibitions by diving-destination companies from around the world. This event is held in late October. Admission is $7 for adults; free for children younger than 12.

Spirits of the Past
Four Mile Historic Park, 715 S. Forest St.
• (303) 399-1859

This Halloween event in Four Mile Historic Park usually is held the third weekend in October. Denver's oldest house, dating from 1859 and spookily decorated, emits a ghostly aura with historically dressed re-enactors in several of the rooms posing as ghosts and doing skits to demonstrate historic lifestyles. Other attractions include a bonfire, hayrides, stagecoach rides and music, all of which make the Historic Park a fun place to hang. The cost is $5 for adults and $3 for children.

Victorian Horrors
Molly Brown House Museum, 1340
Pennsylvania St. • (303) 832-4092

This is a nice way to see the museum. As visitors go tour the house during this last weekend in October, they encounter costumed characters reading selected bits from horror writers like Mary Shelley, Bram Stoker and Edgar Allen Poe. There are refreshments in the carriage house. The cost is $10 per person.

Boo at the Zoo
Denver Zoo in City Park, E. 23rd Ave. and
Steele St. • (303) 331-4110

Celebrate Halloween at the zoo on the last Saturday in October. All kids 12 and younger who wear a costume get in free, but they must be accompanied by a paying adult ($5). Trick-or-treat doors are set up throughout the zoo, and kids get a food or toy item at each door. The zoo sets up a medieval village offering storytelling and face painting.

November

Rocky Mountain Book Festival
Currigan Exhibition Hall, 1324 Champa St.
• (303) 839-8320

About 200 exhibitors sell books at this early November event, and more than 200 authors are on hand to read from or talk about their books. There are panel discussions and activities for kids, including a performance stage. Literary celebrities who attended past events include Judy Blume, Ivan Doig, Barbara Kingsolver and a lot of Colorado authors. The event is free.

Dia De Los Muertos
Mexican Consulate, 48 Steele St.
• (303) 331-1870

The Day of the Dead is an old Mexican tradition celebrating death and the departed, and here in Denver it's an exhibition of morbid arts, crafts and rituals. That doesn't mean morbid in a negative sense — the Mexicans have a lot of fun with it. Although you really have to see it in Mexico to enjoy the full festive force of the occasion, you can have a lot of fun with it in Denver too.

This free event is held sometime close to November 1.

Botanic Gardens Holiday Sale
Denver Botanic Gardens, 1005 York St.
• (303) 331-4000

This is a sale of the organic and the inorganic. Plants are for sale as well as herbs, oils and vinegars that volunteers have been producing all year long. Ornaments are crafted and purchased. You'll also find books on gardening, tools and other botany-related subjects. Held the last weekend in November, the sale is free as is admission to the gardens.

Starlighting
Old Courthouse Square, 301 Wilcox,
Castle Rock • (303) 688-4597

The annual lighting of the Christmas star on top of Castle Rock, the monolith that towers above the City of Castle Rock, is a Saturday evening event that's been going on since 1936. It goes along with a ceremony in Courthouse Square that includes carolers, Santa and hot chocolate. It is followed by a fire-department-sponsored chili supper and dance (indoors), all on the Saturday before Thanksgiving. Everything is free except the chili, which will only set you back a couple of dollars.

Come-Catch-the-Glow Christmas Parade
Throughout downtown Estes Park
• (800) 44-ESTES

The Christmas season starts the Friday after Thanksgiving in this mountain town. Start off this free event by visiting with Santa and various character animals; then watch the evening light parade.

Christmas in the Browns' Neighborhood
Molly Brown House Museum, 1340 Pennsylvania St. • (303) 832-4092

Called an architectural history tour, really it's a walking tour of Molly's neighborhood in which you see three different Victorian homes or businesses, including Molly's. Tickets have previously cost $10. The event is held the last Sunday in November.

Winterfest
Larimer Square, Larimer St. (between 14th and 15th sts.) • (303) 534-2367

Starting the day after Thanksgiving and running through the whole month of December, this festivity attracts the diehards who believe cold weather is another excuse to have fun. An outdoor ice rink ($1 to skate, $3 to rent skates) and Santa's workshop provide hours of fun. In a slightly wacky vein, a tuba concert (actually 225 tubas) provides a little music. Every tuba is decorated for the holiday season.

December

World's Largest Christmas Lighting Display
The City and County Building, between Colfax Ave. and 14th St. (across from Civic Center Park) • (303) 640-3386

If light were music, the Denver City and County Building would be the world's largest pipe organ. About 40,000 colored spotlights turn this huge government building into one big neon sign. It has become a Denver holiday tradition, and it's a delight to go walk around and ogle on a frosty winter evening. Bundle up the kids. The display is up from the first Thursday in December until January 1, and then again during the National Western Stock Show in January (see previous entry).

Continental Divide Hot Air Balloon Festival
Lower parking lot at Breckenridge Ski Area, Breckenridge • (970) 453-6018

Hot-air balloons from all over the nation fill the early morning skies in competition; then they fill the evening skies in a spectacular luminary event. The last night of the festival coincides with the lighting of Breckenridge and officially starts the holiday season. All events are free; look for early December dates.

Olde Golden Christmas
Throughout downtown Golden
• (303) 279-3113

Golden may be spreading out a bit, but it's still one of the last of the Greater Denver communities with a real small-town feel about it. And here's an old-fashioned, small-town Christmas festival. This free event is held the first Friday and the first three Saturdays in December, and Golden is a charming location for holiday festivities that begin with candlelight walks through downtown Golden, in which everybody carries a candle and files down to Clear Creek to see the tree lights ignited. Santa Claus shows up. In the past, the event has featured a dance troupe clogging and kids dancing. Then everybody troops over to the Coors Hospitality Center to check out a train exhibit, angel display, Christmas carolers, sleigh rides and other festivities as well as hot chocolate, cookies and candy. On that day and the first three Saturdays in December, other events include snow sculpting, children's igloo contests, wagon rides, cookie decorating and carolers, and kids sometimes get to make their own Christmas ornaments.

Over at the Clear Creek Living History Ranch, in restored old cabins from the turn of the century, folks serve up cowboy beans, doughnut holes, coffee and great entertainment. At the Pioneer Museum, 923 10th Street, there's live musical entertainment, hot cider, cookies and a big bonfire across the creek.

Parade of Lights
Streets of downtown Denver
• (303) 534-6161

This is truly one of the great public events of Denver's calendar: a night parade that lasts more than an hour and features floats, clowns, marching bands, giant balloon figures and other parade elements, all of them lit up or festooned with lights. Greater Denver has a number of big parades during the year, but this one has a special magic by virtue of being at night during the holiday season with everybody bundled up, with steamy breath and rosy cheeks. The whole event is one big Roman candle of multicolored holiday illumination. You might consider bringing extra wraps, blankets and a thermos of something hot and comforting. And as with all parades, if you want to position a folding chair for a front row seat, get there an hour before the show. The parade is the first Friday and Saturday nights the week after Thanksgiving.

Handel's Messiah
Boettcher Concert Hall, 14th and Curtis sts.
• (303) 98-MUSIC

Holiday music lovers adore this one: classic Christmas music with the Colorado Symphony Orchestra and the Colorado Symphony Chorus performing Handel's *Messiah*. There are Friday and Saturday evening performances where you just listen. Sunday afternoon is the big one — the audience is invited to participate in the performance. What you do is get a copy of the sheet music for the *Messiah* from any respectable music store. But call the Colorado Symphony administrative office, (303) 292-5566, to make sure you get the right arrangement. Even if you're not musical, the sheet music should have the words, and you can join the general caterwauling of fellow amateurs and/or just enjoy the spectacle of *Messiah* buffs around you singing away. This is typically held the first weekend in December. Tickets run from $5 to $38.

Candlelight Tours
Denver Museum of Miniatures, Dolls &
Toys • 1880 Gaylord St. • (303) 322-1053

The museum, in a house built in 1899 and decked out for the holidays, has a nice, old-time Christmas atmosphere in which to take a tour by candlelight in early December. Volunteers provide entertainment, including Christmas music, and food is donated by local businesses. Admission is $6 to $8.

Buffalo Bill's Holiday Celebration
The Buffalo Bill Memorial Museum on
Lookout Mountain, 987½ Lookout
Mountain Rd., Golden • (303) 526-0744

This is the museum's free mid-December Christmas event. Past years included bell ringers, Girl Scouts singing Christmas carols, high school choirs, food, drink and a Buffalo Bill look-alike playing Santa Claus.

Holiday Open House
Four Mile Historic Park, 715 S. Forest St.
• (303) 399-1859

Find an old-fashioned Christmas atmosphere at Four Mile Historic Park during this one-day affair in mid-December. St. Nick, or Father Christmas, will be there; Christmas music will be performed; and sleigh rides (if snow conditions permit) will be offered along with the Park's usual offerings of stagecoach rides and demonstrations of antique arts. The cost is $5 per adult, $3 per child.

Wild Lights
The Denver Zoo in City Park,
E. 23rd Ave. and Steele St.
• (303) 331-4110

This memorable family outing takes place on any one of the 31 nights in December from 6 to 9 PM. Thousands of sparkling lights strung on trees create Christmas light sculptures of colored animals. There's nightly entertainment, storytelling, holiday refreshments and a nightly appearance by Santa Claus (through Christmas). Amid all the lights, it's fun to visit the animals and see what they do with their time on a winter night. Be aware that some of the animals are not out, but the seals and sea lions are a real scream playing on the ice. Admission is $5 per adult, $3 per senior or child.

Blossoms of Lights
The Denver Botanic Gardens,
1005 York St. • (303) 331-4000

Have you seen the lights? During the month of December, the Denver Botanic Gardens does for plants in its Blossoms of Lights what the Denver Zoo does for animals in its Wild Lights (see previous listing). There are giant flowers of Christmas lights and lights draped all over plants and other objects. There's nothing more invigorating than a stroll through a wonderland of lights on a frosty evening, and it's a different way of seeing Denver's beloved Botanic Gardens. Nightly entertainment is included, along with holiday re-

freshments, all for a price of $5 per adult and $3 per child or senior.

Teddy Bear Teas
The Denver Botanic Gardens, 1005 York St.
• (303) 331-4000

Children share the English high-tea experience with a favorite teddy bear. A Barbie or a Power Ranger would probably not be turned away, but it would certainly clash with the ambiance, so go for the teddy bear.

Some parents and grandparents tend to dress their kids like little ladies and gentlemen for these teas. There are also snacks and assorted entertainers such as a storyteller and magician. It takes place on select weekends during the Blossoms of Lights (see previous entry), so there's another attraction. Price for the tea is $15 for adults, $8 per child.

Holiday Concerts
The Denver Botanic Gardens, 1005 York St.
• (303) 331-4000

Holiday concerts at the Botanic Gardens range from 16-piece bands to blues and other types of music during selected evenings in December. Concerts are held inside. Outside, you can see the Blossoms of Lights (see previous entry). Tickets range from $10 to $18.

Christmas Pops Concert
Boettcher Concert Hall, 14th and Curtis sts.
• (303) 986-8742

This is a benchmark in our year, our favorite way to inaugurate the Christmas season as being officially under full steam. The concert, usually held in mid-December (Thursday through Sunday), features The Colorado Symphony Orchestra, the Colorado Symphony

Chorus and the Colorado Children's Chorale. Tickets run from $5 to $38.

Christmas Eve Torchlight Parade
Winter Park Resort, Winter Park
• (970) 726-5514

Watch from the base of Winter Park Ski Area as skiers weave a trail of light down the slopes and then create a Christmas-related formation such as a Christmas tree or star. Fireworks and religious services follow. Held on Christmas Eve (naturally), this is a free event.

First Night Colorado
Various locations in downtown Denver
• (303) 399-9005

From afternoon into the evening, downtown Denver celebrates New Year's Eve with family entertainment, music, dance, storytelling, theater, visual displays and the like. At midnight, pyrotechnics herald in the New Year. In 1998, the indoor program (which is most of it) cost $8 in advance, $10 at the door. For the 5K run in the afternoon, it was $20 to register in advance ($25 day-of), but that included admission to the evening festivities.

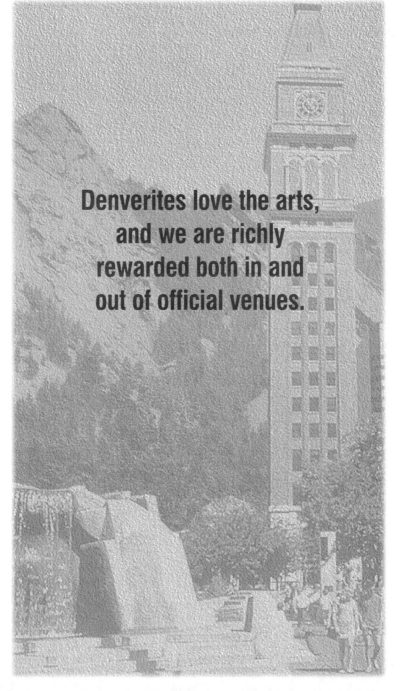

Denverites love the arts, and we are richly rewarded both in and out of official venues.

The Arts

We admit it. We love Denver's cultural scene. In fact, there aren't enough hours in a weekend to do all we'd like. Don't believe us? Consider these offerings on a recent weekend: Ch0ristopher Plummer's one-man show, *Barrymore*, at the Buell Theatre; the annual Colorado Indian Market and Western Art Showcase at Currigan Exhibition Hall; World Class violinist Cho-Liang Lin performing at the beautiful Chautauqua Auditorium in Boulder; and singer-songwriter James Taylor performing at Fiddler's Green outdoor ampitheater.

And that's only a partial list. The point is Denverites love the arts, and we are richly rewarded both in and out of official venues.

In addition to theaters and theater companies, there's a large section on art galleries in this chapter as well as a section on art museums (for other museums see Tours and Attractions.) And given that one person's definition of culture may overlap with another person's idea of popular entertainment, check our Nightlife chapter too. We've put concert venues, both indoor and outdoor, where you buy tickets in advance and sit and listen, in this chapter. Movie houses and bars and restaurants with music or other kinds of entertainment are in the Nightlife chapter.

In this section we begin by describing the Denver Center for the Performing Arts, its theaters and resident performing groups. Next we describe other performing groups, theaters, theater companies and dinner theaters. The following section covers popular music concert venues, and then we move on to community art centers, the most significant of which, the Arvada Center for the Arts and Humanities, is a leader in both performing and visual arts programming. We move on to Greater Denver's art galleries and art museums. Finally we detail the literary arts by describing the many writers' organizations in town.

Performing Arts

Denver Center for the Performing Arts

14th and Curtis sts. • (303) 893-4100 (Box Office), (303) 893-DCPA (Performance Schedule)

Extending over the space of four downtown city blocks, the Denver Center for the Performing Arts (called the Denver Performing Arts Complex on city signage) has 9,000-plus seats and is home to several of Denver's most prominent performing companies, including the Denver Center Theatre Company, the Colorado Symphony Orchestra, the Colorado Ballet and Opera Colorado.

In 1998, the DCPA opened its Donald R. Seawell Grand Ballroom, named for the DCPA's visionary and longtime Board member. The 10,000 square foot, glass and steel ballroom has a maximum capacity of 1,029 persons and can accommodate a variety of functions with many smaller configurations. It is drawing kudos from community leaders and DCPA subscribers who have been the first to see it. Especially popular are its mountain views.

The Theaters

The newest and largest theater in the complex is the **Temple Hoyne Buell Theatre**, which opened in 1991. The theater has 2,800 seats. **Boettcher Concert Hall**, a unique 2,600-seat concert hall-in-the-round, dates from 1978. **The Auditorium Theatre** is a grand old (1908) neoclassical proscenium (traditional stage) house with 2,200 seats. There has been much talk in recent years about renovating the historic venue, but plans — and funds — have yet to be secured. Perhaps 1999 will bring improvements.

The Helen Bonfils Theatre Complex, built in 1979, houses four smaller theaters. **The Stage** (700 seats) is a thrust theater; **The Space** is theater-in-the-round (well, it's actually more of a pentagon) with 450 seats; the **Ricketson Theatre** is a 250-seat informal pros-cenium; and **The Source**, with 200 seats, is an intimate experimental thrust stage. Also in the complex is the **Garner Galleria Theatre**, which presents cabaret shows.

At intermission, patrons spill out into the high, arched, glass-ceilinged galleria to stretch their legs and get some fresh air (or, conversely, to smoke a cigarette). The unique ceiling, which connects the diverse theaters, affords the DCPA the distinction of second-largest theater complex next to New York's Lincoln Center. It's a proud distinction among Denver's cultural set.

The Companies

Denver Center Theatre Company
14th & Curtis sts. • (303) 893-4100

Though Denver Center Attractions brings in touring Broadway shows to the Buell or Auditorium theaters, the Denver Center Theatre Company is the resident troupe, with a season running from October to June. The biggest news for the DCTC in 1998 was winning the Tony Award for Outstanding Regional Theatre. Theater-goers were happy for the troupe, but not surprised given its consistent excellence. In 1998-99, they presented such plays as *Travels with My Aunt*, from the Graham Greene novel, *The Last Night of Ballyhoo*, a funny and poignant tale of a Jewish family, and the hilarious *Sylvia*, a tale about a dog (played by a person). For tickets or information, call the box office or stop in — it's open 10 AM to 6 PM Monday through Saturday. To avoid a service charge, purchase tickets at the box office. Tickets are also available by

phone through TicketMaster at (303) 830-TIXS and at TicketMaster outlets throughout Greater Denver, including the Ticket Bus at 16th and Curtis streets (cash only).

Colorado Symphony Orchestra
821 17th St., Ste. 700
• (303) 98-MUSIC

The Colorado Symphony Orchestra, under the direction of Marin Alsop, plays classical music and popular classics in Boettcher Concert Hall during its season that lasts from September to May. Each season there are also several low-priced "casual classics" concerts, usually on Sunday afternoons.

Colorado Ballet
1278 Lincoln St. • (303) 837-8888

The Colorado Ballet was established as the Colorado Concert Ballet in 1961. The resident company of 25 dancers is under the artistic direction of Martin Fredmann and is the only dance company in the state to perform with a live orchestra. The repertoire includes full-length classical and one-act ballets. Performances are held in either the Buell Theatre or Auditorium Theatre from fall through spring. In 1993, the company made its exciting New York debut and was praised by New York Times dance critic Anna Kisselgoff for its "surprising maturity, presence and solid technique of its performers."

Opera Colorado
695 S. Colorado Blvd., Ste. 20
• (303) 98-MUSIC

Opera Colorado presents three grand operas each winter and spring, two in the round at Boettcher Concert Hall and one on the traditional proscenium stage in the Buell Theatre. It is the only company in the United States producing grand opera in the round. Performances are sung in the original language, with English translations projected onto screens above and around the stage. Opera Colorado director Nathaniel Merrill was resident stage director at the Metropolitan Opera for 28 seasons. Opera Colorado also performs at special holiday concerts and summer festivals throughout the state. The Opera Colorado for Children program includes children's opera workshops, matinee performances for students and an in-school puppet opera.

Colorado Children's Chorale
910 15th St., Ste. 1020 • (303) 892-5600

The Colorado Children's Chorale, a 400-member chorus that tours nationally and internationally, celebrates its 25th anniversary in 1999. Each year it joins the Colorado Symphony Orchestra for a very special, very popular holiday concert.

Denver Young Artists Orchestra
1415 Larimer St., Ste. 301 • (303) 571-1935

The Denver Young Artists Orchestra was formed in 1977 as a means for Colorado's talented young musicians to rehearse and perform under professional standards. The Young Artists Orchestra plays three concerts each year in Boettcher Concert Hall, including a joint concert with the Colorado Symphony. Top admission price at the other two concerts is only $5.

Other Performing Companies

Music

Denver Brass Aries Brass Quintet
2253 Downing St. • (303) 832-4676

Formed in 1981, the 12-member Denver Brass is one of very few symphonic brass ensembles in the country. Concerts feature something for everyone, from splendid brass fanfares to Big Band music. Performances, including an annual Christmas concert, are held at Bethany Lutheran Church, 4500 E. Hampden Avenue, and Montview Boulevard Presbyterian Church, 1980 Dahlia Street.

Also under the same management is Aries Brass Quintet. Founded in 1976, Aries has toured the United States, Europe and South America, performed its fresh and vibrant renditions of chamber music live on National Public Radio and recorded several albums. Aries is a resident company at St. John's Episcopal Cathedral in Denver, 1313 Clarkson Street, and at the Lamont School of Music at the University of Denver.

Dance

Cleo Parker Robinson Dance
119 Park Ave. W. • (303) 295-1759

Cleo Parker Robinson Dance is a multicultural performing arts institution with a professional modern dance company and a dance school based in the historic African Methodist Episcopal Church. The ensemble performs regularly in Denver and extensively around the country and is one of Denver's best-known exports in the arts field. It celebrated its 25th anniversary in 1995. In 1997, the troupe partnered with the DCPA in a move that will help keep Cleo Parker Robinson strong, and help the DCPA reach broader audiences.

David Taylor Dance Theatre
2539 W. Main St., Littleton
• (303) 797-6944

David Taylor Dance Theatre, which marked its 20th season in 1999, is Denver's foremost professional contemporary ballet company. In addition, it's one of the region's major presenters of *The Nutcracker*, which is performed annually at the Arvada Center and on tour throughout the state and the country. The main

---

INSIDERS' TIP

Don't let all the acronyms at Denver's premier theater complex, the Denver Center for the Performing Arts, confuse you. The DCPA is a collection of intimate and grand theaters under one roof. Signage around the complex refers to it as the Denver Performing Arts Complex (DPAC) because that's what city officials dubbed it. But it's all the same place.

focus of the company, however, is original contemporary works. The *Rainforest Ballet* is one of its most popular productions. Although the company is headquartered in Littleton, where it offers ballet classes for children and adults, it performs in different venues throughout Greater Denver from September through May.

Kim Robards Dance
821 Acoma St. • (303) 825-4847

Kim Robards Dance was established in 1987 as Colorado Repertory Dance Company and is an important center for modern dance in Colorado. The dynamic collection of works in KRD's repertoire includes pieces by artistic director Kim Robards along with works by selected international guest choreographers. The professional touring company, which consists of eight to 10 dancers, has performed in New York and California, among other places. Locally, the company presents a winter and spring season at different venues in metro Denver, along with a statewide educational outreach program. The KRD school, established in 1990, offers classes for beginners (ages 4 to adult) and professionals.

Theaters: Variety

Joseph B. Gould Family Paramount Theatre
1631 Glenarm Pl. • (303) 534-8336

The historic Joseph B. Gould Family Paramount Theatre has more than once been on the verge of falling to the wrecker's ball. Built in 1930 by Temple Hoyne Buell, a prominent Denver architect, the theater is the epitome of art deco style and has one of only two Mighty Wurlitzer organs in the country (the other is at Radio City Music Hall in New York City). During the summer of 1994 — under new management yet again — the Paramount underwent extensive remodeling. The Paramount presents a mixed bag of theater, comedy, pop music, children's programming and ballet.

The Bluebird Theater
3317 E. Colfax Ave. • (303) 322-2308

The Bluebird Theater is Denver's newest old movie theater to offer a variety of musical and other programming. Built in 1914 and origi-

nally used to show silent films, the Bluebird fell upon hard times and closed in the late 1980s. The newly restored theater reopened in fall 1994. On Sunday nights, the Bluebird shows cult movie classics and music movies. On Wednesday through Saturday nights, there's a wide variety of live music including rock, reggae, Latin, jazz, folk and blues.

The Ogden Theatre
935 E. Colfax St. 830-2525

A vaudeville-era theater that later became a moviehouse, The Ogden Theatre's newest incarnation is as a concert hall presenting a wide variety of local and national acts.

Theaters and Theater Companies

Avenue Theatre
2119 E. 17th Ave. • (303) 321-5925

The award-winning Avenue Theatre is an intimate space amid 17th Avenue's "restaurant row." Producer John Ashton offers an eclectic schedule of performances that are often comedies but not always. They perform the perennially popular *Murder Most Fowl* — Denver's longest-running play — every holiday season from Thanksgiving to mid-January.

CityStage Ensemble
1553 Platte St. • (303) 433-8082

CityStage Ensemble is in its 12th season at Jack's Theatre in Lower Downtown, an intimate, $3/_4$-round theater. They perform plays by Molière, Shaw and Shakespeare, with a focus on works that address the issues of our times. They also do one original play each season and have a resident playwright.

El Centro Su Teatro
4725 High St. • (303) 296-0219

El Centro Su Teatro was formed in 1971 by students at the University of Colorado at Denver as a forum for those interested in the Chicano movement. It has grown into a multidisciplinary cultural-arts center that sponsors concerts, drama, performance art, dance, festivals, workshops and art exhibitions. The-

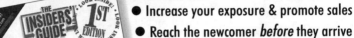

Germinal Stage Denver

Ed Baierlein played to perfection the buffoon role of Major Petkoff in George Bernard Shaw's comedy, *Arms and the Man*, scowling and bellowing, gaping and grinning and lolling his tongue, his face a writhing parade of expressions so foolish that the audience sometimes laughed loudest when he was saying nothing at all.

"That's some play you're running," a fan told him over the telephone one night an hour before the curtain went up. "You're quite a comedian."

"Well, thanks," Baierlein said. "We're doing pretty well. You wanted how many reservations now? Would that be Visa or MasterCard?"

More than a comedian, Baierlein, 53, is also one of the Denver area's most respected serious actors, but that doesn't mean he is above taking reservations, cleaning the theater, maintaining the mailing lists and doing the books at the Germinal Stage Denver theater in northwest Denver.

"The thing that makes Ed unusual is that he's in a category that's almost gone," said Jackie Campbell, theater critic at the *Rocky Mountain News*. "He's manager, producer, director and actor. Because he is all of those things, his theater has his stamp very clearly."

So does Greater Denver. Since its founding in 1973, Germinal Stage has built a faithful audience with more than 130 plays including everything from experimental, first-run productions to Ibsen, Shaw and Shakespeare. Those plays have earned the theater a reputation and influence all out of proportion to its 100-seat facility in an old 5,000-square-foot building.

"The smaller theaters are where the vital theater wells up in any town," says Campbell. "Germinal Stage is certainly the definitive smaller theater in town."

While the large theaters of the Denver Performing Arts Complex are a point of pride and a focus of entertainment on Denver's cultural landscape, Germinal Stage and the more than a dozen other smaller local theaters perhaps provide a truer measure of that landscape's cultural depth.

"In the smaller theaters the artists tend to be in primary control," Baierlein says. "They tend to be more eclectic, with a more specialized audience and repertoire. The problems today are fairly similar to what they were when we started out

Denver's several small performance theaters, such as the Germinal Stage Denver, have attracted faithful audiences of Denverites based on their ability to present a variety of productions from experimental first-runs to Shakespeare.

— continued on next page

— on the one hand, maintaining the integrity of our repertoire, and on the other hand, being popular enough so that people will pay to see your next failure."

Baierlein and Sallie Diamond, 52, his wife and partner in the nonprofit Germinal Stage and one of the area's most versatile and respected actresses, are among the many who came to Denver by chance and stayed by choice.

"I was in the Air Force and was shipped here in 1968 and spent most of my time in the service at Lowry Air Force Base," Baierlein said. "My wife and I decided this was the nicest place we had ever lived. My philosophy is, find a place where you like to live and then make the work happen there."

It was the city that attracted them, Baierlein said. The city is where they and their son Thaddeus, who was born here in 1980, spend most of their time. From their home just a block away from the theater, they take periodic trips to Glenwood Springs, a three-hour drive to the west, to enjoy the world's largest outdoor hot pool.

"That's our favorite vacation, just to let the city seep out of us in the pools," Baierlein said. "We're not great outdoors people. We don't ski, and we don't camp."

Even so, Baierlein said they try to get to the mountains as much as possible, just to enjoy the beauty and solitude that are never far away from the lives and thoughts of even the most urbane of Greater Denverites.

"When you're away from here for any period of time, you really miss just the presence of the mountains," he said. "There's no other place I know where you can have the amenities of a big city and still, in a half-hour, be absolutely isolated in a place where you feel nobody has ever been before."

---

ater performances emphasize original works by Chicano and Latino playwrights, including Su Teatro's director Tony Garcia. El Centro Su Teatro is housed in a former elementary school. In 1997, it celebrated its 25th anniversary.

The Changing Scene
1527½ Champa St. • (303) 893-5775

The Changing Scene is the oldest independent theater in Denver and presents only world premieres, some of which continue on to New York and Europe. In addition to original dramas, The Changing Scene hosts dance, music, film, performance art and events in its small theater — "anything new and fresh," says director Al Brooks.

Arts Theatre of the West
721 Santa Fe Dr. • (303) 595-3800

Established in 1985 as the Denver Civic Theatre, this theater changed its name to the Arts Theatre of the West in August 1997 when managers Frank Carlson and Charles Wingerter came on board. It's been in its present location on Santa Fe Drive since 1991. Under the guidance of Christopher Selbie, the Arts Theatre stages well-known plays, including Broadway musicals and original works, year round. The building was built in 1923 as a movie theater and over the years has been used for many different purposes — it was a meatpacking plant in the 1950s and '60s and later a photographer's studio. Now it houses two theaters: a main stage proscenium with 285 seats and an intimate black box theater that seats 104.

Continuing programs at the Arts Theatre of the West include a theater series for children and a school touring program. The Denver Civic Theatre houses two resident theater companies. The **Compass Theatre Company**, founded by Christopher Selbie in the early 1990s, does primarily the classics, including a great deal of Shakespeare. The other company, **The Industrial Arts Theatre Company**, is known for its staging of classics and contemporary plays.

Denver Victorian Playhouse
4201 Hooker St. • (303) 433-4343

The Denver Victorian Playhouse in northwest Denver is a restored and refurbished 1911 house with a 73-seat theater. Children's shows, a full range of adult comedies, dramas and musicals are performed here year round.

Eulipions Cultural Center
1770 Sherman St. • (303) 863-0026

Founded in 1982, Eulipions's mission is to foster, promote and encourage artistic expression of Denver's diverse cultural communities, with an emphasis on the African-American community. Eulipions has received a mayor's award for excellence in the arts, and in 1989 their production of *Ma Rainey's Black Bottom* won a Denver Critics Circle Award for best theater production.

Germinal Stage Denver
2450 W. 44th Ave. • (303) 455-7108

Germinal Stage Denver was founded by four Denver actors in 1973, making it one of the longest-living small theaters in the region. Performances are held in an air-conditioned, 100-seat converted storefront, five blocks east of Federal Boulevard. The repertoire includes traditional to more arcane and experimental plays. The Germinal has an excellent reputation for producing quality theater.

Hunger Artists Ensemble Theatre
821 Acoma St. • (303) 893-5438

Hunger Artists Ensemble Theatre is a successful 19-year-old acting ensemble. They produce about four plays a year, one per season. An eclectic company, they do primarily contemporary pieces bordering on experimental with some forays into the classics. In 1997, they staged *Angels in America*. Performances are held at two locations: Jack's Theatre at 1553 Platte Street or the Acoma City Center at 1080 Acoma Street.

The Theatre on Broadway
13 S. Broadway
• (303) 860-9360

The Theatre on Broadway presents Denver premieres of new Broadway and off-Broadway shows in a small black-box theater. Artistic director Steven Tangedahl recently announced the formation of The Theatre Group, which governs both the Theatre on Broadway and the newly acquired Phoenix Theatre (formerly the RiverTree Theatre) at 1124 Santa Fe Drive. The Phoenix Theatre opened in April 1997 with *The Compleat Works of Wllm Shkspr (Abridged)*.

The Physically Handicapped Amateur Musical Actors League
P.O. Box 44216, Denver 80201
• (303) 575-0005

The Physically Handicapped Amateur Musical Actors League (PHAMALy) gives physically handicapped actors a chance to perform. This group does only one musical a year, which in recent years has been staged during the summer at the Denver Performing Arts Complex. Performances are always wheelchair-accessible, and arrangements are made to provide assistance to hearing-impaired and visually impaired audience members.

Aurora Fox Arts Center
9900 E. Colfax Ave., Aurora
• (303) 361-2910

From fall to spring, the Aurora Fox Arts Center is home to three performing arts groups: the Aurora Theatre Company, which puts on four plays and a musical each year; the Aurora Singers and the Aurora Symphony, each of which gives four performances a year. In the summer there's a children's theater program, performed for and by children.

Festival Playhouse
5665 Olde Wadsworth Blvd., Arvada
• (303) 422-4090

There's plenty of history behind the Festival Playhouse. The Denver Players Guild, formed in 1936, stages eight plays a year — primarily Broadway comedies — in this converted Grange building in Olde Town Arvada. The Players Guild believes it is the oldest community theater group in the country under the same family management, and the theater is even older. Built in 1874, it's the second-oldest standing Grange hall in Colorado and the oldest building in the city of Arvada.

Dinner Theaters

Country Dinner Playhouse
6875 S. Clinton St., Englewood
• (303) 799-1410

Country Dinner Playhouse is an Equity theater that presents Broadway hits and family entertainment year round, with a buffet dinner preceding the show. There are Saturday and Sunday matinees.

Heritage Square Music Hall
18301 W. Colfax Ave. (U.S. Hwy. 40), Golden • (303) 279-7800

Heritage Square Music Hall is a Victorian-style theater with original comedies with melodramatic overtones and musical revues. A buffet dinner precedes the show, but it's possible to buy a ticket for the performance only. Performances are Wednesday through Saturday evenings, with Sunday matinees.

Popular Music Concerts

Outdoor rock and other popular music concerts are held at Mile High Stadium, Fiddler's Green Amphitheatre and Red Rocks Amphitheatre. Indoor venues include McNichols Sports Arena, the Ogden Theatre and the Paramount Theatre, which are described above in the Theaters section as they're not limited to popular musical events. Tickets for all concerts at virtually all venues are most conveniently purchased at TicketMaster outlets (cash only) or by calling TicketMaster at (303) 830-TIXS, but a trip to the box office can generally (though not always) save you from paying a service charge. You can also purchase tickets for most concerts at Rocky Mountain Teleseat by stopping in any King Soopers or calling (800) 444-SEAT.

Red Rocks and Fiddler's Green are the venues for the Summer of Stars series, which brings major recording artists in for concerts during the summer.

Mile High Stadium
2755 W. 17th Ave. • (303) 458-4850

By far the biggest venue, offering 80,000 seats, Mile High hosts popular summer concerts featuring groups such as the Eagles, Michael Jackson and Bruce Springsteen. In 1997, the KOOL Koncert (KOOL 105 FM) featured 10 bands for 10 bucks, one of the best deals in town. Can't see from the nosebleed seats? No problem. Giant video screens show everything that's happening on the stage so far away.

Fiddler's Green Amphitheatre
6350 Greenwood Plaza Blvd., Englewood • (303) 220-7000

Fiddler's Green Amphitheatre is a huge 18,000-seat amphitheater just west of I-25 between Arapahoe and Orchard roads. You can opt to sit on the lawn, which costs a little less than reserved seats. It's also a little less comfortable. For info on concerts and tickets, call (303) 220-7000.

Red Rocks Amphitheatre
I-70 W. to the Morrison Exit • (303) 640-7334 (recorded information)

Red Rocks Ampitheatre is one of the most spectacular settings anywhere for a concert. About half the size of Fiddler's Green, Red Rocks is a natural red sandstone amphitheater set deep into the Foothills on Hogback Road near Morrison (take I-70 W. to the Morrison Exit and follow the signs). In 1996 it won three major industry awards as "Best Venue."

McNichols Sports Arena
1635 Bryant St. • (303) 640-7300

Home to the Denver Nuggets and the Colorado Avalanche (soon to be replaced by the Pepsi Center), McNichols Sports Arena also hosts big-name shows like Metallica and The Who. The arena seats up to 16,000, and the custom full-range speakers blaring music are crowd-pleasers. Once the Pepsi Center opens

INSIDERS' TIP

Love the theater, hate the high prices? The Denver Center Theatre Company offers one free performance per play — always a Saturday matinee. Tickets are distributed two hours before the performance at the box office at 14th and Curtis streets. No reservations are accepted; it's first come, first served. Watch the *Rocky Mountain News* or *The Denver Post* for notice of when the free performance is held.

in fall 1999, McNichols will be torn down to make way for a new Bronco stadium.

Swallow Hill Music Association
1905 S. Pearl St. • (303) 777-1003

The venerable Swallow Hill Music Association is Denver's center for folk and traditional acoustic music. All concerts at their intimate Pearl Street location are nonsmoking, all-ages events. Swallow Hill also presents concerts elsewhere in the city.

Visual Arts

Art Museums

The Denver Art Museum
100 W. 14th Ave. Pkwy.
• (303) 640-4433 (recording), (303) 640-2793

The Denver Art Museum is the largest art museum between Kansas City and the West Coast and is especially noted for its superb collections of Native American, pre-Columbian and Spanish colonial art. Its seven floors also house impressive displays of American, Asian and contemporary art, and galleries devoted to design, graphics and architecture.

The museum building itself, completed in 1971, is artistically noteworthy. Designed by Milan architect Gio Ponti in association with Denver architect James Sudler, the fortress-like seven-level building has a 28-sided tiled exterior with uniquely shaped windows. Most of the collections have been reinstalled in recent years as part of a seven-year renovation. As of 1997, the museum added a new entrance onto Acoma Plaza and an underground connection with the new Central Library. Also newly opened was the entirely new American and Western Art exhibit on the seventh floor.

In addition to its permanent collections, the museum hosts many traveling exhibitions, some of which travel to very few venues in the United States. Starting in October of 1999, the museum will host "Impressionism: Paintings Collected by European Museums." March of 2000 will feature a special Henri Matisse show.

Choice Tours are free with admission and are scheduled at 1:30 PM daily with an additional tour at 11 AM on Saturday. Tours can be scheduled at other times, so call ahead. Family programs are held every Saturday. The museum has a shop and full service restaurant.

The museum is open 10 AM to 5 PM Tuesday through Saturday (extended hours until 9 PM on Wednesday) and noon to 5 PM on Sunday; it's closed Monday and major holidays. Admission is $4.50 for adults, $2.50 for seniors and students with ID and free for children 5 and younger. Saturdays are free for Colorado residents, thanks to funding provided by the Scientific and Cultural Facilities District. Membership is available to individuals for $30, families for $40.

Museo de las Americas
861 Santa Fe Dr. • (303) 571-4401

Denver's newest museum is the only one in the Rocky Mountain region dedicated to Latin-American art, history and culture. Officially opened in July 1994, the Museo de las Americas showcases art from all the Americas, including the Caribbean, in changing exhibitions. The museum supplements its temporary exhibitions with lectures, workshops and other educational programs and has built a small permanent collection. It has twice shown an exhibition jointly with the Denver Art Museum, with some of the material at the art museum and some at the museo. The museum is open 10 AM to 5 PM Tuesday through Saturday. Admission is $3 for adults $2 seniors and free for kids younger than 10. Memberships are available and cost $20 for individuals and $30 for a family.

INSIDERS' TIP

A funky collection of galleries in fast-changing northwest Denver is a fun and different way to spend a Friday or Saturday evening. Galleries such as Bug and Pirate are located within the 3600 block of Navajo Street. Have dinner at Patsy's Inn Italian Restaurant (3651 Navajo Street) and stroll through the galleries afterward.

Museum of Outdoor Arts
7600 E. Orchard Rd., Englewood
• **(303) 741-3609**

More than 50 outdoor sculptures comprise this "museum without walls" in the 400-acre Greenwood Plaza Business Park area. You can do a self-guided tour, or call to schedule a guided group tour. We recommend the children's art classes that are offered year round. Visitors can view the art on their own during daylight hours for free. For guided tours, the cost is $3 adults, $1 children 17 and younger. Membership costs $30 for an individual, $50 for a family.

Community Art Centers

Arvada Center
for the Arts and Humanities
6901 Wadsworth Blvd., Arvada
• **(303) 431-3939**

The major contender in this category is the Arvada Center for the Arts and Humanities. The Arvada Center has two galleries, which display changing exhibits of contemporary art, folk art, design and crafts. There's also a small historical museum. In addition, the center has both an indoor 500-seat auditorium and an outdoor amphitheatre with 1,200 seats (600 covered, 600 on the lawn).

The Arvada Center keeps up an impressive schedule of performing arts programming that includes children's and adult professional theater, dance and music concerts. One resident company, the Arvada Center Chorale, calls the Arvada Center home, but many groups perform here. It's the site each winter of a cowboy-poetry gathering. A highly regarded deaf-access program makes many programs accessible to the hearing-impaired.

In 1992, the Arvada Center underwent a $10.5 million expansion that added over 59,000 gross square feet, more than doubling its previous size. At this time they installed a controversial "dirt wall" by New York artist Vito Acconci that wends its way through the building.

The Foothills Art Center
809 15th St., Golden • (303) 279-3922

The Foothills Art Center is much smaller than the Arvada Center and does not offer a performing arts program. However, the center is home to two prestigious national exhibitions — the biannual North American Sculpture Exhibition and the annual Rocky Mountain National Watermedia Exhibition. It also hosts the statewide annual Colorado Clay exhibition. The remainder of the center's schedule is composed of changing exhibits of national and regional arts and fine crafts.

Art Galleries

Downtown

Greater Denver's contemporary art galleries tend to be clustered in the Lower Downtown area (LoDo). Working on the assumption that there's strength in numbers, the LoDo galleries have banded together to form a Lower Downtown Arts District (LDAD) and to coordinate openings and other special events. The most significant program to come out of this cooperative effort is First Fridays, in which more than two dozen LoDo galleries stay open until 9 PM the first Friday of each month. Especially in the summer, there's kind of a street festival atmosphere as patrons go from one gallery to the next, stopping to compare notes with friends on the sidewalk. For more information about LDAD and LDAD membership, call (303) 820-3139.

Gallery openings are usually held on Fridays and are, with rare exceptions, free and open to the public. Check *Westword* or the Friday editions of *The Denver Post, Rocky Mountain News* and *Daily Camera* for a list of openings and current exhibit information. Most galleries close on Monday, but this varies, so call ahead to be sure.

Think of art galleries as a wonderful free smorgasbord of exciting things to see. Of course, the bottom line is that galleries must sell art to stay in business, but unlike art dealers in some cities, Denver dealers are notably low-key and happy to educate browsers without pressuring them to buy. Dealers know that the best way to develop customers is to make people feel comfortable, and high-pressure sales tactics aren't going to do that. On the other hand, if you are a serious buyer, you

The glass-topped galleria is part of the Denver Performing Arts Complex.

should be aware that virtually every gallery in town adds the phrase "and by appointment" to its set hours. This may be especially important to visitors whose time in the city is limited.

The heart of Denver's avant-garde arts district is the 1700 block of Wazee Street. You'll find several galleries in the surrounding district. LoDo's high rents forced several galleries to relocate in 1998. Many have chosen the area near the Denver Art Museum for its proximity to downtown, and its exciting urban feel.

Robischon Gallery
1740 Wazee St. • (303) 298-7788

Robischon Gallery is Denver's premier gallery for abstract, representational and symbolistic painting and sculpture. It represents such well-known artists as Robert Motherwell, Christo and Manuel Neri.

The Metropolitan State College of Denver Center for the Visual Arts
1734 Wazee St. • (303) 294-5207

Technically a college gallery, Metro seldom shows student work, but rather, puts on some of the best and most provocative exhibitions in town. Recent exhibitions have included African-American quilts, contemporary Chinese painting and baseball paraphernalia from local collections.

The Sloane Gallery of Art
1612 17th St. • (303) 595-4230

The Sloane Gallery of Art is devoted exclusively to contemporary Russian art by Russian artists. It exhibits oils, acrylics, drawings, pastels and sculpture.

Core New Art Space
1412 Wazee St. • (303) 571-4831

Core New Art Space is a cutting-edge cooperative gallery that primarily features local artists who work in oils, photography, ceramics and papermaking.

Baobab Tree Gallery
1518 Wazee St. • (303) 595-0965

The Baobab Tree Gallery is the place to shop for stone sculptures, wood sculptures, fabric, masks and baskets. This gallery is dedicated to art from all over Africa.

Merrill Gallery of Fine Art Ltd.
1401 17th St. • (303) 292-1401

The Merrill Gallery of Fine Art Ltd. (formerly the Carol Siple Gallery) is an excellent representational art gallery. It offers a blend of traditional and contemporary realism by well-known American artists such as John Asaro, Michael Lynch and Daniel Sprick.

William Matthews Gallery
1617 Wazee St. • (303) 534-1300

The William Matthews Gallery exhibits the Western watercolors of William Matthews. It also features limited-edition prints, posters and notecards.

David Cook Gallery
1637 Wazee St. • (303) 623-8181

David Cook Gallery specializes in historic American Indian art, from Navajo rugs to Pueblo pottery, from beadwork to baskets. You can also find antique jewelry as well as paintings of the Rockies by early Colorado artists.

Old Map Gallery
1746 Blake St. • (303) 296-7725

If you're in the market for antique maps, this is the place. You'll find historic maps, such as ones from the 16th century or maps of Louisiana before it was purchased. Maps range from $35 to several thousand dollars.

Third Canyon Gallery
1512 Larimer St. at Writers Square • (303) 893-3936

The large Third Canyon Gallery has contemporary Southwestern painting and sculpture plus traditional and contemporary Indian jewelry. They exhibit work by minimalist John Axton, Indian painter James Knary and colorist David Parker

Knox Gallery
1632 Market St. • (303) 820-2324

Knox Gallery specializes in realistic bronze sculpture. The gallery represents local and regional painters and sculptors.

Marks and Marks
1338 15th St. • (303) 620-9993

This gallery is one of the newest kids on

the block. It specializes in classic oils and re-creations, but it also carries contemporary art by emerging regional talent. Established artists represented include photographer Norman Lerner and painter Barry Leighton Jones.

Spark Gallery
1535 Platte St. • (303) 455-4435

Over by the Platte River is Spark Gallery, an artists' cooperative (Denver's oldest) that's only open weekends. They feature original paintings, sculpture and photographs sold directly by the artists.

Camera Obscura Gallery
1309 Bannock St. • (303) 623-4059

Near the Denver Art Museum is Camera Obscura Gallery, devoted exclusively to photography. Owner Hal Gould is supremely knowledgeable; spend a little time talking with him, and he'll show you the vintage treasures he keeps upstairs.

Cherry Creek and Other Central Denver Galleries

Most of the galleries in Cherry Creek are more commercial and more geared toward Santa Fe-style art than those downtown. For this reason, we've listed many of them in our Shopping chapter rather than here. However, there are a few exceptions.

Ginny Williams Family Foundation
299 Fillmore St. • (303) 321-4077

Ginny Williams Family Foundation gallery recently changed its format and now exhibits about four shows a year from Ginny Williams' estimable collection of photography, sculpture and other artwork.

Cherry Creek Arts Festival
201 Fillmore St. • (303) 355-2787

Cherry Creek is the site of a hugely popular arts festival every July Fourth weekend. Started in 1991, the Cherry Creek Arts Festival has been astonishingly successful in attaining national recognition. See our Annual Festivals and Events chapter for details.

West of Cherry Creek

Sandy Carson Gallery
123 W. 12th Ave. • (303) 573-8585

The Sandy Carson Gallery used to be in LoDo, but moved in 1998 closer to the Denver Art Museum. It shows contemporary painting, sculpture and photography as well as ceramics and glass. In business for 22 years, this gallery acquires arts from all over the country and also has quite a reputation as art consultants.

Artyard
1251 S. Pearl St. • (303) 777-3219

Artyard is a wonderful, out-of-the-way place that feels like a discovery even when you've been there a dozen times.

The indoor space doubles as a studio for acclaimed kinetic artist Robert Mangold as well as gallery space for a variety of artists; outdoors is a large sculpture garden that features changing exhibitions of sculpture by well-known artists.

Rule Modern and Contemporary Gallery
111 Broadway • (303) 777-9473

The peripatetic Rule Modern and Contemporary Gallery, which used to be on Wazee Street, then on Wynkoop, is now housed on Broadway across from the Mayan Theater. This gallery specializes in modern and contemporary painting, sculpture and photography by regional artists.

Inkfish Gallery
116 S. Broadway • (303) 715-9528

Inkfish shows contemporary art by established local and international artists. The gallery is one of Denver's old-timers — it's been in business 23 years.

1/1 Gallery
1058 Delaware St. • (303) 893-2360

The 1/1 Gallery (say "one over one") also relocated closer to DAM. It specializes in monotypes, which are one-of-a-kind prints. It also displays paintings, generally by regional artists.

Photo: Daily Camera

The Denver Public Library is in downtown Denver.

Westside Galleries

As LoDo has changed and rents have gone up, many artists have moved their studios from the Platte River area to the area just west of I-25. In this transitional neighborhood you'll find the following galleries.

Platte River Art Services
350 N. Santa Fe Dr. • (303) 571-1060

This premier frame shop relocated in 1998, but is the place to go when you want something unusual. The shop offers exquisite frames, including hand-carved, hand-gilded frames and restored antique frames.

Red Shift Framing and Gallery
2201 Larimer St. • (303) 293-2991

The Red Shift Framing and Gallery has been around nine years (although in this new location since 1998) and features the work of local and national emerging artists. The art here — which includes paintings and sculptures — is affordable and original.

Mackey Gallery
2900 W. 25th Ave. • (303) 455-1157

Mackey Gallery shows contemporary art and photography by up-and-coming and established artists. It also offers full-service framing and art workshops for adults and children.

Pirate, A Contemporary Art Oasis
3659 Navajo St. • (303) 458-6058

Pirate, A Contemporary Art Oasis has what are generally regarded as the hippest openings in town. Pirate is only open on weekends, and shows change frequently.

The Bug Performance and Media Arts Center
3654 Navajo St. • (303) 477-5977

The buzz is good on The Bug Performance and Media Arts Center, a renovated movie house that's now an avant-garde showcase for emerging artists and their artwork, including poetry, music, film and new media. Call the Bugline at (303) 477-5977 to find out what's coming.

The Chicano Arts and Humanities Council
772 Santa Fe Dr. • (303) 571-0440

CHAC, the Chicano Arts and Humanities Council, has a gallery that is open Thursday through Sunday from 1 until 4 PM. In addition, CHAC sponsors a number of special events and programs throughout the city, including a Day of the Dead exhibition, the annual Chile Harvest Festival held at the Four Mile Historic Park in August and Las Posadas at the gallery during December.

The Literary Arts

If you love the written word — or the company of those who write — Denver has several writers' organizations that appeal to both beginning and advanced scribes as well as writers in a variety of genres.

Colorado Authors' League
P.O. Box 24905, Welshire Postal Station, Denver 80224 • no phone

Founded in 1931, the Colorado Authors' League is one of the oldest professional writers' organizations in the state. Counting such notable writers as Clive Cussler, Clarissa Pinkola Estes and Joanne Greenberg amongst its ranks, this organization has monthly meetings with speakers on any topic from spotting trends to writing with a collaborator. Dues are $30 a year.

Columbine State Poetry Society
10751 Routt St., Broomfield 80021 • (303) 465-3638

Part of the National Federation of State Poetry Societies, Columbine is the state society that also offers two local chapters. The purpose of this organization is to promote poetry throughout the state and to that end, the society offers contests, workshops and monthly critique groups.

Membership in Columbine (which also includes membership in the national group) is $8 a year. For $20 a year, you can belong to a local chapter (that includes the $8 to belong to the state group) and partake in specific activities.

INSIDERS' TIP

While the Denver Center for the Performing Arts is by far the biggest show in town, small theaters in the metro area offer wonderful productions with fine acting and staging. And theaters like the Germinal Stage and Aurora Fox Arts Center are a bargain in an intimate setting where every seat is a good one.

Mystery Writers of America (Rocky Mountain Chapter)

130 Pearl St. #1901, Denver 80203
• no phone

Monthly meetings and bimonthly programs keep these published and unpublished members of the regional chapter of Mystery Writers of America busy. Members get to attend all bimonthly programs for free. One of the highlights of each year is the Annual Meeting where the featured speaker might be an FBI agent or a judge from a criminal court. National dues are $65, which allows membership locally.

Rocky Mountain Fiction Writers

P.O. Box 260244, Denver 80226
• (303) 331-2608

This popular fiction-writing organization is geared to writers of commercial novels. Its 375 members are both published and unpublished and all enjoy monthly meetings where speakers talk about anything related to writing and researching. Monthly newsletters offer market news, and critique groups are held all over greater Denver. The annual conference in September is a much awaited event; big name writers, six to seven editors and several New York agents attend. Dues are $25 a year.

Women Writing the West

P.O. Box 12, Boulder 80306
• (303) 444-9139

This five-year-old organization already has 450 members from all over the United States, Canada and Australia. The motto here is "We don't do meetings, and we don't do T-shirts." What they do do is work on marketing themselves — all of whom are interested in writing about "a new view of the women's west." Forty dollars a year gets members a quarterly newsletter, displays at booksellers associations and a major opportunity to network.

Denver Woman's Press Club

1325 Logan St., Denver 80203
• (303) 839-1519

Celebrating more than 100 years in existence, this club was formed in 1898 by 19 members whose mission included "functioning as a stimulating gathering place for people in literary journalism and media endeavors." Today it meets regularly for lunch and dinner programs, offers Saturday Seminars for the community at large and afternoon teas featuring authors in town on book tours. Housed in a charming historic landmark, this organization of women writers is the oldest in the state. Dues run $50 a year.

Denver is one of only a few cities that boast five big-league sports teams.

Spectator Sports

Spend a few days in Denver, and you're likely to think the term "sports town" was coined for the Mile-High City. This town is rabid about its sports.

In 1987, when the Denver Broncos lost their second Super Bowl, local media enlisted psychologists to help comfort downtrodden fans through newspapers and radio talk shows. People were encouraged to look at the loss not as a reflection of civic pride but for what it was — a game. (Of course, since the 1997 Super Bowl championship, fans are still pounding their chests.)

When baseball's National League was looking for expansion cities, a majority of metro Denver fans anted up with a tax hike to fund a stadium. "Build it and they will come" became the local mantra. We have Coors Field to show for our efforts.

Today, Denver is one of only a few cities that boast five big-league sports teams: football's Broncos, baseball's Colorado Rockies, hockey's Colorado Avalanche, basketball's Denver Nuggets and soccer's Colorado Rapids.

Denver's two daily newspapers step all over each other to be the best source in sports news. When the Rockies expansion team formed, the *Rocky Mountain News*, which owns part of the team, declared itself the "Official Newspaper of the Rockies." *The Denver Post* quickly followed by dubbing itself the "Official Newspaper of the Fan."

No matter which paper visitors read, they quickly get a sense of Colorado's love of sports. The sour mood at the office on Monday morning is almost palpable if the Broncos lose on Sunday. Fans talk about players like they're family. Broncos quarterback John Elway was once proclaimed "St. Elway" in a *Denver Post* headline.

Even when the favorite teams aren't winning championships, Denver fans remain loyal. Bronco fans are an especially devoted group. Season-ticket holders have reaped thousands of dollars in windfall profits by selling rights in the '80s and '90s that were free in the '60s. Rockies fans refuse to be outdone in their fervor. They broke nearly every attendance record on the books in the Rockies first season: the all-time major league single-season attendance record, the largest opening-day crowd, largest attendance at a single game and fastest team to reach one-, two-, three- and four-million attendance levels. Games continue to be sellouts or near-sellouts year after year.

The newest and most spectacular addition to Denver's sports scene is scheduled to open in the fall of 1999. The Pepsi Center will house the Denver Nuggets and the Colorado

Avalanche. It also will be home to dozens of other events such as concerts, circuses and ice shows. Groundbreaking on the $160 million, 675,000 square foot arena began in 1997. The new structure is located in the Central Platte Valley on the edge of downtown and next to Elitch Gardens Amusement Park (much closer to the downtown action than McNichols Arena). A pedestrian walkway will connect it to Elitch's, and it will feature 17 concession stands, a 236-seat club restaurant, 95 luxury suites and fully upholstered cast-iron arm chairs throughout the arena. It also will be walking distance to lower downtown restaurants and shops.

For those who like playing to win, Greater Denver also has several racetracks. Lots of people would consider the National Western Stock Show and Rodeo the city's premier spectator sports event, but as it only happens once a year, we've covered it in our Annual Events chapter.

Baseball

Colorado Rockies
Coors Field, Blake and 20th sts.
• (303) 762-5437 (ROCKIES)

The Colorado Rockies was one of two expansion teams added to the National League in 1993. Despite a losing inaugural season, they won the hearts of Coloradans and received national media attention for the record-breaking attendance they attracted and for the former player they call "the Cat," Andres Galarraga. With the Cat gone, players such as MVP Larry Walker, infielder Vinny Castilla and outfielder and local sports icon Dante Bichette thrill fans.

After two seasons playing in Mile High Stadium, the Rockies began their 1995 season in their new home, Coors Field, in Lower Downtown at Blake and 20th streets. Designed by Hellmuth, Obata & Kassabaum, a Kansas City firm, the 50,249-seat all-baseball stadium is an updated version of a classic ballpark. Its exterior is built of two shades of red brick, and its seats provide views of the Rocky Mountains. The nation got a good look at Coors Field when Denver hosted the 1998 All-Star Game. The game was a week-long celebration of baseball and lower downtown fun for thousands of local and visiting fans.

With such intense focus on baseball in Colorado, the best game seats are hard to come by. Still, the Rockies organization has vowed to cap the number of season tickets sold so that some seats are always available at every game. Single seats go on sale for all games beginning in February and range from $5 to $33. During the season, purchase tickets at the stadium at Gate C between 20th and 21st streets and Blake Street, or at Rockies Dugout Stores and King Soopers supermarkets. Handicapped seating is available. Day-of-game "Rockpile" seats go on sale at the stadium two hours prior to game time and cost $4 for adults, $1 for kids 12 and younger and seniors 55 and older.

RTD (Regional Transportation District) provides special buses to and from Rockies games from 16 suburban park-and-rides and along Broadway. The fare is $4 round trip for express routes, $2 round trip for the Broadway shuttle. Regular service to and from Market Street Station also brings you within walking distance of the stadium but may not be as conveniently timed for evening games. For

www.insiders.com
See this and many other
Insiders' Guide®
destinations online.
Visit us today!

INSIDERS' TIP

The hottest spot to meet for pre-Broncos game beers, burgers and boasting is Zang Brewing Company, 2301 Seventh Street, visible from Mile High Stadium. If you don't have tickets but want to experience Bronco fever, stop by any number of sports bars, including Jackson's Hole at Sixth and Kipling streets, to cheer on the team via television.

Colorado Rockies Bring Baseball, Big Bucks and Beer to Once-Seedy Lower Downtown

The time is the 1970s, the place is a small section of Denver — dirty, a little rough and definitely seedy.

Brown bags and empty booze bottles litter the streets like bad reminders of the night

before. Graffiti covers plywood, which covers shattered warehouse windows. The only signs of life happen at night, and these aren't the signs of prosperity and possibility. If the place had a disclaimer, it would shout: "Danger: Go Away."

This is no place for America's favorite pastime.

Now fast forward to the mid-1990s. Red brick surrounds gleaming windows in renovated warehouses. Litter is gone, replaced by bustling shops and streets and smiling pedestrians. Tourists lounge on the sunny patios of upscale joints and savor microbrewed beer. Above it all towers Coors Field, home of the Colorado Rockies.

This dramatic turnaround may sound like a scene from a developer's dream, but it's the reality of Lower Downtown Denver's revitalization. Much of the metamorphosis comes compliments of the Colorado Rockies and their new baseball stadium.

The Rockies have done wonders for Denver's economy and, specifically, the revival of the once-blighted area Insiders call "LoDo." An economic impact study done in 1994 estimated the Rockies would prompt nearly $200 million a year in new spending. That's a lot of beer and hot dogs.

Of course, there's more to LoDo than beer and dogs. In fact, unless the beer has a fancy name from one of 11 local brew pubs (Sagebrush Stout, anyone?), and the dogs

— continued on next page

The Colorado Rockies bring more than 4 million people to Downtown Denver during baseball season.

are dressed up with freshly crushed green chile salsa and served in the center of a dazzling food display, it probably isn't in LoDo. Indeed, LoDo (sort of like SoHo, only not quite) is home of the hip, cool and happening.

Development around the stadium in the past few years is remarkable. More than 40 new restaurants and brew pubs have sprung up in LoDo since Coors Field opened.

Residential living also has sprung up around Coors Field. Now that the abandoned warehouses around the stadium have been revived into posh lofts, many of which advertised "Coors Field access," developers have begun ground-up projects elsewhere in LoDo to sate public demand.

Also on the rise are hotel rates, not-so-good news for tourists but good for Denver's economy. Rates since Coors Field opened have climbed from about $90 to about $114 per night. Occupancy rates have gone up as well.

The city of Denver has done its part to build the area. Baseball-related infrastructure improvements include millions in road construction (at least $36 million for the city of Denver alone). Another $5 million has gone toward LoDo economic development projects and streetscaping.

In fairness to the LoDo area, much of the revival was launched pre-Rockies. But nearly everyone agrees the Rockies have stimulated business and interest in LoDo. The Rockies alone bring more than 4 million people to downtown during baseball season (of course, many of those are repeat customers). But the games lure people downtown who might not otherwise have made the trek — like suburbanites who in the '80s stayed away from the city. Those same people, having sampled the excitement and vibrancy of downtown, return to eat, shop and party. In a downtown Denver survey, 37 percent of metro respondents said baseball was the main reason they went downtown.

"It's turned LoDo into a year-round destination," says Ben Wright, chief economist for the Denver Metro Chamber of Commerce.

To some extent, the phenomenon happened out of luck — and lack of parking. A dearth of spaces (only 15,000 spaces for 50,000 fans) was once a negative against Coors Field in its planning stages. But the paucity has forced fans to park in lots all over downtown and walk to the game — passing enticing restaurants and shops along the way.

A recent nationwide survey placed the Rockies and Coors Field 11th on the list of top tourist attractions. LoDo rose in popularity to seventh place. Publications around the nation and even in Canada have hailed the powerhouse effect of the Rockies on breathing economic life into LoDo, says Christian Brixey of the Lower Downtown District Inc. As proof, Brixey cites a drawer full of publications, including *Sunset Magazine*, *USA Today* and *The New York Times*, which have written all about the revival.

"People call me two or three times a week wondering how we did this so effectively," Brixey says. "They wonder how you balance all of this and all of the quality-of-life issues that having a major league team in your back yard brings."

If you're Coors Field and Lower Downtown Denver, you do it with a little luck and a lot of style.

INSIDERS' TIP

There are two "family sections" in Coors Field where alcohol is not served. Ask for sections 141 and 342.

schedules and fare information, call (303) 299-6000, TDD (303) 299-6089.

Basketball

Denver Nuggets
McNichols Sports Arena, off I-25 at W. 17th Ave. • (303) 893-6700

After losing momentum due to the 1998 NBA lockout, the Nuggets finally got moving in 1999 with a couple of big-name free agents — Nick Van Exel of the Los Angeles Lakers and Antonio McDyess, who previously played for the Nuggets. A new slate of younger players round out the Nuggets hopes for revived success: power forward Danny Fortson, University of Colorado guard Chauncey Billups, and Raef LaFrentz (who sat out 1999 with injuries).

The Nuggets play in McNichols Sports Arena (part of the same sports complex as Mile High Stadium). Tickets start at $10.50 and reach as high as $100 for courtside. Average ticket price is $27, and there are a number of special deals, such as family and youth nights, and group discounts. Handicapped seating is available on request. Nuggets tickets are available by calling the number above or through TicketMaster at (303) 830-TIXS.

The Nuggets are scheduled to open the 2000 season in their new arena, the Pepsi Center, in the Platte Valley next to Elitch Gardens. The Colorado Avalanche will share this venue.

Football

Denver Broncos
Mile High Stadium, 2755 W. 17th Ave. • (303) 433-7466

After losing three Super Bowl bids (1986, 1987 and 1989), the Broncos finally granted fans their ultimate wish — the 1997 championship. Broncos fans were joined by legions of John Elway supporters across the country who wanted to see the longtime quarterback win a Super Bowl title.

The city's fans have been beaming ever since. And after widespread rumors, speculation and hand-wringing, John Elway returned for the 1998/99 season, but isn't expected to be around in the fall of '99.

But returning Super Bowl MVP Terrell Davis will be back after signing a 9-year, $56.1 million contract with the Broncos in 1998, making him the highest paid running back ever.

It's no surprise that virtually every home game is a sellout. So if you want to attend, you'll have to call well in advance for tickets and information, or show up at the game and take your chances that someone in the parking lot has a ticket to sell. The Broncos will play at Mile High Stadium until their new stadium opens, tentatively scheduled for fall, 2001. The new stadium comes compliments of metro area voters, who in November 1998 approved partial public funding for Mile High to be demolished and replaced with a state-of-the-art facility.

RTD's BroncoRide services all home games from a number of locations in Greater Denver, with special shuttles available for fans catching the BroncoRide along Federal Boulevard and at the Auraria campus. Call RTD at (303) 299-6000 for schedules and current fare information.

Hockey

Colorado Avalanche
McNichols Sports Arena, 1635 Bryant St. • (303) 893-6700

By mid-1995, Denver could boast of having four major-league teams when it was announced that the company that owns the Nuggets purchased the Quebec Nordiques. By 1996, Denver could really boast — and boast

Coors Field is home-run central for the Colorado Rockies.

it did — when its new Colorado Avalanche won the Stanley Cup. After winning the Cup, the Avs suffered a few losing years. In 1998, former Coach of the Year (1994-95) Marc Crawford was fired and replaced by Bob Hartley, a minor league coach from the Avs organization. In the meantime, players such as center Joe Sakic and goalie Patrick Roy continue to draw fans. The Avs call McNichols Arena home until the new Pepsi Center, which will also house the Nuggets, is built.

Single-game tickets go on sale in early fall, with prices ranging from $12.50 to $100; lower level seats are around $45. Ask about group discounts. Season tickets are available. To purchase tickets, call the number above or TicketMaster, (303) 830-TIXS.

Soccer

The Colorado Rapids
Mile High Stadium, 2755 W. 17th Ave.
• (303) 299-1599

The Colorado Rapids kicked off its first home game in April 1996 and have been gaining momentum ever since. In 1997, the team captured the western conference championship. In 1998, four of its star players made the All-Star lineup: Marcelo Balboa, Chris

INSIDERS' TIP

Official Dugout Stores are the place to buy Rockies fare, from T-shirts and hats to rarities such as broken bats and used jerseys. Call (303) 298-9200 for locations across the Front Range.

Henderson, Paul Bravo and Adrian Paz. Along with the 1997 title, the team also has the distinction of raising its win/loss record from "worst" in 1996 to "first" in 1997. The team is gaining popularity; attendance averages 15,000 per game. Rapids play at Mile High Stadium March through September. Tickets are between $12 and $20, with a limited amount of $7 general admission tickets available on game days. Call the Rapids at the number above or call TicketMaster at (303) 830-TIXS.

Racetracks

Mile High Greyhound Park
6200 Dahlia St., Commerce City
• **(303) 288-1591**

Parimutuel greyhound races take place at Mile High Greyhound Park, 6200 Dahlia Street (at Colorado Boulevard) in Commerce City June through February. Matinee and evening races are scheduled throughout the week, with the exception of Sundays and Thursdays when the Colorado Rapids play the field in the center of the track. General admission is $1; clubhouse admission is $3.

Bandimere Speedway
3051 S. Rooney Rd., Morrison
• **(303) 697-6001,**
  (303) 697-4870 (recording)

Championship drag racing events are held from April to October at Bandimere Speedway, 3051 S. Rooney Road in Morrison (off C-470 between Alameda Avenue and Morrison Road). Events aren't limited to drag racing only and include motorcycle and snowmobile events as well as such unusual shows as "most unique vehicle" and "stereo wars." Admission varies with events.

Colorado National Speedway
I-25 Exit 232, Erie
• **(303) 665-4173**

This speedway has NASCAR and a variety of other races on a paved three-eighths of a mile oval track. Races are held Saturday nights April through September. Colorado National Speedway is in Erie, 20 minutes north of Denver off I-25.

Arapahoe Park Racetrack
26000 E. Quincy Ave., Aurora
• **(303) 690-2400**

Parimutuel thoroughbred, quarter horse and other races take place Thursday through Sunday and holiday Mondays from May through early September at the Arapahoe Park Racetrack, just east of Gun Club Road. General admission is $1, clubhouse admission, $4.

One thing that's fun about daytrips in Colorado is that the roads you travel are usually quite spectacular for their geography.

Daytrips

Just to keep things reasonable, our daytrips are destinations within about 100 miles of Denver. Using the old pi-r² rule, however, that still forces you to choose from more than 3,000 square miles of opportunities. Our recommendations tend to concentrate in the mountains and up and down the Front Range along Interstate 25. That's not a prejudice against the plains but simply a result of the fact that the Front Range and the mountains to the west have historically focused a lot more energy on tourism, and that's where the tourists tend to go. And for most people who come to Denver, a ride to see the scenery seems automatically to mean heading into the mountains.

Anyone who loves the Great Plains knows that few landscapes are more tranquilizing or tremendous than the endless rolling prairie and few things are more magnificent than 180 degrees of sky. Towns and cities on the plains, furthermore, retain much more of their original historic feel because they haven't been so relentlessly populated by newcomers or so dolled-up to attract the tourist trade.

That being said, however, our recommendations are heavily weighted westward, wherein lie attractions on a larger scale connected by drives through flamboyantly awesome scenery. The landscape itself is a daytrip. Anywhere you go in the mountains, you can get out of your car and take a walk. Parking at the top of Berthoud Pass on U.S. Highway 40 between Empire and Winter Park, for example, you may just want to hike eastward up the windswept slope to the top of Colorado Mines Peak for some great views and landscape. Loveland Pass or any other mountain pass in the state offers a similar opportunity to go to great heights and wonderful views from a high-altitude parking spot.

We've mentioned a few scenic driving trips near Denver. But they are virtually infinite, given the combination of roads and off-road experi-

ence. If you're looking for new ideas, you might check the "Minitour" feature that runs in the "Weekend" section of *The Denver Post,* published on Friday.

Do bear in mind, however, that snowstorms can render high mountain roads treacherous, if not impassable, from September through May. You might consider calling (303) 639-1111 for Colorado State Highway Patrol's report on road conditions within two hours of Denver before taking off on a mountain jaunt during these months. Most mountain lovers who've lived in Greater Denver for any period of time can give you a horror story about sliding sideways on a snowy mountain pass, or worse. Particularly treacherous in heavy weather are high-altitude roads such as Berthoud Pass, Loveland Pass over the Continental Divide, the nearby Eisenhower Tunnel under the Continental Divide (on the way to Breckenridge, Arapahoe Basin, Keystone and Copper Mountain ski areas) or Vail Pass (on the way to Vail and Beaver Creek).

If conditions are bad, it's advisable to make sure your vehicle has good snow tires, if not studded tires. Or carry chains. If the chain law is in effect at a particular pass, that means those without chains will be turned back, no matter how good their tires are. And sometimes, the road will just be closed, period; so be aware of that possibility. It's really a pain to pull out of Vail heading east up I-70 and discover that they've swung the gates closed across the interstate.

Another worthwhile tip: I-70 and U.S. Highway 285 are Greater Denver's two main conduits into and out of the mountains. If there's any way to avoid it, do not return to Denver during the Sunday and Monday holiday rush hour, which runs from late afternoon to early evening. These highways become absolutely jammed with traffic, and it kind of sours the mountain experience to spend an hour creeping along bumper-to-bumper. And that's if there isn't an accident, which really clogs the road. This problem is worse in winter, when the ski areas all shut down their lifts from 3:30 to 4 PM. This unleashes a concentrated wave of traffic in often slick conditions when it's already dark. Sometimes you can barely figure out where the lines are that separate your car from the cars hurtling and weaving around you, and there may be driving snow blinding everyone. Return in early afternoon. If you can't, then forget about rushing home for supper. Stop for dinner in the mountains, let the rush pass you by, then have a pleasant drive home.

With the exception of Winter Park, we haven't mentioned the mountain resort areas in this chapter because we've covered those in our Ski Country chapter. But they are certainly wonderful daytrip destinations year round. We've chosen a few of our favorite daytrips with outstanding special features that are sure to make you feel that a day's outing has been worth the drive.

One thing that's fun about daytrips in Colorado is that the roads you travel are usually quite spectacular for their geography. There's always some amazing or strange formation of land and rocks that makes you wonder at how it got there. A good book to have along on any automobile trip is *Roadside Geology of Colorado*, by Halka Chronic. For most any route you travel in the state, the book has a section about why you're seeing what you're seeing along the road and explaining how it got there. The price is around $15, and any bookstore with an acceptable Colorado section should be proud to have it or ashamed not to.

Boulder

A daytrip to Boulder could really turn into a weekend trip — there's so much to do in this college town. Should you decide to stay longer and want more extensive information, check out *The Insiders' Guide® to Boulder*. That said, let's go.

When you're driving up U.S. Highway 36 from Denver to Boulder, watch for the exit to the cities of Louisville and Superior. Don't take

it. Just use it as a benchmark, because a stunning vista is about to punch you in the brain at the top of the next hill. In fact, if you haven't been to Boulder before, you should watch for a sign that says "Scenic Overlook," and take the exit to the right. During the warmer months, the Boulder Convention and Visitors Bureau operates a visitor information center at the overlook. More importantly, you really need to absorb the view to get a full sense of what Boulder is all about, and Davidson Mesa, as this hill is known, is a primo vantage point.

Boulder nestles like a jewel in the scenic bowl of Boulder Valley. On the mountainsides rising from its western edges, you are struck immediately by the sight of the Flatirons, enormous sandstone monoliths that lean against the slopes like a row of fossilized aircraft carriers. Losing that vantage point as you drive down the hill and into town, you encounter a city of tremendous charm and diversity.

Detractors used to call it "the people's republic of Boulder" during the Vietnam era when students at the University of Colorado at Boulder, CU's main campus, added antiwar protests to the already offbeat lifestyles of this university town. Profiles of Boulder in national magazines continue to emphasize the offbeat, and there's plenty of that. Boulder is a national mecca for alternative medicine, natural foods, spirituality and outdoor sports such as bicycle racing, mountain biking and technical climbing.

The **Naropa Institute**, a national center for Buddhist studies, is here. It's the only fully accredited, Buddhist-inspired institution of higher education in North America, including bachelor's and master's degrees. And it's unconventional, colorful and photogenic. It's open all day for those who want to drop in at 2130 Arapahoe Avenue, but it also has tours on weekdays at 2 PM. Call (303) 444-0202 for more information. **Celestial Seasonings**, 4600 Sleepytime Drive, now an international power in the herbal tea business, was founded here and remains headquartered here. Want to take a tour of the company? Call (303) 530-5300.

Celestial Seasonings is only one example

of how Boulder's penchant for individualism and innovation also expresses itself in business entrepreneurism. This is a start-up town, where new companies pop up like spring flowers. Many are high-tech companies, and many have moved outward to other parts of Boulder County as they have grown. Storage Technology Corp., located in Louisville on the edge of Boulder Valley, for example, sprang from the Boulder high-tech community, and its employees have gone on to found numerous other high-tech companies. High-tech spin-offs are a fundamental part of the local culture, and technology here is high indeed, including major federal government laboratories such as the National Center for Atmospheric Research and the National Institute of Standards and Technologies. The University of Colorado, which did more than $143 million worth of research in the 1993-94 fiscal year, is nationally prominent in fields ranging from molecular biology to telecommunications. It's one of the main reasons why high-tech companies locate or start up here, and it works closely with that community. US West Advanced Technologies, the research and development arm of US West Inc., is in the CU Research Park specifically to be close to its university research partners.

Despite the flaky image, often unfairly and shallowly reported by the outside press, Boulder has a wealth of cultural attractions and probably a greater concentration of good restaurants than you'll find in Denver with the possible exceptions of Denver's downtown and Cherry Creek area. Boulder has everything from the fine cuisine of the elegant **Dandelion** restaurant at 101 Walnut Street, (303) 443-6700, to the hearty fare of family restaurants like the **Red Robin Spirits Emporium** at 2580 Arapahoe Avenue, (303) 442-0302. A great place to spend an evening is **Trios Grille and Wine Bar**, 1155 Canyon Boulevard, (303) 442-8400, an intimate place with an extensive wine menu as well as all other bar offerings, including a limited food menu. Live jazz is played Tuesday through Sunday; live blues is played on Monday.

Boulder also belies its offbeat image by the impressive strength of its business community. Boulder County has the state's highest percentage of employment in manufacturing, and it's way ahead in per-capita high-tech manufacturing. But don't expect to see Boulderites walking around in boardroom-elegant suits with grim, nose-to-the-grindstone expressions. Boulderites generally maintain an easygoing attitude. They're avid on the subjects of environmental responsibility and health consciousness.

All this is a rather long dissertation on one daytrip, but Boulder is by far the biggest nearby daytrip in breadth of offerings. The **Pearl Street Mall** is the center of the city. Formerly the main street of old Boulder, it's now a pedestrian mall lined with unique shops, restaurants, art galleries, flower gardens and street performers — a delightful stroll in any but the worst weather, except for the occasional panhandler or bourgeoisie-disdaining misanthrope. South on Broadway from Pearl Street and up the hill is **University Hill**, where you can enjoy a walk around the graceful campus of the University of Colorado at Boulder.

Go farther south on Broadway past the campus to Baseline Road, turn right on Baseline and go up a long hill. Just past Ninth Street you'll find on the left the entrance to **Chautauqua Park & Auditorium**. The auditorium is a lovely setting for a summer evening concert. For information, call the Chautauqua ticket service at (303) 440-7666. One of Boulder's biggest treats is a summer breakfast or lunch on the veranda of the 100-year-old **Chautauqua Dining Hall**, (303) 440-3776, where you can gaze out at the mountains as you munch.

Chautauqua Park is also the city's prime entrance to **Boulder Mountain Parks**, some 8,000 acres of trails and rough climbing including Bear Peak, Green Mountain, Flagstaff Mountain, Mount Sanitas and, of course, the Flatirons.

Another entrance to the park, and an attraction in its own right, is the **National Center for Atmospheric Research**, commonly referred to around Boulder simply as NCAR (say it EN-car). An architectural masterwork by master architect I.M. Pei, it perches like an Italian hill fortress on the redundantly named Table Mesa to the south of Chautauqua with views of the mountains and plains that make it a great spot just for weather gazing. You find it by going still farther south on Broadway from Baseline to Table Mesa Drive. Turn right, and keep going until you stop at NCAR. You may see deer on the way. You can pick up a numbered tour guide in the lobby and take the self-guided tour from 8 AM to 5 PM Monday through Friday and 9 AM to 3 PM on Saturday, Sunday and holidays. There's also a drop-in tour, which takes place at noon Mondays and Wednesdays from September to mid-June. The Exploratorium Museum in San Francisco has also given NCAR six interactive exhibits similar to those in San Francisco. And it's all free, except for the cafeteria, which is open to the public for breakfast and lunch from 7:30 to 9:30 AM and 11:30 AM to 1:30 PM. To find out about NCAR's guided tours and other information, call (303) 497-1174. Outside NCAR, you can hike on 400 acres of the mesa top, including a wheelchair-accessible natural trail leading west behind the lab. And just west of the mesa, you get into the system of Boulder Mountain Park trails.

You can usually see climbers scaling the Flatirons, but the best place for close-up watching of technical climbers is **Eldorado Canyon**. Keep going south on Broadway from Table Mesa Drive until Broadway becomes Colo. Highway 93 as you pass into open country. Watch for the Eldorado Springs Drive turn-off on the right, just more than 5 miles out of Boulder. This is Colo. Highway 170, and about 8 miles of it takes you to **Eldorado Springs**. Back around the turn of the century this resort town used to be called "the Coney Island of Colorado" because of all the people who flocked here for the resort hotels and 76-degree springs. Pass on through it and into

Eldorado Canyon State Park where you'll find a magnificent cut between high cliffs. You'll see little smudges of white all over the rocks, chalk from climbers' hands. In good weather, you'll see people dangling all over the canyon walls.

Colorado Springs

"The Springs," as locals call it, is an hour's drive south, 67 miles from Denver, and the largest single cluster of tourist attractions in our daytrip-defining radius of 100 miles. It doesn't have as many natural wonders as Rocky Mountain National Park, but it has some great ones. And it has plenty of other attractions of human contrivance.

Pikes Peak is the biggest show in town, of course. You can drive to the top by taking U.S. Highway 24 west to Cascade and hanging a left on the same road that brings top auto racers from around the world every year for the Pikes Peak Hill Climb. Or you can do the dizzying trip on the **Pikes Peak Cog Railway**, officially known as the Manitou and Pikes Peak Cog Railway. Reach its terminal by driving west from Colorado Springs on U.S. Highway 24 to the Manitou Exit, west on Manitou Avenue and left onto Ruxton Avenue.

This is the highest cog railway in the world. Established in 1889, it's a historical as well as a sensory experience. During the three-and-a-half-hour round trip, you get more panoramas than you can stuff into your brain, including great views down on Manitou Springs and the Garden of the Gods. You get a great view of Denver on a clear day, just as Denverites can see Pikes Peak on a clear day. You can see a seemingly infinite expanse of mountains to the west, and you can even look into New Mexico.

Do take care not to exert yourself too hard and too long on the 14,110-foot summit: oxygen is scarce up there, and altitude sickness is not a pleasant experience. Besides walking around and taking in the views, you can also unwind in the information center, the gewgaw shop and the concession area.

The railway is only open from April to October and runs every day during that period. Reservations are required, since this is one of Colorado's big attractions. There's a $21.50

Photo: Daily Camera/Vern Walker

Macky Auditorium is one of the historic buildings
on the University of Colorado-Boulder campus.

charge for adults and a $10 charge for children ages 5 through 11. Call (719) 685-5401 for information.

Garden of the Gods Park, 1805 N. 30th Street, (719) 634-6666, is another of Colorado Springs' most famous sights. A drive through the park reveals one of the most spectacular displays of dramatic red sandstone formations in Colorado. It's just northwest of downtown. **Cave of the Winds**, Colo. Highway 24 W. in Manitou Springs, is the biggest commercial cave in Colorado, and well worth taking the tour through the underground passages and caverns. Call for tour information at (719) 685-5444. Cost is $10 for adults and $5 for children ages 6 through 15. There's also an outside laser light show each night at 9 PM, costing $6 for adults and $3 for children, with kids ages 6 and younger getting in free.

If you want to go a bit beyond the 100-mile limit of our daytrip definition, you will certainly enjoy the **Cripple Creek Narrow Gauge Railroad**. Cripple Creek itself is worth visiting, certainly, as one of Colorado's most famous old mining towns and a National Historic District in its own right, although the town has changed somewhat since limited-stakes gambling was legalized here in 1991. But the 4-mile round trip on this old-time steam railroad is rivaled on the Front Range only by the **Georgetown Loop** for cool railroad Americana ($7.50 for adults, $3.75 children ages 3 through 12). Call (719) 689-2640 for information. A little farther out Colo. Highway 115 southeast from Colorado Springs is **Royal Gorge**, about an hour's drive from Colorado Springs, where you can drive across the world's highest suspension bridge 1,053 feet above the Arkansas River. Call Royal Gorge Bridge information at (719) 275-7507. By paying $11 for adults and $8 for children ages 4 through 11, you can drive or walk across the bridge as well as ride an aerial tram across the canyon's history, a minitrain that takes you in the scenic mile circle ride and a carousel. They also have an incline railway, a cagelike ride that takes you all the way down to the bottom of the canyon to the river's edge.

There is so much more to see and do in the Colorado Springs area, including the Victorian town of **Manitou Springs** and its natural hot springs; the **Cliff Dwellings Museum**, (719) 685-5242, 5 miles west of Colorado Springs on U.S. Highway 24; the historic **Broadmoor Hotel**, (719) 634-7711, with its two great 18-hole golf courses; **Santa's Work-**

shop at the North Pole, (719) 684-9432, a little magic village/funland that kids can enjoy from mid-May through Christmas Eve; the **ProRodeo Hall of Fame** and the **Museum of the American Cowboy**, both at (719) 528-4764.

Of all Colorado Springs' attractions, however, the very busiest is the **U.S. Air Force Academy**. You can spend a lot of time touring its 18,000 acres. The Academy doesn't have any one attraction that will blow your socks off, but it's intrinsically interesting simply because of its importance in the military world of aviation. You can take a self-guided driving tour around the grounds or walk the nature trail that winds along the ridge behind the school, with plenty of wind-through-the-pines atmosphere and Academy overlooks with benches. There's a very nice museum on the grounds. The most famous sight is the chapel, which is architecturally striking. Perhaps the best way to experience the Academy is by attending its spring graduation ceremony, where you can see the now-ceremonial tossing of hats in the air by cadets and enjoy a performance by the Thunderbirds, the Air Force's famed jet-acrobatics team. You do need tickets in advance for this event, however. The tickets are free, but they generally come available about two weeks before the ceremony, which is always held on the first Wednesday after Memorial Day. Call the Academy's visitor center at (719) 333-2025 for tickets and other information.

Directly across I-25 from the north gate of the Air Force Academy is a particular favorite of ours, the **Western Museum of Mining and Industry**. It's a nice place for a picnic, with its 27 acres of rolling hills, trees, meadows, streams, beaver ponds and picnic tables. Most important, of course, is the museum itself: more than 15,000 square feet of exhibits in four buildings, along with outdoor displays.

It's a big treat to watch them fire up the 1895 Corliss steam engine and watch the 17-ton flywheel go. You can see mining and milling demonstrations and even pan for gold. Admission is $5 for adults, $4 for seniors and students, and $2 for kids ages 5 to 12. Kids younger than 5 get in free with a paying adult. The museum is open 9 AM to 4 PM Monday through Saturday. For info, call (719) 488-0880. To reach the museum, get off I-25 at Exit 156A, Gleneagle Drive.

Fort Collins

We go to Fort Collins when we need a small-town fix. Just one hour north of Denver on I-25, this college town (home of Colorado State University) feels like Mayberry RFD. You almost expect to see Aunt Bee or Opie sitting on the front porch. Still, there's enough to do here to make you enjoy this small town rather than be bored by it.

As you head north on I-25, take the Harmony Road Exit and go right for a quarter of a mile until you see a farm with all kinds of shiny sculptures. This is the **Swetsville Zoo**, a menagerie of dinosaurs and mythical creatures made by owner Bill Swets. This self-styled artist makes his creatures out of old car parts and farm equipment. With more than 80 sculptures, this "zoo" makes a delightful diversion. Open every day year round, the zoo is free, though donations are appreciated.

Once you're ready to head into town, get back on I-25 and go north to the Mulberry Street Exit. This will take you through town and past it to Roosevelt Street where you'll find City Park. Here you'll find the **Fort Collins Municipal Railway**, a fancy term for a restored trolley car that travels down its original route on Mountain Avenue to downtown. Powered by 600 volts of electricity, the trolley runs on tracks that line the grassy median of one of

---

INSIDERS' TIP

Finding a place to buy snacks and bottled water most anywhere these days is fairly simple, but throwing a little something in a backpack while trekking around is one less thing to worry about. High protein, high carbohydrate snacks like trail mix and string cheese will keep you going while hiking, biking or just driving to view the fall aspen colors. And don't forget the water!

the city's major thoroughfares. Don't be surprised when you reach downtown if the conductor gets out and smokes a pipe before returning to City Park. Remember, this is small-town living, not a New York subway. The 25-minute ride costs $1 for adults and 50¢ for kids 12 and younger.

Like most college towns, Fort Collins offers shopping that transcends the typical mall experience. **Historic Old Town Square** at College and Mountain avenues is a trove of art galleries, shops and outdoor cafes all housed in historic buildings. Like the Pearl Street Mall in Boulder (though much smaller), this is a pedestrian-only area with places to sit and people-watch when you're tired of shopping.

For beer drinkers, a visit to Fort Collins would be incomplete without a free tour of the **Anheuser Busch Brewery**, off of I-25 at Exit 271. Opened in 1988, the world's largest brewery offers free tours from 10 AM to 4 PM Thursday through Monday. The 75-minute tour shows high-tech brewing processes as well as a chance to see the famous Clydesdale horses. Best of all, at the end, you can visit the Hospitality Center to taste a few brews.

We think a trip to Fort Collins must include a visit to the **Colorado State University** (CSU) campus. You might want to stop at the visitors center just south of College Avenue and Laurel Street if you want a map of the campus. Our favorite destination is Johnson Hall, where, in the summer, the CSU Theater Department puts on three plays in repertory. Usually light comedies such as *The Heidi Chronicles*, *On Golden Pond* and *Love Letters*, the plays are performed at the outdoor theater where the audience sits at cabaret tables. The student actors are an enthusiastic bunch, and at $10 a ticket, this is a theatrical bargain. And a wonderful way to end a day in Fort Collins.

Winter Park

Just because you don't ski doesn't mean a daytrip to a ski resort should be crossed off your list — especially in the summer. Come Memorial Day weekend, Winter Park Ski Resort gears up for the onslaught of visitors who want to get the heck out of Dodge — or Denver as the case might be.

To reach Winter Park, located 67 miles northwest of Denver, take I-70 W. to Exit 232 (Highway 40) and follow U.S. Highway 40 over Berthoud Pass to Winter Park. However, if you're really feeling adventurous, consider going down to Union Station and catching the **California Zephyr** to Fraser (the town right next to Winter Park). The train leaves Denver daily at 9:35 AM, arriving in Fraser at 11:30 AM. This is a much more relaxing way to get there and better yet, once you arrive in Fraser, a free shuttle bus will pick you up (it stops at the station at 11:38) and take you to any number of fun destinations. The train costs between $35 and $55 depending on availability and leaves Fraser each afternoon at 4:25 PM, arriving back at Union Station at 7:10 PM.

Once you're there, consider a ride down the **Alpine Slide**, located at the base of Winter Park Mountain. It's the longest alpine slide in Colorado. Then head over to the **Zephyr Express Chairlift** to take a scenic ride to the 10,700-foot summit of the mountain. You can have lunch at the Lodge at Sunspot and then burn those calories off by hiking down to the base.

If you've brought a bike with you (or you can rent one at the resort) consider riding the 5-mile **Fraser River Trail**, built three years ago and perfect for beginners and families. You can get on the road at the base of the mountain and follow it to the Trademark Condos where you'll pick up the Fraser River Trail. If your lungs and legs are in good shape, consider taking the bike to the top of the mountain on the Zephyr Express and choose any number of sky-high trail rides.

Should you happen to be visiting the Winter Park area on a Saturday in July or August, plan to catch some cowboy action at the **High Country Stampede Rodeo**, held at the John Work Arena in Fraser on County Road 73. This little rodeo pits cowboys against bucking broncos. You can even come a bit earlier and enjoy the barbecue dinner before the show.

And if you just want to spend the day shopping, summer is a great time to look for bargains. Look for sidewalk sales of closeout winter clothing and equipment. Also check out the specialty gift shops for items you won't find in a mall.

Georgetown

Georgetown is a historic mining town that has been lovingly maintained and restored with a turn-of-the-century style that makes it look like one of those toy towns on an elaborate model railroad setup. John Denver used it as the site of one of his Christmas specials in the 1980s. It's a National Historic Landmark District that nestles deep in the head of a valley overshadowed by the steep slopes of several 12,000-foot mountains.

The biggest single attraction here is the **Georgetown Loop**, an old Western railroad train that hauls loads of tourists and train and history buffs from Georgetown uphill to Silver Plume, and back, which is about a 3-mile round trip. **Silver Plume**, by the way, is another great historic town to spend some time in. The train ride includes passage over a 100-foot trestle known as Devils Gate Bridge. We can't recommend this trip highly enough, and it's not just the scenery or the fun of riding. It's the historic element and the bits of cinder that fly from the stack of the horrendously puffing old engine and settle on the passengers behind. It's one of the few great antique train rides in Colorado and by far the closest one to Denver. For a special treat, do it in the fall when the aspens are at high color. The railroad costs $11.95 for adults and $7.50 for children ages 4 through 15, with no charge for kids 3 and younger as long as they sit on a parent's lap. The train operates from May to October, and reservations are suggested. For reservations and information, call the Denver metro number, (303) 670-1686, or the Georgetown number, (303) 569-2403.

Georgetown itself went from a mining camp in 1859 to style itself as the "Silver Queen of the Rockies" by the 1870s. Now it's just a fun place to stroll around; it has shops, restaurants, museums, galleries and National Historic Register sites. The museums include the **Hotel de Paris**, the **Hamill House** and the **Georgetown Community Center**, which was recently renovated with help from the State Historic Fund. The Hamill House was built in the 1870s in Gothic Revival Style and has been restored to that period. The Hotel de Paris, owned by Louis Dupuy, included a fine dining room and is open for tours, as are all the museums. Reach Georgetown by taking I-70 Exit 228, about 50 miles west of Denver.

You can also drive out of Georgetown south on the **Guanella Pass Scenic Byway**, which goes all the way to the City of Grant on U.S. Highway 285. The byway peaks out at Guanella Pass, elevation 11,669 feet, where you have wonderful views that include looking up at Mount Bierstadt. This pass is also a good place to get out of the car and look around, but don't stand up too fast in this altitude; the air is thin, and people have been known to faint from small exertions. Find a big rock and have a picnic. Or do some hiking. Heck, you can even hike to the top of Bierstadt. You're already so high that it doesn't take more than a couple of hours, even including the frequent stops to gasp and wheeze. We once encountered a 5-year-old boy on top of Bierstadt. With a parent, of course.

Georgetown has another neat little element. The State of Colorado chose a spot near the lake just east of Georgetown as the state's first **Watchable Wildlife Viewing Station**, although there are others now. Stop and see if you can spot the herd of bighorn sheep on the mountainsides. Often, you can even spot them from I-70 as you're whizzing by, although recently they've been harder to find because the herds went through a decimated-by-disease phase in 1994.

Georgetown visitor information has a toll-free number, (800) 472-8230.

Grand Lake/ Granby Loop

We call this the Grand Lake/Granby Loop drive because those are the two towns that anchor it on the western side of the Continental Divide. *National Geographic Traveler* mentioned this drive in its March/April 1994 edition, in an article called "50 Great Scenic Drives." Nobody around here was surprised.

You can experience Grand Lake/Granby Loop by driving from Denver to Estes Park and over Trail Ridge Road (closed in winter) through Rocky Mountain National Park and down to Granby. Take U.S. Highway 40 from Granby south through Winter Park, over Berthoud Pass, connecting at Empire with I-70 back to Denver. It's almost 200 miles, a full day, especially if you stop along the way, which you should. Or, you may want to take the circle in the other direction. In fact, you may want to head the other direction only as far as Grand Lake, rather than making a full loop, and leave the Boulder, Estes Park and Rocky Mountain National Park stops for a trip of their own some other day.

Grand Lake is both the name of the city and the name of the big lake on the edge of which the city perches. And just south of Grand Lake is Lake Granby. You'll travel along their western edges and, looking east at the mountains rising from the lakes' other sides into Rocky Mountain National Park and Arapaho National Forest, you could almost believe you're in Switzerland. The lakes are huge, deep blue and clear, usually decorated with sailboats and always lined with small resorts. Grand Lake is the state's largest lake created by glaciers. Grand Lake is a quaint historic village with boardwalks along the main street. Walk around and maybe catch a bite to eat. Or, you might buy something and head out for a picnic at Lake Granby's Arapahoe Bay.

Arapahoe Bay is at the far southeastern end of Lake Granby. Its depths are a favorite fishing spot in June for the lake's big Mackinaw, or lake trout. You reach it by taking the first left turn off of U.S. Highway 34 at the southwestern tip of Lake Granby. A long gravel road passes over Granby Dam and skirts the southern edge of the lake. At the end of the bay you'll find campgrounds and some nice short hiking trails. You can follow the trail east past Monarch Lake and go as far as you want up toward or into the Indian Peaks Wilderness. It's a pretty area that makes a pleasant stopping point on your loop.

Head south to meet U.S. Highway 40 just west of Granby. You may want to take an added excursion west, or right, on Highway 40 along the scenic highway toward Steamboat Springs, at least as far as Hot Sulfur Springs, anyway. See our entry below on Hot Sulfur Springs. If not, take a left on Highway 40 to get back to Denver by way of Granby, Tabernash, Fraser, Winter Park, Berthoud Pass and down through Empire onto I-70.

Most people just hustle through **Empire**, but there are some nice places to stop for refreshment there, and it's perhaps most famous as the home of **The Peck House**, Colorado's oldest operating hotel. Driving through Empire from Berthoud Pass, The Peck House, (303) 569-9870, is about three-fourths of the way through town, a half-block off U.S. Highway 40. You'll see it from the highway on your left, a big white building with red trim. It's a moderately priced hotel, ranging from $45 to $80 for a night. Check it out, and maybe dine in its restaurant.

Hot Sulphur Springs

What was once our oddball recommendation is no longer such an oddball. This quaint town of 376 residents has come alive again with the recent major renovation of the 70-acre resort and spa called the **Hot Sulphur Springs Resort**. It reopened full time in August of 1997. To reach this town located 90 miles northwest of Denver, take I-70 to U.S. Highway 40 and head west. U.S. 40 has been widened and resurfaced so slow down when you come to Hot Sulphur Springs.

You'll see the **Riverside Hotel** and the **Stagecoach Bed and Breakfast** on the close side of the Colorado River. Cross the river to get to the Hot Sulphur Springs Resort, which is nestled against 70 acres of sagebrush.

The Ute Indians once "took the waters" here to heal and relax. Today people come for the same reasons. You can soak in any of the 10 pools where 200,000 gallons of hot mineral

---

INSIDERS' TIP

When opening carbonated beverages in the car during high-altitude drives, remember that they have been bottled at a lower altitude/pressure. When opened they can squirt in your face and all over the interior of your vehicle. Some containers have the same effect even down in Denver. Instant coffee crystals, for example, often spray all over your kitchen counter when you break the airtight seal.

Special Summer Events

Denverites don't mind the 45-minute trip to Central City or Boulder for the following summer performing arts events.

The **Central City Opera**, (303) 292-6700, is a favorite summer tradition. Begun in 1932, the opera holds its performances in the historic Opera House in the old mining town of Central City, about 34 miles west of Denver. The incongruously grand opera house was built in 1878 and ceased operations from 1927 to 1932, at which time the

Central City Opera Association took over the building and began restoration and performances. Such notables as Edwin Booth, Mae West, Helen Hayes and Beverly Sills have performed here. The coming of gambling to Central City in 1992 has drastically changed the formerly sleepy nature of the town, but the opera

remains as charming as ever. Three operas are performed each summer, and all are sung in English. Ask in advance about specially priced youth performances, round-trip bus transportation from Lakewood and Cherry Creek and reserved parking — the last is highly recommended if you plan to drive yourself.

The summer concerts at Boulder's **Chautauqua Auditorium** are another reason to head west. Boulder's Chautauqua dates back to 1898, when a national movement

— continued on next page

Photo: Daily Camera

MacDuff lays on to MacBeth at a recent performance of *MacBeth* at the Colorado Shakespeare Festival in Boulder.

brought the arts to numerous Chautauqua summer camps throughout the country. Before the evening concerts in the wonderful wooden auditorium, concertgoers can enjoy a picnic dinner under the big shady trees at the base of the Foothills or a sit-down dinner at the Chautauqua Dining Hall, (303) 440-3776. Chautauqua concerts include both a popular music series, (303) 440-7666 (box office) and the Colorado Music Festival, (303) 449-1397, year round; (303) 449-2413, summer ticketing, which emphasizes classical music.

The **Colorado Shakespeare Festival**, (303) 492-0554, is another summer-only event in Boulder that draws audiences from Denver and beyond. Held at the outdoor Mary Rippon Theatre and indoor University Theatre on the University of Colorado-Boulder campus, the annual event features both traditional and modern renditions of Shakespeare plays and non-Shakespearean classics. Tom Stoppard's *Rosencrantz and Guildenstern Are Dead*, for example, was a big hit of the 1995 season. Film actor Val Kilmer took part in a production one year, and other top performers and directors have likewise been attracted to this highly regarded event. "Falstaff's Fare," a box dinner, can be ordered and eaten on the lawn before the show begins. There are evening and matinee performances as well as special children's nights.

The **Colorado Dance Festival**, (303) 442-7666, is now the third-largest dance festival in the nation. It has earned international recognition for its innovative programs of modern dance and performance art and has featured such acclaimed artists as Trisha Brown, Ralph Lemon and the late, great tap dancer Honi Coles. Some years the CDF organizes its one-month summer season around a theme, other years it's more free-form. Performances are held on the University of Colorado campus in Boulder.

---

waters flow at temperatures of 102-112 degrees F year round. Too darn hot? Go to the kid's pool that runs around 85 degrees F.

This casual resort has private pools, pools with views and cave-like pools. And if you're feeling particularly luxurious, you can go for a massage and a facial too. If you're feeling invigorated, you may want to hike and picnic in the beautiful surroundings. The pools are open year-round from 8 AM to 10 PM. A private pool is $10 per person per hour. If you want to hang out inside or out all day, the cost is $9.75. Either way, you'll return home totally relaxed. For information call (800) 510-6235.

The **Riverside Hotel**, across the bridge from the baths, is a blocky wooden structure that was built in 1908. Abe Renta, the energetically welcoming innkeeper, bought the hotel when it was rundown and had been closed for 1½ years. He spent 10 months sprucing it up and opened for business in 1983. The 19 rooms are old-fashioned in appearance, like the hotel rooms you might see in a cowboy movie or find a bit more fancied up in a modern bed and breakfast. Rates recently went up to $32 for a single room and $42 for a double. The hotel may be closed

Monday through Wednesday in the winter months, when business slows down, and only dinner is served from September to May. The rest of the year, Abe opens for lunch and dinner seven days a week. The dining room has a potbellied stove and looks out on the Colorado River. You'll find mostly American cuisine, with some European accents. Call ahead for reservations, (970) 725-3589.

Idaho Springs

Idaho Springs, 32 miles west of Denver on I-70, is the first resort town and erstwhile mining town you hit on the way west.

It's also the mining town that is most visible as a mining town, thanks to the floes of yellow tailings spilling from holes that dot the mountainsides along I-70 here. If you want a closer look at this phenomenon, take the "Oh My God Road" from Idaho Springs to Central City, a narrow and scary road with even more holes and tailings dotting the hillsides.

Prospector George Jackson launched Idaho Springs in early 1859 when he pulled out nearly $2,000 worth of gold in one week. Miners flocked in, and the town was off. Two of your best choices for a look into the town's mining past are the **Argo Gold Mill** and the **Phoenix Mine**. You can't miss the Argo Gold Mill. It's the biggest structure on the north side of the valley, and the name is printed in large letters on its front. Where much of the local ore was processed in now a museum and National Historic Site that you can tour from May to October. The Phoenix Mine, sunk in 1872, is once again a working mine that you can tour guided by an experienced miner. Learn about the history, geology and the art of gold mining, dig your own ore and pan your own gold. Call (303) 567-0422.

Idaho Springs and the surrounding area have a lot of other attractions, too, and one of them is simply the Clear Creek Ranger District office **Arapaho National Forest**, (303) 567-2901, where you can stop in to find out about other opportunities nearby. It's at 101 Chicago Creek Road. Coming from Denver on I-70, take the Mount Evans Exit, then turn left up Colo. Highway 103 and it's the first brown building on the right-hand side.

And of course, Idaho Springs has natural hot mineral springs. The **Indian Springs Resort,** listed on the National Register as a historic site, offers hot baths and a covered mineral water swimming pool. It's at 302 Soda Creek Road, just east of downtown. Call (303) 567-2191 for information.

For more information on these and other attractions, call the Chamber of Commerce's visitor information line at (800) 685-7785 or the Idaho Springs Visitors Center at (303) 567-4382.

Mount Evans

If you love mountains, this is the best daytrip of them all. Not because there's a resort or town or some paying attraction at the end of it — just because this is the fastest route to the greatest vistas in the region. For out-of-town visitors here on business or some other short stay, with only a morning or afternoon to see the mountains, this is the best

recommendation we can make. For anybody else, it's a must.

It's simple. Colo. Highway 5 to the top of Mount Evans is the highest paved road in the world and your chance to go to the top of one of Colorado's "14ers" without having to huff and puff up thousands of feet of forest and alpine meadow. You park at about 14,260 feet, wander around and look down and out 100 miles in every direction. The view is absolutely magnificent. It's more impressive than the view from Trail Ridge Road where it meets the Continental Divide in Rocky Mountain National Park, and it's just up the hill from Idaho Springs.

Take I-70 west out of Denver to Idaho Springs, about a 30-minute drive. Get off at Exit 240, which features a sign saying Mount Evans, and get on Colo. Highway 103. It winds uphill, to the intersection with Colo. Highway 5 at Echo Lake. This is where rangers will collect the $6 per vehicle fee, newly started in the fall of 1997. The lake, by the way, is a nice place for a picnic and some fishing. Also, either on the way up or on the way down, stop at the **Echo Lake Lodge**, (303) 567-2138, located at the intersection. Pause for a refreshment in their little restaurant, and browse among their gifts and souvenirs. Make sure to look out the window at their hummingbird feeder. In summer, you can expect to see the striking spectacle of ruby-throated hummingbirds swirling and hovering like bees just on the other side of the windowpane.

Head uphill on Colo. Highway 5 for another 14-mile trip to the top. Acrophobics should be warned that this stretch may produce whiter knuckles than any paved road in Colorado. The road is very narrow, especially on the ride down. Looking out from the passenger seat, your can easily imagine the car slipping off the side and cartwheeling into the abyss.

You will probably see mountain goats on the way up, and maybe even bighorn sheep. Several years ago, an ill-trained hunter wounded one near the highway, and tourists were treated to the sight of a bloody sheep

---

INSIDERS' TIP

It's always cool in the mountains at night, even in the summer. Take a sweater, or shiver.

running across the road pursued by the gun-toting hunter. Motorists stopped, and there was a hunter/driver exchange of angry words and fisticuffs.

Once at the parking lot, you can climb a short trail to the highest point and look down to the west on the Continental Divide, east over Denver and the Great Plains, north over the Roosevelt National Forest and south over the Pike National Forest. Bring along a state map; it's fun to try to identify some of the major peaks. If you like boulder fields, there are plenty to scramble around on. If you're a flatlander who hasn't been in Denver for at least three days, however, do bear in mind that there's only about half as much oxygen up here as there is at sea level. Don't exert yourself too hard or too long. Altitude sickness can hit you right away, or it can hammer you after you've been back in Denver for hours. We had one friend from outside Colorado who hiked 2,000 feet lower than this and had to be taken to the emergency room that evening when she got stomach cramps and began vomiting and frantically hyperventilating. Take it easy, drink lots of water and you should do fine. The road to Mount Evans is open only in the warmer months, and even then, weather can turn bad. To check on road conditions or ask other questions, call the **Clear Creek Ranger District of Arapaho National Forest** at (303) 567-2901.

The Peak-to-Peak

The Peak-to-Peak Highway is so called because it follows the eastern slopes of more peaks than you can shake a stick at. It's basically the road that runs below the Continental Divide from the tourist mecca of Estes Park on the north to the historic towns and gambling meccas of Black Hawk and Central City on the south. Along the way there are plenty of turnoffs westward that will get you closer to Longs Peak, Mount Meeker, Chiefs Head Peak, Isolation Peak, Ouzel Peak, Mount Alice, Mount Orton, Mahana Peak and Copeland Mountain — and those are just some of the peaks along the first 10 miles. The highway is about 60 miles long and actually consists, north to south, of Colo. Highway 7, Colo. Highway 72 and Colo. Highway 119.

Many Insiders take their bikes along when daytripping in the mountains.

Take the Peak-to-Peak in either direction. The entire route is a winding road of beautiful vistas and lovely mountainsides. It's a worthwhile tour anytime but an especially great place to take in the views of autumn's golden aspens, generally in September. Ten miles south of Estes Park, you find the well-traveled turnoff for the Longs Peak Trailhead. This may be the most popular ascent of a Colorado "14er." It's a heck of a long slog. See the Hiking section of our Recreation Chapter.

Another 4 miles or so along, you'll find on the right the turnoff for the **Ouzel Falls Trail** at Wild Basin. If you want to get out of your car for a pleasant walk to a gemlike waterfall in the cool forest, this is the opportunity. The falls are only about 3 miles up the trail.

All along the Peak-to-Peak there are not only turnoffs to the west to reach scenic areas and other attractions but also turnoffs to the left that will take you back down to the flatlands in case you decide to bail out of the loop. You can come up these routes and travel only part of the loop. At one of these points, the historic mining town of Ward, you can head east downhill via **Lefthand Canyon** or you can head west up to **Brainard Lake**. This crystalline, high-mountain lake is a beautiful place where you can absorb spectacular views without walking more than a few steps from your car.

Actually, you can just look out through the windshield, but the effect is better if you get out and inhale the mountain breezes.

Pass on south through Nederland (lots of nice drives west from here too) and on down to Rollinsville. A drive west from here on a gravel road will bring you to the Moffat Tunnel, which connects Denver by railroad with points west. A trail up to the east of the tunnel makes a nice hike and is popular with cross-country skiers in winter.

From Rollinsville on down, the big tourist attractions are **Black Hawk** and **Central City**, which have become the places to go and gamble for Denverites since limited-stakes gambling was allowed by Colorado voters in 1991. Call (800) 542-2999 for information on Central City's lodgings and attractions. Also see our Nightlife chapter for more information.

Black Hawk is right next to Central City and was one of the first mining camps around Gregory Gulch, where gold was discovered in 1859. Central City, in the middle of Gregory Gulch, became the prominent population center because of its location, which claims the "richest square mile on Earth." Central City is a great old historic mining town, but a lot of people feel that its historic authenticity has been obliterated by all the new casinos. Well, Central City has become a favorite evening

and weekend excursion for a lot of people looking for a little Las Vegas in their own back yard, but it's still a nice historic district as well. The **Central City Opera House** is still Colorado's reigning opera performance center during its summer season. It was built in 1861, burned in 1874, rebuilt in 1878 and during the latter part of the century was pulling in some of the biggest names in theater. Closed when the silver boom ended, it has been operating since it reopened in 1932. Call the Denver business office at (303) 292-6700 for opera information.

The **Teller House**, next to the opera, is Central City's historic hotel, perhaps most well-known for the "Face on the Barroom Floor." The mystique of that woman's face is probably due more to the faded paint job and her mysterious expression than to its origin, because it doesn't hail from the boom days. It was painted in 1932. The **Gilpin County Historical Museum** is a better bet for a bit of history on this gold and silver town of yore, and it's located right in town. Call (303) 582-5283 for more information about the museum.

Whether gambling has hurt or helped Central City and Black Hawk is a matter of opinion. Historic tourism wasn't paying the bills, many said, and gambling would bolster the economy so the historical aspects could get their just due. Gambling drove real estate sky

Photo: Daily Camera

Many Rocky Mountain cities have balloon festivals.

high, drove out a lot of authentic residents and their businesses and required the gutting of historic buildings for new casinos, say detractors. At any rate, your Peak-to-Peak Highway tour is likely to run into heavy gambler traffic along here, bumper-to-bumper traffic on busy gambling nights. This area is well-patrolled by police.

A short ride down the road will take you to I-70, if you're in a rush to get back home. But if you're here for the scenic route, you're well-advised to take a left on U.S. Highway 6 down scenic Clear Creek Canyon to Golden.

Rocky Mountain National Park

With the possible exception of Yellowstone in Wyoming, Rocky Mountain National Park is the nation's most famous. And you can't say too much about it, since it's Colorado's hugest single immersion in nature that you can experience by auto and/or short walks. It's a chance to see the full spectrum of Rocky Mountain nature in one gulp. You can roam from the darkest subalpine forests below to the sun-sprinkled meadows and granite grandeur of the continent's roof — 265,000 acres of it well-connected by roads and trails.

The best way to do the park by auto, of course, is **Trail Ridge Road**, 48 miles of U.S. Highway 34 that vaults over the park from Estes Park on the east to Grand Lake on the west. The drive over the top is one of the nation's great scenic routes, although its two lanes are well-jammed in the summer season. The opening of Trail Ridge Road by snowplow some time around Memorial Day is an annual Colorado event photographed for the Denver and Boulder papers, and it stays open until October. But you can access the park year round. The east side has plenty of lovely drives and hiking opportunities. To reach the west side in winter, take I-70 west from Denver to U.S. Highway 40 at Empire, then U.S. Highway 40 north to Granby, where you go right on U.S. Highway 34 to the park. Autumn and spring visits are particularly enjoyable. Do check it out on late-summer or early autumn evenings when the elk are bugling, particularly in the Kewuneeche Valley on the western side.

The park headquarters can be reached for questions at (970) 586-1206.

Education

Choices, choices and more choices. That best describes the educational scene in Greater Denver. Your child loves music and dancing? Denver Public Schools offer The Denver School of the Arts. You have a child who's goofing off and not living up to his or her potential? There are numerous private schools that offer a low pupil/teacher ratio and individualized instruction. You want your child to have rigorous college prep courses? Several public schools offer the International Baccalaureate Program. No matter what you're looking for, chances are you'll find it here.

Better yet, Colorado's public schools were made more accessible in 1994 by legislation creating open enrollment statewide, meaning you can enroll your kids in any public school at no extra cost. Got your eye on a school with some real nice programs but live outside the traditional enrollment area? That problem has been eliminated by open enrollment. Of course, local children have priority, so it depends on whether space is available.

The state stands at the educational forefront in many ways. In 1993, for example, Colorado became the third state after Minnesota and California to enact charter schools, which are publicly funded but run by groups of parents, teachers and other individuals who want to devise their own curriculum. Greater Denver now has charter schools in operation or pending in every one of its counties. Whether they opt for charter schools or not, Denver parents are involved in their children's education. Many schools are governed by cooperative decision-making teams, made up of parents, teachers, administrators, students and local business people. And, not surprisingly, in 1997 the end of 25 years of court-ordered busing in Denver Public Schools has already brought a tremendous amount of community support for what will now, once again, be neighborhood schools.

One of the best publications a parent can buy is *The Guide to Metro Denver Public Schools* by Margerie Hicks. It lays out just about everything you could want to know about Greater Denver's 15 public school systems, its school districts and its individual schools and programs. It's available through Denver's Magnolia Street Press, (303) 322-2822, the Metro Denver Chamber of Commerce, (303) 534-8500, and some local bookstores for $14.50. You can always look through a copy at a public library, but it's at least worth contacting Magnolia Street Press to make sure you are looking at the latest annual edition.

A valuable pre-college program for high school students is **Project Upward Bound**, operated by Metropolitan State College of Denver. Small, late-afternoon classes on Metro's Auraria Campus are geared for students from low-income families, students who need better preparation and students recommended by a high school teacher, counselor, principal, adult friend or community person. The program is designed to enhance development of basic skills, creative thinking, effective expression, independence in learning and positive attitudes toward learning. For info call (303) 556-2812.

For the younger set, Greater Denver has more than 60 **Head Start** centers. For information, contact Denver's Region VIII office of the U.S. Department of Health and Human Services, (303) 844-3106.

The state of Colorado has a newcomer's packet to get you started on learning about the state's public schools; it's available through the Department of Education's Communications Center at 201 E. Colfax in Denver, (303) 866-6646. You can also get a free copy of *A Parent's Guide to Colorado Public Schools* by calling the Governor's Office of Policy and Initiatives at (303) 866-2155.

Colorado's colleges and universities in many ways stand among the nation's best. Colorado has one of the highest percentages of the population with bachelor's degrees in the nation.

Higher education is available in a wide variety of forms in Greater Denver, the most obvious choices being the major institutions such as the University of Colorado and the Metro State College of Denver. Private colleges and universities are generally smaller but are numerous and diverse. In many ways the most important part of Greater Denver's higher-education establishment is the community college system. At any one time, around 40,000 students are attending the area's five community colleges. These are public colleges so well-distributed around Greater Denver that no resident is very far from one of them. They tend toward curricula that are career oriented and designed for accessibility by working students.

One handy reference to area colleges and universities is the *LEARN Directory*, produced by the Local Educational Adult Resource Network. You can get a copy by calling the Director of Admissions at National College, (303) 758-6700. This book can be found at many local libraries.

Private elementary and secondary schools are another area of enormous choice, and parents shop carefully when looking into this option. How do you shop for a school? Ask other parents, of course, and research guides such as this one. A more complete guide dedicated entirely to this subject is the $11.50 directory, *Colorado Private Elementary and Secondary Schools*, by Margerie Hicks, published by Magnolia Street Press, (303) 322-2822.

Our list of colleges and universities is by no means a full account of local adult educational opportunities. There are more specialized business, technical and other schools than you can shake your brain at. Colorado has nearly 200 private occupational schools, for example, ranging from the A-Plus Real Estate School to the Xenon International School of Hair Design. The bulk of these are in the Greater Denver area. They're fully listed and described in a handy reference known as the *Directory, Colorado Private Occupational Schools Approved to Do Business in Colorado*. To get a copy, contact the State of

Colorado's Department of Higher Education, Division of Private Occupational Schools, (303) 894-2960.

Whatever educational needs and interests you may have, Greater Denver has an abundance of opportunities to offer. We'll begin with the public school systems.

www.insiders.com
See this and many other **Insiders' Guide®** destinations online.
Visit us today!

Public Schools

Adams County School District No. 1 Mapleton Public Schools
591 E. 80th Ave. • (303) 853-1000

Adams County School District No. 1, more familiar to most as Mapleton Public Schools, lies just north of Denver and includes part of the City of Thornton and some of unincorporated Adams County. With the third-smallest total enrollment in Greater Denver, the system has six elementary schools, two middle schools, one high school and one alternative school. Although this system has Greater Denver's lowest percentage of teachers with advanced degrees, and the highest pupil-teacher ratio, it has one of the area's lower high-school dropout rates.

The district provides a lot of special opportunities for its diverse student body, including programs in back-to-basics, learning enrichment, accelerated classes, bilingual and multi-cultural education, Native American education and open enrollment for all schools based on availability.

Adams 12 Five Star Schools
11285 Highline Dr., Northglenn • (303) 451-1561

The Five Star Schools, Adams County's largest school district and the seventh-largest in the state, includes more than 24,000 students attending 37 schools in a 62-square-mile area serving Northglenn, Federal Heights and parts of Thornton, Broomfield, Westminster and unincorporated Adams County. In addition to 24 elementary schools, it includes six middle schools and three high schools as well as the Bollman Occupational Center, Vantage Point Alternative School and three charter schools — Stargate, for the gifted and talented, the Academy of Charter Schools, a basic school, and the Pinnacle Learning Center. All charter schools use the E.D. Hirsch curriculum.

Per-pupil spending at Five Star Schools is in the mid-range in Greater Denver, as are the graduation and dropout rates. The mission of the district, "Success for each student through shared responsibility," is exemplified by the decentralized approach to shared decision making that exists in the district. Principals work in conjunction with school improvement teams to further student achievement at each school. The district reviewed and approved a strategic plan recently that sets goals for improved graduation rate and a lower dropout rate. Another district goal is an increase in proficiencies for all students. The district honors the diversity of individuals and believes a student's success is linked to a "responsive school community."

Adams County School District 14
4720 E. 69th Ave., Commerce City
• (303) 289-3941

One of Greater Denver's smaller school systems, District 14 has seven elementary schools, two middle schools, one high school and one alternative high school. It also has a full-time preschool. This district pulls students from Commerce City and areas in Thornton and unincorporated Adams County. It's solidly in the mid-range of Greater Denver school districts as far as the education and salaries of its teachers and its spending per pupil. Its high school dropout rate is the highest, and it has Greater Denver's lowest graduation rate and lowest composite ACT scores in the most recent rankings.

At the same time, Adams 14 has a gung-ho attitude about the future with a new commitment to improving its schools under the "Blueprint for Continued Success," a strategic planning document. The blueprint moves the community toward a common plan, with each school devising its own improvement plan. Among its special programs is Cities in Schools/Academy of the Rockies. At Adams City Middle School, 4451 E. 72nd Avenue in Commerce City, it's a personalized alternative instructional program for students at risk of dropping out. Since it was established in 1991, the program has grown to serve 4,610 students and families. With more than 52 percent of its students Hispanic, Adams 14 puts a lot of effort into bilingual education and accommodating cultural diversity.

Adams County School District 50
4476 W. 68th Ave., Westminster
• (303) 428-3511

School District 50 serves the City of Westminster, parts of Arvada and unincorporated Adams County with 15 elementary schools, four middle schools and two high schools. Its average teacher salary is Greater Denver's second-lowest, and its spending per pupil is the lowest. Still, District 50 has a dynamic attitude about its school system. Its mission statement is "to maximize student performance in a safe, orderly learning environment." They've clearly met part of their goal. In 1992, the graduation rate was 64.7 percent. In 1996, it rose to 80 percent.

In 1993 the district began an Odyssey of the Mind League to encourage students to develop creative thinking skills. The district also began the Graphics Communication Cluster, a prototype for a new method of integrating academic and technical education. Offered to 11th and 12th graders, it includes instruction in graphic arts, desktop publishing, video and electronic media, engineering and business.

The district puts out a special tabloid publication, *Focus on Excellence*, that highlights the service of individual teachers to encourage parents to get to know them. Adams County 50 pushes for technological innovation and offers such features as a computer-assisted instruction lab and a Writing-to-Read computer lab in every elementary school. It also has a fully integrated networking system in the District.

INSIDERS' TIP

Greater Denver's largest student populations are not in the City and County of Denver but in Arapahoe and Jefferson counties.

Aurora Public Schools
1085 Peoria St., Aurora • (303) 344-8060

Aurora Public Schools covers most of Aurora, which is Greater Denver's second-largest city. The district's mission is to develop its kids into "lifelong learners who value themselves, contribute to their community and succeed in a changing world."

Strong emphasis is placed on student achievement in basic subjects. The district is committed to preparing students for life in the 21st century by helping them become self-directed learners, collaborative workers, complex thinkers, community contributors and quality producers. Special services and classes are offered for gifted and talented students, special education students and non-English-speaking young parents, preschoolers and adults.

The district has seven elementary schools and two middle schools on year-round schedules. In total, the district has 28 elementary schools, seven middle schools and six high schools, one of which is an alternative high school.

Special classes in 50 skill areas are offered within the district at T.H. Pickens Technical Center, 500 Airport Boulevard, Aurora. Some programs offer credit toward an associate degree from the Community College of Aurora.

Stanford University has designated Aurora Public Schools as a regional center for its Stanford University Accelerated Schools Project. In 1995, William Smith Alternative High School became the first accelerated high school in the country.

Brighton Public Schools
630 S. Eighth Ave., Brighton
• (303) 659-4820

The closest thing to a small-town, country-school district in Greater Denver, Brighton Public Schools (District 27J), serves about 210 square miles of farmland around the 15,000 population of Brighton, the Adams County seat. As a school district, Brighton's enrollment is the second-smallest in Greater Denver. The district has five elementary schools, two middle schools, one high school and an alternative school. Just about half of Brighton's teaching staff has master's degrees. The turnover rate of classroom teachers is 3 percent. In accordance with state law, District 27J is developing content standards for all academic areas. Included in this effort toward Standards Based Education are the improvement of instructional techniques as well as the assessment of skills and knowledge learned. The average composite ACT score for Brighton students is 20, and the dropout rate is on the low side. The district's schools offer enrichment programs including bilingual education, programs in basic skills and accelerated education.

Cherry Creek School District 5
4700 S. Yosemite, Englewood
• (303) 773-1184

Covering Greater Denver's southeastern corner, District 5 encompasses Cherry Hills Village, Glendale, parts of Aurora, Englewood, Greenwood Village and some of unincorporated Arapahoe County. It includes the rapidly growing and well-to-do communities of new businesses and young families along the northern edge of Douglas County and wraps around the Denver Technological Center.

Cherry Creek School District 5 has some impressive statistics, including Greater Denver's highest average teacher salary. It has 30 elementary schools, six middle schools, four high schools and one magnet school. Every year since 1990, The U.S. Department of Education has named one of the elementary schools, Indian Ridge Elementary, and two of the high schools, Smoky Hill High and Cherry Creek High, as Schools of Excellence.

INSIDERS' TIP

The Colorado Free University (which isn't really free, but nearly so) offers a vast array of fun, interesting and informative classes for busy people. Whether it's computers, yoga or wine tasting, CFU has something for everyone. Pick up class schedules at grocery and convenience stores.

In 1996, West Middle School also became a Blue Ribbon School. Smoky Hill High has one of Colorado's International Baccalaureate programs, in which advanced studies give students a jump on college. Every elementary and middle school in the district makes special accommodations for gifted and talented students.

This district has plenty to toot its horn about. Smoky Hill's principal Dr. Mary Jarvis was named the National Principal of the Year in 1996-97. And the 1996-97 Colorado Teacher of the Year was Pamela Schmidt, science teacher at Thunder Ridge Middle School.

Denver Public Schools
900 Grant St. • (303) 764-3200

As the workhorse school system of Denver's central city population, Denver Public Schools has one of Greater Denver's greatest educational challenges. It also provides some of Greater Denver's greatest educational opportunities.

The Denver school system provides parents with a lot of choices, including special programs for the 13,600 or so students in the district who have limited English proficiency. Other choices include the Challenge Highly Gifted program, three fundamental academies, two extended-day schools, a Montessori school, a laboratory school and an International Baccalaureate program, which was the first in the state. The system is still the only area district to have the IBP program at all three levels — elementary, middle and secondary.

Denver's magnet schools are educational venues that parents prize for their kids. Seven elementary schools, four middle schools and three high schools offer the magnet concept, which means that they offer some special programs not ordinarily part of the regular curriculum. The Denver School of the Arts, for example, where arts education is combined with academics, is one of the most sought-after educational venues among Denver parents. Unfortunately, many audition, and many must be turned away. The Computer Magnet program at George Washington High School is another popular program where students extend their knowledge about the use of computers beyond what is available at other schools. Knight Fundamental Academy (which has the highest standardized scores in the district) and Traylor Fundamental Academy teach traditional basics with strict behavioral standards — Knight pulling kids from all schools east of University Boulevard and Traylor pulling from the west. Morey Fundamental, a magnet school newly created in 1994 at Morey Middle School, provides a place where Knight Academy kids can continue in the magnet concept. Denver also has two charter schools.

Denver Public Schools leads Greater Denver in per-pupil spending, but it is still struggling with one of the lowest graduation rates. Still, several schools in the district have received impressive awards.

Mitchell Elementary School and Garden Place Academy were both honored by *Redbook* magazine as two of America's best elementary schools for overall excellence. In 1997, *Reader's Digest* named Hamilton Middle School principal Cheryl Betz one of 12 American Heroes in Education.

Since 1991, every Denver Public School is governed by a collaborative decision-making (CDM) team. Each team is made up of parents, teachers, the principal, students and a business community representative. All told, DPS has 80 elementary schools, 18 middle schools, 10 high schools and two alternative schools. Special facilities include the Fred N. Thomas Career Education Center, 2650 Eliot Street, (303) 964-3000, enrollment 1,000, where secondary students attend half-day career education training. The Emily Griffith Opportunity School at 1250 Welton Street, (303) 572-8218, is the adult education arm of Denver Public Schools, offering more than 350 classes at more than 120 locations.

Douglas County School District
620 Wilcox St., Castle Rock
• (303) 688-3195

This district's 19 elementary schools, one charter school, three middle schools and three high schools cover a far-flung area ranging from the southern edges of Jefferson and Arapahoe counties much of the way to Colorado Springs. Douglas is the fastest-growing county in the United States. The district currently has 25,000 students. Due to a successful $81.2 million bond election in 1993, nine new schools have been funded, including a new high school in Highlands Ranch, another high school in Parker and a replacement middle school in Castle Rock.

The majority of the county's elementary students go to school on a four-track, year-round calendar, a rotation of nine weeks in school followed by three weeks of vacation, throughout the year.

Douglas County has one of the highest graduation rates and the lowest dropout rate. How do they do it? The system overall places a high value on educational excellence. Cherokee Trail Elementary School in Parker was named by *Child Magazine* as one of the 10 best schools in the nation. Greater Denver's first charter school, Academy Charter School, is in Castle Rock. Beginning in the 1994-95 school year, the county approved a teacher-compensation plan linked to performance rather than longevity.

Douglas County is one of four school districts partnering in the Expeditionary Learning School, a K through 9 school that has won national grants and acclaim for its challenging learning program.

Englewood Schools
4101 S. Bannock St., Englewood
• **(303) 761-7050**

Also known as Arapahoe County School District No. 1, this district educates a little more than 4,600 students, Greater Denver's third-smallest enrollment, in the City of Englewood.

Englewood was not shy about its educational ambitions when it adopted a student-created name for its only alternative high school: Colorado's Finest Alternative High School. Either *Redbook* magazine was swayed by the name, or it found the name accurate, because the magazine in 1994 named this school as the best in the state. The school was devised by the Englewood School District for kids at risk of dropping out. Aside from the regular curriculum at Colorado's Finest, the 530 students participate in teacher-run counseling groups of 25 students, complete 20 hours of community service in their senior year and can take college courses for credit. This school accepts students from anywhere in the state.

Englewood's other schools include Englewood Senior High School (where, in 1996, 20 hours of community service became a requirement for graduation) plus two middle schools and five elementary schools.

Jefferson County Public Schools
1829 Denver West Dr., Golden
• **(303) 982-6808**

Jefferson County makes up Colorado's largest school district with more than 86,000 students and a budget of $350 million. Many people seem to want to get their kids into Jefferson County schools. In 1996-97, 1,900 students came from outside the district.

What is it about Jeffco that makes it so desirable? Well, it's a nice place to live, right up against the mountains with a lot of upscale neighborhoods and light-industry, white-collar employment. Also, the school system has Greater Denver's highest percentage of teachers with master's degrees or higher and the second-highest average teacher salary.

Jeffco in 1991 established a task force of parents, staff, students and community members to recommend how student learning could be improved. The task force's efforts have blended with the district's work in 1994-95 to determine what students should know and be able to do. Teams have drafted high, achievable-content standards for students in reading, writing, math, science, history and geography. In 1996-97, standards were also drafted for economics, civics, foreign languages, art, music and physical education.

Jeffco has a "least-restrictive environment" policy for special education students that gives primary responsibility for a special-needs student's education to the neighborhood school. The school district also has a Multicultural Learning Center that provides multicultural resources for teachers across the district.

As of 1995, Jeffco was pursuing these lofty goals in neighborhood schools — 91 elementary schools, 18 middle schools and 16 high schools — as well as a wide range of educational choice programs. These include open enrollment where space is available, schools within a school, alternative schools and self-governing charter schools. A brochure called *Choices* is available from the district's Communications Services office, (303) 982-6808.

Jeffco passed a $325 million bond issue in 1992, the largest general obligation bond issue in the state's history. By spring 1995, 186 projects had expanded or renovated old buildings, replaced four older buildings, and opened eight new schools.

Littleton Public Schools
5776 S. Crocker St., Littleton
• (303) 347-3386

Pulling students from the City of Littleton and neighboring unincorporated zones, Littleton Public Schools is another one of those districts that does a good job with its money. The district serves 16,028 students in Littleton and parts of unincorporated Arapahoe County, including 15 elementary schools, four middle schools, three senior high schools, one alternative middle school, one alternative high school program and one charter school.

LPS students consistently rank above state and national averages on standardized tests. Littleton has one of Greater Denver's highest composite ACT scores in recent rankings, the third-highest average teacher salaries and the third-lowest high school dropout rate. Of LPS's 1,000 teachers, 650 hold master's or doctorate degrees, and more than 600 exceed 10 years of teaching experience.

LPS places a high value on small class sizes, which range from 20 to 27 for elementary and 26 to 32 for middle and high school classes. School choice is available to all district residents through an open enrollment/transfer policy.

LPS also enjoys a high level of community involvement and support. Parents, community members, businesses and senior citizens donated more than 179,000 hours to the schools during 1993-94, the equivalent of 86 full-time employees.

Sheridan School District No. Two
4000 S. Lowell Blvd.
• (303) 761-8640

Greater Denver's smallest school district, Sheridan has a total enrollment of just more than 1,900 in two elementary schools, one middle school and one high school. It serves the City of Sheridan, which surrounds the Englewood Municipal Golf Course and pieces of Englewood. The district's graduation rate is

fourth-highest in Denver. Not surprisingly, it also has the lowest student-teacher ratio.

Private Schools

Not every private school in the area is included here, of course, but you will find the larger, as well as many smaller, schools that come to us by word-of-mouth recommendation. Some accept only one sex, and many of them are religion-based private schools. None of the religious schools profess to turn away students on the basis of their religion or lack of religious commitment. Actually, however, religious schools require students to take religious instruction, and lack of adequate preparation can in some cases disqualify a student. At Herzl Jewish Day School, for example, students need to have a sufficient grounding in the Hebrew language, and the Yeshiva Toras Chaim School is particularly heavy in Talmud and Torah.

Accelerated Schools
2160 S. Cook St. • (303) 758-2003

Students, including the gifted and the learning disabled, study independently through individually prescribed instructional and motivational systems. Heavy use of computer instructional programs increases time spent on prescribed learning tasks and gives immediate feedback with an emphasis on practical business applications. Regular day students are in learning centers from 9 AM to 3 PM. The school offers accelerated reading and college classes for extra credit as well as field trips and other activities. Transportation to and from home is included in tuition. Housing is available for students who need it. The school serves 150 students in grades kindergarten through 12.

Alexander Dawson School
4801 N. 107th St., Lafayette
• (303) 665-6679

This college-prep school is on a 135-acre campus 35 minutes north of Denver. The school has a need-based financial aid program with more than $400,000 in grants, which go to 22 percent of the students. Though the school has historically had boarding students, it has been strictly a day school since 1998.

Colorado Academy students wait for their buses.

The rigorous academic program includes a keen interest in the arts. Alexander Dawson takes part in interscholastic athletic competitions, including canoeing, skiing and horsemanship. Stables with horses are on campus. The school has a new library as well as a $3 million gym and a $2.7 million arts center. It now offers grades kindergarten through 12.

Beacon Country Day School
6100 E. Belleview Ave., Greenwood Village • (303) 771-3990

Beacon Country Day School is a private, nonprofit school on a large acreage in Greenwood Village. The programs use each child's interests to promote learning in classrooms designed for small learning groups. The grounds have a pond and a variety of natural ecology for children to explore. This school also has ponies that the children learn to care for and ride. Offering Pre-K through 8th grade, the school has 150 students and is coed.

Bethlehem Lutheran School
7470 W. 22nd Ave., Lakewood • (303) 233-0401

Bethlehem Lutheran, a coed school, is part of the national network of Lutheran schools, the largest Protestant school group in the country. It offers quality education in a Chris-

tian environment and has received National Lutheran School Accreditation. It has a good music program, computer lab instruction and interscholastic athletics as well as an advanced reading program for students in 3rd through 6th grades. The school's 450 students are in grades Pre-K through 8.

Bishop Machebeuf Catholic School
1958 Elm St. • (303) 322-1819

Formerly Machebeuf Catholic High School, students' "responsibility as children of God in a democratic society" is the underlying theme of education at Machebeuf — that and preparation for college. The school boasts more than 95 percent of its graduates enrolled in college by graduation, and it employs a full-time college admissions counselor. By graduation, the 59 graduates in the class of 1996 had earned more than $1.5 million in scholarships. Three hundred students are in grades 9 through 12.

Christian Way Schools
14700 E. Mississippi Ave., Aurora • (303) 751-2014

Christian Way Schools offers traditional secular academic studies combined with religious instruction. A nonsectarian Colorado corporation, the Christian Way Schools is sponsored by independent, autonomous Christian churches and Churches of Christ in Colorado. The schools profess not to be in rebellion against public education but rather to be an extension of the home and church. At these coed schools, the 150 students are in grades K through 6.

Christ the King Catholic School
860 Elm St. • (303) 321-2123

This school, where boys and girls in grades Pre-K through 8 wear uniforms, adheres to a philosophy that places a high premium on top-quality academic skills along with developing a sense of responsibility all within the framework of the Catholic faith. Along with religion, students are exposed to a core curriculum enhanced by music and art. Extracurricular activities include Junior Great Books, volleyball, basketball and baseball. The school's population is 250.

Colorado Academy
3800 S. Pierce St. • (303) 986-1501

Among Colorado's most respected private schools, Colorado Academy is in southwest Denver on a lovely 75-acre campus. It's a college preparatory program emphasizing a well-rounded education in academics, fine arts and athletics with a 10-to-1 ratio of students to teachers. Bus transportation is available. Seven hundred and twenty five students are in grades Pre-K through 12.

Colorado Catholic Academy
11180 W. 44th Ave., Wheat Ridge
• (303) 422-9549

Near the western edge of Wheat Ridge, this coed Academy offers a traditional curriculum and teaches the Catholic faith to 50 students in grades 1 through 12. Students attend weekly Latin Mass and daily Rosary.

Denver Academy
1101 S. Race St. • (303) 777-5870

The Academy applies a structured, closely supervised and highly personalized approach to educating students who have intellectual aptitude but need help realizing their potential. This school has a 6-to-1 student-teacher ratio. Three hundred boys and girls fill grades 3 through 8.

Denver Christian Schools
2135 S. Pearl St. • (303) 733-2421

Denver Christian Schools was established by a small group that settled here before World War I, many of whom were from the Netherlands and ill with tuberculosis. Since the first classes in 1917, DCS has grown to four schools at three student locations: Denver Christian Middle School and Denver Christian High School, both at 2135 S. Pearl Street; Van Dellen Elementary School, 4200 E. Warren Avenue; and Highlands Ranch Elementary School, 1733 E. Dad Clark Drive. A total of 970 students study in grades K through 12.

Denver International School
2690 S. Holly St. • (303) 290-8461

Denver International School is a French-American, bilingual, multicultural school that attracts students committed to studying in two languages. Founded in 1977, it offers grades K through 8 and prepares its students to thrive in a global society. Ninety students study the usual round of subjects in both English and French. Child care is offered before and after school.

Faith Christian Academy
6210 Ward Rd., Arvada • (303) 424-7310
I-70 and Carr St., Arvada • (303) 424-7310

A unique, charismatic Christian school, Faith is open to anyone interested in a Christian education. The curriculum includes the full range of traditional subjects. Thirteen hundred students study in grades K through 12. The Ward Road address is for kindergarten through 8th grade, and the Carr Street address is for the high school.

Foothills Academy
4725 Miller St., Wheat Ridge
• (303) 431-0920

Valued by alumni and children of alumni, this is one of those schools where word-of-mouth is the best advertising. The small and interactive classes expose 200 boys and girls to basic skills as well as art, music, foreign languages, physical education and an extensive outdoor education program. Foothills emphasizes "experiential learning and exploration," with field trips and visiting artist programs, outdoor experiences and community projects and services. Once a month, they conduct a "mini-society" in which students buy and sell homemade goods, act out the workings of government and simulate success in the real world. The school offers grades K through 12.

Graland Country Day School
30 Birch St. • (303) 399-0390

Among Denver's premier private schools, Graland has a history of fostering academic and personal growth. Its enrollment is limited to maintain small classes and close interaction between teachers and students. Graland is in a residential neighborhood 5 miles south of downtown Denver. Six hundred and fourteen boys and girls study in grades K through 9.

Good Shepherd Catholic School
940 Fillmore St. (Elementary School), 620 Elizabeth St. (Middle School)
• (303) 377-8018

Actually two schools, an elementary and a middle school, Good Shepherd is between Sixth Avenue and East Colfax Avenue, York Street and Colorado Boulevard. It offers a Catholic education along with core educational curriculum. The enrichment program is a before- and after-school program, between 6:45 AM and 6 PM, that includes guided study time, structured play time and extracurricular activities. A Montessori program is also available for age 3 through grade 4. The school offers grades Pre-K through 8 to 425 boys and girls.

Havern Center Inc.
4000 S. Wadsworth Blvd., Littleton
• (303) 986-4587

This is one of the best and oldest schools in the area for learning-disabled students. With a low student/teacher ratio, the school offers kids with learning disabilities individualized instruction, occupational therapy, speech and language therapy as well as self-esteem groups. The goal of Havern is to ultimately reintroduce the child into mainstream education. The school has 78 students ages 5 through 12.

Herzl Jewish Day School
2450 S. Wabash St. • (303) 755-1846

This school's basic approach is an education emphasizing not only the students' connections within the Jewish community but also their connection in the world at large. Along with a primary focus on integrated secular and Judaic education, the school pursues a pluralistic approach to Jewish education, emphasizing respect for both the diversity of Jewish cultures and other religions. Hebrew background is a requirement because Hebrew is taught through all grades, from K through 6. The school is coed and has 285 students.

Holy Family High School
4343 Utica St. • (303) 458-8822

Founded in 1922 as a parish high school, Holy Family's mission statement proclaims a Catholic-Christian learning environment that "stresses academic excellence, fosters mutual respect, demands responsibility and encourages self-growth." Besides the standard high school core curriculum, there are also courses in subjects such as theology, journalism, advanced computer applications, law and drama. Three hundred students study in grades 9 through 12.

Humanex Academy
3222 S. Vance St., Ste. 100, Lakewood
• (303) 985-0050

This alternative high school is for students ages 13 to 21 who may not have been successful in other schools. Humanex is dedicated to the idea that every student can succeed in the proper environment. The school has a student-teacher ratio of 7-to-1, a closed campus,

INSIDERS' TIP

Colorado high school seniors have the opportunity to take college courses at community colleges and state universities and colleges. Not only does this provide a challenging academic experience, but it also reduces the length and expense of college.

progress reports to parents every two weeks and parent notification within 20 minutes after school starts if the student does not show up. Enrollment is at 56 students, male and female.

Kent Denver School
4000 E. Quincy Ave., Englewood
• (303) 770-7660

Kent Denver has roots going back to the founding of the Kent School for girls in 1922 and the founding of the Denver Country Day School for boys. The two schools merged to create the present institution in 1974. Its challenging, college-preparatory curriculum produced an average SAT score of 1,240 in the graduating class of 1996, 227 points above the national average. Kent Denver has a campus of 200 acres with five academic buildings that include 43 classrooms and laboratories, six studios for music, dance and art, two gymnasiums, six tennis courts and 20 acres of playing fields. In grades 6 through 12, there are 590 students.

The Logan School
1836 Logan St. • (303) 830-0326

A school for gifted and creative children ages 4 through 14, The Logan School boasts a stimulating academic program with hands-on learning experiences for its 185 boys and girls. Admission requires a minimum IQ test score of 125.

Lutheran High School
3201 W. Arizona Ave. • (303) 934-2345

Owned by the Colorado Lutheran High School Association, Lutheran High has been operating since 1955 on a 12-acre campus in southwest Denver. It was named in 1991 as one of 222 national recipients (four in the state) of the National Exemplary School award for exceptional educational services with outstanding staff in an atmosphere conducive to achieving excellence. There are 375 students in grades 9 through 12.

Maranatha Christian Center
7180 Oak St., Arvada • (303) 431-5653

A Bible-believing, nondenominational educational center, with Christ-centered academics taught by qualified, born-again staff, Maranatha was opened in 1982 on an agricul-tural piece of land that previously had been occupied by a house and barn. Now its 15 acres include more than 70,000 square feet of classrooms, offices, a gymnasium, locker rooms, a learning center, a library and a computer lab for 935 students in grades Pre-K through 12.

Mile High Adventist Academy
711 E. Yale Ave. • (303) 744-1069

This school dates back to a one-room school established by Seventh-day Adventists in Denver in 1913. The themes here are academic excellence, individual resourcefulness and responsibility, Christian philosophy and making the world a better place within the student's sphere of influence. Three hundred students attend grades K through 12.

Montessori School of Denver
1460 S. Holly St. • (303) 757-6145

The oldest Montessori in Denver (there are five other independent Montessori schools in metro Denver), this one has 85 boys and girls, ages 3 through 12. As with all Montessori schools, this one adheres to the philosophy which allows students "the opportunity to achieve individually, creatively and successfully." The school has a wide parent volunteer base and offers a Montessori curriculum including botany, zoology, language, math, art, physical education and Spanish.

Montclair Academy
212 Syracuse St. • (303) 893-3735

Formerly St. John's Academy, this kindergarten through 8th-grade school serves 150 students. The curriculum has a strong liberal arts emphasis with a variety of enrichment programs including field trips and special classes. A student/teacher ratio of 9-to-1 ensures individualized learning. Extracurricular activities include tae kwon do, woodworking and dance.

Most Precious Blood Parish School
3959 E. Iliff Ave. • (303) 757-1279

You've got your standard curriculum here, along with religious instruction including morning prayer, Mass once a month and religious education. The school also features geography and spelling bees, science and art fairs, speech meets and a "super citizens" program in which grades 3 through 5 choose a supercitizen from their class each month to be honored by the Colorado Optimists Club. From grades Pre-K through 8, there are 460 students.

J.K. Mullen High School
3601 S. Lowell Blvd. • (303) 761-1764

One of Denver's more well-known Catholic private high schools, Mullen was founded in 1931 as a home for orphaned boys. In 1965 it became J.K. Mullen Prep, a college-prep school for boys. It has been coeducational since 1989. It's conducted by the Christian Brothers, a religious teaching order. Today it has a population of 860 students.

Our Lady of Fatima
10530 W. 20th Ave., Lakewood
• (303) 233-2500

Catholicism, of course, is the philosophical bent of this school, with religious instruction in addition to the academic courses one expects. The school has an extensive athletic program as well as special features including a science lab, a reading lab and a computer lab. In the 1995-96 school year, Fatima became the first school in Colorado to link up with the Learn Star program, a California-based, satellite-mediated interactive computer system that allows Fatima students to compete on-line with other schools nationwide on a weekly basis. Five hundred students are in grades Pre-K through 8.

Regis Jesuit High School
16300 E. Weaver Pl., Aurora
• (303) 699-1598

Regis has the Jesuit-school mystique of quality education with a public-service mentality. Special senior projects, volunteerism, student retreats, counseling and peer tutoring are among the additions to regular curriculum here, as well as college credit earned from Regis University. Its population is currently at 790 — men only.

Ricks Center for Gifted Children
2040 S. York St. • (303) 871-2982

As the name implies, Ricks Center is for children who've demonstrated "educational needs in the gifted range." A strong academic curriculum is enhanced with extracurricular activities such as chess, student council, yearbook and Odyssey of the Mind. The school serves 153 students, grades K through 8, and is associated with the University of Denver.

St. Anne's Episcopal School
2701 S. York St. • (303) 756-9481

A state- and nationally accredited school founded in 1950, St. Anne's gives students a broad traditional education with emphasis on balancing academic excellence, artistic endeavor and athletic achievement while engaging students in community service and moral development.

Located on 10 acres in southeast Denver, the school encourages parental involvement. From grades Pre-K through 8, it has a population of 420 students.

St. Francis De Sales School
235 S. Sherman St. • (303) 744-7231

Since 1904 this Catholic school has been serving the same neighborhood south of downtown Denver, combining religious instruction and experiences with a strong basic curriculum and small classes for its 230 students in grades K through 8.

St. James Catholic School
1250 Newport St. • (303) 333-8275

On Denver's eastern side, just northwest of Lowry Air Force Base, St. James tries to provide a values-based education that emphasizes academic excellence, self-direction, responsibility, a genuine love of learning and the wherewithal to become solid Catholic citizens. The school teaches 230 boys and girls in preschool through 8th grade.

St. Louis School
3301 S. Sherman, Englewood
• (303) 762-8307

Mastery of the basics is the focus at St. Louis School, along with art, music, computer training and programs such as Junior Achievement, Great Books and Community Resource. It's a Catholic-sponsored school, but non-Catholics are welcome. There's religious instruction, student-prepared Masses and special sacramental instruction for 200 students in grades K through 8.

St. Mary's Academy
4545 S. University Blvd., Englewood
• (303) 762-8300

St. Mary's Academy is a Catholic, independent school founded in 1864 by the Sisters of Loretto. In 1875, it awarded the first high school diploma in the Colorado Territory. Among its features are its Early Learning Center, at the Denver Tech Center, and the all-girls' high school where the program is based on current research on girls' learning. St. Mary's emphasizes values-based education, small classes, strong curriculum, personalized attention and community service. Coed through 8th grade, St. Mary's serves a total of 705 students.

St. Therese School
1200 Kenton St., Aurora • (303) 364-7494

St. Therese School includes Catholic teaching with its conventional curriculum. It's staffed by Sisters of Charity as well as lay teachers. It includes a reading specialist and full-time teachers in physical education, computer science and music education for 390 students in grades K through 8.

St. Vincent de Paul School
1164 S. Josephine St. • (303) 777-3812

A Catholic parish school, St. Vincent's primary purpose for existence is to pass on the Catholic faith, and it accompanies that mission with all the standard core academic subjects. Special features include a technology program and full-time teachers for computer education, art, music and physical education. The student-teacher ratio is 25-to-1. St. Vincent's starts at preschool and goes up through 8th grade. It serves 530 students.

Sts. Peter and Paul Catholic Elementary School
3920 Pierce St., Wheat Ridge
• (303) 424-0402

One of the west side's better-known Catholic schools, Sts. Peter and Paul provides sound academics and Catholic values and traditions to 420 students from Pre-K through 8th grade. Features of its integrated curriculum include a literature program, computers, art, music, speech and drama, family math and physical education.

Shrine of St. Anne Catholic School
7320 Grant Pl., Arvada • (303) 422-1800

A high-quality, well-rounded curriculum in basic academics is accompanied by daily classes in religion. The school describes itself as a "Christian community witnessing to the gospel message of Jesus Christ." Special features include an education fair, a science fair and a life education program, which tackles real-world issues that students face and will face in life. The school offers a computer lab, science lab and library to its 510 students in grades K through 8.

Silver State Baptist School
875 S. Sheridan Blvd., Lakewood
• (303) 922-8850

Strong in music and orchestra, with daily Bible classes, Silver State has its own mix of standard educational curricula along with educational direction from the Bob Jones Press. The school also participates in interscholastic sports governed by the Colorado High School Sports Athletic Association. Silver State has 380 students in grades K through 12.

Stanley British Primary School
1301 Quebec St. (Elementary School),
350 Quebec Ct. (Middle School)
• (303) 333-9154

Stanley British Primary School (or B.P.S. as it's called locally) teaches 310 students in grades K through 8. Its philosophy is that education should be experiential, and to that end students study where they are developmentally, rather than strictly by age or grade. The curriculum revolves around core subjects, with the inclusion of study skills. This school relies heavily on parental involvement, both in the classroom and in fund-raising.

The Denver Waldorf School
735 E. Florida Ave. • (303) 777-0531

The "Waldorf Movement" emphasizes working with the whole child, not just the mind, everything evolving through art. The school doesn't use textbooks. Rather teachers present the subjects, and students, through what they've learned, create their own narratives and illustrations — their own textbooks. By 8th grade, a lot of them have already had chemistry, biology, geometry and algebra.

Beginning in 1st grade, German and Russian languages are mandatory. The school goes from kindergarten through high school and serves 290 students.

University of Denver High School
2450 S. Vine St. • (303) 871-3313

Founded in 1995, the University of Denver High School accommodates the academically gifted as well as the learning disabled. The course of studies is rigorous, and students have the opportunity to attend some university classes. Teachers here "adopt the role of coach rather than dispenser of information." The school's 60 students have access to several extracurricular activities, including a literary magazine, basketball, Latin club and debate.

Westland Christian Academy
430 S. Kipling St., Lakewood
• (303) 986-5509

"Academic excellence in Christian education" is the motto of this school maintained by Westland Baptist Church. The Christ-centered and Bible-based education has a traditional academic curriculum and daily chapel service. The school has three main classroom buildings on a 4.6-acre campus. The school has 250 students in grades K through 12.

Yeshiva Toras Chaim School
1400 Quitman St. • (303) 629-8200

This private orthodox Jewish high school would be one of many in New York, but here in the Rocky Mountain area it has been unique since its founding in 1967. Half of each day is spent in studying Talmud and Torah, and the other half is spent in secular studies. At least 50 percent of the 85 male students board at the school.

Colleges and Universities

Chapman University
1400 S. Colorado Blvd., Ste 430
• (303) 753-6551

This is an academic center of Chapman University, based in Orange, California, that offers graduate level classes for teacher recertification. The school processes 4,000 to 5,000 students a year, all of whom are teachers taking classes for professional development.

Colorado Christian University
180 S. Garrison St., Lakewood
• (303) 202-0100

As the only major evangelical Christian university in the Rocky Mountain region, Colorado Christian University offers fully accredited undergraduate and graduate courses with 26 undergraduate majors. CCU also offers programs designed to serve the social and spiritual needs of all students. The University has an enrollment of more than 3,000 students in all programs. In addition to its Lakewood campus, CCU administers a Foothills campus in Morrison specializing in graduate-level education in biblical counseling. The School of Graduate and Professional studies offers accelerated evening, weekend and on-site corporate classes (on-site training to company personnel) for adult learners, with centers at Lakewood's main campus, at the Higher Education and Advanced Technology Center at Lowry and in Colorado Springs and Grand Junction. It offers undergraduate and graduate degrees and a teacher-recertification program.

CCU is a division II member of the NCAA, competing in men's and women's basketball, soccer, cross-country and tennis in addition to women's volleyball and men's golf. CCU also owns and operates a radio network consisting of KWBI-Denver, KJOL-Grand Junction and KDHR-Glenwood Springs.

Colorado School of Mines
1500 Illinois, Golden • (303) 273-3000

"Mines," as it's called, is a school of engineering, energy, environment and economics nationally known for academic rigor. Mines was founded in Golden in 1874 because that city was the gateway to Colorado's booming minerals mining industry. A public school, Mines now focuses on areas such as engineering, engineering systems, chemical engineering, petroleum engineering, mining engineering, economics, geology and geological engineering. Degrees are also available in chemistry, geochemistry and physics. Its metallurgical, materials science, environmental

Community College of Denver is one of three colleges on the Auraria campus.

science and engineering programs are among the best in the nation, and not surprisingly, Mines is strong in math and computer science.

Mines also has the benefit of a beautiful location. Golden is nestled against the Foothills behind South Table Mountain from Denver and retains a small-town atmosphere. Mines is on its uphill side, a close walk from downtown. Golden is also connected by I-70 and U.S. Highway 6 directly into Denver, by I-70 into the mountains and by U.S. Highway 6 W. through scenic Clear Creek Canyon into the Gilpin County/Clear Creek County historic mining areas and mountain communities.

Golden claims a higher per-capita concentration of Ph.Ds than Boulder, home of the University of Colorado.

Colorado State University — Denver Center
110 16th St., Ste. 100 • (303) 573-6318

Colorado State University in Fort Collins is the state's most highly esteemed public school after the University of Colorado, and in some ways it stands way out in front. A significant number of its majors are not available anywhere else in the state. It's nationally famous for its College of Natural Resources and its School of Veterinary Medicine. Faculty member Marty Fettman was a space shuttle astro-

naut and the first veterinarian in space. CSU is the state's only land-grant university, and CSU's Agricultural Experiment Station and Cooperative Extension form the education/research backbone of Colorado's agriculture industry.

CSU's Denver-area educational and technical services are found in a single location, the Colorado State University — Denver Center. Located downtown in the Petroleum Building at 16th Street and Broadway are the educational services aimed heavily toward downtown Denver's working population. Housed in the Denver Center are study programs extended from the Fort Collins campus, the Executive MBA program of the College of Business, Cooperative Extension's Denver County office, and the Colorado State Forest Service. Offerings include courses in education, vocational education, business and professional and personal advancement. CSU-Denver offers a master's degree in occupational therapy and in human resources development specialization. This campus specializes in customized training for businesses.

Columbia College
2530 S. Parker Rd., Ste. 300, Aurora
• (303) 755-7561

This is actually an extension center of the Columbia College campus in Columbia, Missouri, but it's a sizeable operation. Some 700 students attend evening classes here, working toward associate and baccalaureate degrees in the liberal arts, business administration, computer information systems, psychology, criminal justice, history, government and other subjects. It's primarily adult education, with an average student age of 32.

Embry-Riddle
Aeronautical University
1059 Yosemite St., Aurora • (303) 340-7194

Since its founding in Cincinnati, Ohio, in 1926, Embry-Riddle has been devoted exclusively to aviation-related education. In addition to residential campuses in Arizona and Florida, it has 100 off-campus centers in the United States and Europe (including the Aurora location) dedicated to working adults in a nontraditional setting. Embry-Riddle is a four-year, regionally accredited institution with bachelor's and master's degrees including bachelor of science in professional aeronautics, management of technical operations, master of aeronautical science and master of business administration in aviation. The Denver center was started in 1993.

The Metropolitan State
College of Denver
1006 11th Ave. • (303) 556-3058

Metro, Colorado's third-largest college, is a cosmopolitan city college on a 175-acre oasis on the edge of Denver's downtown business district. Half of its student body is students of traditional college age (18 to 25), and half consists of nontraditional students — those older than age 25 who have already been in the work force. This, of course, can be a delight to professors who find they are dealing not only with students fresh out of high school but also with professional adults as well. And

it's great for students, because they can learn from their peers as well as their professors. The Met has a reputation as the working student's college, with an emphasis on applied education, and takes pains to accommodate that student with a lot of weekend and evening classes.

The main campus, the Auraria Higher Education Center, is unique. The Metropolitan State College of Denver shares the campus with two other institutions, the Community College of Denver and the University of Colorado at Denver. The three schools together offer a more potent education package than any one could alone because they allow students to cross-register for classes in all three schools and enjoy a combined menu of lectures, concerts, plays and student programs.

The Met offers a full lineup of NCAA intercollegiate athletic competitions in 10 men's and women's sports. The teams use one of the region's best athletic facilities, the Auraria Events Center, which seats more than 3,000 and is used for a variety of campus-wide events.

The Met has all the elements of a traditional university, such as extensive physical education facilities, one of Greater Denver's best libraries and a quiet, tree-lined campus. The historic 19th-century Bavarian-style brewery, the Tivoli, which until recently was an independent shopping center, has been transformed into one of the country's most picturesque student unions. The Tivoli houses shops, the campus bookstore, restaurants, a 12-screen theater, recreation rooms and nightclubs as well as student offices and services.

Although there are not on-campus dormitories, many students get assistance from the campus housing office to live on their own in surrounding apartments. Plus, The Met is just an easy walk from downtown Denver, the Den-

INSIDERS' TIP

The Auraria Campus — shared by The Metropolitan State College of Denver, the University of Colorado at Denver and the Community College of Denver — is a jewel of the metro region not only for its outstanding educational offerings, but also for its accessibility to nontraditional students. Night classes have long been a mainstay for working students, and increases in on-line classes are making things even easier.

The Teacher of the Century and Her School of Unlimited Opportunity

Emily Griffith is still Denver's best-known educator, even though she died more than 60 years ago. As a Denver Public School teacher who taught 8th grade at the Twenty-Fourth Street School during the day, Griffith volunteered at night teaching adults, many of them immigrants, to read and write and acquire basic math skills. But her true goal was to start a school where the age limit was lifted and the hours were flexible, so that a working adult who could spare an hour could come for some job training or self-improvement.

Close-up

In 1916, Denver Public Schools converted the Longfellow School at 13th and Welton streets into the Opportunity School. (It didn't become Emily Griffith Opportunity School until 1934, a year after Emily's death.) Her eponymous school, which has touched more than 1.3 million lives since it opened, had a dream to help people help themselves. On the first day, Emily sat near the front door and personally greeted each student. By the end of the first week, 1,400 students had registered. School was open 13 hours a day, five days a week. Tuition was free. Emily's goal was to provide training wherever it was needed.

One day a man came to look at course offerings. When he started to leave without registering, Emily asked why he hadn't signed up. "There are no courses for sign painters," he told her. Shortly thereafter, the school offered a course in sign painting. Over the years, the course offerings have continued to meet students' — and society's — needs. From radio communications and ambulance driving in World War I to victory gardening and defense work in World War II, the Opportunity School has stayed current with a changing marketplace.

Five years ago, the local grocery stores, including King Soopers, Safeway and Cub Foods, approached the school's administration with a request for a program designed to train workers for bakery and deli work, an area that would continue growing as more people turn to prepared foods for their meals. Thus was born the food-services department, which operates a bistro and restaurant where students can practice their craft.

Though many courses lean heavily toward technology, the school still offers

Photo: Denver Public Schools

Emily Griffith, who founded Denver's Opportunity School in 1916, had a dream to help people help themselves.

classes in areas such as cake decorating, creative sewing, floral design, dental anatomy — even aircraft-accident investigation. In fact, just scanning course offerings makes a good read.

— continued on next page

What has remained constant since 1916 are the high school and continuing education courses for adults who never finished high school and immigrants who wish to become citizens. In 1997, 5,200 students received high school diplomas, GEDs and vocational certificates. While the list of graduates isn't exactly filled with household names, their stories are the stuff of the American dream: A college dropout who took transportation courses at EGOS, went back to college, then law school and is now a transportation lawyer; a man who took automotive mechanics classes and today owns his own transmission shop; a woman who took typing classes, which launched her into the business world, and who eventually become a state senator; the current mayor's sister-in-law who dropped out of high school 24 years ago and who graduated with a GED from EGOS in June of 1997, armed with a certificate in Early Child Care Professions.

Today more than 13,000 students train in 350 classes. Students range from age 17 to 94. Though tuition is no longer free (it was until several years ago), it now costs $1.25 an hour — still a bargain by anyone's standards. Better yet, the school and its students provide a wide range of services to the community at discount prices. Want a filling, inexpensive lunch? Emily's Bistro, which trains the food-service students, offers meals for $3.25 to $4. Need a haircut? A barber student will cut your locks for $2. How about a manicure for $2.40? Having dinner guests but don't have a table decoration? Floral centerpieces are $10.

Consumers benefit from EGOS, but so does Denver's economy. In 1992, it was estimated that aggregate earnings of EGOS students employed in training-related jobs exceeded $9 million dollars, of which approximately 14 percent was returned to the community in tax dollars.

Money aside, Emily Griffith Opportunity School is still a model for adult education. Associate principal Bill Smith says he gets calls from all over the world about programs implemented at EGOS. Emily would be proud. Her dream to "help people help themselves" is very much alive and well.

---

ver Center for the Performing Arts, Six Flags Elitch Gardens, Coors Field, the nightlife and restaurants of Lower Downtown and Mile High Stadium.

Oh yes, and The Met has classes, too, 2,400 of them each fall and spring. The emphasis at The Met is on individual attention, with an average class size of just 23 students. Each class is taught by a master teacher; no student teaching assistants here. Summer offerings are also available.

The Met has 50 majors and 69 minors, in addition to the individual degree program. Degree offerings cover business, performing and visual arts, liberal arts, natural and social sciences, and specialty areas such as criminology, aerospace and aviation and engineering technology.

The Met also operates two other campuses that offer degree programs and specialty classes. Metro South, in Englewood, offers evening and weekend classes to over 1,500 students from southeast Denver. Metro North, in Northglenn, serves the northern suburbs.

National College
1325 S. Colorado Blvd. • (303) 758-6700

Aimed at the career interests of the nontraditional adult student, National's average student age is 30. National College offers bachelor's degrees in accounting, applied management, business administration and computer information systems; associate degrees in accounting, applied management, business administration, computer information systems and travel and tourism; and diplomas in the areas of accounting clerk, business, computer operator, travel and airline careers.

Regis University
3333 Regis Blvd. • (303) 458-4100

Regis University got a nice big PR boost in the summer of 1993 when it was chosen as the spot where President Bill Clinton met with Pope John Paul II on the Pope's historic visit to Denver. Secret Service helicopters buzzed like flies over the surrounding residential neighborhoods. Regis has been around for a long time, founded in 1877, and it has a pretty 90-acre main campus, about 9,800 students and a sterling reputation as an educational institution. It's a Colorado Jesuit university, centered around the Ignatius Loyola philosophy of leaders in service of others. Regis pursues that philosophy in three colleges: Regis College, The School for Professional Studies and The School for Health Care Professions. Regis College itself is a relatively small school, with about 1,100 undergraduate students studying liberal arts, sciences, business and education. The student-faculty ratio is 16-to-1.

The School for Professional Studies has undergraduate and graduate programs in business, education and computer sciences and offers classes in Denver, Colorado Springs, Loveland, Boulder, Sterling, Glenwood Springs, Littleton, and Wyoming.

The School for Health Care Professions is particularly well-known among the Greater Denver nursing community. Its graduate and undergraduate programs include nursing, physical therapy and healthcare administration and management.

University of Colorado
Office of Admissions, Campus Box 30, Boulder • (303) 492-1411

Known in the vernacular as CU, this flagship institution of higher education in Colorado was founded in 1876, the year in which Colorado became a state. Today it is a university of international prominence. The university's campuses in Boulder, Denver and Colorado Springs, (719) 262-3383, have a combined student body of about 45,000, and each campus has its own specific mission.

The University of Colorado at Boulder, or CU-Boulder, is where the university started, and it's still its largest and most important campus. Placed in the beautiful setting of Boulder's University Hill, its 786 acres of rural Italian-style buildings and complexes of Colorado sandstone make it one of the nation's most aesthetically pleasing campuses. A 1991 book, *The Campus as a Work of Art*, by Thomas Gaines, ranked CU-Boulder fourth among 50 of the "most artistically successful campuses in the country." Because of nearby skiing and the many outdoor activities available, and because it's often the campus of choice for wealthy students who want a most excellent place in which to spend their campus years, some people think of CU as a "party school." But CU-Boulder is far more than the place where film actor and director Robert Redford played on the baseball team and waited tables in a local bar.

CU-Boulder excels as both a teaching and a research university. In 1997, *Fiske Guide to Colleges* ranked CU as one of the 21 best buys in higher education. *Success Magazine* voted CU one of the top 25 schools in the country. CU, which received $17 million in NASA funding in 1995-96, has 13 alumni who have flown in space.

CU-Boulder's leading programs include telecommunications, aerospace engineering and atmospheric and space physics. The department of molecular, cellular and developmental biology is ranked among the top 10 national doctoral programs by the National Research Council. The chemistry and biochemistry department boasts 1989 Nobel Laureate Thomas Cech among its teaching faculty. CU-Boulder funneled more than $134 million into research during the 1996-97 fiscal year, and it has a separate 147-acre research park nearby, which includes US West Advanced Technologies as a tenant.

Programs include the schools of law, business and administration, education, journalism and mass communications, arts and science, music, architecture and planning. The schools offer more than 2,500 courses in more than 150 fields of study to some 25,000 students.

Part of the Big 12, the school's sports program is impressive too. The football program is one of the nation's most respected; CU has played in nine consecutive bowl games. And in 1996-97, CU was one of just three schools to be ranked in the nation's top 25 in what are considered the three premier sports: football, men's basketball and women's basketball. Finally, the men's and women's ski team has won 14 national championships, the most recent in 1996.

University of Colorado at Denver
1250 14th St. • (303) 556-3287

Established in 1912 to make the state university available in Denver, this is still Denver's only public university. CU-Denver, or "CU in the City," today has 83 undergraduate and graduate programs. CU-Denver shares the 175-acre Auraria Higher Education Center campus with The Metropolitan State College of Denver and the Community College of Denver. Students can cross-register for classes in all three schools. The more than 6,100 undergraduate students at CU-Denver are therefore part of a much larger student body and enjoy academic and extracurricular opportunities greater than those provided by CU-Denver alone. Undergraduate class size averages 22 students.

A five-minute walk from downtown Denver, CU-Denver makes the opportunities of a state university available to working students in an urban environment. Strong programs include its School of the Arts, business and administration, engineering and applied science, architecture and planning, and education.

University of Colorado
Health Sciences Center
4900 E. Ninth Ave. • (303) 399-1211

This is Colorado's only academic health center and the seat of medical research in the region. The 40-acre campus offers baccalaureate and graduate programs in medicine, nursing, dentistry, pharmacy and health-related fields. It includes two hospitals, University Hospital and the Colorado Psychiatric Hospital, as well as seven research institutes. The center is as prominent nationally in research as it is regionally in medical education and renowned in numerous fields including transplants, cancer, neuroscience, molecular biology, perinatal care and cardiovascular services.

University of Denver
2199 S. University Blvd. • (303) 871-2000

Founded in 1864, this is the oldest independent university in the Rocky Mountain region and the reason why one of Denver's main north/south thoroughfares is named University Boulevard. In a residential area 8 miles southeast of downtown, the University of Denver, called "DU" by locals, is a good combination of big-university experience and small liberal-arts-college atmosphere. The campus includes 100 buildings on 125 acres. Its Lamont School of Music and its College of Law are on the university's Park Hill campus, formerly Colorado Women's College. The student body counts about 8,700 students. About 3,100 of those are graduate students, and plenty of faculty members are at the forefront of research in their fields. Still, the university is a good place to spend one's undergraduate years. The student-faculty ratio is 13-to-1 for undergraduates. Class sizes average 20 students. Undergraduate degrees are available in arts, fine arts, music, music education, science, business administration, accounting, chemistry, electrical engineering and mechanical engineering. Campus Connection, a mentoring program, joins each new freshman with a faculty adviser in his or her major area of study.

University of Phoenix
7800 E. Dorado Pl., Englewood
• (303) 755-9090

This is the Colorado Campus of the University of Phoenix, which is based, of course, in Phoenix, Arizona, but has 47 campuses in 14 states and Puerto Rico. To attend you have to be at least 23 years old and have at least two years of full-time work behind you. This university focuses on degree programs and services for working adults. Students from US West, for example, take classes at their company, and UP designs customized educational programs and seminars for many other companies as well. Degrees range from nursing and business administration to educational administration, computer information systems and technology management. UP has about 4,000 students in metropolitan Denver, Colorado Springs and Grand Junction.

Webster University
12510 E. Iliff Ave., Ste 200, Aurora
• (303) 750-6665

Webster University is based in St. Louis, Missouri, and has about 15,000 students worldwide; about two-thirds of them are graduate students. The Denver Campus in Aurora has about 150 students taking graduate courses in business administration, business, computer

Photo: Daily Camera

Colorado State University is home to many animal science programs.

resources and information management, human resources development, and human resources management. All programs are designed for working adults and offered in the evening format.

Community Colleges

Arapahoe Community College
2500 W. College Dr., Littleton
• (303) 794-1550

Arapahoe Community College's 7,500-plus students attend classes on a 51-acre campus adjacent to Littleton's downtown and just east of the South Platte River, which affords great mountain views to the west. It was established by ballot as Arapahoe Junior College in 1965 as the first two-year college in Greater Denver when south-side residents decided there was a need for a local junior college. It joined the Colorado State System of Community Colleges in 1970 as Arapahoe Community College.

Arapahoe leans toward two-year associate's degrees that help students enhance their careers with a degree or certificate, often while working. Some 50 percent of its students are working students. But courses can also transfer to a four-year college or university. The college has more than 80 degree and certificate programs in both academic and vocational areas, with more than 2,400 classes per year. ACC also offers community education classes for the lifelong learner. The average class size is 17 students, and the average cost of education here is 10 to 60 percent less than most Colorado four-year schools.

The college also operates satellite classrooms at the Denver Tech Center, Parker and Castle Rock.

Community College of Aurora
16000 E. Centretech Pkwy., Aurora
• (303) 360-4700

Community College of Aurora has been the community college of Greater Denver's east side since its founding in 1983. It moved to a new 35-acre campus just west of Buckley Air National Guard Base in 1991 and, with the closing of Lowry Air Force Base, Community College of Aurora opened a second campus

there in the fall of 1994, the Higher Education and Advancement Technology Center. Like other community colleges, it accommodates adult learners. The 5,400 students average 31 years in age.

Community College of Aurora offers the full range of courses needed by students planning to transfer to four-year institutions with associate of arts and associate of science degrees. It has vocational programs that focus on an associate of applied science degree and training for employment certification. And it provides a menu of courses that serves a wide variety of interests by east-siders interested in learning. The college's faculty development program, which trains faculty in better methods of teaching students, has won several national awards and has been used as a model for schools across the country.

Community College of Denver
1111 W. Colfax Ave. • (303) 556-2600

With about 10,000 full-time and part-time students, this is Greater Denver's "inner-city" community college. It shares the Auraria Higher Education Center's 175-acre campus with The Metropolitan State College of Denver (MSCD) and the University of Colorado at Denver. Around 37,000 students can cross-register in the courses of all three schools.

The college offers degree programs in the full range of college subjects, as well as transfer courses for the baccalaureate degree, occupational programs for job entry skills or upgrading, remedial instruction and GED prep, continuing education, community services and cooperative programs with the other schools.

Front Range Community College
3645 W. 112 Ave., Westminster
• (303) 404-5550

The community college of Greater Denver's north side, Front Range Community College is Colorado's largest community college. It has about 18,000 students at its Fort Collins, Longmont, Boulder and Westminster campuses. Front Range has more than 90 degree and certificate programs, including associate's degrees in arts, science and general studies as well as degrees and certificates in applied sciences.

Front Range offers classes for GED, English as a second language, literacy courses and classes for students with learning disabilities. Front Range is the leader among local community colleges in delivering courses at business and industry work sites, including companies such as AT&T in Westminster, Geneva Pharmaceuticals in Broomfield and Rocky Flats in Jefferson County, where Front Range has 600 employee-students. Front Range is also one of the few places in the West teaching hearing people to interpret for the deaf. Its nursing program won acclaim as a 1994 program of excellence, and in addition to its vocational programs, it has 60 courses that transfer to four-year schools. Locals can also take a lot of fun, lifelong learning courses, such as handwriting analysis and garden management.

Red Rocks Community College
13300 W. Sixth Ave., Lakewood
• (303) 988-6160

Red Rocks is among the fastest-growing institutions of higher learning in the state, and given its location, it's not hard to believe. Its 140-acre main campus perches on the western edge of Lakewood, in some of Jefferson County's most beautiful natural settings. It's also near the site where a major developer recently announced plans for a prestige shopping center to rival the Cherry Creek shopping mall, not a bad idea considering all the wealth in the mountain communities to the immediate west. Red Rocks' enrollment of 7,200 students in the winter and 3,500 in the summer represents 62 percent growth over the last six years.

Red Rocks was founded in 1969 as a two-year institution. It also serves northwest metro suburbanites with an Arvada campus and mountain communities with the Mountain Area Center in Conifer.

Its largest enrollments are in math, followed by the sciences, computer information systems, English, multimedia, fire science technology and criminal justice. More than half of the student reasons for attending Red Rocks are job-related. The college has special programs in construction technology, film/video technology, medical assisting and biotechnology. The Red Rocks Institute does customized training for businesses. The Red Rocks OSHA Training Institute is one of four sites in the nation designated by the U.S. Department of Labor for OSHA training. A Computer Access Center trains individuals with disabilities to use adaptive computer technologies.

Colorado is a forerunner in day-care licensing requirements. In fact, the licensing criteria here are equal to accreditation criteria in other states.

Child Care

First, the good news: there are a reasonable number of day-care homes and centers in Greater Denver.

Now, the bad news: the biggest problem (both in Greater Denver and statewide) is finding care for infants. In fact, there are currently three infants for every one spot that opens up. Still, parents of kids a year and older should be heartened to know that currently there's no shortage of choices. Even better, Colorado is a forerunner in day-care licensing requirements. In fact, the licensing criteria here are equal to accreditation criteria in other states.

That said, we know from personal experience that finding the right person for your child can be high on the list of stressful situations. We recommend getting the book *Child Care and PreSchools in Metro Denver*, by Margerie Hicks ($14.95), a comprehensive guide to what's available in the area. Hicks lists only state-licensed child-care centers, preschools, school-age care facilities and day camps in Greater Denver. She also includes information for resources and referral agencies and explains what you can expect under the ADA if you have a special-needs child. Finally, she lists facilities by zip codes — an expeditious way to see what's in your immediate area. Comprehensive as it is, the book carries one pretty standard caveat: some of the facilities may have closed by the time you read it and the newest may not be listed.

For up-to-the-minute referrals, your best bet (if you live in Denver, Arapahoe, Adams or Douglas counties) is to call the **Work and Family Resource Center at Community College of Denver**, the most extensive of local referral agencies. It's a nonprofit agency with a database of all licensed child-care providers in the Greater Denver area, including day-care centers, private child care, before-and-after school programs and preschools. For free referrals and information about choosing quality child care, call them on their Community Line, (303) 534-2625. Go through a voice-messaging question-and-answer session, and they'll call you back with perhaps three to five possibilities that match your criteria; you do the legwork from there. Community Line will continue to provide referrals free until you find what you're looking for. They also have a for-charge "Cadillac" service in which they do all the legwork, but this is a contract service available only to employees of customer companies. In addition, they have the 4 Parents Helpline, (303) 620-4444, that provides information and referrals on a wide spectrum of parent support. Thirty trained volunteers answer questions ranging from teething to teen problems. The line is staffed from 8 AM to 8 PM on weekdays. The Work and Family Resource Center serves parents and child-care providers in 10 counties, including those of Greater Denver.

For referrals in Jefferson County, call **Family Resource and Child Care Education**, (303) 969-9500. This nonprofit agency, housed at Red Rocks Community College, helps families locate quality child care in Jefferson, Gilpin, Park and Clear Creek counties. Its database lists all licensed homes and centers in these counties.

One thing you might want to do, once you've scanned the possibilities and settled on what look like some good ones, is check on day-care providers before you commit by calling the **Colorado Department of Human Services' Licensing Verification**, 1575 Sherman Street, Denver, (303) 866-5958. If you have the correct name and/or street address of the provider, the licensing verification department can look it up on the computer and let you know if the place is licensed and when the license was issued. The department can also provide other general information. Want to know if any complaints have been filed against your candidate day-care providers?

There are many resources to help parents find child care in the metro area.

Call licensing verification and ask to speak to a counselor who can set you up with an appointment to come in and view the file, providing you make a file-review appointment at least 72 hours in advance. It's probably a good idea to double check. Most day-care providers are undoubtedly fine people, but a little paranoia is always a good thing when your kids are involved. Licensing verification only works for day-care providers licensed by the State of Colorado. Unlicensed day care is caveat emptor.

Keep in mind that child-care centers and homes are but one means of solving child-care problems. School-age child-care programs that provide before- and after-school care are becoming recognized by school districts as a way of putting their facilities to better use both in serving the community and in generating revenue. Call your school district to see if the school you want provides such services.

Preschools, part-day educational facilities that take care of kids anywhere from $2\frac{1}{2}$ to 4 hours per day, are increasingly popular for early education, early socialization and helping parents get some extra time off to work or just to keep them sane. The Work and Family

---

INSIDERS' TIP

The local Red Cross, (303) 722-7474, has baby-sitter training courses. You might want to enroll your sitters and pay the nominal fee to make sure they're knowledgeable about such things as CPR and the Heimlich maneuver.

Resource Center can direct you to several in your area.

Finally, if you want a nanny, a good place to find a trained one is **Starkey International Institute**, (303) 832-5510. This is the "Rolls Royce" of nanny-placement agencies in large part because no nanny is placed who doesn't already have two years of college and three years of experience. Many come to Starkey for the Nanny Advancement Program, a five-day, 50-hour course that gives nannies a higher level of polish and professionalism. Want your child to learn social graces? These graduates can teach them. Want your child to learn to handle international etiquette situations? No problem. As you can imagine, Starkey nannies don't come cheap. Typical salaries range from $25,000 to $40,000 a year, but what you get transcends mere baby-sitting. There are other nanny agencies in town (check the Yellow Pages), but you may not be assured of the level of experience you'll get with their referrals.

Then there's the au pair route. A lot of people enjoy having a European au pair for the relatively low cost and the cosmopolitan experience of getting a live-in child-care helper while exposing the kids to a foreign culture. Two referral agencies for au pair services are **Au Pair in America**, (800) 727-2437, and **AuPairCare**, (800) 288-7786.

If your needs go no further than simple baby-sitting services, one of your best options is to advertise through local high schools and churches. Put an advertisement up on their bulletin boards, and it can be the start of a long string of baby-sitters who, as they reach graduation and go on to full-time jobs or college, keep passing down recommendations to subsequent generations of younger sitters from the same institutions.

And, of course, there are your neighbors. People who never bothered to make much effort in neighbor-schmoozing before they had children suddenly find reasons why neighbors are good people to know. Part of it is the sense of security these contacts can provide, and part of it is because the kids often initiate neighborhood relationships and force their parents to get involved. But a real good incentive we've found is all those unidentified teenagers who suddenly become intensely interesting as possible neighborhood baby-sitters.

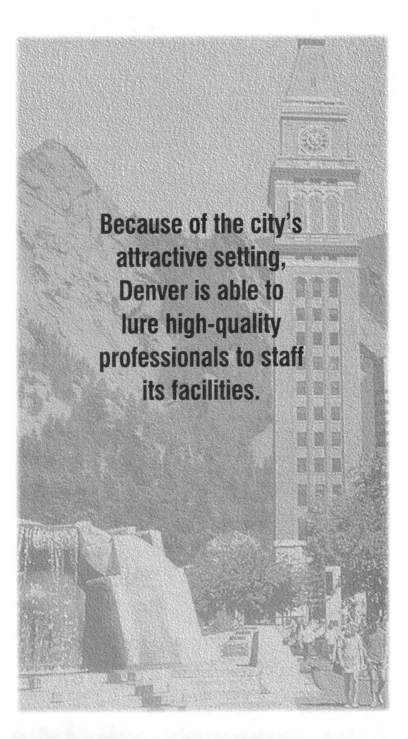

Because of the city's attractive setting, Denver is able to lure high-quality professionals to staff its facilities.

Healthcare

In the past few years, healthcare in Greater Denver has changed faster than Hillary Clinton can say "healthcare reform."

That might be a slight exaggeration, but certainly Denver's healthcare scene — most notably hospital mergers — have kept local headline writers busy and consumers trying to figure out what's what.

Despite all the changes, Denver remains a regional center for high-quality medicine. Three Level I trauma centers serve the region, along with two emergency helicopter companies, AirLife and Flight for Life. (Level I is the highest, most technologically advanced level of trauma care available and includes the highest staffing levels.) The emergency room at Denver General Hospital sees so much gruesome action that it inspired a book called *The Knife and Gun Club*. A number of facilities, including Craig Hospital and National Jewish Medical and Research Center, have earned national and international acclaim for outstanding care and research developments.

In all, Greater Denver has 17 acute-care hospitals and three rehabilitation centers. Two operations, Centura Health and HealthONE, own and operate several facilities. The largest of Denver's hospitals, Presbyterian/St. Luke's just east of downtown, has 676 licensed beds and nearly 1,800 employees. The smallest, Platte Valley Medical Center, north of Denver in Brighton, has 58 licensed beds and about 290 employees.

Because of the city's attractive setting, Denver is able to lure high-quality professionals to staff its facilities. Hospitals and physicians work with university researchers and high-technology companies. University Hospital, at the University of Colorado's Health Sciences Center in Denver, has been ranked as one of the 25 best hospitals in the country in *The Best of Medicine* by Herbert J. Dietrich, M.D., and Virginia H. Biddle.

Pulmonary medicine is one example of a field in which Greater Denver enjoys renown. Many of the city's major hospitals, including National Jewish Medical and Research Center and Swedish and Lutheran medical centers, originally began as tuberculosis treatment centers back in the days when tuberculosis patients came to Colorado for the healthy air. Not surprisingly, Greater Denver is a leader in pulmonary research and technology. Research and expertise at institutions such as National Jewish and the Web-Waring Lung Institute are one of the main reasons why some of the world's most advanced pulmonary technology manufacturers make their homes in the Denver area.

Denver's other research and medical advancement highlights include the Belle Bonfils Blood Center, the Eleanor Roosevelt Institute for Cancer Research, the Barbara Davis Child Diabetes Center and the C. Henry Kempe National Center for the Prevention and Treatment of Child Abuse.

To insure their health, Denverites, like others across the nation, have turned to managed-care companies. Changes in this area happen so fast that only the industry pros can keep it all straight. Managed-care companies appeal to Greater Denver residents' sense of health and outdoor living through advertisements and policies that stress preventative care and healthy lifestyles.

Physician and Hospital Referrals

Clearly, healthcare choices abound in Denver. To find what's right for you, you can go to research extremes and get a directory of Colorado hospitals from the **Colorado Health and Hospital Association**, (303) 758-1630, for $100. CHHA also makes this resource and several others available at all public and academic libraries in the state for free. Other publications include issue papers on such topics as violence, teen pregnancy and smoking. You also can check the phone book under "Hospitals" or "Physicians" for a number of free referral services. **Mile High United Way** is a great place to start when seeking all kinds of community service information, and medical service is no exception. You can call their United Way HelpLine at (303) 433-8900. You can also find Greater Denver's medical and other community services in exhaustive detail by buying Mile High United Way's book, Where to Turn, a value at $30. Call Mile High United Way's HelpLine, or their administrative offices at (303) 433-8383 to find out how to get the book.

Among the referral services to start with:

Children's Hospital physician referral, (303) 861-0123

Ask-A-Nurse, (303) 777-6877

Answer Line at Exempla Health Care, (303) 425-2929

HealthONE, (800) COLUMBIA

Columbia/Rose Resource, (303) 320-7673

Surgical Associated Service, (303) 322-9111

Med Search at Saint Joseph Hospital, (303) 866-8000

Prologue's Rocky Mountain Doctor line, (303) 4-HEALTH

Colorado Health Care Network, (303) 280-3121

Medical Society Metro West, (303) 232-1428

Greater Denver has more than 100 nursing homes and more than a dozen hospices, some operated in association with hospitals. A fine source of local nursing home referrals and information is **Community Housing Services**, (303) 831-4046. A good number to keep on the telephone if you have kids is the **Rocky Mountain Poison Center**, (303) 629-1123 or (303) 739-1127 for the deaf or hearing-impaired.

Hospitals

Denver

Children's Hospital
1056 E. 19th Ave.
• (303) 861-8888

The name says it all. Kids. Children's Hospital is a healthcare system caring for kids with the full spectrum of needs from wellness and prevention through the most complex care. For the third consecutive year, Children's was named in 1997 by *U.S. News & World Report* as one of the top-10 hospitals nationwide in caring for kids, and it was the only hospital so recognized between Chicago and Los Angeles. Serving a 12-state region, Children's has been an innovator in medicine since it was founded in 1908, with firsts including the largest and most successful pediatric heart transplant program, the nation's first pediatric transport system and the discovery of Toxic Shock Syndrome. In 1997 it was designated as a Level I pediatric trauma center, the only one in the region devoted solely to children. Children's mission focuses on clinical care, research, education and advocacy.

Beyond the walls of the hospital, Children's offers pediatric services throughout the metropolitan area, the state and the region through partnerships with other healthcare institutions and clinics. Children's also operates four off-site specialty care centers in Aurora, Arvada, Wheat Ridge and Highlands Ranch. The hospital itself handles about 10,000 inpatient and 250,000 outpatient visits yearly. Children's is also affiliated with the University of Colorado Health Sciences Center to pool pediatrics expertise and enhance treatment and research.

www.insiders.com
See this and many other
Insiders' Guide®
destinations online.
Visit us today!

INSIDERS' TIP

One of the best ways to get a physician reference is to call a hospital. Most of the big ones have their own free physician referral service.

Denver Health Medical Center
777 Bannock St. • (303) 436-6000

This is Colorado's largest public hospital. It is operated by Denver Health, which also runs Community Health Services, the Rocky Mountain Poison Center and Denver CARES Community Detoxification.

The medical center includes 308 staffed beds for a range of inpatient medical and behavioral health services. The center runs the Rocky Mountain Regional Trauma Center — the region's only Level I trauma center certified for both children and adults. It also operates Denver's 911 emergency system, paramedic services and one of the nation's most competitive emergency medicine residency programs.

To a large extent Denver General is the safety net for Denver residents regardless of their social or economic status. Nearly half of all charges for inpatient and outpatient services come from people without health insurance, and more than a third are from people covered by Medicaid and Medicare. Denver General also emphasizes adolescent and adult inpatient psychiatry and handles some 3,000 childbirths a year. Denver General's Rocky Mountain Regional Trauma Center serves the entire Rocky Mountain region. With more than 3,000 trauma patients annually, it is the busiest Level I trauma center in the area. Community Health Services, (303) 436-7420, operates 11 health centers throughout Denver and 10 student health clinics in Denver Public Schools. Denver Public Health monitors communicable diseases such as AIDS, tuberculosis, measles and hepatitis. It operates several outpatient clinics for diagnosis and treatment of these and many other diseases. Through its Environmental Health Division, Public Health also provides a wide range of non-clinical services such as air and water pollution monitoring, restaurant inspections, licensing for day-care facilities and personal boarding-care homes, and operation of the Denver Municipal Animal Shelter.

National Jewish Medical and Research Center
1400 Jackson St. • (303) 388-4461

People with asthma and other chronic respiratory diseases come here from all over the world because National Jewish has an international reputation as a leading — if not *the* leading — medical center for the study and treatment of chronic respiratory diseases, allergic diseases and immune system disorders.

National Jewish's pedigree is impressive. It is ranked among the top 10 independent biomedical research facilities in the world and is the No. 1 private institution in the world for immunology research.

One of those Denver medical centers that began to serve tuberculosis patients, it started in 1899 with the opening of the National Jewish Hospital for Consumptives. Today this nonsectarian medical center's staff of 1,100 serves patients on a sort of modified outpatient basis, in which patients usually stay in hotels or in some cases at another hospital. One out of every five pediatric allergists in the United States was trained here.

National Jewish operates a free telephone information service known as Lung Line to answer questions and forward literature on such subjects as acute bronchitis, asthma, emphysema and pneumonia. Call (303) 355-LUNG if you're in Colorado or (800) 222-LUNG if you're not for the 8 AM to 5 PM service.

Centura Porter Adventist Hospital
2525 S. Downing St. • (303) 778-1955

Formerly Porter Memorial Hospital, this hospital on Denver's southern border is a 368-bed, acute-care hospital that boasts more than 1,200 physicians. A nonprofit organization, it's one of four — along with Platte Valley Medical Center in Brighton, Centura Health Littleton Adventist Hospital and Centura Health Avista Adventist Hospital in Boulder County — affiliated under Rocky Mountain Adventist Healthcare. It was founded in 1930 by Denver pioneer and businessman Henry M. Porter after he was impressed by his treatment at California hospitals that were owned by the Seventh-Day Adventist Church. He and his daughter gave the church $315,000 and 40 acres to start a hospital in Denver. The hospital's mission is "to serve as a continuation of the healing ministry of Christ." Its specialties include cancer care and cancer support, heart care and healthy heart programs, the Clyde G. Kissinger Center for Sight, the Porter Birthplace, Porter Breastcare, a center for treatment of substance abuse and eating disorders, transplant services and education programs in areas such as stress management, weight control and nutrition counseling, smoking cessation and alcohol education. Independence Square helps cardiac rehabilitation patients return to normal activities by simulating situations patients will encounter when discharged from the hospital.

Presbyterian/St. Luke's Medical Center
1719 E. 19th Ave. • (303) 839-6000

A division of HealthONE, this huge medical center has more than 1,000 physicians and more beds and staff than any hospital in Greater Denver. You would be hard put to dispute its claim to being the most comprehensive healthcare provider in the Rocky Mountain West, given its amazing range of services including virtually everything you would traditionally expect of a general hospital to things such as Hospital for Infants and Children (opened in 1998), The Mothers' Milk Bank, the Denver Broncos Sports Medicine Rehabilitation Center, the Sleep Disorders Center, the Colorado Gynecology and Continence Center, the Institute for Limb Preservation, the Senior Citizen's Health Center, the Hyperbaric Medicine Center, psychiatric services, organ and tissue transplants, Addictions Recovery Centers and a wide variety of women's and pediatric services. The list goes on and on.

The Family Birth Place has been named as one of the top-10 maternity units in the United States by Child magazine. Close to Pres/St. Luke, as the locals call it, The Inn at Presbyterian, 2021 High Street, (303) 839-7150, offers convenient lodging at reasonable rates to people undergoing pre-admission testing and to families of patients.

Centura St. Anthony Central Hospital
4231 W. 16th Ave. • (303) 629-3511

St. Anthony Hospital Central was built by the Sisters of St. Francis in 1893. St. Anthony Central operates one of the area's three certified Level I trauma centers and is home base to Flight for Life, probably the best known of Greater Denver's helicopter emergency rescue services. The hospital is an innovator in cardiovascular surgery and services and was one of the first hospitals to provide a chest pain emergency center. It's also one of 11 sites in the nation to offer gamma knife surgery, which entails the use of gamma rays to eliminate deep-seated tumors and other malformations in the brain. St. Anthony Hospital Central has 498 licensed beds.

Rose Medical Center
4567 E. Ninth Ave. • (303) 320-2121

Rose Medical Center is well known to many Greater Denverites as the place where their children, grandchildren, nieces and nephews were born. That's not surprising considering its emphasis on women's health services, education, parent education classes, infertility and high-risk pregnancies. Rose also operates a satellite location in Littleton. The Rose Breast Center performs more mammograms than any other facility in the Denver area. And the Rose Children's Center is strong on inpatient, ambulatory and emergency services for infants, children and adolescents. All this is not to say that Rose is just for women and children. Opened in 1949 and named after Denver World War II hero Gen. Maurice Rose, the Medical Center provided the first comprehensive, primary-care-oriented health program designed especially for men. The special 6th North Suites continue to provide a distinctive level of care, including private chefs. Among the general list of hospital services provided by Rose's 1,400 employees is advanced oncology research and Colorado's first coronary care unit.

With 420 licensed beds, it was also the first adult, acute-care metro medical center to formally affiliate with the nearby University of Colorado Health Sciences Center. Rose also is a teaching hospital. Other Rose special features include a surgical treatment of emphysema program and sports medicine orthopedists, who provide care for professional and weekend athletes alike. Rose in 1994 created what it calls an orthopedic center of excellence, the Rose Institute for Joint Replacement, which is recognized for its model of full-service care. At the new Elaine and Melvin Wolf Ambulatory Surgery Building, Columbia Rose offers cosmetic and laser surgery services, and a minimally invasive breast biopsy technology

Photo: Daily Camera

The Greater Denver area offers basic and emergency medical care, but is a regional healthcare center as well.

that is taught to physicians from around the world. The Travel Medicine Clinic has cared for more than 30,000 business and pleasure travelers.

Exempla Saint Joseph Hospital
1835 Franklin St. • (303) 837-7111

Denver's oldest private hospital, Saint Joseph was founded in 1873 by the Sisters of Charity of Leavenworth, Kansas, and they still own it. It has been designated as one of the top-100 hospitals in the United States by Mercer Management Consulting and Health Care Investment Analysts, and it has a national reputation for the quality of its heart care. It's the busiest childbirth center in Denver and Colorado. With more than 5,000 births per year, Saint Joseph is the birthplace of 10 percent of

Colorado's babies. The hospital's Maternal/Fetal Medicine program and Level III Neonatal Intensive Care Nursery ensure that babies needing extra help get the best care available before and after birth. Saint Joseph excels in other services including oncology, orthopedics, gastroenterology and pulmonology. Saint Joseph also has average patient charges among the lowest of the metro area's hospitals.

Spalding Rehabilitation Hospital
900 Potomac St. • (303) 367-1166

Although Spalding is officially in Denver, it's actually located all over the place. The hospital's 169 licensed beds are in fact located at other hospitals. At each of these, Spalding operates as a wing or unit specializ-

---

INSIDERS' TIP

Need specialized medical attention for your pet? Colorado State University is one of the leading veterinary schools in the nation, and Greater Denverites often take their pets there for chemotherapy or other advanced veterinary needs. Call (970) 491-4477 for information.

ing in the treatment of stroke, brain injury, chronic pain, neck/back injuries, neurological disorders, multiple sclerosis and orthopedic problems. Spalding was founded in 1965 as a stand-alone hospital but sold that facility in 1992 and went the "hospital-within-a-hospital" route to save on costs and also to bring care to people in their own communities. There also is a freestanding facility at the main Potomac location in Aurora where inpatient and outpatient specialty care is offered. Spalding Downtown is now at Presbyterian/St. Luke's Medical Center. Spalding West is at Exempla Lutheran Medical Center. Spalding operates an outpatient unit, Spalding Rehabilitation Center, in Longmont, and a unit at United Medical Center in Cheyenne, Wyoming.

University Hospital
4200 E. Ninth Ave. • (303) 399-1211

If the state of the medical art is what you're looking for, it's said, a research hospital is a good place to go. University Hospital is part of the University of Colorado Health Sciences Center. University Hospital is physically connected with Colorado's major health research base, which pulls in $139 million annually in research and training grants. The University of Colorado, known around here as CU, has its School of Medicine here. The schools of nursing, pharmacy and dentistry are also on site, as is the Colorado Psychiatric Hospital. At any one time, University Hospital provides 393 beds along with outpatient services. University pulled off the nation's first successful liver transplant, and it has plenty of other accomplishments to brag about since it was created in 1921, including its 1998 listing among top hospitals in U.S. News and World Report. Pushing the medical frontiers, CU has given the hospital special expertise in areas ranging from heart surgery to cancer. The hospital's National Cancer Institute-designated Cancer Center, for example, does specialized experimental cancer treatments in conjunction with its research.

Department of Veterans Affairs Medical Center
1055 Clermont St. • (303) 399-8020

Through the VA Med Center, the federal government delivers health services to people who have previously served in the military. With 382 beds in use, it provides medical, surgical, neurological, rehabilitation and psychiatric care. The center also has a 60-bed Nursing Home Care Unit and reaches out to other parts of Front Range Colorado through outlying clinics and a mobile MEDIVAN program. Among their special programs are care and treatment for aging veterans, female veterans, ex-POWs, Vietnam-era veterans and issues relating to Agent Orange and the Persian Gulf. The center is also a major research site, the 14th largest in the Veterans Administration, with projects including a Schizophrenia Center, a VA Alcohol Research Center and an AIDS Clinical Trial Unit.

Adams County

Sunrise-Mediplex Rehab-Denver
8451 Pearl St., Thornton • (303) 288-3000

This is a comprehensive medical rehabilitation facility for adult inpatients and outpatients with traumatic brain injury, stroke, amputation, orthopedic conditions, arthritis, neurological disorders, pulmonary conditions, psychiatric disorders or other disabling conditions. It's a 117-bed facility near I-25 just off the 84th Avenue Exit. Comprehensive brain injury rehab services include coma rehabilitation, acute brain injury rehabilitation and neurobehavioral rehabilitation. Comprehensive rehab includes multiple trauma, neurologic, stroke, orthopedic, amputee, arthritic and neuromuscular rehabilitation. Pulmonary rehab includes ventilator rehab, ventilator management and pulmonary restoration. There's a substance abuse program for people with disabilities.

Platte Valley Medical Center
1850 Egbert St., Brighton • (303) 659-1531

Platte Valley stays busy because of its proximity to U.S. Highway 85 and I-76. It's also the closest hospital to Denver International Airport. Founded as Brighton Community Hospital in 1960, it came under the management of Rocky Mountain Adventist Health Care in 1980. A new hospital was built in 1982, and the name was changed in 1985. With 58 beds, it's one of Greater Denver's smallest acute-care hospitals, but it provides a solid spectrum of general hospital care ranging from coronary care and cardiac rehabilitation to perinatal and pediatric services. In 1997 the Transitional Care Unit opened, which added six beds. Platte Valley is second only to Rose Medical Center in the ratio of childbirths to hospital beds. Generally it serves people from Adams and Weld counties.

Centura St. Anthony North Hospital
2551 W. 84th Ave., Westminster
• (303) 426-2151

One of three major hospitals operated by Centura Health (see St. Anthony Central, in Denver), St. Anthony North was built in 1971 to serve the northern suburbs. This 198-bed hospital is oriented toward the needs of young families in a growing community. The emergency room is one of the state's busiest. Major medical specialties include diabetes management, family practice, pediatrics, cardiology and obstetrics, with advanced intermediate and intensive care nurseries. It also plays an educational role, offering parent education classes, wellness seminars, obstetrics classes, sick child day care and health promotion activities for businesses.

Arapahoe County

The Medical Center of Aurora
1501 S. Potomac St. (South campus),
700 Potomac St. (North campus), Aurora
• (303) 695-2600

Eventually, these two campuses will be combined into one in order to provide the best, most efficient care. About 400 physicians represent nearly every specialty, and almost a quarter of the doctors are female.

Columbia Medical Center offers a full range of services. Programs include comprehensive cardiovascular services; open-heart surgery; a breast diagnostic center; the Colorado Spine Center, providing conservative and surgical care to adults, adolescents and children with degenerative spine disease, trauma, spinal deformities and tumors of the spine; kidney dialysis; Level III trauma; a sleep disorders center; a diagnostic eye center and the east metro area's only radiation therapy unit for cancer treatment.

Craig Hospital
3425 S. Clarkson St., Englewood
• (303) 789-8000

Craig Hospital dates back to 1907 when it was started as a tuberculosis colony by Frank Craig, who himself was a tuberculosis sufferer. Today, Craig Hospital is dedicated exclusively to patients with spinal cord and brain injuries. It is listed in the 1998 *U.S. News and World Report* compilation of top hospitals. Some 10,000 patients have been treated and rehabilitated since Craig converted to a rehabilitation facility in 1956. Another of those Greater Denver hospitals with an international reputation in a specialized niche, Craig pulls the majority of its patients from outside Colorado. It supports that widespread patient base with an air transport team that flies an average of 200,000 miles a year in a specially equipped air-ambulance, a Lear jet and other aircraft. About a mile south of the Denver border in Englewood, Craig tries to maintain a casual, home-away-from-home atmosphere because it's a long-stay hospital that encourages family involvement in a patient's progress. Craig recently opened a $10 million addition to the hospital known as the Transitional Care Facility. In these apartment-like units, patients during the last phase of their inpatient stay can work on adjusting to independent life. The units are designed to hold the patient's family members as well, so family can help with the adjustment. Acute-care patients can be managed almost immediately after injury by Craig physicians and therapists in neurotrauma units at

INSIDERS' TIP

A good jumping-off point for alternative and holistic medicine is local grocery store Alfalfa's, with several locations in the metro area. Nutritionists and other staffers can help steer you toward the right products and services.

The Health Sciences Center is part of the University of Colorado.

adjacent Swedish Medical Center and at St. Anthony Hospital Central in Denver. The hospital is licensed for 89 beds.

Centura Health Littleton Adventist Hospital
7700 S. Broadway, Littleton
• (303) 730-8900

Centura Health Littleton (formerly Littleton Hospital-Porter) was opened in 1989 in response to growing development in south Greater Denver, from Littleton and Englewood to Highlands Ranch and Castle Rock. It's just north of C-470, near the intersection of Broadway and Mineral Avenue. The next hospital to the south is in Colorado Springs. Centura Health Littleton features services including obstetrics and gynecology, pediatrics, surgical services, radiology, cardiopulmonary, rehabilitation and 24-hour emergency care. All of its rooms are private. The hospital's Family Life Center offers a wide selection of classes and programs. In addition, the hospital serves its community with Ask-A-Nurse, a 24-hour, free health information and physician referral service at (303) 777-6871. This 105-licensed-bed hospital is owned by PorterCare Adventist Health System and represents an extension of the Adventist healing mission.

Swedish Medical Center
501 E. Hampden Ave., Englewood
• (303) 788-5000

A division of Columbia HealthONE, Swedish serves as a regional center for the most complex trauma, neurological and infertility cases. It is a nonprofit, 328-bed acute-care hospital. Because it shares its campus with two major regional rehab hospitals, Craig Hospital and Spalding Hospital, it is well-positioned to provide continuum care for victims of spinal cord injury, stroke, neurological disorders and complex orthopedic problems. Critical healthcare includes cardiovascular and pulmonary services, oncology services and emergency and trauma services. Special facilities include the Center for Reproductive Medicine and a Radiation Therapy Department. The Laser Clinic has state-of-the-art treatment for removing port-wine stains, spider veins, birthmarks, moles, tattoos, etc.

Jefferson County

Cleo Wallace Center Hospital
8405 Church Ranch Blvd. • (303) 438-2208

Cleo Wallace Center is Colorado's largest and most comprehensive behavioral healthcare organization dedicated to the treatment of psychiatric, emotional and behavioral problems in children and adolescents. Cleo Spurlock Wallace was a local schoolteacher who saw a need for special services for troubled youth, which was why she started the center in 1943. Today, Cleo Wallace operates two campuses, in Westminster and Colorado Springs. In 1998, it closed its Denver campus, but plans to re-open when a suitable location is found. The centers provide inpatient hospitals, residential facilities, day treatment and outpatient services for children and adolescents with behavioral health concerns and for their families. In all, Cleo Wallace has 248 beds. It runs a school certified by the Colorado Department of Education, each class-

room having both a teacher and a paraprofessional to integrate treatment into education. Cleo Wallace is accredited by The Joint Commission on the Accreditation of Health Care Organizations. John Wayne used to come here for fund-raising events; he was a member of the Sigma Chi fraternity, which selected Cleo's hospital/school as its special charity.

Exempla Lutheran Medical Center
8300 W. 38th Ave., Wheat Ridge
• (303) 425-4500

This community-owned nonprofit health system was founded in 1905. In recent years it has rated among the top 100 hospitals in the nation. Lutheran offers a variety of outpatient and community outreach programs in addition to a 409-bed hospital, inpatient and outpatient psychiatric services, a rehabilitation center, a skilled nursing unit, a residence for seniors and a full-service homecare and hospice division.

ELMC has a long-standing reputation for providing high-quality, low-cost healthcare and stressing preventative medicine. Lutheran owns and operates a wide spectrum of integrated health services. Recently opened was the new Family Birth Center that provides support and education in all aspects of birthing and family planning with a holistic approach. ELMC partners with Rocky Mountain Radiologists, P.C. and Nordstrom department stores to operate a mammography center at Park Meadows shopping center.

ELMC offers a program called EZ Care, a community-based health service designed to meet the needs of the homeless and those with inadequate or no insurance. Its Youth Education Alliance for Health is a collaborative effort with the public school system to enhance science curriculum and improve health and wellness behaviors.

Mental Health

Bethesda Behavioral Health
4400 E. Iliff Ave. • (303) 758-1514

A division of Columbia Bethesda Behavioral Health, this is a psychiatric treatment center that offers the full spectrum of care for adults. Help for children is offered through Cleo

Wallace, which rents space on their campus. Founded in 1910 as a tuberculosis sanatorium, Bethesda now has about 90 inpatient beds and a variety of outpatient programs at its 20-acre campus in a residential area of Denver. Specialty programs include the Center for Trauma and Dissociation and an Eating Disorders Program.

Colorado Mental Health Institute at Fort Logan
3520 W. Oxford Ave. • (303) 761-0220

This is the state psychiatric hospital, charged with providing treatment and services for the mentally ill. It was founded in 1960 and was rather revolutionary for its time as a completely open facility with no locked units. Areas of specialty fall in three treatment divisions: children/adolescents, adult psychiatry and geriatrics. An inpatient-only facility with 222 inpatient and 76 residential beds, this hospital is based on a treatment team approach — a patient's team consists of a psychiatrist, a psychologist, a social worker, psychiatric nurses and mental-health clinicians. The team also has special education teachers for children and adolescents.

Comitis Crisis Center
9840 E. 17 St., Aurora • (303) 343-9890

This privately owned nonprofit is in its 27th year of serving youth awaiting placement into a permanent residential home. This is a short-term residential care facility with a small emergency housing area for homeless kids. Comitis helps get people off the streets and into low-income housing. Its main mission is to care for runaway and throwaway kids.

Adams County Mental Health Center
4371 E. 72nd Ave., Commerce City • (303) 287-8001

Founded in 1957, this center has been serving Adams County residents for emergency and outpatient mental health needs. About 4,000 people a year receive treatment for such things as family preservation, youth needs and vocational counseling. The center also has a school for kids preschool through 18 and five outpatient offices in the Adams County area.

Aurora Community Mental Health Center
14301 E. Hampden Ave., Aurora • (303) 693-9500

Around 15,000 people a year receive help from this center's 19 Denver-area locations. Services include counseling for depression, older adults, divorce, parenting, drugs and alcohol and group therapies. Also offered are residential services from overnight to long-term adjustments.

Denver Alcohol, Drug & Psychiatric Care Emergency
770 Bannock St. • (303) 436-6266

This is the emergency psychiatric facility for Denver Health Medical Center. The center is open 24 hours to serve people who come to Denver General Hospital and are referred for a variety of mental health reasons, including drug and alcohol abuse and crisis situations.

Jefferson Center for Mental Health
5265 Vance St., Arvada • (303) 425-0300

Business at the private, nonprofit Jefferson Center has been so brisk in recent years that the center has expanded across the street to make room. A wide variety of mental health services are offered, including counselors in schools, an older adult program, several residential areas for inpatient services and 24-hour emergency services. In all, Jefferson Center operates 14 satellite locations in Jefferson, Gilpin and Clear Creek counties.

Alternative and Holistic Health

The alternative health scene is growing and gaining notice — and credibility — in Greater Denver. In fact, Denver has more professionals than most comparably sized cities. And nearby Boulder is well known for its array of alternative healers.

Colorado's alternative health doctors got a boost in 1997 when the State Legislature passed a law protecting the ability of M.D.s to do business by prohibiting the state medical board from sanctioning doctors merely for practicing alternative medicine. The stamp of credibility was seen as a sign from lawmakers that alternative medicine is a viable option for thousands of people across the state.

Alternative medicine is generally defined as anything outside the mainstream of Western medicine. Services generally include herbology, acupuncture, massage, counseling, hypnotherapy, nutrition, hydrotherapy, reflexology, homeopathy and chiropractics. Holistic is an approach to healing that views the patient as a whole being with a diverse life and range of reasons for ill-health. Holistic practitioners look for the interconnections of a person's health — not just the source of one given problem.

Colorado doesn't have any central listing of alternative practitioners, nor is there a Yellow Pages listing under "Alternative." But there is a Yellow Pages section under "Holistic Practitioners" with several listings, and practitioners tend to be a close-knit group with knowledge of each other's expertise. People in search of recommendations can try the ones listed, or can contact one of the seasoned pros at local Alfalfa's and Wild Oats markets, grocery stores known for vast offerings of natural foods, vitamins, medicines and friendly staffs who dispense advice on holistic health. The stores also are a good source of publications, from national magazines to local advertising supplements, on alternative healing.

As with many states, Colorado has varying requirements for alternative practitioners. Depending on the specialty, one may be required to be licensed, certified or registered. The following listings are recommended as organizations committed to professionalism and overall health.

Bodymind Healing Arts
217 E. 7th Ave. • (303) 831-1339

This group of holistic practitioners puts out a free quarterly newsletter offering tips on everything from relaxation to skin care to prenatal massage. The newsletter, available by calling the office, is a nice introduction to the center's professional staff members trained in the art of healing the natural way. All are educated and meet state requirements in such areas as acupuncture, herbs, massage, hypnosis, counseling and skin care. Check the office for a calendar of interesting seminars and events designed to boost your health.

Frontier Medical Institute
2801 Youngfield St., Ste. 117, Lakewood
• (303) 233-4247

Two medical doctors and a nutritionist specialize in treating patients with chronic illnesses who've tried everything and been failed by conventional medicine. Special interests include vascular disease and atherosclerosis. Treatments include such things as diet and nutrition, intravenous therapies and homeopathy.

East West Health Centers Inc.
6558 S. Yosemite Cir., Greenwood Village
• (303) 694-5757

This center includes more than 20 practitioners, including an internist and family physician, with both Eastern and Western specialties. Western services include family and sports medicine, preventative medicine and geriatric care, physical therapy, counseling and an OB-GYN. Eastern offerings include acupuncture, herbology, naturopathy, chiropractics, massage, Rolfing, nutrition education, exercise prescription and stress management.

American WholeHealth
5161 E. Arapahoe Rd., Littleton
• (303) 694-2626

This is a physician-supervised holistic health center that offers a broad range of services for kids through seniors. A family practice physician works with the staff that includes an acupuncturist, chiropractor, massage therapist and a nutritional therapist.

Retirement

Forget Wednesday night bingo and mashed potatoes in a dingy dining room. Today's retirement homes are called communities for a reason: they offer residents a place to recreate, socialize and thrive.

Denver's offerings are no exception to the standard that retirement communities should be enticing to those who call them home. Brochures are more likely to sound like a pitch for a vacation than a place to grow old. Auditoriums, fitness centers, restaurants and swimming pools are only a few of the amenities. And with the older generation getting stronger and more prevalent — Denver's 60-and-older population is expected to climb 13 percent by 2013 — housing options are getting better.

Greater Denver isn't exactly a retirement mecca on par with Arizona or Florida. But its sunny, mild climate (belied by our rare but news-making blizzards) has lured thousands over the years, including seniors who want to be closer to relatives or who end their careers in colorful Colorado.

The City and County of Denver has by far the greatest number of independent and assisted-living facilities for seniors in the area, but when you seek word-of-mouth recommendations, Denver's outlying areas, and especially the suburban counties, tend to get the most praise. That may not be fair to Denver's senior communities. It may simply say more about life being more difficult for the elderly in an urban setting.

There are a variety of information sources to aid your decision. Referral agencies such as **Elderly Housing Choices**, (303) 831-4046, are a good place to start. Elderly Housing Choices is part of a nonprofit organization known as Community Housing Services Inc. It provides free housing referrals to use as a start in comparing costs, availability and other factors. Another good one is **Senior Housing Options**, (303) 595-4464, a nonprofit corporation that owns and/or manages 16 assisted-living properties and HUD-subsidized properties.

You can do your own word-of-mouth research by asking other seniors you meet in groups, such as the **American Association of Retired Persons**, which has an office in Denver, (303) 830-2277, and the **Association for Senior Citizens**, (303) 455-9642. The **Aging Services Division of the Denver Regional Council of Governments**, (303) 480-6734, offers information and referral services for seniors, as well as a Nursing Home Ombudsman Program. You can hobnob with seniors at any of Greater Denver's numerous senior centers. For other senior tips as well as just a lot of good ideas about enjoying the area, you might take a look at *Uniquely Denver: A Discovery Guide to the Mile High City For Those Over 50*, written by Virginia Brey and published by American Source Books, Lakewood, Colorado. You might also get a copy of *The Denver Business Journal Top 255 Lists*, an annual publication of *The Denver Business Journal*, (303) 837-3500. We've mentioned it before as a great resource for all kinds of area information. One of its lists ranks the top 25 retirement communities.

And don't forget *The Beacon Review*. This is Greater Denver's biweekly newspaper for "the better side of 40." It has an annual listing of retirement communities, but it's also a great resource for all kinds of senior news and issues in the area. You can pick it up for free at King Soopers stores as well as at various banks, restaurants, senior centers and recreation centers in the five-county area. If you can't find it, call *The Beacon Review* at (303) 692-8940.

Once you know what part of Greater Denver you'd like to live in and have some communities in mind, call their sales offices for brochures and information packages. Then check them out in person. Arriving around meal time gives you a sense of the staff and how well it relates to residents. Of course, most communities have marketing representatives eager to give guided tours.

Vital to picking the right place is the surrounding neighborhood: whether it's clean, pleasant and quiet; whether there are parks and/or shopping within walking distance; and whether the surroundings are congenial to the elderly. Greater Denver's four-lane traffic arteries such as Wadsworth Boulevard can be tough to negotiate, even for speed-walking teenagers. A more docile setting might be best for those with difficulties moving around.

The following entries represent the more-talked-about examples of retirement communities in Greater Denver. But by no means is the list comprehensive or meant to suggest other places aren't equally good. We have tended to look specifically at places with independent and/or assisted living in which seniors have their own homes or apartments. These are the mid-range of a spectrum of senior living and care options ranging from nursing homes to prestigious single-family developments. Assisted living simply means that assistance is available for such needs as medication reminders; help with dressing, grooming and bathing; close-by medical and health monitoring; laundry; in-apartment meal services; and rehabilitation programs. Typically, both independent and assisted-living units have call buttons at strategic locations, so residents can summon help if needed.

Overall, these senior living communities resemble moderate to upscale apartments or condominiums. The difference is in the community feel, which places more emphasis on communal dining and gathering areas, shared activities and services. Typically, at least one meal is included in rent, although this may vary. Housekeeping is a fairly standard service. Virtually every community listed here offers a calendar of social activities; many have their own newsletters; and all of them have their own transportation services to area shopping and other attractions. Residents are likely to have their own garage or carport space and storage lockers. Perhaps best of all: someone else cleans the bathroom and does the dishes!

Canterbury Gardens
11265 E. Mississippi Ave., Aurora
• (303) 341-1412

Canterbury Gardens was the first independent- and assisted-living community for seniors in Aurora when it opened in the late 1970s, and some of the pioneer residents are still there. The Gardens consists of two-story structures built around two ponds in a landscaped courtyard with a gazebo. This community actually consists of two sections: Canterbury Gardens, the independent-living section, and The Inn at Canterbury Gardens, which is assisted-living. Independent-living units are one- and two-bedroom apartments with up to two bathrooms; assisted-living units are studios. Some units have private patios or balconies.

Canterbury is owned and operated by Crossings Corporation of Tacoma, Washington, a company that specializes in developing and managing retirement communities. Canterbury includes a fireside lounge, library, TV and movie lounge, a beauty/barber shop, a full-service dining room with soup and salad bar, private dining, complimentary van service for scheduled trips, an ice cream shop, guest apartments and a hobby and crafts room. Monthly independent-living rent for a single person ranges from $795 to $1,610; assisted-living, $1,065 to $1,950.

Cherry Creek Retirement Village
14555 E. Hampden Ave., Aurora
• (303) 693-0200

Cherry Creek has a nice location in a residential neighborhood and across the street from Aurora's public Meadow Hills Golf Course. The village is in a three-story, buff-colored building with a large circular drive and two atriums for relaxing and entertaining.

Some apartments have patios or balconies. Every unit has a window over the kitchen sink that looks out into one of the halls. Monthly rent — from $800 for a studio to $1,760 for a two-bedroom deluxe apartment — covers amenities ranging from continental breakfast and weekly housekeeping to excursions. Meals and other amenities are available at a nominal charge. The Village has card and game rooms, an exercise room, library, country store, billiards, an arts and crafts area, restaurant-style dining and a private dining room. Independent and assisted living are provided. Cherry Creek Retirement Village is owned by Lifecare Centers of America, Cleveland, Tennessee.

The Courtyard at Lakewood
7100 W. 13th Ave., Lakewood
• (303) 239-0740

Three blocks east of Wadsworth Boulevard and a couple blocks south of Colfax Avenue in Lakewood, the Courtyard is in a quiet residential neighborhood. Every apartment in the three-story building has a view of the center courtyard, where there are flowers, rock gardens and a pond. The Courtyard is managed by two husband-and-wife teams who live on the premises.

Beyond the living quarters, the Courtyard's amenities include a giant-screen TV room, large kitchen for group activities, beauty shop, library, billiards areas and a spa. Single-occupancy units range from $1,250 to $1,750 per month. The Courtyard is owned by Holiday Retirement Corporation.

Dayton Place
1950 S. Dayton St., Aurora • (303) 751-5150

Dayton Place is right on the western edge of the City of Aurora's south side, just off Parker Road, a major thoroughfare that runs northwest to Denver and southeast past the Cherry Creek Reservoir State Recreation Area. Dayton is a three-story complex with an open feel, in part due to its suburban location and perhaps in part due to its setback on large grounds with meandering walkways, gardens and outdoor patios. Dayton Place has a general store, chapel, beauty and barber shop,

TV lounges, a billiards room and a cards and activities room.

Apartments range from $1,540 to $1,840 per month for assisted living. Independent living ranges from $1,195 to $1,620. Dayton Place is owned by CMD Corporation.

Heritage Club
2020 S. Monroe St. • (303) 756-0025

Heritage Club has a good reputation for elegant living at affordable prices. The apartments are luxurious. The dining room really looks like something in an upscale downtown restaurant with a menu to match, and there's a private dining room for special occasions. Heritage Club has a private library, exercise room with whirlpool and spa, a country store and ice cream parlor, billiards room, a cards and games room, an arts and crafts studio and a beauty and barber shop plus shuffleboard, a putting green and horseshoes pit. The bay windows and balconies are nice features, and the community is in the University Park neighborhood, a pleasant part of the city southwest of Colorado Boulevard's intersection with Interstate 25.

Heritage Club is managed by American Retirement Corporation of Brentwood, Tennessee. It has both assisted- and independent-living options, ranging from $2,255 to $3,000 and $1,220 to $3,985 a month, respectively.

Meridian
10695 W. 17th Ave., Westland
• (303) 232-7100
1805 S. Balsam St., Lakewood
• (303) 980-5500
9555 W. 59th Ave., Arvada
• (303) 425-1900
3455 S. Corona St., Englewood
• (303) 761-0300

Denver's western suburbs in Jefferson County have the largest number of retirement communities. One of the most extensive retirement-residence organizations that gets mentioned in a positive light is Meridian, which has four retirement communities in Greater Denver. All of them are owned by LeGan Corporation, a Denver company that also owns a Meridian in Boulder. Each is managed independently, but all are essentially the same: nicely appointed buildings on campus-like settings, with elegant interiors and formal furniture. The only major difference is that the Balsam Avenue Lakewood Meridian and the Englewood Meridian have nursing-home sections, while the other two have independent and assisted living only.

Monthly rents range from $1,780 to $3,550 for the high-end, two-bedroom apartment at the Englewood Meridian; $1,535 to $1,955 at the Arvada Meridian; $1,670 to $2,550 at the Lakewood Meridian; and $1,535 to $1,955 at the Westland Meridian.

www.insiders.com
See this and many other
Insiders' Guide®
destinations online.
Visit us today!

Park Place
111 Emerson St. • (303) 744-1950

In the heart of Denver, this 18-story independent- and assisted-living facility resembles one of those quiet, elegant hotels that get known by word-of-mouth. Its elegance is immediately apparent in the dark wood and rich upholstery of the lobby, lounge and formal dining room, and the atmosphere is maintained throughout. It's next to Hungarian Freedom Park on the south side of Speer Boulevard, south of Denver's downtown and not far from the Cherry Creek shopping area. The Cherry Creek greenbelt and its pedestrian/bicycle path runs along Speer Boulevard out front. Park Place has an indoor swimming pool with a hot tub and exercise room plus a convenience store, beauty and barber shop, library, card lounge, patio dining area and auditorium.

This community doesn't have a rate sheet because the units are quite individualized, but rents range from $1,750 to $3,950 per month and include one meal per day. Park Place is owned and managed by American Retirement Corporation, Brentwood, Tennessee.

Porter Place
1001 E. Yale Ave. • (303) 871-9200

Porter Place is on the campus of PorterCare Hospital in Denver's University Park neighborhood on the northernmost edge of Englewood. In addition to independent and assisted living (with studio, one-bedroom and two-bedroom apartments), it offers small studio apartments at $39 per day for visiting family and friends of residents. Porter Place is affiliated with PorterCare Hospital, Centura Health and PorterCare Hospital-Littleton, but that doesn't mean it looks like a medical facility. The interiors are lovely, from the grand piano and high ceilings of the lobby to the pleasant tranquility of the library. There are flower gardens and outdoor patios, a chapel, activity rooms, a gift shop, beauty and barber shop, big-screen TV room, parlor, card room and craft room. And residents have access to the hospital's Porter Health Club. A recently completed addition boosted the number of apartments to 181 and added a 250-seat auditorium. Single-occupancy prices range from $1,195 to $1,845 monthly; for doubles, add $400 a month.

Shalom Park Cottages and Apartments
14800 E. Bellevue Dr., Aurora
• (303) 680-5000

One of Greater Denver's newest retirement additions is Shalom Park Cottages and Apartments. The 35-acre park offers residents lovely grounds to mill around on as well as an in-house activity department to keep them entertained. There are a total of 104 units, including 44 patio homes and 60 apartments. Any of the 104 units can be assisted- or independent-living, depending on the needs of the occupants. Two-bedroom patio homes start at $1,700 a month, one-bedroom apartments start at $1,200, and two-bedrooms begin at $1,450.

INSIDERS' TIP

Check the fine print when looking for a retirement home. Some communities require long-term leases and large down payments, while others are month-to-month. Decide what's best for you, then take the time to ask good questions.

Springwood
6550 Yank Way, Arvada • (303) 424-6550

The Springwood Retirement Community is a "beautiful facility," and that's according to an administrator of a competing retirement community. It's just off the Yankee Doodle Park in a nice residential section of Arvada. Facilities and services include a full-time social director, dining room, maid service, laundry and dry cleaning, a general store, library, chapel, hair salon, game room and exercise facility. Lutheran Medical Center provides input to Springwood's healthcare and health-promoting activities.

Springwood offers a variety of one-and two-bedroom apartments, with two-way intercom and emergency buzzers, ranging from $1,340 to $1,940 per month for single occupancy, with $250 extra for double occupancy. Springwood also offers assisted living at its Nightingale Suites, which range from $1,595 to $2,295 per month for single occupancy. The cottages at Springwood are 1,100-square-foot residences built on a private cul-de-sac at Springwood's campus. Each includes a foyer, living room, dining room, covered patio, master bedroom with its own bath and oversized walk-in closet, a guest bedroom, second bathroom, laundry/utility room and attached garage. The cottages cost $1,375 per month for one person; $1,525 for two.

Harvard Square Retirement Community
10200 E. Harvard Ave. • (303) 696-0622

Harvard Square's interiors are bright and open yet reminiscent of the club spaces in an Ivy League university, with dark wood and formal, Old World style. The exterior and grounds — overlooked by a second-story deck — also exude a country club air. Harvard Square is in the northwest corner of Denver's Hampden Heights neighborhood, just west of Aurora near the pleasant green spaces of Babi Yar Park and the private Los Verdes Golf Club. Although it's basically an independent-living community, it has a formal Assisted Living Program managed by a professional social worker with nursing support. Under the same roof, Harvard Square also includes a dining room, beauty and barber shop, game room, library and multipurpose room. Apartments range from $995

Retirement communities offer classes and hobby areas.

to $1,785 per month, with assisted-living plans running an additional $450 to $550 per month.

Villas at Sunny Acres
2501 W. 104th Ave., Thornton
• (303) 452-4181

Perhaps the most oft-recommended retirement community by word-of-mouth, the Villas at Sunny Acres is a large facility on a campus-like setting just south of Stonehocker Park in Thornton. The northern suburbs are quiet areas with good mountain views and a lot of remaining open space, and the Villas' landscaped grounds include two fishing lakes as well as gardening areas for residents. To that Sunny Acres adds amenities including home healthcare, 10 libraries, a 3,000-square-foot fitness center, a whirlpool, pool tables, a woodworking and carpentry shop, lounges, dining rooms including a restaurant, a convenience store and beauty and barber shops.

Residents at the Villas pay monthly rent ranging from $850 for one to $1,935 for two. Or they may choose the unique Life Care package, which requires an entry fee starting at $39,000 for one person in addition to a monthly service fee ranging from $705 for one to $2,250 for two. The Life Care entry fee prepays for all future long- and short-term nursing care.

Today, the economy has rebounded, and buyers, sellers and even Realtors are scratching their heads over rising property values.

Neighborhoods and Real Estate

A line charting Denver homes sales over the years looks like a wave — up, down, up, down, up, down. These days the wave is riding high. Denver's housing market historically mirrors the state's "boom/bust" economy. In the late 1980s, for example, Denver was still recovering from a crash in the oil business, and real estate was seemingly impossible to give away. Today, the economy has rebounded, and buyers, sellers and even Realtors are scratching their heads over rising property values. The big — and unfortunate — story in Denver real estate is skyrocketing costs. The recent boom began in 1991 as the economy began its recovery and hasn't slowed since. What used to be an affordable locale to buy a home has now joined the ranks of the nation's most expensive housing markets. Today, home sales continue their rise, posting new record sales and prices seemingly every month. The first quarter of 1999 was strong, bolstered by low interest rates and consumer confidence, according to the Denver Board of Realtors.

The big problem in Greater Denver is the lack of affordable housing (less than $120,000). The average price of a single-family home in Denver shot to $201,134 in February of 1999 — pricing many working-class families out of the market. All for-sale homes, including single-family, condominiums and townhomes, sold in February 1999 reached a new average high of $182,547 — 10 percent more than 1998. Real estate experts predict 1999 will be record-setting year. "It's an incredibly hot market for Denver real estate," Eileen Pettijohn, broker associate at Fuller Towne and Country, told *The Denver Post*. "All of the amenities are here in this state — people want to relocate here."

As prices climb, housing inventory remains low: 9,000 units in the six-county metropolitan region compared to a normal average of 12,000 units.

For a cursory look at Denver's real estate market, turn to the Internet where you can find information on prices, neighborhoods, agents and photos of properties. One caveat: since homes sell so quickly in Denver, properties listed often are sold or under contract. Still, it's an easy way to scan listings.

If what you seek is the offbeat, then "cohousing" might be for you. Specially planned communities that house residents in individual homes but bring them together in jointly owned kitchens, greenhouses, nursery schools, gardens and workshops can be found in at least eight Colorado locations. Closest to the city are two near Boulder and one in Golden. For more information, call (303) 413-8252. Some of Denver's neighborhoods are hotter and more expensive than others. Cherry Creek North, in the shadow of Denver's No. 1 tourist attraction, Cherry Creek Shopping Center, is booming. Tiny, crackerbox houses once occupied by working-class families are being bought, demolished and replaced with expensive townhomes and rowhouses fashioned in the old, East Coast style. Price tags rarely dip below $350,000 and easily climb as high as $1.2 million. (Walking distance to Saks Fifth Avenue has its price.)

Loft living is another hotter-than-hot trend. In the late '80s, developers began transforming rundown warehouses into empty, but very stylish, loft shells for as low as $90,000. You supplied the walls, kitchen, etc. Today's urban palaces command triple digits that reach $950,000, but most cost around $350,000.

New home sales also remain strong, though they've cooled a bit. The vast majority of the new housing market is in the suburbs, where land is plentiful, and opposition to development is minimal. New development in Denver tends to be small, exclusive infill projects on vacant lots.

Two major redevelopment projects currently are being built. Stapleton Airport, which was replaced by Denver International Airport, and Lowry Air Force Base, which was closed by the federal government, will be redeveloped to include a "new urbanism" mix of residential homes, parks, open space and retail. Lowry's redevelopment is ahead of schedule and popular with homebuyers; Stapleton is still mired in planning but is expected to break ground soon.

The corner grocery store has made a strong comeback in Denver and is starting to show up in new development. A housing project outside of Longmont features homes with Victorian Era styling and the amenities of days past. Other developers are watching sales closely to see if buyers will pay more for detailing and a city feel without the city problems. The redevelopment of the former Elitch Gardens site in northwest Denver will incorporate new urbanism concepts. Presales of single and multi-family homes and townhomes began in early 1999.

A full picture of Denver's residential scene, from home prices to ambiance, would require a book much larger than our entire guide. There are more than 70 officially designated neighborhoods in the City and County of Denver alone, and hundreds more in surrounding counties. Nonetheless, we've scanned several to give you an idea of Greater Denver's residential fabric.

The most important factor to remember is that prices within neighborhoods can vary greatly. In Capitol Hill, for instance, a lovely $80,000 Victorian condo can be a mere three blocks from a mansion that commands $800,000. Because "average" prices aren't always an accurate reflection of values, we've also given a range of low to high. Prices reflect activity in the first quarter of 1999.

Neighborhoods

Denver

As Greater Denver's urban center, the City and County of Denver covers the widest range of neighborhood types and home prices, from humble to haughty. The most general statement we can make, aside from highlighting some of Denver's more well-known neighborhoods, is that you can find any level of living you want in the City and County of Denver, from rural ranches to downtown highrises.

Downtown Denver includes the Union Station area on the north, the Auraria neighborhood, the Civic Center area on the southwest and reaches east to Broadway, where it borders the North Capitol Hill and Capitol Hill neighborhoods. This is where you live if you like the downtown lifestyle; and here you almost certainly live in a condo.

Lower Downtown, the red-brick historic area between the central business district and Union Station and the Central Platte Valley, is particularly popular of late. LoDo, as Denverites call it, is hot owing largely to the revitalization of the Central Platte Valley in general and the rise of baseball's Coors Field in particular.

Downtown Denver is très chic, but an anomaly as far as residential opportunities. Condo prices are high, and single-family homes are virtually nonexistent.

The **Uptown** neighborhood, just east of downtown and centered around 17th Avenue, called "restaurant row" for its hip dining spots, is experiencing a revival that includes several new infill projects. Most notable here are three-story, statuesque row houses, mixed with grand mansions that have been turned into law offices, graphic arts studios and single-family homes. The feel is urban elegance. Prices haven't skyrocketed because of its proximity to East Colfax Avenue, known for sleaze and crime. Still, new rowhouse developments command between $180,000 and $400,000.

Just east of downtown Denver, you'll find historic neighborhoods untouched by the revitalization boom shaking Lower Downtown.

North Capitol Hill and **Capitol Hill**, bounded roughly by 20th and Sixth avenues, Clarkson Street and Broadway, were among the first of Denver's housing developments in the 1800s. While those in the working class were making their homes down by the river and in other outlying sections, the aristocrats were populating this area east and upslope from the business district. Here you find most of the historic mansion tours, and a stretch of Grant Street once known as "Millionaires Row." In recent years, people have come to appreciate the historic charm of the area and its accessibility by foot to downtown. Many of Capitol Hill's mansions have been converted to condominiums, offices and bed and breakfast inns, and there are a lot of cultural and fine-dining opportunities close by. Sales of Capitol Hill houses in 1999 averaged $450,000. The same condos that sold for less than $30,000 in the early '90s sold for closer to $80,000 in 1999. The average price was around $100,000 in 1999.

Because of Capitol Hill's overblown reputation for crime, many prefer to live farther east in the Cheesman Park or City Park West neighborhoods. The **Cheesman Park** neighborhood, bounded by University Boulevard and Clarkson Street, Colfax and Sixth avenues, surrounds one of Denver's finer parks, Cheesman Park, and borders one of the city's finest amenities, the Denver Botanic Gardens. Cheesman Park neighborhood contains two historic districts and has a feel of urban gentility with lots of pedestrians, coffee shops and neighborhood gathering spots.

Things start to get more expensive as you move south of Cheesman. Still relatively reasonable is **City Park West**, an urban treasure trove of historic homes going back to Denver's silver boom of 1880 to 1893. Bounded by Clarkson Street, University Boulevard and Colfax and 23rd avenues, it's located between North Capitol Hill and City Park, Denver's largest central park, containing the Denver Zoo and the Denver Museum of Natural History.

It's a moderate walk from the Botanic Gardens, a reasonable walk from downtown, and it has a hospital complex on its northern edge. The 17th Avenue strip of fine restaurants and entertainment runs right through it.

Washington Park is Denver's other big, well-known public green space, and the **Washington Park** neighborhood is one of Denver's most popular living areas. It has a lot of homes built in the early to mid-1900s, with 1999 prices averaging $300, 000. It's convenient to transportation as well, bordering on I-25 to the south and Colorado Boulevard to the east. The Denver Country Club is just north of it, where homes average $650,000 but range beyond $2 million.

Just east of the Denver Country Club is fashionable **Cherry Creek**. Bounded by University Avenue and Colorado Boulevard, Sixth and Alameda avenues, it's an area of large to moderate-size homes, expensive condos and shopping nirvana. It's Greater Denver's premier retail and arts area (see our Shopping chapter). It has a gracious ambiance and is a fun place to visit and shop. Its residences are highly sought-after. Residential sales average $500,000 and range well over $1 million.

Directly east of Cherry Creek is **Hilltop**, another prestigious living area of well-cared-for streets adjacent to the major north/south corridor of Colorado Boulevard. Home sales in Hilltop range from $1755,000 to $1.5 million. **Park Hill**, to the north, just west of City Park, is an area of handsome old homes and large, mature trees. Residential prices average $250,000.

One area that has become particularly interesting of late is the area known as **Far Northeast Denver**. These neighborhoods stand out not only geographically but also as a focus of growth expected as a result of the new airport.

Montbello and **Green Valley Ranch** are established, quiet neighborhoods, although there's been some complaining about noise since the new Denver International Airport opened. The oldest home in Montbello is about 30 years old, and the oldest home in Green Valley Ranch is about 10 years old. These are low-crime areas with panoramic views of the mountains, room for another 9,400 dwellings and a lot of open space. Yet, they're still the extreme edge of Denver's urban fabric, places where residents can take a walk and see a deer or an eagle in flight and maybe even hear coyotes howling at night.

Gateway, between Montbello and Green Valley Ranch and directly bordering the new airport on the north, is where Denver planners envision big-time development. Already launched are the beginning stages of a planned $1 billion Denver International Business Center just a few miles from the terminal. The local media has referred to the Gateway as "our first 21st Century neighborhood," and represented it as a future community of 65,000 people with strong economic links to the airport. Although it was annexed by Denver to link the city with the airport, it's not yet officially a neighborhood. Denver planners envision it as a new employment area on the level of downtown Denver and the Denver Tech Center, which is only one-sixth the size of Gateway.

Southeast Denver is a popular area with a variety of housing options. In general houses tend to be more expensive and newer than their northwest counterparts. However, that doesn't necessarily mean homes are bigger. Southeast Denver offers anything from two-bedroom tiny frame homes on up. Neighborhoods such as Southmoor Park offer quiet residential living with plenty of trees and nearby parks. There also are plenty of upscale apartment, condo and townhome choices.

We've given a lot of mention here to the central and eastern parts of Denver, perhaps more than is fair. But this is where the oldest neighborhoods, the big-name neighborhoods and the well-known neighborhoods are.

INSIDERS' TIP

In the Denver-area real estate market, homes, frequently sell for at or above the asking price. At best, bargaining is reserved for the over-priced or run-down homes. In general, your dollar buys a lot more square footage, and often lot size, in the suburbs.

A lot of people, however, prefer the west side of the city. It's the smaller part of the city, closer to the mountains and generally has a feeling of being near to its country roots.

Northwestern Denver is the city's smallest quadrant, bounded by W. Colfax Avenue on the south and 52nd Avenue on the north, Sheridan Boulevard on the west and the South Platte River on the east. The **Highland** and **Jefferson Park** neighborhoods, stretching west from the high ground above the South Platte, were where Denver put its first residential neighborhoods west of the South Platte. Around the turn of the century, there was a large ethnic Italian neighborhood here. Descendants of truck farmers in what is now the western suburbs still tell of taking their produce downtown for delivery to Italian produce salesmen who would sell their wares in the streets. These neighborhoods now have a rich ethnic mix and some fine restaurants, including Latin American and Vietnamese establishments. This neighborhood is one of the few where buyers can still find a bargain, but they'll have to be willing to wait out the revival of their surroundings as the neighborhood continues to improve.

Sloan Lake, **West Highland**, **Berkeley** and **Regis** are some of the neighborhoods to the west that are pleasantly equipped with quiet streets and the greenery of lawns and parks around small lakes. These northwestern neighborhoods are as old as a lot of east Denver neighborhoods between downtown and Colorado Boulevard, but they're across the river, up the hill and over the ridge from the central city. The feeling here is apart from the urban bustle.

Southwest Denver is larger, more extensive and more dynamic than the west side of the city. Certainly, it has its older neighborhoods close in, such as **Val Verde** and **Sun Valley**. Val Verde, Spanish for "green valley," was a separate town established in 1873 and annexed into Denver in 1902. Bordered by Sixth and Alameda avenues, the South Platte River and Federal Boulevard, it is today an ethnically diverse neighborhood with a large industrial and warehousing base. As you move southwest toward southern **Lakewood**, however, you get a sensation of increasingly newer urban landscape. Not that there haven't been

homes in this area since the 1800s, of course, just that it wasn't developed as early and extensively as the northwest.

One of Denver's few areas where major new development is taking place is the **Marston** neighborhood that juts down into unincorporated Jefferson County on southwest Denver's farthest southwestern point. Near Marston Reservoir you'll find particularly high-quality residential living. Generally, however, southwest Denver vies with northwest Denver for the city's lowest overall housing prices, and a much larger percentage of its population consists of married couples and families.

Adams County

Adams County is often viewed as the area's most blue-collar, working-class county, and that has a lot to do with the heavy industry and warehousing around Commerce City, northeastern Denver and the I-76 corridor leading northeast. **Commerce City**, Adams County's industrial/warehousing heartland, where twice as many people work as live, certainly has some of the county's lowest housing prices.

One of the first things you may notice in driving north on I-25 to Thornton, Westminster and Northglenn is a sensation of climbing to higher ground. **Federal Heights**, a community between Westminster and Thornton, is well-named. From here you're actually looking down at the tops of downtown Denver's highest buildings. Much of this northern area seems to be on high ground, and since there is little in the way of high-rise buildings, Denver's northern suburbs have some of the grandest views of the Rockies.

Westminster is Greater Denver's closest northside city to the mountains. Westminster spreads all over the place, so it isn't easily categorized. It's roughly centered around the Westminster Mall just off U.S. Highway 36, the Boulder Turnpike, at 88th Avenue. To the west, 88th Avenue contains the most extensive complexes of shopping and shopping centers on Greater Denver's north side. To the north, there are attractive housing developments clustered and scattered through a lot of open country with big-sky views. Another arm of Westminster protrudes west to wrap around two sides of Standley Lake, one of Greater Denver's best water recreation resources, on the edge of unincorporated Jefferson County. Westminster has lots of good, upscale townhomes and middle-class neighborhoods as well as established areas with mature trees and big lots. The average low in 1998 was $125,000 and the average high was $250,000.

Westminster's eastern half, near **Northglenn** and **Thornton**, is where you'll find the most condo activity, although availability is limited compared with Denver, Arapahoe and Jefferson counties.

Just north of Westminster, mostly in Boulder County but with a good quarter of its population in Adams County and a smaller portion in Jefferson County, is the City of **Broomfield**. Originally a residential community, it's fast becoming a business development area thanks to its strategic position between Boulder and Greater Denver and the rampant development of business and industrial parks along U.S. Highway 36. Broomfield is popular because it still retains its own identity, separate from Greater Denver, with enduring, solid 1950s brick ranches. This type of living is attractive to people who work in Denver and Boulder and want more affordable living. Broomfield's average price is climbing along with closer-in locales; it now averages over $200,000.

The **North Suburban Central** area, between I-25 on the west and the South Platte River on the east, Denver on the south and 144th Avenue on the north, contains the bulk of the City of Thornton, which has a moderate- to lower-income population and a suburban feel. Some new developments, such as **Hunter's Glen** and **Thorn Creek**, surround golf courses and are more upscale. But the mid-1970s two-story homes still dominate Thornton. Because of its outlying location, prices here haven't climbed as much as elsewhere. Average low is $130,000, and average high is $200,000.

Brighton, the Adams County seat to the northeast, is seeing a lot of growth but still has the benefit of a small-town, rural atmosphere within an easy, 15-mile commuting distance to Denver. Here you'll find homes with acreages and space for horses. Some new developments have a minimum 35-acre requirement. Home prices are moderate, with an average low of $130,000 and an average high of $275,000.

Southeast of Commerce City, the City of **Aurora** has its industrial centers in its northern Adams County side, along the I-70 corridor near the new Denver International Airport. Here in north Aurora, also called "Old Aurora," homes are among Adams County's least expensive, ranging from $80,000 to $300,000.

Arapahoe County

Most of the City of Aurora lies in Arapahoe County. This is where the bulk of the city's office and research and development centers are found. It's also where the homes are higher priced, ranging from $85,000 to $650,000 and averaging $195,000. A typical, moderately priced Aurora development is **Tollgate**, where the homes are new, the neighborhood is clean, and the lawns are well-manicured. The area is close to the Denver Tech Center business area on the south and is well-connected north/south by I-225 to both I-70 and I-25.

Aurora's population is young, with a median age of 31 years. The city has always suffered from a lack of identity, due primarily to its connection to Denver. It's also known for its flat landscape and lack of mature trees, prompting the nickname "Saudi Aurora." But with a good supply of affordable housing, Aurora is popular with young families looking for starter homes or wanting more room for less money.

The region known among Realtors as the

Cherry Creek is one of Denver's most popular neighborhoods.

Suburban Southeast, roughly defined by the Arapahoe County Line, County Line Road on the south and Aurora on the north, contains most of the region's most expensive properties. The northwestern segment contains about half of Greenwood Village and most of Cherry Hills Village.

The bulk of this area lies in unincorporated Arapahoe County east, west and north of Centennial Airport. It includes the Denver Tech Center. Home prices here tend to be skewed rather dramatically upward by prestige pockets such as **Cherry Hills Village**, one of Greater Denver's most upscale communities with residences averaging $1.5 million and ranging from $400,000 to $3.5 million. Cherry Hills Village, for example, has virtually no commercial base, and the only nonresidential features are two private schools and the Cherry Hills and Glenmoor country clubs. **Greenwood Village**, just south of Cherry Hills, wrapping under the Denver Tech Center and up its eastern side, is another highly desired living area with distinctive custom homes. Many are on large lots and are tucked away from the street. Prices range from $450,000 to $1.9 million.

Move a little to the west, and you'll find the area directly below the City of Denver known as the **South Suburban Central** region, which includes the cities of **Littleton**, **Englewood**, about half of Greenwood Village and a substantial patch of unincorporated Jefferson County between Greenwood Village and County Line Road, Littleton and I-25.

The unincorporated part of South Suburban Central is generally an area of clean, new neighborhoods with the kind of convoluted street patterns that make life confusing for pizza deliverers but peaceful for residents. It has a country feel, being the last neighborhood south of Denver before you arrive at Douglas County. There are some good shopping complexes along County Line Road, including the new Park Meadows; the Denver Tech Center is just up I-25; and C-470 (part of this is a toll road) provides fast access west and up to I-70 near Golden.

The City of **Littleton** grew from an old downtown established in 1890 on what is now its northwestern edge along the South Platte River. It still has that old, traditional community atmosphere with ranch homes on big lots, but the city also has its newer areas reaching south to Douglas County and C-470. The South Platte River runs north/south through nearly the entire length of the city, and the extra green spaces make the city a particularly pleasant place to live. Prices range from $135,000 to $410,000.

Englewood, like Littleton, is one of the southern suburbs with an old downtown established in the 1800s along Broadway. Also like Littleton, it has a small-town appeal. But it's closer to Denver, and its business corridor along S. Santa Fe Drive on the city's west side is home to hundreds of manufacturing, industrial and service companies. Homes are smaller, frame structures. On the city's east side, it borders Cherry Hills Village. Prices range from $110,000 to $190,000.

Douglas County

Anyone who has lived in Greater Denver for 10 years or more is likely to be struck by the number of new residences, set well apart like estates speckling the landscape from I-25 south. It's an area of rolling hills and open spaces with views of the mountains and the feel of the Great Plains. At least for now. Dou-

glas County in January 1999 lost its designation as the fastest growing county in the nation, but still ranks among the top five.

Douglas County certainly is the metro area's fastest growing county. It is a huge area, with just a few small towns that have old and well-established downtowns, places like **Larkspur**, **Franktown** and the county seat of **Castle Rock**. Otherwise, you'll find very little in the way of residential buildings that aren't either ranches, farm structures or the large and expensive homes that are popping up like crazy in exclusive planned communities with names like **Castle Pines Village**, **Deer Creek Farm** and **The Meadows**. These are among the 20 to 30 planned communities along the Denver/Colorado Springs corridor that are expected to bring Douglas County's population as high as a half-million by the year 2030.

Highlands Ranch is the Douglas County community best known by Denverites, partly because it now represents a continuum of the Greater Denver urban fabric. It lies on the northern edge of Douglas County directly south from the City and County of Denver. With 25,000 residents and growing like crazy, it's supposed to top out at a population of 90,000 by the year 2020, and it won't be too surprising if at some point it is incorporated as a city. It's already starting to look like one with its well-established schools and community centers; its huge central green space, the Northwest Community Park that branches through the main, western cluster of the community; and the large Highland Heritage Regional Park on the growing eastern cluster. The average single-family home sells for $270,000, with a range of $130,000 to more than $1 million.

Jefferson County

Here is where home buyers can choose from the widest variety of landscapes, simply because Jefferson County has both the bulk of Greater Denver's mountain communities and a large percentage of the area's flatland communities. The mountain communities are a big attraction. After a hot summer day at work in Denver, residents retreat to cool mountain evenings among the pines. Of course, it can be less of a treat in the winter when you have to commute through the severe snow conditions of the mountains. Sport-utility vehicles tend to be popular among mountain community commuters.

Jefferson County's flatland communities, however, still offer the attraction of being near the mountains, and Jefferson County in general has a good reputation for quality-of-life factors such as good schools, relatively low crime and nice neighborhoods. Actually, flatland is a bit of a misnomer here, because Jefferson County's eastern half, being close to the mountains, tends to go up and down across a lot of ridges and valleys. Realtors over in Aurora and far eastern Denver tend to think they've got the same quality of houses and yards as in Jefferson County but for $15,000 to $20,000 less. It may be true that you pay such a premium for being in Jefferson County, but of course it's a big place and cost/benefit depends on where you are. On average, Jefferson County's population is moderately well-to-do and well-educated.

Jefferson County South is the county's most expensive housing region bordering directly on Denver. The vast majority of residences here are in the area bounded roughly by U.S. Highway 285 on the north, Sheridan Avenue on the east and Colorado-470 on the south and west. Bulging into that area on the northeast corner is the City and County of Denver's **Marston** neighborhood, which surrounds Marston Lake. Denver tried to annex most of the rest of this area back in the 1970s but was rebuffed by Jefferson County and the courts. It's an unincorporated area, but one with a lot of consciousness of itself as a unique community right on the edge of the mountains. It has rejected efforts at incorporation as a city, but it holds its own community festivals and has its own organization of homeowners associations known as the Council of Homeowners Organizations for Planned Environment.

South Jeffco also has some nice housing south and west of C-470, in Ken Caryl Valley on the other side of the Dakota Hogback, for example, where there's a mix of everything from townhomes to million-dollar mansions. **Ken Caryl Ranch** is a stable area with lots of horse property, surrounded by Foothills and tucked away from the big city. Houses range from $230,000 up to $800,000, with most around $350,000 to $550,000.

North from Ken Caryl is **Green Mountain**, with stunning city views and prices from $170,000 to $370,000.

The city of **Lakewood** is the giant of Denver's southwest side and the third-most populous city in Greater Denver after Denver and Aurora. Unlike many suburbs, Lakewood is a major employment center, with the Denver Federal Center, strong retail communities and substantial light industry. At the same time, it has a lot of semi-rural areas right inside the city limits. Lakewood's older neighborhoods lie to the east, where the city meets with about half the entire western border of Denver. On the west, it reaches into the Foothills, where its 6,000 acres of parks include Green Mountain and the surrounding William Frederick Hayden Park. Lakewood touches the City of **Morrison**, a Greater Denver small town hidden in one of the red rock-rimmed valleys in the Rocky Mountains' first folds. Lakewood-area homes average $120,000 to $270,000 but can range higher than $600,000.

North of Lakewood is the City of **Wheat Ridge**, also bordering Denver. It has developed largely since World War II. Before that it was a farming area known for fruits, vegetables and carnations. Wheat Ridge also has that uniquely rural flavor characteristic of many suburbs here, with older homes on larger lots. Foxes come up into the neighborhoods at night from the Clear Creek greenbelt. Deer sometimes blunder into busy Wadsworth Boulevard at morning rush hour. Walkers in serene suburban neighborhoods sometimes see people passing on horses. Home sales here average $130,000 to $220,000 and range up to $400,000.

Driving west on 32nd Avenue and passing out of Wheat Ridge as you go under I-70, you are on the way to the City of **Golden**, on the other side of South Table Mountain. Between I-70 and South Table Mountain, however, you notice nicely groomed new neighborhoods primarily on the left. You are on the north side of a loosely defined area known as **Applewood**, which includes bits of Lakewood, Golden and Wheat Ridge but is mostly in unincorporated Jefferson County. Applewood is a name often heard on the lips of westsiders considering a move to a new home, but it also includes older, established homes with mature trees. Applewood prices range from $180,000 to $450,000.

Keep going west on 32nd Avenue, around South Table Mountain, past a row of Adolph Coors Co. subsidiary companies and finally past the brewery itself, and you'll be coming in a sort of back door to Golden. Largely hidden from Denver on the west side of South Table Mountain and with its eastern sides scrunching up against the Foothills, Golden has kept an identity apart from the rest of the metro area. It has an Old West downtown and it is a charming small town. But it's also a big town. Once a Coors-company town, it's now mainly a high-technology and university town, largely influenced by the culture of the Colorado School of Mines just up the hill from Washington Avenue, its main street. New neighborhoods have been climbing up the side of South Table Mountain, growing south toward Heritage Square and Morrison and spreading east toward Lakewood. The level of education among Golden's population is one of the highest in the Greater Denver area. Homes range from $140,000 to $240,000, with many newer ones as high as $500,000.

Northeast of Golden and north of Wheat Ridge is one of the larger cities of Denver's west side, **Arvada**. Looking north from the top of the ridge that is the center of Wheat Ridge, you can see the historic center of Arvada, now known as **Olde Town Arvada**. But Arvada has spread considerably from that historic beginning, out to the "horse country" of the far west side. Arvada's central area consists largely of homes typically built in the 1950s and 1960s. But a rapidly growing high-end development called **West Woods Ranch** offers new homes centered around a golf course. Arvada is known for its family-oriented lifestyle and its easy access to Boulder and Denver. Home prices in Arvada range from $150,000 to $330,000. Custom-made homes in West Woods Ranch climb to $650,000.

Arvada, north of 80th Avenue, and Westminster, west of Sheridan Boulevard, pretty much define the residential majority of the area known as **Jefferson County North**. The parts of the two cities in this area — north,

east and south of Standley Lake — are more like each other than they are like their respective city centers. A lot of new homes have gone in here in the last five or 10 years, primarily tract homes with some high-end custom homes and some of the patio homes preferred by empty-nesters. There are lots of younger families here and a lot of shopping close by, along North Wadsworth Boulevard. The area has a country feel to it because you're looking west across the last prairie before the mountains. It's a short shot north on Wadsworth to Broomfield and U.S. Highway 36 to Boulder.

West beyond Rocky Flats and Golden, off Colo. Highway 93, there are growing mountain developments up side roads such as **Coal Creek Canyon**, **Golden Gate Canyon** and **Crawford Gulch**.

Greater Denver's big mountain communities, though, tend to be off I-70 and U.S. Highway 285. Communities such as **Genesee**, **Evergreen**, **Conifer**, **Aspen Park**, **Indian Hills**, **Kittredge** and **Hidden Valley** offer a lot of new, high-end living across ridge tops with fantastic vistas and hidden, pine-covered valleys and hillsides. The only drawback is the 30-minute commuting time from Evergreen to Denver, assuming no traffic jams, and 45 minutes to an hour from areas farther out. Homes up in this area tend to average around $350,000. There are some older, less-expensive properties, though they're harder to find. But the bulk of opportunities are in burgeoning, although tasteful, developments. **Genesee** homes are considered more in the foothills, with better access to Denver. Homes there range from $400,000 to more than $1 million.

Evergreen is probably the largest, most-established community near I-70, about 8 miles south of it, actually, on Colo. Highway 74. There are more than 7,000 people in the City of Evergreen — 20,000 including the nearby communities of **Kittredge** and **Bergen Park** — and there's even a downtown, just below the dam that holds back Evergreen Lake. Evergreen also has shops, restaurants and the Little Bear bar, which pulls people up from Denver for its great musical evenings and singles scene. Housing here is among the most expensive in the region, ranging from $350,000 to $2 million.

Mountain communities down U.S. Highway 285, in the **Conifer/Aspen Park** area, have Denver commuting times closer to an hour, but here you'll find properties in all price ranges, with some horse properties and more available space. Here prices range from $250,000 to $350,000.

Real Estate Resources

You can get more information on the local real estate market, Realtor licensing and ethics and other information involving the sale or purchase of homes, by contacting the following agencies.

Colorado Association of Realtors Inc., (303) 790-7099

Denver Board of Realtors, (303) 756-0553

Douglas/Elbert Board of Realtors, (303) 688-0941

Evergreen-Conifer Association of Realtors, (303) 674-7020

Jefferson County Association of Realtors, (303) 233-7831

North Metro Denver Realtor Association, (303) 451-5757

South Metro Denver Realtor Association, (303) 797-3700

Home Builders

Colorado's new home building business is doing well after a major slump in the late 1980s. Based on available space, most new home construction — master planned communities and tract-housing developments — is going on in the suburbs. Single units, and smaller townhome or condo developments, make up the bulk of city infill projects. Perhaps the biggest trend continuing in 1999 is the growing number of upscale townhomes and row homes being built on vacant city lots or in the place of rundown existing homes.

On a larger scale, redevelopment of both Lowry Air Force Base, a few miles east of downtown, and the old Stapleton Airport site are major projects that include residential, retail and parks. Work on Lowry is nearing completion, while Stapleton construction will extend beyond 2000.

Another trend hitting Greater Denver is the revival of New Urbanism, in which communities are built to look like the days of old with vintage housing and neighborhood amenities just down the street. The Lowry and Stapleton sites are likely to include New Urbanism, as is development still in the drawing stages in the Central Platte Valley, just west of downtown.

For more information on the hundreds of home builders, call the Home Builders Association of Metropolitan Denver at (303) 778-1400.

Real Estate Firms

The following are among Greater Denver's more well-known real estate brokerages.

The Kentwood Moore Co.
5690 DTC Pkwy., Englewood
• **(303) 773-3399**

Based in the Denver Tech Center, The Kentwood Moore Co. specializes in upper-price homes and does most of its brokerage in the south metro area as well as some of the more-expensive properties in the inner city. It offers the complete range of real estate services, including corporate relocations, condo conversions and new home sales. The company's 35 sales associates average more than 15 years of experience. Average annual sales volume tops $300 million. An office was recently opened in Cherry Creek, (303) 331-1400.

Coldwell Banker/ Moore and Co.
8490 E. Crescent Pkwy., Greenwood Village • **(303) 778-6600**

After a merger in 1999, Coldwell Banker/Moore and Co. became the largest real estate services firm in Colorado, with more than 900 associates. Each office is staffed by experts who know their area, or can help you anywhere across Colorado. One busy office, listed above, is in what's called south suburban central — an area known for its mountain views and mix of suburban living amid open space. Coldwell Banker/ Moore and Co. is active all over the Denver area, north to Loveland and in Breckenridge, Frisco and Winter Park. The company sells new construction as well as resales.

Perry & Butler Realty Inc.
101 University Blvd., Ste. 100
• (303) 394-2221

This Colorado company, founded in 1963, has 350 sales agents and 10 branch offices serving metropolitan Denver, Boulder and Longmont. It has a relocation division and sells residential real estate in the whole spectrum of incomes and price ranges.

RE/MAX Southeast Inc.
8821 E. Hampden Ave.
• (303) 777-7435

RE/MAX Mountain States Inc.
5445 DTC Pkwy., Englewood
• (303) 770-5531

RE/MAX is a real estate giant in the area. RE/MAX has dozens of independently owned and operated offices in Greater Denver. They're all joined together by the RE/MAX International Referral Roster System.

Leonard Leonard
420 Downing St.
• (303) 744-6200

When you see a Leonard Leonard "for sale" sign, you're almost sure to find a top-quality home inside. After 15 years in the business, Leonard Leonard is known for specializing in the heart of Denver. Owner Sonja Leonard Leonard has built a staff of agents whose attention to detail shows in their high-quality properties. And their open house tours, which often feature champagne and munchies at every stop, are a fun way to spend a few hours.

Co-Ka-Ne Consultants Inc.
2041 Colo. Hwy. 83, Ste. A, Box 1049, Franktown • (303) 841-1100
405 Arapahoe St., Kiowa • (303) 841-6100

Two offices (Franktown and Kiowa) specialize in ranch and horse property in the southeast edge of suburban Denver and stretching east into rural territory. Thirteen agents help people looking for a rural lifestyle, many with horses and small animals and some looking for multi-acre ranches.

The Devonshire Company
105 Fillmore St. • (303) 758-7611

The Devonshire Company frequently produces several of the top 10 agents in the Denver area, including past winners Judith Johnson, Mary Ann Lee and Margaret Knowlton. The awards say a lot about the agency's expertise but also about the high-end homes in which it specializes. "Cottages to Castles" is Devonshire's slogan, and in 1998, agents sold over $300 million in real estate with an average price of $455,000.

Metro Brokers Inc.
8400 E. Prentice Ave., Englewood
• **(303) 843-0100**

Metro Brokers Inc. is a trade association of independent brokers that operate all over the state. With 66 offices and more than 1,500 agents, they sold more than $2.3 billion in 1998.

Century 21 Professionals Inc.
550 Wadsworth Blvd., Lakewood
• **(303) 922-2121**

Century 21 is a worldwide company operating in 19 countries. Each of Denver's 20 offices are independently owned. Broker Susan Joslyn owns the Lakewood office and can direct you to an office specializing in any area of the metro region. The Lakewood office includes 60 agents.

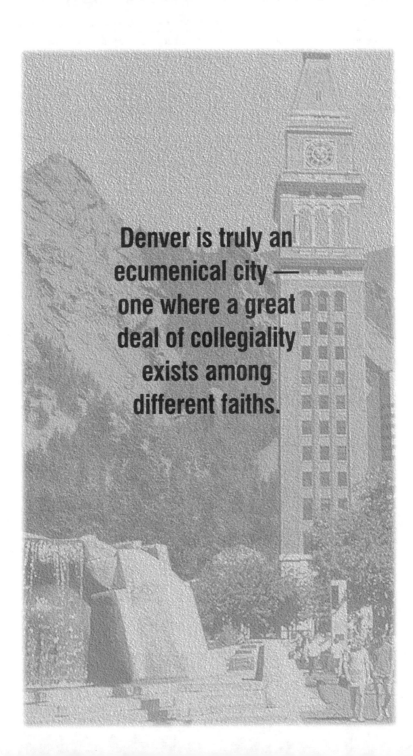

Denver is truly an ecumenical city — one where a great deal of collegiality exists among different faiths.

Worship

Drive around town on Sunday and chances are you'll find church parking lots full. Denver is definitely a "church" town, but in a most laid-back and casual way. Denverites are not only observant (our church attendance average is right up there with national numbers), but also open to new and different spiritual experiences. From traditional services to religious seminars, we fill our spiritual coffers in a variety of ways.

Denver offers every major denomination as well as most of the smaller ones. Catholics make up the largest denomination, though their presence is not a dominant force. Still, with the installation of Archbishop Charles Chaput in April 1997, the Denver Catholic community is likely to enjoy some national attention. Chaput, who is part Native-American, is gregarious, a people person and the kind of religious leader, Insiders say, who will establish himself as a mover and shaker in the national movement of the Catholic Church.

Every branch of Protestantism is also represented, and Denver has active Jewish, Buddhist, Muslim and Mormon communities as well. Chances are, no matter what your beliefs, Denver will have a congregation to satisfy you.

This is truly an ecumenical city — one where a great deal of collegiality exists among different faiths. When graffiti on a synagogue made local news, Christians and Muslims took a little time to publicly show their outrage. Even within a congregation, there is a feeling of acceptance that invites people to check it out, which is good, since Denverites are church consumers. They shop around, looking for a good fit. And churches here have responded to that trend by being open and hospitable.

Denver's religious diversity dates back to before Colorado was a state; by the time of statehood in 1876, 20 religious denominations had been organized in Colorado. St. Joseph Hospital, the first of Denver's many church-affiliated hospitals, was founded in 1873, and Jews and Catholics as well as many Protestants were conducting services in and around Denver at that time. Present-day Congregation Emanuel can trace its beginnings back to its incorporation in 1874 and, even before that, to the establishment of the Hebrew Burial Society in 1859. Similarly, enough Catholics were in Colorado during the territorial period that the Rocky Mountains were removed from the authority of Santa Fe and recognized as a separate vicariate in 1868. The first Bishop of Denver, Joseph Machebeuf, was consecrated in 1887.

Today that diversity still prevails, and Denver is a town fueled by religious energy. In addition to the much heralded 1993 visit by Pope John Paul II for World Youth Day, Denverites eagerly anticipated the visit of the Dalai Lama in the summer of 1997. Sponsored by the Colorado Friends of Tibet and the Naropa Institute in Boulder, the Dalai Lama took part in a four-day spirituality fest held in Denver and Boulder and featured other notables such as Joan Halifax and Huston Smith. The Dalai Lama gave two public talks — one at Macky Auditorium in Boulder; the other, an interfaith ceremony at McNichols Arena.

Meanwhile, for your own immediate religious needs, plan to get out and visit some churches or synagogues. In addition to your hands-on research, read the column "How Coloradans Worship" in the Monday *Rocky*

INSIDERS' TIP

The Denver Post publishes a good religion page on Saturdays that lists upcoming events and special services.

Mountain News, which features a different house of worship each week.

And be sure to check out two of the area's more popular destinations: The Mother Cabrini Shrine and Red Rocks Park.

The **Mother Cabrini Shrine**, *20189 Cabrini Boulevard in Golden, (303) 526-0758*, is where pilgrims go for prayer and contemplation. The shrine is open to the public daily, and mass is celebrated each morning. Take I-70 west to the Morrison Exit 259, then take U.S. Highway 40 (the frontage road) west about a mile.

Also in Morrison, scenic **Red Rocks Park** is the site of an annual nondenominational Easter sunrise service that fills the 9,000-seat natural amphitheater to capacity in good weather. Take I-70 west to the Morrison Exit 259, and turn south toward Morrison; watch for signs marking the entrance to Red Rocks on the right.

There are also several historic houses of worship worth a visit (see our Attractions chapter) for their historical and architectural value.

This brief chapter is merely an overview of the religious scene in the metro area. It would not be practical to list every place of worship in Denver, nor would it be appropriate for us to suggest one rather than another. To find a specific place of worship for yourself and your family, consult the listing of religious organizations at the end of this chapter or the Yellow Pages under churches, mosques, religious organizations and synagogues.

Finally, use the following resource list to guide you in your search:

Catholic Archdiocese of Denver
200 Josephine St. • (303) 388-4411

Church of Jesus Christ of Latter-day Saints
Denver North Mission • 11172 N. Huron St., Ste. 21, Northglenn • (303) 252-7192
Denver South Mission • 2001 E. Easter Ave., Littleton • (303) 794-6457

Colorado Council of Churches
1234 Bannock St. • (303) 825-4910

Colorado Muslim Society
2071 S. Parker Rd., Aurora
• (303) 696-9800

Denver Buddhist Temple
Tri-State Buddhist Headquarters
• 1947 Lawrence St. • (303) 295-1844

Episcopal Diocese of Colorado
1300 Washington St. • (303) 837-1173

Fifth District of the African Methodist Episcopal Churches of Colorado/Shorter Church
3100 Richard Allen Ct. • (303) 320-1712

The Greek Orthodox Cathedral of the Assumption
4610 E. Alameda Ave. • (303) 388-9314

National Baptist Convention
195 S. Monaco Pkwy. • (303) 355-0297

Presbytery of Denver (Presbyterian Church U.S.A.)
1710 S. Grant St. • (303) 777-2453

INSIDERS' TIP

One of the most peaceful and powerful services in Denver is Taize (TEZZ-ay), a communal meditation hour for people of almost any faith. Held on the second Sunday of the month at Calvary Baptist Church, 6500 E. Girard Avenue, (303) 757-8421, the service has no liturgy, no sermon, no apparent plan. It is held by candlelight and involves meditation and music. A how-to sheet helps first-timers with breathing and meditation. People drive from across town to attend this monthly service.

The Dalai Lama happily compared haircuts with high school students
when he visited Denver and Boulder in summer 1997.

**Reorganized Church of Jesus
Christ of Latter-day Saints**
Denver Stake & Regional Office • 9501 Lou
Dr., Westminster • (303) 426-5900

**Rocky Mountain Conference United
Church of Christ**
7000 N. Broadway Building, No. 420,
Westminster• (303) 428-0045

**Rocky Mountain Synod/Evangelical
Lutheran Church in America**
7000 N. Broadway Building, No. 401,
Westminster • (303) 427-7553

**Rocky Mountain United Methodist
Conference**
2200 S. University Blvd. • (303) 733-3736

**Synagogue Council of Greater
Denver**
P.O. Box 102732, Denver 80250
• (303) 759-8485

Unitarian Universalists
1510 Glen Ayr Dr., Ste. 4, Lakewood
• (303) 238-4051

Additional Resources

Faith on the Frontier, a book compiled by
the Colorado Council of Churches in 1976,
was used as the source for much of the historical data in this chapter. *Denver: The City
Beautiful* by Thomas J. Noel and Barbara S.
Norgren (Historic Denver Inc.) contains a brief
section on Greater Denver church architecture and is a wonderful resource for anyone
interested in Denver's architectural history.

Denver is among the few
U.S. cities that still have
two independent daily
newspapers.

Media

Greater Denver is not exactly a media center, at least not in the sense of New York or Los Angeles. It doesn't produce a lot of television programs or magazines, although it does occasionally show up in movies. Still, at least in part because Greater Denver is home to telecommunications industry giants Jones Intercable and Tele-Communications Inc., it may very well become a major stop on the information highway. And Denver does have something that most comparably sized cities don't: two daily newspapers.

Newspapers

Denver is among the few U.S. cities that still have two independent daily newspapers. Over the years, rumor has had it that either *The Denver Post* or *Rocky Mountain News* was on the verge of folding — and although such rumors continue, as of this writing both papers are holding on. They fight each other for readership and advertising, and each has its fans and detractors. In 1995, the *News* made news when it introduced Front Range Plus, which eliminated home delivery in 50 counties outside the Front Range. That strategy created a circulation windfall for the *Denver Post*. Both are morning papers, but while *The Denver Post* is a broadsheet, *Rocky Mountain News* has a tabloid format.

For readers, the newspaper war has meant improved color in both papers and fiercely competitive subscription rates. As in most cities, the dailies have special sections depending on the day of the week. Looking for recipes and food stories? Pick up the Wednesday edition of either paper. Looking for something to do on the weekends? Pullout weekend entertainment guides are published each Friday.

Hate it or love it, many Denverites pick up *Westword*, the city's weekly arts and entertainment paper. Why not — it's free and has comprehensive lists of what's going on around town.

There are also many community papers, too numerous to list here. Specialized publications are always coming into and going out of existence to serve a particular region (downtown) or interest (art).

Dailies

The Denver Post
1560 Broadway • (303) 820-1010

The *Post* has a long and colorful history. It was founded in 1895 by Harry Heye Tammen and Frederick Gilmer Bonfils. The early *Post* was a prime exemplar of sensational journalism, relying on stunts and gossip to attract readership. In the 1920s, Tammen and Bonfils got themselves entangled in one fine mess, the Teapot Dome scandal. Originally vehemently opposed to questionable oil leases in Wyoming, the *Post* dropped the issue when paid to do so. Tammen died of cancer in 1924, and Bonfils resigned in 1926.

After Bonfils died in 1933, ownership passed largely to his daughters. In the 1960s, May Bonfils sold her stock to S.I. Newhouse, head of a chain of newspapers and magazines. Helen Bonfils contested the sale, and after years of litigation, Newhouse finally dropped his bid to gain control of the *Post* in 1973.

The *Post* was sold to the Times Mirror Company, owners of the *Los Angeles Times*, in 1980, and sold again to William Dean Singleton of the Dallas-based MediaNews Group in 1987.

The *Post* switched from evening to morning distribution in 1982. The *Post*, in the past year, has made an effort to emphasize more positive news. This doesn't mean they don't cover "big stories;" rather readers may find themselves reading routine crime stories in the local section instead of the front page. Notable *Post* columnists include sportswriter Woody Paige, editorial writer Chuck Green and society man-about-town Bill Husted. The Sunday "Empire" section is a favorite and focuses on people and places important to the West. Daily circulation for the *Post* is (303) 284,542; Sunday circulation is (303) 456,057.

Rocky Mountain News
400 W. Colfax Ave.
• (303) 892-5000

The first issue of *Rocky Mountain News* — four pages, 500 copies — came out in 1859, published by William N. Byers. In 1901, the first year that accurate measurements could be made, the upstart *Denver Evening Post* surpassed *Rocky Mountain News* in circulation for the first time; the two papers have battled for readership and advertising ever since. The *News* was purchased in 1926 by Scripps-Howard during a decade of particularly acrimonious competition, and in 1928, having disposed of or incorporated their other competitors, the *Post* and the *News* called a truce. But in 1993, when the *News* temporarily dropped the price of its Sunday issue from 75¢ to 25¢, Greater Denver saw the return of the kind of drastic price-cutting that characterized the 1920s.

The *News* is generally more conservative in its editorial viewpoints than the *Post*, but this varies depending on the topic.

The *News* recently added a new Sunday section called "Home Front" that addresses matters related to home decorating, remodeling and food as well as popular features like Dr. Laura, Hints from Heloise and Dear Abby. Popular columnists include old-time Denverite Gene Amole, Norm Clark, who pens the Talk of the Town column, and movie reviewer Rob-

ert Denerstein. Daily circulation is (303) 295,011; Sunday's is (303) 377,882.

Weeklies

In addition to the following non-dailies, weekly newspapers are published for residents of Englewood, Highlands Ranch, Littleton, Evergreen, Golden, Greenwood Village and Westminster. If you live there or are interested in news about these communities, check for these papers at local newsstands.

Westword
1621 18th St. • (303) 296-7744

Owned by New Times, a national publisher of "alternative" papers, *Westword* is known for its muckraking investigative stories and is depended upon for its arts and entertainment coverage. Not everyone admires the weekly paper's zeal in pursuing stories, as is evidenced by heated letters to the editor. But at least a dozen of its articles, such as an investigation of the Rocky Flats grand jury proceedings that examined who should be held responsible for environmental crimes, have won awards and national media attention.

Westword is distributed free throughout Greater Denver and hits the streets late Wednesday afternoon. You can find *Westword* in boxes on street corners all over town. Its art/dining/entertainment listings are superb.

Jefferson Sentinel Newspapers
1224 Wadsworth Blvd., Lakewood
• (303) 239-9890

This company publishes weekly newspapers for residents of Arvada, Lakewood and Wheat Ridge, and an online edition, Jefferson Sentinel Online, through America Online. The papers focus on news relevant to these sub-

urbs and includes quarterly education sections and a yearly garden insert. The papers cost 75¢ a copy.

The Denver Business Journal
1700 Broadway #515 • (303) 837-3500

The weekly *Denver Business Journal* covers local business news in depth and includes a small-business strategy section, along with specialized sections that relate to a variety of topics from healthcare to personal finance. The paper comes out on Friday and is available by subscription or throughout metro Denver for a single-copy price of $1.25

Broomfield Enterprise
1006 Depot Hill Rd., Broomfield • (303) 466-3636

This community paper is owned by Boulder Publishing, which publishes the *Daily Camera*, Boulder's daily newspaper. The *Enterprise* is delivered free to Broomfield residences and businesses and carries news of Broomfield, Greater Denver's most northwestern community. Regular offerings include news and feature stories, editorials and classified ads. Coverage is strong on government, business, schools and sports. The paper also publishes special sections ranging from homes and gardens to election issues.

Magazines and Special-interest Publications

5280
5280 Publishing, Inc. • P.O. Box 40194, Denver 80204 • (303) 832-5280

Denver has seen its share of city magazines come and go. The new kid on the block, *5280*, "Denver's Mile-High Magazine," debuted in 1993. (For those who don't know, 5,280 feet equals a mile.) It's fresh, independent and has a lively design like any city magazine. It covers things of interest to locals — restaurants, getaways and interesting people. *5280* is published bimonthly. Single issues are $3.95 at newsstands throughout the city.

Colorado Homes & Lifestyles
Colorado Business Magazine
Wiesner Publishing • 7009 S. Potomac, Englewood • (303) 397-7600

Two magazines with long track records are *Colorado Homes & Lifestyles* and *Colorado Business Magazine*, both Wiesner Publications. *Colorado Homes & Lifestyles*, published bimonthly, not only includes a wealth of information about home and garden design, but also personality profiles of Colorado residents. The monthly *Colorado Business Magazine* surveys the movers and shakers in the state, with an emphasis on Denver. Single issues of *Colorado Homes & Lifestyles* are $3.50. Singles issues of *Colorado Business Magazine* cost $2.95.

Colorado Expression
New West Publishing • 10200 E. Girard Ave., Ste. 222B • (303) 751-0696

Poised somewhere in terms of longevity — and focus — between *Colorado Homes & Lifestyles* and *5280* is *Colorado Expression*. Every issue features a comprehensive "Dining Guide." And every issue celebrates the Colorado lifestyle — from winter activities to cultural outings. Single copies are $4.

The Bloomsbury Review
1762 Emerson St. • (303) 863-0406

A bimonthly book "magazine" of reviews and interviews, *The Bloomsbury Review* (a.k.a. *TBR*) is printed on newsprint and is available free of charge at many local bookstores. *TBR* has a national audience but emphasizes regional writers. You'll find an occasional bestselling writer profiled in here, but *TBR's* mission is to call attention to good but lesser known wordsmiths.

INSIDERS' TIP

Wednesday is food day in the local papers. *The Denver Post*, *Rocky Mountain News* and Boulder's *Daily Camera* run recipes and food-related articles, often with a local slant.

Colorado Parent Magazine
2430 S. University Blvd., Ste. 205
• (303) 320-1000

Formerly *Denver Parent*, this monthly tabloid magazine includes a comprehensive calendar of events and classes of interest to parents in the Greater Denver area. The free paper comes out the first of each month and can be picked up in about 800 different locations around town, including libraries and bookstores. The folks at *Colorado Parent* also publish an annual A-to-Z directory of local resources for parents each June ($4.95). In July they distribute a free birthday guide with listings of restaurants, party planners, suppliers and the like.

High Country News
119 Grand Ave., Paonia • (970) 527-4898

An environmentally oriented newspaper, *High Country News* is published by the intrepid husband-and-wife team of Ed and Betsy Marston in Paonia, Colorado. The much-praised paper focuses on issues intrinsic to the West, such as use of public lands and water and grazing rights. This sharp biweekly is highly recommended to Greater Denver newcomers who would like to know more about the region they now call home. It's available free at the Tattered Cover Book Store (see our Shopping chapter) and other locations throughout the city.

Out Front Colorado
244 Washington St. • (303) 778-7900

A gay and lesbian newspaper, *Out Front Colorado* is published every two weeks (with a break at Christmas). The paper is free and is available at local bars, restaurants, gay businesses and bookstores. It's noted for its entertainment and nightlife listings. Mail subscription is available for a small charge.

Radio

Nothing but the Rocky Mountain weather changes as much as Denver radio stations. One day you're listening to jazz; the next day the station has gone country-western. Consider that caveat when tuning in to the stations listed subsequently, and for an up-to-date list, check the entertainment pages in *The Denver Post* and *Rocky Mountain News* and the "Friday Magazine" in the *Daily Camera*.

Adult Contemporary
KOSI 101.1 FM
KQKS 107.5 FM (Top-40)

Classical
KCFR 90.1 FM (National Public Radio)
KVOD 92.5 FM

Country
KLMO 1060 AM
KYGO 1600 AM and 98.5 FM
KGLL 96.1 FM
KUAD 99.1 FM
KCKK 104.3 FM

Christian
KLZ 560 AM
KLT 670 AM
KPOF 910 AM (Classical)
KRKS 990 AM and 94.7 FM
KQXI 1550 AM (Music/talk/sports)
KWBI 91.1 FM

Kids
KKYD 1340 AM

Jazz
KUVO 89.3 FM
KHIH 95.7 FM

Mexican/Spanish
KCUV 1150 AM
KBNO 1220 AM
KJME 1390 AM

National Public Radio
KGNU 88.5 FM
KUVO 89.3 FM (Jazz)
KCFR 90.1 FM (Classical)

News/Talk/Sports
KHOW 630 AM
KNUS 710 AM
KTLK 760 AM
KOA 850 AM
KCOL 1410 AM

Oldies

KEZW 1430 AM (1940s-'70s)
KIMN 100.3 FM (1970s-'80s)
KTRR 102.5 FM
KRFX 103.5 FM (Classic rock)
KXKL 105.1 FM (1960s-'70s)

Rock and Progressive

KXPK 96.5 FM
KBCO 97.3 FM
KTCL 93.3 FM
KKHK 99.5 FM
KALC 105.9 FM
KBPI 106.7 FM

Sports Only

KKFN 950 AM

Urban Contemporary

KDKO 1510 AM

Television

Greater Denver is the nation's cable television capital, with industry giants Tele-Communications Inc. (TCI) and Jones Intercable both headquartered here. The Denver area is also home to DIRECTV, a Hughes Communication subsidiary that competes with the cable industry. DIRECTV operates its national direct satellite service out of Castle Rock. As a practical matter, however, cable TV here is like cable TV everywhere: you pay your money; you watch your programs. For service in your area, call the cable companies' customer service numbers: Jones Intercable (Kittredge, Idledale, Evergreen, Brighton, and portions of Littleton), (303) 978-9770; TCI, Mile Hi Cablevision, (Denver), (303) 744-9696; TCI (suburbs), (303) 930-2000.

Major Local TV Stations and Network Affiliates

KWGN Channel 2 (Independent/WB)
KCNC Channel 4 (CBS)
KRMA Channel 6 (PBS)
KMGH Channel 7 (ABC)
KUSA Channel 9 (NBC)
KBDI Channel 12 (PBS)
KTVD Channel 20 (Independent/UPN)
KDVR Channel 31 (Fox)
K38DF Channel 38 (Independent)
KRMT Channel 41 (Independent)
KCEC Channel 50 (Univision)
KWHD Channel 53 (Independent)
KTBN Channel 57 (Trinity)
KUBD Channel 59 (Telemundo)

Religious Television Programming

The sermon from the Riverside Baptist Church, 2401 E. Alcott Street, (303) 433-8665, is broadcast on KWGN Channel 2 at 8 AM each Sunday. Check local listings for other religious programming.

Index of Advertisers

Index